DATE DUE

OC 30 '92		
JE 10 '94		
RENEW JUN 2 3 1994		
SE 23 '94		
~~JA 11 00~~		
AP ~~~~ T '18		

HOW TO READ A FILM

OTHER BOOKS BY JAMES MONACO

HOW TO READ A FILM

The Art, Technology, Language, History, and Theory
of Film and Media

Revised Edition

James Monaco

with diagrams by David Lindroth

New York Oxford
OXFORD UNIVERSITY PRESS
1981

Library of Congress Cataloging in Publication Data

Monaco, James.
  How to read a film.

  Bibliography: p.
  Includes index.
  1. Moving-pictures. I. Title.
PN1994.M59 1980   791.43'01'5   80-16848
ISBN 0-19-502802-3
ISBN 0-19-502806-6 (pbk.)

20 19 18 17 16 15 14 13 12 11

Printed in the United States of America

For Susan
With love

PREFACE

Is it necessary, really, to learn how to read a film? Obviously, anyone of minimal intelligence over the age of four can—more or less—grasp the basic content of a film, record, radio, or television program without any special training. Yet precisely because the media so very closely mimic reality, we apprehend them much more easily than we comprehend them. Film and the electronic media have drastically changed the way we perceive the world—and ourselves—during the last eighty years, yet we all too naturally accept the vast amounts of information they convey to us in massive doses without questioning how they tell us what they tell. *How To Read a Film* is an essay in understanding that crucial process—on several levels.

In the first place, film and television are general mediums of communication. Certain basic interesting rules of perception operate; Chapter 3, "The Language of Film: Signs and Syntax," investigates a number of these concepts. On a more advanced level, film is clearly a sophisticated art—possibly the most important art of the twentieth century—with a rather complex history of theory and practice. Chapter 1, "Film as an Art," suggests how film can be fit into the spectrum of the more traditional arts; Chapter 4, "The Shape of Film History," attempts a brief survey of the development of the art of movies; Chapter 5, "Film Theory: Form and Function," surveys some of the major theoretical developments of the last seventy-five years.

Film is a medium and an art, but it is also, uniquely, a very complex technological undertaking. Chapter 2, "Technology: Image and Sound," is—I hope—a clear exposition of the intriguing science of cinema. Although film is dominant, the development of the electronic media—records, radio, tape, television, video—has proceeded in parallel with the growth of film during this century. The relationship between film and media becomes stronger with each passing year; Chapter 6 outlines a general theory of media (both print and electronic), discusses the equally complex technology of the electronic media, and concludes with a survey of the history of radio and television.

As you can see from this outline, the structure of *How To Read a Film* is global rather than linear. In each of the six chapters the intention has been to try to explain a little of how film operates on us psychologically, how it affects us politically. Yet these twin central dominant questions can be approached from a number of angles. Since most people think of film first as an art, I've begun with that aspect of the phenomenon. Since it's difficult to understand how the art has developed without some knowledge of the technology, Chapter 2 proceeds immediately to a discussion of the science of film. Understanding technique, we can begin to discover how film operates as a language (Chapter 3). Since practice does (or should) precede theory, the history of the industry and art (Chapter 4) precedes the intellectualization of it here (Chapter 5). We conclude by widening the focus to view movies in the larger context of media (Chapter 6).

This order seems most logical to me, but readers might very well prefer to begin with history or theory, language or technology, and in fact the book has been constructed in such a way that the sections can be read independently, in any order. (This has resulted in a small number of repetitions, for which I ask your indulgence.) Please remember, too, that in any work of this sort there is a tendency to prescribe rather than simply describe the complex phenomena under investigation. Hundreds of analytical concepts are discussed in the pages that follow, but I ask that readers consider them just that—concepts, analytical tools—rather than given laws. Film study is exciting because it is constantly in ferment. It's my hope that *How To Read a Film* is a book that can be argued with, discussed, and used. In any attempt at understanding, the questions are usually more important than the answers.

How To Read a Film is the result of ten years spent, mainly, thinking, writing, and talking about film and media. Having tried in the pages that follow to set down a few ideas about movies and TV, I find I am most impressed with the number of questions that are yet to be answered. Appendix II gives a fair sense of the considerable amount of work that has already been done (mainly in the last ten years); there is much more yet to do. Had *How To Read a Film* included all the material I originally wanted to cover it would have been encyclopedic in length; as it is now, it is an admittedly hefty, but nevertheless still sinewy, introduction. More and more it seems to me movies must be considered in the context of media in general—in fact, I would go so far as to suggest that film is best considered simply as one stage in the ongoing history of communications. Chapter 6 introduces this concept. You will find some additional material on both print and electronic media in the Glossary (Appendix I) and the Chronology (Appendix III). A fuller account will have to wait for a second volume.

A few miscellaneous notes: bibliographical information not included in footnotes will be found in the appropriate section of Appendix II. Film titles are in English, unless the original foreign language titles are commonly used. In cases where halftones are direct enlargements of film frames, this has been noted in the captions; in most other cases, you can assume the halftones are publicity stills and may differ in slight respects from the actual images of the film.

I owe a very real debt to a number of people who have helped in various ways. *How To Read a Film* never would have been written without my invaluable experience teaching film at the New School for Social Research. I thank Allen Austill for allowing me to do so, Reuben Abel for taking a chance on a young teacher in 1967, and Wallis Osterholz for her unflagging encouragement and necessary help. I am especially grateful to my students at the New School (and the City University of New York) who, although they may not know it, gave at least as much as they got.

At Oxford University Press I have been particularly fortunate. Editor John Wright, with intelligence, savvy, and humor, has added immeasurably to whatever success the book might enjoy. Ellen Royer helped to make sense out of a manuscript that may have been lively, but was certainly sprawling and demanding. Dana Kasarsky designed the book with care and dealt efficiently with the myriad problems such a complex layout entails. Ellie Fuchs, Jean Shapiro, and Editor James Raimes at Oxford were consistently and dependably helpful. Curtis Church has overseen the production of the second edition with patience and great care. Thanks to all.

David Lindroth has drawn more than three dozen diagrams which I think add considerably to the effect of *How To Read a Film*. If I may say so, I think they are notably superior to comparable illustrations of this sort. David not only translated my scrawls into meaningful conceptions, he also added significantly to the realization of those conceptions. His input was invaluable.

Dudley Andrew and David Bombyk read the manuscript and commented upon it rigorously and in exceptionally useful detail. Their comments were enormously helpful. I also want to thank Kent R. Brown, Paul C. Hillery, Timothy J. Lyons, and Sreekumar Menon for reading and commenting upon the manuscript.

William K. Everson, Eileen M. Krest, and my brother Robert Monaco provided valuable information I was unable to discover for myself, as did Jerome Agel, Stellar Bennett (NET), Ursula Deren (BBC), Kozu Hiramatsu (Sony), Cal Hotchkiss (Kodak), Terry Maguire (FCC), Joe Medjuck (University of Toronto), Alan Schneider (Juilliard), and Sarah Warner (I.E.E.E.). Many thanks.

Marc Fürstenberg, Claudia Gorbman, Annette Insdorf, Bruce Kawin, and Clay Steinman, among others, made suggestions valuable for this revised edition.

Jacques Charrière of l'Avant-Scène, Mary Corliss of the Museum of Modern Art Film Stills Archive, Penelope Houston of Sight and Sound, and Marc Wanamaker (Bison Archives) were particularly helpful in providing illustrations. Shimon Ben Dor (Cameramart), Kent Carroll (Grove Press), Martha Coolidge, Helen Garfinkle (Darien House), Paul Hillery, Jane Iandola (Philadelphia Museum of Art), Jean-Marie Lavalou, Peter Lebensold (Take One), Pat Lyons (New American Library), Rita Myers (Museum of Modern Art), Joe Riccuiti (NBC), Lonnie Schlein (New York Times), Catherine Verret (French Film Office), John Canemaker, and Frederick Wiseman also very kindly provided photographs, as did Allan Frumkin Gallery, Andy Warhol Enterprises, BBC, CBS, Farrar, Straus & Giroux, Films Inc., Granada Television, International Museum of Photography/George Eastman House, M-G-M, NET, New York Public Library, Paramount, Scientific American Inc., W. Steenbeck and Co., David Susskind, Time-Life Picture Agency, United Artists, Universal Pictures, and Warner Bros.

Penelope Houston of Sight and Sound and Peter Lebensold of Take One graciously allowed me to draw on materials originally published in their journals. Virginia Barber, my agent, helped to make it financially possible for me to finish this lengthy project.

Finally, I thank my wife Susan Schenker, who read and commented on the manuscript, talked out difficulties with me, helped write the Appendices, and did so much more. (Acknowledgments are always such a faint reflection of real feelings.)

How To Read a Film is set in Goudy Oldstyle. (The Display type for chapter headings is Pistilli Roman.) Designed by F. W. Goudy, the most prolific American type designer of the early twentieth century, Goudy Oldstyle is modeled on renaissance lettering. In "oldstyle" typefaces the various elements of the individual letters are of fairly uniform weights so that the design is approximately the same color throughout, which makes oldstyle types generally very readable. Frederic Goudy was a printer as well as a designer—a craftsman in the mold of William

Morris—who owned and operated his own "Village" press for many years, as well as completing more than one hundred typefaces, many of which have become standards. According to his contemporary Douglas C. McMurtrie (*The Book*, 1943), "Goudy has a gift for drawing beautiful letters second to no designer of this or any other generation." Goudy's personal, craftsmanlike, eclectic, and democratic approach to the medium of print makes his typeface an especially fitting choice for *How To Read a Film*.

This second edition has been entirely reset.

New York City   J.M.
January 1977
February 1981

CONTENTS

FILM AS AN ART

ONE

THE NATURE OF ART

"Art" is an extraordinarily difficult term to define precisely because it covers a wide range of human endeavor. Over the years the boundaries of its meaning have changed, gradually but significantly. Cultural historian Raymond Williams has cited art as one of the "keywords"—one that must be understood in order to comprehend the interrelationships between culture and society. As with "community," "criticism," and "science," for example, the history of the word "art" reveals a wealth of information about the structure of our civilization. A review of that history will help us to understand how the relatively new art of film fits into the general pattern of art.

The ancients recognized seven activities as arts: History, Poetry, Comedy, Tragedy, Music, Dance, and Astronomy. Each was governed by its own muse, each had its own rules and aims, but all seven were united by a common motivation: they were tools, useful to describe the universe and our place in it. They were methods of approach to an understanding of the mysteries of existence, and as such, they themselves took on the aura of those mysteries. As a result, they were each aspects of religious activity: the performing arts celebrated the rituals; history recorded the story of the race; astronomy searched the heavens. In each of these seven classical arts we can discover the roots of contemporary cultural and scientific categories. History, for example, leads not only to the modern social sciences but also to prose narrative (the novel, short stories, and so forth). Astronomy, on the other hand, represents the full range of modern science at the same time as it suggests another aspect of the social sciences in its astrological functions of prediction and interpretation. Under the rubric of poetry, the Greeks and Romans recognized three approaches: Lyric, Dramatic, and Epic, each of which has yielded modern prose arts.

By the thirteenth century, however, the word "art" had taken on a considerably more practical connotation. The Liberal Arts curriculum of the medieval university still numbered seven components, but the method of definition had shifted. The literary arts of the classical period—History, Poetry, Comedy, and Tragedy—had merged into a vaguely defined mix of literature and philosophy and then had been reordered according to analytical principles as Grammar, Rhetoric, and Logic (the Trivium), structural elements of the arts rather than qualities of them. Dance was dropped from the list and replaced by Geometry, marking the growing importance of mathematics. Only Music and Astronomy remained unchanged from the ancient categories.

Outside the university cloisters, the word was even more flexible. We still speak of the art of war, the medical arts, even the art of angling. By the sixteenth century, "art" was clearly synonymous with "skill," and a wheelwright, for example, was just as much an artist as a musician: each practiced a particular skill.

By the late seventeenth century, the range of the word had begun to narrow once again. It was increasingly applied to activities that had never before been included—painting, sculpture, drawing, architecture, what we now call the "Fine Arts." The rise of the concept of modern science as separate from and contradictory to the arts meant that Astronomy and Geometry were no longer regarded in the same light as Poetry or Music. By the late eighteenth century, the Romantic vision of the artist as specially endowed restored some of the religious aura that had surrounded the word in classical times. A differentiation was made between "artist" and "artisan." The former was "creative" or "imaginative," the latter simply a skilled workman.

In the nineteenth century as the concept of science developed, the narrowing of the concept of art continued, as if in response to that more rigorously logical activity. What had once been "natural philosophy" was termed "natural science"; the art of alchemy became the science of chemistry. The new sciences were precisely defined intellectual activities, dependent on rigorous methods of operation. The arts (which were increasingly seen as being that which science was not) were therefore also more clearly defined. By the middle of the nineteenth century the word had more or less developed the constellation of connotations we know today. It referred first to the visual, or "Fine," arts, then more generally to literature and the musical arts. It could, on occasion, be stretched to include the performing arts and, although in its broadest sense it still carried the medieval sense of skills, for the most part it was strictly used in the context of more sophisticated endeavors. The romantic sense of the artist as a chosen one remained: "artists" were distinguished not only from "artisans" (craftspeople) but also from "artistes" (performing artists) with lower social and intellectual standing.

With the establishment in the late nineteenth century of the concept of "social sciences," the spectrum of modern intellectual activity was complete and the range of art had narrowed to its present domain. Those phenomena that yielded to study by the scientific method were ordered under the rubric of science and were strictly defined. Other phenomena, less susceptible to laboratory techniques and experimentation, but capable of being ordered with some logic and clarity, were established in the gray area of the social sciences (economics, sociology, politics, psychology, and sometimes even philosophy). Those areas of intellectual endeavor that could not be fit into either the physical or the social sciences were left to the domain of art.

As the development of the social sciences necessarily limited the practical, utilitarian relevance of the arts, and probably in reaction to this phenomenon, theories of estheticism evolved. With roots in the Romantic theory of the artist as prophet and priest, the "art for art's sake" movement of the late Victorian age celebrated form over content and changed the focus of the word. The arts were no longer simply methods of approach to a comprehension of the world; they were now ends in themselves. Walter Pater declared that "all art aspires to the condition of music." Abstraction—pure form—became the touchstone of the work of art and the main criterion by which works of art were judged in the twentieth century.*

The impulse toward abstraction accelerated rapidly during the first two-thirds of the twentieth century. In the nineteenth century the avant-garde movement had taken the concept of progress from the developing technology and decided that some art must perforce be more "advanced" than other art. The theory of the avant garde, which has been a controlling factor in the historical development of the arts ever since the Romantic period, expressed itself best in terms of abstraction. In this respect the arts were, in effect, mimicking the sciences and technology, searching for the basic elements of their "languages"—the "quanta" of painting or poetry or drama. The Dada movement of the

---

*I am indebted to Raymond Williams's essay in *Keywords: A Vocabulary of Culture and Society,* pp. 32, 34.

1920s parodied this development. The result was the minimalist work of the middle of this century, which marked the endpoint of the struggle of the avant garde toward abstraction: Samuel Beckett's forty-second dramas (or his ten-page novels), Joseph Albers's color-exercise paintings, John Cage's silent musical works. Having reduced art to its most basic quanta, the only choice for artists (besides annihilation) was to begin over again to rebuild the structures of the arts. This new synthesis began in the 1960s in earnest, even as political and economic culture was, in parallel, discovering the fallacy of progress and developing in its place a "steady state" theory of existence.

The acceleration of abstraction, while it is certainly the main factor evident in the historical development of the arts during the twentieth century, is not the only one. The force that counters this estheticism is our continuing sense of the political dimension of the arts: that is, their direct connection to the community, and their power to explain the structure of society to us. In Western culture, this power of relevance (which led the ancients to include History on an equal footing with Music) has certainly not been dominant, but it does have a long and honorable history parallel with, if subordinate to, the esthetic impulse toward abstraction. Moreover, it is safe to assume, I think, that as abstraction and reductionism continue to decline in importance during the remainder of the twentieth century, the significance of this hitherto secondary political element will increase. In fact, if we examine the recent history of the popular arts (and direct our attention away from the historical development of the elite arts, such as painting and "serious" music) the balance already has shifted. And this leads us to the third basic factor that has determined the course of the history of the arts during the last hundred years—the rise of the technological arts.

Originally, the only way to produce art was in "real time": the singer sang the song, the storyteller told the tale, the actors acted the drama. The development in prehistory of drawing and (through pictographs) of writing represented a quantum jump in systems of communication. Images could be stored, stories could be preserved, later to be recalled exactly. For seven thousand years the history of the arts was, essentially, the history of these representative media: the pictorial and the literary.

The development of recording media, different from representative media in kind as well as degree, was as significant historically as the invention of writing seven thousand years earlier. Photography, film, and sound recording taken together have shifted completely our historical perspective. The representational arts made possible the "re-creation" of phenomena, but they required the complex application of the codes and conventions of languages. Moreover, those languages were manipulated by individuals and therefore the element of choice was and is highly significant in the representational arts. This element is the source of most of the esthetics of the pictorial and literary arts. What interests estheticians is not what is said but how it is said.

In stark contrast, the recording arts provide a much more direct line of communication between the subject and the observer. They do have their own codes and conventions, it's true: a film or sound recording is not reality, after all. But the language of the recording media is considerably simpler and less ambiguous than either written or pictorial language. In addition, the history of the recording arts has been a direct progression toward greater verisimilitude. Color film reproduces more of reality than does black-and-white; sound film is more closely parallel to actual experience than is silent; and so forth. This qualitative difference between representational media and recording media is very clear to those who use the latter for scientific purposes. Anthropologists, for example, are well aware of the advantages of film over the written word. Film does not completely eliminate the intervention of a third party between the subject and the observer, but it does significantly reduce the distortion the presence of an artist inevitably introduces.

The result is that we now have a spectrum of the arts existing on three levels:
- the *performance arts*, which happen in real time;
- the *representational arts*, which depend on the established codes and conventions of language (both pictorial and literary) to convey information about the subject to the observer;
- the *recording arts*, which provide a more direct path between subject and observer: media not without their own codes but qualitatively more direct than the media of the representational arts.

THE SPECTRUM OF ART: MODES OF DISCOURSE

In order to understand how the recording arts established their place in the spectrum, it's necessary first to define some of the basic concepts of that spectrum. There is a wide variety of determinants that interrelate to give each of the classical and modern arts its own particular personality, resulting in complex and elaborate esthetic equations. Two ordering systems, one mainly nineteenth century in origin, the other more contemporary, suggest themselves immediately.

The older of these systems of classification depends for its definition on the degree of abstraction inherent in a particular art. This is one of the oldest theories of art, dating back to Aristotle's *Poetics* (fourth century B.C.). According to the Greek philosopher, art was best understood as a type of mimesis, an imitation of reality dependent on a medium (through which it was expressed) and a mode (the way the medium was utilized). The more mimetic an art is, then, the less abstract it is. In no case, however, is an art completely capable of reproducing reality.

A spectrum of the arts organized according to abstraction would look something like this:

PRACTICAL	ENVIRONMENTAL	PICTORIAL	DRAMATIC	NARRATIVE	MUSICAL
design					
architecture					
	sculpture				
		painting drawing graphics			
		——stage drama——			
				novel story nonfiction	
					poetry dance
					music

Diagram A

The arts of design (clothing, furniture, eating utensils, and so forth), which often are not even dignified by being included in the artistic spectrum, would be found at the left end of this scale: highly mimetic (a fork comes very close to thoroughly reproducing the idea of a fork) and least abstract. Moving from left to right we find architecture, which often has a very low esthetic quotient, after all; then sculpture, which is both environmental and pictorial; then painting, drawing, and the other graphic arts at the center of the pictorial area of the spectrum. The dramatic arts combine pictorial and narrative elements in various measures. The novel, short story, and often nonfiction as well are situated squarely in the narrative range. Then come poetry, which although basically narrative in nature also tends toward the musical end of the spectrum and sometimes in the other direction, toward the pictorial; dance, combining elements of narrative with music; and finally, at the extreme right of the spectrum, music—the most abstract and "esthetic" of the arts. Remember Walter Pater: "All art aspires to the condition of music."

Where do photography and film fit in? Because they are recording arts, they cover essentially the entire range of this classical spectrum. Photography, which is a special case of film, (stills rather than movies), naturally situates itself in the pictorial area of the spectrum, but it has the capability of fulfilling functions in the practical and environmental areas to the left of the position. Film, in general, covers a range from practical (as a technical invention it is an important scientific tool) through environmental, on through pictorial, dramatic, and narrative to music. Although we know it best as one of the dramatic arts, film is strongly pictorial, which is why films are collected more often in art museums than in libraries; it also has a much stronger narrative element than any of the other dramatic arts, a characteristic recognized by filmmakers ever since D.W. Griffith, who pointed to Charles Dickens as one of his precursors. And because of its clear, organized rhythms, as well as its soundtrack, it has close connections with the musical arts. Finally, in its more abstract incarnations, film is strongly environmental as well.

This spectrum of abstraction is only one way to organize the artistic experience; it is not in any sense a law. The dramatic area of the spectrum could easily be subsumed under pictorial and narrative; the practical arts can be combined with the environmental. What is important here is simply to provide an index to the range of abstraction, from the most mimetic arts to the least mimetic.

The second, more modern way to classify the various arts depends on the relationship between the work, the artist, and the observer. This triangular image of the artistic experience directs our attention away from the work itself, to the medium of communication. The degree of abstraction enters in here, too, but only insofar as it affects the relationship between the artist and the observer. We are interested now not in the quality of the work itself, but in the mode of its transmission.

Organized this way, the system of artistic communication would look something like Diagram B. The vertical axis constitutes the immediate experience of an art; the horizontal, the transmission or narration of it. Artifacts, pictorial representations and pictorial records (that area above the horizontal axis) occupy space rather than time. Performances, literature and film records are more concerned with time than with space. (In Diagram A, the space arts occupy the left-hand side of

Figure 1-1. Edward Dayes's painting *Queen Square, London, 1786* offers striking similarities with. . .

the spectrum, the time arts the right.) Note that any single art occupies not a point in Diagram B but rather an area. A painting, for example, is both an artifact and a representation. A building is not only an artifact but also partially a representation and occasionally a performance. (Architectural critics often use the language of drama to describe the experience of a building; as we move through it our experience of it takes

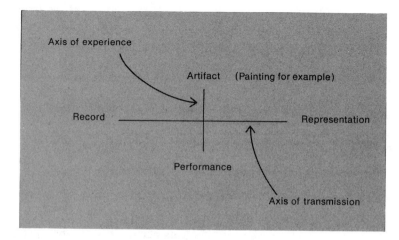

Diagram B

Figure 1-2. . . . this landscape from Stanley Kubrick's *Barry Lyndon*, set in the eighteenth century. Film naturally draws on the historical traditions of the older arts. (*Frame enlargement.*)

place in time.) The recording arts, moreover, often use elements of performance and representation.

The spectrum in Diagram A gives us an index to the degree of abstraction inherent in an art; in other words, it describes the actual relationship between an art and its subject matter. The graph of Diagram B gives us a simplified picture of the various modes of discourse available to the artist. There is one final aspect of the artistic experience that should be investigated: what the French call "rapports de production" (the relationships of production). How and why does art get produced? How and why is it consumed?

Here is the "triangle" of the artistic experience:

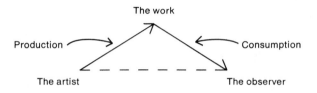

Examination of the relationship between the artist and the work yields theories of the production of art, while analysis of the relationship between the work and the observer gives us theories of its consumption.

(The third leg of the triangle, artist—observer, is potential rather than actual.)

Whether we approach the artistic experience from the point of view of production or of consumption, there is a set of determinants that give a particular shape to the experience. Each of them serves a certain function, and each in turn yields its own general system of criticism. Here is an outline of the determinants, their functions, and the systems of criticism they support:

DETERMINANT:	Sociopolitical	Psychological	Technical	Economic
FUNCTION:	utilitarian	expressive	art for art's sake	careerist product
SYSTEM OF CRITICISM:	ethical/ political	psycho-analytical	esthetic/ formalist	infrastructure

These determinants of the rapports de production function in most human activities, but their operation is especially evident in the arts, since it is there that the economic and political factors that tend to dominate most other activities are more in balance with the psychological and technical factors.

Historically, the political determinant is primary: it is this factor that decides how an art or work of art is used socially. Consumption is more important here than production. Greek and Roman theories of art as an epistemological activity fit under this category, especially when the quest for knowledge is seen as quasi-religious. The ritualistic aspect of the arts as celebrations of the community is at the heart of this approach. The political determinant defines the relationship between the work of art and the society that nurtures it.

The psychological determinant, on the other hand, is introspective, focusing our attention not on the relationship between the work and the world at large, but on the connections between the work and the artist, and the work and the observer. The profound psychological effect of a work of art has been recognized ever since Aristotle's theory of catharsis. In the early twentieth century, during the great age of psychoanalysis, most psychological analysis centered on the connection between the artist and the work. The work was seen as an index of the psychological state of its author—sort of a profound and very elaborate

Rorschach test. Recently, however, psychological attention has shifted to the connection between the work and its consumer, the observer.

The technical determinant governs the language of the art. Given the basic structure of the art—the particular qualities of oil paint, for example, versus tempera or acrylics—what are the limits of the possibilities? How does the translation of an idea into the language of the art affect the idea? What are the thought-forms of each particular artistic language? How have they shaped the materials the artist utilizes? These questions are the province of the technical determinants. The recording arts, because they are grounded in a much more complex technology than the other arts, are especially susceptible to this kind of analysis. Chapter 2 will discuss these factors in depth. But even seemingly untechnological arts like the novel are deeply influenced by technical determinants. The novel, for example, could not exist in the form we know today without the invention of the printing press.

Finally, all arts are inherently economic products and as such must eventually be considered in economic terms. Again, film and the other recording arts are prime examples of this phenomenon. Like architecture, they are both capital-intensive and labor-intensive; that is, they involve large expenditures of money and they often require large numbers of workers.

These four sets of determinants reveal themselves in new relationships at each stage of the artistic process. The technological and economic determinants form the basis for any art. The language of the art and its techniques exist before the artist decides to use them. Moreover, each art is circumscribed by certain economic realities. Film, because it is a very expensive art, is especially susceptible to distortion in this respect. The elaborate economic infrastructure of film—the complex rules of production, distribution, and consumption that underlie the art—set forth strict limitations, a fact that is often ignored in analyses. These economic factors, in turn, are related to certain political and psychological uses to which an art can be put. As an economic commodity, for example, film can often best be understood as selling a service that is essentially psychological in nature: we most often go to movies for the emotional effects they provide.

Artists, confronted with these various determinants, make choices within these sets of established possibilities, occasionally breaking new ground, most often reorganizing and recombining existing factors. As we move down the other leg of the artistic triangle, the determinants reveal themselves in new relationships. Once the work of art has been completed it has, in a sense, a life of its own. It is, first of all, an economic product to be exploited. This exploitation results in certain psychological effects. The end product, as the influence of the film spreads, is political. No matter how apolitical the producer of the work of art may seem, every work has political relevance of some sort.

Historically, the political and psychological determinants have been recognized as important factors in the artistic experience since classical times. In his *Ars Poetica,* for example, Horace declared that the criteria for a work were that it be both utile et dulce, "useful" and "sweet," or "enjoyable." The utilitarian value of the work is governed by the political determinant, its enjoyability by the psychological.

Only recently, however, has serious attention been paid to the technical and economic determinants of the work of art. The approach of semiology is to study arts and media as languages or language systems—technical structures with inherent laws governing not only what is "said" but also how it is "said." Semiology attempts to describe the codes and systems of structure that operate in cultural phenomena. It does this by using a linguistic model; that is, the semiology of film describes film as a "language."

Dialectical criticism, on the other hand, studies the arts in their economic context. Pioneered by the Frankfurt school of German philosophers in the 1930s and 1940s—especially Walter Benjamin, T. W. Adorno, and Max Horkheimer—dialectical criticism analyzes the direct relationships between the work, the artist, and the observer as they are expressed in terms of economic and political structures. The addition of these two modern approaches to the arts—semiology and dialectics—gives us a fuller and more precise understanding of the complex structure of the artistic experience.

It also allows us more freedom in defining its limits. While the image of the artist as priest or prophet reigned, there was no way to disconnect the experience of the work from the production of it. Art depended on artists. But when we recognize the technical and linguistic roots of esthetics, we are more inclined to approach the artistic experience from the point of view of the consumer. In other words, we are free to divorce ourselves from artist/priests and develop a "protestant" theory of art. We have already admitted the practical arts of design into the pantheon. We can go further.

One of the most obvious candidates for admission to the spectrum of the arts is sports. Most sports activities adapt the basic dramatic structure of protagonist/antagonist and can therefore be viewed in dramatic terms. That the "plot" is not preordained simply increases its possibilities and the element of suspense. That the basic "theme" is repeated every time a game is played only reinforces the ritualistic aspects of the drama. Likewise, most sports activities share many of the values of

Figure 1-3. There are two ways to spend exorbitant amounts of money on making movies. For *Apocalypse Now* (above), Francis Ford Coppola reinvented the Vietnam War with the proverbial cast of thousands. The film cost upwards of $30 million in the mid-seventies. The first *Superman* film (below) had a relatively limited cast and no expensive stars except for Marlon Brando, whose salary was dwarfed by the film's quoted $50 million budget. The money—ostensibly—was spent on "special effects" technology, and the biggest cost overrun, reportedly, was connected with the mechanism that allowed Christopher Reeve and Margot Kidder (pictured here) to fly.

dance. Media have not only permitted the recording of sports events for future study and enjoyment but have also significantly decreased the distance between athletes and observers and therefore have heightened our sense of the choreographic aspect of most sports. Imagine a stranger totally unfamiliar with either dance or gymnastics being confronted with an example of each. There is no element of the activities themselves that would permit a differentiation from the point of view of the observer. That sports are "unintentional" (that is, that they are not performed to make a point) simply increases the potential variety of our experience of them.

There are other areas of human endeavor that, like sports, take on new significance when we approach them from the point of view of consumption rather than production—consumables, for example. We experience food and drink (and perfume and possibly other sensual devices) in much the same way that we experience that most esthetic of arts, music. The metaphors we have used to describe the latter (ever since Shakespeare in *Twelfth Night* suggested that "music be the food of love") reinforce this close comparison. True, the quantity of thought in food or drink is often exceedingly low; it is difficult to make a "statement" in, say, the language of green vegetables. But that is only to note that our senses of taste, smell, and touch are different in kind from our senses of sight and hearing. The element of craft in the creation of food or drink is no less sophisticated ideally than it is in music or drawing.

Like music, the art of food and drink comes close to a purely synesthetic experience. One sign of this is that our normal mode of experience of both differs in kind from the narrative arts. We consume music, like food, regularly and repeatedly. Having heard Mozart's Piano Concert #23 once, having drunk a single bottle of Chassagne-Montrachet 1978, we do not think that we have exhausted their possibilities. We also do not think to censure either the concerto or the wine because we cannot discover " meaning" in it. If the pure esthetic is a valid criterion for art, then consumables should be admitted to the spectrum.

What this theory of the art of food is meant to suggest, of course, is that the function of the observer or consumer in the process of art is every bit as important as the function of the artist/producer. If we do not admit wine or baseball to the spectrum of accepted arts, it is not the fault of the producers of those works, but rather a collective decision on the part of consumers—a decision that can be rescinded.

There is a second corollary: if the sum total of the artistic experience includes the consumer as well as the producer, and if we express it as a product:

PRODUCTION × CONSUMPTION

then a novel way of increasing the sum presents itself. Heretofore, when evaluating a work of art, we have concentrated on the production factor. We have judged only the artist's contribution, usually measured against an artificial ideal:

$$\frac{\text{ACHIEVEMENT}}{\text{REQUIREMENT}}$$

a quotient that may have some value in judging other economic activities of a more practical nature (the production of floor waxes or screwdrivers, for example) but that seems to me to be specious as a system of artistic evaluation, since it depends for its validity on the denominator, an artificial "requirement" arrived at arbitrarily. But we can just as easily increase the experience of art by increasing the factor of consumption, both in quality and in quantity.

In quantitative terms, the more people who are exposed to a work of art, the more potential effect it has. In qualitative terms, the observer/consumer does have it within his power to increase the sum value of the work by becoming a more sophisticated, creative, or sensitive participant in the process. This is not a new idea in practice, although it may be so in theory. Indeed, film itself is especially rich in this sort of activity. Film buffs, after all, have trained themselves to discern the thematic, esthetic, even political values inherent in, say, the films of minor directors such as Jacques Tourneur or Archie Mayo. At best, such buffs are the cutting edge of criticism for general students of the subject; at worst, they have discovered a way to extract greater value from poor ore than the rest of us. This is the new ecology of art.

Artists themselves are well aware of the potential of this new, responsive relationship. Found art, found poetry, aleatoric theatre, musique concrète, all are based on an understanding of the potential power of the observer to multiply the value of artistic experience. What the artist does in each of these instances is to act as a preobserver, an editor who does not create, but chooses. The poet Denise Levertov has expressed the basis for this enterprise succinctly:

I want to give you
something I've made

some words on a page—as if
to say "Here are some blue beads"

or, "Here's a bright red leaf I found on
the sidewalk" (because

Figure 1-4. FOUND ART. Andy Warhol's eight-hour-long *Empire* (1964) consists of one image: the Empire State Building viewed through Manhattan smog. The office building as art-object. (*Frame enlargements, Warhol Enterprises.*)

to find is to choose, and choice
is made). . . . *

In eight lines she describes not only the essential artistic drive but also the justification for approaching art not from the point of view of the producer but from that of the consumer: "because to find is to choose, and choice is made."

This means not only that observers can increase their perception of made art works, but also that they can act making choices from the dramatic, pictorial, narrative, musical, and environmental materials that present themselves day by day: choice is made. Moreover, there is an ethical aspect to this new artistic equation, for it implies strongly that the observer is the equal of the artist. The word "consumer," then, is misleading, for the observers are no longer passive but active. They participate fully in the process of art.

The significance of this reappraisal of the roles of artist and observer cannot be underestimated. The most difficult challenge the arts have had to sustain in their seven-thousand-year history has been that posed by the techniques of mass production that grew up with the industrial revolution. While the advantage of mass production has been that it makes art no longer an elite enterprise, it has also meant that artists have had to struggle continuously to prevent their work from being transmuted into pure commodity. Only the active participation of the observer at the other end of the process is guarantee against this.

---

*From Denise Levertov, *Here and Now.* Copyright © 1957 by Denise Levertov. Reprinted by permission of City Lights Books.

Where once the work of art was judged purely according to arbitrary ideals and artificial requirements, now it can be seen as "semifinished" material, to be *used* by the observer to complete the artistic process rather than simply consumed. The question now is not, "does this art work meet the standards?" but rather, "how can we use this art work best?" Of course, we are speaking of an ideal here. In reality, most observers of art (whether popular or elite) still passively consume. But the movement toward participatory artistic democracy is growing.

The spectrum of abstraction, the modes of discourse, the range of determinants, the equation of producer and consumer (and its corollary, the democratization of the process)—these various approaches to the study of the arts are not meant to carry the weight of scientific law, but simply as aids to an understanding of the artistic experience. As conceptual structures, they are useful, but there is a danger in taking them too seriously. In the first place, they have been presented bluntly as if they were preordained principles of art. They are not. They were not derived inductively; rather they are deduced from the artistic experience itself, and they are meant to set that experience in its proper context: as a phenomenon that is comparable at the same time as it appears unique. The experience of art comes first; abstract criticism of this sort is, or should be, a secondary activity.

More important, none of these conceptual structures exists in isolation. The elements are all in continual flux and their relationships are dialectical. The interest lies not in whether or not, say, architecture is an environmental or pictorial art but in the fact that these elements exist in a dialectical relationship with each other within the art. This is the central struggle that enlivens it. Likewise, it isn't so important whether we classify film as being in the mode of record or representation. (It does evince elements of representation—and of performance and artifact, as well). What counts is that the contrasts between and among these various modes are the source of power for the art of film.

Generally, the spectrum of abstraction describes the relationships of the arts to their raw material in reality; the system of modes of discourse explains something about the ways in which the arts are transmitted from artist to observer; the structure of determinants describes the main factors that determine the shape of the arts; and the equation of artist and observer suggests new angles of critical approach to the phenomena of the arts.

FILM, RECORDING, AND THE OTHER ARTS

The recording arts comprise an entirely new mode of discourse, parallel to those already in existence. Anything that happens in life that can be seen or heard can be recorded on film, disc, or tape. The "art" of film, then, bridges the older arts rather than fitting snugly into the preexisting spectrum. From the beginning, film and photography were neutral: the media existed before the arts. "The cinema is an invention without a future," Louis Lumière is often quoted as saying. And indeed it might have appeared so in his day. But as this revolutionary mode of discourse was applied, in turn, to each of the older arts, it developed organically. The earliest film experimenters "did" painting in film, "did" the novel, "did" drama, and so forth, and gradually it became evident which elements of those arts worked in filmic situations and which did not. In short, the art of film developed by a process of replication. The neutral template of film was laid over the complex systems of the novel, painting, drama, and music to reveal new truths about certain elements of those arts. In fact, if we disregard for the moment the crudity of early recording processes, the majority of the elements of those arts worked very well in film. Indeed, for the last hundred years the history of the arts is tightly bound up with the challenge of film. As the recording arts drew freely from their predecessors, so painting, music, the novel, stage drama—even architecture—had to redefine themselves in terms of the new artistic language.

FILM, PHOTOGRAPHY, AND PAINTING

"Moving pictures" are on the surface most closely parallel to the pictorial arts. Until quite recently, film could compete directly with painting only to a limited extent; it wasn't until the late 1960s that film color was sophisticated enough to be considered more than marginally useful as a tool. Despite this severe limitation, the effects of photography and film were felt almost immediately, for the technological media were clearly seen to surpass painting and drawing in one admittedly limited but nevertheless vital respect: they could record images of the world directly. Certainly, the pictorial arts have other functions besides precise mimesis, but ever since the early renaissance mimesis had been a primary value in pictorial esthetics. To people for whom travel was a difficult and risky business, the reproduction of landscape scenes was fascinating and the portrait an almost mystical experience. Inundated now by myriad snapshots, mugshots, newspaper photos, and picture postcards, we tend to downplay this function of the pictorial arts.

Figure 1-5. Daguerreotype by William Shew, circa 1845–50. Although now in poor condition, this portrait still shows the fine detail and range of tones of which Daguerre's process was capable. (*Original size: 3⅛" by 2⅝". Collection, The Museum of Modern Art. New York. Gift of Ludwig Glaeser.*)

Very soon after the invention of a viable means of recording a photographic image was announced to the world on January 7, 1839 in a lecture by François Arago to the French Academy of Sciences the portrait became its chief area of exploitation. The Daguerreotype allowed thousands of ordinary people to achieve the kind of immortality that had hitherto been reserved to an elite. The democratization of the image had begun. Within a few years, thousands of portrait galleries had come into being. But Daguerre's invention was incomplete; it produced an image, but it could not reproduce itself. Only a month after the announcement of Daguerre's unique system, William Henry Fox Talbot described how an image could be reproduced by recording a negative photographic image in the camera and using that to produce, in turn, multiple positives. This was the second important element of the art of photography. When Frederick Scott Archer's collodion process replaced Talbot's rough paper negatives with film, the system of photography, which can both capture images and reproduce them infinitely and precisely, was complete.

Naturally, the new invention of photography was immediately applied to the task where it was most useful: the production of portraits. Painting responded in kind. The years of development and maturation of photography, roughly the 1840s to the 1870s, are just those years in which the theory of painting was quickly developing away from mimesis and toward a more sophisticated expression. Freed from the duty to

Figure 1-6. William Henry Fox Talbot's *Loch Katrine* (Talbottype, c. 1845). The rough paper negative of the Talbottype (or calotype, as it was also known) produced a texture in the image which was not always welcome. The later collodion process, using clear glass negatives, avoided this texture. (*Original size: 6¾" by 8¼". Collection, The Museum of Modern Art, New York. Extended loan from Dr. and Mrs. Irwin Makovsky.*)

imitate reality, painters were able to explore more fully the structure of their art. There is certainly no simple cause-and-effect relationship between the invention of photography and these developments in the history of art. Joseph Turner, for example, was producing "antiphotographic" landscapes thirty years before Daguerre perfected his invention. But their connection is more than coincidental.

More directly, the very quality of the photogrpahic image seems to have had a direct effect on the thinking of painters like the Impressionists (Monet and Auguste Renoir, in particular), who worked to capture the immediate and seemingly accidental quality of the mechanically derived image. In moving away from the idea of a painting as an idealization and toward immediate scientific realism, the Impressionists produced images that must be understood as logically connected with photography. Because the camera now existed, painters were motivated to rediscover the immediacy of the moment and the peculiar quality of light, two factors that loom large in the esthetic formula of still photography. When Monet put a number of these moments side by side, as in his series of paintings of cathedrals and haystacks at different times of the day, he took the next logical step: his painterly "flip-books" are intriguing precursors of the movies.

Still photographers themselves in the mid-nineteenth century also seem on occasion to be looking toward motion—the time element—as the fulfillment of their art. Not long after the portrait and the landscape had established the documentary value of photographs, experimenters like Oscar G. Rejlander and Henry Peach Robinson in England merged the two forms by staging elaborate tableaux not unlike those common in the popular theaters of the day. They used actors and often achieved their effects by painstakingly piecing together collages of negatives. Certainly these photographic dramas are a response to painters' ideas first (they are strongly reminiscent of pre-Raphaelite work), but with the benefit of hindsight we can discern in Rejlander's and Robinson's elaborate images the roots of the dramatic element that was to become paramount once pictures began to move. If Rejlander and Robinson were sentimental pre-Raphaelites, so too was the great director of cinema, D.W. Griffith.

There are many instances of these subtle interrelationships between the developing technology of photography and the established arts of painting and drawing in the nineteenth century, and the next major development in the esthetics of painting, in the early twentieth century, corresponded with the rise of the moving picture. Again, there is no way we can make a precise correlation. It's not as if Marcel Duchamp went to see a showing of The Great Train Robbery, cried, "Aha!" and next day sat down to paint Nude Descending a Staircase. But again, the coincidences cannot be ignored.

From one perspective, the movements of Cubism and Futurism can be seen as direct reactions to the increasing primacy of the photographic image. It's as if artists were saying: since photography does these things so well, we shall turn our attention elsewhere. Cubist painting deliberately eschewed atmosphere and light (the areas in which the Impressionists competed directly—and successfully—with the rising photographers) in order to break radically and irrevocably with the mimetic tradition of Western painting. Cubism marked a significant turning point in the history of all the arts; the artist was freed from a dependence on the existing patterns of the real world and could turn attention to the concept of a work of art separate from its subject.

From another perspective, Cubism was moving parallel with the development of film. In trying to capture multiple planes of perspective on canvas, Picasso, Braque, and others were responding directly to the challenge of film that, because it was a *moving* picture, permitted—even encouraged—complex, ever-changing perspectives. In this sense, *Nude Descending a Staircase* is an attempt to freeze the multiple perspectives of the movies on canvas. Traditional art history claims that the most important influence on Cubism was African sculpture and this is no doubt true, since the Cubists were probably more familiar with those sculptures than with the films of Edwin S. Porter or Georges Méliès, but structurally the relationship with film is intriguing. One of the important elements of Cubism, for example, was the attempt to achieve on canvas a sense of the interrelationship between perspectives. This doesn't have its source in African sculpture, but it is very much like the dialectic of montage—editing—in film. Both Cubism and montage eschew the unique point of view and explore the possibilities of multiple perspective.

The theoretical interrelationship between painting and film continues to this day. The Italian Futurist movement produced obvious parodies of the motion picture; contemporary photographic hyperrealism continues to comment on the ramifications of the camera esthetic. But the connection between the two arts has never again been as sharp and clear as it was during the Cubist period. The primary response of painting to the challenge of film has been the conceptualism that Cubism first liberated and that is now common to all the arts. The work of mimesis has been left, in the main, to the recording arts. The arts of representation and artifact have moved on to a new, more abstract sphere. The strong challenge film presented to the pictorial arts was certainly a function of its mimetic capabilities, but it was also due to the one factor that made film radically different from painting: film moved.

In 1819, John Keats had celebrated the pictorial art's mystical ability to freeze time in an instant in his "Ode On A Grecian Urn."

> Thou still unravish'd bride of quietness,
>   Thou foster child of silence and slow time . . .
> Heard melodies are sweet, but those unheard
>   Are sweeter . . .

Figure 1-7. During the 1870s and 1880s, the experiments of Étienne Jules Marey in France and Eadweard Muybridge in America paved the way for the development of the motion picture camera. Muybridge was particularly interested in the movement of humans and animals. This plate, *Woman Kicking*, was shot with three cameras each with twelve taking lenses, all connected to an electrical clock mechanism switch. The three strips show the same action from side, front, and back views. (*Plate 367, from* Animal Locomotion, *1887. Collotype, 7½" by 20¼". Collection, Museum of Modern Art, New York. Gift of the Philadelphia Commercial Museum.*)

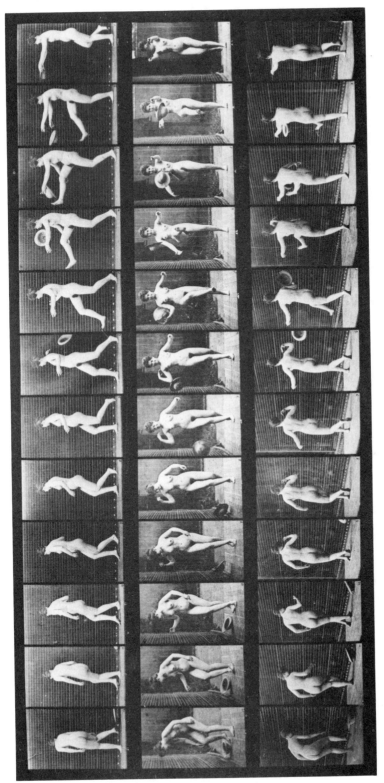

Figure 1-7.

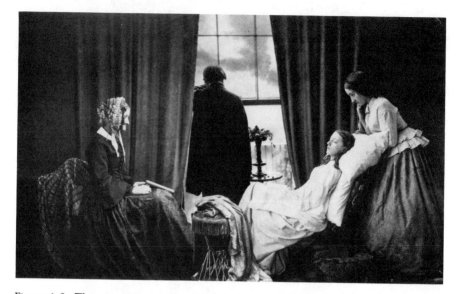

Figure 1-8. The composite photographs of photo-artists like Rejlander and Robinson were in part a response to the relative inflexibility of the medium in the nineteenth century. This particular composition, Henry Peach Robinson's *Fading Away* (1858), is a collage of five negatives. The system allowed the artist to capture foreground details as well as the back light through the window. The composite technique is a direct precursor of modern cinematic matte processes (see pp. 109–13). *International Museum of Photography, George Eastman House.)*

Ah, happy, happy, boughs! that cannot shed
　Your leaves, nor ever bid the Spring adieu
And, happy melodist, unwearied,
　For ever piping songs for ever new;
More happy love! more happy, happy love!
　For ever warm and still to be enjoy'd,
　　For ever panting, and for ever young . . .

There is something magical and intoxicated about the frozen moment of a still work of art that captures life in full flight. But there is an instructive irony in Keats's poem, for it is almost certain that the sort of urn he was hymning had friezelike illustrations, and friezes are among the major attempts of the still pictorial arts to tell a story, to narrate events, to exist, in short, in time as well as space.

In this sense, movies simply fulfill the destiny of painting. Richard Lester made this point nicely in the end credits of *A Funny Thing Happened On the Way to the Forum* in 1966. The film, based on a musical, based on a play by Plautus (thus the classical connection), ends with a shot of Buster Keaton as Erronius running confidently once again around the seven hills of Rome. The image gradually turns into an animated frieze against which the credits are projected. The ultimate freeze-frame ending! Keats's happy boughs, happy piper, and happy, happy lovers likewise in their original incarnation on the surface of the urn would move if they could.

FILM AND THE NOVEL

The narrative potential of film is so marked that it has developed its strongest bond with the novel, not with painting, not even with drama. Both films and novels tell long stories with a wealth of detail and they do it from the perspective of a narrator, who often interposes a resonant level of irony between the story and the observer. Whatever can be told in print in a novel can be roughly pictured or told in film (although the wildest fantasies of a Jorge Luis Borges or a Lewis Carroll might require "special effects" work). The differences between the two arts, besides the obvious and powerful difference between pictorial narration and linguistic narration, are quickly apparent.

First, because film operates in real time, it is more limited. Novels end only when they feel like it. Film is, in general, restricted to what Shakespeare called "the short two hours' traffic of our stage." Popular novels have been a vast reservoir of material for commercial films over the years. In fact, the economics of the popular novel is such now that the possibility of recycling the material as a film is a prime consideration for most publishers. It almost seems, at times, as if the popular novel (as opposed to elite prose art) exists only as a first draft trial for the film. But commercial film still can't reproduce the range of the novel in time. An average screenplay, for example, is 125 to 150 pages in length; the average novel twice that. Almost invariably, details of incident are lost in the transition from book to film. Only the television serial can overcome this deficiency. It carries with it some of the same sense of duration necessary to the large novel. Of all the screen versions of *War and Peace*, for example, the most successful by far seems to me to have been the BBC's twenty-part serialization of the early 1970s; not necessarily because the acting or direction was better than the two- or six-hour film versions (although that is arguable), but because only the serial could reproduce the essential condition of the saga—duration.

At the same time as film is limited to a shorter narration, however, it naturally has pictorial possibilities the novel doesn't have. What can't be transferred by incident might be translated into image. And here we come to the most essential difference between the two forms of narration.

Novels are told by the author. We see and hear only what he wants

Figure 1-9. Marcel Duchamp's *Nude Descending a Staircase, no. 2.* (*1912. oil on canvas, 58" by 35". Philadelphia Museum of Art. Louise and Walter Arensberg Collection.*)

Figure 1-10. The visual conventions of Cubism were utilized by a number of avant-garde film artists. The theory of Cubism has been even more pervasive. Ingmar Bergman's 1966 film *Persona* is an eloquent example of Cubist perspective. The points of view of actress Elizabeth Vogler (Liv Ullmann, left) and her nurse (Bibi Andersson, right) are in such tense balance (as shown here) that at the climax of the film (in another shot) the images of their faces merge together on screen. (*Frame enlargement.*)

us to see and hear. Films are, in a sense, told by their authors too, but we see and hear a great deal more than a director necessarily intends. It would be an absurd task for a novelist to try to describe a scene in as much detail as it is conveyed in cinema. (The contemporary novelist Alain Robbe-Grillet has experimented in just this way in novels like *Jealousy* and *In the Labyrinth*). More important, whatever the novelist describes is filtered through his language, his prejudices, and his point of view. With film we have a certain amount of freedom to choose, to select one detail rather than another.

The driving tension of the novel is the relationship between the materials of the story (plot, character, setting, theme, and so forth) and the narration of it in language; between the tale and the teller, in other words. The driving tension of film, on the other hand, is between the materials of the story and the objective nature of the image. It's as if the author/director of a film were in continual conflict with the scene he is

Figure 1-11. During the 1960s and 1970s, a kind of Realist backlash took place among the older, nonrecording arts. The French "nouveau roman" had close links with cinema, just as American "Hyperrealism" or "Photo-realism" looks to photography for its esthetic base. Here, Philip Pearlstein's *Female Model Reclining on Bentwood Love Seat* (1974, oil on canvas, 48″ by 60″. Allan Frumkin Gallery. Photo: Eric Pollitzer).

shooting. Chance plays a much larger part, and the end result is that the observer is free to participate in the experience much more actively. The words on the page are always the same, but the image on the screen changes continually as we redirect our attention. Film is, in this way, a much richer experience.

But it is poorer, as well, since the persona of the narrator is so much weaker. There has only been one major film, for example, that tried to duplicate the first-person narration so useful to the novel, Robert Montgomery's *Lady in the Lake* (1946). The result was a cramped, claustrophobic experience: we saw only what the hero saw. In order to show us the hero, Montgomery had to to resort to a battery of mirror tricks. Film can approximate the ironies that the novel develops in narration, but it can never duplicate them.

Naturally, then, the novel responded to the challenge of film by

Figure 1-12. Audrey Totter and Robert Montgomery in *Lady in the Lake*. "First-person" narration in film, strictly construed, must make ingenious use of mirrors if the narrator/ hero is to be seen. (*Museum of Modern Art/Film Stills Archive.*)

expanded activity in just this area: the subtle, complex ironies of narration. Like painting, prose narrative has in the twentieth century turned away from mimesis and toward self-consciousness. In the process it has bifurcated. What was once in the nineteenth century a unified experience, the main form of social and cultural expression, and the chosen art of the newly literate middle classes, has in the twentieth century divided into two forms: the popular novel (Irving Wallace, James Michener, Leon Uris, et al.), which is now so closely connected with film that it sometimes begins life as a screenplay; and the elite novel, where the "artistic" avant-garde work is being done.

This high art novel, since James Joyce, has developed along lines parallel to painting. Like painters, novelists learned from the experience of film to analyze their art and conceptualize it. Vladimir Nabokov, Jorge Luis Borges, Alain Robbe-Grillet, Donald Barthelme, and many others write novels about writing novels (as well as other things) just as many painters now paint paintings about painting paintings. Abstraction has progressed from a focus on human experience, to a concern for ideas about that experience, finally to an interest mainly in

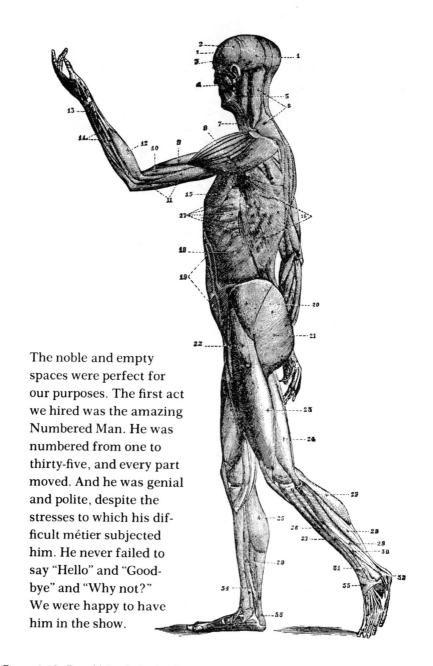

The noble and empty spaces were perfect for our purposes. The first act we hired was the amazing Numbered Man. He was numbered from one to thirty-five, and every part moved. And he was genial and polite, despite the stresses to which his difficult métier subjected him. He never failed to say "Hello" and "Goodbye" and "Why not?" We were happy to have him in the show.

Figure 1-13. Donald Barthelme's "fictions" are not quite novels, not quite poems. He often experiments by integrating old lithographs and drawing with his texts. Here, a page from his story "Flight of Pigeons From the Palace" (*Sadness*, Farrar, Straus & Giroux, 1972). Despite their abstraction, Barthelme's stories have lent themselves to dramatization because they have a visual as well as aural reality.

the esthetics of thought. Jean Genet, playwright and novelist, has said: "Ideas don't interest me so much as the shape of ideas."

In what other respects has the novel been changed by film? Since the days of Defoe, one of the primary functions of the novel, as of painting, was to communicate a sense of other places and people. By the time of Sir Walter Scott, this pictorial service had reached its zenith. After that, as first still, then motion picture photography began to perform this function, the descriptive element of the novel declined. More important, novelists have learned to narrate their stories in the smaller units common to film. Like contemporary playwrights, they think now more often in scenes than in more elaborate acts.

Finally, one of the novel's greatest assets is its ability to manipulate words. Films have words too, of course, but not usually in such profusion and never with the concrete reality of the printed page. If painting under the influence of film has tended toward design, then the novel is approaching poetry as it redoubles its attention to itself and celebrates its material: language.

FILM AND THEATER

On the surface, theatrical film seems most closely comparable to stage drama. Certainly the roots of the commercial film in the early years of this century lie there. But film differs from stage drama in several significant respects: it has the vivid, precise visual potential of the pictorial arts; and it has a much greater narrative capability.

The most salient difference between staged drama and filmed drama, as it is between prose narrative and film narrative, is in point of view. We watch a play as we will; we see a film only as the filmmaker wants us to see it. And in film we also have the potential to see a great deal more. It has become a truism that a stage actor acts with his voice, while a film actor uses his face. Even in the most intimate situation, an audience for a stage play (note the word we use—"audience," hearers— not spectators) has difficulty comprehending all but the broadest gestures. Meanwhile, a film actor, thanks to dubbing, doesn't even require a voice; dialogue can be added later. But the face must be extraordinarily expressive, especially when it is magnified as much as a thousand times in closeups. A film actor will often consider a day well spent if he's accomplished one good "look." When we consider in addition that films can be made with "raw material," nonprofessional actors, even people who aren't aware they're being filmed, the contrasts between stage acting and film acting appear even greater.

Just as important as the difference in acting styles is the contrast

Figure 1-14. "THE LOOK." John Wayne as J. B. Books in Don Siegel's 1976 Western, *The Shootist*. Even in this still photograph, the face speaks volumes.

between dramatic narration in film and on stage. In Shakespeare's time, the unit of construction for the stage was the scene rather than the act. A play consisted of twenty or thirty scenes rather than three to five much longer acts. By the nineteenth century, this had changed. As theater moved from the thrust stage to the proscenium arch, and as realism became an important force, the longer, more verisimilitudinous unit of the act took precedence. During a half-hour act, audiences could suspend their disbelief and enter into the lives of the characters; the shorter unit of the scene made this more difficult.

Film grew up just at the time this sort of stage realism was at its height. And just as painting and the novel had relinquished the function of mimesis to film, so did the stage. The scene returned as the basic unit of construction. Strindberg and others developed an expressionistic (at times almost Cubist) use of the stage space. Pirandello analyzed the structure of stage art in detail, and in the process abstracted the experience of the stage for a generation of future playwrights. By the late twenties, avant-garde theater was in a position to challenge the upstart film seriously. There was no point in realistic stage sets after the style of David Belasco when film could show real locations; no sense in subtlety of gesture when it couldn't be seen past the first row, and audiences could go around the corner to see silent actresses like Gish and Garbo do extraordinary and wonderful things with their faces without seeming to move a muscle. When sound and dialogue joined the image on the screen, film was even more closely comparable to stage drama.

But theater has one advantage over film, and it is a great one: theater is live. If it is true that film can accomplish a great many effects unknown in the theater simply because it is shot discontinuously, it is also true that the people who perform in film are, quite simply, not in contact with the audience.

In their own ways, two very different theorists of theater made use of this incontrovertible fact. In the late twenties and thirties, both Bertolt Brecht and Antonin Artaud (still the most influential theorists of drama in the modern period) developed concepts of theater that depended on the continuing interaction between audience and cast. Artaud's so-called "Theatre of Cruelty" required a more demanding and intimate relationship between performer and observer than had ever before existed in the theater. Artaud's aim was to involve the audience deeply in a direct way, as they never could be in the cinema.

In his manifesto *The Theatre and Its Double* Artaud wrote:

> We abolish the stage and the auditorium and replace them by a single site, without partition or barrier of any kind, which will become the theatre of the action. A direct communication will be re-established between the spectator and the spectacle [p. 93f].

Artaud conceived a kind of frontal assault on the spectator, a total theater in which all the forces of expression would be brought to bear. He redefined the language of the theater as consisting

> of everything that occupies the stage, everything that can be manifested and expressed materially on a stage and that is addressed first of all to the senses instead of being addressed primarily to the mind as is the language of words . . . such as music, dance, plastic art, pantomime, mimickry, gesticulation, intonation, architecture, lighting, and scenery [pp. 38–39].

We can see here that the new language of the stage as conceived by Artaud is influenced by the language of film, even as it counters the rising dominance of the new art. Film, because it had no set rules, no traditions, no academicians, had logically and quickly discovered the value of each of the components Artaud suggests: plastic art, music, dance, pantomime, et cetera. Once again, one of the older arts finds itself in a love-hate relationship with the new technology. But Artaud never loses sight of his one significant advantage: "theatre is the only place in the world where a gesture, once made, can never be made the same way twice" [p. 75].

Brecht took the opposite tack. His theory of Epic Theatre is more complex—and some would say more sophisticated—than Artaud's Theatre of Cruelty. Recognizing the same basic value as Artaud—the immediacy and intimacy of the theatrical performance—Brecht thought to re-create the relationship between actor and audience as a dialectic. No longer would the audience willingly suspend disbelief. That is so much easier in a movie theater.

Epic Theatre, Brecht wrote,

> turns the spectator into an observer, but arouses his capacity for action, forces him to take decisions. . . [In the old, dramatic theater] the spectator is in the thick of it, shares the experience, the human being is taken for granted, he is unalterable, [while in the new, Epic Theatre] the spectator stands outside, studies, the human being is the object of the inquiry, he is alterable and able to alter. . .[Brecht on Theatre, p. 37].

All this is accomplished by a device Brecht labeled the Estrangement Effect (Die Verfremdungseffekt), whose object, in Brecht's words, was to "alienate the social gest underlying every incident. By social gest is meant the mimetic and gestural expression of the social relationships prevailing between people" [p. 139]. This is clearly more than just a theory of drama. Brecht's Epic Theatre and its Verfremdungseffekt can be applied to a wide range of arts, not least of which is film itself. And, indeed, Brecht's ideas have a major place in the development of film theory.

What Brecht did for the theater was to heighten the spectator's participation, but in an intellectual way, whereas Artaud had specifically rejected intellectual approaches in favor of theater as "a means of inducing trances." Both theories, however, were distinctly antimimetic.

Because of their structural similarities, theater and film interact more often than do other arts. If in France it is true that many of the more celebrated contemporary novelists are filmmakers (Alain Robbe-Grillet, Marguerite Duras), in England, Italy, Germany, and the U.S. (to a lesser extent) people who work in film are more likely to split their careers between screen and stage. The stage (together with dance) is the only art that regularly uses film per se within its own context. The relationship has been fruitful. As the theories of Brecht and Artaud have matured over the last forty years, the theater has developed along the lines they forecast; no radically new theories of theater have superseded them. From Artaud's work, contemporary theater gets its renewed interest in the ritual aspect of the dramatic experience and the sense of communal celebration that has always been basic to theater. Much of this is accomplished by the intense emphasis of contemporary dramatic theater on mise en scène as opposed to text. On the other hand, contemporary theater also looks toward the spoken word as a source of energy. British playwrights especially have developed the concept of theater as conversation that has roots in Brecht. Harold Pinter, John Osborne, Edward Bond, and Tom Stoppard, among others, have created a theater of verbal performance that succeeds on an intimate stage as it never could on film.

The close parallelism between the forms of theater and feature film could very well have meant disaster for the older art. Arts have "died" before: the narrative or epic poem was superannuated by the invention of the novel in the seventeenth century, for example. But theater has responded to the challenge of film with a new vitality, and the interaction between the two forms of art has proved to be one of the major sources of creative energy in the mid-twentieth century.

FILM AND MUSIC

Film's relationship with music is altogether more complex. Until the development of the recording arts, music held a unique position in the spectrum of the arts. It was the one art in which time had strict and real significance. Novels and theater exist in time, it is true, but the observer controls the "time" of a novel and, as important as rhythms are in the performing arts, they are nevertheless not strictly controlled. A playwright or director can indicate pauses, but these are, generally speaking, only the crudest of time signatures. Music, the most abstract of arts, allows a precise control of the time element. If melody is the narrative facet of music, and rhythm the unique, temporal element, then harmony in a sense is the synthesis of the two. Our system of musical notation indicates this relationship. Three notes read from left to right form a melody. When they are set in the context of a time signature, rhythms are overlaid on the melody. When we rearrange them vertically, however, harmony is the result.

Painting can set up harmonies and counterpoint both within a picture and between pictures, but there is no time element. Drama occasionally experiments with counterpoint—Eugene Ionesco's doubled dialogues are a good example—but only for minor effects. Music, however, depends on the interrelationship between "horizontal" lines of melody, set in rhythms, and "vertical" sets of harmonies.

Abstractly, film offers the same possibilities. The mechanical nature of the medium allows strict control of the time line: narrative "melo-

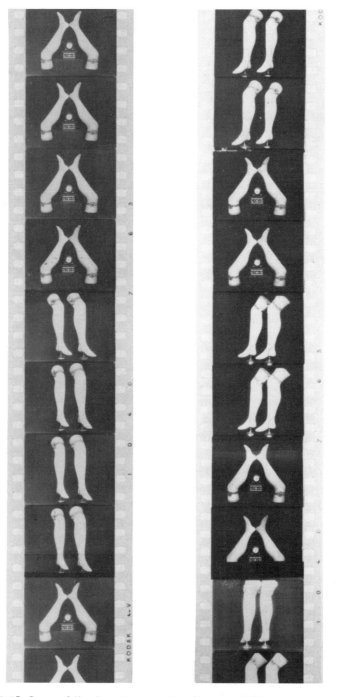

Figure 1-15. Strips of film from Léger's *Ballet Mécanique* (1924–25). Each group of four frames would last ¹/₆ second on screen. The effect would be of a rhythmic double exposure. (MOMA/ FSA *Life-size*.)

dies" can now be controlled precisely. In the frame, events and images can be counterposed harmonically. Filmmakers began experimenting with the musical potential of the new art very early on. Ever since René Clair's *Entr'acte* (1924) and Fernand Léger's *Ballet Mécanique* (1924–25), in fact, abstract or "avant garde" film has depended on musical theory for much of its effect. Even before sound, filmmakers had begun to work closely with musicians. Hans Richter's *Vormittagsspuk (Ghosts Before Breakfast,* 1928) had a score by Hindemith, played live. Walter Ruttmann's *Berlin—Symphony of a City* (1927) had a live symphonic score as well.

Music had quickly become an integral part of the film experience; silent films were normally "performed" with live music. What is important to note is that the experimental filmmakers of the silent period were already discovering the musical potential of the image itself. By the late 1930s Sergei Eisenstein, for his film *Alexander Nevsky,* constructed an elaborate scheme to correlate the visual images with the score by the noted composer Prokofiev. In this film as in a number of others, such as Stanley Kubrick's *2001: A Space Odyssey* (1968), music often determines images.

Because film is projected normally at a rate of twenty-four frames per second, the filmmaker has even more precise control over rhythms than the musician. The shortest semihemidemiquaver that could be written in the Western system of notation would last $1/32$ of a second—but it would be impossible to play notes at that rate. The $1/24$ of a second unit, which is the lowest common denominator of film, effectively exceeds the quickest rhythms of Western music. The most sophisticated system of rhythm in music, the Indian tals, approaches the basic unit of film rhythm as an upper limit. We are ignoring, of course, music that is produced mechanically or electronically. Even before systems of sound recording had matured, the player piano offered an opportunity to musicians to experiment with rhythmic systems that were humanly impossible. Conlon Nancarrow's "Studies for Player Piano" (the earliest dating from 1948) are modern explorations of these possibilities.

Film thus utilizes a set of musical concepts expressed in visual terms: melody, harmony, and rhythm are long established values in film art. While film itself has had no particularly strong effect on the older art of music, the techniques of sound recording, specifically, have revolutionized it. The influence was felt in two waves.

The invention of the phonograph in 1877 radically altered the dissemination of music. No longer was it necessary to attend a performance, a privilege that was, over the centuries, limited to a very small elite. Bach's *Goldberg Variations,* written as bedtime music for a single wealthy individual, Count Kaiserling, former Russian Ambassador at the court of the Elector of Saxony, to be played by his personal harpsichordist, Johann Gottlieb Goldberg, were now accessible to millions of people who couldn't afford private musicians on twenty-four-hour call. Recordings and, later, radio broadcasts quickly became the main means of the dissemination of music, parallel with performance but superseding it, and this had a profound effect on the nature of the art. Just as the invention of movable type had opened up literature to the masses, so recordings democratized music. The historical significance cannot be underestimated. There was a negative aspect to the mechanical reproduction of music, it is true. The importance of folk music, the art people created for themselves in the absence of professional musicians, was greatly attenuated. But this was a small price to pay for the vast new channels of dissemination and, in fact, the new musical literacy that recordings helped to create later redounded to the benefit of the popular musical arts, which have in the twentieth century become the focal point of the musical world as they never were in earlier times.

While the invention of the phonograph had a profound sociological effect on music, it had a very minor technical effect. There were good technological reasons for this having to do with the limitations of Edison's system, which will be discussed in the next chapter. As a result, it was not until the late 1940s and early 1950s—when magnetic tape began to replace the phonograph record as the main means of recording, and electrical transcription yielded to electronic methods—that music technique came under the influence of the recording arts. Again, the effect was revolutionary. Musicians had been experimenting with electronic instruments for years before the development of magnetic tape, but they were still bound by the limits of performance. Tape freed them, and allowed the possibility of editing music. Film soundtracks, which were optical rather than magnetic, had predated tape by twenty years, but in the context of film they had always been relegated to practical functions.

Once tape entered the recording studio, sound recording was no longer simply a means of preserving and disseminating a performance: it now became a main focus of creativity. Recording is now so much an integral part of the creation of music that even popular music (to say nothing of avant-garde and elite music) has become since the early fifties a creature of the recording studio rather than performance. The Beatles' *Sergeant Pepper's Lonely Hearts Club Band* (1967), a milestone in the development of the practical recording arts, was not reproducible in performance. There had been many earlier examples of this shift of focus, dating back at least as early as the popular records of Les Paul and

Mary Ford in the early fifties, but the Beatles' record is generally regarded as the coming of age of recording as one of the primary creative musical forces. The balance has altered so radically that "performances" of popular music (to say nothing of avant-garde performances) now often integrate recordings. If the techniques of visual recording had had as great an effect on theater, then a standard popular theatrical performance today would consist in large part of film and avant-garde theater would consist almost entirely of film!

Clearly, the relationship between sound recording and the musical arts is very complex. We have described only the bare outlines of the new dialectic here. It may be most significant that, unlike the technique of image recording, the technique of sound recording was quickly integrated with the art of music. Film was seen from the very beginning as a separate art from theater and painting and the novel; but sound recording even today is still subsumed under the category of music. Partially, this is the result of the mode of recording—discs—that pertained until twenty years ago. Unlike film, discs could simply record and reproduce their material, not re-create it. But the development of tape and electronic technology added an element of creativity to sound recording. If anything, sound recording is now more flexible and sophisticated than image recording. It may be only a matter of time before sound recording is seen as a separate art. If radio had survived the invention of television, this would have happened sooner, but coincidentally, just as sound recording was emerging as an art in its own right around 1950, radio art was being submerged by television. It is only now beginning to recover its flexibility. Significantly, sound recording as an integral component of cinema also languished during those years and has itself only recently begun to re-emerge. Ideally, sound should be the equal of image in the cinematic equation, not subservient, as it is now. In short, film has only begun to respond to the influence of the art of music.

FILM AND THE ENVIRONMENTAL ARTS

If there is one category of art that has been relatively immune to the influence of film and the recording arts, it is architecture. Unlike the novel, painting, and music, the environmental arts have not responded directly to the new mode of discourse. In fact, we can discern a more fruitful relationship between drama and architecture than between film and architecture. Not only has the function of the theater as a building had a direct effect on the art produced inside it, but architectural constructions themselves have become a part of performance. This phenomenon dates back at least as far as the Masques of the early seventeenth century, whose elaborate "strange devices"—especially those of the architect Inigo Jones—held pride of place. More recently, the movement toward environmental theater, with its concurrent theory that the audience should participate physically in the space of a production as well as in its narration, has led to an even more intimate union of drama and theatrical architecture.

But, as Brecht and Artaud understood, the Achilles heel of film art lies precisely here: we cannot enter into the world of the image physically. Images of film can surround us, overwhelm us psychologically, but we are still structurally separate. Even the most advanced systems of three-dimensional photography, such as holography, won't change this fact. We cannot interract with film. Meanwhile, architecture—more than any other art—insists on and requires interaction. Its function is to serve practical aims, and its form follows from that.

So the relationship between film and the environmental arts remains metaphorical rather than direct. Film can give us a record of architecture (as it can give us a record of any of the other arts), but this hardly constitutes a dialectical relationship. The theory of film montage may have had some slight effect on architectural theory, but it's safe to say this influence was minimal, at best. Likewise, although our sense of film as a "constructed" work is strong, it is the metaphor of construction rather than the actual craft of building design that governs it.

But while this has been true in the past, the future may hold some surprises. "Pop" architecture—the Las Vegas esthetic—comes closer to comparing with the structure of cinema than does the kind of elite architecture with formal artistic intentions that has until recently occupied exclusively the attention of architectural critics and historians. As a social and political expression of the culture, architecture may be more closely parallel with film than it seems at first glance. In the late sixties (especially in *2 or 3 Things I Know About Her,* 1966) Jean-Luc Godard first exlored these admittedly tenuous connections. More recently, architect/critics Robert Venturi, Denise Scott Brown, and Stephen Izenour have approached the film/architecture connection from the opposite point of view. In an exhibition they designed called "Signs of Life: Symbols in the American City" (Renwick Gallery, Washington, D.C., 1976), the Venturis utilized a system of electronically controlled painting developed by the 3M Company to produce life-size, vividly realistic evocations of city scenes that they then integrated with actual constructions. The ramifications of this technique could be considerable. Insofar as architecture is an art of environment rather than simply a system of construction, the objective visual component might very well be susceptible to photographic—and possibly cinematographic—production. Thomas Wilfred's landmark "lumia" light sculptures, as well as the "light shows" common as accompaniment to rock music performances in the late sixties, also point to interesting applications of cinematic techniques to environmental situations.

While it's hard to see how the integration of photography and architecture could lead to anything more than simple trompe-l'oeil effects, this growing concern with the artificiality of the visual environment has been foreshadowed by contemporary developments in what we might call "sound architecture." Just as architects have always been concerned with the physical environment we experience, usually as it is transmitted to us visually, so now the aural environment is drawing their attention. The near ubiquitous Muzak of modern elevators, shopping centers, and office buildings is only the crudest example of aural environment. The "Environment" series of electronically constructed or modified recordings produced by Syntonic Research, Inc. offer more elaborate examples. Computer-designed reconstructions of natural sounds such as ocean waves, rain, and birdsong, they provide psychologically affective aural backgrounds. Some recent experimental video art is also basically environmental in intent.

Socially, the omnipresence of radio and many types of television perform a similar function: they serve as backgrounds, aurally and visually, against which we play out our everyday lives. At present, the art of such cultural elements is of a very low grade. But the time may not be far off when architects become deeply involved in the sort of environment that can be produced by recordings—both aural and visual—and these modes become integrated as a matter of course with the physical, concrete design of our environment.

THE STRUCTURE OF ART

Film, sound recording, and video, then, have had profound effects on the nature and development of nearly all the other, older arts and have in turn to a considerable extent been shaped by them. But while the spectrum of arts is wide, the domain of film and the recording arts is even wider. Film, records, and tapes are media: that is, agencies or channels of communication. While art may be the main use to which they are put, it is clearly not the only use. As we shall see in the next chapter, film is an important scientific tool that has opened up new areas of knowledge. It also provides the first significant general means of communication since the invention of writing more than seven thousand years ago.

As a medium, film needs to be considered as a phenomenon very much like language. It has no codified grammar, it has no enumerated vocabulary, it doesn't even have very specific rules of usage, so it is very clearly not a language *system* like written or spoken English; but it nevertheless does perform many of the same communicative functions as language does. It would then be very useful if we could describe the way film operates with a degree of logical precision. As we shall see in Chapter 5, the desire to describe a rational—even scientific—structure for film has been one of the main motivations of film theorists for more than half a century.

Recently, semiotics has presented an interesting approach to the logical description of the languagelike phenomenon of film and the other recording arts. The linguist Ferdinand de Saussure laid the groundwork for semiology in the early years of this century. Saussure's basic, yet elegant, idea was to view language as simply one of a number of systems of codes of communication. Linguistics, then, is simply one area of the more general study of systems of signs—semiology, or semiotics. Film may not have grammar, then, but it does have systems of codes. It does not, strictly speaking, have a vocabulary, but it does have a system of signs. It also uses the systems of signs and codes of a number of other communicative systems. Any musical code, for instance, can be represented in the music of film. Most painterly codes, and most narrative codes, can also be represented in film. Much of the preceding discussion of the relationship between film and the other arts could be quantified by describing the codes that exist in those other arts that can be translated into film as opposed to those that cannot. Robert Frost once described poetry as "what you can't translate." Similarly, the genius of an art may be just those codes that don't work well in any other art.

Yet while the code system of semiotics goes a long way toward making possible a more precise description of how film does what it does, it is limited in that it more or less insists that we reduce film, like language, to basic discrete units that can be quantified. Like linguistics, semiotics is not especially well adapted to describing the complete, metaphysical effect of its subject. It describes the language, or system of communication, of film very well. But it does not easily describe the artistic activity of film. A term borrowed from literary criticism may be useful in this respect: "trope."

Generally, in literary criticism the term "trope" is used to mean "figure of speech": that is, a "turn" of phrase in which language is bent so that it reveals more than literal meanings. The concepts of code and sign describe the elements of the "language" of an art; the concept of trope is necessary to describe the often very unusual and illogical way those codes and signs are used to produce new, unexpected meanings. We are concerned now with the active aspect of art. "Trope," from the Greek *Tropos* (via Latin *Tropus*) originally meant "turn," "way," or "manner," so even etymologically the word suggests an activity rather than a static definition.

Rhythm, melody, and harmony, for example, are essential codes of music. Within each of these codes there are elaborate sets of subcodes. A syncopated beat, such as that essential to the idiom of jazz, can be considered as a subcode. But the peculiar, exciting, idiosyncratic syncopations of Thelonius Monk's music are tropes. There is no way to quantify them scientifically; and that, precisely, is the genius of Thelonius Monk. Likewise, in painting, form, color, and line are generally regarded as the basic elements of the artistic system. Hard edges and soft edges are subcodes of that system. But the precise, exquisite lines of a painting by Ingres, or the subtle soft edges of a study by Auguste Renoir, are idiosyncratic tropes. In stage drama, gesture is central to the art, one of its basic codes. The offering of a ringed hand for the kiss of devotion is a specific subcode. But the way Laurence Olivier performs this gesture in *Richard III* is very peculiarly his own: a trope.

The system of an art can generally be described in semiological terms as a collection of codes. The unique activity of an art, however, lies in its tropes. Film can be used to record most of the other arts. It can also translate nearly all the codes and tropes common to narrative, environmental, pictorial, musical, and dramatic arts. Finally, it has a system of codes and tropes all its own, unique to the recording arts.

Its own codes and tropes stem from its complex technology—a thoroughly new phenomenon in the world of art and media. For an understanding of how film is *un*like all the other arts—the second stage of our investigation—it is necessary to take a very close look at that technology, and this is the subject of Chapter 2.

TECHNOLOGY: IMAGE AND SOUND

TWO

ART AND TECHNOLOGY

Every art is shaped not only by political, philosophical, and economic factors, but also by its technology. The relationship isn't always clear: sometimes technological development leads to a change in the esthetic system of the art; sometimes esthetic requirements call for a new technology; often the development of the technology itself is the result of a confluence of ideological and economic factors. But until artistic impulses can be expressed through technology, there is no artifact.

Usually the relationships are crude: the novel never could have come into being without the printing press, but the recent rapid increases in the technology of printing (discussed briefly in Chapter 6) have had little discernible effect on the esthetic development of the novel. What changes have occurred in its three-hundred-year history find their root causes in other historical factors, mainly the social uses of the art. Stage drama was radically altered when new lighting techniques allowed it to be brought indoors and sheltered behind the proscenium arch, but the contemporary reversion to the thrust stage is mainly due not to developments in technology but to ideological factors. Bach played on the harpsichord of his own day sounds quite different from Bach performed on the modern "well-tempered clavier," but Bach is still Bach. The invention of oil paint provided painters with a medium of wonderful versatility, but if oil paint had never been invented, it's likely there would have been other techniques that would have allowed the historical development of painting to proceed along pretty much the same lines. In short, although there has been a communion between art and technology that consists of more than an occasional genius like Leo-

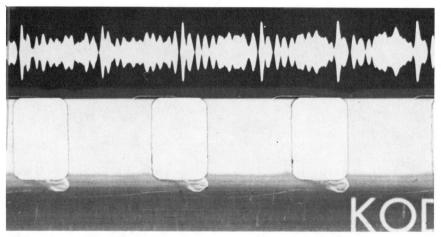

A Soundtrack. Magnification: 6.0x.

B Record groove. Magnification: 2.2x.

C Audiotape. Magnification: 5.3x.

Figure 2-1 AURAL AND VISUAL RECORDING SYSTEMS. In order to record and reproduce sounds and images, recording technology must translate aural and visual information into physical or electronic "language-systems." The variable-area soundtrack (A) translates the frequency (pitch) and amplitude (volume) of sounds into regular patterns of light. The section shown represents one frame of film, or $1/24$ second. The loudest sound is represented by the widest light bands. There are approximately 6.3 cycles for this dominant sound in this $1/24$-second section of soundtrack, so the actual frequency of the sound represented is approximately 150 cycles per second, or "Hertz." This is approximately D below middle C on the piano scale. The variable-area soundtrack is an elegant visualization of wave mechanics. (See Chapter 6, pp. 366, 368).

50

Record grooves (B) translate audio information into physical waveforms rather than light. This section of a modern 33⅓ rpm longplaying disc is approximately 5 cm by 2 cm in reality. Each groove section pictured carries about ¼-second of music (in this case, Duke Ellington), and since this is a stereo record, each groove carries two channels of information, one on each side of the groove.

Magnetic audiotape (C) encodes information eletromagnetically; as a result, the signal cannot be seen here as it can in A and B above. The visible lines are simply signs of wear. The section shown could carry slightly more than ¹/₂₀ second of information at a normal speed of 7½ inches per second. In normal stereo recording this ¼-inch-wide tape might carry four parallel channels.

Visual information is far more complex than aural information and therefore more difficult to encode. In general, visual encoding is more or less binary. In other words, each "bit" of information can have either of two values: "yes" or "no," "black" or "white."

The most flexible of the three common systems of visual encoding is photography. Figure D is an enlargement of a section of standard 8″ × 10″ black-and-white print, 1.5 cm high. The grain is clearly visible. (Remember that in order to reproduce the photograph as you see it, a printer's halftone screen has had to be imposed.)

Figure E shows the same section of the same photograph as it was reproduced in a book. The halftone screen analyzes the variable information present in the photographic grain into binary black-and-white dot patterns. In this case, the screen size was 133 lines per inch. Notice that the white mark in the black area to the right (an imperfection in the photograph) has nearly disappeared in the halftone reproduction.

Figure F shows a section of color television screen. A standard American television screen is com-

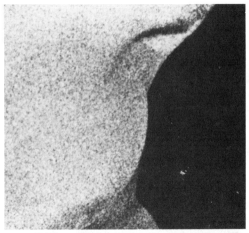
D Photographic grain. Magnification: 4.0x

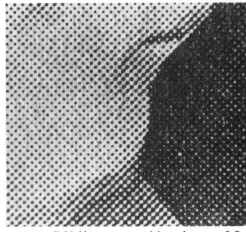
E Halftone screen. Magnification: 5.7x

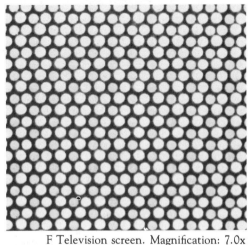
F Television screen. Magnification: 7.0x

posed of 210,000 of these bits of information, red, green, and blue dots arranged in patterns of 30 to 90 lines per inch—much cruder than the halftone screen in E.

nardo da Vinci combining good work in both fields, a communion that belies the modern conception of the two fields as mutually antagonistic, nevertheless one can study the history of painting without ever having gained any knowledge of how oils differ from acrylics, and students of literature can certainly succeed in mastering the basic history of literature without having studied the operation of the linotype or the offset press.

This is not the case with film. The great single artistic contribution of the industrial age, the recording arts—film, sound recording, and photography—are inherently dependent on a complex, ingenious, and ever more sophisticated technology. No one can ever hope to comprehend fully the way their effects are accomplished without a rudimentary understanding of the scientific and systemic procedures that make them possible.

Figure 2-2. This version of the camera obscura reflected the incoming light to a screen at the top of the box so that an artist could trace the image. If the pinhole is sufficiently small, an image will be projected. The optical principle is described in Figure 2-8. (*International Museum of Photography, George Eastman House.*)

IMAGE TECHNOLOGY

The invention of photography in the early nineteenth century marks an important line of division between the pretechnological era and the present. The basic artistic impulses that drive us to mimic nature were the same, essentially, both before and after that time, but the augmented technical capacity to record and reproduce sounds and images of the twentieth century presents us with an exciting new set of choices. Previously we were limited, in a sense, by our own physical abilities: the musician created sounds by blowing or strumming or singing; the painter who captured real images depended entirely on his own eye to perceive them; the novelist and the poet, not engaged in strictly physical arts, were nevertheless limited in describing events or characters by their own powers of observation. The technology of sound and image now offers us the opportunity of recording sounds, images, and

Figure 2-3. The camera lucida consisted of a lens arrangement that enabled the artist to view subject and drawing paper in the same "frame," and thus simply outline the image that seemed projected on the paper. (*International Museum of Photography, George Eastman House.*)

events and transmitting them directly to the observer without the inter-
position of the artist's personality and talents. A new channel of communication has been opened, equal in importance to the development
of written language.

Although the camera did not come into practical use until the early
nineteenth century, efforts to create such a magical tool, which would
record reality directly, dated from much earlier. The camera obscura
(Figure 2-2), the grandfather of the photographic camera, dates from
the Renaissance. Da Vinci had described the principle, and the first
published account of the usefulness of the invention dates from 1558,
the year in which Giovanni Battista della Porta published his book,
Natural Magic. There are even references dating back as far as the
tenth-century Arabic astronomer Al Hazen. The camera obscura (literally "dark room") is based on a simple optical rule, but it it includes all
the elements of the basic contemporary photographic camera except
one: film, the medium on which the projected image is recorded. Louis
Daguerre is usually credited with the first practical development of such
a medium in 1839, but his colleague Joseph Nièpce had done much
valuable work before he died in 1833, and may be credited, as Beaumont Newhall has noted, with the first "successful experiment to fix
the image of nature" in 1827. William Henry Fox Talbot was working
simultaneously along similar lines: modern photography has developed
from his system of negative recording and positive reproduction. Da-

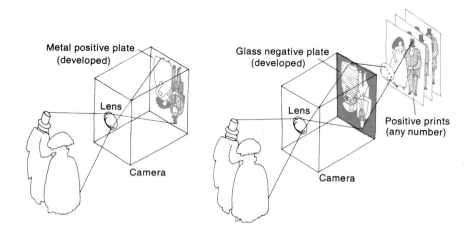

Figure 2-4. PHOTOGRAPHIC SYSTEMS. The negative-positive system (right) of the Tal-
bot-type, Collotype, and modern photography permits infinite reproduction of the
image. The direct positive system of the early Daguerreotype (left) creates a single,
iconic image. Contemporary "instant photograph" systems such as Polaroid SX-70 also
produce direct positives and are therefore comparable to the Daguerreotype.

Figure 2-5. THE ZOETROPE. The cylinder was spun; the images on the inside of the drum were viewed through the slots opposite them, creating the illusion of motion. (MOMA/FSA.)

guerre, whose recording photographic plate was positive and therefore not reproducible (except through being photographed itself), had reached a dead-end; the Daguerreotype marked the end of a line of technological development, not the beginning of one. But Fox Talbot's negative permitted infinite reproductions. The paper negative was soon replaced by the flexible collodion film negative, which not only marked a distinct improvement in the quality of the image but also suggested a line of development for the recording of motion pictures.

Like the still camera, the motion picture camera was not without its antecedents. The Magic Lantern, capable of projecting an image onto a screen, dates from the seventeenth century and was quickly adapted to photographic use in the 1850s. The production of the illusion of motion was made possible in a very crude way by the so-called Magic Discs of the 1830s and the more sophisticated Zoetrope (Fig. 2-5), patented in 1834 by William Horner (although precursors of the Zoetrope may date to antiquity). In the 1870s Eadweard Muybridge, working in California, and Étienne Jules Marey, in France, began their experiments in making photographic records of movement. Emile Reynaud's Praxinoscope (1877) was the first practicable device for projecting successive images on a screen. In 1889, George Eastman applied for a patent on his flexible photographic film, developed for the roll camera, and the last basic element of cinematography was in place. By 1895, all these elements had been combined and movies were born.

SOUND TECHNOLOGY

The technology of sound recording developed more rapidly. Edison's phonograph, which does for sound what the camera/projector system does for images, dates from 1877. In many ways it is a more extraordinary invention than cinematography, since it has no antecedents to speak of. The desire to capture and reproduce still pictures predated the development of moving pictures by many years, but there is no such thing as a "still" sound, so the development of sound recording, of necessity, took place all at once. Equally as important as the phonograph, although not often mentioned in histories of the recording arts, is the telephone of Bell (1876). It presages the regular transmission of sounds and images whose technology provided us with radio and television but, more important, Bell's invention also shows how electrical signals can be made to serve the purposes of sound recording. Edison's original phonograph was an entirely physical-mechanical invention, which gave it the virtue of simplicity but also seriously delayed technological progress in the field. In a sense, the purely mechanical phonograph, like Daguerre's positive photograph, was technically a dead-end. It was not until the mid-1920s that Bell's theories of the electrical transmission of sound were united with the technology of the mechanical phonograph. At almost precisely the same time, sound recordings were united with image recordings to produce the cinema as we know it today. It is interesting to conjecture whether there would have been any period of silent cinema at all had Edison not invented a mechanical phonograph: in that case it's quite possible that Edison (or another inventor) would have turned to Bell's telephone as a model for the phonograph and the electrical system of recording sound would have developed much earlier, more than likely in time to be of service to the first cinematographers.

It is worth noting that Thomas Edison himself conceived of his kinetograph as an adjunct to the phonograph. As he put it in 1894:

> In the year 1887, the idea occurred to me that it was possible to devise an instrument which should do for the eye what the phonograph does for the ear, and that by a combination of the two all motion and sound could be recorded and reproduced simultaneously.*

---

*Quoted in W.K.L. Dickson, "A Brief History of the Kinetograph, the Kinetoscope, and the Kineto-Phonograph," in Raymond Fielding's A Technological History of Motion Pictures and Television, p.9.

William Kennedy Laurie Dickson, an English assistant to Edison who did much of the development work, describes Edison's first conception of the kinetograph as parallel in structure and conception with his successful phonograph:

> Edison's idea . . . was to combine the phonograph cylinder or record with a similar or larger drum on the same shaft, which drum was to be covered with pin-point microphotographs which of course must synchronize with the phonograph record.

This configuration, of course, did not succeed, but the ideal union of sound and image was suggested. Indeed, after Dickson had turned to the new perforated Eastman film, he continued to think of the moving pictures as necessarily joined with the sound record; his first demonstration of his success to Edison on October 6, 1889 was a "talkie." Dickson called this device a "kinetophone." Edison had just returned from a trip abroad. Dickson ushered him into the projecting room and started the machine. He appeared on the small screen, walked forward, raised his hat, smiled, and spoke directly to his audience:

> "Good morning, Mr. Edison, glad to see you back. Hope you like the kinetophone. To show the synchronization I will lift my hand and count up to ten."

These words, less well known, should certainly rank with Bell's telephonic "Mr. Watson, come here, I want to see you" and Morse's telegraphic "What hath God wrought?"

Because of the technical problems posed by Edison's mechanical recording system—mainly synchronization—the effective marriage of sound and image did not occur until thirty years later, but the desire to reproduce sound and image in concert existed from the earliest days of cinematographic history.

By 1900 all the basic tools of the new technological arts had been invented: the visual artist had the alternative of the still camera; the musical artist the alternative of the phonograph; and the narrative artist was presented with the exciting possibilities of motion pictures. Each of these records could be reproduced in large quantities and therefore reach large numbers of people. Although the technology of broadcasting was still a few years in the future, workable methods of instantaneous communication had been demonstrated by the telephone and the telegraph; in fact we are now realizing, as cable technology develops, that radio wave broadcasting may have been in a sense just a preliminary stage to wired transmission. In the latter third of the twentieth

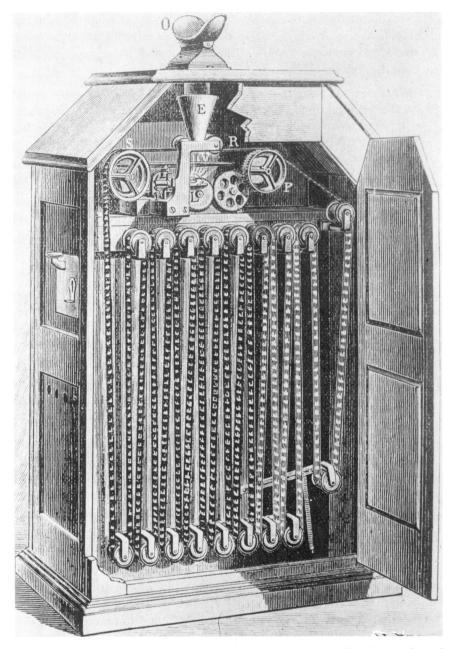

Figure 2-6. Edison's Kinetoscope was a private viewing machine. The film was formed in a continuous loop. (MOMA/FSA.)

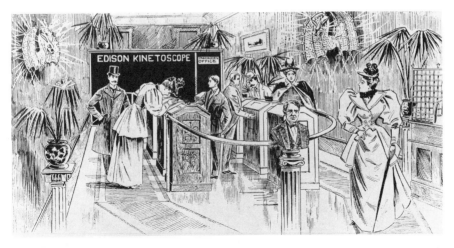

Figure 2-7. An engraving of a Kinetoscope parlor located on Broadway near 28th Street, New York, c. 1895. A bust of the inventor is in the foreground. (MOMA/FSA.)

century, line transmission of sounds and images should become the rule rather than the exception.

This flow chart indicates the various stages of the process of film:

VISUAL:	lens	camera	filmstock	editing laboratory	projection

AURAL:	microphone	recorder	tape, film, or record	editing & mixing	playback

At any one of these stages variables can be introduced to give an artist more control over the process. Within each area of the chart there is a large number of factors, each of which has a discernible effect on the finished product, and these factors interact with each other, and between areas, to create an extraordinarily complex technology. Indeed, no small part of the appreciation of the activity of filmmaking as well as the product lies in an understanding of the technical challenges that filmmakers must surmount.

THE LENS

The earliest of cameras, the camera obscura, consisted of a light-tight box with a pinhole in one side. Contemporary cameras, both still and motion picture, operate on the same principle: the box is more precisely machined; photosensitive, flexible film has replaced the drawing paper as the "screen" upon which the image falls; but the greatest changes have taken place in the pinhole. That crude optical device has evolved into a complex system of great technical sophistication. So much depends upon the glass eye of the lens through which we all eventually view a photograph or a film that it truly should be regarded as the nexus of the photographic art.

The impressive developments in the technology of optics during the last hundred years now offer filmmakers a wide latitude of possibilities. Because light travels at different speeds in different mediums, light rays bend when they pass from one medium to another. Lenses made out of glass or other transparent materials can then focus those rays. While the lens of the human eye is continuously variable, changing in shape each time we unconsciously refocus from one object to another, photographic lenses can only perform the specific tasks for which they are painstakingly designed.

A photographer has three basic types of lenses available to him, although the differences between these three types are relative rather than absolute. Lenses are generally classified according to their focal lengths: the distance from the plane of the film to the surface of the lens. Although a lens is usually chosen specifically for the subject it must photograph, there are various ancillary characteristics to each lens that have become valuable esthetic tools for the photographer. For cameras that use 35 mm film, the "normal" lens has a focal length of between 35 and 50 mm, roughly. This lens is the most common choice for the photographer because it distorts least and therefore most closely mimics the way the human eye perceives reality.

The wide-angle lens, as its name indicates, photographs a wide angle of view. A photographer finding himself in a cramped location would naturally use this lens in order to photograph as much of the subject as possible. However, the wide-angle lens also has the effect of greatly emphasizing our sense of depth perception and often, as well, distorting linear perception. The fish-eye lens, an extremely wide-angle lens, photographs an angle of view approaching 180°, with corresponding distortion of both linear and depth perception. Generally, for 35 mm photography, any lens shorter than 35 mm focal length is considered a wide-angle lens.

The telephoto or long lens acts like a telescope to magnify distant objects, and this of course is its most obvious use. Although the long lens does not distort linear perception, it does have the sometimes useful effect of suppressing depth perception. It has a relatively narrow

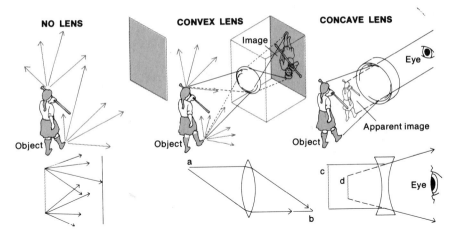

Figure 2-8. LENSES. If there is no lens to focus the rays of light coming from the subject, no image will be produced (left): all rays from all points will strike all parts of the photosensitive plate or film. The convex lens (center) bends the rays from each single point so that they converge on the "focus plane" a certain distance behind it. The image created is reversed right to left and top to bottom. (A transparent negative can then be turned to create the proper left-right orientation in the print.) A pinhole, if it is small enough, will act like a convex lens to give a rough focus. This is the elementary principle which led to the invention of the Camera Obscura (see Figure 2-2). The concave lens (right) causes the rays to diverge in such a way that an observer perceives an "apparent," or "virtual," image which seems smaller than the actual object. The diagrams below the drawings schematically indicate the optical effects of each.

angle of view. Normally, any lens longer than 60 mm is considered a telephoto lens, the effective upper limit being about 1200 mm. If greater magnification were desired, the camera would simply be attached to a standard telescope or microscope.

It should be noted that these lenses are not simply solid pieces of glass, as they were in the eighteenth century, but rather mathematically sophisticated combinations of elements designed to admit the most amount of light to the camera with the least amount of distortion. Within the last fifteen or twenty years zoom lenses, in which these elements and groups of elements are movable, have gained considerable popularity. The zoom lens has a variable focal length, ranging from wide-angle to telephoto, which allows a photographer to change focal lengths quickly between shots and, more important cinematographically, also to change focal lengths during a shot. This device has added a whole new set of effects to the vocabulary of the shot. Normal zoom lenses (which can have a focal length range from 10 to 100 mm) naturally affect the size of the field photographed as focal length is shifted (since longer lenses have a narrower angle of view than do

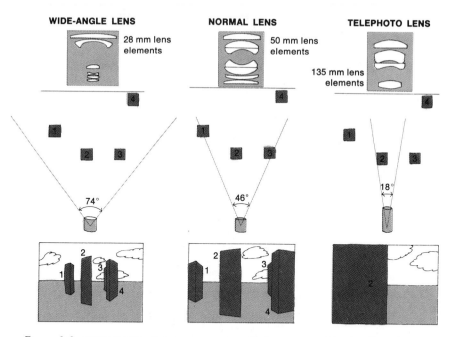

Figure 2-9. WIDE-ANGLE, "NORMAL," AND TELEPHOTO LENSES. Nearly all modern photographic lenses are more complicated than the simple lenses shown in Figure 2-8. Most are composed of sets of elements, such as those which are schematized at the top of this Figure. The 28 mm, 50 mm and 135 mm lenses are common wide-angle, "normal," and "telephoto" lenses in 35 mm photography, whether motion picture or still. Each of the three lenses diagrammed in the middle of the Figure is seeing the same arrangement of four columns from the same distance and perspective. The frames at the bottom are exact visualizations of the various images of the scene each lens produces. The wide-angle lens image appears to be taken from a greater distance; the telephoto image is greatly magnified. Notice the slight linear distortion in the wide-angle image and the "flat" quality of the telephoto image. In 35 mm photography, the 50 mm lens is considered "normal" because it best approximates the way the naked eye perceives a scene. (Compare Figure 3-50.)

shorter lenses), and this effect permits the zoom shot to compete with the tracking shot (see Figure 3-50).

Due to computer techniques and advances in the chemistry of optics, the photographic lens is now an instrument of considerable flexibility; we have reached a point where it has become possible to control individually most of the formerly interrelated effects of a lens. In 1975, for example, optics specialists at the Canon company developed their "Macro Zoom lens" in which elements of the Macro lens (which allows closeup photography at extreme short ranges), combined with a zoom configuration, allow zooms that range in focus from one mm to infinity.

Only one major problem in lens technology remains to be solved. Wide-angle and telephoto lenses differ not only in angle of view (and therefore magnification) but also in their effect on depth perception. No one has yet been able to construct a lens in which these two variables can be controlled separately.

Alfred Hitchcock spent decades working on this problem before he finally solved it in the famous tower shot from *Vertigo* by using a carefully controlled zoom combined with a track and models. Hitchcock laid the model stairwell on its side. The camera with zoom lens was mounted on a track looking "down" the stairwell. The shot began with the camera at the far end of the track and the zoom lens set at a moderate telephoto focal length. As the camera tracked in toward the stairwell, the zoom was adjusted backwards, eventually winding up at a wide-angle setting. The track and zoom were carefully coordinated so that the size of the image appeared not to change. (As the track moved in on the center of the image, the zoom moved out to correct for the narrowing field.) The effect relayed on the screen was that the shot began with normal depth perception which then became quickly exaggerated, mimicking the psychological feeling of vertigo. Hitchcock's shot cost $19,000 for a few seconds of film time.

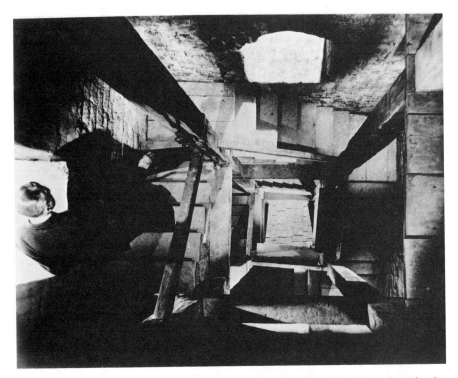

Figure 2-10. Providing a sort of ultimate emblem for Hitchcock's life and work, the tower scene from *Vertigo* forged a union of technology and psychology.

Figure 2-11. WIDE-ANGLE DISTORTION. Anna Karina in Jean-Luc Godard's *Pierrot le fou* (1965). (*l'Avant-Scène. Frame enlargement.*)

To summarize: the shorter the lens, the wider the angle of view (the larger the field of view), the more exaggerated the perception of depth, the greater the linear distortion; the longer the lens, the narrower the angle of view, the shallower the depth perception.

Standard lenses are variable in two ways: the photographer adjusts the focus of the lens (by varying the relationship between its elements), and he controls the amount of light entering the lens. There are three ways to vary the amount of light that enters the camera and strikes the film: the photographer can interpose light-absorbing material in the path of the light rays (filters do this and are generally attached in front of the lens), he can change exposure time (the shutter controls this), or he can change the aperture, the size of the hole through which the light passes (the diaphragm controls this aspect). Filters are generally used to alter the quality of the light entering the camera, not its quantity, and are therefore a minor factor in this equation. Aperture and exposure time are the main factors, closely related to each other and to focus.

The diaphragm works exactly like the iris of the human eye. Since film, more so than the retina of the eye, has a limited range of sensitivity, it is necessary to be able to control the amount of light striking the film. The size of the aperture is measured in f-stops, numbers derived by dividing the focal length of a particular lens by its effective aperture (the ratio of the length of a lens to its width, in other words). The

Figure 2-12. TELEPHOTO DISTORTION. A shot from Robert Altman's *Buffalo Bill and the Indians* (1976). Bill's posse is at least a half mile from the camera.

Figure 2-13. This frame enlargement from Godard's "Camera-Eye" (1967) clearly shows the effect of rapid zooming. The blurred lines aim toward the center of the image. Most zooms do not occur quickly enough to blur individual frames like this. (*l'Avant-Scène.*)

Figure 2-14. THE DIAPHRAGM. One of the simplest elements of the photographic system, as well as one of the most important, the diaphragm is constructed of wafer-thin, spring-loaded metal leaves—usually five or six in number—which overlap each other so that the size of the aperture can easily be adjusted.

result of this mechanical formula is a series of standard numbers whose relationship, at first, seems arbitrary:

f1	f1.4	f2	f2.8	f4	f5.6	f8	f11	f16	f22

These numbers were chosen because each successive f-stop in this series will admit half the amount of light of its predecessor; that is, an f1 aperture is twice as "large" as an f1.4 aperture, and f2.8 admits four times as much light as f5.6. The numbers have been rounded off to a single decimal place; the multiplication factor is approximately 1.4, the square root of 2.

The speed of a lens is rated by its widest effective aperture. A lens 50 mm long that was also 50 mm wide would, then, be rated as an f1 lens; that is, a very "fast" lens that at its widest opening would admit twice as much light as an f 1.4 lens and four times as much light as an f 2 lens. When Stanley Kubrick decided that he wanted to shoot much of *Barry Lyndon* (1975) by the light of a few eighteenth-century candles, it was necessary that he adapt to movie use a special lens the Zeiss company had developed for NASA for space photography. The lens was rated at f0.9, while the fastest lenses then in general use in cinematography were f1.2s. The small difference between the two numbers (0.3) is

Figure 2-15. Ten candles provide all the light for this scene from Kubrick's *Barry Lyndon* (1975). Murray Melvin and Marisa Berenson. (*Frame enlargement.*)

deceiving for, in fact, Kubrick's NASA lens admits nearly twice as much light as the standard f1.2

The concept of the f-number is rather awkward, not only because the series of numbers that results doesn't vividly indicate the differences between various apertures, but also because, being a ratio of physical sizes, the f-number is not necessarily an accurate index of the actual amount of light entering the camera. The surfaces of lens elements reflect small amounts of light, the elements themselves absorb small quantities; in complex multielement lenses (especially zoom lenses) these differences can add up to a considerable amount. In order to correct for this, the concept of "T-number" has been developed. The T-number is a precise electronic measurement of the amount of light actually striking the film.

Changing the size of the diaphragm—"stopping down"—because it effectively changes the diameter of the lens also changes the depth of field: the smaller the diameter of the lens opening, the greater the precision of focus. The phrase "depth of field" is used to indicate the range of distances in front of the lens that will appear satisfactorily in focus. If we were to measure depth of field with scientific accuracy, a lens would only truly be in focus for one single plane in front of the camera, the focus plane. But a photographer is interested not so much in scientific reality as in psychological reality, and there is always a

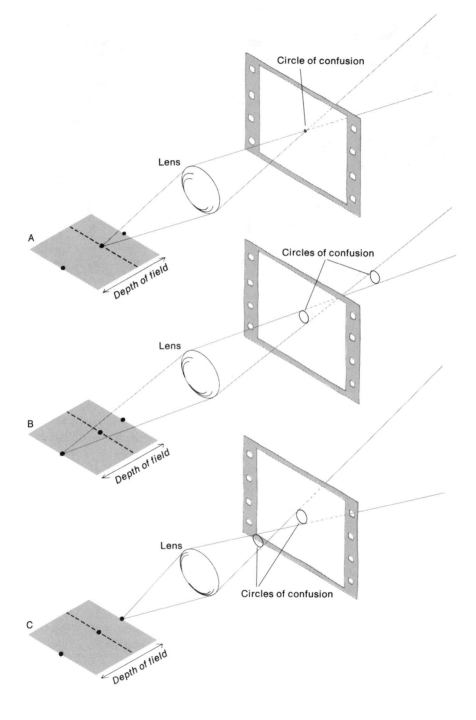

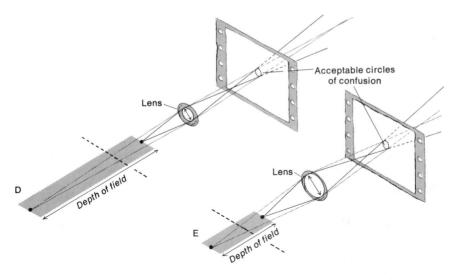

Figure 2-16. FOCUS AND DEPTH OF FIELD. Lenses bend light rays in such a way that only one plane in front of the lens is truly and accurately in focus. The dotted line in these five drawings represents that true focus plane. However, psychologically a certain range of distances in front and in back of the focus plane will appear satisfactorily in focus. This "depth of field" is represented here by the shaded areas. In A, an object point on the precise focus plane produces the narrowest "circle of confusion" on the film plane behind the lens. In B, an object point at the far end of the range of depth of field produces the largest acceptable circle of confusion. For objects beyond this point, the circle of confusion is such that the eye and brain read the image as being "out of focus." In C, an object point at the near boundary of depth of field produces a similarly acceptable circle of confusion. Objects nearer to the lens than this will produce an out of focus circle of confusion.

D and E illustrate the effect of aperture size (diaphragm setting) on depth of field. The narrower aperture in D yields a greater depth of field, while the larger aperture in E limits the depth of field. In both illustrations, points at the near and far end of the depth of field range produce equal, acceptable circles of confusion.

In all five drawings, it should be noted, depth of field has been slightly reduced for illustrative purposes. The calculation of the depth of field of a particular lens and aperture is a simple matter of geometry. Generally, depth of field extends toward infinity. It is much more critical in the near range than the far.

range of distances both in front of and behind the focus plane that will appear to be in focus.

We should also note at this point that various types of lenses have various depth-of-field characteristics: a wide-angle lens has a very deep depth of field, while a telephoto lens has a rather shallow depth of field. Remember, too, that as each particular lens is stopped down, as the aperture is narrowed, the effective depth of field increases.

Filmmakers and photographers are thus presented with a complex set of choices regarding lenses. The style of photography that strives for sharp focus over the whole range of action is called deep focus photography. While there are a number of exceptions, deep focus is generally

Figure 2-17. SHALLOW FOCUS. Characters are sharply in focus, background is blurred in this shot from Kubrick's *Paths of Glory* (1957). (MOMA/FSA.)

closely associated with theories of realism in film while shallow focus photography, which welcomes the limitations of depth of field as a useful artistic tool, is more often utilized by expressionist filmmakers, since it offers still another technique that can be used to direct the viewer's attention. A director can change focus during a shot either to maintain focus on a subject moving away from or toward the camera (in which case the term is follow focus) or to direct the viewer to shift attention from one subject to another (which is called rack focus).

THE CAMERA

The camera provides a mechanical environment for the lens, which accepts and controls light, and the film, which records light. The heart of this mechanical device is the shutter, which provides the second means available to the photographer for controlling the amount of light that strikes the film. Here, for the first time, we find a significant difference between still and movie photography. For still photographers, shutter speed is invariably closely linked with aperture size. If they want

Figure 2-18. DEEP FOCUS. One of the more extraordinary deep-focus shots photographed by Gregg Toland for Orson Welles's *Citizen Kane* (1941). The focus reaches from the ice sculptures in the near foreground to the furniture piled up behind the table at the rear. (MOMA/FSA.)

to photograph fast action, still photographers will probably decide first to use a fast shutter speed to "freeze" the action, and will compensate for the short exposure time by opening up the aperture to a lower f-stop (which will have the effect of narrowing the depth of field). If, however, the effect of deep focus is desired, the photographer will narrow the aperture ("stop down"), which will then require a relatively long exposure time (which will in turn mean that any rapid action within the frame might be blurred). Shutter speeds are measured in fractions of a second and in still photography are closely linked with corresponding apertures. For instance, the following linked pairs of shutter speeds and apertures will allow the same amount of light to enter the camera:

F-STOP:	1	1.4	2	2.8	4	5.6	8	11	16
SHUTTER SPEED	$\frac{1}{1000}$	$\frac{1}{500}$	$\frac{1}{250}$	$\frac{1}{125}$	$\frac{1}{60}^{*}$	$\frac{1}{30}$	$\frac{1}{15}$	$\frac{1}{8}^{*}$	$\frac{1}{4}$

*approximately

In motion picture photography, however, the speed of the shutter is determined by the agreed-upon standard twenty-four frames per second necessary to synchronize camera and projector speed. Cinematographers, therefore, are strictly limited in the choice of shutter speeds, although they can control exposure time by using a variable shutter, which controls not the time the shutter is open but rather the size of the opening. Clearly, the effective upper limit in cinematography is $1/24$ second. Since the film must travel through the projector at that speed, there is no way in normal cinematography of increasing exposure time beyond that limit. This means that cinematographers are effectively deprived of one of the most useful tools of still photography: there are no "time exposures" in normal movies.

Focal length, distortion of linear perspective, distortion of depth perspective, angle of view, focus, aperture, depth of field, and exposure time: these are the basic factors of photography, both movie and still. A large number of variables are linked together, and each of them has more than one effect. The result is, for example, that when a photographer wants deep focus he decreases the size of the aperture, but that means that less light will enter the camera so that he must add artificial light to illuminate the subject sufficiently, but that might produce un-

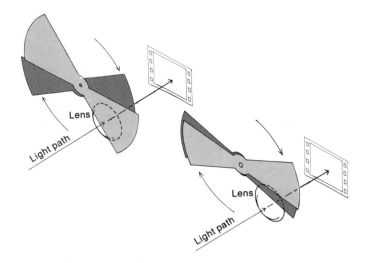

Figure 2-19. THE VARIABLE SHUTTER. In still photography, the shutter is simply a spring-loaded metal plate or fabric screen. In motion-picture photography, however, the time of exposure is limited by the 24-frame-per-second standard speed. The variable shutter allows some leeway in exposure time. Although it revolves always at the same 24 fps speed, the size of the "hole" and therefore the time of the exposure can be varied by adjusting the overlapping plates.

desirable side effects, so, to compensate, he will increase exposure time, but this means that it will be more difficult to obtain a clear, sharp image if either the camera or the subject is moving, so he may decide to switch to a wider angle lens in order to include more area in the frame, but this might mean that he will lose the composition he was trying to achieve in the first place. In photography, many decisions have to be made consciously that the human eye and brain make instantly and unconsciously.

In movies, the camera becomes involved in two variables that do not exist in still photography: it moves the film, and it itself moves. The transport of the film might seem to be a simple matter, yet this was the last of the multiple problems to be solved before motion pictures became feasible. The mechanism that moves the film properly through the camera is known as the "pull-down mechanism" or "intermittent motion mechanism." The problem is that film, unlike audio tape, for example, cannot run continuously through the camera at a constant speed. Films are series of still pictures, twenty-four per second, and the intermittent motion mechanism must move the film into position for the exposure of a frame, hold it in position rock steady for almost $1/24$ second, then move the next frame into position. It must do this twenty-four times each second, and it must accomplish this mechanical task in strict synchronization with the revolving shutter that actually exposes the film.

In the U.S., Thomas Armat is usually credited with inventing the first workable pull-down mechanism in 1895. In Europe, other inventors—notably the Lumière brothers—developed similar devices. The pull-down mechanism is literally the heart of cinema, since it pumps film through the camera or projector. The key to the success of this system of recording and projecting a series of still images that give the appearance of continuous movement lies in what Ingmar Bergman calls a certain "defect" in human sight: persistence of vision. The brain holds an image for a short period of time after it has disappeared, so it is possible to construct a machine that can project a series of still images quickly enough so that they merge psychologically and the illusion of motion is maintained. Al Hazen had investigated this phenomenon in his book, *Optical Elements,* as early as the tenth century. Nineteenth-century scientists such as Peter Mark Roget and Michael Faraday did valuable work on the theory as early as the 1820s. During the early years of this century Gestalt psychologists further refined this concept, giving it the name "phi-phenomenon."

As it happens, a speed of at least twelve or fifteen pictures per second

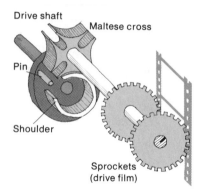

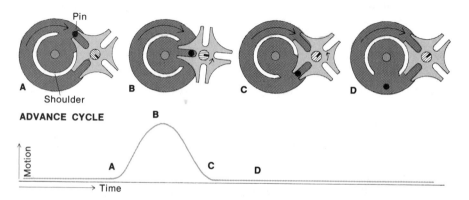

Figure 2-20. THE MALTESE CROSS MECHANISM. The drive shaft rotates at constant speed. At the beginning of the cycle (A), the pin engages the maltese cross gear which is connected by a shaft to the sprockets which drive the film. So long as the pin is engaged in the maltese cross (A,B,C), the film is moving. Through most of the cycle, the pin is *not* engaged and the shoulder holds the cross (and the film) steady (D). The graph describes cross and film movement throughout the full cycle.

is necessary, and a rate of about forty pictures per second is much more effective. Early experimenters, W.K.L. Dickson for one, shot at speeds approaching forty-eight frames per second in order to eliminate the "flicker" effect common at slower speeds. It quickly became evident, however, that the flicker could be avoided by the use of a double-bladed projection shutter, and this has been in common use since the early days of film. The effect is that, while the film is shot at twenty-four frames per second, it is shown in such a way that the projection of each frame is interrupted once, producing a frequency of forty-eight "frames" per second and thus eliminating flicker. Each frame is actually projected

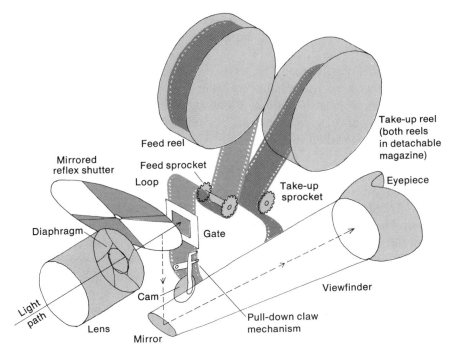

Figure 2-21. THE REFLEX CAMERA. The feed and take-up reels are housed in a separate magazine which can be changed easily and quickly. The feed and take-up sprockets run continuously. Intermittent motion in this machine is provided by a cam-mounted claw mechanism, rather than the more complicated maltese cross system illustrated in Figure 2-20. The heart of the reflex camera is the mirrored shutter. Tilted at a 45° angle to the light path, this ingenious arrangement permits the camera operator to see precisely the same scene through the viewfinder that the film "sees." When the shutter is open, all light strikes the film. When the shutter is closed, all light is redirected into the viewfinder. The reflex camera has almost entirely replaced earlier systems with separate viewfinders, both in still and motion picture photography. Compare Figure 2-26.

twice. During the silent period—especially during the earliest years when both cameras and projectors were hand-cranked—variable speeds were common: both the cameraman and the projectionist thus had a degree of control over the speed of the action. The average silent speed was between sixteen and eighteen frames per second, gradually increasing over the years to twenty and twenty-two frames per second. Twenty-four frames per second did not become an immutable standard until 1927 (although even now it is not entirely universal: European television films are shot at twenty-five frames per second in order to synchronize with the European television system whose frequency is twenty-five frames per second). When silent films are projected at "sound speed," as they often are nowadays, the effect is to make the speeded-up action appear even more comical than it was originally.

The genius of the device Armat invented is that it alternately moves the film and holds it steady for exposure in such a way that there is a high ratio between the amount of time the film is held still and the amount of time it is in motion. Obviously, the time during which the frame is in motion is wasted time photographically. The sequence of operations is described in Figure 2-20. Considering the smallness of the frame, the fragility of the film, and the tremendous forces to which the tiny sprocket holes are subjected, the motion picture camera and projector are formidable mechanisms indeed.

The speed of the camera introduces another set of variables that can be useful to filmmakers, and it is in this area that cinema finds its most important scientific applications. By varying the speed of the camera (assuming the projector speed remains constant), we can make use of the invaluable techniques of slow motion, fast motion, and time-lapse (extreme fast motion) photography. Film, then, is a tool that can be applied to time in the same ways that the telescope and the microscope are applied to space, revealing natural phenomena that are invisible to the human eye. Slow motion, fast motion, and time-lapse photography make comprehensible events that happen either too quickly or too slowly for us to perceive them, just as the microscope and the telescope reveal phenomena that are either too small or too far away for us to perceive them. As a scientific tool, cinematography has had great significance, not only because it allows us to analyze a large range of time phenomena, but also as an objective record of reality. The sciences of anthropology, ethnography, psychology, sociology, natural studies, zoology—even botany—have been revolutionized by the invention of cinematography. Moreover, filmstocks can be made that are sensitive to areas of the spectrum outside that very limited range of frequencies, or colors, which our eyes perceive. Infrared and other similar types of photography reveal "visual" data that have hitherto been beyond our powers of perception.

The terms "slow motion" and "fast motion" are fairly self-explanatory, but it may nevertheless be useful to describe exactly what happens in the camera. If we can adjust the speed of the pull-down mechanism so that, for example, it shoots 240 frames per second instead of the standard twenty-four, then each second of recording time will stretch out over ten seconds of projected time, revealing details of motion that would be imperceptible in real time. Conversely, if the camera takes, say, three frames per second, projected time will "happen" eight times more quickly than real time. The term "time lapse" is used simply to

Figure 2-22. Slow motion is occasionally useful in narrative films, as well. This frame from the sequence in extreme slow motion that climaxes Michelangelo Antonioni's *Zabriskie Point* (1969) captures some of the ironic, lyrical freedom of the explosion fantasy. (*Frame enlargement.* Sight and Sound.)

refer to extremely fast motion photography in which the camera oper-ates intermittently rather than continuously—at a rate of one frame every minute, for example.

It doesn't take many viewings of slow and fast motion films made with primarily scientific purposes in mind before it becomes obvious that the variable speed of the motion picture camera reveals poetic truths as well as scientific ones. If the slow motion love scene has become one of the hoariest cliches of contemporary cinema while the comedic value of fast motion early silent movies has become a truism, it is also true that explosions in extreme slow motion (for example, the final sequence of Antonioni's *Zabriskie Point,* 1969) become symphonic celebrations of the material world, and time-lapse sequences of flowers in which a day's time is compressed into thirty seconds of screen time reveal a natural choreography that is stunning, as the flower stretches and searches for the life-giving rays of the sun.

The camera itself moves, as well as the film, and it is in this area that cinema has discovered some of its most private truths, for the control over the viewer's perspective that a filmmaker enjoys is one of the most salient differences between film and stage. There are two basic types of camera movement: the camera can revolve around one of the three imaginary axes that intersect in the camera; or it can move itself from one point to another in space. Each of these two types of motion implies an essentially different relationship between camera and subject.

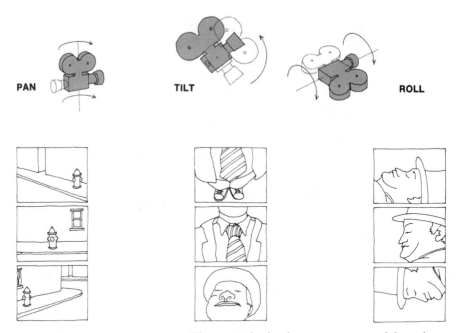

Figure 2-23. PAN, TILT, AND ROLL. The pan is by far the most common of these three elementary movements. The roll, since it disorients rather than providing new information, is least common.

In pans and tilts, the camera follows the subject as the subject moves (or changes); in rolls, the subject doesn't change but its orientation within the frame is altered; in tracks (also known as "dollies") and crane shots, the camera moves along a vertical or horizontal line (or a vector of some sort) and the subject may be either stationary or mobile. Because these assorted movements and their various combinations have such an important effect on the relationship between the subject and the camera (and therefore the viewer), camera movement has great significance as a determinant of the meaning of film.

The mechanical devices that make camera movement possible are all fairly simple in design: the tripod panning/tilting head is a matter of carefully machined plates and ball-bearings; tracking (or travelling) shots are accomplished simply by either laying down tracks (very much like railroad tracks) to control the movement of the camera on its mount, or using a rubber-tired dolly, which allows a bit more freedom; the camera crane that allows a cinematographer to raise and lower the camera smoothly is merely a counterweighted version of the "cherry-pickers" that telephone company linesmen use to reach the tops of poles. (See Figure 3-51.)

As a result, until relatively recently, technical advances in this area were few. Two stand out. First, in the late 1950s, the Arriflex company developed a 35 mm movie camera that was considerably lighter in weight and smaller in dimension than the standard Mitchell behemoths that had become the favored instruments of Hollywood photographers. The Arriflex could be hand-held, and this allowed new freedom and fluidity in camera movement. The camera was now free of mechanical supports and consequently a more personal instrument. The French New Wave, in the early sixties, was noted for the creation of a new vocabulary of hand-held camera movements, and the lightweight camera made possible the style of cinéma vérité documentary common today.

For nearly fifteen years hand-held shots, while inexpensive and popular, were also obvious. Shaky camera work became a cliché of the sixties. Then, in the early seventies, a cameraman named Garrett Brown developed the system called "Steadicam" working in conjunction with engineers from Cinema Products, Inc. During the last few years this method of filming has gained wide popularity. A vest is used to redistribute the weight of the camera to the hips of the camera operator. A spring-loaded arm damps the motion of the camera, providing an image steadiness comparable to much more elaborate (and expensive) tracking and dolly shots. Finally, a video monitor frees the camera operator from the eyepiece, further increasing control of the hand-held walking shot.

Even a lightweight camera, however, is a bulky device when placed on a standard crane. In the mid-seventies, French filmmakers Jean-Marie Lavalou and Alain Masseron constructed a device they call a "Louma." Essentially a lightweight crane very much like a microphone

Figure 2-24. The Steadicam system.

Figure 2-25. Ingmar Bergman with bulky Mitchell camera on the set of *Hour of the Wolf* (1966), Liv Ullmann to the left.

boom, it allows full advantage to be taken of lightweight cameras. The Louma, precisely controlled by servo-motors, enables the camera to be moved into positions that were impossible before and frees it from the presence of the camera operator by transmitting a video image of the scene from the viewfinder to the cinematographer's location, which can be simply outside a cramped room, or miles away, if necessary.

Devices such as the Kenworthy snorkel permit even more minute control of the camera. As the Louma frees the camera from the bulk of the operator, so the snorkel frees the lens from the bulk of the camera. With the advent of these devices, most of the constraints imposed upon cinematography by the size of the machinery necessary have been eliminated, and the camera approaches the ideal condition of a free-floating, perfectly controllable artificial eye. The perfection of fiber optics technology has extended this freedom to the microscopic level; the travels through the various channels of the human body that were science fiction when they were created by means of special effects in 1967 for the film *Fantastic Voyage* could, by the mid-seventies, be filmed "on location" for the documentary *The Incredible Machine*.

Figure 2-26. Stanley Kubrick "hand-holding" a small Arriflex: the rape scene from *A Clockwork Orange* (1971). Malcolm McDowell wears the nose.

THE FILMSTOCK

The fundamental chemical principle on which all chemical photography is based is that some substances (mainly silver salts) are photosensitive: that is, they change chemically when exposed to light. If that chemical alteration is visible and can be fixed or frozen, then a reproducible record of visual experience is possible. Daguerreotypes were made on metal plates and required long periods of exposure, measured in minutes, in order to capture an image. Before motion pictures were technically possible, it was necessary that a flexible base to carry the photographic emulsion be developed, and that this emulsion be sensitive or "fast" enough so that it could be properly exposed within a time period something like $1/20$ second. The speed of standard, popular emulsions is now such that $1/1000$ second is more than adequate exposure time under normal conditions.

Not all image-fixing is chemically photographic, however. Television images are electronically produced (although the nature of photosensitive and phosphorescent chemicals plays a part) and systems used in

Figure 2-27. (above). Shooting a simple automobile scene can be a time-consuming and complex job. Lights, camera, reflectors, diffusers,
and other paraphernalia are all mounted on the
car for this scene from *Not a Pretty Picture*
(1976). Director Martha Coolidge is at right.
(Compare the simple studio rear projection arrangement in Figure 6-19.) (*Photo: Jack Feder.*)
Inset, the scene as it appeared in the film.

photocopying (Xerox) machines are also quite different from traditional
chemical silver-salt photography. The silver scare of early 1980 when,
for a brief period, the price of the metal quintupled, focused renewed
attention on non-silver means of photography. In the future, even
family snapshots may be electrophotographically reproduced, like pho-
tocopies. Even now, a number of graphic artists regulary use photocopying machines in their work for special effects.

NEGATIVES, PRINTS, AND GENERATIONS

Since the salts on which chemical photography is based darken when
exposed to light, a curious and useful quirk is introduced into the system.
Those areas of the photograph that receive most light will appear darkest
when the photograph is developed and put through the chemical baths
that fix the image permanently. The result is a negative image in which
tones are reversed: light is dark and dark is light. A positive print of this
negative image can easily be obtained by either contact printing the

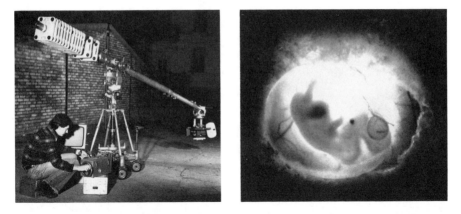

Figure 2-28 (left). THE LOUMA CRANE. The operator controls the movement of crane and camera via servo-mechanisms while observing the image the camera is taking by television monitor. The crane is capable of very precise changes in direction. A zoom motor attached to the camera can also be remote-controlled. (*Photo: P. Brard.*)

Figure 2-29 (right). Fiber optics cinematography: a human fetus in the womb. From *The Incredible Machine (PBS, 1975).*

negative or projecting it on similar filmstock or photographic paper. This makes possible the replication of the image. In addition, when the negative is projected the image can be enlarged, reduced, or otherwise altered—a significant advantage. Reversal processing permits the development of a direct, projectable positive image on the "camera original"—the filmstock in the camera when the shot is made. Negatives (or reversal positives) can also be printed directly from a reversal print.

The camera original is considered to be first generation; a print of it would be second generation; a negative or reversal copy of that, in turn, is third generation. With each successive step, quality is lost. Since the original negative of a film is usually considered too valuable to use in producing the ten to one thousand prints that might be required for a major release of a feature, the print one sees in a theater is often several generations removed from the original:

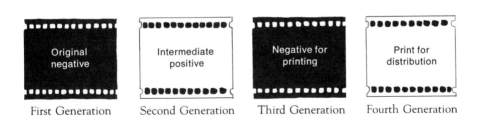

Original negative	Intermediate positive	Negative for printing	Print for distribution
First Generation	Second Generation	Third Generation	Fourth Generation

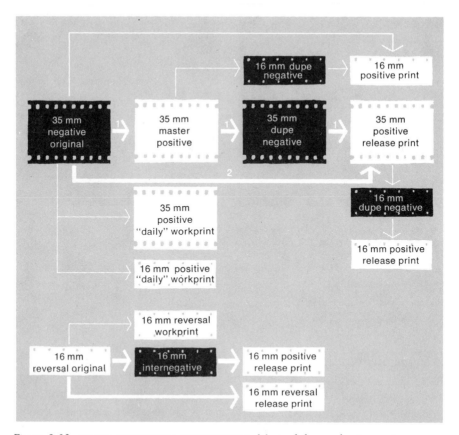

Figure 2-30. STOCK, PROCESSING, GENERATIONS. Most of the production systems commonly in use today are outlined in this flowchart. American theatrical films usually follow path 1, which means that the print audiences see is fourth generation. European theatrical films often are produced by system 2: audiences thus see a second generation print of significantly better quality. A third basic system, not shown here, interposes a "Reversal Intermediate" between the negative and the print. Although 16 mm film production can follow the same patterns, it is also common—especially in television news work—to use Reversal originals, which can be screened directly. All negatives, positives, and reversals shown here are color film. Black and white negatives and prints can can also be derived from color originals if needed.

If complicated laboratory work is required, then several more generations may be added. "CRI" stock (color reversal intermediate), developed especially for the purpose of bridging the intermediate positive stage, has lessened the number of generations in practice. When large numbers of prints and laboratory work are not needed, reversal stocks provide a very useful alternative. The reversal stock that a television newsman shoots at 4:00 P.M., for example, might be developed at 5:00

and go directly into the film chain, still wet, for broadcasting at 6:00. Amateur cinematographers almost always use reversal films such as Kodachrome or Ektachrome.

This is a broad outline of the basic choices of filmstock available to the filmmaker. In practice, the variety is much greater. The Eastman Kodak company has very nearly a monopoly position in the professional filmstock market in the U.S. (even if it has some distant challengers in the amateur and still film markets) and is dominant, as well, abroad. But Kodak enjoys that monopoly partly because it produces a large number of very useful products. And while the professional filmmaker is effectively limited to Eastman Kodak raw materials, there is a wide range of processing techniques available (see the discussion of color below). Yet all these processes reveal basic similarities, since they all must deal with the particular chemistry of the filmstock Eastman supplies. One of the main reasons the company holds such a strong position in the industry is this close connection between stock and processing. A private laboratory will invest hundreds of thousands of dollars in equipment to process a particular stock. Naturally, such large investments require a degree of financial caution on the part of the labs, especially when the technology is developing rapidly and the useful life of the equipment may be no more than six or eight years. Eastman's 5254 stock, for example, introduced in 1968, was technically superior to color stocks that had existed before then, but it lasted only six years before it was replaced by 5247 in 1974. Now the standard color stock of professional cinematography, 5247 has an entirely different chemistry from its predecessor.

For these reasons and others, Kodak enjoys a monopolistic position that is in some ways similar to the situation of I.B.M. in the computer industry. It was George Eastman who developed the first flexible, transparent roll film stock in 1889. Like I.B.M. in its field, Eastman's company has largely defined the languages and systems that must be used by the great majority of their customers. Film is an art, but it is also an industry. Kodak's revenues each year are approximately double the revenues of the entire American feature-film industry.

While economic and logistical decision play a large part in the choice of filmstock and process, there are other, more esthetic, decisions that are integrally involved in these choices. The esthetic variables of filmstock include: gauge, grain, contrast, tone, and color. Intimately involved with these variables, especially the first two—although it is not truly a function of the film stock used—is the aspect ratio, or frame size of the film when projected.

ASPECT RATIO

The ratio between the height of the projected image and its width—the aspect ratio—is dependent on the size and shape of the aperture of the camera (and of the projector) and, as we shall see, on the types of lenses used. But it is not solely a function of the aperture. Early in the history of film, an arbitrary aspect ratio of four to three (width to height) became popular and was eventually standardized by the Academy of Motion Picture Arts and Sciences (so that it is now known as the "Academy aperture" or "Academy ratio"). This ratio, more often expressed as 1:1.33 or simply as the 1.33 ratio, while it was undeniably the most common ratio, was never really the sole ratio in use. Filmmakers—D.W. Griffith is especially noted for this—often masked off part of the frame in order to change the shape of the image temporarily. When sound was developed and room had to be made for the soundtrack on the edge of the film, the square ratio was common for a while. A few years later the Academy shrank the amount of space within the potential frame that was actually used in order to regain the 1.33 ratio, and this standard gradually developed a mystical significance, even though it was the result of an arbitrary decision.

Most film textbooks, even today, connect the 1.33 ratio with the Golden Section of classical art and architecture, a truly mystical number expressive of a ratio found everywhere in nature, often in the strangest places (in the arrangement of the seeds of a sunflower, for example, or the shape of a snail's shell). The Golden Section is derived from the formula $a/b = b/(a+b)$, where a is the length of the shorter side of the rectangle and b is the length of the longer. While it is an irrational number, the Golden Mean can be closely approximated by the expression of the ratio of height to width as 1:1.618. This is very close to the most popular European widescreen ratio in use today, but it is certainly a far cry from the 1.33 ratio of the Academy aperture. While the Academy ratio, arbitrary as it is,* was really only dominant for twenty years or so (until 1953), it was during this time that the television frame was standardized on its model; and that, in turn, continues to influence film composition.

Since the 1950s, filmmakers have been presented with a considerable range of screen ratios to choose from. Two separate methods are used to achieve the widescreen ratios in use today. The simplest method is to mask off the top and bottom of the frame, providing the two most

---

*Cynics will note that the Academy aperture is an expression of Pythagoras's theorem, but that is an abstract ideal while the Golden Mean is a natural, organic one!

common "flat" widescreen ratios: 1.66 (in Europe) and 1.85 (in the U.S.). Masking, however, means that a much smaller portion of the available film frame is used, resulting in diminished quality of the projected image. In the 1.85 ratio, 36 percent of the total frame area is wasted. The second method of achieving a widescreen ratio, the anamorphic process, became popular in the mid-fifties as "Cinemascope." The first anamorphic process was Henri Chrétien's "Hypergonar" system, which was used by Claude Autant-Lara in 1927 for his film *Construire un feu.* In the same year, Abel Gance, working with André Debrie, developed a multiscreen system not unlike Cinerama for the conclusion of his epic *Napoleon.* He called this three-projector system Polyvision. A year previously, for their film *Chang,* Merian C. Cooper and Ernest B. Schoedsack had experimented with "Magnascope," which simply enlarged the entire image, much as a magnifying glass would.

An anamorphic lens squeezes a wide image into the normal frame dimensions of the film and then unsqueezes the image during projection to provide a picture with the proper proportions. The standard squeeze ratio for the most common anamorphic systems (first CinemaScope, now Panavision) is 2:1; that is, a subject will appear in the squeezed frame to be half as wide as in reality. The height of the subject is unchanged. Using nearly all the area of the frame available, the earlier anamorphic process obtained a projected image aspect ratio of 2.55; this was later altered to 2.35, which is now standard, in order to make room for an optical soundtrack.

While the anamorphic system is considerably more efficient than masking, since it utilizes the full frame area available, anamorphic lenses are much more sophisticated optical devices, much more expensive, and more limited in variety than spherical (nonanamorphic) lenses. This results in certain practical limitations placed on the cinematographer using an anamorphic system. In addition, although it seems as if an anamorphic negative contains twice as much horizontal information as a standard negative, the unsqueezing process does amplify grain and inconsistencies along with the image. In other words, the anamorphic lens simply stretches a normal amount of information to fill a screen twice as wide.

The age of widescreen began in September 1952 with the release of *This Is Cinerama,* a successful spectacle whose subject was, in fact, the system that was used to shoot it. Employing stereophonic sound, Cinerama, the invention of Fred Waller, used three cameras and three projectors to cover a huge, curved screen. Like many widescreen systems, it had its roots in a World's Fair exhibit, Waller's "Vitarama," which was used at the 1939 Fair in New York and later evolved into the

Flexible Gunnery Trainer of World War II. In 1953, the first Cinema-Scope film, Twentieth Century-Fox's *The Robe*, was released. An ana-morphic process rather than a multiprojector extravaganza, Cinema-Scope quickly became the standard widescreen process of the 1950s. Techniscope, developed by the Technicolor company, employed an interesting variation on the anamorphic process. The Techniscope negative is shot with spherical lenses masked to give a widescreen ratio. The camera employs a two-hole pull-down mechanism rather than the standard four-hole, thus halving filmstock costs. The negative is then printed through an anamorphic lens, providing a standard anamorphic four-hole pull-down print for projection purposes.

While filmmakers had experimented with widescreen systems for many years, it was the economic threat that television posed in the early fifties that finally made widescreen ratios common. Having be-queathed the arbitrary 1.33 ratio to the new television industry, film studios quickly discovered that their most powerful weapon against the new art was image size. Because it was so unwieldy, Cinerama quickly fell into disuse. Single camera systems, like CinemaScope and later Panavision, became dominant. Cinerama also engendered the short-lived phenomenon of "3-D" or stereoscopic film. Again the system was too inflexible to be successful and was never more than a novelty attraction. What was undoubtedly the best film shot in the two-camera 3-D process, Hitchcock's *Dial M for Murder* (1954), wasn't released in 3-D until 1980.

Ironically, 3-D attempted to exploit an area of film esthetics that was already fairly well expressed by two-dimensional "flat" film. Our sense of the dimensionality of a scene depends, psychologically, upon many factors other than binocular vision: chiaroscuro, movement, focus are all important psychological factors. (See Chapter 3, p. 160.) Moreover, the three-dimensional technique produced an inherently distortive ef-fect, which distracted attention from the subject of the film. These are the twin problems that holography, a much more advanced system of stereoscopic photography, will have to overcome before it can ever be considered a feasible alternative to flat film.

The development of the various trick processes of the 1950s had some useful results, however. One of the systems that competed with CinemaScope in those years was Paramount's VistaVision, which intro-duced two new concepts that have outlived the system itself. VistaVi-sion turned the camera on its side to achieve a wide image with an eight-sprocket-hole pull-down (more precisely, a "pull-across"). The frame, then, was twice the size of normal 35 mm photography and used all the image area available without tricky anamorphic lenses. Release

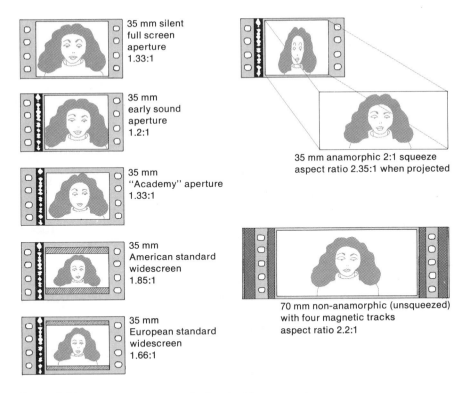

Figure 2-31. ASPECT RATIOS: standard and widescreen systems.

prints were made in normal 35 mm configurations. (Technirama, a later development, used this system with an anamorphic taking lens with a 1.5 squeeze ratio). VistaVision suggested two profitable lines of development: first, that the film itself if it were larger would permit widescreen photography with equal clarity (this led to the development of 65 mm and 70 mm stocks, which had been experimented with as early as 1900); second, that the system used for photographing the film did not have to be the system used for distribution and projection. The result is the complex array of potential aspect ratios—some for photography, some for distribution prints, some for both—outlined in Figure 2-31.

GRAIN, GAUGE, AND SPEED

The development of fast filmstocks has given filmmakers unrivalled freedom to photograph scenes by "available light," at night or indoors. Whereas huge, expensive arc lights were once standard in the industry and greatly restricted the process of filmmaking, fast color and black-

and-white filmstocks now give film almost the same sensitivity that our eyes have. The exposure speed of a filmstock is closely linked with its definition or grain, and varies inversely: what is gained in speed is generally lost in definition. Faster films are grainier; slower films give sharper, fine-grain images. Grain is also a function of the gauge or size of the filmstock. A standard frame of 35 mm film has an area of slightly more than half a square inch. If it is projected onto a screen that is forty feet wide, it has to fill an area that is 350,000 times larger than itself—a prodigious task; a frame of 16 mm film (since the stock is a little more than half as wide as 35 mm, the area of the frame is four times smaller), if it were to fill the same screen, would have to be magnified 1,400,000 times. The graininess of a filmstock, which might never be noticeable if the frame were enlarged to the standard 8 × 10 inches in still photography, will be thousands of times more noticeable on a motion picture screen. The distance between the observer and the image comes into play here, too. From the back row of a very large theater with a small screen, the image of a 35 mm movie might appear in the same perspective as an 8 × 10 print held one foot in front of the observer. In that case, the grain would appear to be more or less equivalent.

The standard width for motion picture stock has been 35 mm. Introduced many years ago as suitable only for the amateur filmmaker, 16 mm stock has become a useful alternative within the last twenty years, as filmstock and processing have become more sophisticated. It is widely used in television film work, especially in Europe, and it is becoming increasingly usable for shooting feature films. The "super 16" format, developed in the early seventies, measurably increases the area of the frame and thus the definition of the image. Also, 8 mm film, which has heretofore been restricted entirely to amateur use, is now also finding some applications in commercial filmmaking, especially in the areas of television news and industrial filmmaking. Whatever problems of definition and precision exist in 35 mm will be multiplied by a factor of four in 16 mm and a factor of sixteen in 8 mm, since we are concerned with areas rather than linear dimensions.

By the same arithmetic, a wider filmstock will greatly ameliorate those problems. Hence, 70 mm filmstocks are valuable for productions that need a feeling of panoramic detail and power on a large screen. While the possibilities of the wider stocks are intriguing, it is the increasing sophistication of 16 mm and even 8 mm gauges that will be most influential and beneficial in the immediate future. The significant factor here is cost: 16 mm stock is two to four times cheaper than 35 mm and therefore opens up filmmaking to a much larger number of

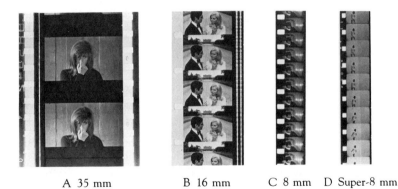

A 35 mm   B 16 mm   C 8 mm   D Super-8 mm

Figure 2-32. GAUGE. These four samples of standard film gauges are reproduced life-size. The 35 mm image is four sprocket holes high. These frames, from Michelangelo Antonioni's *Red Desert* (1964), are masked to produce an aspect ratio of 1.79. The projector's mask will adjust this to one of the standard ratios. The soundtrack is the thin line to the left.

The 16 mm frames (from a television commercial by Richard Lester) and the 8 mm and Super-8 mm frames (from films by Paul Hillery) are each one sprocket high. In addition, 8 and 16 mm release prints have only one row of sprockets. The 16 mm soundtrack is to the right of the image. (There are no soundtracks on the 8 and Super-8 mm samples.) The smaller sprocket holes of Super-8 mm film provide an image area approximately 35 percent larger than with regular 8 mm stock.

potential filmmakers. It not only makes it possible for more people to afford to make films, it also means that more films can be made for the same money, so that professional filmmakers will be less reliant on the vagaries of the venture capital market.

Finally, it should be noted that the gauge of a filmstock is a double variable: as with widescreen processes, the gauge in which the film is shot need not be the same gauge in which it is distributed. For the most part, the gauge of the projected print is important only insofar as the size of the screen it must fill, while the gauge of the negative camera original will affect the clarity of the film throughout the several processes it will undergo.

CONTRAST, TONE, AND COLOR

Until relatively recently, the theory persisted that black-and-white film was somehow more honest, more esthetically proper, than color film. Like the idea that silent film was purer than sound film, or the notion that 1.33 was somehow the natural ratio of the screen dimensions, this theory of black-and-white supremacy seems to have been invented after the fact, more an excuse than a premise. Filmmakers were experimenting with color, as with sound, from the earliest days of cinematography; only the complicated technology of color film held them back. Between 1900 and 1935, dozens of color systems were introduced and some gained moderate success. The great majority of "black-and-white" films in the twenties, moreover, used tinted stock to provide a dimension of color. Eastman's Sonochrome catalogue of the late twenties listed such elegant shades as Peach-blow, Inferno, Rose Doree, Candle Flame, Sunshine, Purple Haze, Firelight, Fleur de Lis, Azure, Nocturne, Verdante, Acqua Green, Argent, and Caprice!

It was 1935, however, before the Technicolor three-strip process opened up color photography to the majority of filmmakers.* This system used three separate strips of film to record the magenta, cyan, and yellow spectrums. In processing, separate relief matrix films were made from each of these negatives, and then were used to transfer each color to the release print in a process very similar to ink printing. The three-strip system was soon replaced by the "tri-pack" system, in which all three negatives were combined in layers on one strip. In 1952, Eastman Kodak introduced a color negative material with a system of masking that improved color renditions in the final print, and Technicolor negatives quickly became obsolete. The Technicolor dye-transfer printing process remained in use, however, since many cinematographers felt that the dye-transfer technique produced better and more precise colors than Eastman's chemical development. The difference between an Eastman chemical print and a Technicolor dye-transfer print is even today evident to professionals. The Technicolor print has a cooler, smoother, more subtle look to it than has the Eastman system print. Moreover, the dye-transfer print will maintain color values for a far longer time.

Ironically, Technicolor closed the last of its dye-transfer labs in the U.S. in the late 1970s. The only place the system is now regularly employed is in China, where Technicolor built a plant soon after the recognition of China by the U.S. At almost the same time that the dye-transfer process was being phased out in the Western world, film archivists and technicians were becoming aware of significant problems with the Eastmancolor process. The colors fade very quickly and never in the same relationship to each other. Unless Technicolor dye-transfer prints, or expensive three-strip black-and-white color records have been

---

*The first Technicolor three-strip film was *La Cucaracha* (1935); the first Technicolor feature was *Becky Sharp*, also in that year.

Figure 2-33. CONTRAST RANGE. This series of photographic prints displays a wide range of contrasts from very subtle, narrow grays to nearly pure black and white.

preserved, most color films of the fifties, sixties, and seventies will soon deteriorate beyond help—if they haven't already. Certain laser processes recently invented will be able to reconstruct an approximation of the original color values of an aged print, but this will be expensive. Most color films of the last thirty years are living under an immutable death sentence.

Before 1952, black-and-white was the standard format and color was reserved for special projects. Between 1955 and 1968, the two were about equal in popularity. Since 1968, when much faster, truer color stock became available, color has become the norm and it is a rare American film that is shot in black-and-white. The reasons for this have as much to do with economics as with esthetics. The popularity of color television in the seventies has made it risky for film producers to use black-and-white, since the resale value to television is affected.

If we limit ourselves for the moment to a discussion of black-and-white photography, we can better isolate two other dimensions of film-stock that are signficant: contrast and tone. When we speak of "black-and-white," we are not really talking about a two-color system, but rather about an image deprived entirely of color values. What remains

Figure 2-34. HIGH CONTRAST. Blacks and whites are extreme values; the range of grays between is limited. Ingrid Thulin, Jörgen Lindström in Ingmar Berman's *The Silence* (1963).

in the so-called "black-and-white" picture are the related variables of contrast and tone: the relative darkness and lightness of the various areas of the image and the relationship between the darks and the lights. The retina of the human eye differs from film, first in its ability to accommodate a wide range of brightnesses, and second in its ability to differentiate between two or more close shades of brightness. Film is a limited medium in both respects. The range of shades of brightness, from pure white to pure black, which a particular filmstock can record is technically referred to as its latitude. Its ability to differentiate between close shades is called the gamma of the film stock. The fewer the number of shades that the stock can separate, the cruder the photograph will be. At its most extreme limit, only black and white will be seen and the film will represent all the shadings in between as either one or the other. The more discriminating the ability of the stock is, the more subtle will be the tone of the photography. Figure 2-36 shows this graphically: a low contrast photograph is one in which the scale of tonal values is very narrow. Tone and contrast are closely associated with grain, so that the best range of tonal values is seen in filmstocks with the finest grain and therefore the highest resolution power.

Figure 2-35. LOW CONTRAST. No pure blacks or whites; grays predominate. Romy Schneider in Luchino Visconti's "The Job" (*Boccaccio 70*, 1963).

Figure 2-36. GAMMA. The curved line here is called the "characteristic" of a film emulsion. A perfect emulsion would have a characteristic curve which was a straight line. That is, for every equal increase in exposure there would be an equal increase in the density of the negative obtained. No emulsion, however, has such a curve, and most emulsions in use today show a similarly curved line. The area in which the curve is relatively flat is the usable contrast range of the emulsion. More important, the slope of this curve is a measure of the "contrastiness"—or potential contrast—of the emulsion. The emulsion represented by curve a, for example, has

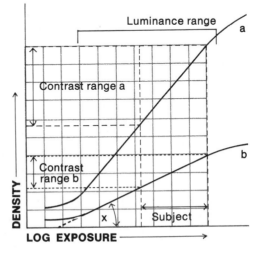

a greater potential contrast than that of curve b. In other words, emulsion a will better be able to distinguish between two similar luminance values. The gamma of an emulsion, precisely, is equal to tan x (the tangent of the angle of the slope).

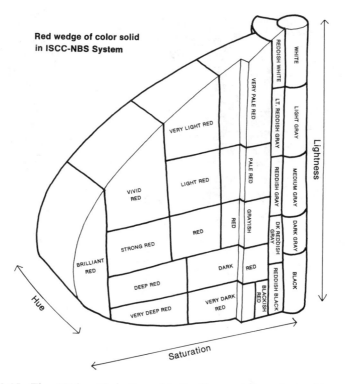

Figure 2-37. The "Color Wedge" graphically illustrates the relationships among the three major variables of color theory. This is a section of the full color solid which covers the entire spectrum.

Recent advances in processing techniques have greatly expanded the latitude of standard filmstocks. Although a particular stock is designed to produce the highest quality image within certain chemical parameters such as development time, it had become common practice by the late sixties to "push" film in development when greater sensitivity was needed. By developing for a longer time than the standard, a laboratory can effectively stretch the latitude of the stock to make it two or even three times more sensitive than its exposure rating might indicate. Grain increases when this is done, and with color stocks there are extra problems with color rendition, but Eastman Color Negative, for example, has enough inherent latitude so that it can be pushed one stop (doubled in sensitivity) or even two stops (quadrupled) without significant loss in image quality. The greatest loss in sensitivity, as one might expect, occurs at the point in the contrast scale where there is least light available—in the shadows of a scene, for example.

A more sophisticated way to cope with this problem is the technique of flashing. First used by cinematographer Freddie Young for Sidney

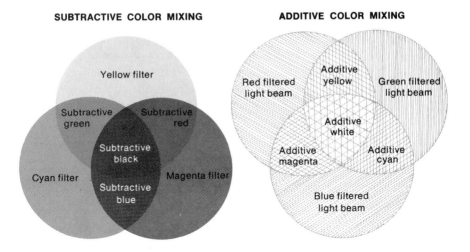

SUBTRACTIVE COLOR MIXING

Yellow filter

Subtractive green

Subtractive red

Subtractive black

Cyan filter

Magenta filter

Subtractive blue

ADDITIVE COLOR MIXING

Red filtered light beam

Additive yellow

Green filtered light beam

Additive white

Additive magenta

Additive cyan

Blue filtered light beam

Figure 2-38. PRIMARY COLOR THEORY. For psychological reasons all colors of the visible spectrum can be reproduced by the combination of three so-called "primary" colors. The "additive" primaries are red, blue, and green. The "subtractive" primaries are magenta (red-blue), cyan (blue-green), and yellow. All the colors of the spectrum together produce white light, just as complete absence of color yields black. If both magenta and yellow are subtracted from a beam of white light, the result is red. If both red and green beams are added together, the result is yellow, and so on.

Lumet's 1967 film A *Deadly Affair,* flashing entails exposing the film, before or after the scene is shot, to a neutral density gray light of a predetermined value. By in effect boosting even the darkest areas of the image into that area of the gamma scale where differentiations between close shades are easily made, flashing extends the latitude of any film stock. It also has the potential advantage of muting color values and thereby giving the filmmaker some measure of control over the color saturation of the image. In 1975, the TVC labs introduced a chemical process called Chemtone (developed by Dan Sandberg, Bernie Newson, and John Concilla) that is a much more sophisticated version of flashing. Chemtone was used on such films as *Harry and Tonto* (1974), *Nashville* (1975), and *Taxi Driver* (1976).

Contrast, tone, exposure latitude are all important factors in the matter of film lighting. With the advent of high speed color filmstock and the techniques of pushing, flashing, and Chemtone, the technology of cinematography has reached a point, after more than three-quarters of a century, where film may approximate the sensitivity of the human eye. It is now possible for filmmakers to shoot under almost any conditions in which they can see. But this was hardly the case during the first seventy-five years of film history. The earliest black-and-white emulsions were "monochromatic"—sensitive only to blue, violet, and ultraviolet light. By 1873, a way had been found to extend the spectrum of sensitivity to green. This was the so-called Orthochromatic film. Panchromatic film, which responds equally to all the colors of the visible spectrum, was developed in 1903, but it was not until more than twenty years later that it became standard in the film industry. Among the first films to use panchromatic stock were Robert Flaherty's *Moana* (1925) and Cooper and Schoedsack's *Chang* (1926). Without panchromatic film, warm colors, such as facial tones, reproduced very poorly, so the filmmaker had need of a light source in the blue-white range. Besides the sun itself, the only source of this kind of light was the huge, expensive arc lamp. As black-and-white stock become more sensitive and panchromatic emulsions were introduced, cheaper and more mobile incandescent lamps became usable; but when filmmakers began working with color, they had to return to arc lamps—both because the color stock was much slower and because it became necessary, once again, to maintain strict control of the color temperature of the light source.

Color temperature, or hue, is only one of the variables that must be calculated for color stock in addition to brightness, tone, and contrast. The others are saturation and intensity. The range of visible hues runs from deep red (the warmest) to deep violet (the coolest), through orange, yellow, green, blue, and indigo. The saturation of the color is a measure of its amount—the same hue of a color can be either weak or strong; the intensity, or lightness, is a measure of the amount of light transmitted (color shares this element with black-and-white).

As with contrast and latitude in black-and-white photography, the filmmaker has only limited parameters within which to work in color. The source of the light used to illuminate the subject, until very recently, had to be rigidly controlled. We make unconscious adjustments for the color temperature of a light source, but the filmmaker must compensate for these variations directly. A color stock balanced for 6000° Kelvin (the color temperature of an overcast sky) will produce an annoyingly orange picture if used with standard incandescent light sources with a color temperature of 3200°K. Likewise, a stock balanced for 3200°K will produce a very blue image when used outdoors under a 5000°K or 6000°K sky. As amateur photographers know, filters can be used to correct these imbalances, to some extent.

THE SOUNDTRACK

Before examining the post-production phase of filmmaking—editing, mixing, laboratory work, and projection—we should investigate the production of sound. Ideally, the sound of a film should be equal in importance with the image. Sadly, however, sound technology in film lags far behind not only the development of cinematography but also the technology of sound recording that has developed independently from film.

The recording of sound is roughly parallel to the recording of images: the microphone is, in effect, a lens through which sound is filtered; the recorder compares roughly with the camera; both sound and picture are recorded linearly and can be edited later. But there is one significant difference: because of the contrasting manners in which we perceive them, sound must be recorded continuously while pictures are recorded discretely. The concept of "persistence of vision" does not have an aural equivalent, which is one reason why we don't have "still sounds" to compare with still pictures. Sound must exist in time.

A corollary of this is that we cannot apply sound recording devices to aural information in the same way we can apply cinematography to visual information. Film can stretch or compress time, which is useful scientifically, but sound must exist in time and it is useless to compress or stretch it. Recent computer techniques allow the division of a sound recording into discrete particles that can then be played back at a faster or slower rate, but generally when we change the speed of a recording we change the quality of the sound, as well.

The union of sound and image, the original dream of the inventors of cinematography, was delayed for technological and economic reasons until the late 1920s. So long as image was recorded in a linear, discontinuous mode and sound was recorded in a circular, continuous mode, the problem of synchronization of sound and image was insurmountable. Lee De Forest's audion tube, invented in 1906, made it possible for the first time to translate sound signals into electrical signals. The electrical signals could then be translated into light signals that could be imprinted on film. Then, the two prints—sound and image—being parallel, could easily be "married" together so that they were always and forever synchronous, even if the film broke and had to be spliced. This was essentially the German Tri-Ergon system that was patented as early as 1919. This optical sound system has existed more or less unchanged to the present.

For twenty years after the sound film was born in 1926, filmmakers were hampered by the bulky and noisy electromechanical equipment necessary to record sound on the set. Even though portable optical recorders were soon available, recording on location was discouraged. In the late forties, however, the technology of film took another quantum leap with the development of magnetic recording. Tape is easier to work with than film, more compact, and, thanks to transistors, the recording devices themselves are now small and lightweight. Magnetic tape, in general, also produces a much better quality signal than an optical soundtrack does. Today, magnetic recording has entirely replaced optical recording on the set, although the optical soundtrack is still much more common than the magnetic soundtrack in theaters. There is good reason for this: optical soundtracks can be printed quickly and easily along with image tracks, while magnetic soundtracks must be recorded separately. Recent developments in optical soundtrack technology, moreover, suggest that some of the advantages that magnetic recording now enjoys over optical recording might be matched: variable density and variable hue optical soundtracks will eliminate the effects of rough handling, providing a higher fidelity, and can also be adapted to stereophonic and multiphonic systems. Because of its advantages in handling, editing, and mixing, however, magnetic tape will remain the medium of choice on the set and in the laboratory.

The microphone, the lens of the sound system, acts as the first gate through which the signal passes. Unlike the optical lens, however, it also translates the signal into electronic energy, which can then be recorded magnetically on tape. (Playback systems work exactly the reverse: magnetic potential energy is translated into electrical energy that is further translated into physical sound by the loudspeaker.) Since sound is being recorded on a tape physically separate from the filmed image, there must be some method of synchronizing the two. This is accomplished either by a direct mechanical linkage, or by electrical cable connections that carry a timed impulse, or by the increasingly common crystal sync generator, which produces a precisely timed pulse by using crystal clocks. This pulse regulates the speeds of the two separate motors, keeping them precisely in sync. The sound record is then transferred to magnetically coated film, where the sprocket holes provide the precise control over timing that is necessary in the editing process. Finally, the print of the film that is projected carries the signal, usually in the optical mode, but sometimes magnetically. Stereophonic and "quintaphonic" sound systems common to 70 mm systems almost always use magnetic tracks.

The variables that contribute to the clear and accurate reproduction of sound are roughly comparable to the variables of filmstock. The factor of amplitude can be compared to the exposure latitude of filmstock: the amplitude is the measure of the strength of a signal. Tape, recorder, and microphone working in concert should be able to reproduce a wide range of amplitudes, from very soft to very loud.

Next in importance is the frequency range, directly comparable to the scale of hues reproducible in color film. The normal range of fre-

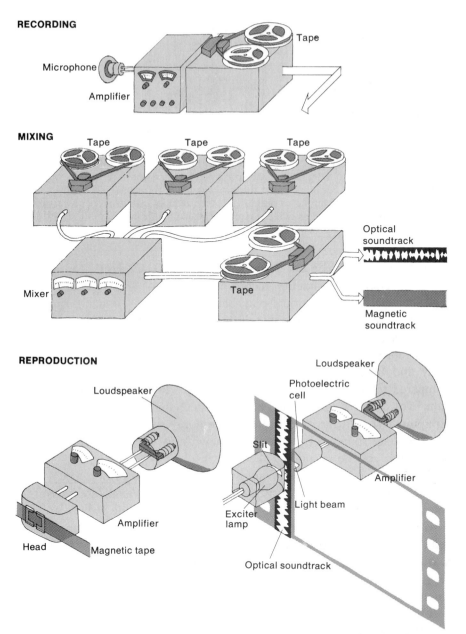

Figure 2-39. SOUND. Tracks from several sources (dialogue, music, effects, for example) are mixed to produce a master tape which is then used to produce the actual sound-track, which is usually optical, sometimes magnetic. The magnetic track is read by the miniature electromagnetic "head" which senses variations in the magnetic signal. The optical soundtrack is read by a photoelectric cell which senses variations in the amount of light transmitted through the soundtrack. The exciter lamp is the uniform light source.

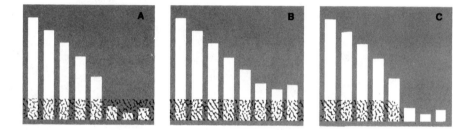

Figure 2-40. THE DOLBY EFFECT. A certain amount of basic surface noise is inherent in any recording medium (A). It presents no problem when the level of the recorded signal is high enough, but it masks out the weaker parts of the signal. The Dolby system boosts the weaker signal during recording (B), then reduces it to its proper level during playback, thus reducing the recorded surface noise along with it (C).

quencies to which the ear responds is 20 to 20,000 Hertz (cycles per second). Good high fidelity recording equipment can reproduce this range adequately, but optical playback systems have a much more limited range of frequency response (100 to 7,000 Hertz, on the average).

The recording medium and the equipment should also have the ability to reproduce a wide range of harmonics, those subtones that give body and life to music and voices. The harmonics of sound can be compared to the tonal qualities of an image. The signal should be free from wow, flutter, and other kinds of mechanical distortion, and the equipment should have a satisfactory response time: that is, the ability to reproduce sounds of short duration without mushiness. This is the "resolution" of the sound signal.

While stereoscopic images are subject to special psychological and physical problems that significantly reduce their value, stereophonic sound is free of these problems and therefore highly desirable. We are used to hearing sound from every direction. Although we engage in selective attention to sounds, we don't focus directly on a sound the way we focus on an image. Film sound should have the ability to reproduce the total aural environment. In the early sixties, the recording industry changed over completely from monophonic to stereophonic recording, yet film sound—with a few exceptions—is still largely monophonic, despite the fact that the application of stereophonic techniques is much simpler and cheaper in film than in the record industry. Quadraphonic reproduction, a problem that engaged recording engineers and audiophiles in the mid-1970's, is also relatively easy and cheap to adapt to film.

Although film sound at present is of comparatively poor quality, recent technological developments point to rapid advances in this area in the next few years. The assimilation of multitrack recording techniques developed in the music industry has already expanded the horizons of the art of film sound—for example, such highly sophisticated soundtracks as Coppola's *The Conversation* (1974) and Altman's *Nashville* (1975), produced on an eight-track system. The application of Dolby techniques of noise reduction and signal enhancement in the mid-seventies has greatly increased the potential fidelity of film sound, as well. Roughly comparable to the flashing of filmstock, the Dolby electronic circuitry reduces the background noise inherent in even the best tape stock, thereby significantly enhancing the latitude. It does this by selecting out the area of the sound spectrum in which the noise occurs and boosting the signal level in that area during recording; when the signal is reduced to normal levels during playback, the noise is reduced along with the audio signal.

POST-PRODUCTION

Film professionals divide the process of their art into three phases: pre-production, shooting, and post-production. The first phase is preparatory—the script is written, actors and technicians hired, shooting schedules and budgets planned. In another art, this period of preparation would be relatively uncreative. But Alfred Hitchcock, for example, regardèd this period of the film process as paramount: once he had designed the film, he used to say, the execution of its was comparatively boring. Moreover, in this most expensive of arts, intelligent and accurate planning often spells the difference between success and failure. It must be clear by now that the equation of film art is complex and intricate—so much so that modern systems design has had a measurable positive effect on the process. The elaborate, carefully organized systems Stanley Kubrick creates for his film projects, for example, are one of the most intriguing aspects of his work.

Nearly all the discussion in this chapter on film technology has so far centered on the second phase of film production: shooting. Yet there is a sense in which this area of the process can be seen as preparatory, too. Shooting produces the raw materials that are fashioned into finished products only in the third stage of the process. Editing is often regarded as the fulcrum of film art, since it is in this process that film most clearly separates itself from competing arts. The theory of film editing will be discussed in Chapters 3 and 5; here we will outline the system and describe the equipment involved.

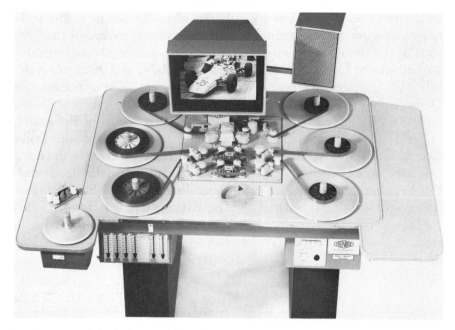

Figure 2-41. Flatbed editing tables, such as the Steenbeck pictured here, permit comparisons between as many as three or four picture and sound tracks. This particular table is set up for one picture track and two soundtracks. (*W. Steenbeck and Co.*)

Three jobs generally proceed more or less concurrently during postproduction: sound mixing and looping; editing; and laboratory work, opticals, and special effects. A film could conceivably be edited, mixed, and printed within a few hours; assuming both the sound track and the picture in their raw state were satisfactory, the editing would be simply a matter of splicing a few takes end to end. But very few films are this simple, and post-production work often takes longer than the actual shooting of the film.

EDITING

The shot is the basic unit of film construction; it is defined, physically, as a single piece of film, without breaks in the continuity of the action. It may last as long as ten minutes (since most cameras only hold ten minutes of film); it may be as short as $1/24$ second (one frame). Hitchcock's *Rope* (1948) was shot to appear as if it were one continuous take, most of Miklós Jancsó's films are composed of full-reel shots (ten or twelve per film), but the standard fictional feature is comprised of as many as five hundred or a thousand separate shots. Each of the shots must be physically spliced with cement or tape to the shots that precede and follow it. The craft of editing consists of choosing between two or more takes of the same shot, deciding how long each shot should last and how it should be punctuated, and matching the soundtrack carefully with the edited images (or vice versa, if the soundtrack is edited first).

In America, until the mid-sixties, this work was accomplished on an upright editing machine generically known by the major brand name, Moviola. Another, much more versatile configuration—the horizontal, or flat-bed, editing table had been pioneered by the UFA studios in Germany in the twenties and was widely used throughout Europe before World War II. The table, as opposed to the upright, allowed the film editor to handle pieces of film much more easily and quickly. The development after the war of the revolving prism to replace the intermittent-motion pull-down mechanism further enhanced the versatility of the editing table, allowing speeds up to five times the normal twenty-four frames per second. During the sixties, partly due to the influence of documentary filmmakers who were among the first to recognize its great advantages, the editing table (Steenbeck and Kem are two important brand names) revolutionized the process of montage. Because the film rests horizontally on plates in the table configuration rather than vertically on reels, it is much easier to handle physically. Modern editing tables also permit instantaneous comparison of as many as six separate picture and sound tracks, thereby vastly shortening the time needed to make a choice of shots. Documentarists, who often have huge amounts of footage to examine while editing, saw the advantages immediately. The editors of the film *Woodstock* (1970), for example, were confronted with hundreds of hours of footage of that epochal concert. Even using split-screen techniques as they did, it was necessary to edit that raw material down to four hours, a feat that would have been very difficult indeed without the speed and multiple abilities of the editing table. (A normal fictional feature might be shot in a ratio of ten to one: that is, ten feet of film shot for every foot finally used.)

MIXING AND LOOPING

The editing of a soundtrack differs somewhat from the editing of images. First, for various reasons, the sound recorded on the set at the same time as the picture may not be usable. While a bad take of the picture is totally useless and must be reshot, a bad take of the sound can be much more easily repaired or replaced. In the process called post-dubbing, or looping, a few seconds of film are formed into a loop that is projected in a sound studio and repeated many times so the actors can catch the rhythm of the scene and then mouth their dialogue in synchronization with the image. This is then recorded and spliced into the original soundtrack.

This process was formerly much more common than it is today because sound recording techniques have been vastly simplified by the introduction of magnetic tape. On-location recording has become the rule rather than the exception. It is still the practice in Italy, however, to post-dub the entire film. Federico Fellini, for one, is renowned for occasionally not even bothering to write dialogue until after the scene has been shot, directing his actors instead to recite numbers (but with feeling!). Post-dubbing has generally been a useful technique for translating films into other languages. Usually, a soundtrack produced this way has a noticeable deadness and awkwardness to it, but the Italians, as might be expected, since their practice is to post-dub all films, have produced some quite passable foreign-language dubbing jobs.

Once the tedious job of dubbing has been completed, the soundtrack can be mixed. This process has no real equivalent with images for, although split-screen techniques and multiple exposures can present us with more than one image at a time, those multiple images are seldom combined. Matte techniques and rear projection (see pp. 111-14) offer more directly comparable equivalents to sound mixing, but they are relatively rarely used.

By 1932, sound technology had developed to the point where rerecording was common, and it was possible to mix as many as four optical tracks. For many years, mixing consisted simply of combining pre-recorded music, sound effects (a crude term for a sophisticated craft), and dialogue. However, the multiple-track magnetic recorder has greatly expanded the potential of sound mixing. A single word or sound effect can easily be spliced in (this was relatively difficult with optical soundtracks), the quality of the sound can be modified, reinforced, or altered in a great many different ways electronically, and as many as sixteen separate tracks can be combined, with the sound mixer in total control of all the esthetic variables of each track.

SPECIAL EFFECTS

"Special effects" is a rather dull label for a wide variety of activities, each of which has direct creative potential. The craft of special effects rests on three premises: 1) film need not be shot continuously, each frame can be photographed separately; 2) drawings, paintings, and models can be photographed in such a way that they pass for reality; 3) images can be combined.

The first premise makes possible the art of animation. The precursors of animation were the zoetrope and the age-old "flip book," in which a series of drawings were bound together so that if the pages were flipped quickly the image appeared to move. But animation is not dependent on drawings, even though most animated films are cartoons. Models and even living figures can be animated by photographing frames individually and changing the position of the subject between frames. This special technique is called pixillation. As for cartoon animation, the cell technique in which various sections of the cartoon are drawn on separate transparent sheets (cells) makes the process much more flexible than one might at first think. Approximately 14,400 separate drawings must be made for a ten-minute animated film, but if the background remains constant then it can be painted on a separate cell and the artist need draw only those subjects that are meant to be seen in motion. During the last twenty years, computer video techniques have made animation even more flexible, since a computer can be programmed to produce a wide variety of line-drawings instantaneously and to change their shape accurately and with proper timing.

The second premise yields a series of special effects known as miniature or model shots and glass shots. The success of miniature photography depends on our ability to run the camera at faster than normal speeds (called "overcranking"). A two-inch wave, travelling at normal speed but photographed at four times normal speed, will appear to be approximately four times larger when it is projected at the standard rate (and therefore slowed down by a factor of four). The rule of thumb in miniature photography is that the camera speed be the square root of the scale; that is, a quarter-scale model will require a camera speed twice normal. In practice, the smallest miniatures that work are $1/16$-size, and even $1/4$-size miniatures present some problems of verisimilitude.

Glass shots are possibly the simplest of special effects. The technique involves placing a glass several feet in front of the camera and in effect painting over the area of the scene that must be changed. The effect depends of course on the talent of the painter, but surprisingly realistic examples of this simple technique exist.

The third premise is possibly the most fruitful for contemporary filmmakers. The simplest way to make use of the idea is to project another image—the background—on a screen behind the actors and the foreground. Thousands of Hollywood taxi rides were filmed this way by the aid of rear projection, introduced in 1932. (See Figure 2-45) The advent of color made rear projection obsolete, however. Color photography required a greater amount of light on the subject, which tended to wash out the rear-projected image. More important, the color image

Figure 2-42. CELL ANIMATION. Classical animation
uses the cell technique for efficiency and accuracy.
The image is divided into layers of movement and each of those layers is drawn on a
separate transparent sheet called a "cell." Thus, the stationary background need be
drawn only once for a scene, simple movements can be executed rapidly, and special
attention can be paid to isolated, complex movements. In this scene from independent
filmmaker John Canemaker's *The Wizard's Son,* four cells—the figure, the pillow, the
globe, and the cat—are overlaid on the background. (*Copyright © John Canemaker
1981; reproduced with permission.*)

Figure 2-43. COMPUTER ANIMATION. Since animation involves managing large quantities of data, computers are often useful. The programs, of varying degrees of sophistication, can take a line drawing though its animated paces, as in this compressed history of
evolution from Carl Sagan's *Cosmos* (1980). The drawing moves continuously and
smoothly from stage to stage. (*James Blinn, Pat Cole, Charles Kohlhase, Jet Propulsion
Laboratories Computer Graphics Lab.*)

provides more visual information, which makes it much more difficult to match foreground and background. Two techniques were developed to replace rear projection.

Front projection utilizes a directional screen composed of millions of tiny glass beads that act as lenses which enable the screen to reflect as much as 95 percent of the light falling on it back to the source. As can be seen in Figure 2-46, this requires that the source be on the same axis as the camera lens, a position that also eliminates shadows on the screen. This positioning is achieved by using a half-silvered mirror set at a 45° angle. Front projection was perfected for Stanley Kubrick's *2001: A Space Odyssey* (1968). (That film, in fact, is a catalogue of modern special effects.)

Glass shots and rear and front projection are techniques that combine images and are accomplished on the set. Matte shots and blue screen (or travelling matte) shots, however, are produced in the laboratory. Stationary matte shots produce an effect similar to the glass shot. In the laboratory, the film is projected on a white card and the artist outlines the area to be matted out and paints it black. This black outline (see Figure 2-48) is then photographed and the film, after it is developed, is packed together with the original shot in the projector and a copy is

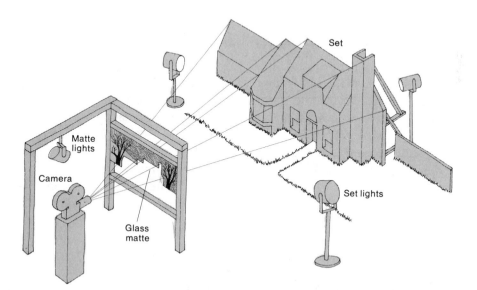

Figure 2-44. GLASS SHOTS. The bottom part of the glass is left clear; the top part has been painted. The glass is situated far enough from the camera so that both it and the set are in focus. Set lights and matte lights are adjusted to balance. The camera is mounted on a solid base to prevent vibration.

made in which the proper area is matted out in each frame. The scene to be added to this area (together with a reversal of the first matte) is then printed onto the copy of the original scene and the print is developed.

Travelling matte shots replace front and rear projection shots and came into use when color film began to dominate the industry. The process, essentially, is this: a deep blue screen is placed behind the foreground action, and the scene is photographed. Because the background color is uniform and precise, "male" and "female" mattes can be made by copying the film through filters. A blue filter would let through only the background light, leaving the foreground action blank and producing a "female" matte; a red filter would block out the background and expose only the foreground, producing a black silhouette, the male matte. The female matte can then be used, as in the stationary matte technique, to block out the blue background when a copy of the original film is made, the male matte will block out precisely the right areas of the background scene that has been chosen, and the matted background and matted foreground can then be combined. This is a difficult and exacting process in film, but the technique has been carried over to television, where it is called chroma key, and there it can be achieved electronically simply by pressing a button. It has become a basic tool of television, used constantly in news and sports to integrate the announcer with the action.

OPTICALS AND THE LABORATORY

The laboratory performs two basic jobs for the filmmaker: the first is to adjust the image so that it more closely approximates what the filmmaker had in mind while shooting; the second is to add a number of effects called "opticals," usually for purposes of punctuation.

In color work, the role of the laboratory is critical. While the brain automatically and unconsciously corrects for variations in lighting and color, film does not. The laboratory technician must "time" the print, adjusting the colors of various scenes shot at different times and under widely varying conditions to conform to some agreed-upon standard. As we have already noted, some compensation can be made for differences in the color temperature of the light source during filming, yet timing is almost always necessary. At the same time, the lab might have to correct for under- or overexposure by over- or underdeveloping the filmstock. In order to save footage that might otherwise be unusable, the film can also be flashed at this point. Some methods of flashing have been tried (notably by Gerry Turpin for *Young Winston*, 1973) that add a wash of color to the print at this point. This is a return to one of the oldest devices in film

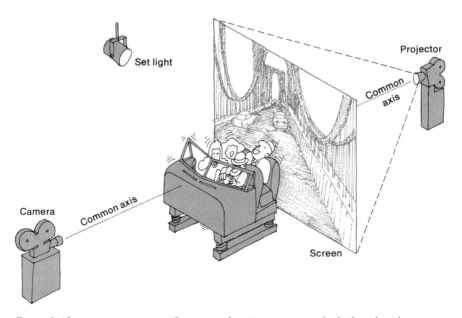

Figure 2-45. REAR PROJECTION. Camera and projector are interlocked so that the projector projects a frame at precisely the same time the camera takes one. The actors in the car mock-up in front of the screen are lit in such a way that the translucent screen behind them does not reflect; it only transmits the light from the projector. This is an artist's conception of the scene being filmed in Figure 6-19. Note the springs which support the car mock-up in order to simulate movement.

history, for black-and-white films of the twenties were often printed on tinted stock to add emotional value to a scene.

In addition to timing the print and correcting for exposure differences, the laboratory also executes a number of punctuational devices known collectively as "opticals," including fades, wipes, dissolves, freezes, and masks. These are discussed in detail in the next chapter. A number of other optical effects are available. Ghosts (visual echoes achieved by double-printing frames), multiple images (split-screen and the like), and superimpositions (double exposures) are the most common.

Finally, the laboratory is equipped to enlarge or reduce the size of the image. The whole film might be enlarged or reduced so that it can be released in a different gauge, or a single shot might be altered by enlarging part of it on the optical printer, the machine on which most of these effects are accomplished. When a Panavision print is prepared for television, for example, a technique known as "pan and scan" is used so that at least the major part of the action shows up within the 1.33 television frame. As the film is printed down to the Academy

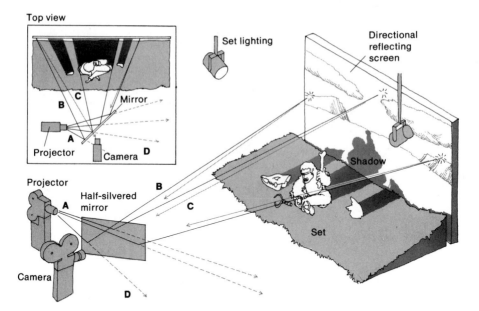

Figure 2-46. FRONT PROJECTION. The essential element of the front projection system is the half-silvered mirror, which both transmits and reflects light. This makes it possible for the projector to project the background image onto the screen behind the set and actor along precisely the same axis that the camera views the scene. Thus, the camera cannot see the shadows which the actor and set cast on the screen. Set lighting is adjusted so that it is just bright enough to wash out the background image which falls on the actor and set. The screen is highly directional, reflecting a great deal more light from the projected image along the axis than off to the side and thus providing a bright enough image. The projected scene travels from the projector (A), is reflected off the half-silvered mirror onto the screen (and set and actor) (B), and then back into the camera, *through* the mirror (C). Some of the light from the projector is also transmitted through the mirror (D). See the final effect in Figure 2-47.

aperture, artificial cuts and pans from one side of the widescreen image to the other are added on the optical printer. Nearly all these laboratory effects will add extra generations to the printing process and therefore affect the quality of the image. As a result, the practice at present is to avoid them as much as possible.

THE USES OF VIDEO

The technologies of television and videotape will be discussed in detail in Chapter 6, but here we can examine the courtship now taking place between film and television. In nearly every stage of film production,

Figure 2-47. Front projection from *2001*. Kubrick and his staff of special effects specialists perfected the system for the film. (*Frame enlargement.*)

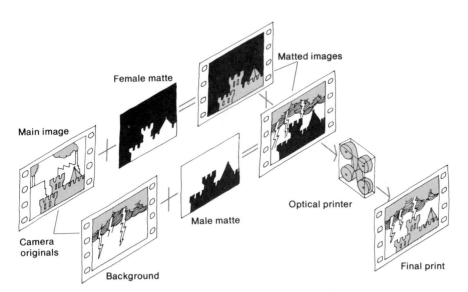

Figure 2-48. MATTES. Both male and female mattes are derived from the main image. In the stationary matte technique they are drawn; in the travelling matte system, the main image would be backed up by a blue screen (not shown here) and the mattes would be derived optically.

Figure 2-49. A matte shot from *2001*. The scenery of the moon has been matted in. The images on the tiny screens below the windows have been rear-projected. (*Frame enlargement.*)

from preparation to shooting to post-production, video can serve useful functions. The most obvious advantage of videotape over film is that tape is immediately available for review; it need not be processed first. In addition, whereas the camera operator is the only person who has a clear view of the image while a film is being shot, a video image can be instantaneously transmitted to a number of receivers. As a result, video-tape is finding a number of applications on the set. It frees the operator from the camera, as in the Louma process described on p. 79. In normal cinematography, a video camera can be attached to a film camera by means of a semireflectant mirror, and can see the same image the operator sees. The director (and other technicians) can then observe on a receiver placed elsewhere the precise image being shot. If the scene is taped, it can immediately be played back so that actors and technicians can check to make sure the take went as planned, thus greatly reducing the need for additional takes.

Video also has applications in the editing process. Electronic editing, especially when it avails itself of computer memories and programming, is far quicker and simpler than the physical splicing of film. A film can easily be transferred to videotape for editing with one channel of the tape (or one section of the computer's memory) being reserved for frame numbers. Once the tape has been edited satisfactorily, the frame num-bers can be recalled, providing a foolproof guide for the actual splicing of the film. Computer technology allows an editor to put together a sequence of shots instantaneously, ask the computer to remember the sequence, then "recut" it just as quickly, compare the two versions, and

Figure 2-50. A model shot of the moon landing station from *2001*. The small portholes in the model spherical landing capsule as well as the bright rectangular areas to the left and right were matted with live-action scenes to increase the illusion of the model. Most of the exquisite detail is lost in this reproduction. (*Frame enlargement.*)

recall the one that is most effective. The problem of storage and retrieval of thousands of pieces of film is vastly simplified. Disc storage of the electronic signal offers immediate random access to any shot.

While film-to-tape transfer has been in wide use in television almost since its inception (a production is shot on film, then transferred to tape for exhibition), the reverse process (shooting on tape for transfer to film) is only now finding applications. Before the perfection of video-tape, the only means of preserving a live television show was to film it as it appeared on a monitor—the so-called "kinescope." Anyone who has seen one of these records is familiar with their poor quality. But a much sharper video image, especially produced for tape-to-film transfer and enhanced by electronic techniques, can provide quite a serviceable film image. Frank Zappa's *200 Motels* (1971) is one commercial film that was shot this way. Videotape cameras and recording equipment of professional quality only recently began to rival film equipment in efficiency and portability, and the video image still does not have the fineness of resolution of the film image, so a working marriage of film and video is still some years away.

PROJECTION

One final step remains before the chain of film technology is complete: projection. This is, in a way, the most crucial step, since all the work done in the earlier stages must funnel through this one before a film reaches an observer. Ironically, the film projector is the single piece of film equipment that has changed least during the last fifty years. Except for the addition of the optical or magnetic head, which reads the soundtrack, and adapters necessary to project anamorphic prints, the projector is basically the same machine used in the early 1920s. Indeed some projectionists think antique machines from the thirties work better than many manufactured today.

Any projector is, simply, a camera that operates in the reverse mode: instead of taking a picture, it shows it—but this one difference is significant. The amount of light necessary to record an image is easily obtained, while the even larger amount of light necessary to project a picture must be provided by a source small enough to fit behind the lens of the projector, and it must be able to enlarge the ½-square-inch 35 mm frame 300,000 times or more to fill the screen. Until recently, the light source of commercial projectors was a carbon arc lamp that could provide the intense light of 5000° or 6000°K. that is necessary. An arc of high-voltage current between two carbon rods was the direct source. The difficulty with the carbon arc lamp (the same sort used to illuminate sets in earlier days) was that the rods were consumed in the process and had to be continually adjusted. In addition, the lamps needed powerful ventilation systems. Carbon arc lamps have generally been replaced by xenon lamphouses, which last longer, need not be continually adjusted, and don't require special ventilation.

While a film negative runs only once through a camera and once through an optical printer, the print of a film is subjected to far more stress, normally being run thirty-five or forty times per week in a commercial movie theater. This is the second salient difference between camera and projector: the latter must treat the film more gently. Because so few advances have been made in projector design, however, prints are subjected to much unnecessary damage. The result is that a filmmaker's work is very seldom observed under ideal conditions. A writer can be fairly sure that his publisher and printer will represent his intentions to his reader; a filmmaker has no such assurance from distributors and exhibitors. Damage to the film means that splices will be made excising parts of the film. Cuts are also made simply to shorten the running time (as well as to eliminate politically or sexually objectionable material). A reader already knows if a copy of a book has been altered—page numbers will be missing. A film viewer seldom knows just what relationship the print he is seeing bears to the original. Film is often thought to be a permanent medium: on the contrary, it is exceptionally fragile. The recent development of the Hollogon Rotary projec-

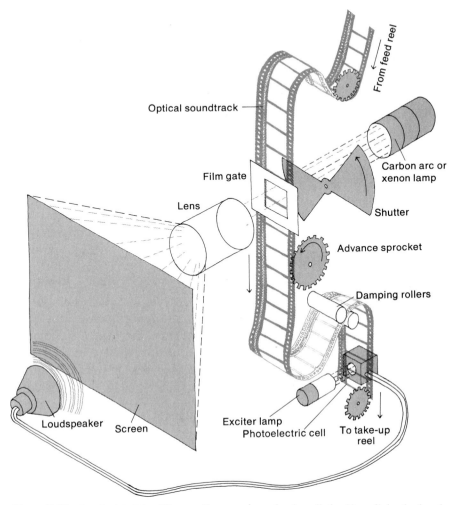

Figure 2-51. THE PROJECTOR. The smaller sprocket wheels pull the film off the feed reel and feed it to the take-up reel. The main sprocket advances the film intermittently. It is connected to the maltese cross gear (see Figure 2-20). A series of rollers damps the intermittent motion of the film before it reaches the sound head, so that the soundtrack can be read continuously and smoothly.

tion system—the first radical redesign of projection machinery in seventy-five years—promises a considerable advance. The Hollogon system utilizes a revolving twenty-four-sided prism like those used in high-speed cameras and modern editing tables to reduce strain on the print. Instead of a complicated system of sprocket wheels, pull-down mechanisms, damping rollers, and sound heads, the Hollogon projector consists simply of two continuously revolving wheels, constantly in sync. As the frame image moves around the picture wheel, it is kept steady on the screen optically by the multifaceted prism.

Besides keeping the projector in working order, the projectionist has two other responsibilities: to keep the image in focus and, through a proper combination of lenses and masks, to show the film in the proper aspect ratio. Standards are as slack here as elsewhere in projection. Although scientifically precise means of focusing are readily available (and at one time were usually found in projection booths), the average contemporary projectionist prefers to improvise, relying on the naked eye. Generations have grown up not knowing what a well-focused film looks like. The problem of masks is even more acute. Few theaters keep a complete range of masks and concomitant lenses on hand. Many theaters have only the contemporary standard 1.85 American wide-screen mask and the basic anamorphic lens. If a 1.66 film arrives—or, even worse—a movie in the Academy aspect ratio, the projectionist shows it with whatever mask is at hand. Heads are lopped off with abandon and whatever composition the director originally had in mind is a matter of conjecture. Finally, there is sound: few theater sound systems are any better in quality than many of the mediocre soundtracks they must reproduce; many are considerably worse, using equipment that dates back thirty or forty years. In major cities one may find first-run theaters that are equipped to handle stereophonic or quinta-phonic sound, Dolbyized tracks, even magnetic tracks. But the large majority of the audience for a major studio release that uses these techniques hears the soundtrack of the film on a sound system that is little better than one of the earliest AM radios.

It is clear that filmmaking is not (as ads directed to amateur photographers have tried to convince us for years) simply a matter of looking through the viewfinder and pressing the button. Filmmaking requires a degree of technical knowledge and expertise far surpassing that of any other art. While it is true that there are certain areas in which the technology of film has not yet caught up with the aspirations of film-makers, it is equally true that there are areas where the technology offers a potential that cinéastes have yet to explore. The technology and the esthetics of film are interlocked: where one pulls the other must follow. So a full understanding of the technological limitations and interconnections is necessary before one can begin to comprehend the ideal world of film esthetics, which is the subject of the following chapter.

THREE

THE LANGUAGE OF FILM: SIGNS AND SYNTAX

Film is not a language in the sense that English, French, or mathematics is. It is, first of all, impossible to be ungrammatical in film. And it is not necessary to learn a vocabulary. Infants appear to understand television images, for example, months before they begin to develop a facility with spoken language. Even cats watch television. Clearly, it is not necessary to acquire intellectual competence in film in order to appreciate it, at least on the most basic level.

But film is very much like language. People who are highly experienced in film, highly literate visually (or should we say "cinemate"?), see more and hear more than people who seldom go to the movies. An education in the quasi-language of film opens up greater potential meaning for the observer, so it is useful to use the metaphor of language to describe the phenomenon of film. In fact, no extensive scientific investigation of our ability to comprehend artificial sounds and images has as yet been performed, but nevertheless we do know through research, that while children are able to recognize objects in pictures long before they are able to read, they are eight or ten years of age before they can comprehend a film image the way most adults do. Moreover, there are cultural differences in perception of images. In one famous 1920s test, anthropologist William Hudson set out to examine whether rural Africans who had had little contact with Western culture perceived depth in two-dimensional images the same way that Europeans do. He found, unequivocally, that they do not. Results varied—there were some individuals who responded in the Western manner to the test—but they were uniform over a broad cultural and sociological range.

121

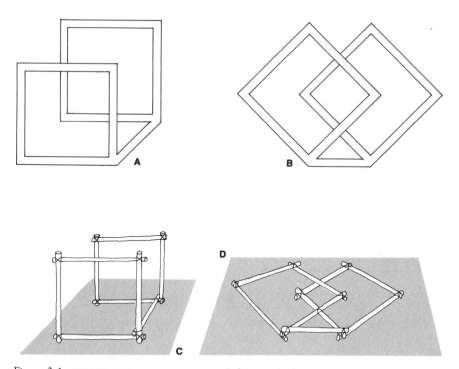

Figure 3-1. CONSTRUCTION-TASK FIGURES. Subjects asked to reconstruct these figures in three dimensions using sticks or rods, respond in different ways. People from Western cultures, trained in the codes and conventions that artists use to convey three-dimensionality in a two-dimensional drawing, see A as three-dimensional and B as two-dimensional. The operating code for three-dimensionality here insists that the dimension of depth be portrayed along the 45° oblique line. This works well enough in A, but not in B, where the oblique lines are not in the depth plane. Subjects from African cultures tend to see both figures as two-dimensional, since they are not familiar with this Western three-dimensional code. Figures C and D illustrate the models of A constructed by Western and African observers, respectively. (*From, "Pictorial Perception and Culture," Jan B. Deregowski. © 1972 by Scientific American, Inc. All rights reserved.*)

The conclusions that can be drawn from this seminal experiment and others that have followed are two: first, that every normal human being can perceive and identify a visual image; second, that even the simplest visual images are interpreted differently in different cultures. So we know that images must be "read." There is a process of intellection occuring— not necessarily consciously—when we observe an image, and it follows that we must have learned, at some point, how to do this.

The "ambiguous Trident," a well-known "optical illusion," provides an easy test of this ability. It's safe to say that the level of visual literacy of anyone reading this book is such that observation of the trident will be confusing to all of us. It would not be for someone not trained in

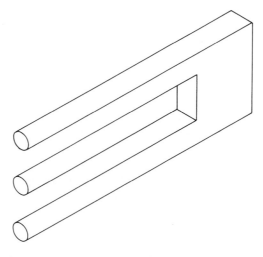

Figure 3-2. THE AMBIGUOUS TRI-
DENT. The illusion is intriguing
only because we are trained in
Western codes of perspective. The
psychological effects is powerful:
our minds insist that we see the object in space rather than the drawing on a plane.

Western conventions of three-dimensionality. Similarly, the well-
known optical illusions in Figures 3-3 and 3-4 demonstrate that the
process of perception and comprehension involves the brain: it is a
mental experience as well as a physical one. Whether we "see" the
Necker Cube from the top or the bottom or whether we perceive the
drawing in Figure 3-4 as either a young girl or an old woman depends
not on the physiological function of our eyes but on what the brain does
with the information received. The word "image," indeed, has two
conjoined meanings: an image is an optical pattern; it is also a mental
experience, which is why, we can assume, we use the word "imagine"
to describe the mental creation of pictures.

So there is a strong element of our ability to observe images, whether
still or moving, that depends on learning. This is, interestingly, not
true to a significant extent with auditory phenomena. If the machines
are sophisticated enough, we can produce recorded sounds that are
technically indistinguishable from their originals. The result of this
difference in mode of the two systems of perception—visual and audi-

Figure 3-3. THE NECKER CUBE. Devised in 1832 by L. A. Necker, a
Swiss naturalist. The illusion depends, once again, on cultural
training.

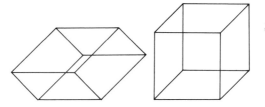

Figure 3-4. "My Wife and My Mother-in-law," by cartoonist W. E. Hill, was published in *Puck* in 1915. It has since become a famous example of the phenomenon known as the multistable figure. The young woman's chin is the old woman's nose. The old woman's chin is the young woman's chest. (*New York Public Library.*)

tory—is that whatever education our ears undergo in order to perceive reality is sufficient to perceive recorded sound, whereas there is a subtle but significant difference between the education necessary for our eyes to perceive (and our brain to understand) recorded images and that which is necessary simply to comprehend the reality that surrounds us. It would serve no purpose to consider phonography as a language, but it is useful to speak of photography (and cinematography) as a language, because a learning process is involved.

THE PHYSIOLOGY OF PERCEPTION

Another way to describe this difference between the two senses is in terms of the function of the sensory organs: ears hear whatever is available for them to hear; eyes choose what to see. This is true not only in the conscious sense (choosing to redirect attention from point A to point B or to ignore the sight altogether by closing our eyes), but in the unconscious as well. Since the receptor organs that permit visual acuity are concentrated (and properly arranged) only in the "fovea" of the retina, it's necessary for us to   stare directly at an object in order to have a clear image of it.   ●   You can demonstrate this to yourself by staring at the dot in   the center of this page. Only the area immediately surrounding it will be clear. The result of this foveated vision is that the eyes must move constantly in order to perceive an object of any size. These semiconscious movements are called "saccades" and take approximately $1/20$ second each, just about the interval of persistence of vision, the phenomenon that makes film possible.

The conclusion that can be drawn from the fact of foveated vision is that we do indeed read an image physically as well as mentally and psychologically, just as we read a page. The difference is that we know how to read a page—in English, from the left to right and top to bottom—but we are seldom conscious of how precisely we read an image.

A complete set of physiological, ethnographic, and psychological experiments might demonstrate that various individuals read images more or less well in three different ways:

- physiologically: the best readers would have the most efficient and extensive saccadic patterns;
- ethnographically: the most literate readers would draw on a greater experience and knowledge of various cultural visual conventions;
- psychologically: the readers who gained the most from the material would be the ones who were best able to assimilate the various sets of meanings they perceived and then integrate the experience.

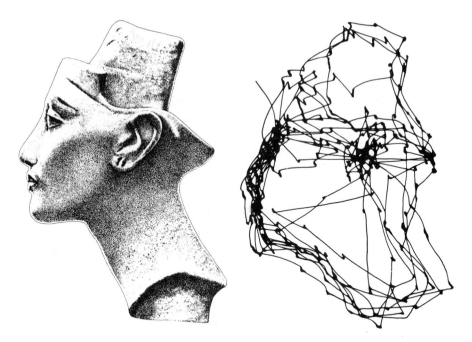

Figure 3-5. SACCADE PATTERNS. At left, a drawing of a bust of Queen Nefertiti; at right, a diagram of the eye movements of a subject viewing the bust. Notice that the eye follows regular patterns rather than randomly surveying the image. The subject clearly concentrates on the face and shows little interest in the neck. The ear also seems to be a focus of attention, probably not because it is inherently interesting, but rather because it is located in a prominent place in this profile. The saccadic patterns are not continuous; the recording clearly shows that the eye jerks quickly from point to point (the "notches" in the continuous line), fixing on specific nodes rather than absorbing general information. The recording was made by Alfred L. Yarbus of the Institute for Problems of Information Transmission, Moscow. (*From "Eye Movements and Visual Perception," by David Noton and Lawrence Stark, June 1971. Copyright © 1971 by Scientific American, Inc. All rights reserved. Reproduced by permission.*)

The irony here is that we know very well that we must learn to read before we can attempt to enjoy or understand literature, but we tend to believe, mistakenly, that anyone can read a film. Anyone can see a film, it's true, even cats. But some people have learned to comprehend visual images—physiologically, ethnographically, and psychologically—with far more sophistication than have others. This evidence confirms the validity of the triangle of perception outlined in Chapter 1, uniting author, work, and observer. The observer is not simply a consumer, but an active—or potentially active—participant in the process.

Film is not a language, but is like a language, and since it is like language, some of the methods that we use to study language might profitably be applied to a study of film. In fact, during the last ten years,

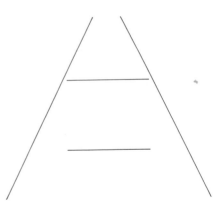

Figure 3-6. THE PONZO ILLUSION. The horizontal lines are of equal length, yet the line at the top appears to be longer than the line at the bottom. The diagonals suggest perspective, so that we interpret the picture in depth and conclude, therefore, that since the "top" line must be "behind" the "bottom" line, further away, it must then be longer.

this approach to film—essentially linguistic—has grown considerably in importance. Since film is not a language, strictly linguistic concepts are misleading. Ever since the beginning of film history, theorists have been fond of comparing film with verbal language (this was partly to justify the serious study of film), but it wasn't until a new, larger category of thought developed in the fifties and early sixties—one that saw written and spoken language as just two among many systems of communication—that the real study of film as a language could proceed. This inclusive category is semiology, the study of systems of signs. Semiologists justified the study of film as language by redefining the concept of written and spoken language. Any system of communication is a "language"; English, French, or Chinese is a "language system." Cinema, therefore, may be a language of a sort, but it is not clearly a language system. As Christian Metz, the well-known film semiologist, pointed out: we understand a film not because we have a knowledge of its system, rather, we achieve an understanding of its system because we understand the film. Put another way, "It is not because the cinema is language that it can tell such fine stories, but rather it has become language because it has told such fine stories" [Metz, *Film Language*, p. 47].

For semiologists, a sign must consist of two parts: the signifier and the signified. The word "word," for example—the collection of letters or sounds—is a signifier; what it represents is something else again—the "signified." In literature, the relationship between signifier and signified is a main locus of art: the poet is building constructions that, on the one hand, are composed of sounds (signifiers) and, on the other, of meanings (signifieds), and the relationship between the two can be fascinating. In fact, much of the pleasure of poetry lies just here: in the dance between sound and meaning.

But in film, the signifier and the signified are almost identical: the sign of cinema is a short-circuit sign. A picture of a book is much closer to a book, conceptually, than the word "book" is. It's true that we may have to learn in infancy or early childhood to interpret the picture of a book as meaning a book, but this is a great deal easier than learning to interpret the letters or sounds of the word "book" as what it signifies. A picture bears some direct relationship with what it signifies, a word seldom does.*

It is the fact of this short-circuit sign that makes the language of film so difficult to discuss. As Metz put it, in a memorable phrase: "A film is difficult to explain because it is easy to understand." It also makes "doing" film quite different from "doing" English (either writing or speaking). We can't modify the signs of cinema the way we can modify the words of language systems. In cinema, an image of a rose is an image of a rose is an image of a rose—nothing more, nothing less. In English, a rose can be a rose, simply, but it can also be modified or confused with similar words: rose, rosy, rosier, rosiest, rise risen, rows (ruse), arose, roselike, and so forth. The power of language systems is that there is a very great difference between the signifier and the signified; the power of film is that there is not.

Nevertheless, film is *like* a language. How, then, does it do what is does? Clearly, one person's image of a certain object is not another's. If we both read the words "rose" you may perhaps think of a Peace rose you picked last summer, while I am thinking of the one Laura Westphal gave to me in December 1968. In cinema, however, we both see the same rose, while the filmmaker can choose from an infinite variety of roses and then photograph the one chosen in another infinite variety of ways. The artist's choice in cinema is without limit; the artist's choice in literature is circumscribed, while the reverse is true for the observer. Film does not suggest, in this context: it states. And therein lies its power and the danger it poses to the observer: the reason why it is useful, even vital, to learn to read images well so that the observer can seize some of the power of the medium. The better one reads an image, the more one understands it, the more power one has over it. The reader of a page invents the image, the reader of a film does not, yet both readers must work to interpret the signs they perceive in order to complete the process of intellection. The more work they do, the better the balance between observer and creator in the process; the better the balance, the more vital and resonant the work of art.

---

*Pictographical languages like Chinese and Japanese might be said to fall somewhere in between film and Western languages as sign systems, but only when they are written, not when they are spoken, and only in limited cases. On the other hand, there are some words—"gulp," for example—that are onomatopoeic and therefore bear a direct relationship to what they signify, but only when they are spoken.

B.

Figure 3-7. A rose is not necessarily a rose. (A) James Rosenquist's roses: *Dusting Off Roses*. 1965. (*Lithograph, printed in color, 30¾" by 21 ¹¹/₁₆". Collection, Museum of Modern Art, New York. Gift of the Celeste and Armand Bartos Foundation.*) (B) Jean-Luc Godard's rose, from *Pravda* (1969). (*Frame enlargement.*)

A.

The earliest film texts—even many published recently—pursue with shortsighted ardor the crude comparison of film and written/spoken language. The standard theory suggested that the shot was the word of film, the scene its sentence, and the sequence its paragraph. In the sense that these sets of divisions are arranged in ascending order of complexity, the comparison is true enough; but it breaks down under analysis. Assuming for the moment that a word is the smallest convenient unit of meaning, does the shot compare equivalently? Not at all. In the first place, a shot takes time. Within that time span there is a continually various number of images. Does the single image, the frame, then constitute the basic unit of meaning in film? Still the answer is no, since each frame includes a potentially infinite amount of visual information, as does the soundtrack that accompanies it. While we could say that a film shot is something like a sentence, since it makes a statement and is sufficient in itself, the point is that the film does not divide itself into such easily manageable units. While we can define "shot" technically well enough as a single piece of film, what happens if the particular shot is punctuated internally? The camera can move; the scene can change completely in a pan or track. Should we then be talking of one shot or two?

Likewise, scenes, which were defined strictly in French classical theater as beginning and ending whenever a character entered or left the stage, are more amorphous in film (as they are in theater today). The term scene is useful, no doubt, but not precise. Sequences are certainly longer than scenes, but the "sequence-shot," in which a single shot is coterminous with a sequence, is an important concept and no smaller units within it are sequential.

It would seem that a real science of film would depend on our being able to define the smallest unit of construction. We can do that technically, at least for the image: it is the single frame. But this is certainly not the smallest unit of meaning. The fact is that film, unlike written or spoken language, is not composed of units, as such, but is rather a continuum of meaning. A shot contains as much information as we want to read in it, and whatever units we define within the shot are arbitrary.

Therefore, film presents us with a langauge (of sorts) that:

a) consists of short-circuit signs in which the signifier nearly equals the signified; and

b) depends on a continuous, nondiscrete sytem in which we can't identify a basic unit and which therefore we can't describe quantatively. The result is, as Christain Metz says, that: "An easy art, the cinema is in constant danger of falling victim to this easiness." Film is too intelligible, which is what makes it difficult to analyze. "A film is difficult to explain because it is easy to understand."

DENOTATIVE AND CONNOTATIVE MEANING

Films do, however, manage to communicate meaning. They do this essentially in two different manners: denotatively and connotatively. Like written language, but to a greater degree, a film image or sound has a denotative meaning: it is what is and we don't have to strive to recognize it. This factor may seem simplistic, but it should never be underestimated: here lies the great strength of film. There is a substantial difference between a description in words (or even in still photographs) of a person or event, and a cinematic record of the same. Because film can give us such a close approximation of reality, it can communicate a precise knowledge that written or spoken language seldom can. Language systems may be much better equipped to deal with the nonconcrete world of ideas and abstractions (imagine this book, for example, on film: without a complete narration it would be incomprehensible), but they are not nearly so capable of conveying precise information about physical realities.

By its very nature, written/spoken language analyzes. To write the word "rose" is to generalize and abstract the idea of the rose. The real power of the linguistic languages lies not with their denotative ability but in the connotative aspect of language: the wealth of meaning we can attach to a word that surpasses its denotation. If denotation were the only measure of the power of a language for example, then English—which has a vocabulary of a million or so words and is the largest language in history—would be over three times more powerful than French—which has only 300,000 or so words. But French makes up for its "limited" vocabulary with a noticeably greater use of connotation. Film has connotative abilities as well.

Considering the strongly denotative quality of film sounds and images, it is surprising to discover that these connotative abilities are very much a part of the film language. In fact, many of them stem from film's denotative ability. As we have noted in Chapter 1, film can draw on all the other arts for various effects simply because it can record them. Thus, all the connotative factors of spoken language can be accommodated on a film soundtrack while the connotations of written language can be included in titles (to say nothing of the connotative factors of dance, music, painting, and so forth). Because film is a product of culture, it has resonances that go beyond what the semiologist calls its diegesis (the sum of it denotation). An image of a rose is not simply that when it appears in a film of *Richard III*, for example, because we are aware of the connotations of the white rose and the red as symbols of the houses of York and Lancaster. These are culturally determined connotations.

In addition to these influences from the general culture, film has its own specific connotative ability. We know (even if we don't often remind ourselves of it consciously) that a filmmaker has made specific choices: the rose is filmed from a certain angle, the camera moves or does not move, the color is bright or dull, the rose is fresh or fading, the thorns apparent or hidden, the background clear (so that the rose is seen in context) or vague (so that it is isolated), the shot held for a long time or briefly, and so on. These are specific aids to cinematic connotation, and although we can approximate their effect in literature, we cannot accomplish it with cinematic precision or efficiency. A picture is, on occasion, worth a thousand words, as the adage has it. When our sense of the connotation of a specific shot depends on its having been chosen from a range of other possible shots, then we can say that this is, using the langue of semiology, a *paradigmatic* connotation. That is, the connotative sense we comprehend stems from the shot being compared, not necessarily consciously, with its unrealized companions in the paradigm, or general model, of this type of shot. A low-angle shot of a rose, for example, conveys a sense that the flower is for some reason dominant, overpowering, because we consciously or unconsciously compare it with, say, an overhead shot of a rose, which would diminish its importance.

Conversely, when the significance of the rose depends not on the shot compared with other potential shots, but rather on the shot compared with actual shots that precede or follow it, then we can speak of its *syntagmatic* connotation; that is, the meaning adheres to it because it is compared with other shots that we do see. These two different kinds of connotation have their equivalents in literature. A word alone on the page has no particular connotation, only denotation. We know what it means, we also know potentially what it connotes, but we can't supply the particular connotation the author of the word has in mind until we see it in context. Then we know what particular connotative value it has because we judge its meaning by conscious or unconscious comparison of it with (a) all the words like it that might fit in this context but were not chosen, and (b) the words that precede or follow it. (See p. 341.)

These two axes of meaning—the paradigmatic and the syntagmatic—have real value as tools for understanding what film means. In fact, as an art, film depends almost entirely upon these two sets of choices. After a filmmaker has decided what to shoot, the two obsessive questions are how to shoot it (what choices to make: the paradigmatic) and how to present the shot (how to edit it: the syntagmatic). In literature, in contrast, the first question (how to say it) is paramount, while the second (how to present what is said) is quite secondary. Semiotics, so far, has concentrated on the syntagmatic aspect of film, for a very simple reason: it is here that film is most clearly different from other arts, so that the syntagmatic category (editing, montage) is in a sense the most "cinematic."

Film draws on the other arts for much of its connotative power as well as generating its own, both paradigmatically and syntagmatically. But there is also another source of connotative sense. Cinema is not strictly a medium of intercommunication. One seldom holds dialogues in film. Whereas spoken and written languages are used for intercommunication, film, like the nonrepresentational arts in general (as well as language when it is used for artistic purposes), is a one-way communication. As a result, even the most utilitarian of films is artistic in some respect. Film speaks in neologisms. "When a 'language' does not already exist," Metz writes, "one must be something of an artist to speak it, however poorly. For to speak it is partly to invent it, whereas to speak the language of everyday is simply to use it." So connotations attach to even the simplest statements in film. There is an old joke that illustrates the point: two philosophers meet; one says "Good Morning!" The other smiles in recognition, then walks on frowning and thinking to himself: "I wonder what he meant by that?" The question is a joke when spoken language is the subject; it is however, a perfectly legitimate question to ask of any statement in film.

Is there any way we can further differentiate the various modes of denotation and connotation in film? Borrowing a "trichotomy" from the philosopher C.S. Peirce, Peter Wollen, in his highly influential book *Signs and Meaning in the Cinema* (1969), suggested that cinematic signs are of three orders:

- The Icon: a sign in which the signifier represents the signified mainly by its similarity to it, its likeness;
- The Index: which measures a quality not because it is identical to it but because it has an inherent relationship to it;
- The Symbol: an arbitrary sign in which the signifier has neither a direct or an indexical relationship to the signified, but rather represents it through convention.

Although Wollen doesn't fit them into the denotative/connotative categories, Icon, Index, and Symbol can be seen as mainly denotative. Portraits are Icons, of course, but so are diagrams in the Peirce/Wollen system. Indexes are more difficult to define. Quoting Peirce, Wollen suggests two sorts of Indexes, one technical—medical symptoms are Indexes of health, clocks and sundials are Indexes of time—and one metaphorical: a rolling gait should indicate that a man is a sailor. (This is the one point where the Peirce/Wollen categories verge on the connotative.) Symbols, the third category, are more easily defined. The way Pierce and Wollen use it, the word has a rather broad definition: words are Symbols (since the signifier represents the signified through convention rather than resemblance).

These three categories are not mutually exclusive. Especially in photographic images, the Iconic factor is almost always a strong one. As we have noted, a thing is itself even if it is also an Index or a Symbol. General semiological theory, especially as it is put forth in Christian Metz's writings, covers the first and last categories—Icon and Symbol—fairly well already. The Icon is the short-circuit sign that is so characteristic of cinema; the Symbol is the arbitrary or conventional sign that is the basis of spoken and written language. It is the second category—the Index—that is most intriguing in Peirce and Wollen's system: it seems to be a third means, halfway between the cinematic Icon and the literary Symbol, in which cinema can convey meaning. It is not an

Figure 3-8. ICON. Liv Ullmann in Ingmar Bergman's *Face to Face* (1975). This image is what it is.

arbitrary sign, but neither is it identical. It suggests a third type of denotation that points directly toward connotation, and may in fact not be understandable without the dimension of connotation.

The Index seems to be one very useful way in which cinema can deal directly with ideas, since it gives us concrete representations or measurements of them. How can we convey the idea of hotness cinematically for instance? In written language it's very easy, but on film? The image of a thermometer quickly comes to mind. Clearly that is an Index of temperature. But there are more subtle Indexes, as well: sweat is an Index, as are shimmering atmospheric waves and hot colors. It's a truism of film esthetics that metaphors are difficult in cinema. Comparing love with roses works well enough in literature, but its cinematic equivalent poses problems: the rose, the secondary element of the metaphor, is too equivalent in cinema, too much present. As a result, cinematic metaphors based on the literary model tend to be crude and static and forced. The Indexical sign may offer a way out of this dilemma. It is here that film discovers its own, unique metaphorical power, which it owes to the flexibility of the frame, its ability to say many things at once.

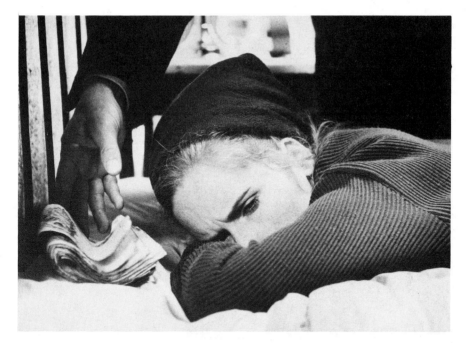

Figure 3-9. INDEX. Liv Ullmann in Bergman's *Shame* (1968). The offer of money—the roll of cash on the pillow—is an index of prostitution and, hence, of Eva's shame.

The concept of the Index also leads us to some interesting ideas about connotation. It must be clear from the above discussion that the line between denotation and connotation is not clearly defined: there is a continuum. In film, as in written and spoken language, connotations if they becme strong enough are eventually accepted as denotative meanings. As it happens, much of the connotative power of film depends on devices that are Indexical; that is, they are not arbitrary signs, but neither are they identical.

Two terms from literary studies, closely associated with each other, serve to describe the main manner in which film conveys connotative meaning. A metonymy is a figure of speech in which an associated detail or notion is used to invoke an idea or represent an object. Etymologically, the word means "substitute naming" (from the Greek *meta,* involving transfer, and *onoma* name). Thus, in literature we can speak of the king (and the idea of kingship) as "the crown." A synecdoche is a figure of speech in which the part stands for the whole or the whole for the part. An automobile can be referred to as a "motor" or a "set of wheels"; a policeman is "the law."

Both of these forms recur constantly in cinema. The indexes of heat

Figure 3-10. SYMBOL. Bergman often uses coffins and corpses as symbols in his films. Here, Ullmann again in *Face to Face*. . .

mentioned above are clearly metonymical: associated details invoke an abstract idea. Many of the old clichés of Hollywood are synecdochic (close shots of marching feet to represent an army) and metonymic (the falling calendar pages, the driving wheels of the railroad engine). Indeed, because metonymical devices yield themselves so well to cinematic exploitation, cinema can be more efficient in this regard than literature can. Associated details can be compressed within the limits of the frame to present a statement of extraordinary richness. Metonymy is a kind of cinematic shorthand.

Just as, in general, our sense of cinema's connotations depends on understood comparisons of the image with images that were not chosen (paradigmatic) and images that came before and after (syntagmatic), so our sense of the cultural connotations depend upon understood comparisons of the part with the whole (synecdoche) and associated details with ideas (metonymy). Cinema is an art and a medium of extensions and indexes. Much of its meaning comes not from what we see (or hear) but from what we don't see or, more accurately, from an ongoing process of comparison of what we see with what we don't see. This is

Figure 3-11. . . .and Max von Sydow in *Hour of the Wolf* (1966).

ironic, considering that cinema at first glance seems to be an art that is all too evident, one that is often criticized for "leaving nothing to the imagination."

Quite the contrary is true. In a film of strict denotation, images and sounds are quite easily and directly understood. But very few films are strictly denotative; they can't help but be connotative, "for to speak [film] is partly to invent it." The observer who adamantly resists, of course can choose to ignore the connotative power of film, but the observer who has learned to read film has available a multitude of connotations. Alfred Hitchcock, for example, has made a number of very popular films during the past half-century. We could ascribe his critical and popular success to the subjects of his films—certainly the thriller strikes a deep responsive chord in audiences—but then how do we account for the failed thrillers of his imitators? In truth, the drama of film, its attraction, lies not so much in what is shot (that's the drama of the subject), but in how it is shot and how it is presented. And as thousands of commentators have attested, Hitchcock was the master par excellence of these two critical tasks. The drama of filmmaking in large part lies in the brainwork of these closely associated sets of deci-

Figure 3-12. METONYMY. In *Red Desert* (1964), Michelangelo Antonioni developed a precise metonymics of color. Throughout most of the film, Giuliana (Monica Vitti) is oppressed psychologically and politically by a gray and deathly urban industrial environment. When she manages to break away from its grip on several occasions, Antonioni signals her temporary independence (and possible return to health) with bright colors, which is a detail associated with health and happiness not only in this film but in general culture as well. In this scene, Giuliana attempts to open her own shop. The gray walls are punctuated with splotches of brilliant color (the attempt at freedom), but the shapes themselves are violent, disorganized, frightening (the relapse into neurosis). In all, complicated set of metonymies.

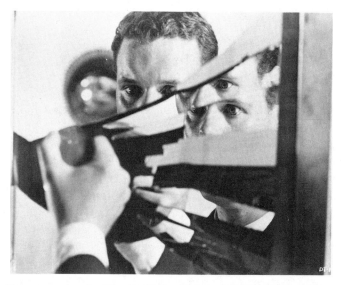

Figure 3-13. METONYMY. In Claude Chabrol's *Leda* (1959), André Jocelyn portrays a schizophrenic character. The image in the cracked mirror is a simple, logical metonymy.

Figure 3-14. SYNECDOCHE. Giuliana in *Red Desert*, again, this time surrounded and nearly overwhelmed by industrial machinery, a "part" that stands for the "whole" of her urban society. It isn't this factory, these particular machines, that oppress her, but the larger reality they represent.

Figure 3-15. SYNECDOCHE. Juliet Berto in Godard's *La Chinoise* (1967) has constructed a theoretical barricade of Chairman Mao's "Little Red Books," parts that stand for the whole of Marxist/Leninist/Maoist ideology with which the group of "gauchistes" to which she belongs protect themselves, and *from* which they intend to launch an attack on bourgeois society.

The terms "synecdoche" and "metonymy"—like "Icon," "Index," and "Symbol"—are, of course, imprecise. They are theoretical constructs that may be useful as aids to analysis; thay are not strict definitions. This particular synecdoche, for example, might very well be better classified as a metonymy in which the little red books are associated details rather than parts standing for the whole. (The decision itself has ideological overtones!) Likewise, although this image seems easiest to classify as Indexical, there are certainly elements of the Iconic and Symbolic in it.

sions. "Literate" filmgoers appreciate Hitchcock's superb cinematic intelligence on a conscious level, illiterate filmgoers on an unconscious level, but the intelligence has its effect, nevertheless.

One more element remains to be added to the lexicon of film semiology: the trope. In literary theory, a trope is a "turn of phrase" or a "change of sense"—in other words, a logical twist that gives the elements of a sign—the signifier and the signified—a new relationship to each other. The trope is therefore the connecting element between denotation and connotation. When a rose is a rose is a rose it isn't anything else, and its meaning as a sign is strictly denotative. But when a rose is something else, a "turning" has been made and the sign is opened up to new meanings. The map of film semiology we have described so far has been static. The concept of the trope allows us to view it dynamically, as actions rather than facts.

As we have noted in earlier chapters, one of the great sources of power in film is that it can reproduce the tropes of most of the other arts. There is also a set of tropes that it has made its own. We have described the way they operate in general in the first half of this chapter. Given an image of a rose, we at first have only its Iconic or Symbolic denotative meaning, which is static. But when we begin to expand the possibilities through tropes of comparison, the image comes alive: as a connotative Index, in terms of the paradigm of possible shots, in the syntagmatic context of its assocaitions in the film, as it is used metaphorically as a metonymy or a synecdoche.

There are undoubtedly other categories of film semiology yet to be discovered, analyzed, propogated. In no sense is the system shown in the chart on pp. 144–45 meant to be either exhaustive or immutable. Semiology is most definitely not a science in the sense that physics or biology is a science. But it is a logical, often illuminating system that helps to describe how film does what it does. Film is difficult to explain because it is easy to understand. The semiotics of film is easy to explain because it is difficult to understand. Somewhere between lies the genius of film.

SYNTAX

Film has no grammar. There are, however, some vaguely defined rules of usage in cinematic language, and the syntax of film—its systematic arrangement—orders these rules and indicates relationships between them. As with written and spoken languages, it is important to remem-

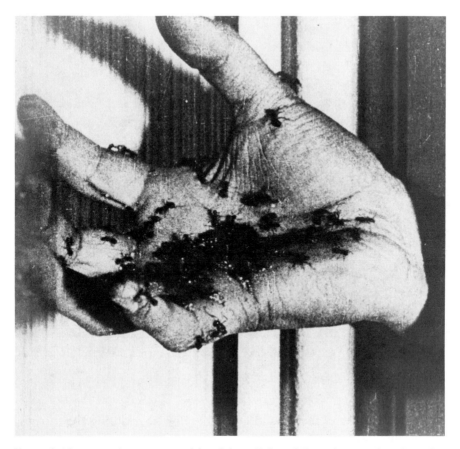

Figure 3-16 TROPE. An ant-covered hand from Dali and Buñuel's surrealist classic *Un Chien Andalou* (1928). Another very complex image, not easily analyzed. Iconic, Indexical, and Symbolic values are all present: the image is striking for its own sake; it is a measure of the infestation of the soul of the owner of the hand; it is certainly symbolic of a more general malaise, as well. It is metonymic, because the ants are an "associated detail"; it is also synecdochic, because the hand is a part that stands for the whole. Finally, the source of the image seems to be a trope: a verbal pun on the French idiom, "avoir des fourmis dans les mains," "to have ants in the hand," an expression equivalent to the English "my hand is asleep." By illustrating the turn of phrase literally, Dali and Buñuel extended the trope so that a common experience is turned into a striking sign of decay. (I am indebted to David Bombyk for this analysis. MOMA/FSA.)

ber that the syntax of film is a result of its usuage, not a determinant of it. There is nothing preordained about film syntax. Rather, it evolved naturally as certain devices were found in practice to be both workable and useful. Like the syntax of written and spoken language, the syntax of film is an organic development, descriptive rather than prescriptive, and it has changed considerably over the years. The Hollywood Gram-

Figure 3-17. METONYMIC GESTURE. Max von Sydow in Ingmar Bergman's *Hour of the Wolf* (1967). . .

mar described below may sound laughable now, but during the thirties, forties, and early fifties it was an accurate model of the way Hollywood films were constructed.

In written/spoken languge systems, syntax deals only with what we might call the linear aspect of construction: that is, the ways in which words are put together in a chain to form phrases and sentences, what in film we call the syntagmatic category. In film, however, syntax can also include spatial composition, for which there is no parallel in language systems like English and French—we can't say or write several things at the same time.

So film syntax must include both development in time and development in space. In film criticism, generally, the modification of space is referred to as mise en scène. The French phrase literally means "putting in the scene." The modification of time is called montage (from the French for "putting together"). As we shall see in Chapter 4, the tension between these twin concepts of mise en scène and montage has been the engine of film esthetics ever since Lumière and Méliès first explored the practical possibilities of each at the turn of the century.

Over the years, theories of mise en scène have tended to be closely

Figure 3-18. . . . and in the same director's *Shame* (1968). Gesture is one of the most communicative facets of film signification. "Kinesics," or "body language," is basically an Indexical, metonymic system of meaning. Here, von Sydow's pose conveys the same basic meaning in each film: the hand covers the face, shields it from the outside world: the knees are pulled up close almost in the fetal position, to protect the body; the ego has shrunk into a protective shell, a sense further emphasized in the shot from *Shame* by the framed box of the wooden stairway von Sydow is sitting on. Texture supports gesture in both shots: both backgrounds—one exterior, one interior—are rough, barren, uninviting. The differences between the shots are equally as meaningful as the similarities. In *Hour of the Wolf*, von Sydow's character is relatively more open, relaxed: so is the pose. In *Shame*, the character (at this point in the narrative) is mortified: a sense emphasized by both the tighter pose and the more distanced composition of the shot.

associated with film realism, while montage has been seen as essentially expressionistic, yet this pairing is deceptive. Certainly it would seem that mise en scène would indicate a high regard for the subject in front of the camera, while montage would give the filmmaker more control over the manipulation of the subject, but despite these natural tendencies, montage can be the more realistic of the two alternatives, and mise en scène on occasion of the more expressionistic

Take, for example, the problem of choosing between a pan from one subject to another and a cut. Most people would agree that the cut is more manipulative, that it interrupts and remodels reality, and that therefore the pan is the more realistic of the two alternatives, since it

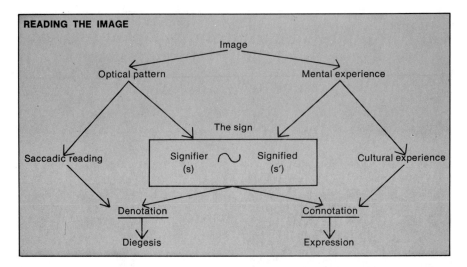

READING THE IMAGE: The image is experienced as both an optical and mental phenomenon. The optical pattern is read saccadically; the mental experience is the result of the sum of cultural determinants, and is formed by it. Both optical and mental intellection combine in the concept of the sign, where signifier (s) is related to signified (s'). The signifier is more optical than mental; the signified more mental then optical. All three levels of reading—saccadic, semiological, and cultural—then combine with each other in various ways to produce meaning, either essentially denotative or essentially connotative.

preserves the integrity of the space. Yet, in fact, the reverse is true if we judge panning and cutting from the point of view of the observer.

When we redirect our attention from one subject to another we seldom actually pan. Psychologically, the cut is the truer approximation of our natural perception. First one subject has our attention, then the other; we are seldom interested in the intervening space, yet the cinematic pan draws our attention to just that.*

It was André Bazin who, more than anyone, developed the connections between mise en scène and realism on the one hand, and montage and expressionism on the other. At about the same time, in the middle

---

*It has been suggested that the zip pan, in which the camera moves so quickly that the image in between the original subject and its successor is blurred, would be the most verisimilitudinous handling of the problem. But even this alternative draws attention to itself, which is precisely what does not happen in normal perception. Perhaps the perfect analogue with reality would be the direct cut in which the two shots were separated by a single black frame (or better yet, a neutral gray frame), which would duplicate the time (approximately $1/20$ of a second) each saccadic movement of the eye takes!

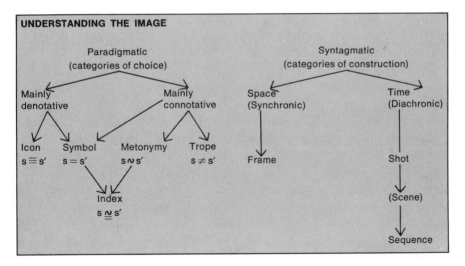

UNDERSTANDING THE IMAGE

UNDERSTANDING THE IMAGE: We understand an image not only for itself, but in context: in relation to categories of choice (paradigmatic) and in relation to categories of construction (syntagmatic). The categories of choice are variously denotative or connotative, and each variety, none of whose boundaries are sharply defined, is characterized by the relationship between signifier and signified. In the Iconic image, signifier is identical with signified. In Symbols the signifier is equal to the signified, but not identical. In metonymies and synecdoches, signifier is similar in some way to signified, while in tropes, the signifier is not equal to (distinctly different from) the signified. Here the relationship is considerably more tenuous. In Indexes, signifier and signified are congruent.

Syntagmatic relationship (categories of construction) operate either in space or in time: synchronic phenomena happen at the same time, or without regard to time, while diachronic phenomena happen across time, or within it. (Here, the words "synchronic" and "diachronic" carry their simplest meanings. They are also used with more specific definitions generally in semiology and linguistics, in which case synchronic linguistics is descriptive, while diachronic linguistics is historical.)

Finally, it must be noted that many of the concepts expressed in this chart are true for sounds as well as images, although usually to a considerably lesser extent. While it is true that we do not read sounds saccadically, we nevertheless focus psychologically on particular sounds within the total auditory experience just as we "block out" unwanted or useless noise. While sound must seem, in general, far more denotative and Iconic than image, it is nevertheless possible to apply the concepts of Symbol, Index, metonymy, synecdoche, and trope, if the necessary changes are made.

fifties, Jean-Luc Godard was working out a synthesis of the twin notions of mise en scène and montage that was considerably more sophisticated than Bazin's binary opposition. For Godard, mise en scène and montage were divested of ethical and esthetic connotations: montage simply did in time what mise en scène does in space. Both are principles of organization, and to say that mise en scène (space) is more "realistic" than montage (time) is illogical. In his essay "Montage, mon beau souci" (1956) Godard redefined montage as an integral part of mise en scène.

Setting up a scene is as much an organizing of time as of space. The aim of this is to discover in film a psychological reality that transcends physical, plastic reality. There are two corollaries to Godard's synthesis: first, mise en scène can therefore be every bit as expressionistic as montage when a filmmaker uses it to distort reality; second, psychological reality (as opposed to verisimilitude) may be better served by a strategy that allows montage to play a central role. (See Chapter 5, pp. 328–38.)

In addition to the psychological complexities that enter into a comparison of montage and mise en scène, there is a perceptual factor that complicates matters. We have already noted that montage can be mimicked within the shot. Likewise, montage can mimic mise en scène. Hitchcock's notorious shower murder sequence in *Psycho* is an outstanding example of this phenomenon. Seventy separate shots in less than a minute of screen time are fused together psychologically into a continuous experience: a frightening and graphic knife attack. The whole is greater than the sum of its parts (see Figure 3-20).

CODES

The structure of cinema is defined by the codes in which it operates and the codes that operate within it. Codes are critical constructions— systems of logical relationship—derived after the fact of film. They are not pre-existent laws that the filmmaker consciously observes. A great variety of codes combine to form the medium in which film expresses meaning. There are culturally derived codes—those that exist outside film and that filmmakers simply reproduce (the way people eat, for example). There are a number of codes that cinema shares with the other arts (for instance, gesture, which is a code of theater as well as film). And there are those codes that are unique to cinema. (Montage is the prime example.) The culturally derived codes and the shared artistic codes are vitally important to cinema, naturally, but it is the unique codes, those that form the specific syntax of film, which most concern us here. Possibly "unique" is not a completely accurate adjective. As you will see, not even the most specifically cinematic codes, those of montage, are truly unique to cinema. Certainly, cinema emphasizes them and utilizes them more than other arts do, yet something like montage has always existed in the novel. Any storyteller is capable of switching scenes in midstream. "Meanwhile, back at the ranch," is clearly not an invention of cinema. More important, for more than three-quarters of a century film art has had its own strong influence on the older arts. Not only did something like montage exist prior to 1900 in prose narrative, but since that time novelists, increasingly influenced by film, have learned gradually to make their narratives even more like

Figure 3-19. Mise en scène or montage? A crucial scene in Bergman's *Face to Face*, this was shot from a hallway giving a "split screen" view of two rooms. Instead of cutting from the action in one to the action in the other, Bergman presented both simultaneously while keeping the action in each separate. The cross-cutting dialectic of montage is thus made an integral element of mise en scène. (*Frame enlargement.*)

cinema. The point is, simply, that codes are a critical convenience—nothing more—and it would be wrong to give them so much weight that we were more concerned with the precise definition of the code than with the perception of the film.

Taking the shower scene in *Psycho* once again as an example, let's derive the codes operating there. It is a simple scene (only two characters—one of whom is barely seen—and two actions—taking a shower and murdering) and it is of short duration, yet all three types of codes are evident. The culturally derived codes have to do with taking showers and murdering people. The shower is, in Western culture, an activity that has elements of privacy, sexuality, purgation, relaxation, openness, and regeneration. In other words, Hitchcock could not have chosen a more ironic place to emphasize the elements of violation and sexuality in the assault. Murder, on the other hand, fascinates us because of motives. Yet the dimly perceived murderer of *Psycho* has no discernible motive. The act seems gratuitous, almost absurd—which makes it even more striking. Historically, Jack the Ripper may come to mind, and this redoubles our sense of the sexual foundation of the murder.

Since this particular scene is so highly cinematic and so short, shared codes are relatively minor here. Acting codes hardly play a part, for instance, since the shots are so brief there isn't time to act in them, only to mime a simple expression. The diagonals that are so important in establishing the sense of disorientation and dynamism are shared with the other pictorial arts. The harsh contrasts and backlighting that obscure the murderer are shared with photography. The musical code of Bernard Herrmann's accompaniment also exists outside film, of course. In addition, we can trace the development of the use of the culturally derived codes in cinema and allied arts: Hitchcock's murder scene might be contrasted with the murder of Marat in his bath (in history, in the painting by Jacques-Louis David, and in the play by Peter Weiss), the bathtub murder scene in Henri-Georges Clouzot's *Les Diaboliques* (1955), or that in *The Last of Sheila* (1973), written by Stephen Sondheim and Anthony Perkins (who played in *Psycho*), or the direct homages to *Psycho* in Mike Hodges's *Terminal Man* (1974) or Brian De-Palma's *Dressed to Kill* (1980).

As we have already noted, the specifically cinematic codes in Hitchcock's one-minute tour de force are exceptionally strong. In fact, it's hard to see how the montage of the sequence could be duplicated in any other art. The rapid cutting of the scene may indeed by a unique cinematic code.

Hitchcock manipulates all these codes to achieve a desired effect. It is because they are codes—because they have meaning for us outside the narrow limits of that particular scene: in film, in the other arts, in the general culture—that they affect us. The codes are the medium through which the "message" of the scene is transmitted. The specifically cinematic codes together with a number of shared codes make up the syntax of film.

MISE EN SCÈNE

Three questions confront the filmmaker: what to shoot, how to shoot it, how to present the shot. The province of the first two questions is mise en scène, that of the last, montage. Mise en scène is often regarded as static, montage as dynamic. This is not the case. Because we read the shot, we are actively involved with it. The codes of mise en scène are the tools with which the filmmaker alters and modifies our reading of the shot. Since the shot is such a large unit of meaning, it may be useful to separate a discussion of its components into two parts.

The Framed Image

All the codes that operate within the frame, without regard to the chronological axis of film, are shared with the other pictorial arts. The number and range of these codes is great and they have been developed and refined in painting, sculpture, and photography over the course of thousands of years. Basic texts in the visual arts examine the three determinants of color, line, and form, and certainly each of the visual codes of film fits within one of these rubrics. Rudolf Arnheim, in his highly influential study *Art and Visual Perception,* suggests ten areas of concern: Balance, Shape, Form, Growth, Space, Light, Color, Movement, Tension, and Expression. Clearly, a full exposition of the codes operating in the film frame would be a lengthy undertaking. We can, however, describe briefly the basic aspects of the syntax of the frame. Two aspects of the framed image are important: the limitations that the frame imposes, and the composition of the image within the frame (and without necessary regard to it).

Since the frame determines the limit of the image, the choice of an aspect ratio suggests the possibilities of composition. With the self-justification that has been endemic to the elusive subject of film esthetics, early theoreticians waxed eloquent over the value of the Academy aperture, the 1.33 ratio. When widescreen ratios became popular in the 1950s, the classical estheticians bemoaned the destruction of the symmetry they perceived in the Academy aperture, but, as we demonstrated in the last chapter, there was nothing sacred about the ratio of 4:3.

The point is not which ratio is "proper" but rather which codes yield themselves to exploitation in which ratios? Before the mid-fifties, it seems, interiors and dialogue dominated American and foreign screens. After the introduction of the widescreen formats, exteriors, location shooting, and action sequences grew in importance. This is a crude generalization, but there is some useful truth to it. It's not important whether there was a cause-and-effect relationship between the two historical developments, only that wide screens permitted more efficient exploitation of action and landscape codes.

Cinemascope and Panavision width ratios (2.33 and above) do make it more difficult, as the Hollywood estheticians had suggested, to photograph intimate conversations. Whereas the classic two-shot of the 1.33 screen size tended to focus attention on speaker and listener, the very wide anamorphic ratios cannot avoid also photographing either the space between them or beside them and therefore calling attention to their relationship to the space surrounding them. This is neither "better" nor "worse" ideally; it simply changes the code of the two-shot.

The filmmaker can also change the dimensions of the frame during

Figure 3-20. THE BATHTUB/ SHOWER CODE. Hitchcock's spellbinding shower murder in *Psycho* (1959) has become notorious over the years for its vertiginous editing, yet the bathroom murder was not a new idea. (*From* Psycho. © *1974. Ed. by Richard J. Anobile. Frame enlargement.*)

Figure 3-21. Several years earlier. Henri-Georges Clouzot's *Diabolique* had shocked audiences with an altogether quieter but no less eerie murder scene. (Paul Meurisse is the victim.) (*Walter Daran. Time/Life Picture Agency. © Time, Inc. Frame enlargement.*)

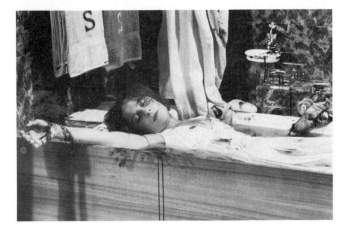

Figure 3-22. *Psycho's* star, Anthony Perkins, cowrote the script for Herbert Ross's *The Last of Sheila.* Joan Hackett attempts suicide in an elegant shipboard bath.

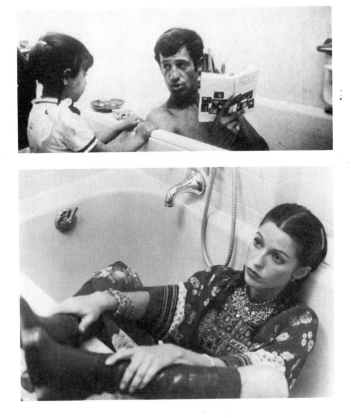

Figure 3-23. Murder isn't the only activity that takes place in tubs. In Godard's poetic master-piece *Pierrot le fou* (1965), Jean-Paul Belmondo relaxes in a tub as he shares some thoughts on the painter Velázquez with his daughter. (*l'Avant-Scène. Frame enlargement.*)

Figure 3-24. In Jean-Charles Tacchella's *Cousin, cousine* (1975), Marie-France Pisier finds the empty tub a pleasant place to think.

the course of the film by masking, either artificially or naturally through composition. This has been an important aspect of the syntax of frame shape ever since D. W. Griffith first explored its possibilities.

Just as important as the actual frame size, although less easily perceived, is the filmmaker's attitude toward the limit of the frame. If the image of the frame is self-sufficient, then we can speak of it as a "closed form." Conversely, if the filmmaker has composed the shot in such a way that we are always subliminally aware of the area outside the frame, then the form is considered to be "open." Open and closed forms are closely associated with the elements of movement in the frame. If the camera tends to follow the subject faithfully, the form tends to be closed; if, on the other hand, the filmmaker allows—even encourages—the subject to leave the frame and reenter, the form is obviously open. The relationship between the movement within the frame and movement of the camera is one of the more sophisticated codes, and specifically cinematic. Hollywood's classic syntax was identified in part by a relatively tightly closed form. The masters of the Hollywood style of the

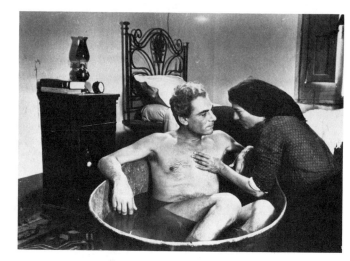

Figure 3-25. Gian Maria Volonté finds some surcease from exile in a remote Italian village in an old-fashioned tub. Irene Papas assists. (Francesco Rosi's *Christ Stopped at Eboli.*)

thirties and forties tried never to allow the subject to leave the frame (it was considered daring even if the subject did not occupy the center of the 1.33 frame). Recently, filmmakers like Michelangelo Antonioni have been equally faithful to the open widescreen form because it emphasizes the spaces between people.

Most elements of compositional syntax do not depend strictly on the frame for their definition. If the image faded at the edges like a vignette (which itself is one of the minor techniques of the framing code), such codes as intrinsic interest, proximity, depth perception, angle of approach, and lighting would work just as well as they do in frames with sharply defined limits.

The filmmaker, like most pictorial artists, composes in three dimensions. This doesn't mean necessarily that he is trying to convey three-dimensional (or stereoscopic) information. It means that there are three sets of compositional codes: one concerns the plane of the image (most important, naturally, since the image is, after all, two-dimensional); one deals with the geography of the space photographed (its plane is parallel with the ground and the horizon); the third involves the plane of depth perception, perpendicular to both the frame plane and the geographical plane. Figure 3-33 visualizes these three planes of composition.

Naturally, these planes interlock. No filmmaker analyzes precisely how each single plane influences the composition, but decisions are made that focus attention on pairs of planes. Clearly, the plane of the frame must be dominant, since that is the only plane that actually exists

Figure 3-26. In the late seventies, the bath became a focus of contemporary California life with the rise in popularity of the hot tub. Stacey Nolkin takes a call in *Serial* (1980).

on the screen. Composition for this plane, however, is often influenced by factors in the geographical plane since, unless we are dealing with animation, a photographer or cinematographer must compose for the frame plane in the geographical plane. Likewise, the geographical plane and the plane of depth perception are coordinated, since much of our ability to perceive depth in two-dimensional representations as well as three-dimensional reality depends upon phenomena in the geographical plane. In fact, perception of depth depends on many important factors other than binocular stereoscopic vision, which is why film presents such a strong illusion of three-dimensional space and why stereoscopic film techniques are relatively useless.*

Figure 3-34 illustrates some of the most important psychological factors strongly influencing depth perception. Overlapping takes place in the frame plane, but the three others—convergence, relative size, and density gradient—depend on the geographical plane. We've already discussed in Chapter 2 how various lens types affect depth perception (and linear distortion, as well). A photographer modifies, suppresses, or reinforces the effects of lens types through composition of the image within the frame.

---

*If so-called 3-D film techniques simply added the one remaining factor to depth perception, there would be no problem with them. The difficulty is that they actually distort our perception of depth considerably, since they don't allow us to focus on a single plane as we do naturally and since they tend to produce disturbing pseudostereoscopic and pseudoscopic stereoscopic images (see Glossary).

Figure 3-27. The Academy aperture two-shot. Spencer Tracy and Katharine Hepburn in George Cukor's *Pat and Mike* (1952). More intimate and involving than. . .

Here are some other examples of how the codes of the compositional planes interact:

Proximity and proportion are important subcodes. Stage actors are forever mindful of them. Obviously, the closer the subject the more important it seems. As a result, an actor in the theater is always in danger of being "upstaged" by other members of the company. In film, of course, the director has complete control over position, and reverse angles help to redress the balance.

Figure 3-35, a classic shot from *Citizen Kane* (1941), gives us a more sophisticated example of the significance of proximity and proportion. Kane enters the room at the rear; his wife is in bed in the mid-ground; a bottle of sleeping medicine looms large in the foreground. The three are connected by their placement in the frame. Reverse the order and the medicine bottle disappears into the background of the shot.

One of the aspects of composition that differentiates Baroque from Late Renaissance painting is the shift from the "square" orientation of the geographic plane to the oblique. There were several reasons for this—one was the quest for greater verisimilitude: the oblique composi-

Figure 3-28. . . .the widescreen two-shot. Jean-Claude Brialy and Anna Karina in Jean-Luc Godard's *A Woman is a Woman* (1961). The still life on the table is carefully composed, both to fill the middle space of the frame and to connect the characters.

tion emphasized the space of the painting, whereas the symmetrical Renaissance compositional standard emphasized its design. The net effect, however, was to increase the psychological drama of the design: geographical obliques translate into the plane of the frame as diagonals, which are read as inherently more active than horizontals and verticals. Here, as in the earlier examples, there is a relationship between compositional factors in separate planes.

Eventually, the geographic and depth planes "feed" information to the plane of the frame. This is truer in painting and photography, which don't have the ability film does to move physically into the pictorial space, but it is still generally true in cinema as well. The frame plane is the only "real" plane. Most elements of composition, therefore, realize themselves in this plane. The empty frame, contrary to expectations, is not a tabula rasa. Even before the image appears, we invest the potential space of the frame with certain qualities, ones which have been measured scientifically: our natural tendency to read depth into the two-dimensional design, for instance. Latent expectations determine intrinsic interest. Figures 3-36 and 3-37 demonstrate this. In 3-36, both verticals are precisely the same length, yet the left-hand line looks much longer. This is because we read the angles at top and bottom as representative of corners, the left receding, the right intruding. If both lines *seem* to be equal, we then calculate that the line on the left *must*

Figure 3-29. Michelangelo Antonioni is well known for his sensitivity to architectural metaphor. This naturally masked shot from *Eclipse* (1962) both isolates Alain Delon and Monica Vitti and calls attention to the comparison to be made between Vitti and the portrait on the wall behind her.

be longer, since it is "further away." In Figure 3-37, which stairway ascends and which descends? The "correct" answers are a ascends and b descends. The trick is in the verbs, of course, since stairs always go both up and down. But since Westerners tend to read from left to right, we see stair a ascending and stair b descending.

So, even before the image appears, the frame is invested with meaning. The bottom is more "important" than the top, left comes before right, the bottom is stable, the top unstable; diagonals from bottom left to top right go "up" from stability to instability. Horizontals will also be given more weight than verticles; confronted with horizontal and vertical lines of equal length, we tend to read the horizontal as longer, a phenomenon emphasized by the dimensions of the frame.

When the image does appear, form, line, and color are impressed with these latent values in the frame. Form, line, and color also have their own inherent values of weight and direction. If sharp lines exist in the design of the image, we tend to read along them from left to right. An object with a "light" inherent significance (Mrs. Kane's medicine bottle) can be given "heavy" significance through shape. And color, of course, adds an entirely new dimension. Hitchcock begins *Marnie* (1964) with a close shot of his heroine's bright yellow pocketbook. The other color values of the scene are neutral. The sense is of the pocket-

Figure 3-30. This shot from Jean Renoir's *Boudu Saved from Drowning* (1932) isolates the forlorn figure of Boudu, about to jump into the Seine, by vignetting the image. The masking has a literal function as well: Boudu (Michel Simon) is seen through a telescope in this shot. (*l'Avant-Scène. Frame enlargement.*)

book carrying the woman rather than vice versa, just the effect Hitchcock wants, considering that the yellow bulge contains the money Marnie had just stolen and that her life, as we later see, is dominated by her kleptomania. Before we learn any of this narratively, we "know" it. (*Marnie* is also an excellent example of other types of color dominance, since the subject of the film is color symbolism: Marnie suffers from rosophobia.) Elements of form, line, and color all carry their own intrinsic interests, significant weights that counteract, reinforce, counterpoint, or balance each other in complex systems, each read against our latent expectations of the frame and with the senses of composition in depth and planar design combined.

Multiple images (split screen) and superimpositions (double exposures, et cetera), although they are seldom used, can multiply the intrinsic weights by factors of two, three, four, or more. Texture, although it is not often mentioned when speaking of film esthetics, is also important, not only in terms of the inherent texture of the subject, but also in terms of the texture or grain of the image. One illustration will suffice: we have learned to associate graininess with enlargement, and

Figure 3-31. CLOSED FORM. The notorious stateroom scene from *A Night At The Opera* (Sam Wood, 1935) must be the zenith of Hollywood-style closed form! The frame drastically limits the space of the scene.

with documentary. The filmmaker therefore has this code at his command. A grainy image signifies a "truthful" one. The grain of enlargement and its significance as a barrier to comprehension provided the basic subtext of Antonioni's 1966 film, *Blow-up*.

Perhaps the most important tool the filmmaker can use to modify the meanings of form, line, and color, and their intrinsic interests is lighting. In the days when filmstock was relatively insensitive (before the 1960s), artificial lighting was a requisite, and filmmakers made a virtue of necessity, as always. The German Expressionists of the twenties borrowed the code of chiaroscuro from painting to dramatic effect—it allowed them to emphasize design over verisimilitude. The classical Hollywood cinematographic style wanted a more natural effect and so developed a system of balanced "key" lights and "fill" lights (see Figure 3-42) that provided thorough but not overt illumination and therefore presented a minimal barrier between observer and subject. At its best, this sophisticated system was capable of some extraordinary, subtle effects, yet is was inherently unrealistic; we seldom observe natural scenes that have both the very high light level and the carefully balanced fill

Figure 3-32. OPEN FORM. Macha Meril in Godard's *A Married Woman* (1964). The taxi is moving to the left out of the frame, Meril is walking to the right out of the frame and looking back toward the left; the car in the background is moving diagonally up out of the frame. The design elements of the shot conspire to make us aware of the continuous space beyond the limits of the frame. (*French Film Office.*)

that mark the Hollywood style (and that is perpetuated today in many television productions).

The development of fast filmstocks permitted a new latitude in the code of lighting, and today most cinematographers work for verisimilitude rather than classic Hollywood balance.

Needless to say, all the lighting codes that operate in photography operate in film as well. Full front lighting washes out a subject; overhead lighting dominates it; lighting from below gives it a lugubrious appearance; highlighting can call attention to details (hair and eyes most often); backlighting can either dominate a subject or highlight it; sidelighting is capable of dramatic chiaroscuro effect.

Aspect ratio; open and closed form; frame, geographic, and depth planes; depth perception; proximity and proportion; intrinsic interest of color, form, and line; weight and direction; latent expectation; oblique versus symmetric composition; texture; and lighting. These are the major codes operating within the static film frame. In terms of the diachronic shot, however, we have just begun.

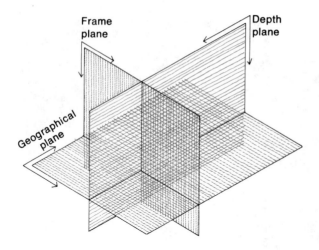

Figure 3-33. THE THREE
PLANES OF COMPOSITION.

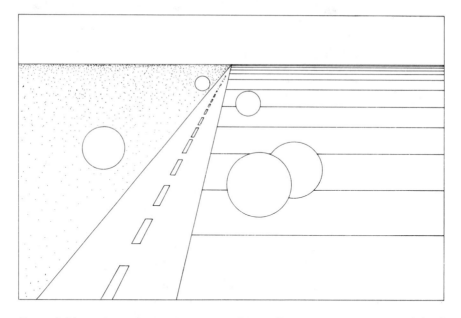

Figure 3-34. CONVENTIONS OF DEPTH PERCEPTION. Four major conventions of depth perception are illustrated here: convergence (the boundaries of the road), relative size (the near and far balls), density gradient (of dots on the left, of lines on the right), and overlapping (the balls on the right).

Figure 3-35. Dorothy Comingore (in shadow), Orson Welles, and Joseph Cotten in Welles's *Citizen Kane* (1941). It is not the material of the shot but its design that tells the story. (*Sight and Sound.*)

The Diachronic Shot

Filmmakers use a wealth of terminology in regard to the shot. The factors that now come into play include distance, focus, angle, movement, and point of view. Some of these elements also operate within the static frame, but all are more appropriately discussed as dynamic qualities. Shot distance is the simplest variable. So-called "normal" shots include the full shot, three-quarter shot, medium shot (or midshot), and head-and-shoulders shot—all defined in terms of the amount of subject viewed. Closeups, long shots, and extreme long shots complete the range of distances. Note that none of these terms has anything to do with the focal length of the lens used. As we saw in Chapter 2, in addition to being defined in terms of distance from the subject, shots are also named for their lenses. Note, too, that in practice these terms are loosely used. One person's closeup in another's "detail shot," and no Academy of film has (so far) sat in deep deliberation deciding the precise point at which a medium shot becomes a long shot, or a long shot metamorphoses into an extreme long shot. Nevertheless, within limits, the concepts are valid.

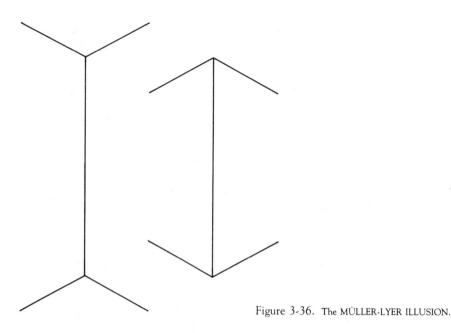

Figure 3-36. The MÜLLER-LYER ILLUSION.

A film shot mainly in closeups, Carl Dreyer's *The Passion of Joan of Arc* (1928), for example, deprives us of setting and is therefore disorienting, claustrophobic. The effect can be striking. On the other hand, a film shot mainly in long shot (many of Roberto Rossellini's recent historical essays, for instance) emphasizes context over drama and dialectic over personality. The code of shot distance is simple—may seem crude, even—but to a large extent it controls the shape of many of the other codes of film.

Focus is the next most important variable in the syntax of the shot. There are two axes in the determination of focus: the first choice is between deep focus, in which foreground, middle ground, and background are all relatively sharp focus, and shallow focus, in which the focus emphasizes one ground over the others. Shallow focus obviously allows the filmmaker greater control over the image. Deep focus, on the other hand, is one of the prime hallmarks of esthetics which emphasize mise en scène. (It is much easier to "put things in the scene" when all three grounds are in focus, since the scene is then much larger, more accomodating.) (See Figures 2-17, 2-18.)

The second axis of focus is the continuum between sharp and soft focus. This aspect of the shot is related to texture. Soft focus is generally associated with so-called romantic moods. Sharp focus is more closely associated with verisimilitude. These are generalizations that specific instances often contradict. Soft focus is not so much romantic

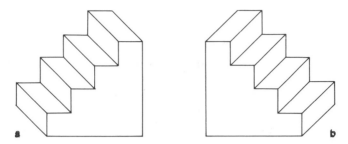

Figure 3-37. THE UPSTAIRS/DOWNSTAIRS ILLUSION.

as it is mollifying. It smoothes out the identifying details of an image and distances it.

Surely focus is a function of the still frame as well as of the diachronic shot. It is intimately associated with the compositional planes, since it permits concentration on a single ground. But it also tends toward movement. By maintaining relatively shallow focus and changing focus during the shot, the filmmaker can shift the intrinsic interest

Figure 3-38. Mischa Auer in Orson Welles's Mr. Arkadin (1955): a typical Welles tilted composition. That the line of the table moves down from left to right disorients us even further. The observer in the frame strains, stretches his neck to see. The low angle of the shot increases our sense of foreboding. Most important, the trope of the magnified eye is doubled and redoubled with typically Wellesian irony by the echoing circles of the top hat and the light above. The joke here of course is that the magnifying glass is positioned for our use, not Auer's. (l'Avant-Scène. Frame enlargement.)

of the frame from one ground to another, which in a way parallels the effect of the pan, zoom, or tracking shot but does so within the frame and without moving the camera.

Focus changes within the shot are of two basic sorts: follow focus, in which the focus is changed to permit the camera to keep a moving subject in focus; and rack focus, in which the focus is changed to direct attention away from one subject and toward another in a different ground. Follow focus was one of the basics of the Hollywood style, admired for its ability to maintain attention on the subject. Focus, then, is one of the codes that connect the codes of composition with those of movement.

The third aspect of the diachronic shot, angle, also reaches back toward static composition and forward toward the movement of the shot. Because the relationship between camera and subject exists in three-dimensional space, there are three sets of separate angles that determine the shot. We have already discussed one of these, the angle of approach (squarely symmetrical or oblique), in the previous section. In order to understand the relationships among the three types of angle, it may be useful to visualize the three imaginary axes that run through the camera (Figure 2-23). The pan axis (vertical) is also the axis of the angle of approach; it is either square or oblique. The tilt axis (horizontal from left to right) determines the elevation of the shot: overhead, high-angle, eye-level, low-angle are the basic terms used here. It goes without saying that high-angle shots diminish the importance of the subject while low-angle shots emphasize its power. Interestingly, the eye-level shot, the least obtrusive, is not always so easily defined. The Japanese filmmaker Yasujiro Ozu is well known for the constant low-angle of his style, yet Ozu isn't really trying to distort the basic design of his image: he is merely shooting from the eye level of a Japanese observer seated on a tatami mat. "Eye-level," of course, depends on the eye of the beholder. Even in European and American cinema, the subtle differences between eyelevels, although not immediately remark-able, can have significant effect over the course of the film.

The third angle variable, roll, is determined by the movement of the camera around the last remaining axis, the horizontal that parallels the axis of the lens. Possibly because this axis represents the metaphysical bond between the observer (or camera) and the subject, possibly because roll destroys the stability of the horizon, the camera is very seldom revolved around this axis. The only common roll movement that comes to mind is that sometimes used to mimic the movements of the horizon as seen from the boat in heavy seas. Roll movement (or the oblique horizon of a static shot from a camera position other than

Figure 3-39. Multiple exposure is one of the most unnatural codes of cinema (we seldom see two images at the same time in real life) but it can also be one of the most meaningful. Here, three multiple exposures from various films by Orson Welles, in increasing order of complexity. The first, from *Citizen Kane*, simply connects Susan Alexander (Dorothy Comingore) with her image in the press, a common use of the double exposure code. (*l'Avant-Scène. Frame enlargement.*)

Figure 3-40. The second, from *The Magnificent Ambersons* (1942), suggests two levels of reality. (*l'Avant-Scène. Frame enlargement.*)

Figure 3-41. The third, from *The Lady from Shanghai* (1947), is from the famous mirror sequence in that film: will we survive the nightmare? (*l'Avant-Scène. Frame enlargement.*)

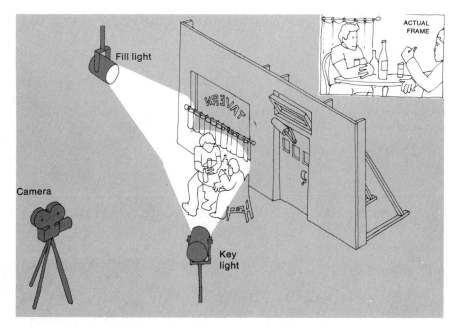

Figure 3-42. KEY LIGHTS AND FILL LIGHTS. The key light, usually at a 45° angle to the camera-subject axis, provides the main source of illumination. The smaller fill light softens the shadows in this classic Hollywood lighting technique.

vertical) is the only change of camera angle that does not significantly alter the focus of attention. To pan or to tilt is to change images; to roll is simply to alter the original image.

The camera not only revolves around these three axes, it is also moved from one point to another: hence tracking shots (also called trucking or dolly shots) and crane shots. The zoom shot, in addition, mimics the effect of a track in or track back, but not precisely. In the zoom, since the camera does not move, the relationships between objects in different planes remain the same; there is no sense of entering into the scene; our perspective remains constant, even if the image is enlarged. In the track, however, we do move physically into the scene; the spatial relationships between objects shift, as does our perspective. Although the zoom is often an inexpensive alternative to the tracking shot, its effect is strangely distancing: we seem to move closer without getting any nearer, and that is disorienting, since we have no such experience in real life for comparison.

Just as a debate has evolved between proponents of deep focus and shallow focus, and between champions of mise en scène and montage, so too the moving camera has its adherents and detractors. Because it

Figure 3-43. HOLLYWOOD LIGHTING. Margaret O'Brien and Judy Garland in Vincente Minnelli's *Meet Me in St. Louis* (1944). The set is vibrantly, thoroughly lit. There are only the faintest hints of shadows, even in the back room, which is out of focus. Since this was a technicolor film, the lighting is even stronger than it might have been in black-and-white.

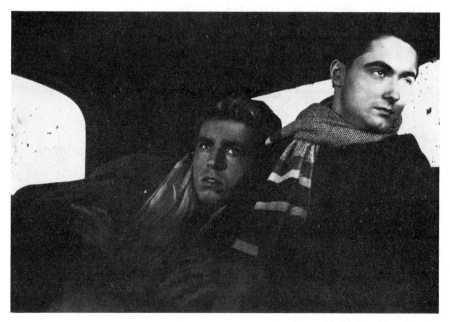

Figure 3-44. HIGHLIGHTING. Jean-Pierre Melville's and Jean Cocteau's *Les Enfants terribles* (1950). The eyes are specially lit.

Figure 3-45. Backlighting is one of the more interesting lighting codes taken from painting. Here, a relatively early example from painting, Constance Marie Charpentier's *Mlle Charlotte du val d'Ognes* (c. 1801). The light source highlights the subject's hair and the folds of her dress. Although there is no perceivable light source from the front, details are nevertheless evident and the shadows are soft and elegant. (*Oil on canvas, 60½" by 50⅜", The Metropolitan Museum of Art, The Mr. and Mrs. Isaac D. Fletcher Collection. Bequest of Isaac D. Fletcher, 1917.*)

continually changes our perspective, the tracking shot significantly increases our perception of depth. More important, the moving camera has an inherent ethical dimension. It can be used in two essentially different ways (like focus shifts, pans, and tilts): either to follow the subject or to change it. The first alternative strongly emphasizes the centrality of the subject of the film; the second shifts interest from subject to camera, from object to filmmaker. As André Bazin has pointed out, these are ethical questions, since they determine the human relationships between and among artist, subject, and observer.

Although some estheticians insist that the moving camera, because it calls attention to the filmmaker, is somehow less ethical than the stationary camera, this is as specious a differentiation as the earlier dichotomies between mise en scène and montage and deep and shallow focus. A tracking or crane shot need not necessarily shift interest from subject to camera: it can, rather, call attention to the relationship between the two, which is arguably both more realistic and more ethical, since there is in fact a relationship.

Figure 3-46. Jean-Luc Godard, among others, is a filmmaker who has been intrigued by this code. By the time of *Weekend* (1968), from which this shot comes, he had abstracted the backlit shot to the extreme of silhouette. The lighting is harsh, bold, and over-whelms the subject. In order to search out detail in the shot we have to work, which makes us feel, faced with the bright win-dow, not unlike voyeurs—ex-actly the effect Godard wants. It is interesting to note that the women's poses are comparable, as well. Jean Yanne and Mireille Darc in *Weekend* (1968). (*Frame enlargement.*)

F. W. Murnau and Max Ophüls loom large in the history of the moving camera. Their use of it was, essentially, humanistic—to create a lyrical celebration of their subjects and to involve their audiences more deeply. Stanley Kubrick, a contemporary filmmaker closely identified with tracking shots, also uses camera movement to involve his audi-ence, but in a colder, more intellectual way. Michael Snow, an impor-tant contemporary abstract filmmaker and artist, has—in a series of three seminal films—explored in great depth the significatory potential of the moving camera. *Wavelength* (1967) is an obsessive zoom, lasting forty-five minutes, which takes us from an image of a rather large New York loft in its entirety to, in the end, a detail shot of a photograph hanging on the wall at the opposite end of the large room. The poten-tial of the simplest pan from left to right and back again is explored in ↔ (1968–9), also called "Back and Forth." Snow set up his camera in an empty classroom, then panned continuously and quickly over a sector of about 75° and in periods ranging from fifteen cycles per minute to sixty cycles per minute. *La Région Centrale* (1970–71), Snow's masterwork lasting more than three hours, gives us an obsessive "map" of the complete sphere of space that surrounds the camera on all sides. Snow constructed a servo-mechanism control head for his camera, set it up in a remote and rocky region of Northern Quebec, and controlled its patterns of movement from behind a hill. The camera swoops, swirls, gyrates, twirls, tilts, zigzags, sweeps, arcs, and performs figure eights in a multitude of patterns while nothing is visible except the barren land-scape, the horizon, and the sun. The effect is the thorough liberation of the camera from both subject and photographer. The global space that

Figure 3-47. Woody Allen achieved an entirely different feel in this equally harshly backlit shot from *Manhattan* (1979). The silhouettes of Diane Keaton and Allen are instantly recognizable at a cocktail party in the garden of the Museum of Modern Art.

surrounds it becomes raw material for Snow's complex patterns of movements; movement is all.

The liberated, abstract quality of Snow's images leads us directly to a consideration of the last of the five shot variables: point of view. Unlike the first four, this is more a matter of metaphysics than of geometry. The point of *La Région Centrale,* for example, is that is has no point of view, or rather that its point of view is abstract and global. Most narrative films, however, do show some sort of subjective point of view. This varies from the objective point of view of long shots, deep focus, and static camera, to the more subjective approach of closeups, shallow focus, and moving camera. We've already noted that the moving camera has an ethical aspect to it. The question of point of view is at the heart of this ethical code, and critics and semiologists are only now beginning to investigate the phenomenon specifically. Considering the structure of the artistic experience we set up in Chapter 1 (pp. 10–12), the ethics of film—the quality and shape of the relationships between filmmaker, subject, artwork, and audience—is elemental: all other ideas about film must stem from it and relate back to it.

Point of view is easier to describe in prose narrative: novels are either

A Sylvia Bataille in Jean Renoir's *Partie de campagne* (1936).

B Bibi Andersson, Gunnar Björnstrand, Liv Ullmann in Bergman's *Persona* (1966).

C Renée Longarini, Marcello Mastroianni in Fellini's *La Dolce Vita* (1959).

D Giulietta Masina in Fellini's *Nights of Cabiria* (1957).

E Masina in Fellini's *Nights of Cabiria* (1957).

F Masina in Fellini's *Juliet of the Spirits* (1965).

Figure 3-48. SHOT COMPOSITION. In practice, shot distance is much more idiosyncratic than the terminology suggests. Both A and B, for example, are somewhere in between closeups and detail shots. Both give us half a woman's face, yet in A the face takes up nearly the whole frame while in B it is part of a three-shot. The aspect ratio of the frame is an important consideration, too. Both C and D are, more or less, mid-shots, yet C, in the scope ratio, has an entirely different effect from D, in the standard Academy ratio. C includes a lot more action than D; D is more like a closeup in effect. Composition is a major element, as well. Shots E and F both must be classified as long shots—same actress, same director. In each, Giulietta Masina takes up three-quarters of the height of the frame, more or less. Yet in E, Fellini has composed a shot in which the other design elements—the road, the statues, the horizon—work to focus attention on Masina. Psychologically, the image of her is more impressive here. In F, composition (and her posture) works to deemphasize her presence. (All shots, *l'Avant-Scène. Frame enlargements.*)

Figure 3-49. A typical low-angle shot from Yasujiro Ozu's *The End of Summer* (1961). The angle doesn't seem so striking because the subjects are seated on the floor. (*New Yorker Films.*)

narrated by someone in the story—the first-person narrator—or by someone outside it—the omniscient narrator. The first-person narrator may be either a major or minor figure in the events; the omniscient narrator is sometimes developed as a separate character, sometimes characterless, except insofar as he represents the character of the author. In its totality, film can fairly well duplicate these fictional models. Most films, like most novels, are told from an omniscient point of view. We see and hear whatever the author wants us to see and hear. But when we come to the first-person mode—which has proved so useful in prose fiction because of the resonances that can be developed between events and the character or persona of the narrator—problems arise in film. It's easy enough to allow a film character to narrate the story. The difficulty is that we see what is happening as well as hear it. In the novel, in effect, we only hear it. As we've noted earlier, Robert Montgomery's *Lady in the Lake* (1945) is the most famous example of rigid adherence to the first-person rule applied to cinema—and the most obvious demonstration of its failure. (See pp. 30–31.)

In *Stage Fright* (1950), Alfred Hitchcock discovered, to his chagrin, that the first-person point of view in film is fraught with problems even when it is used perfunctorily. In that film, Hitchcock had one of his characters narrate a flashback—and lie. Audiences saw the lie on screen and when they later found out that it was false they reacted angrily. They weren't able to accept the possibility that the *image* would lie, although they would have been quite willing to believe that the *character* had lied. The image on the screen is simply invested with an immutable aura of validity.

By the early 1940s, Hollywood had evolved a very smooth, efficient, and clearly understood idiom of point of view. The establishing shot—a long shot—established place, often time, and sometimes other necessary information. Hitchcock was a master of the establishing shot. The opening pan and track of *Rear Window* (1954), for example, tells us where we are, why we are there, whom we are with, what is going on now, what has happened to get us there, who the other characters of the story are, and even suggests possible ways the story might develop—all effortlessly and quickly and without a spoken word! Paragraphs of prose are condensed into seconds of film time.

The Hollywood dialogue style is equally efficient: we normally begin with a shot of both speakers (an establishing two-shot), then move to a montage of one-shots as each of the participants variously speaks and listens. Often these are "over-the-shoulder" shots, an interesting use of the code since it suggests the speaker's point of view but is also physically separate from it. The shot of the first character from (approximately) the second character's point of view is usually termed a reverse-angle shot. The rhythms of this careful, insistent, and intimate shot-countershot technique are often intoxicating: we surround the conversation. This is the ultimate omniscient style, since it allows us to see everything from the ideal perspective. More contemporary techniques, which tend to emphasize the separateness and individuality of the camera, may allow us to "see everything," but always from a separate, distinct point of view. Antonioni's camera, for instance, often holds on a scene that a character has either not yet entered or already left. The effect is to emphasize environment over character and action, context over content. We might call this the third-person point of view: the camera often seems to take on a personality of its own, separate from those of the characters.

In either omniscient style—the Hollywood or the modern—the point-of-view shot (abbreviated "pov") has its uses. And soundtrack narration is often able to strengthen the sense of the character's perspective of events. Yet the psychologically insistent, ever-present image attenuates this perspective. In print we need not always be "looking" at

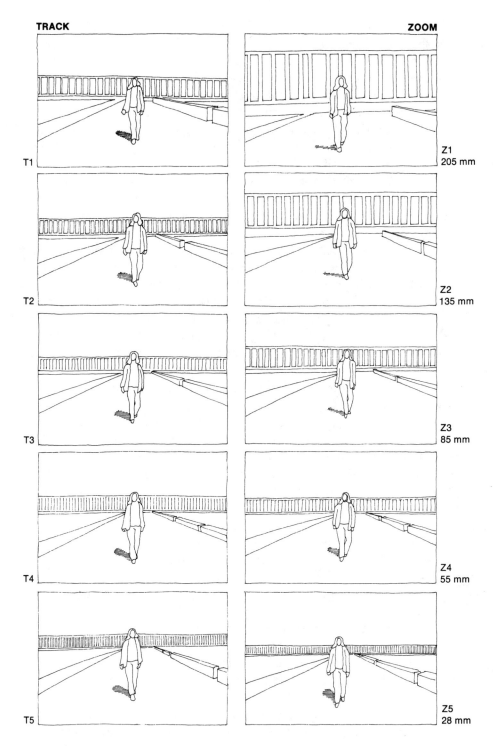

Figure 3-50.

Figure 3-51. THE MOVING CAMERA. On the set of Jean-Luc Godard's *One Plus One* (1968). The typical camera at right is a "prop" in the film. (The red and black flags are *not* standard equipment.) The camera platform is counterbalanced by weights out of the frame. In the middle ground can be seen tracks laid for a camera that is barely visible at the extreme left. In the foreground, a third camera is mounted on a special truck.

Figure 3-50. TRACKING VERSUS ZOOMING. These ten frames from parallel tracking and zoom shots illustrate the significant differences between the two techniques. In both series, the woman is walking towards the camera, covering a distance of approximately fifty yards between frame 1 and frame 5. The track was shot first, with a 55 mm lens. (Thus frames T4 and Z4 are identical.) The zoom was then shot to correspond to the track. The relationship between subject and background is dramatically different in the zoom. As the lens changes from telephoto (205 mm) to wide-angle (28 mm) focal lengths, depth perception changes from suppressed to exaggerated, and perspective undergoes a slight moderation as well. In the tracking shot, the distance between subject and camera is constant from one frame to another, and the building is far enough in the background so as not to change greatly between frames. In the zoom, the distance between subject and camera is constantly changing, and the relative size of the background building is magnified in the telephoto shots and distanced, or minimized in the wideangle frame. Notice, too, that the angle of the shadow changes in the zoom. See Figure 2-9.

Figure 3-52. ROLL. Pans, tilts, and tracks are common enough cinematic codes, but rolls are relatively rare. The reason is obvious: pans, tilts, and tracking shots mimic common, everyday movements, but we seldom "roll" our heads (tilt them sideways), so this is often a striking perspective. While shots are often made at a *static* rolled angle (see the illustrations from Orson Welles films in Figures 3-38, 3-41) the *movement* of rolling is unusual. Here, Fred Astaire performs an entire dance routine in one unedited shot, gradually moving up the wall, across the ceiling, and down the opposite wall. The film is Stanley Donen's *Royal Wedding* (1951). The precisely choreographed routine was accomplished on a set mounted within a drum. The furniture and the camera were secured. As Astaire moved from floor to wall, from wall to ceiling, the set turned and the camera turned with it.

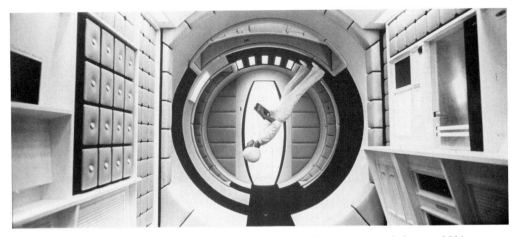

Figure 3-53. Stanley Kubrick used a similar apparatus for many unusual shots in *2001: A Space Odyssey*. This particular shot was a setpiece to show off the device. The flight attendant walked full circle, supposedly using Velcro slippers on the special path. (*Frame enlargement.*)

Figure 3-54. TRACKING. Murnau's set for *Sunrise* (1927). The long tram ride has earned a place in history. In this case, the tracking shot is purely verisimilitudinous: there is no other way to ride a tram than on tracks. (MOMA/FSA.)

Figure 3-55. Max Ophüls was unusually fond of the moving camera. This is a still from a long lyrical, and very complex crane shot in *La Ronde* (1950). Anton Walbrook at left, Simone Signoret on the carousel. (MOMA/FSA.)

Figure 3-56. If the tracking shot was logical and realistic for Murnau, lyrical and romantic for Ophüls, it became, by 1968, a tool of intellectual analysis (as well as a grand joke) for Jean-Luc Godard. This frame comes from the middle of the ten-minute-long tracking shot of the traffic jam in *Weekend*. Godard's camera moves slowly and inexorably past a seemingly endless line of stopped autos. Drivers and passengers honk incessantly, argue with each other, and fight, or stop for an impromptu picnic, play ball from car to car (as here) or test their gear on trailer-mounted sailboats. The poplar trees that line the road at regular intervals divide this magnificent continuous shot into segments that function as separate framing devices. (*Frame enlargement.*)

a scene: writers don't always describe or narrate, they often explain or theorize. In film, however, because of the presence of the image, there is always the element of description—even when the soundtrack is used concurrently for explanation, theorizing, or discussion. This is one of the most significant differences between prose narrative and film narrative. Clearly, the only way to circumvent this insistent descriptive nature of the film image is to eliminate it entirely, in which case the soundtrack can duplicate the abstract, analytical potential of written language. Jean-Luc Godard experimented with just this technique in his highly theoretical films of the late sixties. Sometimes the screen is simply black, while we listen to the words on the soundtrack.

SOUND

While the fact of the image is a disadvantage of a kind in terms of point of view in film narrative, the fact of sound—its ever-presence—is a distinct advantage. Christian Metz identifies five channels of informa-

Figure 3-57. Michael Snow's *Wavelength* (1967) treats the tracking shot as a structural law, the subject of the film. This is a frame from about the middle of the forty-five minute zoom. By the end of the film, Snow's camera has moved into a closeup of the middle of the photograph tacked to the wall above the chair. The image? Waves, of course. (MOMA/FSA. *Frame enlargement.*)

tion in film: (1) the visual image; (2) print and other graphics; (3) speech; (4) music; (5) noise (sound effects). Interestingly, the majority of these channels are auditory rather than visual. Examining these channels with regard to the manner in which they communicate, we discover that only two of them are continuous—the first and the fifth. The other three are intermittent—they are switched on and off—and it is easy to conceive of a film without either print, speech, or music. The two continuous channels themselves communicate in distinctly separate ways. We "read" images by directing our attention; we do not read sound, at least not in the same conscious way. Sound is not only omnipresent but omnidirectional. Because it is so pervasive, we tend to discount it. Images can be manipulated in many different ways and the manipulation is relatively obvious; with sound, even the limited manipulation that does occur is vague and tends to be ignored.

It is the pervasiveness of sound that is its most attractive quality. It acts to realize both space and time. It is essential to the creation of a locale; the "room sound," based on the reverberation time, harmonics, and so forth or a particular location, is its signature. Sound also actualizes time. A still image comes alive when a soundtrack is added that can create a sense of the passage of time. In a utilitarian sense, sound shows

Figure 3-58. Michael Snow's ultimate pan/tilt/roll machine, with camera, set up to shoot *La Région Centrale*. Snow operated the camera from behind the rock at right so as not to appear in the picture. (MOMA/FSA.)

its value by creating a ground base of continuity to support the images that usually receive more attention. Speech and music naturally receive attention because they have specific meaning. It is the so-called "noise" of the soundtrack—"sound effects"—that is paramount. This is where the real construction of the sound environment takes place.

But "noise" and "effects" are poor labels indeed for a worthy art. Possibly we could term this aspect of the soundtrack "environmental sound." The influence of environmental sound has been felt—and noticed—in contemporary music, especially in that aspect of it known as 'musique concrète." Even recorded speech has been affected by this new ability. In the great days of radio, "sound effects" were limited to those that could be produced physically. The advent of synthesizers, multitrack recording, and other electronic devices has now made it possible for the sound effects expert to re-create an infinite range of both natural and entirely new artificial sounds. Much of the best contemporary sound drama (which appears mainly on records, and a few public interest radio stations) has recognized the extraordinary potential of what used to be known simply as sound effects.

Film, too, has recognized sound's new maturity. In the early days of the sound film, musicals, for instance, were extraordinary elaborate visually. Busby Berkeley conceived intricate visual representations of musical ideas in order to hold an audience's interest. Now, however,

Figure 3-59. Grace Kelly and James Stewart in Hitchcock's *Rear Window* (1954). Stewart, a photographer, is immobilized in his apartment on Tenth Street in Greenwich Village. The "Cinemascope" picture windows of the building across the courtyard intrigue him. He becomes deeply involved in the stories they tell. (MOMA/FSA.)

the most successful film musical form is the simple concert. The soundtrack carries the film; the images are dominated by it.

We can conceive of nonmusical cinema in this vein as well. In England, where radio drama lasted longer than in the U.S., a tradition of aural drama has been maintained since the *Goon Shows* of the fifties. In the U.S., Francis Ford Coppola's fascinating *Conversation* (1974) did for the aural image what *Blow-up* (1966), had done for the pictorial image eight years earlier. Much of the best comedy in this country has been almost exclusively aural since the days of vaudeville: beginning with the masters Jack Benny, George Burns, and Fred Allen, this elegant if unsung tradition has given us Nichols and May, Mel Brooks, and the complex "cinematic" constructions of The Firesign Theatre, The National Lampoon, and Albert Brooks. Much of this recent comedy isn't essentially comic: aural artists have moved into more complex modes. Yet the "comedy album" is the single accepted channel of distribution for work of this sort.

In cinema, while the soundtrack can certainly support greater emphasis than it has been given, it cannot easily be divorced from images. Much of the language we employ to discuss the codes of soundtracks treats of the relationship between sound and image. Siegfried Kracauer suggests the differentiation between actual sound, which logically connects with the image, and commentative sound, which does not. Dialogue of people in the scene is actual, dialogue of people not in the scene is commentative. (A filmmaker sophisticated in sound, such as Richard Lester, often uses commentative dialogue of people who are in the shot, but not part of the action of the scene.) Director and theorist Karel Reisz uses slightly different terminology. For Reisz, who wrote the standard text on editing, all sound is divided into synchronous and asynchronous. Synchronous sound has its source within the frame (the editor must work to synchronize it). Asynchronous sound comes from outside the frame.

Combining these two continuums, we get a third* whose poles are parallel sound and contrapuntal sound. Parallel sound is actual, synchronous, connected with the image. Contrapuntal sound is commentative, asynchronous, and opposed to or in counterpoint with the image. It makes no difference whether we are dealing with speech, music, or environmental sound: all three are at times variously parallel or contrapuntal, actual or commentative, synchronous or asynchronous.

The differentiation between parallel and contrapuntal sound is perhaps the controlling factor. This conception of the soundtrack as working logically either with or against the image provides the basic esthetic dialectic of sound. The Hollywood sound style was strongly parallel. The programmatic music of thirties movies nudged, underlined, emphasized, characterized, and qualified even the simplest scenes so that the dullest images as well as the most striking were thoroughly pervaded by the emotions designed by the composers of the nearly continuous music track. Erich Wolfgang Korngold and Max Steiner were the two most egregious examples.

More recently, contrapuntal sound has given an ironic edge to the contemporary style. Often the soundtrack is seen as equal, but different from, the image. Marguerite Duras, for example, has experimented with commentative soundtracks completely separate from the image, as in *India Song* (1975). Programmatic music still exists (television is especially fond of it), but more often the music is used commentatively. Rock, for example, offers filmmakers a repertoire of instant keys to contemporary ideas and feelings, as George Lucas's *American Graffiti* (1973) demonstrated clearly. Ironically, music—which used to be the most powerfully asynchronous and commentative element of the soundtrack—has now become so pervasive in real life that a filmmaker can

---

*I am indebted to Win Sharples, Jr.: "The Aesthetics of Film Sound," *Filmmakers Newsletter* 8:5, for this synthesis.

maintain strict synchronicity of actual sound and still produce a complete music track. The ubiquitous transistor radio and Muzak have made life a musical.

MONTAGE

In the U.S., the word for the work of putting together the shots of a film is "cutting" or "editing," while in Europe the term is "montage." The American words suggest a trimming process, in which unwanted material is eliminated. Michelangelo once described sculpture similarly as paring away unneeded stone to discover the natural shape of the sculpture in a block of marble. One edits or cuts raw material down. "Montage," however, suggests a building action, working up from the raw material. Indeed the classic style of Hollywood editing of the thirties and forties—what the French call découpage classique—was in fact marked by its smoothness, fluidity, and leanness. And European montage, ever since the German Expressionists and Eisenstein in the twenties, has been characterized by a process of synthesis: a film is seen as being constructed rather than edited. The two terms for the action express the two basic attitudes toward it.

Whereas mise en scène is marked by a fusion of complexities, montage is surprisingly simple, at least on the physical level. There are only two ways to put two pieces of film together: one can overlap them (double exposure, dissolves, multiple images) or one can put them end to end. For images, the second alternative dominates almost exclusively, while sounds lend themselves much more readily to the first, so much so that this activity has its own name: mixage.

In general parlance, "montage" is used in three different ways. While maintaining its basic meaning, it also has the more specific usages of:

- a dialectical process that creates a third meaning out of the original two meanings of the adjacent shots, and
- a process in which a number of short shots are woven together in order to communicate a great deal of information in a short period of time.

This last is simply a special case of general montage; the dialectical process is inherent in any montage, conscious or not.

Découpage classique, the Hollywood style of construction, gradually developed a broad range of rules and regulations over the years: for example, the practice of beginning always with an establishing shot, then narrowing down from the generalization; or, the strict rule of thumb for editing dialogue scenes with master shots and reverse angles. All the editing practices of the Hollywood grammar were designed to

permit seamless transitions from shot to shot and to concentrate attention on the action at hand. What helped to maintain immediacy and
the flow of the action was good, what did not was bad.

In fact, any kind of montage is in the end defined according to the
action it photographs. Still pictures can be put together solely with
regard to the rhythm of the succeeding shots. Diachronic shots, inherently active, demand that the movements within the shot be considered
in the editing. The jump cut provides an interesting example of the
contrasting ways in which découpage classique and contemporary editing treat a problem.

In Hollywood cinema, "invisible cutting" was the aim, and the jump
cut was used as a device to compress dead time. A man enters a large
room at one end, for instance, and must walk to a desk at the other
end. The jump cut can maintain tempo by eliminating most of the
action of traversing the long room, but it must do so unobtrusively. The
laws of Hollywood grammar insist that the excess dead time be
smoothed over either by cutting away to another element of the scene
(the desk itself, someone else in the room) or by changing camera angle
sufficiently so that the second shot is clearly from a different camera
placement. Simply snipping out the unwanted footage from a single
shot from a single angle is not permitted. The effect, according to
Hollywood rules, would be disconcerting.

Contemporary style, however, permits far greater latitude. In *Breathless* (1959), Jean-Luc Godard startled some estheticians by jump cutting
in mid-scene. The cuts had no utilitarian value and they were disconcerting. Godard himself seldom returned to this device in later films,
but his "ungrammatical" construction has been absorbed into general
montage stylistics and jump cuts are now allowed for rythmic effect.
Even the simple utilitarian jump cut has been streamlined: edited from
a single shot (single angle), it can be smoothed by a series of quick
dissolves.

It's important to note that there are actually two processes going on
when shots are edited. The first is the joining of the two shots. Also
important, however, is determining the length of any individual shot,
both as it relates to shots that precede and follow it and as it concerns
the action of the shot. Découpage classique demands that a shot be cut
so that the editing doesn't interfere with the central action of the shot.
If we plot the action of each shot so that we get a rising then a falling
curve, Hollywood grammar demands a cut shortly after the climax of
the curve. A contemporary director like Michelangelo Antonioni, however, reverses the logic, maintaining the shot long after the climax,
throughout the period of aftermath. The last shot of *The Passenger*
(1975) is an excellent example.

The rhythmic value of editing is probably best seen in the code of accelerated montage, in which interest in a scene is heightened and brought to a climax through progressively shorter alternations of shots between two subjects (often in chase scenes). Christian Metz points to accelerated montage as a uniquely cinematic code (although Charles Ives's antagonistic brass bands provided an illustration of this kind of cross-cutting in music). Accelerated montage points in the direction of a second type of editing.

Montage is used not only to create a continuity between shots in a scene but also to bend the time line of a film. Parallel montage allows the filmmaker to alternate between two stories that may or may not be interrelated, cross-cutting between them. (Accelerated montage is a special type of parallel montage.) The flashback and the flash-forward permit digressions and forecasts. Involuted montage allows a sequence to be narrated without particular regard for chronology: an action can be repeated, shots can be edited out of order. Each of these extensions of the montage codes looks toward the creation of something other than simple chronology in the montage itself, a factor very little emphasized in classic découpage continuity cutting. Possibly the most common dialectic device is the match cut, which links two disparate scenes by the repetition of an action or a form or the duplication of mise-en-scène factors. Stanley Kubrick's match cut in *2001: A Space Odyssey*, between a prehistoric bone whirling in the air and a twenty-first-century space station revolving in space, is possibly the most ambitious match cut in history, since it attempts to unite prehistory with the future anthropologically at the same time as it creates a special meaning within the cut itself by emphasizing the functions of both bone and space station as tools, extensions of human capabilities.

The codes of montage may not be as obvious as the codes of mise en scène, but that doesn't mean that they are necessarily less complex. Few theorists have gone further than differentiating among parallel montage, continuity montage, accelerated montage, flashbacks, and involuted montage. In the 1920s, both V.I. Pudovkin and Sergei Eisenstein extended the theory of montage beyond these essentially practical concerns. Pudovkin identified five basic types of montage: contrast, parallelism, symbolism, simultaneity, and leit-motif. He then developed a theory of the interaction between shots variously called "relational editing" or "linkage." Eisenstein, on the other hand, saw the relationship between shots as a collision rather than a linkage, and further refined the theory to deal with the relationships between elements of individual shots as well as the whole shots themselves. This he called the "montage of attractions." Both theorists are discussed in greater detail in Chapter 5.

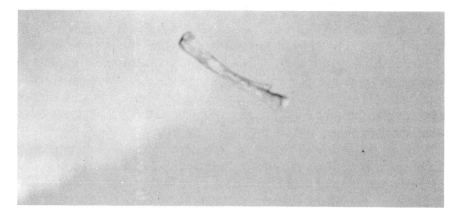

Figure 3-60A. Kubrick's transcendent match cut. (*Frame enlargements.*)

In the late sixties, Christian Metz attempted to synthesize all these various theories of montage. He constructed a chart in which he tried to indicate how eight types of montage were connected logically. There are a number of problems with Metz's categories, yet the system does have an elegance all its own and it does describe most of the major patterns of montage. More important, despite it idiosyncrasies and occasional confusions, it remains the only recent attempt to comprehend the complex system of montage.

Note that Metz is interested in narrative elements—syntagmas—that can exist within shots as well as between them, an important refinement since, as we have already indicated, the effects of many types of montage can be accomplished within a shot without actually cutting. If the camera pans for example, from one scene to another, those two scenes exist in relationship to each other just as they would if they were cut together.

Metz's grand design may seem forbidding at first glance, but it reveals a real and useful logic when studied. He begins by limiting himself to autonomous segments of film. These must be either autonomous shots—which are entirely independent of what comes before and after them—or what he calls "syntagmas": that is, units that have meaningful relationships with each other. (We might call these "scenes" or "sequences," but Metz reserves those terms for individual types of syntagma.) At each stage of this binary system, a further differentiation is made: the first bracket differentiates between autonomous shots and related shots, clearly the primary factor in categorizing types of montage. Either a shot is related to it surrounding shots, or it is not.

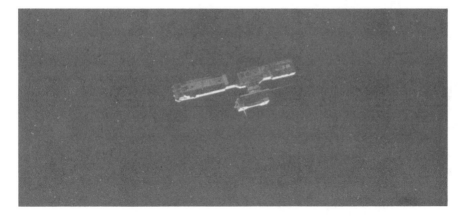

Figure 3-60B.

The second bracket differentiates between syntagmas that operate chronologically and those that do not. In other words, editing either tells a story (or develops an idea) in chronological sequence, or it does not. Now, on the third level, the differentiations branch out. Metz identifies two separate types of achronological syntagmas, the parallel and the bracket. Then he differentiates between two types of chronological syntagmas: either a syntagma describes or it narrates. If it narrates, it can do so either linearly or nonlinearly. If it does so linearly, it is either a scene or a sequence. And, finally, if it is a sequence, it is either episodic or ordinary.

The end result is a system of eight types of montage, or eight syntagmas. The autonomous shot (1) is also known as the sequence shot (although Metz also places certain kinds of inserts—short, isolated fragments—here). The parallel syntagma (2) has been discussed above as the well-known phenomenon of parallel editing. The bracket syntagma (3), however, is Metz's own invention or discovery. He defines it as "a series of very brief scenes representing occurrences that the film gives as typical examples of a same order or reality, without in any way chronologically locating them in relation to each other" [Metz, p. 126]. This is rather like a system of allusions. A good example might be the collection of images with which Godard begins A Married Woman (1964). They all allude to a concept of modern attitudes toward sex. Indeed, Godard in many of his films seems to be particularly fond of the bracket syntagma, since it allows film to act something like the literary essay.

The descriptive syntagma (4) merely describes. The relation between its elements is spatial rather than temporal. Almost any establishing

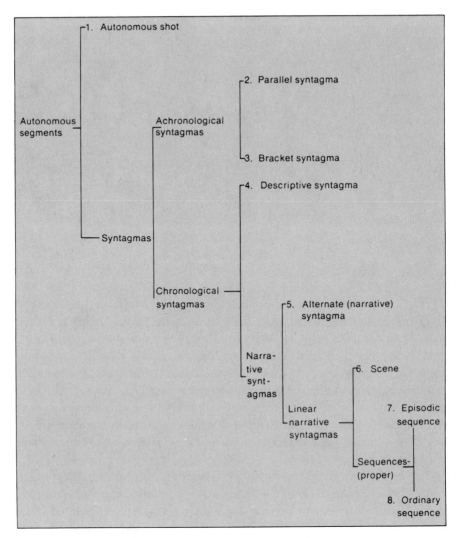

METZ'S SYNTAGMATIC CATEGORIES.

sequence (such as the one already discussed in *Rear Window*) is a good example of the descriptive syntagma. The alternate syntagma (5) is very much like the parallel syntagma except that the parallel syntagma offers two separate scenes or sequences that do not have a narrative connection while the alternate syntagma offers parallel or alternating elements that do. The effect here is of simultaneity, as in chase scenes in which the montage alternates between shots of pursuer and pursued.

If events do not happen simultaneously, they happen one after the other, in linear sequence, and this brings us to Metz's remaining three categories of montage—the scene (6) and two types of sequence—episodic (7) and ordinary (8). There has always been a great deal of confusion in the vocabulary of film criticism between the concepts of scene and sequence, and Metz's elaborate system is valuable for the precise definitions he offers. Metz takes his definition of scene from theatrical parlance. In the scene, the succession of events—the linear narrative—is continuous. In the sequence, it is broken up. It is still linear, it is still narrative, it is still chronological, it is still related to other elements, but it is not continuous. Metz's last differentiation, between the episodic sequence and the ordinary sequence, is a bit arbitrary. In the episodic sequence the discontinuity is organized; in the ordinary sequence it is not. A good example, then, of the episodic sequence is the one in *Citizen Kane* in which Orson Welles portrays the progressive deterioration of Kane's marriage by a set of successive episodes at the breakfast table. In fact, we might call this a "sequence of scenes," and this is a major characteristic of the episodic sequence—that its elements are organized so that each of them seems to have an identity of its own.

Some of these differentiations might still not be clear. For most film viewers, the concepts of the bracket syntagma and the descriptive syntagma are so close that differentiation may seem specious. Parallel syntagma and alternate syntagma present the same difficulty, as do episodic and ordinary sequences. Yet, despite its problems, Metz's system remains a helpful guide to what is, as yet, relatively uncharted territory: the ever-shifting, complex, and intricate syntax of film narrative. Whether or not his eight categories seem valid, the factors of differentiation that he defines are highly significant and bear repeating:

- Either a film segment is autonomous or it is not.
- Either it is chronological or it is not.
- Either it is descriptive or it is narrative.
- Either it is linear or it is not.
- Either it is continuous or it is not.
- Either it is organized or it is not.

We have only to describe the punctuation of cinema to complete this quick survey of the syntax of mise en scène and montage. Because punctuation devices stand out and are simply defined, they often take pride of place in discussions of cinematic language. They are useful, no doubt, as are, well, commas, for example, in written language. The simplest type of punctuation is the unmarked cut. One image ends,

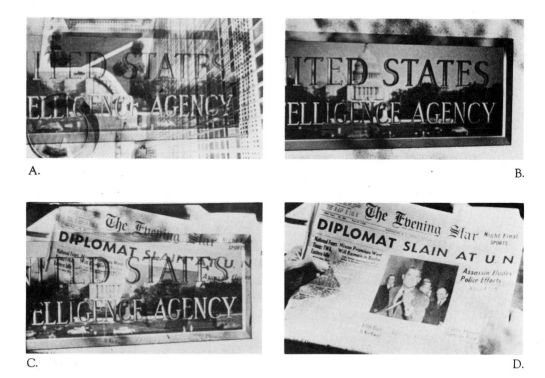

A.

B.

C.

D.

Figure 3-61. This sequence of three shots is a double dissolve from Alfred Hitchcock's *North by Northwest* (1959). At first it seems no more than a highly economical transition from the previous scene at the UN building, in which Roger Thornhill (Cary Grant) has been mistaken for a murderer, to a conference at the CIA in Washington, at which this turn of events is discussed. Hitchcock segues from his striking overhead shot of the antlike Thornhill running away from the slab of the UN Secretariat (barely visible in A) to the building nameplate in B. Since Hitchcock has had the foresight to use a mirrored surface for the sign, it can reflect the Capitol building, thus identifying the city as well as "company" and neatly saving an extra shot. He then dissolves to the newspaper headline in D, which tells us that (1) time has passed, (2) Thornhill has been identified, and (3) he has so far eluded capture. The newspaper is being held by the head of the intelligence agency. Hitchcock pulls back from the paper and goes on with the conference scene.

At the same time, however, there is some extraordinary metaphorical information in this elegant little dissolve for, if we analyze these still images, we can see that the CIA imposes itself on the UN, that the Capitol is a reflection of the CIA (or that the intelligence agency has superimposed itself over the seat of government), and finally, that the CIA gives birth to the newspaper headlines that include, in addition to the one conveying the necessary information: "National Fears Tieup" and "Nixon Promises West Will Remain in Berlin." (*Frame enlargements.*)

another begins. The fade calls attention to the ending or the beginning, as does the iris (a favorite of early filmmakers that has now fallen into disuse). The wipe, in which one image removes another in a dizzying variety of ways (flips, twirls, pushovers, spirals, clock hands), was a favorite in the thirties and forties. Optical houses offered catalogues of scores of patterns for wipes. Now it is used in film only for nostalgic effect, although it has found new life in television where electronic special-effects generators permit new variations on the theme, sometimes shifting the preceding image so that it looks like a page of a book is being turned, in three dimensions.

Intertitles were an important mark of punctuation in the silent cinema and are still used on occasion today. The freeze frame has become popular since it was used to such effect by François Truffaut in *The 400 Blows* (1959). (Truffaut, by the way, is the C. S. Lewis of film punctuation.) Filmmakers today have modernized some of the old forms, fading to colors instead of black (Ingmar Bergman) or cutting to blank, colored frames (Godard). There is even a not uncommon mark of punctuation that has no workable name: this is the effect of going slowly out of focus at the end of the shot, or in focus at the beginning.

All these various marks are periods, end points. A fade out/fade in may suggest a relationship, but it is noticeably not a direct link. The dissolve, however, which superimposes fade out and fade in, does connect. If there is a comma in film amongst this various catalogue of periods, it is the dissolve. Interestingly, it serves a multitude of purposes: it is commonly employed to segue or lead into a flashback, it is also used in continuity montage with the jump cut, while at the same time it can represent the passage of long periods of time, especially when it is sequential. It is the one mark of punctuation in cinema that mixes images at the same time as it conjoins them.

THE SHAPE OF FILM HISTORY

French theorists are fond of making the differentiation between "film" and "cinema." The "filmic" is that aspect of the art concerning its relationship with the world around it; the "cinematic" deals strictly with the esthetics and the internal structure of the art. In English, we have a third word for "film" and "cinema"—"movies"—which provides a convenient label for the third facet of the phenomenon: its function as an economic commodity. These three aspects are closely interrelated, of course: one person's "movie" is another's "film." But in general we use these three names for the art in a way that closely parallels this differentiation: "movies," like popcorn, are to be consumed; "cinema" (at least in American parlance) is high art, redolent of esthetics; "film" is the most general term with the fewest connotations.

This history of movies/film/cinema, although it spans less than a century, exhibits a compressed, intricate structure of development. Film history is a matter of decades and half-decades. Partly this is a result of the explosive nature of the phenomenon of film—as a medium of communication it was immediately apprehensible to large numbers of people; partly it is a matter of the geometric progression of technology in the twentieth century coupled with economic cycles, which demanded that film develop or die out.

At the same time that we speak of three approaches—movies, film, and cinema—it is good to remember that within each approach there is a corresponding spectrum of function, ranging from documentary and nonfiction on the left, through the massive popular narrative commercial cinema that occupies the middle ground, on to avant-garde and abstract film on the right. The major part of this historical discussion will dwell on the middle ground, since it is here that the politics and economics of film have had their most significant effect.

Interesting parallels exist between the history of the art form of the novel during the course of the past three hundred years and the development of film during the past eighty years. Both are, above all, popular arts, depending on large numbers of consumers in order to function economically. Each began with roots in journalism—that is, as a medium of record, developed through an early stage marked by invention and freshness, soon reached a commanding position in which it dominated other arts, and evolved an intricate system of genres that served a variety of disparate audiences—then, as it was challenged by a new medium (film for the novel, television for film), entered into a later period of consolidation, identified by a stronger concern for elite, esthetic values over those of popular entertainment. Just as novels have fed films, providing a rich lode of material, so now films feed television. Indeed, it may no longer be possible to make explicit differentiations among these three forms of narrative entertainment. Commercially, the novel, movies, and television are more closely intertwined than ever before.

The development of film differed, however, in two important respects from the precedent of the novel. Before prose narrative could reach a wide popular audience, it was necessary for a culture of literacy to develop. Film had no such problem. On the other hand, film is highly technological. Although the novel depends on the technology of printing, that technology is comparatively simple, and the development of the form of the novel has been affected only in minor ways by technological developments. We can speak of the history of the novel as being audience-intensive—that is, it is closely linked with the development of its audiences' capabilities—while the history of film is technology-intensive—it does not depend on audience capability so much as technical capability.

All histories of film mark the obvious division between silent and sound periods. While any structure more complex than this simple bifurcation is to a certain degree arbitrary, it seems useful to attempt greater precision. Each of the seven periods outlined has its own coherence. Although we tend naturally to identify these periods by esthetic differences ("cinema"), it's interesting to note that they are defined rather by economic developments ("movies").

- The period of film's prehistory includes the development of all the precursors of the Cinématographe as well as the evolution of certain aspects of the other arts that have a significant effect when applied to film (the qualities of Victorian melodrama, for example, or the values of the photographic portrait).

- The years between 1896 and 1912 saw cinema evolve from a side-show gimmick into a full-fledged economic art. The end of this period is marked by the advent of the feature-length film.
- The years 1913 to 1927 comprise the silent period.
- Between 1928 and 1932, world cinema was in a state of transition. This interval holds no unusual esthetic interest for us, but it does suggest itself economically and technologically as a significant stage.
- The period from 1932 to 1946 was the great age of Hollywood domination; during this era, the movies had their greatest economic success.
- Immediately after World War II, film had to begin confronting the challenge of television. The years 1947 to 1959 were characterized by this response, concurrent with a growing internationalism. Esthetically, if not economically, Hollywood now no longer dominated.
- The growth of the New Wave in France in the early sixties signaled the beginning of the seventh period of film history, 1960–1980. Technological innovations, a new approach to the economics of film production, and a new sense of the political and social value of film have combined to form numerous "new wavelets" in Eastern Europe, Latin America, Africa, Asia, and eventually even the United States and Western Europe.
- 1980 seems as good a point as any to mark the end of the "New Wave" period of world film history and the beginning of another. During this present era, movies are best seen as part of a varied panoply of entertainment and communications media clearly dominated by television in all its forms. As a member of the group that includes audio recordings, videotapes and discs, and various types of print as well as broadcast, satellite, and cable television, film now no longer exercises the economic leverage it once did. Movies still serve as prestigious models for these other forms of media, but increasingly film must be understood in this general context. Theatrical feature filmmaking is simply one of the numerous facets of this media system.

Indeed, we now need a new term to indicate the generalized production of audiovisual communications and entertainment. Whether this unnamed but pervasive form is produced on filmstock or magnetic tape (or someday, perhaps, on laser disc or magnetic bubble memory), whether it is distributed through theaters, via broadcast, "narrowcast," cable, disc, or tape—our core experience of it amounts to the same thing. Now, when we speak about movies/film/cinema we usually mean to infer all of these various media forms to some extent.

Contemporary film can be seen, in a sense, as a synthesis of the forces that each at one time or another seemed to dominate the cinematic formula. It is most important to an understanding of film history, however, to see how each of these social, politial, economic, cultural, psychological, and esthetic factors involves the others in a dynamic relationship. Film history is best comprehended as the product of a wide range of contradictions. This can be seen on every level, from the most specific to the most general. An actor's performance, for example, is the result of the conflict between the role and the actor's own persona. At times the personality dominates, at times the character's role, but in either case the sum is a third thing, a logical conclusion—performance—which then becomes one of the elements involved in the larger unit, the film. A particular film, likewise, is the product of a number of oppositions: director versus screenwriter, ideal script versus practical realities of shooting, shadow versus light, sound versus image, character versus plot, and so on. Each film then becomes an element in the larger systems of oppositions: genre contrasts with the individuality of scripts, studio styles are in logical opposition to personal directorial styles, thematic tendencies contrast with the concrete physical reality of the medium. Finally, each of these larger elements is involved in one or more contradictions that together give the general history of film its overall shape and substance.

What must be remembered is that in very few cases are phenomena in film history correctly described in terms of simple cause and effect. For the purposes of discussion, the brief survey of film history that follows has been organized according to the three principal forces involved—economics, politics (including psychology and sociology), and esthetics. But none of these factors is clearly and ultimately dominant. If film is essentially an economic product, nevertheless there have been numerous filmmakers who have worked without any conceivable regard to the realities of the marketplace and have managed to survive. If certain types of film are best seen in terms of their political and social effects, it must be remembered that the causes of these effects may not be political at all, but rather highly personal and esthetic. In short, our aim should not be to decide, simplistically, "what caused what" in the history of film, but rather to gain an understanding of "what is related to what." For every interesting phenomenon in film history, there are at least three plausible explanations. It's not so important which of these explanations is true, as it is to see how they relate to each other, and to the world around them.

Like any art, only more so because of its all-encompassing and popular nature, film reflects the changing relationships of the social contract. That is why it is useful to look first at the economic and technological foundations of the medium (what economists and intellectual historians would call its "infrastructure"), then to discuss some of the major political, social, and psychological implications of the art (its "structure"), and finally to conclude with a brief survey of the development of film esthetics (its "superstructure"). Any one of these three aspects of film history could easily serve as the organizing principle for a hefty volume. What follows is only the barest outline of some of the major issues involved. Moreover, film has not developed independently of the other arts and media. Its history should be seen in context with the growth of the other technological media (sketched in Chapter 6) and in relationship to developments in the older nontechnological arts. A number of these connections have been outlined in Chapter 1.

"THE MOVIES": ECONOMICS

More so than most of the other technological innovations that form the panoply of modern electric and electronic modes of communication, film was a communal invention. Unlike the telephone, telegraph, or even wireless, film depended upon a whole series of small inventions, each attributable to a different inventor. Even single concepts had multiple authors, In the U.S., Thomas Edison is usually given major credit for inventing the movies, and indeed, much of the important work of development was performed in his New Jersey laboratories. But considering Edison's demonstrated talents and obvious understanding of the problems involved in producing a workable camera/projector system, what is surprising is that he personally didn't achieve more. An Englishman, William Kennedy Laurie Dickson, was the chief experimenter working on the project for Edison. He demonstrated a crude system of projection as early as 1889, but Edison seems to have conceived of movies as more a personal than a communal experience. He was more interested in producing a private viewing system than one to project an image for the entertainment of large groups. He called his individual viewer the "Kinetoscope." It was in production in the early 1890s—one of the first short programs was the famous *Fred Ott's Sneeze*—and it soon became a common fixture of side shows and carnivals. The Kinetoscope inspired a number of European and American inventors and businessmen to apply their talents to the solution of the remaining problems. In England, the Frenchman Louis Augustin Le Prince and the Englishman William Friese-Greene both developed workable portable camera/projection systems in the late 1880s, although nothing came of them.

The key to the main problem of projection for a large audience was the intermittent motion mechanism. Louis and Auguste Lumière in France and Thomas Armat in America came up with this device in 1895. Armat sold out to Edison. The Lumières went into production and, on December 28, 1895, in the basement of the Grand Café, number 14 Boulevard des Capucines, Paris, showed the first projected films to a paying audience. During the next year, the Lumiére Cinèmatographe was demonstrated in most major European cities. Edison's first formal public performance of large-screen communal cinema took place on April 23, 1896, at Koster and Bial's Music Hall, 34th Street and Sixth Avenue, New York. The Lumières' decision to concentrate on the projection of film for large groups had a far-reaching effect. If the development of the technology had progressed along the lines Edison had laid down, the result would have been a medium much more like television, experienced privately, eventually in the home. This quite different mode of distribution and exhibition would undoubtedly have affected the types of films produced. As it happened, Edison's Kinetoscope rather quickly yielded to the Lumières' Cinématographe (and Edison's very similar Kinetograph projector) and the future of public, communal cinema was assured for at least the next eighty years. It is only recently, with the development of videocassettes and discs and home players, that the private, individualized Kinetoscope mode has been revived.

During the next year or two, a number of competitors joined the field. The Italian Filoteo Alberini had taken out several significant patents before 1896; in Germany, Max and Emil Skladanowsky developed their Bioskop; in England, Robert W. Paul was projecting films (with his version of the Edison machine) within weeks after the Lumières' première. In 1896 and 1897, the use of the Cinématographe, Edison's Kinetograph, and similar machines spread widely. It soon became evident that there was considerable profit potential in the invention. In the U.S., Dickson left Edison's employ to form (with partners) the American Mutoscope and Biograph Company, which not only produced a better peepshow machine (the Mutoscope) than Edison's Kinetoscope, but a better projector as well. The Biograph Company was soon to dominate American film. J. Stuart Blackton, like Dickson of English origins, formed the Vitagraph Company. Both the Biograph and the

Vitagraph offices were located near New York's theatrical neighborhoods (Biograph on East 14th Street near Fifth Avenue, Vitagraph in the Chelsea district), which gave them easy access to stage actors—who would surreptitiously spend an afternoon filming before reporting to work in the theater.

In France, Georges Méliès, a stage magician, saw the illusionary power of the medium and entered production, while Charles Pathé began a ruthless campaign to dominate the fledgling industry. He was fairly successful. Unlike his competitors, Pathé was able to find large amounts of capital backing, which he used to establish a near-monopoly, vertically integrated. He controlled the French film industry from the manufacture of equipment to the production of films (in his large studio at Vincennes) to distribution and exhibition, and his influence was widely felt in other countries, as well, during the early years of this century. As a result, French film dominated world screens in the years prior to the first World War. Before 1914, Pathé commonly distributed twice as much film in the U.S. alone as did the whole American industry. For other, more esthetic reasons, Italian influence in those years was also widespread.

By 1905, the concept of the film theater was established. The Lumières had opened the first establishment devoted strictly to the showing of movies in 1897. In 1902, Thomas L. Tally's Electric Theatre (prophetically located in Los Angeles) became the first American film theater. Within a few years, the concept spread rapidly. By 1908, there were more than 5000 "Nickelodeons" across the country ("nickel" because that was the price of admission; "odeon" from the Latin for a small building used for the presentation of musical and dramatic programs). The last link in the chain—manufacture, production, distribution, exhibition—was complete. No company or individual had complete control over the system, however.

Thomas Edison set out to rectify that oversight. In 1897, he had begun a long series of suits against interlopers. Armat, who felt he had been double-crossed by Edison, started his own legal proceedings. Biograph, who had some important patents of their own, prepared countersuits. In all, more than five hundred legal actions were instituted during the first decade of the history of the film industry. These were temporarily resolved with the foundation in January 1909 of the Motion Picture Patents Company, a monopoly consortium of the nine major producers—Edison, Biograph, Vitagraph, Essanay, Selig, Lubin, Kalem, Méliès, and Pathé—with the distributor George Kleine. All patents were pooled, Edison received royalties on all films produced, and George Eastman agreed to supply his filmstock only to members of the company. (Pathé had had the foresight to monopolize Eastman's filmstock in France years earlier.) No distributors who handled films of other companies were permitted to distribute Patent Company films. Most of the distributors were soon merged in their own trust, the General Film Company. But several distributors understandably rebelled against these blanket monopoly agreements. The solution was to produce their own films, and several renegade production companies sprang up, the most important being Carl Laemmle's Independent Motion Picture Company ("Imp"), which would later become Universal Studios.

Antitrust suits replaced patent suits, and the American film industry was off on another ten-year round of legal battles. Eventually, the Motion Picture Patents Company was ruled an illegal trust, but by that time most of the original members of the Company had gone out of business. None of them survived the twenties. By 1912, the Patent Company and the General Film Company controlled more than half of the ten thousand exhibition outlets—Nickelodeons—in the country, but this still left the independents room to maneuver. Their greatest weapon against the trust was not the legal fight but rather an innovation in film form. The trust and the Nickelodeons were geared to one- and two-reel films only (a reel is approximately ten minutes in length). The independents, borrowing a concept pioneered by Italian and French filmmakers, introduced the longer, "feature" film. Within a few years, the Patent Company and its short films were obsolete.

Ironically, D. W. Griffith, the filmmaker who had done most to assure the success of Biograph, the most important of the trust components, was also the first American, after his break with Biograph, to explore the potential of the feature film form. The unprecedented financial success of *The Birth of a Nation* (1915) assured the future of the new form. It also set the pattern for the "blockbuster," the film project in which huge sums of money are invested in epic productions with the hope of even huger returns. *Birth of a Nation*, costing an unprecedented and, many believed, thoroughly foolhardy $110,000, eventually returned $20 million and more. The actual figure is hard to calculate because the film was distributed on a "State's Rights" basis in which licenses to show the film were sold outright. The actual cash generated by *Birth of a Nation* may have been as much as $50 to $100 million, an almost inconceivable amount for such an early film. The focus of film activity had clearly moved out of the Nickelodeon into the legitimate theater to the detriment of the trust companies.

The urge to monopolize, however, was irrestible. The Great War immobilized film production in the European countries, and the domi-

Figure 4-1. *Puck's* view of the fantasy world of early Hollywood, 1913.

nance of France and Italy was soon overcome. The new independent American companies moved quickly to supply world markets and consolidate their position at home by a series of mergers. Adolph Zukor acquired Paramount Pictures Corporation, a distribution and exhibition company, and merged it with his own production organization (Famous Players in Famous Plays) and another company owned by Jesse Lasky. Carl Laemmle founded the Universal Film Manufacturing Company around the nucleus of Imp. William Fox, an exhibitor and distributor, formed his own production company in 1912, later to become Twentieth Century-Fox. Marcus Loew, a successful theater owner, acquired Metro Pictures Corporation (whose chief executive was Louis B. Mayer) in 1920, then merged it with Goldwyn Pictures (founded by Samuel Goldfish—later Goldwyn—and Edward Selwyn) to form Metro-Goldwyn-Mayer in 1924. The four Warner Brothers, exhibitors and distributors, started producing films in 1912. Their company later absorbed First National (which had also started in distribution) and the last of the trust companies to survive, Vitagraph.

By 1920, the "independents" had achieved an informal, low-profile monopoly that would have been the envy of the more belligerent trust companies. Each of them controlled a major section of the industry, each was vertically integrated, active in every link of the film "chain": production, distribution, and exhibition. Not until the late forties was this de facto monopoly challenged successfully in court. Even then the majors were only required to divest themselves of their theater chains. They were allowed to maintain control over distribution, the heart of the system. All five companies survive today (although M-G-M played only a minor role throughout the 1970's) and still exert extraordinary influence on the shape and direction of the film industry.

One of the modern production/distribution organizations, however, had different roots. United Artists was formed in 1919 by Charles Chaplin, Mary Pickford, Douglas Fairbanks, and David W. Griffith as a corporate shelter for their own activities. Surrounding this constellation of six major companies in the twenties, thirties, and forties were a number of minor producers, the so-called "poverty row" companies. Several of them, such as Republic and Monogram, specialized in "B" pictures, which found a niche as the second halves of double bills. By the mid-fifties, the market for such "programmers" had all but disappeared and the companies that supplied them went out of business. They were in a sense replaced by such independent low-budget producers as American International Pictures and, in the sixties, Roger Corman's New World, specializing in "exploitation" films mainly directed to the youth market.

One poverty row company that survived to become a "major" was Columbia Pictures, which evolved in 1924 out of an earlier company founded by Harry Cohn, a vaudeville performer and song-plugger, his brother Jack, and a friend, Joe Brandt. Like United Artists, one of the "little two" for many years, Columbia moved to the ranks of the majors in the late forties. By the late fifties it was one of the more significant producers of international features. During the thirties and forties RKO, which had been formed by a series of mergers to provide an outlet for the RCA sound system that was in competition with Western Electric for the market in the new technology, was also considered one of the "big five." Disney, Selznick, and Goldwyn all released through RKO at its peak. In 1948, Howard Hughes bought most of the stock. In 1953, RKO ceased production and its studios were sold to Desilu for television production.

National cinemas in Europe were also subject to monopoly pressures. The French organizations—Pathé and Gaumont—continued to dominate national distribution after the war. In Germany, the formation in 1917 of Universum Film A.G. ("UFA," with one-third of its capital supplied by the state) effectively merged the major film companies. The Soviet film industry was nationalized in 1919. In Great Britain, the U.S. companies supplied the majority of the product. Exhibition was controlled by British interests. Gaumont-British and Associated British Picture Corporation (who also produced through its subsidiary British International Pictures) controlled 300 theaters each (out of a total of 4400) in 1936. In Italy, the continued growth of what had once been one of the world's most successful cinemas was esthetically damped by the Fascist regime, although it continued to produce films popular at home if not abroad. When the Nazis took power in Germany in 1933, the influence of German cinema on world screens effectively came to an end.

It was not only the debacle of World War I and the rise of Fascist governments in Italy and Germany that assured the international dominance of the American corporations. More important, perhaps, were the industrial aspects of the American system of production. In Europe, the concept of cinema as art had appeared early and developed in tandem with the concept of cinema as business. The *film d'art* movement in France dated from 1908. Its earliest successes, many starring Sarah Bernhardt in the re-creation of her stage roles, pointed toward the creation of the feature film. *Film d'arte italiana* followed quickly. After the war, avant-garde experiments liberally punctuated French cinema and theorists began to treat the medium more seriously, as coequal with literature and the fine arts.

In the U.S., however, "cinema" was "movies." Even the earliest

Figure 4-2. The Warner Bros./First National/Vitaphone studios in Burbank, California, August 1931, one of the best-equipped film production plants at the time. The large, hangarlike buildings are sound stages. To the rear can be seen a number of standing sets—western towns, New York City streets, and the like—on the back lot. In the foreground, to the left, are administration offices and technical support facilities. (*Marc Wanamaker/Bison Art Ltd.*)

production companies—Biograph and Vitagraph especially—considered their studios to be factories, involved in the production of a commodity rather than the creation of an art. D. W. Griffith's company of actors and technicians began wintering in Los Angeles in 1910. Other companies soon followed. Independents appreciated the isolation of the west coast, where they were insulated to some extent from the strong-arm tactics of the Patent Company. By 1914, the locus of filmmaking had shifted from New York to Hollywood. The Los Angeles area provided much sunshine, good weather, and a wide variety of contrasting locales—in short, the raw materials of filmmaking—together with an attractive labor pool. The film industry located in Hollywood for the same reasons that the auto industry located in Detroit: proximity to materials and labor.

Three thousand miles from the cultural capital of the nation, American filmmakers were even more effectively isolated from prevailing artistic influences. Moreover, the men who established the major production companies had minimal experience of established literary culture. They were for the most part first- or second-generation immigrants from Germany, Poland, and Russia, who had started out as merchants, had moved into sideshow film exhibition, and from there to film distribution. They became film producers in order to provide products for their theaters.

More important, the tremendous popularity of film demanded quick expansion in the industry, which, in turn, required large amounts of capital investment. The "moguls" turned to the banks and became increasingly dependent on them. By the time they were forced to retool for sound, they were deeply in debt. Film historian Peter Cowie has written, "By 1936 it was possible to trace major holdings in all eight companies to the two powerful banking groups of Morgan and Rockefeller." Similar relationships between banking interests and film companies were developing in European countries—especially Germany, where the Deutsches Bank took effective control of UFA after the war.

European national cinemas had to contend with the overpowering flow of product from the American factories. Great Britain was most vulnerable in this respect. Although there was an upsurge in British production immediately following World War I, it was cut short by the unstable economic conditions of the early twenties. In 1927, Parliament passed the Cinematograph Act, which forbade block booking (the standard practice of requiring an exhibitor to take a year's worth of product from a single studio) and imposed a nominal five percent quota in order to guarantee that British exhibitors would show at least a few British-made films each year. By this time, however, the American companies had already invested in British branches and were able to recycle their British funds by producing "quota quickies" themselves. Even when they farmed out the business to native British producers, they imposed a contract limit of £6000 per film and kept the films as short as the law permitted (6000 feet—a little more than one hour). The German and French governments instituted similar safeguards, with similar lack of success.

The American companies clearly dominated the world market from 1920 on. As the films flowed out, the artists flowed in, as the studios widened their search for new talent. In one of the earliest instances of the "brain drain," European filmmakers made their way to Hollywood. Ernst Lubitsch was one of the first to arrive. He was followed later in the twenties by several fellow German directors, Fritz Lang, F. W. Murnau, Paul Leni, and E. A. Dupont among them. The two most important Swedish directors, Mauritz Stiller and Victor Sjöström, both emigrated to Hollywood. Stiller brought his star, Greta Garbo, with him. Indeed, many of the most successful American stars of the silent film era were European émigrés, Garbo and Rudolph Valentino being the most prominent.

With the switch to sound, the demand for foreign-born filmmakers grew. It was common practice before 1932, when the postdubbing system was put into practice, to shoot a major film in parallel versions (usually English, French, Spanish, and German). Native directors were useful for the foreign-language versions. Many of the most effective contract directors of the thirties were emigrés, including William Dieterle (German), Edgar Ulmer (Austrian), Robert Florey (French), and Michael Curtiz (Hungarian), as well as Lubitsch, Murnau, and Lang. Sternberg and Stroheim, both Austrians, had emigrated as children.

By the mid-twenties, silent film was well established as a major form of entertainment. No longer were films shown in storefront Nickelodeons or on the bottom half of vaudeville bills. Now they commanded ornate pleasure domes of their own. The picture palaces accommodated thousands of patrons at a time, rather than scores. Possibly the most elaborate of these ornate constructions were the theaters operated by Roxy Rothapfel in New York, which was still the capital of exhibition, if not of production. The Roxy opened in 1927, to be followed in 1932 by Radio City Music Hall, the ultimate movie cathedral, and one of the few still standing (although it no longer shows movies on a regular basis).

All the important technical modifications that the film process has undergone—the addition of sound, color, and widescreen—were first demonstrated to the public at the Paris exposition of 1900, albeit in primitive forms. Color films, for example, were mostly handpainted, hardly a commercially viable process. Sound could be produced by the primitive nonelectronic phonograph, but synchronization was very difficult and sound level was problematic. Lee De Forest's invention of the audion tube in 1906 (see Chapter 6, pp. 366, 369) pointed the way to the workable electronic sound amplifier. By 1919, the German Tri-Ergon process had been patented and film sound was a distinct potential alternative. In the late 1920s, confronted with the growing public interest in radio and responding to what may have seemed like a saturated market for silent films, the production companies turned hesitantly to sound.

By 1932, the technological shakedown period for sound was over and the outlines identifying the Hollywood system were clear. Except for the manufacture of equipment and filmstock, the studios exerted complete control over the film process from production to distribution to exhibition. The system of block booking and the close ties between

Figure 4-3. Radio City Music Hall, one of the great Art Deco movie palaces built in the thirties. (MOMA/FSA.)

most of the studios and large theater chains meant that nearly any film the studio chose to produce would be shown—not a disadvantage artistically. At its peak, M-G-M, the most powerful of the studios, produced forty-two feature films a year on twenty-two sound stages and one hundred acres of backlot standing sets.

The studios operated as efficiently run factories. Properties were acquired, script writers set to work remodelling them for production, set design and costume design departments turned out the required physical elements of the production. Technicians were on salary, working regular shifts, as did actors and directors. Today, it is unusual if a director makes more than one film per year. Between 1930 and 1939, Michael Curtiz shot 44 films, Mervyn Leroy 36, and John Ford 26. After the film was shot, the raw material was turned over to the post-production department for editing, mixing, and dubbing. Studio executives made the final decisions. The most prestigious directors sometimes were allowed to be involved in post-production, but few indeed could follow a film from inception to première.

The result was that studios developed individual styles that often superimposed themselves on the weaker styles of the filmmakers.

Figure 4-4. Throughout most of the thirties and forties, Warner Bros. films were noticeably more realistic in style—gutsier—than the films of the competing studios. Here, a scene from one of Warner's best-known socially conscious movies, Mervyn Leroy's *I Am a Fugitive from a Chain Gang* (1932). Star Paul Muni leans against the post. (MOMA/ FSA.)

M-G-M was noted for its glossy production values and middle-brow subject matter. Even though it was produced independently by David O. Selznick (and released through M-G-M), the 1939 epic, *Gone With the Wind,* is the epitome of the M-G-M style. Romantically melodramatic, expensively produced, with a lush score, it treated epic subject matter while doing relatively little to illuminate its themes. Paramount, which employed more than its share of emigrés, exhibited a European sensibility, both in terms of design and subject matter. Universal specialized in horror films, Republic in westerns. Warner Brothers, a major competitor of M-G-M and Paramount but leaner and hungrier, developed—quite unintentionally—a reputation for realism. To save money, the Warner brothers often filmed on location.

In this tightly organized production system, individual contributors—whether directors, cinematographers, screenwriters, or designers—could not easily assert themselves. Not only did the mass of films exhibit a studio style, they also displayed a surprising degree of intellectual conformity. We can discern a difference between M-G-M's gloss and Paramount's sophistication, but there is no significant contrast in terms of the political and social consciousness they each evinced. Always concerned with the essential commodity value of the films they produced, the moguls of the golden age of Hollywood preferred to produce films that were like other films—not different from them. As a result, very few of the thousands of films produced during these years strike us as unique. The study of Hollywood is more a matter of identifying types, patterns, conventions, and genres amongst a great many films than of intently focusing on the qualities of each individual movie. This doesn't make Hollywood films necessarily any less interesting than the more personal works of cinematic invention. In fact, because these films were turned out on an assembly-line basis in such massive numbers, they often are better indexes of public concerns, shared myths, and mores than individually conceived, intentionally artistic films are.

As the studios moved into the forties, these qualities became even more striking. Actively involved in propaganda and education even before the United States entered the war, the major studios displayed their particular styles even in such propaganda instruments as "Freedom Comes High" (Paramount) and "You John Jones" (M-G-M).

Hollywood thrived during the war. In 1946, its best year, box office grosses amounted to $1.7 billion. In a sense, World War II had delayed the moment of truth for the Hollywood film factories by making impossible the introduction of commercial television, which had been successfully demonstrated in the thirties. In addition, the war effectively limited competition from European countries. In the twenties, Germany had been a major competitor, producing films that were not only popular but carried with them the cachet of art. In the thirties, a handful of French directors gained widespread respect for that nation's industry. Great Britain, despite the pressure of English-language films from Hollywood, produced 225 films in 1936, the second highest output in the world. The war ended these threats even though it also closed many export markets, hurting some small companies.

The effect of television when it did come in the early 1950s was devastating. Television grew out of radio rather than film, and naturally employed radio people. Instead of realizing that they could just as easily produce film product for television as for theatrical distribution, the studios tried to fight. For years, they refused to capitalize on their huge backlog of product. Indeed, with very unbusinesslike shortsightedness, they often destroyed old films rather than pay for storage. The effect of this strategy was to allow television production companies time to develop, seriously weakening the tactical position of the studios. The same thing had happened forty years earlier, when the trust companies had proved unwilling or unable to move from Nickelodeon shorts to theatrical features.

The process of adapting to the new conditions was slow and painful, but it needn't have been. It was fifteen years or more before the studios began dimly to understand how best to operate in the new situation. Aging owners and production heads rigidly clung to the old methods of mass production in studio complexes with enormous overhead costs. Psychologically, this may have been due to their shared roots long ago as exhibitors. Although exhibition was always the weakest link in the Hollywood monopoly chain, it held a peculiar fascination for them.

In 1946, a ruling under the antitrust laws required Paramount Pictures (and by implication the other studios) to divest themselves of their theater chains. The studios appealed, but to no avail, entering into a consent decree in 1951. This wasn't as drastic a change as it might seem. Since the studios were still permitted to maintain their distribution arms, they continued to exert actual if not legal control over exhibition. Had the studios analyzed their situation more carefully the antitrust decision would have had a minor effect. They would simply have tightened their belts and shifted their attention from the theatrical market to the new, increasingly profitable television channels. This did not happen immediately (although now the major studios, having seen the light, are responsible for most network programming).

As their assets shrank, as the original founders died off or retired, the studios were merged into the developing interindustrial conglomerates of the fifties and sixties or sold outright. Desilu bought the RKO studios, Revue took over the Republic soundstages. At the same time, more sensible independent distributors were making quiet fortunes serving as middlemen between the aggressive television networks and the paralyzed film studios.

Eliot Hyman was probably the most astute of these traders. He first bought the Warner Brothers backlog, traded in it for a while, then sold it to United Artists. He then acquired rights to a good number of Fox films. By 1967 his company, Seven Arts, was in a position to purchase Warner Brothers outright. In the early fifties, Howard Hughes had sold RKO to the General Tire and Rubber company who liquidated it, and Universal had been acquired by the American subsidiary of the Decca Record organization. The Music Corporation of America (MCA), originally a talent agency, acquired the Paramount backlist, profits from which helped it finance the purchase of Decca and, with it, Universal. Paramount was absorbed into Gulf + Western Industries in 1966. Shortly thereafter, United Artists was taken over by Transamerica Corporation, a typical contemporary multinational conglomerate who own, in addition to United Artists and its subsidiaries, Budget Rent-a-Car, Transamerica Computer Services, Pacific Finance Loans, Occidental Life Insurance Co., Transamerica Insurance Co., Cinegraphics, Inc., Transamerica Airlines, a capital fund, an investor's fund, a relocation service, a title insurance company, a microfilm service, a moving and storage company, and a real estate tax service.

In 1969, Warner Brothers-Seven Arts was merged with Kinney National Services, which later became Warner Communications, Inc. Shortly thereafter, a controlling interest in Metro-Goldwyn-Mayer, formerly the most powerful and prestigious of studios, was acquired by Kirk Kerkorian, a Los Vegas real estate dealer. In 1974, M-G-M was effectively liquidated, the studio sold, and the distribution organization closed. Throughout the 1970s M-G-M was best known as the owner of the M-G-M Grand Hotel in Las Vegas (named for the M-G-M movie of 1932). While the company dabbled in film production and television (with no great success), healthy profits accrued from the gambling operations. In 1979, perhaps regretting his earlier decision to shift M-G-M's capital assets from the film industry to the gambling industry, Kerkorian attempted to buy a controlling interest in Columbia Pictures Industries. The deal fell through (there was talk of antitrust prosecution) and shortly thereafter it was announced that the M-G-M company, with the permission of its stockholders, would split in two, the original company to continue running the casino operations (now extended to Reno and Atlantic City) while the "new" company aggressively re-entered film production and distribution.

This novel strategy in effect admitted that the conglomerate psychology that had operated in Hollywood for the past fifteen years had been detrimental to film production. What M-G-M was announcing corporately was that it wasn't efficient for a company whose basic interests lay in one economic field of endeavor to participate in another, such as the movie business. There is no record of the reactions of executives at Transamerica, Gulf + Western, Warner Communications, Inc., or MCA, Inc.

The M-G-M developments were only the last in a continuing series of events that shook the conglomerate headquarters of Hollywood during the late 1970s. In 1977, David Begelman, then head of production at Columbia, was charged with embezzling $60,000 in a sordid case that received wide publicity coverage, and engendered much talk about various shady business practices in Hollywood (none of which, by the way, were new). Alan J. Hirschfield, then president of Columbia, attempted to fire Begelman on ethical grounds and was himself dismissed. Many observers felt that the management of Columbia Pictures Industries cared more for Begelman's fabled knack for making profitable pictures than for Hirschfield's moral stance. Begelman was eventually convicted and fined—and hired as head of production at M-G-M. Hirschfield also landed on his feet, as president of Twentieth Century-Fox.

Early in 1978, the five chief executives of United Artists resigned en masse in a dispute with parent Transamerica over management prerogatives and executive compensation. Arthur Krim and Robert Benjamin had taken over the moribund distribution company in the early fifties and molded it into one of the leading film companies of the sixties and seventies. Then, in 1967 they had sold it to Transamerica. Now, they regretted their decision. Together with president Eric Pleskow, treasurer William Bernstein, and production chief Mike Medavoy, they formed Orion Pictures Corp., an entity that was something more than just another production company, but less than a full-fledged studio. Their unprecedented agreement with Warner Communications allowed them full control over the marketing and advertising of their films through the Warners distribution system. Orion thus added a new and significant element to the structure of Hollywood conglomerate control.

Within sixteen months Orion had been joined at this new power level by The Ladd Company, formed when Alan Ladd, Jr. and some of his associates left Twentieth Century-Fox after several financially successful years. As the television networks re-entered feature film production and distribution in 1979 and 1980 (they had failed at this in the late sixties), and as new, more powerful production companies like Lorimar and EMI joined the Hollywood ranks at levels of power slightly lower than Orion and The Ladd Company, the structure of control of the American film industry began to change rapidly.

In 1977, six men—the heads of production at the six major studios—effectively controlled what was seen on America's movie screens. Within three years that number had almost doubled—and the heads of production with the power to say "yes," to guarantee a film satisfactory distribution arrangements, were no longer all male, as Sherry Lansing at Fox became the first woman production chief in modern times.

While there is measurably more room for independent producers to operate now than there was in the mid-1970s, conglomerates still dominate the Hollywood system. Each of them has moved to secure a position as a horizontal (rather than vertical) monopoly. Most of the entertainment and leisure companies that operate under the names of the old studios also own paperback book publishing companies, record companies, and television production companies, as well as the occasional wild animal preserve. A property, once acquired, can now be exploited in five or more media: films, books, records, broadcast television, and videodisc and tape.

The people who run the studios are often former talent agents—people trained in putting together "packages" of stars, script, and financing. Since they no longer have players and technicians under contract, the studios have shifted to concentrate on distribution. To a lesser extent, they also operate as financiers. In the early seventies, tax shelter arrangements that guaranteed a paper profit, if not an actual one, were widely used to draw outside money from investors into film financing. The real work of film production is now split up among a number of independent producers, many of whom are also directors or stars as well—what the new Hollywood jargon calls "hyphenates." The result is a much smaller output of product, but—at least potentially—a wider variety of movies.

The studios arrived at this point by a process of trial and error, even though the structure of the post-television film market could easily have been predicted early on. Television was clearly designed to fulfill cinema's function as the mass entertainment medium. If theatrical film was going to survive, it would have to shift to serving specialized audiences. This is, in fact, what has happened. The movie palaces have been replaced by more intimate theaters seating an average of two hundred patrons. These small theaters are often bunched together in "triplexes" and "fourplexes" to provide a wider choice as well as cut overhead expense.

Yet, despite a brief flirtation with the new freedom in the late sixties, the conglomerate studios have been loath to exploit these possibilities. Instead, they turned increasingly in the seventies to the blockbuster film (usually of the disaster genre), presold through books and aided by massive saturation television advertising, absorbing huge amounts of capital in the process. Since the technocrats who run the film companies now are more interested in making money than in making movies, this strategy has a certain logic to it. However, since the majors still dominate the all-important channels of distribution, and therefore indirectly determine which films shall be financed and which shall not, even independent producers with other ideas in mind are effectively prevented from reaching the general audience. It remains to be seen whether or not Orion, Ladd, and other new distribution entities will have a positive effect on this state of affairs.

The blockbuster system is not new; Hollywood often relied on it in the past for major releases. But it is now operated with computer efficiency. A number of independent companies such as National General and Sun International did well in the mid-seventies by applying market research strategies. Having identified a target market not being effectively served by the major companies, they designed films statistically to this market's taste, filmed them cheaply, then rented theaters (rather than leasing prints)—a process known as "four-walling"—engaged in saturation advertising, and sat back to count the profits.

Internationally, the death of the old studio system had positive effects, simply because it opened up world markets to more strenuous competition for a while. In the early fifties, the French and the Italian governments established quasi-official export sales organizations (Unifrance, Unitalia) that have been instrumental in softening up markets for those countries' films (Unifrance having been much more active than its Italian counterpart). The growth of film festivals in most major film-producing countries was effective in this respect as well.

Two important positive factors in the film production equation in many countries were government subsidy plans and television coproduction. Although the British and the French film industries have minimal subsidy plans that aid in small ways, the model for this new method of finance was the Swedish Film Institute, founded in 1963 to distribute monies collected from a ten percent tax on all cinema admissions, partly on the basis of gross receipts, partly on the basis of quality. The Swedish plan has encouraged the vigorous growth of an exportable film industry in a very small country.

European film production was aided, too, in the fifties and the sixties by American location productions abroad, designed to take advantage of lower costs. This temporary internationalism came to an end in 1970, as prices equalized and as the American companies found themselves in a monetary bind. The British film industry, which had depended heavily on American capital in the sixties, was nearly decimated by the withdrawal. But film's loss was television's gain. Many of the best British filmmakers now work in television.

By 1980, the American companies had regained effective control of the world's screens, challenged only occasionally and weakly by European conglomerates such as Lord Grade's ITC or the Siemens-Phillips combine, Polygram.

As videodisc and tape systems gain in popularity over the next decade, the film industry will find itself responding to still another challenge from an allied but separate medium (see Chapter 6, pp. 375, 413). Paradoxically, the new generation of technocrats who control the major distribution organizations may respond more intelligently than did the previous generation of moguls. The potential exists for a system of distribution as precise and flexible as that enjoyed by the print media, as the technologies of film and video continue to merge. Both movies and television as channels of information and entertainment have, until the present, been characterized by limited access: in the U.S., between five and seven studios have controlled film distribution; three commercial networks have controlled access to television. The videodisc may possibly open up these channels to vast numbers of people who were heretofore denied access. On the other hand, the various competing videodisc and tape technologies are financed and dominated by entertainment conglomerates like MCA, RCA, and Phillips. Whether or not these companies license their systems cheaply enough to make them available to a wide range of producers remains to be seen.

While the disc promises more fluid means of distribution, the production phase still poses a problem. Despite inherently less expensive video production techniques, films and tapes (and discs) still require extraordinary amounts of capital. In the future, the locus of control will shift from distribution to production. This may open up the media to greater numbers of people, but access will nevertheless still be limited only to those with sufficient capital resources. Until a means is developed to provide funding for those without private sources of capital, film and its allied arts will remain a relatively closed system, and the independent movie, tape, or disc will continue to be the prized exception rather than the acknowledged rule.

"THE FILM": POLITICS

The economics of film determines its infrastructure—its foundations— and therefore its potential. The politics of film determines its structure: that is, the way it relates to the world. We understand film, experience it, and consume it from two different perspectives. The "sociopolitics" of film describes how it reflects and is integrated with human experience in general. Film's "psychopolitics" attempts to explain how we relate to it personally and specifically. Because film is such a widespread popular phenomenon, it has played a very important part in modern culture, sociopolitically. Because it provides such a powerful and convincing representation of reality, film has also had a profound effect on members of its audience, psychopolitically. The two aspects are closely interrelated, of course, yet the differentiation is useful, since it focuses attention on the very real difference between the general effect of film and its specific personal effect.

Whichever way we look at it, film is a distinctly political phenomenon. Indeed, its very existence is revolutionary. In his landmark essay on the subject, "The Work of Art in the Age of Mechanical Reproduction," the critic Walter Benjamin wrote:

> One might generalize by saying: the technique of reproduction detaches the reproduced object from the domain of tradition. . . . it substitutes a plurality of copies for a unique existence. And in permitting the reproduction to meet the beholder or listener in his own particular situation, it reactivates the object reproduced. These two processes lead to a tremendous shattering of tradition. . . . Both processes are intimately connected with the contemporary mass movements. Their most powerful agent is the film. Its social significance, particularly in its most positive form, is inconceivable without its destructive, cathartic aspect, that is, the liquidation of the traditional value of the cultural heritage [*Illuminations*, p. 221].

Benjamin's prose is a bit abstruse, but the points he makes are basic to an understanding of the way film (and other mechanically reproduced arts) function in society. The most significant difference, Benjamin is saying, between film and the older arts is that the new art can be mass produced, reaching the many rather than the few. (This is the sociopolitical aspect.) This has a revolutionary effect: not only is the art available on a regular basis to large numbers of people, but it also meets observers on their home grounds, thereby reversing the traditional relationship between the work of art and its audience. These two facts about film—(a) that it is plural rather than unique, (b) that it is infinitely reproducible—directly contradict romantic traditions of art and therefore invigorate and purify. (This is the psychopolitical aspect.)

Film has changed the way we perceive the world and therefore, to a lesser extent, how we operate in it. Yet while the existence of film may be revolutionary, the practice of it most often is not. Because the channels of distribution are limited, because costs prohibit access to film to all but the wealthiest the medium has been subject to strict, if subtle, control. In America between 1920 and 1950, for example, the movies provided the main cultural format for the discovery and description of our national identity (television gradually replaced movies after 1950). Historians argue whether the movies simply reflected the national culture that already existed or whether they produced a fantasy of their own that eventually came to be accepted as real. In a sense, the point is moot. No doubt the writers, producers, directors, and technicians who worked in the large studio factories during the great age of Hollywood were simply transferring materials they had picked up in "real life" to the screen. No doubt, too, that even if those materials weren't consciously distorted toward political ends, the very fact that the movies amplified certain aspects of our culture while attenuating others had a profound effect.

Thus, two paradoxes control the politics of film: on the one hand, the form of film is revolutionary; on the other, the content is most often conservative of traditional values. Second, the politics of film and the politics of "real life" are so closely intertwined that it is generally impossible to discover which is the cause and which is the effect.

This discussion mainly involves American movies. The relationship between politics and film is no less intriguing in other contexts, but it was the homogeneous factory system of the studios that most subtly reflected (or inspired) the surrounding political culture. Because Hollywood movies were mass-produced, they tended to reflect the surrounding culture—or, more accurately, the established myths of the culture—more precisely than did the work of strongly individual authors. Indeed, many of the most notable auteurs in film history stand out precisely because their work goes against the establishment grain, politically: Chaplin, Stroheim, Vidor, Eisenstein, Renoir, Rossellini, Godard, for example.

The central truism of film history is that the development of the art/industry is best seen as a product of the dialectic between film realism and film expressionism: between film's power to mimic reality and its power to change it. The earliest film artists—the Lumière brothers and Georges Méliès—succinctly demonstrate this dichotomy between realism and expressionism. Yet, underlying the dialectic of mimesis/expression is another, more basic, premise: that the definition of film style depends on the film's relationship with its audience. When a filmmaker decides on a realist style, he or she does so to decrease the distance between viewer and subject; the expressionist style, on the other hand, looks to change, move, or amuse the observer through the technique of film. Both these esthetic decisions are essentially political, since they insist on relationships (among filmmaker, film, subject, and observer) rather than idealized abstract systems. In this way, too, film is inherently and directly political: it has a dynamic relationship with its audiences.

To summarize, every film, no matter how minor it may seem, exhibits a political nature on one or more of the three levels:

- ontologically, because the medium of film itself tends to deconstruct the traditional values of the culture;
- mimetically, because any film either reflects reality or re-creates it (and its politics);
- inherently, because the intense communicative nature of film gives the relationship between film and observer a natural political dimension.

Figures 4-5, 4-6. STARS. Both Fairbanks (left) and Chaplin (right) are "out of character" in these publicity shots, but because they had become celebrity personalities by this time, even off the set they carry with them some of the aura of the star. (MOMA/ FSA.)

A political history of film might very well then be three times as complex as an esthetic history, since we should trace the development of all three political facets. We have space to examine only a few of the most salient features of film politics.

Ontologically, the best evidence we have that film has radically altered traditional values lies in the phenomenon of celebrity. Previously, heroic models for society were either purely fictional creations or real people of accomplishment (whom we knew only at one remove). Film fused the two types: real people became fictional characters. The concept of the "star" developed—and stars are quite different from "actors." The most important role Douglas Fairbanks played was not Robin Hood or Zorro, but "Douglas Fairbanks." (In fact, Douglas Fairbanks was played by Douglas Ullman—his original name.) Likewise, Charles Chaplin played, not Hitler or Monsieur Verdoux, but always

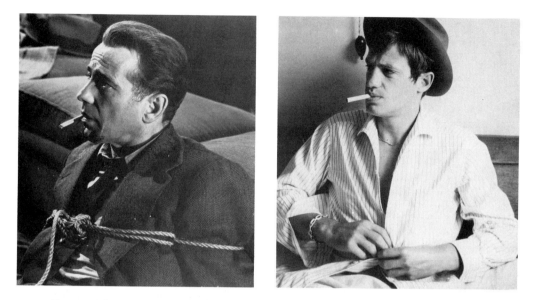

Figures 4-7, 4-8. Humphrey Bogart (left) as Philip Marlowe in *The Big Sleep* (Howard Hawks, 1946). (MOMA/FSA.) Jean-Paul Belmondo (right) as Michel Poiccard mimicking Bogart in *Breathless* (Jean-Luc Godard, 1959). One of the subjects of the film is the interrelationship between film and life.

"Charlot," the tramp, and Mary Pickford (with Chaplin and Fairbanks the United Artists, the preeminent stars of their day) was forever typecast as "Little Mary." When she tried in the late twenties to change her public image, her career came to an end.

Early film producers seem to have been well aware of the potential phenomenon of stardom. They insisted that their actors work in anonymity. In 1912, however, the first fan magazines appeared, identifying "the Biograph Girl" and "Little Mary." A few years later, having been liberated from anonymity, Chaplin and Pickford were vying to see which of the two would be the first to sign a million-dollar contract. Clearly, Little Mary and Charlot had struck responsive chords in audiences. The complex relationship between stars and the public has been a prime element of the mythic, and hence political, nature of film ever since.

"Stars" act out their personas through nominal character roles. "Celebrities" appear mainly as "themselves" and are known, in Daniel Boorstin's phrase, "for their well-knownness." We tend to downplay the significance of this phenomenon, yet stars are extraordinary psychological models of a type that never existed before. We can trace the development of the phenomenon of celebrity back to the lecture circuits of the nineteenth century, where intellectual heroes such as Charles Dickens and Mark Twain (a "character," by the way, created by Samual Clemens) played themselves to adoring audiences. Yet, until the "age of mechanical reproduction," these celebrities reached few people. The public outpouring of grief over the death of Rudolph Valentino in 1926, after his short and undistinguished career as a film actor, exceeded in intensity and dimension the reaction to any similar public death up to that time. It was only after politicians became celebrities as well that victims of assassination elicited such universal mourning.

Although studio moguls tried to construct stars of this magnitude artifically, they seldom succeeded. Stars were—and still are—the creation of the public: political and psychological models who demonstrate some quality that we collectively admire.* Clark Gable was objectively no more physically attractive than dozens of other young leading men of the thirties, yet there was something in the persona he projected that touched a responsive chord. Humphrey Bogart was not a particularly good actor and certainly not handsome by Hollywood standards, yet he became a central role model not only for his own generation but for their children. As the actors became stars, their images began to affect audiences directly. Star cinema—Hollywood style—depends on creating a strong identification between hero and audience. We see things from his point of view. The effect is subtle but pervasive.

Nor is this phenomenon peculiar to Hollywood. In the sixties, European cinema demonstrated some of the same power of identification. When Jean-Paul Belmondo models himself on Humphrey Bogart in Jean-Luc Godard's Breathless (1960), he is announcing a second generation of celebrity, one that demonstrates an historical consciousness. Marcello Mastroianni became the epitome of existential European manhood. Jeanne Moreau was the model for wise, self-assured European womanhood, Max von Sydow and Liv Ullmann the Swedish versions of the two models.

But these people are actors as well as stars, so the effect is muted. There are occasions in their careers when individual roles supersede star personas. As American films came back to life in the sixties, a new generation of stars like the Europeans developed, displaying critical intelligence as well as powerful personas. Politically, this is an important advance. At its most deleterious, the Hollywood star system worked to outlaw psychologically roles that did not fit its own images. It

---

*Few film critics and historians have written cogently about stars. David Thomson's Biographical Dictionary of Film offers a wealth of intelligent and telling sketches. Richard Schickel's His Picture in the Papers is a useful introduction to the subject. See also Celebrity, edited by James Monaco, and Stars, by Richard Dyer.

Figure 4-9. James Dean in a publicity still for *Rebel Without a Cause* (Nicholas Ray, 1955). Within a year, he was dead in an auto accident at the age of twenty-four. Although he only completed three major films before his death (*East of Eden* and *Giant*, as well as *Rebel*), Dean touched a responsive chord in audiences of the fifties, and the outpouring of grief at his death was reminiscent of the hysteria surrounding Rudolph Valentino's death thirty years earlier. There is even a film about the effects of his death on some teenagers in a small southern town: James Bridges's *September 30, 1955* (1977). (MOMA/FSA.)

was acceptable to act like Bogart, Gable, or John Wayne, but until the late 1960s there was no male star who was not a tough guy (like this trio) or sophisticated and urbane (like Fred Astaire or Cary Grant). The critical element of contemporary celebrity permits audiences a much greater degree freedom in this respect.

To a large extent, at least in nations in which film is dominant, the cinema helps to define what is permissible culturally: it is the shared experience of the society. Because its role models are so psychologically powerful, those roles for which it provides no models are difficult for individual members of society even to conceive, much less act out. Like folktales, films express taboos and help to resolve them. The cause-and-effect relationship is, as we noted, not very clear, but it is interesting to note that the quasi-revolutionary mores of the 1960s in America were predated by more than five years by the two major star personas of the 1950s—Marlon Brando and James Dean—both of which were notably rebellious. More specifically, Jean-Luc Godard's film *La Chinoise*, which portrayed a group of revolutionary students from the University of Nanterre, predated the uprising of May–June 1968 by precisely a year and, indeed, students from Nanterre were in the vanguard during the aborted real revolution, just as they had been in Godard's fictional rebellion. In the age of mechanical reproduction fiction has a force it never had before.

Because it is so much more pervasive, television has taken over a large part of the folktale function of cinema, at least in the U.S., where

Figures 4-10, 4-11. Brando in the fifties. A *Streetcar Named Desire* (Elia Kazan, 1951) with Vivien Leigh. Brando, too, projected an image of rebellion that caught the public imagination of the fifties. But in twenty years the sexual energy had modified to produce the quirky, desolate image of . . . (MOMA/FSA.)

. . . Brando in the seventies. Here in *Last Tango in Paris* (Bernardo Bertolucci, 1972). The eyes, the look, the gestures, the relationships with women are similar, but more seasoned after twenty years. Brando was the first of the great stars to develop an image as a thoughtful actor as well as a personality.

popular rather than "artistic" programs are the norm. In Haskell Wexler's *Medium Cool* (1969), an incisive, even brilliant, analysis of the relationship between media and politics, a group of Black militants challenge a TV reporter: "You put him on the six, the ten, *and* the twelve o'clock news," they demand for one of the characters, "*then* he be real." The function of media in determining the validity of an action, person, or idea was one of the central truths of radical politics in the sixties (and still is).

This unusual ability of film to "validate" reality is its most important mimetic political function. For example, one of the most telling social criticisms provided by the Black Power movement of the 1960s was its historical analysis of the inherently racist characterizations to which Blacks had been subjected as a matter of course throughout the history of film and television. In this respect, too, the media faithfully reflected the values of the society. But they also exaggerated the real situation. In general (there were significant exceptions), films pictured Blacks in servile roles. More important, Blacks were used only to play Blacks— that is, in roles in which race was a significant element. One of the greatest accomplishments of the Black movement of the 1960s was to break through this barrier. Black lawyers, doctors, businessmen—even heroes are now validated by the media, if only on an intermittent basis. It is still rare for a casting director to hire a Black to play a lawyer, for

Figures 4-12, 4-13. By the late seventies, Brando's persona had been concentrated to such an extent that it was only necessary for him to make the briefest of appearances in a film in order to imprint it with his cachet. His most notable quintessential cameo was as the corpulent Kurtz in *Apocalypse Now,* but he also set the tone as the ultimate father figure in *Superman.*

instance, unless the script specifies "Black lawyer." (The same infuriating barrier confronts women.)

Racism pervades American film because it is a basic strain in American history. It is one of the ugly facts of film history that the landmark *The Birth of a Nation* (1915) can be generally hailed as a classic despite its essential racism. No amount of technical expertise demonstrated, money invested, or artistic effect should be allowed to outweigh *The Birth of a Nation*'s militantly anti-Black political stance, yet we continue in film history as it is presently written to praise the film for its form, ignoring, or at best paying lip service to, its disastrous content.

This is not to imply that Griffith's masterpiece was anomalous. Until the late fifties, racial stereotypes were pervasive in film, then in television. There had been liberal acts of conscience before—films such as King Vidor's *Hallelujah* (1929) or Elia Kazan's *Pinky* (1949)—but even these were almost without exception marked by subtle condescension. It was not until the late sixties that Blacks began to take on nonstereotypical roles in American film.

We are speaking here of Hollywood. A thriving if limited Black film industry, separate and unequal, dated from the 1920s producing films about Blacks, by Blacks, for Blacks. But, of course, general audiences never saw these films.

American Indians were as poorly served until very recently. Since they were integral to the popular genre of the Western, they were seen on screen more often than Blacks, but the stereotypes were just as damaging. There were a few exceptions in this regard. Possibly because the battle had already been won against the Indians, films were occasionally produced that portrayed them in a positive, human light. Thomas Ince's *The Indian Massacre* (1913) is an early example, John Ford's *Cheyenne Autumn* (1964) a late instance.

The image of women in American film is a more complex issue. It seems likely that in the twenties movies did much to popularize the image of the independent woman. Even sirens such as Clara Bow and Mae West, while serving as male fantasies, were at the same time able to project a sense of independence and a spirit of irony about their stereotyped roles. Moreover, the image of women in films of the thirties and forties, on the whole, was very nearly coequal with that of men. A sensitive feminist can detect numerous stereotypical limitations in the films of that period, it is true, but for most of us to compare the thirties in film with the sixties or seventies is to realize that despite the awakened consciousness of contemporary women, cinematically we have only recently regained the level of intelligence of the sexual politics of even the mid-thirties. Actresses like Katharine Hepburn, Bette Davis, Joan Blondell, Carole Lombard, Myrna Loy, Barbara Stanwyck, Irene Dunne, and even Joan Crawford projected images of intelligence, independence, sensitivity, and egalitarian sexuality the likes of which were rarely seen thereafter.

All this ended in the early fifties with the advent of the personas projected by stars Marilyn Monroe (the childwoman seductress) and Doris Day (the virginal girl-next-door). Of the two, the image projected by Day and similar actresses was to be preferred. She never achieved real independence, but she was often more than simply a male fantasy like Monroe. It wasn't as if actresses of the caliber of the earlier stars didn't exist. Sidney Lumet's *The Group* (1966), for example, starred not one but eight young actresses at least seven of whom showed talent. Yet only Candice Bergen achieved any real success thereafter. With the advent of the "buddy" film in the late sixties (the most popular early example of which was *Butch Cassidy and the Sundance Kid*, 1969), what few major roles there were for women very nearly disappeared entirely.

The recent sexual politics of American movies is one clear case in

Figure 4-14. Lucia Lynn Moses in *The Scar of Shame* (1927), produced by the Colored Players Film Corp., and directed by Frank Peregini. (MOMA/FSA.)

which film does not simply reflect the politics of reality. This may have been true to a certain extent in the fifties, when our national culture was intent upon coaxing women who had gained a measure of independence during the war back into the home. But it was certainly a false picture of the real world in the seventies, when millions of women were becoming involved in feminism. One of the first films of the seventies, for instance, which was praised for its "feminist" approach is Martin Scorsese's *Alice Doesn't Live Here Anymore* (1975), yet that film presented us with a woman who, when deprived of the creature comforts of domesticity, couldn't survive on her own and, in the end, happily submitted to the role of helpmate once again. Why otherwise intelligent critics regarded *Alice* as in any way feminist is difficult to say, unless it was simply that the situation had deteriorated so drastically that any film that gave a woman a central role, no matter what its politics, had to be regarded as an advance.

Despite a lot of hype, the feminist position in film didn't advance much in the late seventies. Such vaunted women's films as *An Unmarried Woman, The Turning Point,* and *Julia* (all 1978) did, it's true, use

Figures 4-15, 4-16. "America's Sweetheart," Little Mary Pickford (c. 1920): sausage curls, gingham, and cute puppies. (*Marc Wanamaker/Bison Art Ltd.*)

Judy Garland as Dorothy (1939): pigtails, more gingham, and childhood fantasies: America's second-generation sweetheart. (*Marc Wanamaker/Bison Art Ltd.*)

Figures 4-17, 4-18. Louise Lasser as "Little" Mary Hartman (1976): braids, calico, and adult fears. The third-generation American sweetheart struggled violently—and unknowingly—against the little-girl image that has been handed down from generation to generation.

In *10* (1979) Bo Derek impersonated Blake Edwards's fantasy of feminine perfection, 1980s-style. The pigtails have metamorphosed into tight cornrow braids, and the image is altogether tougher than it ever was before. Perhaps it is even "macho." Derek set the fashion for hairstyles in 1980, the first time a film actress had done this since Debbie Reynolds's pigtails of the mid-fifties. For 25 years, television had controlled such matters.

women as central characters, but with no discernible raised consciousness. Ironically, the recent film that has shown the most sophisticated understanding of sexual politics has been Robert Benton's *Kramer vs. Kramer* (1979), in which the woman (Kramer, played by Meryl Streep) is, if not actually the villain, then certainly the source of the problem, and the focus is almost entirely on the sensitive and painful reaction of the man (Kramer, Dustin Hoffman) to a classic feminist-inspired situation of the seventies. No film in recent years has shown anything approaching this sensitivity and concern for the woman's point of view.

If we are to judge from Hollywood's evidence, the effect of the contemporary woman's movement has been to free men from male stereotypes. This is true, but it is not anywhere near the whole truth.

Yet, despite the fact that we can't point to many specific films that have mirrored the new feminism, nevertheless the situation certainly improved vastly in the seventies. It is now no longer unusual for an actress to be able to prolong her career as female lead well into her forties: Jane Fonda, Shirley MacLaine, Anne Bancroft, Jill Clayburgh, and Barbra Streisand have suffered no decrease in earning power as they have passed into maturity. And there is an undefinable sense that the balance between men and women is slowly but inexorably being redressed.

The question of sexual politics in film is closely connected with what we might call the "dream function" of the movies. Much of the avant-garde criticism of the late seventies treats of this aspect of the film experience. The strong identification we make with cinematic heroes is one simply observed evidence that film operates on our psyches not unlike dreams. This is the inherent aspect of film politics: how do we interrelate with films? Since the early days, filmmakers have been in the business of selling fantasies of romance and action—or, to use the contemporary synonyms, sex and violence. In this respect, film is not much different from literature. Popular films, like popular novels, depend upon the motivating forces of these twin libidinal impulses. The issue is complex: film satisfies the libido not only by giving a kind of life to fantasies, but also more formally—the style of a film, its idiom, can be either romantic or active, sexual or violent, without any regard to its content. In addition, it is far from clear what precise effect this particular function of film has on the people who experience it. Does it take the place of real experience? Or does it inspire it? This is a particularly interesting dilemma when expressed strictly in terms of political action. A film in which the hero wins the day may simply convey to audiences that "business is being taken care of"—that there is no need to act—while a film in which the hero loses may be taken as a sign that action is futile. How can a political filmmaker, then, create a structure in which the audience is involved, but not to such an extent that the characters serve as surrogates? How can it be made clear that action is both possible and still necessary in real life? There are no simple answers.

The question of surrogate action is more easily explained in terms of romance and sex. Here the characters are clearly surrogates for the audience and there is no real intent to suggest that the drama of the film be carried over into real life. In fact, the verisimilitude of the film experience suggests the opposite: that the experience of the film can to a great extent replace the experience of reality. We speak of film "fans" and film "buffs," but there is a subculture of film addicts, as well: people with such a strong need for the dream experience of film that it might very well be physiological as well as psychological. These crucial effects of film have not as yet been studied in any sufficient detail. Much of the most interesting work in film theory during the next few years will concern such topics.

The libidinal effect of film as dream also has a more practical aspect. Ever since Edison's Kinetoscope loop, the John Rice-May Irwin *Kiss* (1896), movies have excited outpourings of moralism, which in turn have led to censorship. While in Continental countries film censorship has most often been political in nature, in the U.S. and Britain it has been moral and puritanical, a vestige of native puritanism and Victorian attitudes toward sex. In 1922, in response to supposed public moral outrage at a recent spate of sex scandals involving film actors (notably the Fatty Arbuckle affair), Hollywood founded the Motion Picture Producers and Distributors of America organization (M.P.P.A.), colloquially known as the "Hays Office" after its first president. The Hays Office performed no formal censorship, preferring to counter bad publicity with good, but gradually guidelines were issued. The first production code dates from 1930. When Joseph Breen joined the M.P.P.A. in 1934, the code began to be strictly enforced. (The Catholic Legion of Decency was founded the same year and exerted a distinct puritanical influence until the early sixties.) The code made absurd demands on filmmakers. Not only were outright acts of sex and violence strictly prohibited, but a set of guidelines was laid down (and strictly enforced) that prohibited the depiction of double beds, even for married couples, and censored such expletives as "God," "hell," "damn," "nuts"—even "nerts." The effect was profound. One of the greatest surprises awaiting a student of film first experiencing precode movies is the discovery that in the late twenties and very early thirties films had a surprisingly contemporary sense of morality and dealt with issues, such as sex and drugs, that were forbidden thereafter until the late sixties. The effect is curiously disorienting. We have grown up with late thirties, forties, and fifties Hollywood through the wide exposure of the films (usually recen-sored) on television. To experience some of the realistic films from the precode era is to discover a lost generation. One of the last vestiges of precode relevance, for example, was the cycle of Gangster films—*Public Enemy* (1931) and *Scarface* (1932) among them—that attempted to treat political issues directly.

In Britain, self-censorship, by the British Board of Film Censors, is more strict, and dates from 1912. Yet, interestingly, the British system of censorship has had a less marked effect than the American code. Until 1951, British films were rated U, A, or H (for Universal, Adults, and Horrific—prohibited to children under sixteen). The object has been to protect young children from undue exposure to extreme vio-lence (which is what "horrific" meant), an unobjectionable aim. In 1951, as sex became more important in film, H was replaced with X.

The American code was useful to producers throughout the Hollywood period. Although it set up maddeningly arbitrary rules, it also freed the studios from any ethical pressure to deal with relevant political and sexual subjects or even to treat milder subjects with a degree of sophisti-cation. Hollywood settled comfortably in the mid-thirties into a style of filmmaking that generally eschewed relevance in favor of the highly prized, often hollow, fantasy "entertainment values" of the Golden Age.

It was not only the direct prescriptions of the code that were signifi-cant. The code also had a general chilling effect on an industry that was particularly susceptible to economic pressure. In addition, this vulnera-bility yielded another type of censorship. The studios produced nothing that would offend powerful minorities in the audience. They were also very eager to please when the political establishment made suggestions. The lawlessness of the prohibition era, for example, led to a cycle of proto-fascist movies in the early thirties—*Star Witness* (1931), *Okay America* (1932), and *Gabriel Over the White House* (1934) are examples. During World War II, naturally, Hollywood rose to the occasion, not only by producing thousands of training and propaganda films, (the most famous example being Frank Capra's *Why We Fight* series), but also by quickly erecting in fiction films a myth of the conflict that played no small part in uniting the country behind the struggle. A perfect example of this technique is Delmer Daves's *Destination Tokyo* (1943), which displays the usual varied ethnic group united against the common enemy. As leader, Cary Grant stops in mid-picture to write a letter home to his wife in the midwest. The sequence takes a good ten minutes. As Grant writes, justifying the war, documentary shots illus-trate his lecture, the gist of which is that the Japanese and the Germans are racially despicable, while our allies, the Chinese and the Russians, are genetically destined to win and historically peace-loving people very much like ourselves! Later, this didn't fit very well with the mythology of the cold war. By design or accident, many of the current prints of *Destination Tokyo* lack this powerful sequence. As the war came to an end, there were occasional realistic treatments of combat that could almost be called antiwar in approach. *The Story of G. I. Joe* and *They Were Expendable* (both 1945) are two notable examples.

After the war, Hollywood dutifully followed along as the national myths of the cold war developed. In the quasi-documentary spy films produced by Louis de Rochemont (*The House on 92nd Street*, 1945; *13 Rue Madeleine*, 1947; *Walk East on Beacon*, 1952), we can trace a smooth progression as Commies replaced Nazis as villains, without any alteration of the style or the structure of the films. During the fifties, the cold war mentality was pervasive. There were cycles of spy films and films glorifying cold-war institutions like the Strategic Air Command and the F.B.I. But more abstractly, we can also discern cold-war psychology in the popular genre of science fiction during the 1950s. *Invasion of the Body Snatchers* (1956) is perhaps the prime metaphor for the political paranoia of those years, while *Forbidden Planet* (1956) provides a more sophisticated analysis. In this latter film, the monsters are not insidious, implacable otherworldly beings against whom there is no defense short of complete mobilization, but rather creatures of our own ids, reflections of our own elemental fears. Once the characters of *Forbidden Planet* learn to deal with their own subconsciouses, the monsters evaporate.

Obviously, the purge and the blacklist that occurred at the urging of House Un-American Activities Committee in the late forties had a deeply disturbing effect. But this in itself is not enough to explain the widespread, nearly unanimous ideology exhibited by Hollywood films in the 1950s. Filmmakers were seized by the same paranoia that held the rest of the country in its grip. It was as if, having found a spirit of unification and purpose in the war against fascism, we desperately desired another enemy of equal danger to bring us together. When cold-war myths disintegrated in the sixties, coincidentally, forces for social change were partially liberated. American films reflected these changes as well.

In Europe, the effects of the war were, paradoxically, positive. In the quiet, more sensible and reasonable propaganda of films like *In Which We Serve* (Noel Coward, 1943), English filmmakers found a sense of purpose. As the documentary techniques of Grierson and his associates were applied to fiction, England discovered a national cinematic style for the first time. Politically conscious, historically intelligent, that style was reborn for a brief period in the late fifties and early sixties, as the so-called Angry Young Men of the theater had their effect on film.

In Italy, the long drought of fascism was ended by a flood of politically active, esthetically revolutionary films known collectively as Neorealism. Rossellini's *Open City* (1945) and *Paisan* (1946), De Sica's *Bicycle Thief* (1948) and *Shoeshine* (1946), Visconti's *Ossessione* (1942) and *La Terra Trema* (1947) set standards that inspired filmmakers around the world for decades after. But the political relevance that marked both British and Italian cinemas during the forties did not survive long in the fifties. Not until the late sixties was it revived, in a series of French and Italian muckracking films that have had proven political effect. The main exponents of this style have been Constantin Costa-Gavras (Z, 1969; *State of Siege*, 1973) in France and Francesco Rosi (*Salvatore Giuliano*, 1962; *The Mattei Affair*, 1972) in Italy. There have been very few examples of this muckraking style of cinema in the U.S. *The China Syndrome* (1979) is the most notable example, a film released only weeks before the near-meltdown at Three Mile Island mimicked its plot.

Like all forms of mass entertainment, film has been powerfully mythopoeic even as it has entertained. Hollywood helped mightily to shape—and often exaggerate—our national myths and therefore our sense of ourselves. It has likewise had a profound effect abroad. For the New Wave in France in the early 1960s, the phenomenon of American filmic cultural imperialism was an important subject of study. As recently as 1976, for example, a full forty percent of West German box office receipts was garnered by American films. American cinema is even more dominant in England, Italy, and France, and these are all major film-producing nations. In smaller countries in Europe, and especially in the Third World, the situation is even more unbalanced. In 1975, for example, only 18 percent of Dutch film income went to native producers.

At present, the overwhelming dominance of American films in the world marketplace is being challenged from several directions. Some countries have instituted quota systems. Third World filmmakers have worked to counteract Hollywood myths with their own. A number of filmmakers have attempted a more radical approach, questioning the very premise of the Hollywood film: entertainment. This new approach, sometimes called dialectical film, involved reconceiving the entertaining consumer commodity as an intellectual tool, a forum for examination and discussion. This is a view of film that not only admits the relationship between film and observer but hopes to capitalize on it to the viewer's benefit by bringing it out into the open. Like the plays of

Figure 4-19. LUMIÈRES' REALITY. *Leaving the Factory* (1895): the fact of existence. (MOMA/FSA. *Frame enlargement.*)

Bertolt Brecht (see pp. 35–37), these films want to involve their observers intellectually as well as emotionally. It is necessary, then, that the viewers participate intellectually in the experience of the film; they must work, in other words. As a result, many people who don't understand the new ground rules are turned off. Waiting for the film to do all the work, to envelop them in the expected heady fantasies, they find that dialectic films—Jean-Luc Godard's work, for example—are boring. Yet this approach, when properly understood, offers one of the most exciting possibilities for the future development of cinema.

Ontologically, the power of film to deconstruct traditional values is enhanced and put to use. *Mimetically,* film becomes not simply a fantastic reflection of reality, but an essay in which we can work out the patterns of a new and better social structure. *Inherently,* the political relationship between the film and the observer is recognized for what it is and the observer has, for the first time, a chance to interact, to participate directly in the logic of the film. Hollywood film was a dream—thrilling, enthralling, but sometimes a political nightmare. Dialectic film can be a conversation—often vital and stimulating.

Figure 4-20. MÉLIÈS'S FANTASY. *The Kingdom of the Fairies* (1903): the expressive narrative. (*MOMA/FSA. Frame enlargement.*)

"THE CINEMA": ESTHETICS

While film esthetics should always be considered in the context of economic, political, and technological developments, when isolated they display some attractive, often informative patterns. Perhaps the best way to describe each period of cinema history is to identify the characteristic esthetic dialectic operating therein. Of course, a great many other forces are working to shape film style at any one time, but these dialectical oppositions offer a convenient handle.

It's nearly impossible to offer a comprehensive history of film styles and filmmakers in a single volume (much less an individual chapter). Much of what follows, therefore, may seem no more than listmaking. For this, I beg your indulgence. The alternative—to ignore the names of individual films and filmmakers—would greatly distort our sense of film history, which is very much a matter of individuals, and individual efforts.

CREATING AN ART: *LUMIÈRE VERSUS MÉLIÈS*

The most elemental dichotomy of film esthetics is that between the early work of the Lumière brothers, Auguste and Louis, and Georges Méliès. The Lumières had come to film through photography. They saw in the new invention a magnificent opportunity to reproduce reality, and their most effective films simply captured events: a train leaving the station at Ciotat, workers leaving the Lumière photographic factory. These were simple yet striking proto-films. They told no story, but they reproduced a place, time, and atmosphere so effectively that audiences paid eagerly to view the phenomena. On the other hand, Méliès, a stage magician, saw immediately film's ability to change reality—to produce striking fantasies. His *Voyage to the Moon* (1902) is the best-known example of Méliès's thoroughly cinematic form of illusion, and one of the most elaborate early films. Significantly, many of Méliès's films had the words "nightmare" or "dream" in their titles. The dichotomy represented by the contrasting approaches of the Lumières and Méliès is central to film and is repeated through the years in a variety of guises.

At the same time in the U.S., Thomas Edison's company was turning out simpler films, which seldom exhibited the ingrained cinematic sense of his French contemporaries. *Fred Ott's Sneeze* and the John Rice-May Irwin *Kiss* are two prototypical examples of Edison's diffident approach. In 1897, Edwin S. Porter, a salesman, joined Edison's company. For the next eleven years, he was the most important filmmaker on the American scene. After an apprenticeship filming newsreel footage, Porter produced in 1903 two films—*The Life of an American Fireman* and *The Great Train Robbery*—which are classics in film history. Porter is known for his fluid parallel montage (indeed, he is often considered the "inventor" of film editing), and while it is true enough that both of these films are inventive, his reputation as one of the fathers of film technique raises the first serious problem in the history of film esthetics. Porter's later films never fulfilled his early promise. Moreover, other filmmakers were exhibiting much the same fluency at the same time in England and France. In fact, the memorable parallel editing of *The Life of an American Fireman* may have been partly accidental, since one of Porter's aims in making the film was to use some leftover footage he had discovered in the Edison factory. Yet Porter is praised in standard film histories as an innovator. One of the major difficulties with film history to date is this uncontrollable urge to discover "firsts," to create a sort of *Guinness Book of World Records* in film.

The truth is that it would have been memorable if Porter (or someone else) had *not* "discovered" the potential of the cut. It is inherent in

Figure 4-21. THE SENNETT CHASE: The Keystone Cops in action on the streets of old Los Angeles.

the physical nature of film; even for this, supposedly the most cinematic of devices, there are models in the other arts, and any intelligent practitioner of the art should have been able to make the necessary logical jump. Porter's parallel cutting, Griffith's closeups, tracking, and panning were all devices that cried out to be discovered and used; judged by the standards of the established arts, they were hardly innovative. In film, however, it was very easy to set records if you were among the first to play the game.

In England in the early years of this century, Robert W. Paul and Cecil Hepworth were doing more interesting work than Porter. Hepworth's *Rescued by Rover* (1905) is a better illustration of the potential of editing than the American classics. In France in the latter half of the decade, Ferdinand Zecca (at Pathé) and Louis Feuillade (at Gaumont) were actively exploring numerous film possibilities, and Max Linder (Pathé) became the first successful film comedian. Émile Cohl was beginning to explore the possibilities of the animated film. In Italy, Filoteo Alberini was shooting some of the earliest historical dramas. Clearly, the first period of film history is the story of European accomplishments.

D. W. Griffith first entered films as an actor in 1907. During the

Figure 4-22. D. W. Griffith: *The Musketeers of Pig Alley* (1912). Lillian Gish as "the girl." Famous for its documentary image of New York, *The Musketeers of Pig Alley* was one of Griffith's most popular Biograph films. It was shot on location on West Twelfth St. and at the Biograph studios on East Fourteenth St. in September 1912. (MOMA/ FSA. *Frame enlargement.*)

succeeding six years, he directed hundreds of one- and two-reelers for Biograph and in the process established a reputation as the leading film artist of the day. Griffith was particularly effective with actors and theatrical devices—especially lighting. He used closeups, tracks, pans, and parallel editing with great aplomb. He made films that were emotionally profoundly affecting, even if they nearly always operated within the conventions of Victorian melodrama. He certainly deserves his reputation as the "father" of the feature film. Yet there are a number of serious problems.

It is not necessary to compare Griffith's work in film with developments in the other arts of the period—Picasso in painting, Conrad, Joyce, and Dreiser in the novel, Strindberg, Chekhov, and Shaw in the theater. That comparison is certainly unfair, since film was still a fragile enterprise that depended very much on its popular audience. Yet other filmmakers at about the same time were doing fresh and interesting work, unhampered by the clichés of the nineteenth-century theater. A good part of Griffith's reputation as the patriarch of film art is due to a kind of esthetic inferiority complex, which has marked film history until quite recently. Griffith, who had begun his career in the theater, wanted very much to make films that were "respectable." He wanted to liberate film from its "bad object" status. Yet much of the vitality and power of film lies in just that area. By 1911, Mack Sennett, who had begun by acting and writing for Griffith, was making his first comedies, which show a sense of freedom and a gusto that are also evident in the best of Griffith, but which he often seems to be working against. Griffith's art looked backward; Sennett's looked forward, toward Dada and Surrealism. The problem with Griffith's reputation is twofold: we don't yet take cinema seriously enough, so that we tend to denigrate slapstick; and at the same time we take film too seriously, so that we yearn for the respectable father, the role that Griffith played so well. Similar attitudes reveal themselves in the study of American literature, where we tend to overemphasize writers who offer a neat parallel with British literature and neglect native American work as not quite respectable. When the balance is redressed, Griffith's reputation will benefit, since we will be able to accept the faults with the successes. We will also understand better why his early promise led to the grandiose schemes of later years and, eventually, failure.

Central to both Griffith's melodrama and Sennett's farce was the concept of the chase, still a dominant element of popular film. Dating from the early examples of Porter and Hepworth, with antecedents in the conventions of Victorian theater, the chase was the single great element of narrative dramaturgy that film did not share with theater. It brought theater out of the proscenium arch (real or ideal) and into the world, and it became a quintessential model of the battle between protagonist and antagonist that drives all dramatic narrative. When Griffith is at his best, in such films as *The Lonedale Operator* (1911), *The Musketeers of Pig Alley* (1912), the closing sequence of *Intolerance* (1916), or *Way Down East* (1920), the chase is often the device (real or metaphorical) that allows him to free himself from the stasis of Victorian sentiment to discover the power inherent in melodrama. Likewise, Sennett's reeling chases in the bleak streets of early Los Angeles provide some of the most inventive cinematic moments of early film history.

THE SILENT FEATURE: REALISM VERSUS EXPRESSIONISM

The spectacle, melodrama, and sentiment we associate with Griffith were commercially valuable during the period of the silent feature, as the successful career of Cecil B. DeMille attests. We can also divine at least the last two elements in the phenomenal popularity of Mary Pickford's films during the late teens and twenties. But esthetically, it was the Sennett tradition that flowered profusely and eloquently during these years. Silent film in the U.S. is, primarily, a matter of comedy. Charles Chaplin, Buster Keaton, Harold Lloyd, Harry Langdon, and Mack Sennett and Hal Roach as producers dominate the period, as well they should. The personas invented by Chaplin, Keaton, and Lloyd are among the most significant creations in film history. Sennett had built his earliest films around a simple structural idea: there was no moral to his stories; they were simply collections of gags. The great comic actors of the late teens and twenties added an ethical or political dimension that raised the slapstick film from the level of mechanical competence to the level of metaphor and meaning. Interestingly, Chaplin reveals nearly as much Victorian sentiment as Griffith, but he expresses it in contemporary terms. All the silent comedians translated a basically political problem—how can the individual cope with industrial civilization and power politics?—into physical terms and audiences responded—still respond—with visceral understanding. If Lloyd was the most mechanical and abstract of the silent comedians, Chaplin was the most human and political, but all of them to varying degrees made the connection between mechanics and morality. Probably the quintessential example of the styles and concerns of silent comedy is Chaplin's masterpiece, *Modern Times* (although made in 1936 it has no dialogue, only music), a film about machines and men that is just as relevant today.

Apart from the comic tradition, the most interesting esthetic force operating in American cinema in the twenties was the exploration of the possibilities of film realism. Erich von Stroheim, struggling against the developing commercial trend, managed to complete only a small number of films. More often than not, his conceptions were drastically reedited by studios, but he nevertheless had a profound influence on the course of American cinema. *Foolish Wives* (1921), *Greed* (1923), and *The Wedding March* (1928)—all savaged by studio heads—nevertheless survive as legends and object lessons on the vital power of realist techniques such as deep focus, complex mise en scène, and location shooting. Filmmakers are still exploring the potential of these devices. Stroheim was among the first to recognize that the observer of a film had to be given freedom to operate in concert with the creator.

Nor was Stroheim alone during the twenties in exploring the possibilities of the camera as communicator rather than manipulator. Working outside the Hollywood system, Robert Flaherty became the first notable documentarist with such films as *Nanook of the North* (1922) and *Moana* (1926). F. W. Murnau, who had had a successful career in

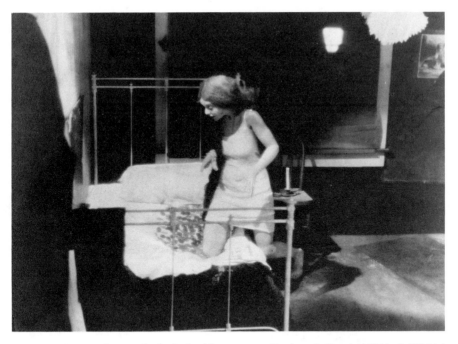

Figure 4-23. Zasu Pitts and a bed of gold coins: von Stroheim's *Greed* (1923). (MOMA/FSA.)

Germany in the early twenties, arrived in America in 1926. *Sunrise* (1927) and *Tabu* (1929, 1931, with Flaherty) remain fine examples of how theatricality can be fused with realism. To a lesser extent, King Vidor's *The Big Parade* (1925) and *The Crowd* (1928), as well as the later *Our Daily Bread* (1934), stand as examples of political realism.

While in America in the twenties film was rapidly industrializing, in Europe it was a business that was also seen as art. Filmmakers in general worked more closely with established painters, musicians, and playwrights. In London, the Film Society was founded in 1925 to promote the art of film. In France, Louis Delluc became the first important esthetic theorist of film, and such filmmakers as Abel Gance, Jean Epstein, Germaine Dulac, René Clair, Luis Buñuel and Salvador Dali, Man Ray, and Marcel Duchamp provided practical examples of film as art while the commercial cinema produced little of value. In Germany, UFA set about consciously raising the esthetic standards of German film. The result was one of the major efflorescences of talent in cinema history: German Expressionism. Writer Carl Mayer, designer/painters Hermann Warm, Walter Röhrig, and Walter Reimann played signifi-

Figure 4-24. German Expressionist chiaroscuro: Robert Wiene's *Raskolnikow* (1923). The play of light and shade was a major code. (MOMA/FSA.)

cant roles in the movement, as did directors Robert Wiene (*The Cabinet of Dr. Caligari*, 1919), Fritz Lang (*Dr. Mabuse*, 1922; *Metropolis*, 1927), Murnau (*Nosferatu*, 1922; *The Last Laugh*, 1924), and Paul Leni (*Waxworks*, 1924, and in Hollywood *The Cat and The Canary*, 1927). Meanwhile, G. W. Pabst (*The Joyless Street*, 1925) explored realist alternatives. As fascinating as this period of film history is, only Lang and Murnau proved to be major artists, and only Lang survived to produce any considerable body of work.

While German Expressionism had a far greater effect worldwide, interesting, productive traditions were developing in Sweden and Denmark as well during the teens and early twenties. Swedish directors Mauritz Stiller and Victor Sjöström shared backgrounds in the theater. From its earliest days through the career of Ingmar Bergman, Swedish film has been closely associated with the theatrical world. Stiller at first specialized in witty comedies (*Love and Journalism*, 1916; *Thomas Graal's Best Film*, 1917) before moving on to more literary projects (*Gösta Berling's Saga*, 1924), and finally emigrating to Hollywood with his star, Greta Garbo. Sjöström, an actor, is best known for his poetic social commentary (*The Outlaw and His Wife*, 1917; *Körkalen*, 1921).

Danish director Carl Theodor Dreyer's career spanned more than fifty years, although he directed relatively few films. His *Passion de Jeanne D'Arc* (1928) has become one of the standard masterpieces of world film, as have *Vampyr* (1932) and *Gertrud* (1964). Dreyer's cinema is notable for its transcendental simplicity and fascination with cruelty, humiliation, and suffering.

The twenties are also the great age of Soviet cinema. Lev Kuleshov and Vsevolod Meyerhold had established separate but parallel theories that were taken up and greatly elaborated upon by Sergei Eisenstein (*Strike*, 1924; *Potemkin*, 1925; *October*, 1927), V. I. Pudovkin (*Mother*, 1926; *The End of St. Petersburg*, 1927), and Alexander Dovzhenko (*Arsenal*, 1929; *Earth*, 1930). These films remain major landmarks in the history of cinema, especially *Potemkin*, probably the clearest example of Eisenstein's influential theories of montage. Eisenstein saw film as a dialectical process and his technique in *Potemkin* demonstrates the effectiveness of that approach. Using "types" rather than fully developed characters, he created a forceful, incessant logic for this story of the 1905 mutiny of the crew of Battleship Potemkin. The Odessa Steps sequence (see Figures 5-1 to 5-4) is one of the most famous examples of his celebrated montage technique, building both drama and significance through the juxtaposition of shots.

At the same time, Dziga Vertov was developing his theory of "film-truth" in such films as *Kino-Pravda* (1922–25), *Kino-Eye* (1924), and *Man With a Movie Camera* (1929). As the Germans had investigated the expressiveness of artifical setting and mise en scène, so the Soviet revolutionary filmmakers explored the powerful expressive nature of montage. Their theories, among the most important in cinema, will be discussed in the following chapter.

HOLLYWOOD: GENRE VERSUS AUTEUR

By the early thirties, American cinema had achieved a position of dominance on world screens. Between 1932 and 1946, the history of film is, with two exceptions, the history of Hollywood. The exceptions are the group of directors in France sometimes linked together under the rubric "Poetic Realism," and the beginnings of the British documentary tradition with John Grierson and his group in England. Grierson, who made only one film himself, acted as producer, organizer, and herald for the British documentary tradition in the thirties, a movement whose effect on the future development of British cinema was more important than the actual films that issued from it. Although not associated with Grierson, Humphrey Jennings produced possibly the most

Figure 4-25. Dziga Vertov's *Man With a Movie Camera* (1929): idiosyncratic kino-pravda. (*MOMA/FSA. Frame enlargement.*)

enduring examples of this genre during the war: *Listen to Britain* (1942), *Fires Were Started* (1943), *A Diary for Timothy* (1945) are all personal statements as documentary from a former poet and painter.

As Alfred Hitchcock dominated British fiction film in the 1930s, so Jean Renoir towered over the French film scene of that decade. Less appreciated then than now (when he is regarded as one of acknowledged masters of world cinema), Renoir, in an extraordinary series of films— *Boudu Saved From Drowing* (1932), *Toni* (1934), *The Crime of M. Lange* (1935), *Grand Illusion* (1937), and *The Rules of the Game* (1939)— created a new fusion of modes that combined the humanism of such silent artists as Chaplin with realist technique. The effects of his humane, politically sensitive, drolly comic style are still being felt.

At the same time in France, a number of other strong and very personal styles were developing: Marcel Pagnol directed a series of popular, lyrical, and diffident studies of French provincialism. René Clair, whose reputation has suffered with the years, directed several amusing, if lightweight, films. Marcel Carné was responsible for a number of highly theatrical witty dramas, culminating in *Children of Paradise* (1944). Jacques Prévert was his frequent collaborator. Most memorable, perhaps, are the two major films made by Jean Vigo before he died at

Figure 4-26. The Arizona Jim Collective celebrates their communal good fortune in Jean Renoir's *The Crime of M. Lange* (1935). (*l'Avant-Scène. Frame enlargement.*)

the age of twenty-nine, *Zero for Conduct* (1933), and *L'Atalante* (1934), masterpieces exhibiting Vigo's clear-eyed, virtuoso cinema.

There were few such clearly identifiable personal signatures in Hollywood at the time. Alfred Hitchcock, who had matured in England, has certainly been the most obvious of the Hollywood auteurs since he arrived in 1940. He has dominated the genre of the thriller for half a century.

He should, he invented it. In a number of films made during his first years in America, Hitchcock further refined the basic sense of political paranoia with which he had experimented in England in the 1930s. *Foreign Correspondent* (1940) is a film of subtle reversals and correspondences that points toward the future. *Saboteur* (1942) was the first of his films to spread the American landscape before us in a coast-to-coast chase. In it he developed some interesting ideas about the relationship between the individual and the State in wartime. *Shadow of a Doubt* (1943), from a script by the playwright Thornton Wilder, contrasts small-town life with the criminal personality and is generally regarded as one of the major films of the Hitchcock canon. *Spellbound* (1945) seems simplistic today, but was one of the earliest introductions of Freudian concepts in American film. *Notorious* (1946) paired Cary

Figure 4-27. In the early thirties Howard Hawks made the classic gangster film *Scarface* for producer Howard Hughes before moving on to other genres. Ann Dvorak and George Raft starred.

Grant and Ingrid Bergman in an intensely personal exploration of the effects of paranoia on a relationship.

Josef von Sternberg left his mark in a series of visually elaborate romances (*The Blue Angel, Morocco,* 1930; *Shanghai Express,* 1932; *The Scarlet Empress,* 1934). Busby Berkeley invented a peculiarly cinematic form of musical (*Gold Diggers of 1935,* 1935; *The Gang's All Here,* 1943). John Ford made the form of the Western sing with new resonance (*Stagecoach,* 1939; *My Darling Clementine,* 1946) and extended many of the metaphorical significances of that essentially American genre in other directions in the scores of other films he directed.

Howard Hawks left his imprint on a wide variety of genres, his films always impressive for their wit, good nature, and richness of texture, among them so-called Screwball Comedies (*Twentieth Century,* 1934; *Bringing Up Baby,* 1939; *His Girl Friday,* 1939), dramas (*To Have and Have Not,* 1944), and Westerns (*Red River,* 1948; *Rio Bravo,* 1959). Hawks's *The Big Sleep* (1946) is a classic Film Noir detective story, based on Raymond Chandler's novel and starring Humphrey Bogart and Lauren Becall. It is also a near-perfect model of all that is best in the Hollywood film. Chandler, Hawks, Bogart, and screenwriters William

Figure 4-28. Lauren Bacall, Humphrey Bogart: *The Big Sleep* (Howard Hawks, 1945): a more balanced relationship between women and men than is common today. (MOMA/ FSA.)

Faulkner, Leigh Brackett, and Jules Furthman combined talents to produce a tightly woven fabric of their various concerns and styles. What is significant is that the film, being the product of a number of artistic personalities, nevertheless impresses with its unity. As entertainment, it has few equals in the Hollywood canon. The electric Bogart-Bacall relationship merges with Hawks's witty mise en scène, Chandler's laconic, poetic existentialism, and the tough, rich, humorous dialogue and elegantly complicated plot provided by the screenwriters (under Hawks's direction). The result is an extraordinarily effective machine for entertainment.

But *The Big Sleep*, like all of Hollywood's best films, is more as well, almost unconsciously. Hawks's gallery of women is unmatched for the depth of characterization and, more important, the strength and the intelligence they exhibit. (And this from a director known best for his treatment of male friendships!) The balanced tension between the men and the women in the film gives it a special psychological relevance. At the same time, *The Big Sleep* is representative of the Hollywood style in a less admirable way: most of the directly political material of Chan-

Figure 4-29. GENRES: THE MUSICAL. At Warner Bros. in the thirties, Busby Berkeley made the elaborately choreographed geometric dance number famous, but it was not solely his invention. Here a scene from the first Fred Astaire-Ginger Rogers musical, RKO's *Flying Down to Rio* (1933, directed by Thornton Freeland). It combines the vivid star work of the Astaire-Rogers team with the pas de milles famous in Berkeley's work. The choreographer was Dave Gould. (MOMA/FSA.)

dler's novel has been cut out so that the film is, in this respect, a pale shadow of its original source. It was nearly thirty years before *Chinatown* (1974), written by Robert Towne and directed by Roman Polanski, explored on the screen the same political subjects of decay and corruption that Raymond Chandler discussed in nearly all his novels, including *The Big Sleep,* but which were only hinted at in the film versions of his stories made in the 1940s.

Hitchcock, Ford, Hawks, von Sternberg, and a few others may have been able to maintain a recognizable personal signature from film to film during the great age of Hollywood. For the most part, however, Hollywood cinema was the product of numerous craftspeople: directors, actors, cinematographers, writers, designers, producers. Directors such as William Wellman, Lewis Milestone, Leo McCarey, and John Huston display personal styles, no doubt, and are proper studies of auteurist critics, yet the structure of the Hollywood system was such that even powerful directorial personalities were more often than not submerged in a sea of studio styles, actor's styles, producers' requirements, and writers' idiosyncrasies.

One of the more interesting exceptions to this rule was Preston Sturges. A playwright in the twenties, he, like so many of his colleagues, migrated from New York to Hollywood with the advent of sound. He enjoyed a successful career as screenwriter during the 1930s. *Easy Living* (1937, directed by Mitchel Leisen) is probably the best of his scripts from this period. He began directing in 1940, and for almost a decade was able to maintain a large measure of control over his films, writing all his own scripts and working regularly with a group of character actors. His eccentric, pointed satire is best represented by *The Lady Eve* (1941), *Sullivan's Travels* (1942), and *The Miracle of Morgan's Creek* (1944).

It was this dialectic between genre and auteur that drove the Hollywood cinema: the clash between an artist's sensibility and the classic mythic structures of the story types that were identified and popular. Probably the most important of these was the Western, since it embodied so many of the myths—the frontier, individualism, the land, and law and order versus anarchy—upon which the national psychology of the United States depends. Musicals were probably second in popularity, whether the geometric exercises of Berkeley's Warner Brothers series or the sophisticated, light comedies of Fred Astaire at RKO. Comedy remained strong in the thirties, as the Broadway writers of the twenties were imported en masse to provide dialogue for sound films. Again, it was the performers who led the way, as it had been in the silent era. The Marx Brothers, Mae West, and W. C. Fields (who had begun in silents) produced some of the most intriguing comic personas, the Marxes setting a mode of illogic that was to last through the seventies. The quick patter and insouciance of Broadway in the twenties gave rise to the Screwball Comedy, the genre that probably best identifies the 1930s on American screens. Gangster films, Horror films, Historical Romances, and embryonic Thrillers were all important genres, as well.

In the forties, the mood changed. War films, of course, were added to the genre catalogue and, beginning in the late forties, the peculiar blend of urban cynicism, downbeat subject matter, and dark shadows known as "Film Noir" made its appearance.

Throughout the Hollywood period, the genres refined themselves; by the end they were nearly self-parodies. Yet they proved engrossing in two respects: on the one hand, by their nature genres were mythic. To experience a Horror film, a Gangster film, or a Screwball Comedy was cathartic. The elements were well known: there was a litany to each popular

Figure 4-30. Tim Holt, Ann Baxter, Joseph Cotten, Dolores Costello, and Agnes Moorehead with "The Original Morgan Invincible" in Welles's *The Magnificent Ambersons* (1942). A less startling film than *Citizen Kane* (1941), *Ambersons* was no less perceptive about the American condition and—in its commentary on the effect of the automobile on American society—strangely prophetic. In his first two films, Welles described the two major controlling factors—the media and the automobile—of twentieth-century America. (*MOMA/FSA.*)

genre. Part of their pleasure lay in seeing how those basic elements would be treated this time around. On the other hand, individual examples of a genre were also often specific statements. For the more knowledgeable observer, there was an equal interest in the multiple clash of styles in the film—styles of the studio, the director, the star, the producer, occasionally even the writer or designer or cinematographer. Genres offered infinite combinations of a finite number of elements.

In the middle of this often confusing forest of genres, styles, auteurs, and stars stands the monument of Orson Welles's *Citizen Kane* (1941), possibly the most important American movie ever made. Welles's classic belongs to no specific genre, but it operates like genre films by tapping mythic resonances in history and shaping them to dramatic ends. The saga of Charles Foster Kane, media baron and politician, public figure and private man, is an emblem of American life in the first half of this century. Moreover, Welles—with the aplomb of a master—

Figure 4-31. Aldo Fabrizi as Don Pietro in Rossellini's monumental Neorealist document *Rome, Open City* (1945). (MOMA/FSA. *Frame enlargement.*)

shapes his narrative in sublimely cinematic terms. It was as if the stranger
to Hollywood, child of New York theater and radio, had viewed objectively all the various strands of film technique of thirties Hollywood and
woven them all together. His notorious ego, which he exerted as co-
writer, producer, director, and star, also makes Welles's film a prime
example of auteurship. His second film, *The Magnificent Ambersons*
(1942), was never released in the version he had prepared and Welles
never again matched his success with *Citizen Kane.* This union of the
strong auteur and strong genre elements was a singular phenomenon.

NEOREALISM AND AFTER: HOLLYWOOD VERSUS THE WORLD

Television was not the only force working to counter the dominance of
the Hollywood studios during the late forties and fifties. Cinemas in
other countries were maturing, becoming more powerful, or reorganizing
after the paralysis of fascism and the war. The 16 mm equipment perfected for use during the war permitted an alternate system of distribution
that grew slowly, coming of age in the sixties. Film festivals and film

societies bloomed, providing effective promotional tools to filmmakers who did not have the resources of the great Hollywood business combines behind them. Recognizing film as an export commodity, France, for example, built the Cannes festival into the major international marketplace and established the Unifrance promotion organization.

In terms of esthetics, this more aggressive and fluid economic situation allowed major artists, even in small countries, to find an international market. If Hollywood had to battle television economically in order to survive the fifties, it had to contend esthetically with a worldwide flowering of new talent during the late forties, fifties, and sixties. The old genres remained, a few new ones were added—most notably Film Noir; the craftspeople grew older. But in Europe and Asia a new type of cinema was coming to the fore: personal, nongeneric, related directly to the contemporary historical situation.

The first group of these films appeared in Italy just at the end of the war, the product of the Neorealist movement. Cesare Zavattini, a critic and writer, had established the ground rules for Neorealism and was responsible for the scripts of several important films (*Shoeshine*, 1946; *Bicycle Thief*, 1948; *Umberto D*, 1952). Vittorio De Sica, who had been a leading romantic star of the thirties, directed these three scripts (and several others by Zavattini), thereby making an important contribution to Neorealism, before falling back into more commercial, less interesting work in the mid-fifties. Luchino Visconti directed one of the earliest Neorealist films, (*Ossessione*; 1942), a classic during the height of the movement (*La Terra Trema*, 1948), as well as one of the latest examples of the style (*Rocco and his Brothers*, 1960), although most of his work was closer in style to his first love, opera, than to Neorealism. Most important was the work of Roberto Rossellini (*Rome, Open City*, 1945; *Paisan*, 1946; *Germany—Year Zero*, 1947; *Stromboli*, 1949), for he was the only one of the three major directors to build upon the experience of Neorealism. His work throughout the fifties and in television, to which he turned in 1960 (*The Rise to Power of Louis XIV*, 1966; *Acts of the Apostles*, 1968; *Socrates*, 1970), established the foundation for materialist cinema, the direct descendant of Neorealism.

Rome, Open City remains one of the major landmarks of film history. Secretly planned during the German occupation of Rome, the film was shot soon after the allies took the city. The conditions under which it was shot add much to its sense of urgent realism. The story of a resistance leader and a priest who are arrested and killed by the Gestapo, *Rome, Open City* is marked by an urgency and intensity that are directly related to the time and place in which it was filmed. Rossellini shot with whatever filmstock he could find, often leftover portions of reels. Working under such conditions, there was no possibility that the film could be given a professional gloss, even if Rossellini had wanted to do so. Professional actors Anna Magnani and Aldo Fabrizi worked with a cast that was otherwise entirely nonprofessional. The result was an authenticity of performance that is rivalled only in true documentaries. The style of the film was highly influential. Ever since, the elements of Realist film technique have been an integral part of world film esthetics.

The Neorealists were working for a cinema intimately connected with the experience of living: nonprofessional actors, rough technique, political point, ideas rather than entertainment—all these elements went directly counter to the Hollywood esthetic of smooth, seamless professionalism. While Neorealism as a movement lasted only until the early fifties, the effects of its esthetics are still being felt. In fact, Zavattini, Rossellini, De Sica, and Visconti defined the ground rules that would operate for the next thirty years. Esthetically, Hollywood never quite recovered.

Meanwhile, back at the southern California ranches, business proceeded much as usual. There was room in Hollywood neither for the political relevance of Neorealism nor for the personal, nongeneric style that was developing throughout Europe. While there were occasional surprises, such as Frank Capra's *It's a Wonderful Life* (1947), the most interesting of his series of populist sentimental dramas and a crisp, direct lesson in the benefits of cooperative social and economic organizations, the political mood of Hollywood, as we noted earlier, was reactionary.

The most intriguing esthetic result of this dark, paranoiac mood was the cycle of Films Noirs of the late forties and early fifties. A vaguely defined genre (as the name announces, it was first noticed by the French), Film Noir is one of the more complex and intelligent Hollywood styles. Part detective story, part gangster, part urban melodrama, Film Noir was identified best by its dark and pessimistic undercurrents. While many examples of the genre had cold-war overtones, this was not necessarily a condition: if the genre had a literary source it was in the detective novels of Dashiell Hammett and Raymond Chandler, both of whom evinced sympathies with the Left. In fact, one of the earliest examples of Film Noir is Hawks's *The Big Sleep* (1946), a film of Raymond Chandler's novel. Combine the weary cynicism of Chandler's hero Philip Marlowe with the Freudian aspects of another memorable Film Noir, Raoul Walsh's *White Heat* (1949), and you have a good model for the genre. Combine the titles for those two films and we have, interestingly, *The Big Heat* (1953), one of Fritz Lang's most deeply fatalistic movies and a central film of the genre.

Jacques Tourneur's *Out of the Past* (1947) is one of the most neglected and most beautiful Films Noirs, Nicholas Ray's *They Live By Night* (1948) one of the best remembered. Jules Dassin's *The Naked City* (1948) and John Huston's *The Asphalt Jungle* (1950) make eloquent use of the urban settings that were such an important element, as does Samuel Fuller's *Pickup on South Street* (1953), a film that also shows how cold-war psychology could be adapted to the form of the Film Noir. Orson Welles's *Mr. Arkadin* (1955) gives us the essence of the mood of the genre. Robert Rossen's short career included two outstanding Films Noirs: *Body and Soul* (1947) and the latter-day *The Hustler* (1961).

The definition of Film Noir can be stretched to include most of the films of the "tough guy" directors, who came to the fore in the 1950s: Samuel Fuller (*House of Bamboo*, 1955; *China Gate*, 1957; *Shock Corridor*, 1963), Robert Aldrich (*Kiss Me Deadly, The Big Knife*, both 1955), Phil Karlson (*Kansas City Confidential*, 1952; *The Phenix City Story*, 1955; and a latter-day example: *Walking Tall*, 1974), and Don Siegel (*Riot in Cell Block 11*, 1954; *Crime in the Streets*, 1956). Visually, Siegel took the genre to its extremity in *Escape From Alcatraz* (1979), a film made with so little light that it must set a record of some sort. The Film Noir mode also had a pervasive effect on television programming throughout the fifties, sixties, and even seventies, as the urban, downbeat detective genre continued to grow in importance. *Kojak* and *Columbo* both had roots in fifties Film Noir. Robert Benton's *The Late Show* (1977) gave us Art Carney's version of the gumshoe anti-hero thirty years on.

Two other popular genres of the fifties, the Western and the Science Fiction film, also exhibited the downbeat mood of Film Noir, each in its own way. The Western began to treat more serious and more pessimistic themes; the Science Fiction film developed a number of objective correlatives for the cultural paranoia of the decade. Delmer Daves, one of the more underrated of Hollywood craftsmen, directed *Broken Arrow* in 1950, the first Western since silent days to allow Indians some measure of self-respect. He was also responsible for *3:10 to Yuma* (1957). John Sturges made a number of interesting Westerns, including *Gunfight at the O.K. Corral* (1957), *Last Train From Gun Hill* (1958), and *The Magnificent Seven* (1960). Anthony Mann developed a cult reputation with such films as *Winchester 73* (1950), *The Far Country* (1954), and *The Man From Laramie* (1955). Two of the first "Adult" Westerns were Fred Zinnemann's *High Noon* (1952) and George Stevens's *Shane* (1953). John Ford weighed in with *The Searchers* (1956), possibly his best Western, and *Two Rode Together* (1961). Henry King directed *The Gunfighter* (1950), Henry Hathaway *From Hell to Texas* (1958). Arthur Penn's first film was *The Left-Handed Gun* (1958). The

Figure 4-32. John Ford's two favorite Western stars: John Wayne and Monument Valley, as they appeared in one of Ford's most intriguing Westerns, *The Searchers* (1956). A "revisionist" Western, *The Searchers* critically examined elements of the Western myth that had hitherto been taken for granted as truths. Wayne's Ethan Edwards is a hero in the contemporary mold: lonely and obsessive as well as heroic, neurotically compulsive as well as faithful. The underlying text of racism is brought to the surface in *The Searchers*. Westerns would never be the same afterwards. (MOMA/FSA.)

sixties saw such significant Westerns as Marlon Brando's *One-Eyed Jacks* (1961), John Huston's *The Misfits* (1961), David Miller's *Lonely Are the Brave* (1962), and a number of films by Sam Peckinpah, notably *Ride the High Country* (1962) and *The Wild Bunch* (1969). In Italy, meanwhile, the "Spaghetti" Western had come of age. Sergio Leone reworked the elements of the genre in films like *A Fistful of Dollars* (1964) and *The Good, The Bad, and The Ugly* (1967), starring an American, Clint Eastwood.

Science Fiction films of the fifties were fascinating psychoanalytic documents: paranoid fantasies of moving blobs, invading pods, reified ids, and metamorphoses. Among the most important were: *The Thing* (1951, Christian Nyby), *The Day The Earth Stood Still* (1951, Robert Wise), *The Invasion of the Body-Snatchers* (1956, Don Siegel), *Forbidden Planet* (1956, Fred Wilcox), *The Incredible Shrinking Man* (1957, Jack Arnold), *The Fly* (1958, Kurt Neumann), and *The Time Machine* (1960, George Pal).

The Musical, like the Western, benefited greatly from the technologies of color and widescreen and enjoyed a renaissance during the fifties under the sponsorship of producer Arthur Freed at M-G-M. Vincente Minnelli directed *An American in Paris* (1951), and *Gigi* (1958). Stanley Donen worked with Gene Kelly in *On The Town* (1949) and *Singin' in the Rain* (1952) and with Fred Astaire in *Royal Wedding* (1951) and *Funny Face* (1957, produced by Roger Edens for Paramount). Astaire also starred in Rouben Mamoulian's *Silk Stockings* (1957, produced by Freed). Mamoulian had been responsible for one of the very first significant Hollywood musicals, *Applause* (1929). In just a few films he left an indelible mark on the genre. His films were characterized by a rare wit and an unusually sophisticated sense of place.

Despite the continued dominance of genres, a few American directors of the late forties and fifties managed to convey a strong sense of personal style in their films. Among these auteurs were Elia Kazan (*Gentleman's Agreement*, 1947; *Viva Zapata!* 1952; *On The Waterfront*, 1954; *East of Eden*, 1955), Otto Preminger (*Laura*, 1944; *The Man with the Golden Arm*, 1955; *Anatomy of a Murder*, 1959), and—more important—Nicholas Ray (*Johnny Guitar*, 1954; *Rebel Without a Cause*, 1955; *Bigger than Life*, 1956) and Douglas Sirk (*All that Heaven Allows*, 1955; *Written on the Wind*, 1956). Both Ray and Sirk were taken up as heroes by the generation of younger European filmmakers in the next two decades: Ray by the French in the sixties, Sirk by the Germans in the seventies.

Despite these interesting currents and eddies in the flow of Hollywood product, American film experienced a slow but steady decline throughout the fifties. Real innovations in cinema were occurring elsewhere as the art split into popular and elite factions, the latter served by the growing number of "art" houses.

World audiences were discovering the Asian cinema for the first time. Japanese cinema had a long tradition to draw upon, including one of the more interesting styles of silent film in which "Reciters" were used to describe and explain the action—a device borrowed from Kabuki theater. Filmmakers outside Japan were unaware of these accomplishments until the success of Akira Kurosawa's *Rashomon* at the Venice Film Festival of 1951. Although it was Kurosawa's Samurai films that gained the most attention, he made many films in modern settings as well. Among his most important films are *Ikiru* (1952), *Seven Samurai* (1954), *Throne of Blood* (Macbeth, 1957), and *Yojimbo* (1961). Kurosawa's success led to the release of other Japanese films in the 1950s. Kenji Mizoguchi, whose career dates from 1922, directed a number of films in the fifties that became classics of the world repertory: *The Life of O-Haru* (1952), *Ugetsu Monogatari* (1953), *Sansho the Bailiff* (1954),

Figure 4-33. Yasujiro Ozu's *Tokyo Story* (1953). With characteristic Japanese clarity, sensitivity, and respect, Ozu's films most often deal with family relationships between generations. The old couple of *Tokyo Story* find on a visit to their children in the capital that the younger generation, busy with its own endeavors, no longer has much time for their parents. (*New Yorker Films.*)

Chikimatsu Monogatari (1954), and *Princess Yang Kwei Fei* (1955) among them. The last of the Japanese directors to be "discovered" in the West was Yasujiro Ozu, possibly the most interesting of the group. An unusual stylist, Ozu contemplated locales and seasons with a very un-Western sensitivity and tranquillity, whereas the films of Kurosawa are much more easily understood by Occidentals. Among Ozu's most important films are the "season" series: *Late Spring* (1949), *Early Summer* (1951), *Early Spring* (1956), *Late Autumn* (1960), *Early Autumn* (1961), and *An Autumn Afternoon* (1962), as well as *Tokyo Story* (1953), his most popular film in the West.

Like Japan, India has long had a prolific film industry. The staple of Indian cinema is the lengthy, highly stylized Musical, which still remains to be introduced to the world market. In the late fifties, however, one filmmaker—Satyajit Ray—began producing films with more universal appeal. The Apu Trilogy (*Pather Panchali*, 1955; *Aparajito*, 1957; *The World of Apu*, 1959) was immediately appreciated in the

West and Ray has become a favorite of film festivals and art houses with such films as *The Music Room* (1958), *Kanchenjunga* (1962), *Days and Nights in the Forest* (1970), and *Distant Thunder* (1973).

During the 1950s England gave world screens the series of priceless Alec Guinness comedies (*The Man in the White Suit*, *The Lavender Hill Mob*, 1951; *The Horse's Mouth*, 1959), which were followed by the Peter Sellers comedies of the sixties (*I'm All Right Jack*, 1959; *Only Two Can Play*, 1961; *Heavens Above!*, 1963) and the Music-Hall low comedy series of *Doctor . . .* and *Carry On* farces. German cinema didn't recover from the experience of the war and Nazism until 1970.

In the fifties, French screens were dominated by what the young critic François Truffaut termed the "cinéma du papa," an overly literary and—Truffaut thought—stultifying style, but the New Wave was about to break and at least three independent, contrasting auteurs—Jean Cocteau, the poet; Jacques Tati, the comedian; and Robert Bresson, the ascetic esthete—were producing interesting work. Cocteau completed *Orpheus* in 1950 and *The Testament of Orpheus* a decade later. Tati directed and starred in *M. Hulot's Holiday* (1953) and *Mon Oncle* (1958). Bresson, a meticulous craftsman, finished *Diary of a Country Priest* (1950), *A Man Escaped* (1953), and *Pickpocket* (1959).

At about the same time Max Ophüls, whose career had begun in Germany in the early thirties and wound its way through France and Italy to Hollywood in the fifties, returned to France to produce three films which have been highly influential: *La Ronde* (1950), *Madame de . . .* (1953), and *Lola Montès* (1955). Ophüls is best known for these ironic love stories and for his long, fluid, exhilarating tracking shots, which were the hallmark of his style. (See Figure 3-55.)

The movement of film esthetics toward personal art and away from collectively produced genres reached a climax in the middle fifties with the maturation of two profoundly idiosyncratic filmmakers—Ingmar Bergman and Federico Fellini. These two, together with Alfred Hitchcock, whose work in the fifties represents the summit of his career, dominated film esthetics in the late fifties and prepared the way for the cinéma d'auteur, which became the rule rather than the exception in the sixties. Interestingly, all three deal in one way or another with the anxiety that also motivated the popular genres of the period and that the poet W. H. Auden had declared the principal emotion of the age. For Bergman, *angst* was expressed in psychoanalytic and religious terms; for Hitchcock, anxiety was a matter of stylized paranoia of everyday life; for Fellini, *angoscia* was a social problem as much as it was personal.

Bergman had begun making films in the mid-forties, but it wasn't until *Smiles of a Summer Night* (1955), *The Seventh Seal* (1957), *Wild*

Figure 4-34. Victor Sjöström comes to terms with his past in Bergman's *Wild Strawberries* (1958). Sjöström, one of the fathers of Swedish film, capped his career with this film. It was not by accident that Bergman chose a fellow director to play the central role of Professor Isak Borg, for *Wild Strawberries* also marks an important stage in Bergman's own struggle with his past.

Strawberries (1958), and *The Virgin Spring* (1959) that he gained world renown. *The Seventh Seal* was especially effective in this respect. Its symbolism was immediately apprehensible to people trained in literary culture who were just beginning to discover the "art" of film, and it quickly became a staple of high school and college literature courses. Based on Bergman's own play, *The Seventh Seal* stars Max von Sydow, who was to become the main actor in Bergman's extraordinary repertory company of the 1960s. Antonius Blok, a medieval knight returning from the Crusades, undergoes a series of encounters with death. Sweden is ravaged by the plague. Each of the real encounters—with a group of strolling players, a witchburning, flagellating peasants—is paralleled by a symbolic encounter with the black-clad figure of death, with whom Blok is engaged in a running chess game, the stakes of which are life itself. Images of stark blacks and whites effectively convey the medieval mood of the film, which is further enhanced by Bergman's visual and dramatic references to medieval painting and literature. Unlike Holly-

Figure 4-35. Like Bergman's films of the period, Federico Fellini's also reflect a basically introspective nature. 8½ (1962) examines the existential dilemma of a film director, Guido (Marcello Mastroianni), who is not unlike Fellini. The film begins at a spa where the diaphanous, quasi-mythical Claudia Cardinale offers Guido the purifying waters. It is an image of innocence that constantly recurs in Fellini's films. . . . (l'Avant-Scène. Frame enlargement.)

wood "movies," *The Seventh Seal* clearly was aware of elite artistic culture and thus was readily appreciated by intellectual audiences. Bergman's best work lay ahead in the sixties, after the religious symbolism had been exorcised and he was able to concentrate on more personal, less general situations. *Wild Strawberries*, one of his best films, points in this direction.

Federico Fellini had first entered the film world during the Neorealist period of the late forties. With his countryman, Michelangelo Antonioni, he remains the major talent of that period. He first directed a film in 1950. *La Strada* (1954) had nearly as profound an effect on world screens as *The Seventh Seal* had a few years later. *Nights of Cabiria* (1956) was also widely hailed, while *La Dolce Vita* (1959) marked the opening of a new period in cinema history. A sprawling, widescreen, three-hour fresco of life among the upper classes in the Rome of the late 1950s, *La Dolce Vita* contrasts ironically with *Rome, Open City.* Fellini's film takes the form of the Renaissance peripatetic epic poem, stringing a series of tableaux and adventures together, uniting them by the figure of Marcello (Marcello Mastroianni), a gossip columnist. The "sweet life" is empty and meaningless, but the film about it is a rich and ironic tapestry of manners and morals. Fellini sharply prefigured the mood of the "swinging sixties" and the film was very successful outside of Italy, even in the U.S.

Figure 4-36. . . . *La Dolce Vita* (1959) had ended with this image of unreachable innocence. At the seashore, the journalist Marcello (Mastroianni, again) found it impossible to communicate with this young woman. (*l'Avant-Scène. Frame enlargement.*)

Figure 4-37. Fellini had been obsessed with this imagery (and the emotions it represents) throughout the 1950s. In *La Strada* (1954) and *The Nights of Cabiria* (1957), he had built whole films around it as it was personified by his wife, Giulietta Masina, here shown as Gelsomina in *La Strada*. (See also Figure 3-48.) (*l'Avant-Scène. Frame enlargement.*)

A generation older than Bergman and Fellini, Alfred Hitchcock remains the one director to have made exceptionally personal films working entirely within the genre factory system. He had, in a sense, not one but four careers (in silent film, in sound film in Britain, in Hollywood in the forties and since 1952 in color), any one of which would guarantee his position in the history of cinema. Arguably, his most representative films (and many of his best) date from the 1950s, the period in which he consolidated his position, becoming the one director whose name was known to almost every filmgoer in America. In *Rear Window* (1953), *Vertigo* (1958), and *North by Northwest* (1959), he constructed three masterpieces of anxiety—as perceptual, as psychosexual, and as psychopolitical. The last of these, *North by Northwest*, was exceptionally prescient: an emblem for America in the sixties and seventies. Roger O. Thornhill (Cary Grant) is mistaken one afternoon for a mysterious Mr. Kaplan and chased, north by northwest, across most of the nation by foreign agents. Kaplan, it turns out, is the fictional invention of a government agency—Hitchcock suggests strongly that it is the C.I.A.—see Figure 3-61)—which is quite happy to find a real person acting out the invented role. The film ends with a spectacular chase across the foreheads of the fathers of the country at Mount Rushmore. As Grant runs for his life, the national symbols stare ahead, unblinking and unseeing. A pleasant and witty thriller directed with consummate skill, *North by Northwest*, written by Ernest Lehman, took on new dimensions of meaning a decade after it was released, when the antagonism between the people of the U.S. and its government came out into the open.

This period, in which film as art established its precedence worldwide, came to a notable climax. The year 1959, give or take six months, was an annus mirabilis: an extraordinary conjunction of talents existed. In France, Truffaut, Godard, Chabrol, Rohmer, Rivette, and Resnais all made their first films—the New Wave was established. In Italy, Fellini took a new path with *La Dolce Vita*, and Michelangelo Antonioni with *L'Avventura*. In England, the Angry Young Men of the theater were moving into film production. In America, the personal, independent, auteur-oriented cinema was established as the way of the future with one of its first significant productions, John Cassavetes's *Shadows*.

THE NEW WAVE AND THE THIRD WORLD: FILM AS ENTERTAINMENT VERSUS FILM AS COMMUNICATION

The New Wave in France signalled a markedly different attitude toward film. Born after the development of the sound film, these filmmakers had a sense of film culture and film heritage; the movies they made

Figure 4-38. The challenge and the grandeur of the wide open spaces of the Western (see Figure 4-32) had become a paranoid nightmare by the late 1950s. Here advertising-man-in-the-gray-flannel-suit Roger Thornhill (Cary Grant) runs for his life through desolate midwestern cornfields, chased by a faceless assassin flying a crop-duster, an ecological portent! Thornhill's suit and tie are peculiarly but aptly out of place in the heart of the country.

exhibited that sense. Claude Chabrol, François Truffaut, Jean-Luc Godard, Eric Rohmer, and Jacques Rivette had all written for *Cahiers du Cinéma* in the 1950s and been influenced by the theories of André Bazin. Louis Malle and Alain Resnais did not begin as critics, but nevertheless exhibited parallel attitudes. Truffaut's early classics, *The 400 Blows* (1959), *Shoot The Piano Player* (1961), and *Jules and Jim* (1962), were the first great popular successes of the group. In each of those three disparate films he displayed a virtuosity, humanity, and depth of feeling that quickly won audiences worldwide. After that early period he retreated to more personal concerns, beginning a series of films that were studies in genre: *The Soft Skin* (1964), *Fahrenheit 451* (1966), and *Mississippi Mermaid* (1969) attempted, as he put it, "to explode genres by combining them." This was a cinema that came close to insisting that viewers shared with the filmmaker an understanding of past forms and conventions.

Figure 4-39. Charles Aznavour as Charlie Kohler in Truffaut's *Shoot the Piano Player,* an essay in genres. Like most of the New Wave, Truffaut was fascinated by American films. Here he combined elements of Film Noir and the Western and Gangster films with a notably French philosophical attitude. The mixture of cultures was exhilarating.

Godard also began with a number of personal versions of genre films: the Gangster film (*Breathless,* 1960), the Musical (*A Woman Is a Woman,* 1961), two Films Noirs (*Le Petit Soldat,* 1960; *My Life to Live,* 1962)— even a star-filled Hollywood melodrama (*Contempt,* 1963). His first film, *Breathless,* was an extraordinarily iconoclastic study that immediately marked him as one of the most innovative and thoughtful members of the new generation of filmmakers. Ignoring the established conventions of narrative, which even such personal filmmakers as Bergman and Fellini more or less observed, Godard operated on a number of levels simultaneously. *Breathless* was at one and the same time a Gangster story and an essay *about* Gangster films. Michel Poiccard, played by Jean-Paul Belmondo, kills a cop, meets up with an American woman named Patricia (Jean Seberg), hangs out in Paris for a while, evading the police, and is eventually betrayed by Patricia and shot down. Poiccard is fascinated by the image of Humphrey Bogart as he knows it from the old Hollywood films. He invents a pseudonym for himself. He isn't so much a Gangster as he is a young man acting out the role of Gangster that he has learned from American films. Patricia, for her part is compared visually by Godard to a number of artistic images of women, notably those by Picasso. She is not so much a character, the "moll," as she is an esthetic image of woman on the model of the paintings in the film. Even the death of Michel that closes the film is played at one remove, Michel doing his best

Figure 4-40. American and French culture met for the first time in the New Wave on the Champs Élysées in *Breathless*. Michel Poiccard (Jean-Paul Belmondo), a devotee of Bogart and the Gangster mythos, falls for New York *Herald Tribune* newspapergirl Patricia Franchini (Jean Seberg), the archetypal American girl in Paris in the early sixties. Maybe it was the tee-shirt. (*l'Avant-Scène. Frame enlargement.*)

to die a heroic death as he has learned it from the movies, while Patricia persists in her emotional isolation, never quite understanding the potential drama of the plot.

As Godard's career progressed, he turned more and more to the essay form, eventually abandoning fictional narrative altogether. In an extraordinary series of films in the mid- and late sixties, he established an approach to filmmaking that has had worldwide influence. *A Married Woman* (1964), *Alphaville*, *Pierrot le Fou* (both 1965), *Masculine-Feminine*, *2 or 3 Things I Know About Her* (both 1966), *La Chinoise* (1967), and *Weekend* (1968) explored cinema as personal essay conscientiously and with exhilaration. In these films, Godard set up a direct communication with the viewer, using the conventions of genre to his own ends and avoiding the distractions of the well-made, absorbing dramatic experience. In the late sixties, Godard withdrew into an even more personal, political cinema under the shelter of the "Dziga-Vertov Group" for a series of films that lacked all pretense as finished products and were meant clearly as works in progress. The result of this period of

Figure 4-41. Olga Georges-Picot and Claude Rich on the beach in Alain Resnais's *Je t'aime, je t'aime* (1968), one of Resnais's most complex studies in time and memory. This scene, repeated many times throughout the film in varying versions, is the focal point of Rich's science-fiction odyssey through his past. Resnais uses the fiction of a journey by time machine to experiment with the repetition of scenes and the disjuncture of narrative. The result is extraordinary. (*French Film Office.*)

cinematic contemplation was *Tout va bien* (1972). Godard then turned his attention to video, before returning to theatrical screens with *Sauve Qui Peut la vie* in 1980.

Unlike Truffaut and Godard, Claude Chabrol confined his attention to one genre. Strongly influenced by Hitchcock, the subject of a study he wrote with Eric Rohmer, Chabrol redefined the Hitchcockian universe in French terms and contributed, beginning in the late sixties, a fine series of parodic thrillers that effectively satirized bourgeois values as they celebrated them. *Les Biches* (1968), *La Femme Infidèle* (1969), *Le Boucher* (1970), *Just Before Nightfall* (1971), and *Red Wedding* (1972) stand out.

Eric Rohmer brought to cinema familiarity with a literary culture hundreds of years old. His series of "Moral Tales"—including *La Collectionneuse* (1967), *My Night at Maud's* (1968), *Claire's Knee* (1970), and *Chloë in the Afternoon* (1972)—demonstrated that many of the literary pleasures of narrative, setting, and reasoned analysis could be derived in film.

While Rohmer's cinema is influenced by the novel, Jacques Rivette's is influenced by stage drama. The last of the *Cahiers* group to come to prominence, Rivette is obsessed with the structures of dramatic narrative. In *L'Amour fou* (1968), *Out One* (1971), and *Céline et Julie vont en bateau* (1973), he examined the phenomena of duration and psychological intensity that shape our fictional world.

Alain Resnais also brought some of the avant-garde complexity of the New Novel to cinema. Always working in close collaboration with novelists (several of whom—Alain Robbe-Grillet and Marguerite Duras, for example—later turned to filmmaking themselves), Resnais has explored the function of time and memory in narrative with stunning effect in such films as *Last Year at Marienbad* (1962), *La Guerre est finie* (1965), and *Je t'aime, je t'aime* (1968). Louis Malle, like Resnais trained as a technician, has been the most eclectic of the New Wave: *The Lovers* (1968) was a highly romantic drama, *Zazie dans le Metro* (1960) a Screwball Comedy, *India* (1969) an idiosyncratic documentary, and *Lacombe Lucien* (1973) one of the best of the then-current cycle of films about the Nazi occupation of France. Agnès Varda brought a documentary sensibility to the New Wave. Her *Cleo From 5 to 7* (1961) is a central film of the days of the early New Wave. *Le Bonheur* (1965) remains one of the more interesting experiments in color prior to 1968 and an unusual romantic essay. *Daguerreotypes* (1975) is a witty and insightful homage to Varda's neighbors in the rue Daguerre.

The New Wave had been fascinated by Hollywood cinema, but in the 1960s little of major interest was happening in America. Hitchcock continued with *Psycho* (1960), *The Birds* (1963), *Marnie* (1964), and *Topaz* (1969), all interesting films if not as important as his major work in the fifties. Hawks and Ford made minor contributions. Generally, however, the sixties were years of transition in American cinema. Esthetically, the most interesting developments in the U.S. were taking place underground, where a strong avant-garde tradition was bearing fruit in the films of Kenneth Anger, Ron Rice, Bruce Baillie, Robert Breer, Stan VanDerBeek, Stan Brakhage, Gregory Markopoulos, Ed Emshwiller, Jonas and Adolfas Mekas, James and John Whitney, Jordan Belson, and many others. Above-ground, Andy Warhol's Factory produced a number of "Underground" films that were commercially successful.

Hollywood felt the first thrust of the television esthetic as a number of directors trained in television turned to film. Among the most prominent were Arthur Penn (*Bonnie and Clyde*, 1967; *Alice's Restaurant*, 1969; *Night Moves*, 1976). Sidney Lumet (*The Group*, 1966; *Dog Day Afternoon*, 1975; *Just Tell Me What You Want*, 1980), John Frankenheimer (*The Manchurian Candidate*, 1962), Martin Ritt (*Hud*, 1963; *Sounder*, 1972; *The Front*, 1976; *Norma Rae*, 1979), and Franklin Schaffner (*The Best Man*, 1964; *Patton*, 1969).

Perhaps the most far-reaching development in the U.S. was seen not on movie screens but on television. The perfection of lightweight, adaptable 16-mm equipment in the late fifties and early sixties made possible a new style of documentary, so different from the traditional, highly "worked," and often semifictional style as to deserve a new name: Direct Cinema. Filmmakers became reporters, with nearly as much freedom as print journalists, and television was the place to view their work. Robert Drew headed a group, Drew Associates, that produced a number of important films for television. Working with him were Richard Leacock and Donn Pennebaker, Albert and David Maysles. *Primary* (1960) was the first major result of Direct Cinema techniques. Pennebaker's *Don't Look Back* (1966) was a portrait of Bob Dylan. The Maysles brothers adapted the techniques to theatrical release in a series of films they called "nonfiction features," most notably *Salesman* (1969), *Gimme Shelter* (1970, about a Rolling Stones concert), and *Grey Gardens* (1975).

The principal theory of Direct Cinema was that the filmmakers not involve themselves in the action. Gone were the well-phrased narrations of earlier documentaries. The camera was all-seeing: hundreds of hours of film were shot in order to capture a sense of the reality of the subject. Frederick Wiseman, trained as a lawyer, brought this technique to perfection in a well-received series of studies of institutions for Public Television, among them *Titicut Follies* (1967, about a mental institution), *High School* (1968), *Hospital* (1970), *Primate* (1974), and *Meat* (1976).

In France during the sixties, a parallel style of new documentary was developing. Called "cinéma vérité," it differed from Direct Cinema in that it admitted that the presence of the camera made a difference and indeed traded on that fact. *Chronique d'un été* (1960), by anthropologist Jean Rouch and sociologist Edgar Morin, was the first and still classic example of cinéma vérité. Because cinéma vérité and Direct Cinema both measurably expand the boundaries of the permissible in film, they have had a profound effect out of all proportion to the number of films actually identified as being in those styles. The traditional musical, for example, has been superseded by the filmed concert, which in its turn has become a dramatic event. More important, our sense of what is "correct" in narrative has been drastically altered as the profusion of nonfiction films has prepared us for the rhythms of real time. We no longer insist on Hollywood's découpage classique. In the late forties, the French critic Alexandre Astruc (see pp. 331–32) had composed a manifesto in which he called for a cinema built around the "Caméra-Stylo" ("Camera-Pen"), which would be just as flexible and personal as literature. To a large extent, his wish was fulfilled in the fifties, as cinema

Figure 4-42. Frederick Wiseman's *Welfare* (1975). Wiseman's films combine the insistent, relentless shooting techniques of Direct Cinema with a lawyer's sense of social structures in order to investigate the inner workings of significant contemporary institutions. (*Zipporah Films.*)

shifted from assembly-line product to personal statement. What he did not foresee was that the flexibility of the Caméra-Stylo would also lead to a new level of film realism: the new equipment encouraged the filmmaker to get closer to the world around him, film on location rather than in the studio, and shoot actualities rather than actors. Direct Cinema and cinéma vérité were only two evidences of this radical change in attitude. Cinema had become a medium with a wide range of applications.

In England there was a brief burst of activity in the sixties. In 1958, John Osborne, the major figure of the stage renaissance taking place at that time, formed Woodfall Films in collaboration with the director Tony Richardson. Much of the best British cinema of the sixties was closely connected with the vital theater of that period. Tony Richardson began with two adaptations of plays by John Osborne: *Look Back in Anger* (1959) and *The Entertainer* (1960), and continued with an adaptation of Shelagh Delaney's *A Taste of Honey* (1961), before turning to Alan Sillitoe's novel *Loneliness of the Long Distance Runner* (1962).

Richardson won an Oscar for *Tom Jones* (1963), from Henry Fielding's eighteenth-century novel. Karel Reisz directed one of the more interesting "kitchen-sink" films, *Saturday Night and Sunday Morning* (1960, also written by Sillitoe), then turned to *Morgan* (1966), and *Isadora* (1968) before moving to the U.S. where he directed *The Gambler* (1974) and *Who'll Stop the Rain* (1978). John Schlesinger's more interesting films include *A Kind of Loving* (1962), *Billy Liar* (1963), *Darling* (1965, written by Frederic Raphael), and *Sunday, Bloody Sunday* (1971, written by film critic Penelope Gilliatt). In the U.S. he directed *Marathon Man* (1976), then he returned to England for *Yanks* (1979). Lindsay Anderson may be the most ambitious director of this group. His films include *This Sporting Life* (1963, from a novel by David Storey), *If . . .* (1968), *Oh Lucky Man* (1973), and *In Celebration* (1975, from the Storey play).

All the earlier films shared an interest in working-class subjects. As they matured, all four directors turned toward more middle-class concerns. With few exceptions, their later films are either pretentious or uninteresting. Anderson, Reisz, and Richardson were associated with the Free Cinema documentary movement in the fifties. The Documentary tradition continued to have an effect on British cinema in the sixties. Peter Watkins's strident *The War Game* (1966), about the effects of atomic war, was considered too convincing to be broadcast on the BBC. Kevin Brownlow and Andrew Mollo's *It Happened Here* (1963) documented an equally fictitious historical event: the German occupation of Britain during the Second World War.

More interesting in England during the sixties was the work of several American exiles. Joseph Losey, blacklisted in Hollywood, directed a number of mediocre films, but the ones written by Harold Pinter—*The Servant* (1963), *Accident* (1967), and *The Go-Between* (1971)— manage to capture Pinter's droll, warped view of bourgeois society.

Stanley Kubrick had made several interesting minor films in the U.S. before he settled in England. *Dr. Strangelove* (1963) remains a superb satire of the cold-war mentality. It's significance increases with each passing year. *2001: A Space Odyssey* (1968) is a masterful blending of cinematography with scientific and religious theory. It set the style for a decade of popular and remunerative science fiction. *A Clockwork Orange* (1971), a striking celebration of violence, remains perhaps the most prescient film about the 1970s yet made. *Barry Lyndon* (1975) was not only a superbly accurate evocation of time and place (eighteenth-century Europe), but also adventurous in narrative style: a very expensive commercial proposition, it nevertheless eschews all the Hollywood rules of pace. *The Shining* (1980) is Kubrick's attempt to succeed at a highly profitable, if ethically suspect, genre.

Figure 4-43. Julie Christie, George C. Scott in Richard Lester's *Petulia* (1967). Not highly popular when it was released, *Petulia* is now generally regarded as one of the landmark films about America in the sixties. Returning from fifteen years in Europe, Lester was able to see us as we could not see ourselves, and the jaundiced vision of the hip society he projected held more truth than the counterculture myths of the time.

Richard Lester began his career directing television in Philadelphia, moved to London in the mid-fifties, and became involved with Peter Sellers and the Goon Show people. He first gained attention as a director with the Beatles films (*A Hard Day's Night*, 1964; *Help!*, 1965) and was typecast by most critics thereafter for his supposedly frenetic "TV" editing style. Nevertheless, his *A Funny Thing Happened on the Way to the Forum* (1965) remains one of the best film adaptations of stage musicals; *Petulia* (1967), shot in San Francisco, was as prescient as it was sharply ironic—one of the two or three best American films of the period; while *How I Won the War* (1967) and *The Bed-Sitting Room* (1968) are among the few English-language films to employ Brechtian techniques successfully. These latter two films were commercially unsuccessful. Lester was inactive for more than five years, finally returning to the cinema with less ambitious, commercially safer projects such as *The Three Musketeers* (1973), *Juggernaut* (1974), *Robin and Marian* (1978), and *Cuba* (1979).

When sources of funding dried up in the late sixties, British filmmakers had two choices: to leave the country, or to turn to television. Directors like John Boorman and Peter Yates came to the U.S., where

Figure 4-44. Neville Smith, Ann Zelda, and Charles Gormley in Maurice Hatton's witty, sardonic investigation of the contemporary British film scene, *Long Shot* (1979).

they established themselves as effective craftsmen. Ken Loach (*Poor Cow*, 1967; *Kes*, 1969; *Family Life*, 1972) had always considered television as important as cinema. His films demonstrate sophisticated refinements of realist techniques, as do his television efforts (notably the series *Days of Hope*, 1976).

Maurice Hatton, like Loach, has chosen to stick close to his English roots. His first feature, *Praise Marx and Pass the Ammunition* (1970), is one of the rare films that combine politics with humor successfully. It is only now beginning to attract the audience it deserves outside of Britain. Hatton's more recent *Long Shot* (1979) applies the same mordant wit to the moribund British film industry. A film about the difficulties of remaining a filmmaker in Britain in the late 1970s, *Long Shot* was made entirely independently: an extraordinary economic, as well as artistic, achievement.

Ken Russell and Nicolas Roeg are among the few British filmmakers to survive the withdrawal of American capital in the late sixties. Russell, who first gained attention with a series of unusual biographies of musicians done for the BBC, continued in feature films to specialize in cinematic biography, although his approach became progressively more eccentric (*The Music Lovers*, 1970; *Mahler*, 1974). His lurid, pop art, comic strip style was probably shown to best advantage in *Tommy*

(1975). Roeg, a former cinematographer, has produced several films that are stunningly photographed although less interesting in other respects (*Walkabout*, 1971; *Don't Look Now*, 1973; *The Man Who Fell to Earth*; 1976).

During the late 1970s, a new generation of British filmmakers—most of them trained in television commercials—found commercial success in the international market. After *Bugsy Malone* (1976), an unusual musical about children for children, but for adults also, Alan Parker filmed *Midnight Express* (1978), far more lucrative, and as exploitative as his earlier film had been charming. Similarly, Ridley Scott tested the waters with the romantic *The Duellists* (1977), then delivered the highly manipulative (and profitable) *Alien* (1979). Like nearly all financially successful British films of the last ten years, these four examples depended on American stars, American money, and American audiences. Hybrids, they are signs of things to come.

In Italy, Fellini and Antonioni, two influential masters, held sway throughout the sixties. Fellini completed several major films, including 8½ (1962), *Juliet of the Spirits* (1965), and *Fellini-Satyricon* (1969), before turning his attention to television, where he produced a series of semiautobiographical essays that eventually culminated in the theatrical films *Roma* (1972) and *Amarcord* (1973). Antonioni came into his own with *L'Avventura* (1960), the first film of a trilogy that included *La Notte* (1961) and *L'Eclisse* (1962), which redefined basic concepts of film narrative. *Red Desert* (1964) and *Blow-up* (1966) continued his experiments with narration and perception in an existential setting. *The Passenger* (1975) is the epitome of Antonioni's very special cinema, a film redolent of existential *angst*, constructed in long, periodic, hypnotic rhythms.

Luchino Visconti's latter films (*The Damned*, 1970; *Death in Venice*, 1971; *Conversation Piece*, 1975) were as languorously decadent as his earlier Neorealistic films had been alert and pointed. "The Job" (from *Boccaccio 70*, 1962; see Figure 2-35) and *The Leopard* (1963) were more successful if less remarkable. Pietro Germi, who had been one of the leading directors of the Neorealist movement (*In the Name of the Law*, 1949), but who had never had much success outside of Italy, established an international comic style for the sixties with two assured comedies of manners. *Divorce Italian Style* (1961) and *Seduced and Abandoned* (1963).

Pier Paolo Pasolini, poet and theorist, turned to film in the sixties and completed *Accattone* (1961), *The Gospel According to St. Matthew* (1964), *The Hawks and the Sparrows* (1966), and a number of other symbolic exercises before his death in 1976. Francesco Rosi, most underrated of contemporary Italian directors, directed a number of intri-

Figure 4-45. Vanessa Redgrave, David Hemmings. A typical, highly designed shot from Antonioni's *Blow-Up* (1966). The plot of the film concerned the mystery of images. (MOMA/FSA.)

guing political films, including *Salvatore Giuliano* (1962), *Le Mani Sulla Citta* (1963), *The Mattei Affair* (1972), *Lucky Luciano* (1973), and *Christ Stopped at Eboli* (1979).

Of the younger Italian filmmakers, Bernardo Bertolucci was the first to attract attention with *Before the Revolution* (1964), *The Conformist* (1970), and *Last Tango in Paris* (1972). Bertolucci quickly fell into a Visconti-like fascination with the shapes and surfaces of bourgeois decadence, which he ostensibly criticized. *Last Tango in Paris* achieved a certain international reputation for its clever combination of star (Marlon Brando) and frank sex. In his five-hour epic *1900* (1976) Bertolucci seemed to return to his earlier political concerns, while actively continuing the bourgeois trend of *Last Tango*. This was confirmed by *Luna* (1979). Marco Bellocchio, at least as interesting as Bertolucci, received far less international attention with his ideologically stronger films— *Fists in the Pocket* (1965), *China Is Near* (1967), *In the Name of the Father* (1971), and *Slap the Monster on Page One* (1973). In the seventies, Lina Wertmüller took center stage for a brief moment with a series of sardonic sex comedies flavored with a suspicion of politics, including *Love and Anarchy* (1972), *The Seduction of Mimi* (1973), *Swept Away* (1974), and *Seven Beauties* (1975).

While directorial stars such as these rose with regularity on the Ital-

Figure 4-46. Ermanno Olmi's *The Tree of the Wooden Clogs*, filmed with a kind of anthropological perspective, set a style for such investigations in the eighties.

ian horizon, there were a number of less spectacular directors whose work never received its international due. Most of their films have strong political implications; the political melodrama pioneered by Rosi and Costa-Gavras has been most successful in Italy. Some of the directors in this neglected group are: Mario Monicelli (*The Organizer*, 1963), Giuliano Montaldo (*Sacco and Vanzetti*, 1971), Elio Petri (*Investigation of a Citizen Above Suspicion*, 1970; *The Working Class Goes to Heaven*, 1971), Gillo Pontecorvo (*The Battle of Algiers*, 1965; *Burn*, 1968), Gianni Amico (*Tropici*, 1968; *Ritorno*, 1973), Nelo Risi (*Diary of a Schizophrenic Girl*, 1969), Marco Leto (*Black Holiday*, 1974), and Ermanno Olmi (*Il Posto*, 1961; *Un Certo Giorno*, 1969; *Durante l'Estate*, 1971). Olmi's *The Tree of the Wooden Clogs* (1978), a deeply felt, mesmeric three-hour evocation of peasant life at the turn of the century, is one of the more outstanding films from Italy during the last few years. Like *1900* and the Taviani brothers' *Padre, Padrone* (1976), *The Tree of the Wooden Clogs* is representative of a newly rediscovered Italian fascination with peasant habits and rhythms. Fellini's *Amarcord* and Rosi's *Christ Stopped at Eboli* should also be included in this interesting genre.

Like Wertmüller before him, Franco Brusati gained some surprising international audiences with deceptively intellectual bourgeois dramas

Figure 4-47. Liv Ullmann, Max von Sydow, and money in Jan Troell's *The New Land* (released 1973).

in the late seventies, including *Bread and Chocolate* (1976) and *To Forget Venice* (1978).

In addition, it should be noted that Italian television is second only to British television in quality, and many filmmakers besides Roberto Rossellini have done interesting work for the state network, RAI. Many of the recent films cited above were originally RAI productions.

In Sweden, Ingmar Bergman completed a regularly spaced string of films, working with what amounted to a repertory group of actors and technicians. From this period dates his finest cinema: *Through a Glass Darkly, Winter Light,* and *The Silence* form the trilogy in which Bergman exorcized God from his consciousness (1961–63). *Persona* (1966) remains possibly his most imaginative and daring film. The series of films with Liv Ullmann and Max von Sydow (*Hour of the Wolf,* 1967; *Shame,* 1968; *The Passion of Anna,* 1969) forms one of the most striking accomplishments in the cinema of the sixties. In the seventies, Bergman withdrew to firmer ground. His television series *Scenes From a Marriage* (1973), however, compares with his best work. In 1976, after a Kafkaesque encounter with tax authorities, he left Sweden to make films elsewhere for the first time.

Younger Swedish directors found an international audience in the sixties, as well. Jörn Donner (*To Love*, 1964), Bo Widerberg (*Elvira Madigan*, 1967), Vilgot Sjöman (*I Am Curious-Yellow*, 1967), and most notably, Jan Troell, whose trilogy of emigration and resettlement—*The Emigrants*, *The New Land* (both 1970), and *Zandy's Bride* (1974)—brought a new freshness of vision and historical perspective to a classic theme.

In Eastern Europe, the state film schools nurtured a new wave of talent in the sixties: in Poland, Roman Polanski (*Knife in the Water*, 1962), who left to become an international director of facile, often empty, vaguely supernatural thrillers; Jerzy Skolimowski (*Walkover*, 1965; *Barrier*, 1966; and in London, *Deep End*, 1970); and Krzysztof Zanussi, whose quiet, searching studies of scientists and engineers (*Behind the Wall*, 1971; *Illumination*, 1973) are unique in world cinema. In Hungary, Miklós Jancsó became one of the foremost Structural filmmakers, intent on the relationship between camera and subject rather than the subject itself (*The Red and the White*, 1967; *Winter Wind*, 1969; *Electreia*, 1974). Marta Meszarós gained an international festival following with a number of precisely realized essays, mainly on the roles of women, including *Nine Months* (1976), *Women* (1977), and *The Heritage* (1980).

Perhaps the most significant development in Eastern Europe was the Czech Renaissance which flowered unexpectedly for a few brief years in the middle sixties. Miloš Forman (*Loves of a Blonde*, 1965; *The Fireman's Ball*, 1967), Ivan Passer (*Intimate Lighting*, 1966), Jiří Menzel (*Closely Watched Trains*, 1966), and Věra Chytilová (*Daisies*, 1969) evolved a vivid humanist realism, invested with humor and respect for their subjects, which was cut horribly short by the Soviet invasion of the country in 1968 and the subsequent return to Stalinism. Forman and Passer moved to the United States, where they have done interesting work, but never on the level of their earliest films. Forman's *Hair* (1979) is, however, a notable recent musical.

As for the Soviet Union, an occasional film of interest escapes, but for the most part the strict state control of the art instituted during the earliest days of the Stalinist period has stifled completely what was once one of the world's leading political cinemas. Sergei Paradjanov, director of *Shadows of Our Forgotten Ancestors* (1964) and *Sayat Nova* (1969), two of the more interesting Soviet films of the sixties, was imprisoned and sent to a labor camp, ostensibly for homosexuality, in January

1974. Dušan Makavejev, the best-known Yugoslav filmmaker of the 1960s (*Love Affair, or the Case of the Missing Switchboard Operator*, 1967) ran into censorship problems as well because he mixed politics with sex in an intriguing but officially unacceptable way. *WR: Mysteries of the Organism* (1971) was banned in Yugoslavia.

Clearly the most far-reaching development in world cinema during the last fifteen years has been its extension beyond the boundaries of the U.S., Japan, and Europe into the developing countries collectively known as the "Third World." Often rough and angry, Third World cinema is also usually vital and relevant. Like the nonfiction filmmakers of the West, Third World cinéastes generally see film as a powerful medium of communication, a medium they employ with passion.

The most productive Third World movement has been the Brazilian Cinema Novo, which got underway in the early sixties and, although slowed by the right-wing millitary junta that took power in 1964, has nevertheless been able to survive, partly because of the symbolic styliza-tion most of the films employ. Glauber Rocha (*Barravento*, 1961; *Antonio das Mortes*, 1969) has been the most visible of the group. Other important directors are: Ruy Guerra (*Os Fuzis*, 1964), Nelson Pereira dos Santos (*How Tasty Was My Little Frenchman*, 1971), Joaquim Pedro de Andrade (*Macunaima*, 1969), Carlos Diégues (*Os Herdeiros*, 1971), all of whom share to some degree Rocha's commitment to political allegory.

Mexico, like Brazil, produces more than fifty features per year. For many years Mexican cinema was dominated by the imposing figure of Luis Buñuel. Buñuel, who had made two important surrealist films with Salvador Dali in Paris in the late twenties (*Un Chien Andalou*, 1928; *L'Âge d'or*, 1930), spent the next twenty years on the fringe of the film industry before finding a home in Mexico in the late forties. He di-rected a number of essentially commercial films during the next ten years. It was not until he returned to his native Spain in 1961 to film his first feature there, *Viridiana*, that he finally achieved the worldwide attention that was his due. Although Buñuel was born in 1900, the center of his career lies in the sixties. Making films mainly in France, he produced a masterful series of surrealist allegories (*Diary of a Chambermaid*, 1964; *Belle de Jour*, 1967; *The Milky Way*, 1969, *Tristana*, 1970; *The Discreet Charm of the Bourgeoisie*, 1972; *The Fantôme of Liberty*, 1974) that assured his position in the international pantheon of the art film. Buñuel's more personal Mexican films are: *Nazarín* (1958), *The Exterminating Angel* (1962), and *Simon of the Desert* (1965), antireli-gious allegories all. Recently, the young Mexican director Arturo Rip-

Figure 4-48. A series of surrealistic blackout sketches, Buñuel's *The Discreet Charm of the Bourgeoisie* (1972) is droll, good-natured satire. Here, a dinner party ends in discreet embarrassment as the guests are machine-gunned.

stein (*Castle of Purity,* 1974; *Foxtrot,* 1976) has impressed with a style like Buñuel's. Paul Leduc (*John Reed: Insurgent Mexico,* 1972) has also done some interesting work.

The destruction of the young phenomenon of Chilean film by the Fascist military putsch of 1973 in that country is one of the most tragic developments in recent film history. Four films of special interest that were produced during Chile's brief experience with democratic socialism are available in the West: *Valparaiso, Mi amor* (1970) and *Praying Is Not Enough* (1972), directed by Aldo Francia, and *The Jackal of Nahueltoro* (1969) and *The Promised Land* (1973), directed by Miguel Littin. Committed, passionate, direct, expressive, and lyrical, Chilean cinema might have been one of the more rewarding had it survived. Of special interest is the three-part documentary *The Battle of Chile* produced outside the country after the coup, mainly from footage shot before.

The situation has been brighter in Cuba. Since the revolution, the Cuban Institute of Cinematic Art and Industry (ICAIC) has nurtured an active and interesting cinema. Several admired films available outside Cuba include: *Memories of Underdevelopment* (Tomás Gutiérrez

Alea, 1968), a new wave-like exploration of the psychological condition of Cuban intellectuals at the time of the revolution; *Lucia* (Humberto Solas, 1969), a widely praised three-part study of Cuban womanhood; and *First Charge of the Machete* (Manuel Octavio Gomez, 1969), a highly stylized depiction of the uprising of 1868.

Other Latin American countries have contributed to the repertory of Third World classics on a more limited scale. Notable are *Blood of the Condor* (Bolivia, Jorge Sanjines, 1969) and *The Hour of the Furnaces* (Argentina, Fernando Solanas and Octavio Getino, 1968).

English-language Canadian cinema has always suffered from the proximity of the United States. It wasn't until 1974 that a native English-language Canadian feature (Ted Kotcheff's *The Apprenticeship of Duddy Kravitz*) was able to gross enough in Canadian theaters to pay its own way. French-language cinema, however, enjoyed some success in the sixties and early seventies. Claude Jutra's *À Tout Prendre* (1963) was a landmark film, as was his *Mon Oncle Antoine* (1971), one of the first Québecois films to enjoy some popularity outside Canada. Jean-Pierre Lefebvre has earned a reputation as an interesting stylist with such films as *Q-bec My Love* (1970) and *Les Maudits Sauvages* (1971). André Forcier's *Bar Salon* (1974) brought a sense of humor to the typical depressive Canadian setting; Jacques Leduc's *Ordinary Tenderness* (1974) was an interesting experiment in materialist cinema; Gilles Groulx's *Le Chat Dans Le Sac* (1964) was a landmark of Quebec's political awakening; and Michel Brault's *Les Ordres* (1975) was one of the more relevant political films of recent years.

A few English-language Canadian films are notable as well, mainly Irvin Kershner's *The Luck of Ginger Coffey* (1964); Paul Almond's *Act of the Heart* (1970); Don Owen's *Nobody Waved Goodbye* (1964); Allan King's *Warrendale* (1967) and *A Married Couple* (1969), two influential documentaries; and Donald Shebib's *Goin' Down the Road* (1970). The avant-garde filmmaker Michael Snow, who has often worked in the U.S., is probably the best known Canadian filmmaker. His most important films are *Wavelength* (1967), ↔ (1969), and *La Région Centrale* (1970)—this last shot in Canada. (See Figures 3-57, 3-58.)

The business (although not necessarily the art) of Canadian film experienced explosive growth during 1978 and 1979 when tax laws made it profitable to invest in Canadian productions. By selling public subscriptions in the stock of the film (much as if the movie were a new manufacturing venture), Canadian producers pioneered a form of financing which will become increasingly popular throughout the Western world in the next few years. Most of the films produced under this system were unexceptionable internationalist grist, but a few, like Dar-

Figure 4-49. Donald Sutherland collects colorful Canadian banknotes during the heist in *A Man, a Woman, and a Bank,* (1979) a typical Canadian film of the late seventies made in the American style with U.S. participation and directed to the U.S. market.

ryl Duke's *Silent Partner* (1979) attracted critical attention as well, and the tax breaks that were granted to investors who lost money on Canadian productions at least resulted in a large number of Canadian actors and technicians being able to work at home.

Perhaps the most surprising development during the late 1970s was the international success of the new Australian cinema. Filmmakers had been working on that continent for many years, but their productions seldom if ever made the ocean crossing (even if, occasionally, Americans and Europeans journeyed to Australia to exploit its natural wonders). An active government program instituted in the mid-seventies, however, soon resulted in a number of interesting Australian talents coming to international attention at festivals, then in commercial distribution. The most financially successful of the new group has been Peter Weir, whose apocalyptic fantasies, *The Last Wave* (1978) and *Picnic at Hanging Rock* (1977), provided fashionable metaphors for the peculiar, stereotyped psychology that non-Australian audiences like to think characterizes the edge of the world. Of more lasting interest are Phillip Noyce's *Newsfront* (1977), an unusual film, part documentary, part fiction, that describes the lives of newsreel cameramen during the forties and fifties, and Gill Armstrong's *My Brilliant Career,* based on an

Figure 4-50. Judy Davis in Gill Armstrong's *My Brilliant Career*, one of the new wave of Australian films to garner worldwide attention.

autobiographical novel about a young woman's fantasies of civilized success while growing up in the wild outback at the turn of the century. Both *Newsfront* and *My Brilliant Career* suggest that Australian cinema might yet develop a style that is really new to world screens.

The African cinema has so far produced one filmmaker of international standing, Ousmane Sembène, whose films are regularly seen in Europe and the U.S. Among the most important are: *Black Girl* (1965), *Mandabi* (1970), and *Xala* (1974). Senegalese, Sembène is a novelist as well as filmmaker. Sarah Maldoror's *Sambizanga* (Angola, 1972) and Med Hondo's *Soleil-O* (Mauritania, 1972) are two other interesting African films. Film industries of considerable size exist in Algeria and Egypt, and Nigeria and Tunisia are actively involved in production. *Countdown at Kusini* (1976), directed by Ossie Davis, was the first Black American-Nigerian coproduction. Black cinema in the U.S. can also be considered an element of Third World cinema, but since it has strong connections as well with U.S. commercial cinema, we shall discuss it later in that context.

Japanese cinema has continued to expand during the sixties and seventies. Kurosawa completed *High and Low* in 1963, *Red Beard* in 1965, *Dodeskaden* in 1970, and *Dersu Uzala* in 1975. Among the more inter-

Figure 4-51. Ousmane Sembène's *Xala* (1974), from the director's own novel, satirizes and criticizes the growth of a pompous, venal governmental bourgeoisie in emerging African nations. It created a furor when it was released in Senegal. (*New Yorker Films.*)

esting younger directors of the sixties and seventies is Hiroshi Teshiga-hara, whose *Woman in the Dunes* (1964) quickly became a classic of allegorical cinema and whose *Summer Soldiers* (1971) was a unique cross-cultural attempt at treating the subject of American deserters from Vietnam residing in Japan. Nagisa Oshima may be the first Japanese filmmaker to have made a complete break with the past. He is certainly one of the most important of the new generation. His films include *Diary of a Shinjuku Burglar* (1968), *Boy* (1969), and *The Ceremony* (1971). His international fame, however, is based on his 1977 *succès de scandale*, the sexually exploitative *In the Realm of the Senses*. A good example of the new independent political cinema of Japan is Shinsuke Ogawa's *Peasants of the Second Fortress* (1971).

Asian cinema has blossomed elsewhere in the sixties and seventies. Filipino blood epics regularly make money in the U.S. and Europe. Occasional Chinese films reach the West. Most noticeable has been the Hong Kong cinema, mainly devoted to the martial arts genre, an enor-mously successful type of film worldwide during the late sixties and seventies. King Hu (*Dragon Gate Inn*, 1966; *A Touch of Zen*, 1969, 1975; *The Fate of Lee Khan*, 1970) is one of the few directors who has managed to make a personal mark.

The most important effect of the New Wave was not so much esthetic as it was practical. Godard, Truffaut, Chabrol, and the others had demonstrated that it was possible to make films inexpensively, whether directed toward a commercial audience or toward a minority audience. (Indeed, Godard continued to finance his films in the late sixties and early seventies without any commercial distribution to speak of. He reportedly made *Numéro 2* for the same amount of money as his first film, *Breathless.*) The spread of cinema into countries that previously could never have afforded the capital expense is one salient result of the new economy of film. Another, perhaps even more telling, is the vigorous eclecticism that has sprung up in French cinema since the New Wave.

The list of interesting French directors who have made their first films during the last decade is numerous and encouraging. There is space here to name only a few of those who at present seem to have the greatest potential. Nothing like the fascination with genres and Hollywood cinema that bound together the New Wave identifies this later amorphous group. But most French film since 1968 shows the effects, one way or another, of the student-worker uprising of that year. In general, French film has discovered a political sense that it had always lacked and, in the process, it has gained a new vitality. In a sense, it has undergone the same change of viewpoint as British theater and film did in the 1950s, widening its interests beyond the narrow bounds of the *haute bourgeoisie.*

Marcel Ophuls's extraordinary historical document, the 4½-hour *The Sorrow and The Pity* (1971), is a landmark of this new awareness. Documenting with panache and intelligence the true nature of French collaboration with their Nazi occupiers during World War II, it had a deep effect on French sensibilities. One of the results was a whole cycle of Occupation films during the early seventies, most interesting of which (together with Malle's *Lacombe Lucien*) was Michel Mitrani's *Les Guichets du Louvre* (1974). Ophuls's *Memory of Justice* (1976), an investigation into the Nuremberg trials which followed World War II, was an equally subtle film essay. On a more fundamental level, the events of May and June 1968 led to direct political organization in film, notably in the work of the Groupe Medvedkine collective and the SLON collective surrounding filmmaker Chris Marker.

Jean Eustache's *The Mother and the Whore* (1973) was as vital an experience fictionally as Ophuls's film had been historically. Eustache was able, during 3½ hours of intense cinema, to capture, examine, and parody not only many of the conventions of the now old New Wave, but also that particular atmosphere that surrounds and sometimes suffocates French intellectuals. *The Mother and the Whore* was, esthetically,

Figure 4-52. "Neo-New Wave": Jean Eustache's *The Mother and the Whore* (1973): two actors whose careers began in the early days of the New Wave, Bernadette Lafont and Jean-Pierre Léaud, in a rigorous, demanding, witty psychodrama. (*New Yorker Films.*)

the last of the New Wave films. Maurice Pialat, middle-aged when he made his first film, *L'Enfance nue* (Me, 1968), has quietly become one of the most innovative directors working in commercial cinema. *La Gueule ouverte* (1975) and *Nous ne vieillirons pas ensemble* (1972) are two absorbing studies of the way we live now. Nelly Kaplan's films, including *A Very Curious Girl* (1969), are also of interest in this respect.

Jean-Louis Bertucelli has directed several of the most interesting "new realist" films. *Ramparts of Clay* (1970), *Paulina 1880* (1972), and *Mistaken Love Story* (1974) dealt with a variety of political situations (respectively Algeria at the point of independence, nineteenth-century feminist concerns, and contemporary sexual politics) with unusual intelligence. Marin Karmitz formed a collective of more than one hundred workers and filmmakers to shoot *Coup pour coup* (1972) about the occupation of their factory by a group of workers—a semidocumentary surprisingly close to Godard's *Tout va bien* in plot and theme. Pascal Aubier, in *Valparaiso, Valparaiso* (1971) and *Le Chant du départ* (1975), extended allegorical techniques to political subjects.

A number of other directors have turned to a mode of filmmaking

Figure 4-53. The Jerry Lewis-style open set for Godard's *Tout va bien* (1972) becomes a concrete representation of the structure of a factory organization. The poster declares: "It's right to lock up the bosses, UNLIMITED STRIKE." *Tout va bien* was the practical result of Godard's five-year period of experimentation with film form with his "Dziga-Vertov Group." (*New Yorker Films. Frame enlargement.*)

based on politics. Among these are Jean-Daniel Simon (*Il Pleut toujours ou c'est mouillé*, 1974), Philippe Condroyer (*La Coupe à dix francs*, 1974), Jacques Doillon (*Les Doigts dans la tête*, 1974), and Edouard Luntz (*Loulou*, 1975).

At the same time, several young filmmakers have returned to more traditional, humanistic portraits. Pascal Thomas (*Les Zozos*, 1973; *Don't Cry With Your Mouth Full*, 1974) and Claudine Guilmain (*Véronique, ou l'été de mes treize ans*, 1975) were among the most promising. While the films of these and many other young directors have received some criticial attention, it is sobering to remember that the French and international box office has been dominated by a different sort of cinema—the type of bourgeois romance that French filmmakers have always done very well, if to no particular end. Jean-Charles Tacchella's *Cousin, cousine* (1975) when it was released in the U.S. two years later broke the box-office record of *A Man and a Woman* that had stood for more than ten years. This extraordinary performance was exceeded in 1979 by Edouard Molinaro's *La Cage aux Folles*, an amusing but small story about a homosexual ménage.

Bertrand Tavernier also garnered some international success with a

Figure 4-54. The visual block of the chorus in Jean-Marie Straub and Danièle Huillet's film of Schönberg's opera, *Moses and Aaron* (1975): structuralist cinema. (*New Yorker Films.*)

quick series of more-or-less well-mounted melodramas in the late seventies. Tavernier's first successful export was released in 1975 as *The Clockmaker*. The screenwriters for that film were two men named Jean Aurenche and Pierre Bost—precisely the two whom, twenty years earlier, François Truffaut had castigated in his famous essay on the cinéma du papa. The irony was lost on the new generation of filmgoers who responded just as nicely to this current wave of well-made *petits drames* as their parents had to similar fare in the fifties. Esthetically, the most important French innovator has been Jean-Marie Straub who, with his wife and collaborator Danièle Huillet, has developed a type of materialist cinema that has had a strong effect on the avant garde. Although French by birth, Straub has worked in the German language and mainly with German money. *The Chronicle of Anna Magdalena Bach* (1967), *Othon* (1970), *History Lessons* (1972), and *Moses and Aaron* (1975), his version of Schönberg's opera, are austere experiments in narrative modes and essays in esthetic theory that, although they have never been appreciated by general audiences, nevertheless served as an inspiration to the filmmakers of Das Neue Kino, the new German cinema that came into being in the late sixties and gained quite a reputation through film festivals in the seventies.

Alexander Kluge was the first of this informal group to turn to film. *Yesterday Girl* (1966), *Artists Under the Big Top: Perplexed* (1968), and more recently *Part-time Work of a Domestic Slave* (1974) and *Strongman Ferdinand* (1975) exhibited a political drive couched in cold wit. Volker Schlöndorff's cinema is also broadly political in nature, but Schlöndorff exhibits both a greater cinematic facility and less simplistic logic. *Young Törless* (1966) was a version of the Robert Musil psychological novel; *The Sudden Wealth of the Poor People of Kombach* (1971), a Brechtian medieval morality tale. Working with his wife, Margarethe von Trotta, Schlöndorff next made *Strohfeuer* (*A Free Woman*, 1972), a Liberationist film that enjoyed some commercial success. Their next film, *The Lost Honor of Katharina Blum* (1975, from the novel by Heinrich Böll), was a major document of contemporary German politics and a distinct popular success because it confronted the right-wing, jingoist press lord Axel Springer directly. In 1979, Schlöndorff completed his film version of *The Tin Drum*, Günter Grass's classic postwar novel. Schlöndorff's elegant and inspired version of that parabolic masterpiece met with due

Figure 4-55. Angela Winkler in Schlöndorff's and von Trotta's *The Lost Honor of Katharina Blum* (1975): the political facet of new German cinema.

international acclaim, including the first U.S. Academy Award ever granted a German film. In a dramatic acceptance speech, Schlöndorff accepted the Oscar not only for himself and for the young generation of German filmmakers, but also, as he put it movingly, "for Fritz Lang, Billy Wilder, Lubitsch, Murnau, Pabst—you know them all! You welcomed them!"

Other films of the young German cinema are less specifically political. Rainer Werner Fassbinder is probably the best known practitioner of Das Neue Kino. Combining careers in the theater, television, and cinema, he has completed more than thirty films in fifteen years. His earlier, more political films—*Why Did Herr R. Run Amok?* (1969), *The Merchant of Four Seasons* (1971), for example—may be of greater interest than *The Bitter Tears of Petra von Kant* (1972), *Fears Eats the Soul* (1973), *Fox* (1974)—which, although more popular, show more of the camp influence of Douglas Sirk and are generally more involuted. After numerous television films, Fassbinder made his first English-language film in 1978: *Despair,* from a screenplay by Tom Stoppard of the novel by Vladimir Nabokov. Despite those impressive literary antecedents it

Figure 4-56. R.W. Fassbinder's *The Marriage of Maria Braun* (1979) experimented with narrative forms in a way that still left the plot of the film accessible to general audiences. Hanna Schygulla and Elisabeth Trissenaar.

did not establish him as an international director. In 1979, *The Marriage of Maria Braun* (in German once again) enjoyed considerable success and appealed to more general audiences. Fassbinder is nothing if not prolific.

Werner Herzog is the least classifiable of the group. *Even Dwarfs Started Small* (1970) and *Fata Morgana* (1971) are ineffable experiments, while *Land of Silence and Darkness* (1971) and *Every Man for Himself and God Against All* (*Kaspar Hauser*, 1974) are much more lucid, the former a study of the world of the deaf-mute, the latter Herzog's version of the wolf child/noble savage legend. Herzog concentrates on human beings in extreme situations, almost as if he were an experimental anthropologist. *Aguirre, the Wrath of God* (1972) studies an obsessive Spanish explorer in the New World on a trip up an increasingly alien river. Many critics compared it favorably to its not dissimilar, but far more expensive successor, *Apocalypse Now,* as a study of the psyche under pressure. *Heart of Glass* (1977) is a hermetic, abstract essay on the mysteries of medieval glass-workers, while *Stroszek* (1977) is a much more accessible portrait of a simple-minded European confronting American culture.

The most underrated of the group of new German directors is probably Wim Wenders. Direct rather than cloying (as Kluge, Herzog, and especially Fassbinder sometimes seem to be), Wenders has made a number of low-key yet intense films in which human concerns rather than style hold center stage. Among these are *The Goalie's Anxiety at the Penalty Kick* (1971) like *Wrong Movement,* from a script by playwright Peter Handke), *Alice in the Cities* (1974), and *Kings of the Road* (1975). Wenders's most successful film to date has been *The American Friend* (1977), an international coproduction that deftly summarizes his themes of alienation and American-European cultural intercourse. Shortly after completing this remarkable film, Wenders was "discovered" by Francis Ford Coppola, who signed him to direct *Hammett*—and also named a San Francisco restaurant after "Wim."

Coppola was also instrumental in gaining some critical and popular attention for Hans-Jürgen Syberberg, certainly the most abstruse of new German filmmakers. In 1979, Syberberg's magnum opus, *Our Hitler: A Film from Germany,* seven hours in length, more or less, was screened to eager audiences in San Francisco and New York. Entirely lacking in discipline and only at times exhibiting the shadow of intelligence, *Our Hitler* amounts to very little beyond its avant-garde hype.

The renaissance of Swiss cinema was one of the more attractive developments of the seventies. The films of Alain Tanner (*Charles, Mort ou vif,* 1969; *La Salamandre,* 1971; *Retour d'Afrique,* 1973; *The*

Figure 4-57. Alain Tanner's *Jonah Who Will Be 25 in the Year 2000* remains one of the most significant films of the seventies, a warm, heartfelt investigation of the way we live now—and the way we might.

Middle of the World, 1974) display a unique mixture of traditional dramatic narrative and sophisticated mise en scène. *Jonah, Who Will Be 25 in the Year 2000* (1976), a wry, humane, and very wise political allegory, is a most accomplished film and one of the most important social documents of the 1970s, considering its perceptive comments on the cultural and political fallout of the events of 1968. Claude Goretta's films (*L'Invitation,* 1972; *Pas si méchant que ça,* 1975) are shaggy dog stories of particular charm. Michel Soutter manages to combine a bit of Goretta's charm with Tanner's politics in *James ou pas* (1970), *Les Arpenteurs* (1972), and *L'Escapade* (1973). The films of all three directors are curiously and pleasantly reminiscent of the spirit of the early New Wave.

American cinema has also seen an explosion of talent in the late sixties and early seventies, but unlike French and German new cinema it is most often couched in highly commercial terms. The concept of genre is still strong. Gangsters and Musicals nowadays are hard to find, but they have been replaced by a whole series of new genres, including the

Figure 4-58. New Black cinema: Bill Gunn and Duane Jones in Gunn's remarkable *Ganja and Hess* (1973), part vampire movie, part anthropological analysis of the myth. (MOMA/FSA.)

Chase film, the Road film, the Nostalgia film, the Hollywood film (about the golden days of yesteryear), the Martial Arts film (usually imported—*Variety* calls this genre "Chop Socky"), the respectable Porn film ("sexploitation"), and—most profitable of all in the mid-seventies—The Disaster film. Significantly, none of these contemporary genres offers as wide an opportunity for self-expression as, say, the Western or the Film Noir. Probably the most innovative of these new genres is the Black film, a wide category that includes a great deal of cheap material ("Blaxploitation" in *Variety*'s parlance) but also several films of lasting value.

Melvin van Peebles, deciding that he wanted to be a filmmaker, went to France in order to accomplish his aim. After making one film there (*Story of a Three-Day Pass*, 1967) he returned to the U.S. and was able, having proved himself abroad, to obtain a Hollywood contract. The result was a very poor comedy, *The Watermelon Man* (1969). His third film, however, the independently produced *Sweet Sweetback's Baaadasssss Song* (1970) is still the purest Black film, in terms of esthetics, that has yet been made—a shriek of pain that is also an object lesson in Black survival in America. Van Peebles then turned his attention to the stage.

Gordon Parks, Sr. had been a widely respected photographer for *Life* magazine when he decided to break the race barrier in film. His first film, based on his autobiography, *The Learning Tree* (1968), was a visually stunning essay on his Kansas childhood, but too static for audiences accustomed to regularly timed stimulation. Parks satisfied that commercial requirement with his next film, *Shaft* (1970), which was the founding example of the Black action genre that was commercially so popular in the early seventies. After a few more similar ventures, Parks returned to a more personal subject with *Leadbelly* (1976), a biography of the Blues singer and a major film in the short history of the new Black cinema.

Playwright Bill Gunn is responsible for one of the most original and exciting films of the seventies—*Ganja and Hess* (1973)—which started out as a Black vampire exploitation vehicle but became much more than that. Sadly, the film was shelved by its distributor and has hardly been seen.

In the late sixties, it looked as if a new generation of young American filmmakers would be able, like their European counterparts, to move onward to a more personal cinema. Building on the examples of independent directors like Arthur Penn (*Bonnie and Clyde*, 1967; *Alice's Restaurant*, 1969; *Little Big Man*, 1970; *Night Moves*, 1975) and Frank and Eleanor Perry (*David and Lisa*, 1962; *Diary of a Mad Housewife*, 1972), the younger Americans, many of them trained in film schools, looked toward a cinema that would be less dominated by commercial considerations than Hollywood had been in its great days. At first this seemed to be possible; the earliest films of the directors now dominant in the U.S. were independent in outlook, but few of them were able to maintain that spirit of independence.

The films produced by the independent company BBS were among the first to announce a new style: *Easy Rider* (1969, directed by actor Dennis Hopper), *Five Easy Pieces* (1970, Bob Rafelson), *A Safe Place* (1971, Henry Jaglom), *Drive, He Said* (1971, Jack Nicholson). Yet the commercial success of *Easy Rider* led only to the short-lived Youth genre, and even Rafelson, the most accomplished of the group, was only able to complete two films in the next seven years: *The King of Marvin Gardens* (1972) and *Stay Hungry* (1976). Monte Hellman, another director associated with the BBS group, had been responsible for two remarkable Westerns in the mid-sixties (*The Shooting, Ride the Whirlwind*) and made one of the best films of the seventies—and certainly the superior Road film—in *Two-Lane Blacktop* (1970), but was able to put together only one project in the six years that followed.

Figure 4-59. Martin Sheen in *Apocalypse Now:* "The horror, the horror." But emotional trips up the river of symbolism into the heart of darkness accompanied by swarms of Huey helicopters aren't enough. By 1979, Americans wanted a more intelligent investigation of the war in Vietnam.

Filmmakers who maintained a personal vision while attempting to work more closely with the studios had better success at getting their films made but were slowly worn down by the requirements of the conglomerate entertainment industry.

Martin Scorsese began with two unusual independent productions (*Who's That Knocking at My Door?*, 1969 and *Mean Streets*, 1973) but then produced two films that, while seemingly independent in style, nevertheless fit Hollywood patterns neatly: *Alice Doesn't Live Here Anymore* (1974) and *Taxi Driver* (1976). *New York, New York* (1977) was an ambitious attempt to rework 1940s Musical style that never found an audience while *The Last Waltz* (1978), an elegantly filmed record of The Band's farewell concert, achieved some critical and commercial success.

The model for the new generation of Hollywood directors has been Francis Ford Coppola who went to work for Roger Corman straight out of film school in the 1960s, achieved some success as a screenwriter, produced and directed several personal films, including *The Rain People*

(1969) and *The Conversation* (1974). Concurrently, he was responsible for one of the most profitable films of the early seventies, *The Godfather* (1972) which along with its sequel (1975) is regarded by many critics as the most significant American film of the decade. That combination of commercial and artistic success is extremely rare. Coppola next spent close to four years and more than $30 million on *Apocalypse Now* (1979), a stunningly conceived and elegantly filmed attempt to wring some meaning out of Joseph Conrad's *Heart of Darkness* set in the context of the Vietnam war. Critics and audiences seemed to agree that the attempt was not successful. Despite its vividly felt metaphors for the malaise of the American experience in Vietnam—perhaps because of its brilliantly constructed images and sounds—*Apocalypse Now* doesn't seem to tell us very much about Vietnam. In 1968, when the idea first occurred to Coppola and Milius, such a film would have had revolutionary impact. More than ten years later, the postwar generation needed more than the nightmare of war; they needed an understanding of its specific causes and effects. It may be asking too much of three hours of film to provide such an analysis, but *Apocalypse,* throughout its agonizing production schedule, seemed to promise a great deal that it eventually didn't deliver. *Apocalypse Now* needed an American Jean-Luc Godard—but there is none.

Undaunted, Coppola picked himself up quickly and in the spring of 1980 bought the former Samuel Goldwyn Studios in Hollywood. Ten years earlier he had tried with middling success to found an alternative studio in San Francisco. His challenge to the Hollywood power structure—"American Zoetrope"—succeeded mainly behind the scenes as Coppola supported the budding careers of several younger filmmakers. Renamed more ambitiously, "Omni Zoetrope," the new studio may succeed in the new decentralized Hollywood.

Ironically, one of Coppola's earliest protégés, George Lucas, was able to realize his mentor's corporate dream first. After his debut with *THX 1138,* a science-fiction film produced by Zoetrope that earned very little at box offices, Lucas turned in 1973 to *American Graffiti,* one of the most popular films of the seventies. He followed it in 1977 with *Star Wars,* as of this writing the most profitable film of all time and, through its lucrative licensing rights (dolls, games, toys, t-shirts, et cetera), the foundation of Lucas's own empire, called Lucasfilm Ltd. Lucas has apparently left the director's chair to concentrate on managing this company. He has reportedly planned eight sequels to *Star Wars* (to be directed by others) and is involved in numerous other projects.

The film itself remains an extraordinary catalogue of Hollywood history. Most of its popular elements have direct antecedents in classics of

Figure 4-60. *The Empire Strikes Back* (1980) was the second of George Lucas's projected nine-film triple trilogy of Star Wars blockbusters. Intent on creating a modern mythology for children Lucas rivals Jim Henson, creator of the Muppets, who himself radically altered the mythos of childhood worldwide in the eighties through various television shows. A. A. Milne and Beatrix Potter don't stand much of a chance against the combined forces of modern audiovisual technology.

numerous genres that characterized the Golden Age of Hollywood. *Star Wars* isn't just a science-fiction film, it's a Western, at times, a war movie, a historical romance, and so forth. Considering the many details, styles, and tricks of the trade Lucas borrowed from his illustrious predecessors, or paid homage to, it seems only fitting that *Star Wars* has earned more than any film in American history.

Close on the heels of Lucas and Coppola has been Steven Spielberg. *Jaws* (1975) held first place on *Variety*'s list of all-time highest "grosses" for a while before it was displaced by *Star Wars*, and Spielberg's own science-fiction effort, *Close Encounters of the Third Kind*, released at the end of 1977, seven months after *Star Wars*, also ranks near the top of the list. *1941* (1979), an attempt at comedy set in that year and an even more expensive film, brought Spielberg down to earth as it failed completely at the nation's box offices.

Older by a generation than these three director/moguls, Robert Altman has survived in uneasy alliance with the studios, somehow managing to make his own films his way. He is one of the most original of

Figure 4-61. Carol Burnett, Paul Dooley, Mia Farrow, Dennis Christopher, and Amy Stryker as the happy wedding party in Altman's A Wedding (1978), an ebullient, adventurous movie that was significantly underrated. A year later, the "father-son" team of Dooley and Christopher achieved greater success in another midwestern town in Breaking Away (directed by Peter Yates).

contemporary filmmakers. His cinema is adventurous: M.A.S.H. (1970) set the tone for a generation (and secured Altman's artistic freedom in the process). McCabe and Mrs. Miller (1971) was certainly the primary Western of the period, just as The Long Goodbye (1972) and Thieves Like Us (1974) represented original versions of their genres, the Detective film and Film Noir, respectively. But Altman's greatest achievement was Nashville (1975), an extraordinarily original film that touched mythic roots in the Bicentennial consciousness. Buffalo Bill and the Indians (1976) also raised some interesting questions about the American way of life. Perhaps Altman's main contribution to the "New Hollywood" has been his method of working. While star directors painstakingly labor over their would-be masterpieces for years on end, Altman churns out movies at the rate of one every nine months. They seldom make much money, but on average they pay for themselves. Sometimes they are interesting (A Wedding, 1978), sometimes they are charming (A Perfect Couple, 1979), and occasionally they're abysmally arty (Quintet, 1978), but they are almost always infused with a love of the medium and a humane intelligence—and there are so many of them!

John Cassavetes, who had foreshadowed the independence of con-

Figure 4-62. Paul Mazursky's *Willie & Phil* (1980): Michael Ontkean (left), Ray Sharkey, and Margot Kidder in the eternal triangle: a social history of the 1970s.

temporary directors with his *Shadows* (1959), returned to independent production ten years later with *Faces* (1968). He followed it with *Husbands* (1970), *Minnie and Moskowitz* (1971), and *A Woman Under the Influence* (1974), his most popular film to date, then several exercises seen only by conscientious Cassavetes devotees (among them *The Killing of a Chinese Bookie*, 1976, a film of some interest). Despite a difficult style, dependent on improvisation and intense relationships between actors, Cassavetes has usually been able to finance and complete his films without recourse to studio money.

Michael Ritchie and Paul Mazursky are two other important contemporary filmmakers who have managed to live more or less successfully within the conglomerate system. One of the most underrated directors, Ritchie—in *Downhill Racer* (1969), *The Candidate* (1972), *Smile* (1975), *Bad News Bears* (1976), and *Semi-Tough* (1977)—combines documentary techniques with fictional structures to achieve an unusual blend. Like Ritchie, Mazursky is intent upon conveying the human element of his films. *Bob & Carol & Ted & Alice* (1969), *Blume in Love* (1973), *Harry and Tonto* (1974), and *Next Stop, Greenwich Village* (1976) all display a quiet humor at the same time as they treat contemporary life styles. *An Unmarried Woman* (1978) was Mazursky's most popular film, catching the feminist wave at its crest. *Willie and Phil* (1980) is a summary of his concerns and an interesting

Figure 4-63. Woody Allen's black-and-white romantic fantasy of his home town, *Manhattan* (1979), emphasized the mythic elements of New York: bridges, and rivers, and tow-away zones.

attempt to comment upon its spiritual source, Truffaut's classic *Jules and Jim.*

Equally successful at controlling the content and form of his films is Woody Allen, who after completing a string of comic successes in the early seventies (*Bananas,* 1971; *Sleeper,* 1973; *Love and Death,* 1975), discovered new resonance and new critical attention in 1977 with *Annie Hall.* He followed this with an ill-advised "serious" mock-European essay in intellectual angst, *Interiors* (1978)—whose main effect was to make it difficult to take mentor Ingmar Bergman seriously—but snapped back into form with *Manhattan* (1979).

While Cassavetes, Coppola, Lucas, Spielberg, Altman, Allen, Scorsese, Ritchie, and Mazursky—the pantheon of American filmmakers in the seventies—seem to rise above the general run of American directors, there are others whose work bears study. Alan J. Pakula, Sydney Pollack, John Korty, Philip Kaufman, Hal Ashby, Paul Schrader, and Mel Brooks all fall into this category.

The documentary fared well in the seventies, too. Besides the filmmakers already mentioned above, Haskell Wexler, Saul Landau, Peter

A.

B.

C.

D.

Figure 4-64. American documentary filmmakers in the late seventies discovered new sources of power by combining historical footage with straight nonfiction action. Les Blank's *Always for Pleasure* (A) is one of this filmmaker's most lively and sympathetic films about American music and customs. When Blank shows the film himself he usually cooks up some New Orleans food for the audience. Lorraine Gray's *With Babies and Banners* (B), Stewart Bird's and Deborah Shaffer's *The Wobblies* (C), and William Miles's *Men of Bronze* (D) provide invaluable insights into forgotten and neglected areas of American history at the same time that they survey our present attitudes to past events. B: The Great General Motors Sit-Down Strike of 1937. C: Funeral for the victims of the Everett Massacre, 1916. D: Soldiers of the 369th Infantry Regiment in the front-line trenches, Champagne, France, July, 1918.

Davis, and Emile De Antonio should be cited. Wexler, an accomplished cinematographer, directed one of the most significant films of the 1960s, *Medium Cool* (1969), which skillfully combined the real heartbreak of the 1968 Democratic Convention in Chicago with a very incisive essay on the relationship between the media and politics. Landau has been responsible for a number of salient nonfiction films (*Interview with President Allende, Report on Torture in Brazil,* both 1971), often working with Wexler. De Antonio has specialized in the compilation film, building politically pointed essays out of material shot by other people: *Point of Order* (1963), on the Army-McCarthy hearings, *Millhouse* (1971), about Richard Nixon, and *Painters Painting* (1972), his only nonpolitical film. De Antonio and Wexler combined to film *Underground* in 1976, a film about Weather organization fugitives.

Peter Davis's documentary essay about the painful relationship between the U.S. and Vietnam, *Hearts and Minds* (1975), annoyed some viewers because it seemed to be partisan, but remains one of the most remarkable American nonfiction films since 1960. It not only presented much important information visually, but because it is passionate about its subject it had an emotional as well as intellectual effect upon its audiences. Sadly, the film was seen only in the last months of the war, when it was already finally clear, after ten years, that U.S. intervention had been a tragic and obscene mistake.

The documentary format also proved to be a comfortable ground for a number of women directors in the seventies: Joyce Chopra, Martha Coolidge, Julia Reichert, Amalie Rothschild, Claudia Weill, Nell Cox, and Cinda Firestone, among others. Most of these directors found the autobiographical format useful to investigate feminist issues. In 1978, Claudia Weill made an impressive feature debut with *Girl Friends*, an independent production that displayed the sort of direct sensitivity and unvarnished style that marked the independent nonfiction film in the late seventies.

Among the wealth of nonfiction films made both for theatrical distribution and television airing in the late 1970s three historical studies might be singled out for special attention.

Barbara Kopple's 1976 *Harlan County, U.S.A.* gave us a vivid and moving portrait of the women and men who still struggle for better working conditions in that mining center forty years after the great labor struggles of the thirties earned their county the nickname "Bloody Harlan." Kopple doesn't use the people to make political points, she gives them the freedom within the film to discover their own view of the truth to us and in the process, ordinary people (albeit with extraordinary stamina, dedication, and humor) become real movie stars for a brief time.

With Babies and Banners (1978, Lorraine Gray, Anne Bohlen, Lyn Goldfarb) documents the story of the Women's Emergency Brigade during the General Motors sitdown strike of 1937 with rare historical footage and affectionate interviews with the same women forty years later at a reunion.

The Wobblies (1979, Stewart Bird, Deborah Shaffer) similarly combines historical footage and contemporary interviews to shed new light on the Industrial Workers of the World and its struggles during the early years of this century. The survivors Bird and Shaffer discovered were by then almost all over eighty. Both films show how the medium can be used to great effect for historical purposes.

Although the historical essay form was perhaps the leading form of nonfiction film in the late 1970s, other types of independent film also thrived. The straight essay form resulted in numerous vital and absorbing studies of the way we live now. *The American Game* (1978, Jay Freund, David Wolf) gave us a simple but thoroughly ingratiating portrait of two young basketball players, a white Indianan and a Black Brooklynite. Warrington Hudlin's *Streetcorner Stories* (1979) recorded the images, voices, and attitudes of Black residents of New Haven and showed how their streetcorner raps had roots in the age-old oral storytelling traditions of Black Americans. Alfred Guzzetti's *Family Portrait Sittings* (1978) was an outstanding example of a very popular form in the late seventies—a type of anthropological essay set close to home and comparable to the form of home movies.

Independent fictional features took on new life beginning in 1976 and 1977, as well. Certainly, many of the independent fiction films produced during the last few years are neither any better or any worse than studio commercial product—simply different in form and budget. Yet a film like Jan Oxenberg's bitingly refreshing *Billy in the Lowlands*, the story of a working-class kid in Boston, shows the potential for this sort of filmmaking, as does Claudia Weill's already mentioned *Girl Friends*. Penny Allen's *Property* (1978) is as closely tied to its geographical location, Oregon, as *Billy* and *Girl Friends* are to theirs (Boston, New York). Independent filmmaking now has a strongly regional cast, a phenomenon which should grow even more important in the eighties.

THE EIGHTIES AND BEYOND:
DEMOCRACY AND TECHNOLOGY: END OF CINEMA

By 1980 it was clear that it was no longer possible to make a distinct separation between what we call film and what we know as video, or television. These various forms of audiovisual narrative had been seen as separate—even antagonistic—for more than thirty years. Now, they must be regarded as parts of the same continuum. Indeed we need a new word to embrace both film and tape forms. As video technology has grown in sophistication and flexibility, "film"makers increasingly find the choice of format simply a matter of economics and technology—no longer related to esthetic considerations.

Despite its well-publicized economic gains in the seventies, commercial fiction filmmaking has grown ever closer to the television industry. In fact, a balanced view of film and television now should describe the former as a subcategory of the latter. The majority of companies that make films also make television programs, and vice versa. The theatrical release film industry realizes approximately $3 billion in annual sales each year while the network television industry has revenues three times as large. In 1980, more than 100 so-called "made-for-television" films were in production while theatrical features lagged far behind. Before the early seventies most critics and audiences would have regarded "made-for-tv" productions as notably less prestigious and adventurous than theatrical movies. By 1980, this stigma no longer applied. Many of the most interesting and relevant subjects are now first exploited in made-for-tv movies. The TV films still don't have quite the aura of their more expensive theatrical cousins, but actors and technicians now no longer regard made-for-tv movies as a professional step down.

Even within the relatively circumscribed area of theatrical filmmaking, television looms ever larger in the economic equation. During the late seventies a number of films originally conceived as theatrical productions skipped that stage of distribution to find some measure of success in television immediately. The string of distribution possibilities now looks something like this:

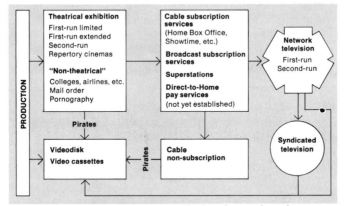

One or more of these stages can easily be skipped with no necessarily significant loss of revenue. In fact, pirating of videotapes and film prints is growing so rapidly that studios are now forced into the tape and disc market almost immediately after a film is released theatrically (and certainly after it has been shown on HBO, whose widespread exploitation offers videotape pirates irresistible opportunities).

Network television gets pushed further back in the string making it necessary for those companies to pour more money and talent into

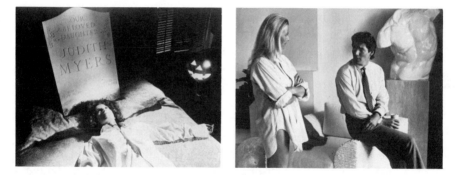

Figures 4-65, 4-66. As the eighties began, American film presented a complex array of possibilities. The blockbuster entertainment machine was still a focus of industry attention, represented here by a shot from John Carpenter's very-low-budget but very-high-profit horror thriller *Halloween*. Yet a number of filmmakers in the New Hollywood were capable of quite sophisticated esthetics. Here, Richard Gere, clothed elegantly by Giorgio Armani, meets with his former procurer Nina van Pallandt in Paul Schrader's *American Gigolo* (1979), a highly stylized film that was actually able to turn a profit while quoting Robert Bresson. More important, however. . . .

made-for-television product (since that is the one type of filmed entertainment over which they still have a degree of control). They can no longer depend, as they did for twenty years, on broadcast of theatrical films to provide the linchpin of their programming schedules. This is also a prime reason that networks have re-entered theatrical production within the last few years.

While commercial, conglomerate filmmakers find themselves confronting a new world of anarchic dimensions, thanks to the unplanned effects of technological developments, independent filmmakers can look forward to dramatically increased possibilities in the eighties and beyond. As late as 1978 a filmmaker who wished to distribute his or her film theatrically had, basically, six choices: the major Hollywood studios.

More important, the new, aggressively marketed technologies of videotape and videodisc, cable and satellite distribution offer entirely new possibilities for the independent filmmaker. It soon will be not only possible, but perhaps advisable for a filmmaker (or tapemaker) to skip theatrical distribution entirely. New television services will require large amounts of new product. And tape and disc offer a direct channel to the public very similar to book publication and record production. The independent still must fight against the expensive hype of competing conglomerate products, but at least the potential exists for a far more democratic system of distribution.

A.

B.

C.

D.

E.

Figure 4-67. . . . was the significant movement just as the decade changed, to films with more human subject matter—movies that eschewed visceral thrills to bask in character and the trials and pleasures of everyday life. Robert Benton's *Kramer vs. Kramer* (A) helped to set the tone for such movies in 1979. Dustin Hoffman and Justin Henry are pictured here. There were dozens of others, large and small, made by established filmmakers and newcomers: James Caan and Jill Eikenberry in *Hide in Plain Sight* (1980, directed by Caan) (B), a working-class *Kramer*. Jameson Parker, Karen Allen, and Brad Davis (C) in *A Small Circle of Friends* (1980, directed by Rob Cohen), a truthful, thoughtful film about the sixties. The Dance class in *Fame* (D), Alan Parker's feverish musical about high-school kids (1980). Tatum O'Neal and Kristy McNichol enjoy a food fight in *Little Darlings* (1980, directed by Ronald F. Maxwell).

During the 1960s and 1970s, the production of film became significantly more democratic as prices were reduced through technological developments. In the 1980s, the process of distribution, once the bottleneck, will undergo the same sort of democratization. This wasn't planned. In fact, it is nothing more than a (very welcome) side effect of the exploitation of new hardware in a market which had been approaching the saturation point. Nevertheless, it marks an important turning point in the history of film, not only in the U.S. but abroad.

Economically, the trend has been and continues to be toward greater access. American studios may still dominate the international film market, but at least the potential exists for other countries to battle against such cultural exploitation—not by banning American films, which becomes increasingly difficult as technology democratizes the process of distribution, but by attacking American studios on their own ground, understanding the economic multiplier effects of the export of culture, and making collective decisions to engage aggressively in the development and export of their own culture.

Technologically, the visual media continue to develop their powers of precision, further opening up the mysterious technological process to new groups of artists. What was once a massive undertaking, requiring vast investments of capital is now very close to being that personal, flexible instrument of communication that Alexandre Astruc called the "camera-pen." At the same time, new technologies of distribution should allow markedly increased access to an ever wider and more varied public—a public, by the way, who will have far greater control over media experiences than they have had in the past.

Esthetically, the confluence of these forces is producing a more varied range of cinematic product. The gap between "elite" and "mass" cultures continues to narrow. And the bourgeois concept of the "avant garde" becomes less important with each passing year.

Finally, it seems that the sum of these forces suggests that it may be a good time to announce the end of movies/film/cinema—at least as we have known them (it). From now on, "film" is simply a raw material, one of the possible choices, along with disc and tape, available to the media artist; "movies" are an integral part of a new, encompassing art, technology, and industry for which we do not yet have a name—other than "movies-and-television"; and "Cinema"? After eighty-five years, a long and tempestuous and rewarding life, cinema has passed away. For the sequel to this story proceed to Chapter 6.

FIVE

FILM THEORY: THEORY: FORM AND FUNCTION

In Mel Brooks's and Ernest Pintoff's funny and insightful short film *The Critic* (1963), we watch abstract animated shapes perform on the screen as we hear the voice of Brooks, an old man, puzzle his way happily through the significance of this "art":

> Vot da hell is dis?!
> Mus' be a cahtoon.
> Op . . . Mus' be boith. Dis looks like boith. I remembeh when I was a boy in Russia . . . biology.
> Op! It's born. Whatever it is, it's born. . . . Look out! Too late. It's dead already. . . . Vot's dis? Usher! Dis is cute. Dis is cute. Dis is nice. Vot da hell is it? Oh. I know vot it is. It's gobbage. Dat's vot it is! Two dollas I pay for a French movie, a foreign movie, and now I gotta see dis junk!

The first shape is joined by a second, and Brooks interprets:

> Yes. It's two. . .two *things* dat, dat, dat—they like each other. Sure. Lookit da sparks. Two things in love! Ya see how it got more like?—it envied the other thing so much. Could dis be the sex life of two *things*?

The scene changes again and Brooks's old codger begins to lose interest:

> Vot is dis? Dots! Could be an eye. Could be anything! It mus' be some symbolism. I t'ink . . . it's symbolic of . . . junk! Uh-oh! It's a cock-a-roach! Good luck to you vit ya cock-a-roach, mister!

As the artistic short comes to a close, the critic passes final judgment:

> I dunno much about psych'analysis, but I'd say dis is a doity pictcha!

The Critic is humorous partly because Brooks manages, in the short space of his three-minute monologue, to touch on a number of vital truths about criticism. "Two dollas" we pay for a movie; what do we get for it? How do we determine cinematic value? How do we know what's "symbolic of junk?" There are others in the audience with Mel Brooks's critic who seem to be enjoying the film. Are values, then, entirely relative? Are there any true universal "rules" for film art? What does film do? What are its limits?

Questions like these are the province of film theory and criticism, two related but not identical activities that have as their common end an increased understanding of the phenomenon of film. Theory, in general, is more abstract than criticism, which is more practical in nature. At the lowest end of the scale, we find the kind of criticism a reviewer practices: more reportage than analysis. The reviewer's function is to describe the film and evaluate it, two relatively simple tasks. At the upper end of the scale is the kind of film theory that has little or nothing to do with the actual practice of film: an intellectual activity that exists primarily for its own sake, and often has its own rewards, but doesn't necessarily have much relation to the real world. In between lie the vast expanses of general criticism and theory.

A number of important dichotomies govern the work of film theory. The first, the contrast between the practical and the ideal, is suggested by the difference between criticism (practical) and theory (ideal). Closely associated with this is the contrast between prescriptive and descriptive theory and criticism. The prescriptive theorist is concerned with what film should be, the descriptive theorist only with what film is. Prescriptive theory is inductive; that is, the theorist decides on a system of values first, than measures actual films against his system. Descriptive theory, in contrast, is deductive: the theorist examines the entire range of film activity and then, and only then, draws tentative conclusions about the real nature of film. Theorists and critics who prescribe are naturally concerned about evaluation; having strong systems of values, they logically measure real films against their requirements and judge them.

The third and most important governing dichotomy is that between theory and practice. The fact is, no filmmaker need study theory in order to practice the art. Indeed, until recently, very few filmmakers had any interest in theory. They knew (or did not know) instinctively what had to be done. Gradually, however, as film art became more sophisticated, a bridge between theory and practice was established. Many of the more interesting contemporary filmmakers, unlike their predecessors, now proceed from strong theoretical bases.

Before advancing further, it is worth taking a moment to examine the inherent effects of these governing dichotomies. It's a curious fact that the Hollywood style, which to a great extent still dominates film history, never produced a codified body of theory. On the face of it, the Hollywood film of the thirties and forties depended on a complex and powerful esthetic system, yet there is no Hollywood theory as such. Clearly, then, film—like all the other arts—needs no theory. Edison had none, Lumière had none, nor did Méliès. The best that D.W. Griffith (who inspired so many theorists) could come up with was an embarrassing, cock-eyed idea that the "human pulse beat" was the secret metronome of effective filmmaking. In "Pace in the Movies" (*Liberty* Magazine, 1926), he wrote:

> The American school . . . makes an effort to keep the tempo of the picture in tune with the average human heartbeat, which, of course, increases in rapidity under such influences as excitement, and may almost stop in moments of pregnant suspense.

Much of this sort of after-the-fact cogitation was the result of film's own inferiority complex as the youngest of the arts. Christian Metz suggests that the function of such criticism, psychoanalytically, is to rescue film from its "bad-object" status. More simply, the thinking went: if film can support a weighty system of theory, then it must be just as respectable as any of the other, older arts. This may seem a rather childish motive for film theory, but it was not so long ago that film was commonly regarded by educated people as not to be taken seriously. In the U.S., for example, film did not become a generally accepted subject for study in colleges and universities until about 1970. So the impetus for much of early film theory was to gain a degree of respectability.

As a result, many of the earliest works of film theory were prescriptive: often quite pretentiously so, as we shall see, but sometimes intriguingly elaborate. Continuing the psychoanalytic metaphor, we can think of this as the ascendance of film's "superego"—its sense of the artistic community's standards of behavior and respectability—as it struggled to be treated as an equal, and mastered its natural libidinous impulses. "Standards" were necessary, and film theorists provided them. Now that film theory has matured, it is much less likely to insist on rules and regulations often derived from outside the domain of film itself and instead concentrates on developing its own more flexible and more sophisticated values.

Within any specific film theory, there are a number of oppositions at work. Is the theory mainly esthetic or mainly philosophical? Does it deal with the relationships of parts of cinema to each other, or the parts of a specific film to each other? Or does it concern itself with the relationship between film and culture, film and the individual, film and society? Sergei Eisenstein, still the most fecund of film theorists, used cinematic terminology to describe the difference between various approaches to film study. In his 1945 essay "A Close-up View," he described "long shot" film theory as that which deals with film in context, which judges its political and social implications. "Medium shot" film criticism, meanwhile, focuses on the human scale of the film, which is what most reviewers concern themselves with. "Closeup" theory, however, " 'breaks down' the film into its parts," and "resolves the film into its elements." Film semiotics and other theories that attempt to treat the "language" of film, for example, are closeup approaches.

The essential concept here is the classic opposition between form and function. Are we more interested in what a film is (form) or in how it acts upon us (function)? As we shall see, it was quite a while before film theory turned from a focus on the form of the art to the more difficult and meaningful analysis of its function. Gradually, prescription has yielded to more scientific methods of investigation as film theory had become less demanding and more inquisitive.

THE POET AND THE PHILOSOPHER: Lindsay and Münsterberg

The first film theorists, as we have noted, were mainly interested—some more consciously than others—in providing a respectable artistic cachet for the young art. In 1915, just as the feature film was rising to prominence, Vachel Lindsay, at that time a well-known poet, published *The Art of the Moving Picture*, a lively, naïve, often simplistic but nevertheless insightful paean to the wild, youthful popular art. The very title of his book was an argumentative proposition: he challenged his readers to consider this sideshow entertainment as a real art. Working on the model of the established narrative and visual arts he identified three basic types of "photoplays," as movies with pretensions to art were then called: "The Photoplay of Action," "The Intimate Photoplay," and "The Motion Picture of Splendor," three categories that serve well to triangulate the Hollywood cinema of the next fifty years. In each case, Lindsay had noticed and formulated elements of narrative in which film could not only rival but often surpass the other arts: Action, Intimacy, and Splendor were all strong (sometimes crude), direct values—and still are.

Working intuitively from his lively passion for the movies, Lindsay then further compared the potential of film with the accomplishments of the older arts, discussing film as, in turn, "sculpture-in-motion," "painting-in-motion," and "architecture-in-motion." He concluded his basic outline of the esthetics of film with two chapters, each in its own way suprisingly prescient. At the time he wrote, those few films taken seriously by the cultural Establishment were the ones that mimicked the stage—the so-called "photoplays." Yet Lindsay understood very early on—after *The Birth of a Nation* (1915) but before *Intolerance* (1916)—that the real strength of film might lie in precisely the opposite direction. In "Thirty Differences Between Photoplays and the Stage," he outlined an argument that was to become a major concern of film theorists throughout the twenties and into the thirties as he explained how the two seemingly parallel arts contrasted. This was the dominant theme as film theorists tried to establish a separate identity for the adolescent art.

Lindsay's last chapter on esthetics, "Hieroglyphics," is even more insightful. "The invention of the photoplay," he wrote, "is as great a step as was the beginning of picture-writing in the stone age." He then goes on to treat film as a language and, although his analysis may be, as he suggests, "a fanciful flight rather than a sober argument," it nevertheless points directly to the most recent stage of development in film theory—semiotics—quite an achievement in 1915 for an antiacademic poet enamored of the "barbaric yawp" and untrained in the scholarly disciplines. Nor does Lindsay stop with the internal esthetics of film. The third section of his book is devoted to the extrinsic effects of the "photoplay." Again, the discussion is not so important for its concrete contributions to our understanding of the medium as it is as an early historical marker, yet one of Lindsay's most idiosyncratic theories—always dismissed by later theorists and critics—bears further examination. Lindsay suggests that the audience should engage in conversation during a (silent) film rather than listen to music. No one took his suggestion seriously; if they had, we might have developed a cinema that was communal and interactive much earlier than we did. Many recent Third World films (as well as those of Godard) are designed, despite their soundtracks, as first statements in conversation between filmmaker and observer. In short Vachel Lindsay as poet and passionate lover of film intuited a number of truths that more academic theorists, limited by their rigid systematic thinking, never could have understood.

A year after Lindsays's paean to movies first appeared, it was joined by another major contribution—directly opposed in style, approach, and tone, but just as valuable: Hugo Münsterberg's seminal *The Photoplay: A Psychological Study* (1916). Münsterberg, of German origin, was a professor of philosophy at Harvard and, like his sponsor William James, one of the founders of modern psychology. Unlike Lindsay, the populist poet, Münsterberg brought an academic reputation to his work.

He was not a "movie fan" but rather a disinterested academician who only a year before his book was published had little or no experience of the rowdy popular art. His intellectual analysis of the phenomenon not only provided a much needed cachet, but also remains even today one of the more balanced and objective outlines of film theory. Münsterberg was committed to bridging the gap between professional theory and popular understanding. "Intellectually the world has been divided into two classes," he wrote, "—the 'highbrows' and the 'lowbrows.' " He hoped that his analysis of the psychology of film would "bring these two brows together." Sadly, his book was ignored for many years and has only recently (1969) been rediscovered by film theorists and students.

Like Lindsay, Münsterberg quickly understood that film had its own special genius and that its esthetic future did not lie in replicating the kind of work that was better done on stage or in the novel. Like the poet, the professor also understood that film theory must take into account not only implicit esthetics but also explicit social and psychological effects. He calls these two facets the "Inner" and the "Outer" developments of motion pictures, and he begins his study with a discussion of them.

His most valuable contribution, however, predictably lies in his application of psychological principles to the film phenomenon. Freudian dream psychology was a useful tool for many popular theories of cinema from the twenties on. Münsterberg's approach, however, is pre-Freudian, which is one good reason why it was ignored for so long, but at the same time he is an important precursor of Gestalt psychology, which makes his approach seem surprisingly contemporary. Freudian film psychology emphasizes the unconscious, dreamlike nature of the experience, and therefore concentrates on the passive attitude toward the medium. Münsterberg, in contrast, develops a conception of the relationship between film and observer as interactive.

He begins by describing how our perception of movement in moving pictures depends not so much on the static phenomenon of persistence of vision as on our active mental processes of interpretation of this series of still images. Thirty years later, this active process became known as the phi-phenomenon. Münsterberg had described it (without labeling it) in 1916. In chapters dealing with "Attention," "Memory and Imagination," and "Emotions," he then develops a sophisticated theory of film psychology that conceives of film as an active process—a strongly mental activity—in which the observer is a partner with the filmmaker. In a second section, dealing with "The Esthetics of the Photoplay," he investigates some of the ramifications of this state of affairs. In shifting attention away from the passive phenomenon of persistence of vision and toward the active mental process of the phi-phenomenon, Münsterberg established a vital logical basis for theories of film as an active process. Yet, in at least one important respect, this theory was prescriptive rather than descriptive. As we shall see, during the first thirty or forty years of film theory, the concept of the medium as essentially passive and manipulative is dominant, as it is in film practice. Yet Münsterberg's understanding of the medium as at least potentially interactive would eventually be redeemed.

Curiously, Lindsay's and Münsterberg's books were the last really significant works of film theory produced in the U.S. until quite recently. It seemed as if the film theory was beside the point once Hollywood began to dominate film practice. By the early twenties, the focal point of film theory had shifted to Europe and has for the last fifty years been dominated by French, German, and Eastern European thinkers. Like the British tradition, the American line of development of theory/criticism has been mainly practical—concerned with concrete criticism rather than abstract theory. Ideally, it is not a less valuable tradition because of this practical orientation, but because it is diffuse it is not so easy to describe or to study. Concentrated single volumes of abstract theory lend themselves to analysis much more readily, a fact that should be remembered, since it tends to distort our conception of the shape of developing film theory.

Paradoxically, one of the first signs of the growing vitality of film theory in Europe in the twenties was found in the work of Louis Delluc who, although he produced several volumes of theory (*Cinéma et cie*, 1919: *Photogénie*, 1920), is best remembered as a practicing daily film critic, filmmaker, and founder of the ciné-club movement. Together with Léon Moussinac, he established film reviewing as a serious undertaking in direct contrast to the reportage and puff publicity then common. Delluc died in 1924, before his thirty-fifth birthday, but by that time the European tradition of the art film (and the film of art) was solidly established.

EXPRESSIONISM AND REALISM: Arnheim and Kracauer

In his useful introduction to the subject, *The Major Film Theories* (1976), J. Dudley Andrew adopts categories derived from Aristotle to analyze the structure of film theory. He approaches various theories by four avenues: "Raw Material," "Methods and Techniques," "Forms and Shapes," and "Purpose and Value." We can further simplify the categories if we realize that the two central ones—"Methods and Techniques" and "Forms and Shapes"—are simply opposite facets of the same phenomenon, the first practical, the second theoretical. Each of these categories focuses on a different aspect of the film process, the chain connecting material, filmmaker, and observer. The way in which a theory arranges these relationships to a large extent determines its aim, and is a direct function of its underlying principles. Those theories that celebrate the Raw Material are essential realist. Those that focus first on the power of the filmmaker to modify or manipulate reality are, at base, expressionist: that is, they are more concerned with the filmmaker's expression of the raw materials than with the filmed reality itself.

These two basic attitudes have dominated the history of film theory and practice ever since the Lumière brothers (who seemed to be obsessed with capturing raw reality on film) and Méliès (who obviously was more fascinated by what he could do to his raw materials). It is only recently that the third facet of the process, the relationship between film and observer (in Aristotle's terms, "Purpose and Value"), has begun to dominate film theory, although it was always implicit in both realist and expressionist arguments. The semiotics of film and the politics of film both begin with the observer and work back through the art of the filmmaker to the reality of the raw materials on the other side. The center of interest has shifted from generative to receptive theories. We are now no longer so concerned with how a film is made as with how it is perceived and what effect it has in our lives. Münsterberg's work (and even Lindsay's) had foreshadowed this shift of emphasis. Moreover, it must be remembered that all three of these interrelated elements were evident during the practical development of film, even if theory at various points tended to emphasize one to the exclusion of the others.

Expressionism dominated film theory throughout the twenties and thirties. D. W. Griffith described two major "schools" of film practice, the American and the German. The American School, he told his audience, "says to you: 'Come and *have* a great experience!' Whereas the German school says: 'Come and *see* a great experience!' " Griffith's purpose was to suggest that American cinema in the twenties was more active and energetic than German cinema, as indeed it was. Yet although we speak of "German Expressionism" in the twenties and seldom use the word in an American context, nevertheless both of Griffith's schools focus on the essentially expressionist aim of the "great experience." As Griffith describes his theory of pacing in the movies, it is a tool for the manipulation of the spectators' emotions. "For a quick, keen estimate of a motion picture," he wrote, "give me a boy of ten and a girl of fifteen—the boy for action, the girl for romance. Few things have happened in their lives to affect their natural reactions." What Griffith and Hollywood wanted were pure reactions to their stimuli; the art of film accordingly, lies almost entirely in the design of effective stimuli. There is little or no sense of the observer actively involved in the process.

Realism was a common, if subordinate, strain in film practice throughout the first four decades of film history; it didn't come into its own theoretically until the late thirties (in the practical work of the British documentarists led by John Grierson) and the forties (with Italian Neorealism). There were good reasons for this late blooming: first, since realist theory naturally implied that film itself was of lesser importance (that reality was more important than "art"), this led both filmmakers and theorists toward expressionist positions. Expressionism not only made the filmmaker more important in the general scheme of things, it was also a natural outgrowth of the early efforts to achieve for film "art" a certain degree of respectability. During the early twentieth century, every one of the other, older arts was moving toward greater abstraction, less verisimilitude—"less matter with more art." Why shouldn't the adolescent upstart, film, move in this direction as well? Moreover, if film was in fact to be considered a mature art, it was necessary to show that the activity of the art of film was just as complex and demanding as, say, the activity of painting. Expressionism, by placing emphasis on the manipulative power of the filmmaker, served this function nicely.

More important, perhaps, is the second reason theories of expressionism dominated the first fifty years of film theory: there was very little room for private or personal art in film. Because it was so expensive, cinema had to be a very popular form. Theories of realism demand that we see the observer as a participant in the process. If film is strictly a commodity, how could we justify "making the consumer work" for his entertainment? As a product film had to be manipulative: the more "effect" the film had, the better value for the money the consumer had spent. In fact, most popular film is still judged by this simple rule: witness the success in the seventies of such "mind-blowers" as *The Exorcist* (1973), *Jaws* (1975) and *Alien* (1979). In this economic sense, movies are still a carnival attraction—rides on roller coasters through chambers of horror and tunnels of love—and realism is totally beside the point.

The two standard, most succinct, and colorful texts describing the contrasting expressionist and realist positions are Rudolf Arnheim's *Film as Art* (published first in German in 1933 as *Film als Kunst* and translated into English almost immediately) and Siegfried Kracauer's *Theory of Film: The Redemption of Physical Reality* (first published in 1960). Both books are strongly—almost belligerently—prescriptive. Both present "revealed truths" as if film theory were a matter of pronouncements rather than investigations. Yet both remain memorable and have become classics of the literature of film, not only because they each neatly summarize the positions of their respective schools, but also in no small part because they are so sententious: more complex, less determinist theories of film are obviously not so easily remembered.

Arnheim has had a distinguished career as a psychologist (he is the author of *Art and Visual Perception: A Psychology of the Creative Eye*, 1954), so it is no surprise to discover that the basic tenets of *Film as Art* are psychological. But unlike his predecessor, Münsterberg, he is more concerned with how film is made than with how it is perceived. The thrust of his small volume can be described quite succinctly: he proceeds from the basic premise that the art of film depends on its limitations, that its physical limitations are precisely its esthetic virtues. As he himself summarizes his position in his preface to the 1957 edition: "I undertook to show in detail how the very properties that make photography and film fall short of perfect reproduction can act as the necessary molds of an artistic medium." It is a curious proposition, yet in a sense correct, since logically each art must be formed by its limitations. The problem is that Arnheim suggests that it should not exceed those limitations and that technological developments—sound, color, widescreen, and so forth—that do push the limits further out are not to be welcomed. He finds film at its height artistically in the late silent period, a position that, although understandable enough in 1933, he continues to maintain in the 1957 edition.

After listing a number of ways in which film representation differs from reality, Arnheim proceeds to enumerate how each of these differences—these limitations—yields artistic content and form. The gist of his argument is that the closer film comes to reproducing reality, the less room there is in which the artist can create his effects. The success of this theory rests on two assumptions that are certainly problematic:

a) that art equals effect, or expression; that the magnitude of a work of art is directly related to the degree of the artist's manipulation of materials; and

b) that the limitations of an art form only generate its esthetics and do not restrict them.

"The temptation to increase the size of the screen," he writes, for example, "goes with the desire for colored, stereoscopic, and sound film. It is the wish of people who do not know that artistic effect is bound up with the limitations of the medium. . . ." Yet as those new dimensions were added to the repertoire of film art, filmmakers discovered more freedom, not less, and the range of possible artistic effects expanded considerably.

Basically, the difficulty with Arnheim's theory of limitations is that he focuses all too narrowly on the production of film and doesn't take into account the liberating and complicating factor of its perception. Many of the limitations he lists (aside from the technological)—the framing of the image, film's two-dimensionality, the breakup of the space-time continuum by editing—are far less important in terms of how we perceive a film than in terms of how we construct one. By ignoring the total scope of the film process, Arnheim produces a strictly ideal prescription for film art that has less to do with the actual phenomenon of practical film than it might at first appear. In any event, his pure, limited conception of film was quickly overtaken by events as technology developed and practical filmmakers discovered the possibilities of new variables.

The conflict between realism and expressionism that colors nearly all film theory is not so direct, explicit, and nicely balanced as it might at first seem. The relationship is more dialectical than dichotomous, so that realist theory grows out of expressionist theory just as expressionist theory had, in its turn, grown out of the urge to build an artistic reputation for film. Siegfried Kracauer's magnum opus, *Theory of Film: The Redemption of Physical Reality*, coming twenty-seven years after Arnheim's elegant, lean prescription, is in contrast a sprawling, sometimes blunt, often difficult investigation into wide-ranging theories of realism that had been developing slowly over a period of more than twenty years. Expressionism, because it is self-limiting and self-defining, is relatively easy to outline. Realism, on the other hand, is a vague, inclusive term that means many things to many people. All students of literature have run into the "problem" of realism before. Is Jane Austen, who wrote precisely about a very narrow segment of society, a realist? Or is breadth as important as depth to the realist sensibility? Is Naturalism, rather easily defined as an artistic form based on Determinist philosophy, a kind of realism, an offshoot from it, or in direct opposition to it? In film, too, "realism" is a slippery term. The Rossellini of *Open City* (1945) is a "realist," but what about the Rossellini of *The Rise to Power of Louis XIV*? Or Fellini? Are politics necessary to realism? What about acting? Are documentaries always more "realistic" than fiction films? Or is it possible to be a realist and still a story-teller? The catalogue of questions about the nature of film realism is endless.

Kracauer covers many of them, but his book is by no means a complete survey of the quirky definitions of the word. It is *a* theory of film, not *the* theory of film. Like Arnheim's essay, it chooses a single central fact of the film experience as crucial, then builds a prescription that leads to a specific conclusion. Like Arnheim, too, Kracauer was writing mainly after the fact. If the great age of film expressionism was the twenties, then the central period of film realism was the forties and fifites. The most important realist trend of the sixties, for instance, occurred in documentary—an area of film activity about which Kracauer has very little to say.

While Kracauer has the reputation of being the foremost theorist of film realism, he was actually only one among many. André Bazin, for instance, is also generally considered a "Realist," yet although he offered a much richer investigation of the phenomenon during the fifteen years preceding Kracauer's book, his work was never so clearly codified as Kracauer's and therefore hasn't until recently had the direct impact of his successor's. Throughout most of film history, realism has been of more interest to practical filmmakers than theoretical critics. Dziga Vertov in the Soviet Union in the 1920s, Jean Vigo in France, and John Grierson in England in the 1930s, Roberto Rossellini, Cesare Zavattini, and the Neorealists in Italy in the 1940s, all developed realist positions in opposition to expressionist theories. It was as if the filmmakers reacted against the potential abuse of power of their medium, instead searching for a more "moral" position in realism.

At the center of Arnheim's theory had been the limitations of the technology and the form of film art. The kernel of Kracauer's theory is the photographic "calling" of film art. Simply because photography and film do come so close to reproducing reality, they must emphasize this ability in their esthetics. This premise is diametrically opposed to Arnheim's. "Film," Kracauer wrote, "is uniquely equipped to record and reveal physical reality and, hence, gravitates toward it." Therefore, he suggests, content must take precedence over form. He then develops what he calls a material esthetic rather than an esthetic of form. Because theories of art depend so heavily on formalism, then, film becomes for Kracauer a kind of antiart. "Due to its fixed meaning," he concludes, "the concept of art does not, and cannot, cover truly 'cinematic' films—films, that is, which incorporate aspects of physical reality with a view to making us experience them. And yet it is they, not the films reminiscent of traditional art works, which are valid esthetically."

This is the third stage of the psychological development of film as art. After having established itself as respectable in its adolescence, then having joined the community of the arts in its young adulthood by showing how like them it really was, it now moves into maturity, exerting its "ego integrity" by separating itself from the community and establishing its own personal system of values. If film doesn't fit the definition of art, then the definition of art must be changed.

Having celebrated film's uniqueness, Kracauer then makes a crucial logical jump. Since it can reproduce reality so well, he suggests, it *ought* to. It is at this point that his theory is most open to contradiction. It would be just as easy to propose (as Arnheim does in a way) that, since film and reality have such a close and intimate connection, film ought to exercise this mimetic power in the opposite way: by contradicting, molding, forming, shaping reality rather than reproducing it. Nevertheless, after these first significant pronouncements, Kracauer moves on into a more general and more objective study of the medium of film. The logical endpoint of his primary contention about the close relationship of flim and reality would be to elevate the film record, the nonfiction film, and the documentary over the film of fiction. Yet Kracauer, as we have noted, pays relatively little attention to strict factual film and instead focuses on the most common type of film: the narrative. He finds the ideal film form to be the "found story." Such films are fiction, but they are "discovered rather than contrived." He continues, explaining the difference between this quasi-fictional ideal form and the fully developed "artwork":

> Since the found story is part and parcel of the raw material in which it lies dormant, it cannot possibly develop into a self-contained whole—which means that it is almost the opposite of the theatrical story. [p. 246].

As his theory develops and broadens, it becomes clear that Kracauer has no great objections to form—so long as it serves the purpose of content. And here we get to the heart of Kracauer's true contribution to film theory: film serves a purpose. It does not exist simply for itself, as a pure esthetic object; it exists in the context of the world around it. Since it stems from reality it must also return to it—hence the subtitle of Kracauer's theory: *The Redemption of Physical Reality.* If this sounds vaguely religious, the connotation is, I think, intended. For Kracauer, film has a human, ethical nature. Ethics must replace esthetics, thereby fulfilling Lenin's prophecy, which Jean-Luc Godard was fond of quoting, that "ethics are the esthetics of the future." Having been divorced from physical reality by both scientific and esthetic abstraction, we need the redemption film offers: we need to be brought back into communication with the physical world. Film can mediate reality for us. It can both "corroborate" and "debunk" our impressions of reality.

This seems an admirable goal.

MONTAGE: Pudovkin, Eisenstein, Balázs, and Formalism

The words "expressionism" and "Formalism" are often used interchange-ably in film criticism to denote those tendencies generally opposed to "realism." Both expressionism and Formalism are also labels attached to specific periods of cultural history: Expressionism was the major force in German culture—in theater and painting as well as film—during the 1920s, just as, during the same period, Formalism marked the burgeon-ing cultural life—both literary and cinematic—in the Soviet Union. Essentially, the difference between the two movements depends on a slight but significant shift of focus. Expressionism is a more generalized, romantic conception of film as an expressive force. Formalism is more specific, more "scientific," and more concerned with the elements, the details that go to make up this force. It is more analytic and less synthetic, and it also carries with it a strong sense of the importance of function as well as form in art.

During the 1920s, the period immediately following the Russian Revolution, the Soviet cinema was among the most exciting in the world, not only practically but theoretically. There is no doubt that the Soviet filmmaker-theorists wanted not only to capture reality, but to change it. Realism, at least esthetically, is not particularly revolution-ary: as we have noted, it tends to deny the power of the filmmaker and therefore makes film seem to be less powerful as a tool to effect social change. During this period—before Stalin imposed the doctrine of So-cialist Realism (which is neither Realist nor especially Socialist)—two filmmakers, V. I. Pudovkin and Sergei Eisenstein, produced not only a number of exceptional films but also an amorphous body of Formalist theory that has had a profound impact on the course of development of film theory. At the same time, the Hungariam writer, critic, and film-maker Béla Balázs was pursuing a line of Formalist thinking that, al-though it is less well known than those of Pudovkin and Eisenstein, nevertheless deserves to be ranked with theirs.

Unlike Arnheim and Kracauer, Pudovkin, Eisenstein, and Balázs were practicing filmmakers who wanted to describe their art rather than prescribe for it. Their theoretical work was not compressed into single volumes, but rather spread out in individual essays over a period of many years. It was organic, developing, on-going rather than closed, complete, and final. It is thus much less easy to summarize quickly: it is also much more useful and insightful.

Very soon after the revolution of 1917, a filmmaker named Lev Kuleshov was put in chage of a workshop. Pudovkin was one of his students as was, briefly, Eisenstein. Unable to find enough filmstock to fuel their projects, they turned to reediting films already made, and in the process discovered a number of truths about the technique of film montage. In one experiment, Kuleshov linked together a number of shots made at varying times and places. The composite was a unified piece of film narrative. Kuleshov called this "creative geography." In probably their most famous experiment, the Kuleshov group took three identical shots of the well-known prerevolutionary actor Moszhukin and intercut them with shots of a plate of soup, a woman in a coffin, and a little girl. According to Pudovkin, who later described the results of the experiment, audiences exclaimed at Moszhukin's subtle and affective ability to convey such varied emotions: hunger, sadness, affection.

In his two major works, *Film Technique* (1926) and *Film Acting* (1935), Pudovkin developed from the elemental root of his experiments with Kuleshov a varied theory of cinema centered on what he called "relational editing." For Pudovkin, montage was "the method which controls the 'psychological guidance' of the spectator." In this respect, his theory was simply expressionist: that is, mainly concerned with how the filmmaker can affect the observer. But he identified five separate and distinct types of montage: contrast, parallelism, symbolism, simultaneity, and leitmotif (reiteration of theme). Here we have the basic premise of film Formalism: Pudovkin discovered categories of form and analyzed them. Moreover, he was greatly concerned with the importance of the shot—of mise en scène—and therefore displayed an attitude that we have come to regard as essentially realist. He saw montage as the complex, pumping heart of film, but he also felt that its purpose was to support narrative rather than alter it.

Eisenstein set up his own theory of montage—as collision rather than linkage—in dialectical opposition to Pudovkin's theory. In a series of essays beginning in the early twenties and continuing throughout most of his life, he worked and reworked a number of basic concepts as he struggled with the shape and nature of cinema. (These essays are collected in *The Film Sense* and *Film Form* and in a number of other volumes.) For Eisenstein, montage has as its aim the creation of ideas, of a new reality, rather than the support of narrative, the old reality of experience. As a student, he had been fascinated by Oriental ideograms that combined elements of widely different meaning in order to create entirely new meanings, and he regarded the ideogram as a model of cinematic montage. Taking an idea from the literary Formalists, he conceived of the elements of a film being "decomposed" or "neutralized" so that they could serve as fresh material for dialectic montage.

Figure 5-1. Eisenstein's *Potemkin* (1925): the Odessa Steps sequence. As the people of Odessa gather to hail the rebellious soldiers on the battleship *Potemkin* in the harbor, soldiers appear. The crowd runs down the steps in horror as the soldiers fire. A young boy is hit and killed. His mother picks him up in her arms and turns to face the soldiers at the top of the steps. . . .

Figure 5-2. . . . As she advances, pleading with them, they prepare to fire. The officer lowers his saber and a volley is fired, cutting down the mother and child. The crowd runs down the steps, trampling those who have fallen. . . .

Figure 5-3. . . . As they reach the pathway at the bottom, they are attacked by mounted Cossacks. The people are caught in the pincers between the rank of soldiers relentlessly advancing down the steps, and the Cossacks who whip and trample them. Eisenstein cuts back and forth between shots of the victims and shots of the oppressors. A woman with a baby carriage is hit near the top of the steps. As she falls, she nudges the carriage over the first step. . . .

Figure 5-4. . . . It careens down the steps over corpses, as people watch in terror, until it reaches the bottom step and overturns.

Figure 5-5. Eisenstein's *Alexander Nevsky* (1938): the Battle on the Ice. The Russian army is in position to defend against the German invaders. Battle scenes, with their strong visual oppositions, were among Eisenstein's most striking sequences. (*All stills l'Avant-Scène. Frame enlargements.*)

Even actors were to be cast not for their individual qualities but for the "types" they represented.

Eisenstein extended this concept of dialectics even to the shot itself. As shots related to each other dialectically, so the basic elements of a single shot—which he called its "attractions"—could interrelate to produce new meanings. Attractions as he defined them included

> every aggressive moment . . . every element . . . that brings to light in the spectator those senses or that psychology that influence his experience—every element that can be verified and mathematically calculated to produce certain emotional shocks in a proper order within the totality . . . [*Film Sense*, p. 231].

Because attractions existed within the framework of that totality, a further extension of montage was suggested: a montage of attractions. "Instead of a static 'reflection' of an event with all possibilities for activity within the limits of the event's logical action, we advance to a new plane—free montage of arbitrarily selected, independent . . . attractions . . . " [p. 232]. This was an entirely new basis for montage, different in kind from Pudovkin's five categories.

Later, Eisenstein developed a more elaborate view of the system of attraction in which one was always dominant while others were subsidiary. The problem here was that the idea of the dominant seemed to conflict with the concept of neutralization, which supposedly prepared all the elements to be used with equal ease by the filmmaker. There are a number of such seeming contradictions in Eisenstein's thought: a good sign that his theory of film was organic, open and healthily incomplete.

Possibly the most important ramification of Eisenstein's system of attractions, dominants, and dialectic collisional montage lies in its implications for the observer of film. Whereas Pudovkin had seen the techniques of montage as an aid to narrative, Eisenstein reconstructed montage in opposition to straight narrative. If shot A and shot B were to form an entirely new idea, C, then the audience had to become directly involved. It was necessary that they work to understand the inherent meaning of the montage. Pudovkin, whose ideas seem closer in spirit to the tenets of realism, had paradoxically proposed a type of narrative style that controlled the "psychological guidance" of the audience.

Eisenstein, meanwhile, in suggesting an extreme Formalism in which photographed reality ceased to be itself and became instead simply a stock of raw material—attractions, or "shocks"—for the filmmaker to rearrange as he saw fit, was also paradoxically describing a system in which the observer was a necessary and equal participant. The simplistic dichotomy between expressionism and realism thus no longer holds. For Eisenstein it was necessary to destroy realism in order to approach reality. The real key to the system of film is not the artist's relationship with his raw materials, but rather his relationship with his audience. A hypothetical film that might show the greatest respect for photographed reality might at the same time show little or no respect for its audience. Conversely, a highly Formalist, abstract film expression—Eisenstein's own *Potemkin* (1925), for instance—might engage its audience in a dialectical process instead of overpowering them with a calculated emotional experience.

Eisenstein's basic conception of the film experience was, like his theories, open-ended. The process of film (like the process of theory) was far more important than its end, and the filmmaker and observer were engaged in it dynamically. Likewise, the elements of the film experience which was the channel of communication between creator and observer were also connected logically with each other. Eisenstein's wide-ranging theories of film thus foreshadow the two most recent developments of cinematic theory,, since he is concerned throughout not only with the language of film but also with how that language can be used by both filmmakers and observers.

Like Eisenstein, Béla Balázs worked out his description of the structure of cinema over a period of many years. Hungarian by birth, he left his native country after the Commune was overthrown in 1919 and spent time thereafter in Germany, the Soviet Union, and other Eastern European countries. His major work, *Theory of the Film: Character and Growth of a New Art* (1948), summarizes and comments on a lifetime of theorizing. Because he had practical experience in the art and because he developed his theory over a number of years, *Theory of the Film* remains one of the most balanced volumes of its kind. Sharing many of the basic Formalist principles of Eisenstein and Soviet literary critics of the twenties, Balázs manages to integrate these concepts with certain realist principles. He was fascinated by the "secret power" of the closeup to reveal details of fact and emotion and developed a theory of the true province of film as "micro-dramatics," the subtle shifts of meaning and the quiet interplay of emotions that the closeup is so well equipped to convey. His earliest book on film had been entitled *The Visible Man, or Film Culture* (1924). It made this essentially realist point strongly and probably influenced Pudovkin.

But while he celebrated the reality of the closeup, Balázs also situated film squarely in the economic sphere of influence. He realized that the economic foundation of film is the prime determinant of film esthetics, and he was one of the earliest film theorists to understand and explain how our approach to any film is molded and formed by the cultural values we share. Predating Marshall McLuhan by many years, he anticipated the development of a new visual culture that would resurrect certain powers of perception that, he said, had lain dormant. "The discovery of printing," he wrote, "gradually rendered illegible the faces of men. So much could be read from paper that the method of conveying meaning by facial expression fell into desuetude." That is changing now that we have a developing, reproducible visual culture that can match print in versatility and reach. Balázs's sense of film as a cultural entity subject to the same pressure and forces as any other element of culture may seem obvious today, but he was one of the first to recognize this all-important aspect of film.

MISE EN SCÈNE: Neorealism, Bazin, and Godard

Like Eisenstein, André Bazin was engaged in a continual process of revision and revaluation as his short career progressed from the mid-

1940s to his early death in 1958 at the age of thirty-nine. Unlike nearly all other authors of major film theories, Bazin was a working critic who wrote regularly about individual films. His theory is expressed mainly in four volumes of collected essays (*Qu'est-ce que le cinéma?*) published in the years immediately succeeding his death (selected and translated in two volumes: *What Is Cinema?*). It is deeply imbued with his practical, deductive experience. With Bazin, for the first time film theory becomes not a matter of pronouncement and prescription, but a fully mature intellectual activity, well aware of its own limitations. The very title of Bazin's collected essays reveals the modesty of this approach. For Bazin, the questions are more important than the answers.

With roots in his background as a student of phenomenology, Bazin's theories are clearly realist in organization, but once again the focus has shifted. If Formalism is the more sophisticated, less pretentious cousin of expressionism, perhaps what Bazin is after should be called "Functionalism" rather than simply realism, for running throughout his argument is the important idea that film has significance not for what it is but for what it does. For Bazin, realism is more a matter of psychology than of esthetics. He does not make a simple equation between film and reality as does Kracauer, but rather describes a more subtle relationship between the two in which film is the asymptote to reality, the imaginary line that the geometric curve approaches but never touches. He began one of his earliest essays, "The Ontology of the Photographic Image," by suggesting: "If the plastic arts were put under psychoanalysis, the practice of embalming the dead might turn out to be a fundamental factor in their creation." The arts arose, he contends, because "other forms of insurance were . . . sought." That primal memory of embalming lives on in photography and cinema which "embalm time, rescuing it simply from its proper corruption." This leads to an elegantly simple conclusion: "If the history of the plastic arts is less a matter of their aesthetic than of their psychology then it will be seen to be essentially the story of resemblance, or, if you will, of realism."

If the genesis of the photographic arts is essentially a matter of psychology, then so is their effect. In "The Evolution of the Language of Cinema," Bazin traces the roots of film realism back to Murnau and Stroheim in the silent cinema, and quickly and elegantly describes how a series of technological innovations pushed film ever closer, asymptotically, to reality. But while technology was the source of this particular power, it was used for psychological, ethical, and political effects. This tendency blossomed in the movement of Italian Neorealism just at the end of and directly after World War II—a cinematic era for which Bazin felt a great affinity. "Is not neorealism primarily a kind of humanism," he concludes, "and only secondarily a style of filmmaking?" The real revolution, he thinks, took place more on the level of subject matter than of style.

Just as the Formalists had found montage to be the heart of the cinematic enterprise, so Bazin claims that mise en scène is the crux of the realist film. By mise en scène he means specifically deep focus photography and the sequence-shot; these techniques allow the spectator to participate more fully in the experience of film. Thus Bazin finds the development of deep focus to be not just another filmic device, but rather "a dialectical step forward in the history of film language." He outlines why this is so: depth of focus "brings the spectator in closer relation with the image than he is with reality." This implies consequently "both a more active mental attitude on the part of the observer and a more positive contribution on his part to the action in progress." No more the "psychological guidance" of Pudokvin. From the attention and the will of the spectator, the meaning of the image derives. Moreover, there is a metaphysical consequence of deep focus: "montage by its very nature rules out ambiguity of expression." Eisenstein's attractions are what they are: they are strongly denotative. Neorealism, on the other hand, "tends to give back to the cinema a sense of the ambiguity of reality." Free to choose, we are free to interpret.

Closely associated with this concept of the value of ambiguity are the twin concepts of the presence and reality of space. Bazin, in a later essay, suggests that the essential difference between theater and cinema lies in this area. There is only one reality that cannot be denied in cinema—the reality of space. Contrariwise, on the stage space can easily be illusory; the one reality that cannot be denied there is the presence of the actor and the spectator. These two reductions are the foundations of their respective arts. The implications for cinema are that, since there is no irreducible reality of presence, "there is nothing to prevent us from identifying ourselves in imagination with the moving world before us, which becomes *the* world." Identification then becomes a key word in the vocabulary of cinematic esthetics. Moreover, the one irreducible reality is that of space. Therefore, film form is intimately involved with spatial relationships: mise en scène, in other words.

Bazin did not live long enough to formulate these theories more precisely, but his work nevertheless had a profound effect on a generation of filmmakers, as did Eisenstein's, but as Arnheim's and Kracauer's prescriptions did not. Bazin laid the groundwork for the semiological and ethical theories that were to follow. More immediately, he inspired a number of his colleagues on *Cahiers du Cinéma*, the magazine he founded with Jacques Doniol-Valcroze and Lo Duca in 1951. The most influential film journal in history, *Cahiers* provided an intellectual home during the fifties and early sixties for François Truffaut, Jean-Luc Godard, Claude Chabrol, Eric Rohmer, and Jacques Rivette, among others. As critics, these men contributed significantly to the development of theory; as filmmakers, they comprised the first generation of cinéastes whose work was thoroughly grounded in film history and theory; their films—especially those of Godard—were not only practical examples of theory but often themselves theoretical essays. For the first time, film theory was written in film rather than print.

This fact itself was evidence that the vision of critic and filmmaker Alexandre Astruc was being realized. In 1948, Astruc had called for a new age of cinema, which he identified as the age of caméra-stylo (camera-pen). He predicted that cinema would "gradually break free from the tyranny of what is visual, from the image for its own sake, from the immediate and concrete demands of the narrative, to become a means of writing just as flexible and subtle as written language."* Many earlier theorists had spoken of film's "language"; the concept of the caméra-stylo was significantly more elaborate. Astruc not only wanted film to develop its own idiom, he wanted that idiom to be capable of expressing the most subtle ideas. Except for Eisenstein, no previous film theorist had conceived of film as an intellectual medium in which abstract concepts could be expressed.

Nearly all theorists naturally assumed that the proper province of the recording medium of film was the concrete. Even Eisenstein's dialectical montage depended thoroughly on concrete images—we might call it a dialectic of objective correlatives. Astruc wanted something more. In an offhand reference to Eisenstein, he noted: "the cinema is now moving towards a form which is making it such a precise language that it will soon be possible to write ideas directly on film without even having to resort to those heavy associations of images that were the delight of silent cinema." Astruc's caméra-stylo was a doctrine of function rather than form. It was a fitting complement to the developing practice of Neorealism that so influenced Bazin.

It would be more than ten years before Astruc's 1948 vision would be realized in the cinema of the New Wave. Meanwhile, Truffaut, Godard, and the others set about developing a theory of critical practice in the pages of *Cahiers du Cinéma*. Always the existentialist, André Bazin was working to develop a theory of film that was deductive—based in practice. Much of this work proceeded through identification and criti-

---

*The New Wave, edited by Peter Graham, contains two essays of note: "The birth of a new avant-garde: La caméra-stylo," by Alexandre Astruc; and "La politique des auteurs," by André Bazin; both of which are quoted in this section.

cal examination of genres. "Cinema's existence precedes its essence," he wrote. Whatever conclusions Bazin drew were the direct results of the experience of the concrete fact of film.

François Truffaut best expressed the major theoretical principle that came to identify *Cahiers du Cinéma* in the fifties. In his landmark article, "Une certaine tendance du cinéma français" (*Cahiers du Cinéma*, January 1954), Truffaut developed the "politique des auteurs," which became the rallying cry for the young French critics. Usually translated as "auteur theory," it wasn't a theory at all but a policy: a fairly arbitrary critical approach. As Bazin explained several years later in an essay in which he tried to counter some of the excesses of the policy: "The *politique des auteurs* consists, in short, of choosing the personal factor in artistic creation as a standard of reference, and then of assuming that it continues and even progresses from one film to the next."

This led to some rather absurd opinions on individual films, as Bazin points out, but by its very egregiousness the politique des auteurs helped to prepare the way for a resurgence of the personal cinema of authors in the sixties who could wield Astruc's caméra-stylo with grace and intelligence. Cinema was moving from theories of abstract design to theories of concrete communication. It was not material realism or even psychological realism that counted now, but rather intellectual realism. Once it was understood that a film was the product of an author, once that author's "voice" was clear, then spectators could approach the film not as if it were reality, or the dream of reality, but as a statement by another individual.

More important than Truffaut's politique, though much less influential at the time, was Jean-Luc Godard's theory of montage, developed in a series of essays in the middle fifties and best expressed in "Montage, mon beau souci" (*Cahiers du Cinéma* 65, December 1956). Building on Bazin's theory of the basic opposition between mise en scène and montage, Godard created a dialectical synthesis of these two theses that had governed film theory for so long. This is one of the most important steps in film theory. Godard rethought the relationship so that both montage and mise en scène can be seen as different aspects of the same cinematic activity. "Montage is above all an integral part of *mise en scène*," he wrote. "Only at peril can one be separated from the other. One might just as well try to separate the rhythm from a melody. . . . What one seeks to foresee in space, the other seeks in time." Moreover, for Godard, mise en scène automatically implies montage. In the cinema of psychological reality that derived from Pudovkin and influenced

"THE SIGN FORCES US TO SEE AN OBJECT THROUGH ITS SIGNIFICANCE."
FIVE STILLS FROM LATER GODARD FILMS.

Figure 5-6. Juliet Berto, in *Weekend* (1968), is caught between the two unruly forces of the film, sex and energy, a bra ad and the Esso tiger.

the best of Hollywood, "cutting on a look is almost the definition of montage." Montage is therefore specifically determined by mise en scène. As the actor turns to look at an object the editing immediately shows it to us. In this kind of construction, known as "découpage classique," the length of a shot depends on its function and the relationship between shots is controlled by the material within the shot—its mise en scène.

Godard's synthesis of the classic opposition is elegantly simple. It has two important corollaries: first, that mise en scène can thus be every bit as untruthful as montage when a director uses it to distort reality. Second, that montage is not necessarily evidence of bad faith on the part of the filmmaker. No doubt, simple plastic reality is better served by mise en scène, which in the strictest Bazinian sense is still more honest than montage. But Godard has redefined the limits of realism so that we now no longer focus on plastic reality (the filmmaker's concrete relationship with his raw materials) nor on psychological reality (the filmmaker's manipulative relationship with the audience), but on intellectual reality (the filmmaker's dialectical, or conversational, relationship with the audience). Techniques like mise en scène and montage then cease to be of main interest. We are more concerned with the

Figures 5-7. Recalling the long tracking shot in *Weekend* (see Figure 3-56) past the endless line of stalled autos, this opening sequence from *British Sounds* (1969) objectively follows the construction of a car on the assembly line. The soundtrack is a screech of machinery, as the workers are seen only as parts of the larger machine. The fabrication of the car is as painful as traffic accidents. In both *Weekend* and *British Sounds* tracking shots, mise en scène becomes an ideological tool: it is experience and thus *felt*, whereas montage is analytical; because it summarizes for us, it does not permit us to work out our own logic. Montage draws conclusions; mise en scène asks questions.

"voice" of a film: is the filmmaker operating in good faith? Is he speaking directly to us? Has he designed a machine of manipulation? Or is the film an honest discourse?

Godard has redefined montage as part of mise en scène. So to do montage is to do mise en scène. This presages the semiotic approach that was to develop in the sixties. Godard was fond of quoting the apothegm of one of his former teachers, the philosopher Brice Parain: "The sign forces us to see an object through its significance." Plastic or material realism deals only with what is signified. Godard's more advanced intellectual or perceptual realism includes the signifier. Godard was also in the habit of quoting Brecht's dictum that "Realism doesn't consist in reproducing reality, but in showing how things *really* are." Both of these approaches concentrate the realist argument on matters of perception. Christian Metz later elaborated this concept, making an

Figure 5-8. In *Vladimir and Rosa* (1971), Godard (left) and his collaborator Jean-Pierre Gorin (right) set up the "dialectic of the tennis court". The elements of the dialectic are, variously: Vladimir (Lenin) and Rosa (Luxemburg), Jean-Luc (Godard) and Jean-Pierre (Gorin), sound and image, American experience and French experience, film-makers (here) and filmwatchers (also here, by implication).

important differentiation between the reality of the substance of a film and the reality of the discourse in which that substance is expressed. "On the one hand," he wrote, "there is the *impression* of reality; on the other the *perception* of reality. . . ."

Godard continued his examination of these theoretical problems after he became a filmmaker. By the mid-sixties, he had developed a form of filmed essay in which the structure of ideas usually superseded the classic determinants of plot and character. Most of these films—*The Married Woman* (1964), *Alphaville* (1965), *Masculine-Feminine* (1966), *Two or Three Things that I Know about Her* (1966), for example—dealt with general political and philosophical questions: prostitution, marriage, rebellion, even architectural sociology. By the late sixties, however, he was once more deeply involved in film theory, this time the politics of film. In a series of difficult, tentative, experimental cinematic essays, he further developed his theory of film perception to include the political relationship between film and observer.

Figure 5-9. An essay on the trial of the Chicago 8, *Vladimir and Rosa* pays close attention to the function of the media. "Bobby X" (Godard/Gorin's character for the real-life Bobby Seale) is gagged and bound in the courtroom (as he was in real life). To demonstrate the absence of Bobby X for the media, the group of revolutionaries in the movie set up a press conference for him. But he can't appear. He speaks from a tape recorder set up on a red chair. Looking for a dramatic *story,* the television cameras are forced to cover a less exciting *idea* the struggle between sound and image. In this shot, sound finally gets its own image!

The first of these, and the most intense, is *Le Gai Savoir* (1968), in which Godard deals with the acute problem of the language of film. He suggests that it has become so debased by being used manipulatively that no film can accurately represent reality. It can only, because of the connotations of its language, present a false mirror of reality. It must therefore be presentational rather than representational. While it cannot reproduce reality honestly and truthfully, it *may* be able to produce itself honestly, In order for the language to regain some of its force, Godard suggests, it will be necessary for filmmakers to break it down, to engage in what literary critic Roland Barthes called "semioclasm"—the revivifying destruction of signs—in order to "return to zero" so that we may begin again.

During the following five years, before Godard turned his attention to video, he completed a number of 16 mm films in which he attempted

Figure 5-10. The tracking shot in the supermarket at the end of *Tout va bien* is equally as long (and as exhilarating) as the earlier shot in *Weekend*. Godard's cameras moves inexorably past a huge rank of twenty-four cash registers, most of them clanging away, as the group of young gauchistes stages a political event in the market: production versus consumption—of images as well as products. (*All stills frame enlargements.*)

to return to zero. In *Pravda* (1969) he investigated the ideological significance of certain cinematic devices; in *Vent d'est* (1969) he explored the ideological meaning of film genres; in *British Sounds* (1969) and *Vladimir and Rosa* (1971) he examined among other things, the relationship of sound and image. Sound, he thought, suffers under the tyranny of image; there should be an equal relationship between the two. Eisenstein and Pudovkin had published a manifesto as early as 1928 declaring that sound should be treated as an equal component of the cinematic equation and allowed to be indepedent of image. But for forty years film theorists had given only the most perfunctory attention to the element of the soundtrack. Godard hoped the imbalance could be redressed.

Tout va bien and *Letter to Jane* (both 1972) are probably the most important of Godard's theoretical works during this period. The former summarizes what he had learned from his experiments; the latter is, in part, an autocritique of the former. *Tout va bien* involves a filmmaker and a reporter (husband and wife) in a concrete political situation (a strike and the worker occupation of a factory) and then studies their reaction to it. From this it builds to an analysis of the entire filmic process of production and consumption. Godard reworks his earlier synthesis of montage and mise en scène in economic terms, seeing cinema not as a system of esthetics but as an economic, perceptual, and political structure in which the "rapports de production"—the relationships between producer and consumer—determine the shape of the film experience. The emphasis is not on how cinema relates to an ideal system (esthetics) but rather on how it directly affects us as viewers. Film's ethics and politics therefore determine its nature.

This was not a particularly new idea; Balázs was aware of this dimension of film. In the thirties and forties, the Frankfurt school of social criticism (Walter Benjamin, Theodor Adorno, and Max Horkheimer, mainly) had examined film in this context, most notably in Benjamin's very important essay "The Work of Art in the Age of Mechanical Reproduction." Benjamin had written: "For the first time in world history, mechanical reproduction emancipates the work of art from its parasitical dependence on ritual. . . . Instead of being based on ritual, it begins to be based on another practice—politics." Benjamin, however, was speaking of an ideal. Godard had to show how commercial cinema had usurped what Benjamin had termed film's unique ability to shatter tradition, tamed it, and made it serve the purposes of a repressive establishment. It was this subliminally powerful idiom that Godard knew had to be broken down.

Letter to Jane, a forty-five-minute essay about the ideological significance of a photo of Jane Fonda (one of the stars of *Tout va bien*), carries out this process in detail. Working with Jean-Pierre Gorin, Godard attempted to analyze the signification of the esthetic elements of the photo: the angle, design, and relationships between components, Godard showed, have delicate but real ideological significance. By the time of *Letter to Jane*, Godard was by no means alone in this dialectic, semiotic approach to film.

FILM SPEAKS AND ACTS: Metz and Contemporary Theory

While Godard was studying on film the consequences of the idea that "the sign forces us to see an object through its significance," Christian Metz and others were studying in print the ramifications of that dictum. In two volumes of *Essais sur la signification au cinéma* (the first of which has appeared in English translated as *Film Language: A Semiotics of the Cinema*) published in 1968 and 1972, and in his major work *Language*

and Cinema (1971), Metz has outlined a view of film as a logical phenomenon that can be studied by scientific methods. The main points of
Metz's thesis have already been discussed in Chapter 3. It will suffice
here simply to outline the broad principles of what is the most elaborate, subtle, and complex theory of film yet developed.

Semiotics is a general term that covers many specific approaches to
the study of culture as language. With strong roots in the linguistic
theories of Ferdinand de Saussure, it uses language as a general model
for a variety of phenomena. The approach first took shape in the
cultural anthropology of Claude Lévi-Strauss in the fifties and early
sixties. This "Strucutralism" quickly became accepted as a general
worldview. Michael Wood has described the nature of this intellectual
fashion succinctly:

> Structualism is perhaps best understood as a tangled and possibly unname-
> able strand in modern intellectual history. At times it seems synonymous
> with modernism itself. At times it seems to be simply one among several
> twentieth-century formalisms. . . . And at times it seems to be the in-
> heritor of that vast project which was born with Rimbaud and Nietzsche,
> spelled out in Mallarmé, pursued in Saussure, Wittgenstein, and Joyce,
> defeated in Beckett and Borges, and is scattered now into a host of
> helpless sects: what Mallarmé called the Orphic explanation of the earth,
> the project of picturing the world not *in* language but *as* language [*New
> York Review of Books,* March 4, 1976].

In short, structuralism, with its offspring, semiotics, is a generalized
worldview that uses the idea of language as its basic tool.

Metz's approach to film (like all film semiotics) is at once the most
abstract and the most concrete of film theories. Because it intends to be
a science, semiotics depends heavily on the practical detailed analysis of
specific films—and parts of films. In this respect, semiotic criticism is
far more concrete and intense than any other approach. Yet at the same
time, semiotics is often exquisitely philosophical. The semiological description of the universe of cinema, in a sense, exists for its own sake: it
has its own attractions, and the emphasis is often not on film but on
theory. Moreover, semioticians—Metz especially—are noted for being
elegant stylists in their own right. Much of the pleasure of reading
semiotic studies has to do with the pure intellectual creativity and the
subtlety of technique of its practitioners. Metz, for example, has a droll,
eloquent sense of humor that does much to meliorate his often florid
theorizing.

Umberto Eco, next to Metz the most prominent of current film
semioticians, has outlined four stages of the development of the science

since the early sixties. The first stage, which according to Eco lasted until the early seventies, was marked by what he calls "the overevaluation of the linguistic mode." As semiotics struggled to achieve legitimacy, it clung tightly to the accepted patterns of the study of linguistics that had preceded it. (In the same way, the earliest stages of film theory had mimicked that of the older arts.) The second stage began when semioticians started to realize that their system of analysis was not so simple and universal as they would have liked to believe at first. During the third stage—the early seventies—semiotics concentrated on the study of one specific aspect of the universe of meaning in film: production. The semiotics of the process, of the making of texts, was central here, and political ideology became part of the semiotic equation. The fourth stage—beginning in 1975—saw attention shift from production to consumption, from the making of texts to the perception of them. In this stage, film semiotics was greatly influenced by the approach to Freudian psychology of the French sage Jacques Lacan. Having begun with a quasi-scientific system that purported to quantify and offered the prospect of complete and exact analysis of the phenomenon of film, semiotics has gradually worked its way backwards to the basic question that has puzzled all students of film: how do we know what we see? Along the way, by rephrasing old questions in new ways, semiotics has contributed significantly to the common struggle to understand the nature of film.

We now might want to add a fifth stage—especially in England and the United States: the academic establishment of semiotics. During the past few years, this once elegant system of thought has produced little of real intellectual value. At the same time, it has become a useful tool for academic careerists interested more in publishing before they perish than in increasing our understanding of film theory. Because it is inherently, defiantly abstruse, semiotics is especially dangerous in this regard. In the hands of elegant stylists like Metz, Eco, or Roland Barthes, the tools of semiology can produce attractive and enlightening discursions. But lesser acolytes can get away with a lot, here. Anyone intending to read semiotics should be forewarned: just because you can't understand it doesn't mean it means anything.

Much of Christian Metz's earliest work was concerned with setting up the premises of a semiotics of film. It would seem that the fact of montage offers the easiest comparison between film and language in general. The image is not a word. The sequence is not a sentence. Yet film is *like* a language. What makes film distinctly separate from other languages is its shortcircuit sign, in which signifier and signified are nearly the same. Normal languages exhibit the power of "double articulation": that is, in order to use a language one must be able to understand its sounds and meanings, both its signifiers and its signifieds. But this is not true of film. Signifier and signified are nearly the same: what you see it what you get.

So Christian Metz quickly left behind the structures of linguistics that had served as models for all the various semiological studies of film, literature, and other areas of culture. He turned to the analysis of specific problems. Although he didn't agree that montage was the governing determinant of film language, he felt that the use of narrative was central to the film experience. The motivation of cinematic signs, he felt, was important to define: the difference between denotation and connotation in cinema is important. (See pp. 130–32.) The second important differentiation in narrative, he felt, was between syntagmatic and paradigmatic structures. Both of these are theoretical constructions rather than practical facts. The syntagma of a film or sequence shows its linear narrative structure. It is concerned with "what follows what." The paradigm of a film is vertical: it concerns choice—"what goes with what." Now Metz felt he had a system of logic that would permit the real analysis of the film phenomenon. Montage and mise en scène had been thoroughly redefined as the syntagmatic and paradigmatic categories. These Cartesian coordinates determined the field of film.

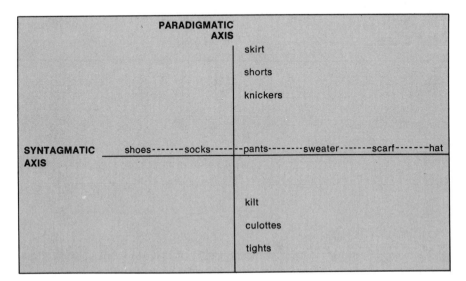

Syntagmatic and paradigmatic structures of clothing.

Metz next turned, in *Language and Cinema,* to a thorough exposition of the system of codes that govern cinematic meaning. Within the syntagmas and paradigms of film theory, what determines how we acquire meaning from a film? Contemporary mathematical set theory plays an important part in his elaborate structure of codes. Making the differentiation between "film" and "cinema" that we noted in Chapter 4, Metz explained that the concept of codes transcends the limits of film. Many codes that operate in film come from other areas of culture. These are "nonspecific" codes. Our understanding of the murder in *Psycho* (1960), for example, does not depend on specifically cinematic codes. The way in which Hitchcock presents that murder, however, is an example of a "specific" cinematic code. Finally, there are those codes that cinema borrows from or shares with other media. The lighting of the shower sequence in *Psycho* is a good example of such a shared code. We thus have our first series of overlapping sets.

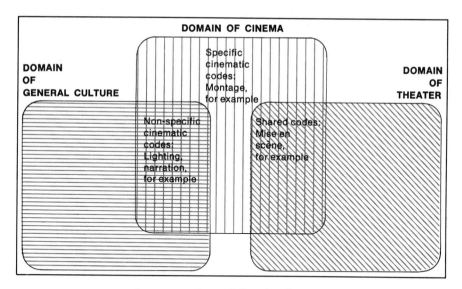

CODE SET THEORY: specific, nonspecific, and shared codes.

The next differentiation of codes follows logically. If some codes are specific to cinema and some are not, then of those specific codes some are shared by all films and some by only a few, while others are unique to certain individual films. The diagram visualizes this logic:

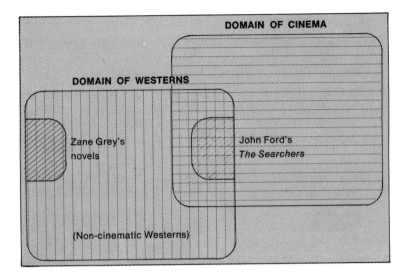

CODE SET THEORY: Generality of codes.

Finally, codes—any codes—can be broken down into subcodes; there is a hierarchy of codes. The system is elegantly simple: film is all the possible sets of these codes: a specific film is a limited number of codes and sets of codes. Genres, careers, studios, national characters, techniques, and every other element ever suggested by previous film theorists, critics, historians, and students can be broken down into code systems. Codes are the things we read in films.

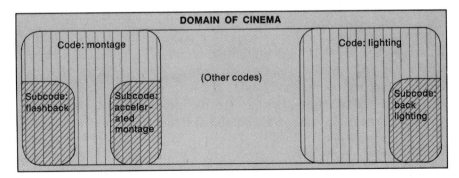

CODE SET THEORY: codes and subcodes.

Along with other semioticians, Metz in the late seventies moved on to a discussion of the psychology of filmic perception, most successfully in his long essay, "The Imaginary Signifier," which appeared simultaneously in both French and English in 1975. Drawing on basic Freudian theory as rephrased by Jacques Lacan, he psychoanalyzed not only the cinematic experience, but cinema itself. Because of its great debt to Freud, whose theories are now much less highly regarded in America than they once were, this latest trend in film semiotics has elicited much less interest among English-speaking followers of semiology than among its French practitioners.

While Metz has received the most attention, he is by no means alone in his semiological pursuits. The movement remains strong in France. Roland Barthes, although mainly a literary critic, contributed significantly to the debate in cinema before his death in 1980. Raymond Bellour has written widely; his two extended studies of sequences from Hitchcock's *The Birds* and *North by Northwest* are of special interest. In Italy, Umberto Eco and Gianfranco Bettetini have made significant contributions, and Pier Paolo Pasolini, although as he put it an "amateur" theorist, produced some interesting analyses before his untimely death. In England, semiotics found an early and receptive home in the journal *Screen* and led to the establishment of the English school of "Ciné-Structuralism." Peter Wollen's *Signs and Meaning in the Cinema*, the major argument of which is outlined in Chapter 3, pp. 133–36, has been the most important English-language contribution to the broad outline of semiotic theory so far.

In the U.S., semiotics has had little effect so far, although the growth of film scholarship in colleges and universities, as we have noted, is now providing a fertile seedbed for this egregiously academic theory of film. Highly intellectualized, abstract theories of cinema have never been popular in America. We can, however, discern a strong native tradition of more practical criticism, often with a social if not exactly political orientation, stretching from Harry Alan Potamkin and Otis Ferguson in the thirties through James Agee and Robert Warshow in the forties to Dwight Macdonald, Manny Farber, and Pauline Kael in the sixties and seventies. Andrew Sarris, although he doesn't fit into this sociological tradition, has had a marked effect on the course of film criticism in the U.S. in the last twenty years through his work in popularizing the auteur policy.

The main tradition of American criticism, however, has preferred to see films not so much as products of specific authors, but as evidence of social, cultural, and political currents. Recently, especially in the work of Kael, Molly Haskell, and others, this strain of social criticism has been modified to include an intensely personal focus. Practically, American criticism is not so far removed from the French theoretical tradition at the moment. Both are strongly concerned with the problem of perception. The difference is that the Europeans, as has been their wont, prefer to generalize and to develop elaborate theories, while the Americans, true to tradition, are more interested in the everyday experience of specific phenomena.

This personal, perceptive orientation may be superseded in the immediate future by a more strongly political view of the cinematic experience. Concurrent with the growth of semiotics on the Continent, for example, has been a revival of Marxist criticism. The French journals *Cahiers du Cinéma* and *Cinéthique* managed to combine the semiotic and the dialectic traditions in the late seventies. In England, too, semiotics often has a distinctly political cast. In America, many of the younger critics see film as a political phenomenon. Of the major English-language film journals, for example, only *Film Comment* and *American Film* cannot be characterized as politically oriented. *Sight and Sound* is eclectic in approach but usually evinces a political bent, while smaller-circulation magazines—notably *Cinéaste, Jump Cut,* and *Film Quarterly*—are strongly political in orientation. Some exciting work in film criticism is being published in their pages.

More important, perhaps, is the developing theory of film in the Third World. A major document here is "Toward a Third Cinema," by Fernando Solanas and Octavio Getino (*Cinéaste* IV:3, 1970). More a manifesto than a theory, the South American filmmakers' essay suggests that the "first cinema"—Hollywood and its imitators—and the "second cinema"—the more personal style of the New Wave or "author's" cinema—will yield to the "third cinema," a cinema of liberation that will consist of "films that the System cannot assimilate and which are foreign to its needs, or . . . films that directly and explicitly set out to fight the System."

In the U.S. these various currents—semiotic, psychoanalytic, dialectical, and politically proscriptive—have each gained their adherents as film theory has become attractive to academicians. Our own native strain of practical criticism continues to develop, too. In the last few years it has centered on a study of narrativity—the ways in which the stories of film are told. Such scholars as Frank McConnell (*Storytelling and Mythmaking in Film and Literature*, 1979) have pointed the way to some fertile areas for inquiry.

The great value of such theories of narration is, paradoxically that they deflect attention from the specially cinematic qualities of film. If film is seen first as narrative then we almost immediately infer the corollary that film is simply one of several different modes of narrative. And that observation, in turn, leads us to consider film in the context of the continuum of media. Both practically and theoretically, this will be a necessity from now on.

What seems clear in general about the present course of film theory is that description as an attitude, which reached its apex in the early days of film semiotics, has in a sense merged with the prescription that characterized the earliest film theories. People who think about film are no longer content simply to describe an ideal system of esthetics or political and social values, nor do they see their main aim as finding a language to describe the phenomenon of film. The job of film theory now is profoundly dialectical: cinema is an enormous and far-reaching set of interrelating oppositions: between filmmaker and subject, film and observer, establishment and avant garde, conservative purposes and purposes of liberation, psychology and politics, image and sound, dialogue and music, montage and mise en scène, genre and auteur, literary sensibility and cinematic sensibility, signs and meaning, culture and society, form and function, design and purpose, sex and violence, syntagmas and paradigms, image and event, realism and expressionism, language and phenomenology . . . a never-ending set of codes and subcodes that raises fundamental questions about the relationships of life and art, reality and language.

MEDIA

One of the most succinct analyses of the differences that separate the various techniques of communication known collectively as "the media" lies in a series of pieces written by Samuel Beckett in the sixties. In *Play, Film, Eh Joe, Cascando,* and *Word and Music,* the playwright/novelist/poet/critic, who writes in both French and English, captured the essence of each form.

Play presents three characters immobilized on stage in urns. As the stream-of-consciousness dialogue flows back and forth from one to the other, a sharp, precise spotlight follows the "action" or comments upon it. Beckett's abstract design of the stage focuses attention on the element of choice that the observer controls in this medium while it emphasizes the minor importance of physical action. For Beckett, the stage play is deep focus mise en scène, not controlled montage.

Film, on the contrary, develops the dialectic between filmmaker and subject that Beckett sees as inherently essential in that medium. As directed by Alan Schneider and acted by Buster Keaton, *Film* is the silent abstract representation of the drama that goes on not between characters, but between filmmaker and actor. Alone on the screen throughout most of the film. Keaton is nevertheless not alone in the narrative, for the camera is made to appear as a very real presence, and Keaton's struggle to avoid its all-seeing eye is theme of the dramatic design. *Play* emphasizes the interaction between and among characters and the relative freedom of the observer to mold the experience. *Film,* on the other hand, emphasizes the solitude of the subject, the drama between subject and artist, and the observer's relative lack of involvement in the process.

Eh Joe, a teleplay, is an equally sophisticated analysis of the essential elements of television. Lasting about forty-five minutes, the piece con-

Figure 6-1. George Rose in Beckett's *Eh, Joe.* (New York Television Theatre, April 18, 1966. Producer: Glenn Jordan; director: Alan Schneider.) (*Grove Press, Frame enlargement of kinescope recording.*)

trasts the audio and the video components of the television experience. "Joe," the subject of the play, is seen on the screen in a single sequence shot that progresses over the course of the play from a relatively long shot showing most of the room that is the set, to full shot, to mid-shot, and finally to a long, extremely slow tracking closeup that gradually and inexorably moves from a full head shot to an extreme closeup of eyes, nose, and mouth. On the soundtrack, a woman's voice, speaking to Joe, intones a continuing stream-of-consciousness monologue. The design of *Eh Joe* subtly emphasizes the two essential elements of television that separate it from film on the one hand and the stage play on the other: the separate, parallel monologue, as it creates the basic atmosphere and tone of the piece, reinforces our sense of the relatively greater significance of sound in television, while the extraordinary, intense sequence shot from long shot to extreme closeup cannily emphasizes the unusual psychological intimacy of this medium.

Cascando and *Words and Music* are both radio plays. The structure of this often-ignored dramatic form is considerably simpler than are the structures of the stage play, film, and television. Beckett isolates the essential elements of radio art—"words and music", the background noise of civilization. The product of the dynamic between them is the "falling," "tumbling" "cascando" of the radio experience. In each of these analytical pieces, Beckett sets up a dramatic tension, not between characters but between elements of the structure of the various arts: for the stage, audience choice versus the flow of dialogue; for film, the director's control and the subject's integrity; for television, the intense nature of audio versus the psychological intimacy of the image; and for radio, more simply, words and music, information and background.

Esthetically, Beckett's series of analytical plays comprises an elegant summary of the differences between and among media. But the political, social, and technological factors in the media equation may very well supersede the esthetic determinants. The connotations of the word "media" in fact, suggest that we regard the phenomenon as having a latitude much more extensive then the limits of esthetics would suggest. The media, essentially, are means of communication: all more or less technological systems designed to transmit information without regard to the natural limits of space and time. They have come to be used in a variety of manners that combine elements of information and entertainment. They are, moreover, exceptionally powerful socializing forces, as the root of the word "communication" strongly suggests: to "communicate" in a sense is to forge a "community."

PRINT AND ELECTRONIC MEDIA

Written language is the prototype for all media. For seven thousand years, it has provided a workable and flexible method for getting information from one person to another. But it was not until the invention of movable type by Johann Gutenberg in the fifteenth century that "written" messages could be mass-produced so the author could communicate with a large number of other individuals simultaneously. This multiple reproducibility is a prime factor in the structure of media. Between 1500 and 1800, the production of books developed into a major industry. It was the concept of the newspaper or journal, quickly produced and appearing on a regular schedule, that suggested the second vital element of the media—the open channel of communication. Books are produced in quantity, but they are each singular events, limited to their subjects. Newspapers and magazines are open, in both time and space, to continuing and various uses.

Although print was immediately recognized as a socially revolutionary force, it was not until the nineteenth century and the rise of a massive literate middle class that printing realized its full potential as a medium. (Significantly, the rise of the electronic media in the twentieth century was much more rapid, since no particular skills were required for comprehension.) Print media also benefited from technological advances in the latter half of the nineteenth century. The steam-powered press had been developed by Friedrich König in 1810; rotary presses, which operated continuously rather than discretely, date from the 1840s through the 1860s. Richard March Hoe is credited with inventing the first rotary press in 1846. Twenty years later, the stereotype printing plate was first patented in England. The combination of steam-power, rotary configuration, and one-piece stereotype plates greatly increased the speed and flexibility of presses. The typewriter, invented by C.L. Sholes in 1867 and first produced by Remington in 1874, and the linotype typesetting machine, invented in 1884 by Ottmar Mergenthaler, made the preparatory processes much more efficient.

In 1880, the *New York Graphic* printed the first halftone photographs, although it was a decade and more before this important technique gained wide acceptance among newspapers and magazines. Earlier technological developments in printing had been quantitative: they increased the speed and flexibility of the process, but they did not affect its basic nature. The halftone process, on the other hand, was a qualitative advance, making the reproduction of photographs an integral part of the technique of printing. The basic problem with reproducing photographs in print was that the photographic process produces a continual and infinitely variable range of tones from white through gray to black, while the printing process is essentially "binary"—any given space on a printed page is either white or black. The technique of the halftone solved this problem in an ingenious manner: the continuous space of the photograph was broken up into discrete particles—as many as two hundred per inch—which could be translated into the binary language of print. If fifty percent of a given area was actually printed, then that area would appear a medium gray; if 100 percent was printed, it would be black, et cetera.

In its way, the concept of the halftone was as important as the recognition of the uses of the phenomenon of persistence of vision was in the development of motion pictures: both utilized basic physiological facts of perception in simple yet productive ways. Moreover, the concept that underlies the halftone process—the translation of a continuous range of values into a discrete binary system—was to become one of the most significant and widely effective intellectual devices of the twentieth century: television, phototelegraphy, telemetry, and—most important—computer technology, all rest on this basic binary concept.

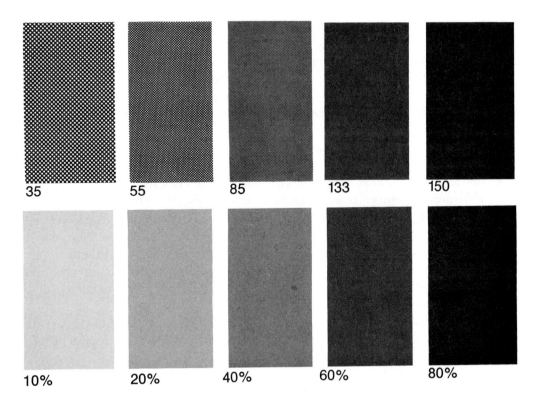

35   55   85   133   150

10%   20%   40%   60%   80%

Figure 6-2. HALFTONE SCREENS. The 35 lines per inch and 55 lines per inch screens are too coarse to be used for anything except special effects. The 85 screen is the standard for newspapers. 133 is the most common screen for books. (All the photographs in *How to Read a Film* were reproduced with this screen.) The 150 screen is used in special applications—such as medical illustrations—where the finest detail is essential.

The various shadings at the bottom of the illustration are used in design. The diagrams in this book, for example, include 20 percent, 40 percent, and 60 percent screens. The shading is accomplished not by changing screen size, but by increasing the size of each dot within the pattern. See also Figure 2-1E.

Many of the social and semiological effects of the electronic revolution were foreshadowed during the great age of newspapers and magazines in the nineteenth century. It became clear very quickly that the media would provide a version of reality, a record of history—sometimes even an alternate reality, and that this mediating function would have a profound effect on the organization of life. As economic entities, newspapers and magazines began by selling mainly material—information and entertainment—then gradually progressed to a more complex mode in which they also sold advertising space to other economic organizations who wanted to communicate with the readership. In other words, publishers of magazines and newspapers moved from selling an object to selling a service, the medium that they controlled providing a means of access for advertisers to the general public.

Since about 1930, this service has been refined considerably. Marketing survey techniques enable the publisher to offer a particular audience rather than simply crude space to an advertiser. The advertiser had always been aware generally of the shape of the audience he was reaching, but the rise of the erstwhile science of "demographics" enabled the publisher to pinpoint specific valuable sectors of the general audience. A modern magazine such as *Time,* for example, breaks its readership down into a number of geographic, social, and class sections and then publishes a number of separate (if nearly identical) editions so that it can offer an advertiser a finely tuned audience for his message at the most efficient "cost per thousand." In recent years, the sophistication of the demographic approach has meant that general audience magazines, even those with large circulations, have yielded to smaller, special interest journals that can offer advertisers smaller but more susceptible audiences for their products.

Advertising—central to the efficient operation of a capitalist economic system—has, according to many observers, had an enormous effect on life patterns during the past hundred and fifty years. Because the permanent record of the society is kept in the media it quickly became evident that not only manufacturers but also politicians and public figures had to advertise if their ideas were to be taken seriously by large numbers of people. This led to the development of the publicity and public relations industries, which are closely allied with advertising, but directed toward creating favorable images for companies, individuals, and ideas rather than directly selling consumable products. Moreover, advertising itself has become such a sophisticated industry that the tail now often wags the dog: ad agencies participate directly in the creation of products, sometimes inventing markets for new products where none existed before by establishing a sense of need in consumers.

Caught up in this complex economic system are the secondary, noneconomic functions of the media: the distribution of news, entertainment, and information. The "news hole"—that space in a newspaper or magazine set aside for actual news reports—is often as small as twenty-five percent of the total space available. In other words, three-quarters of the communicating ability of a print medium in the U.S. is often devoted to advertising. This veritable deluge is a major factor in determining shared systems of values in contemporary societies. Communication used to take place mainly on a personal level: the largest number of people one was able to reach was determined by the capacity of the

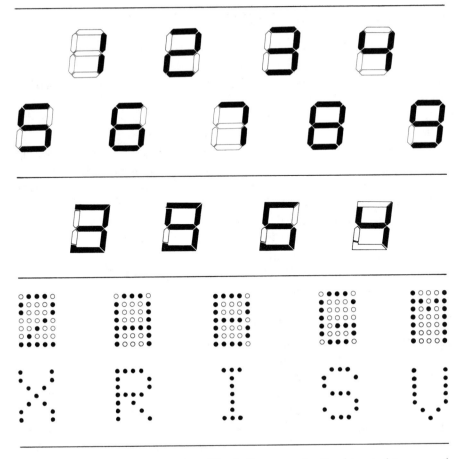

Figure 6-3. LED'S AND DOT MATRIXES. The halftone was the first historical instance of the merger of print and visual technology. It set a pattern for future development. By the early seventies, for example, when computer electronic readouts were developed for consumer and professional applications two versions of digitalized alphanumeric representations were standardized. Above, the seven-segment LED ("light-emitting diode") made possible readable numbers composed of only seven switchable elements, a considerable simplification. Such a system wouldn't work for the more complex alphabet, however, so the dot matrix printer (below) was developed to display Roman letters in readable form. The most common version uses 35 dots arrayed 5 × 7 to produce all the letters of the alphabet. Notice that in the third row of LED examples the design of the elements has been modified slightly to improve the readability of the numbers.

meeting place. But the rise of the print media greatly increased the potential for communication. Not only could one reach a far greater number of people, none of whom had to be in the same place at the same time, but—significantly—communication became for the most part unidirectional: that is, the members of the "audience" now had no chance to interact with the "speaker."

The development of the mechanical and electronic media generally followed the pattern set by the growth of the print media during the preceding 150–200 years. There were, however, some significant differences. Unlike the print media, film, radio, television, and records did not require that their audiences be highly trained to perceive and understand their messages. In this sense, at least, it is perfectly true that one does not have to learn to "read" a film. On the other hand, the mechanical and electronic media developed at a significantly higher level of technological sophistication. "Literacy" might not be necessary, but equipment is. Film developed as a public rather than a private experience, mainly because of the cost and complexity of the equipment involved in projecting the image. Significantly, it is the only one of the modern media that has maintained a public nature. It may not offer its audiences a chance for interaction with performers (as all public meetings and stage performances had done before it), but it still maintains, at least, the communal sense of the experience.

All the other contemporary media, however, developed as private "enterprises," for an interesting reason. The gradual shift from product to service discernible in the history of the print media is even more highly developed with the electronic and mechanical media. Two patterns interlock: in the first, the medium begins as a professional activity for which a high degree of expertise is necessary, then shifts to a semiprofessional activity as groups of fairly knowledgeable devotees learn the techniques. Finally, it becomes an everyday activity in which anyone can engage with a minimum of training.

This third stage is usually a result of the influence of the second pattern of development, which is economic. Except for motion pictures, each of the contemporary media began as a product—specifically, in the language of economics, a "consumer durable." Like central heating, refrigerators, gas or electric lighting, or even indoor plumbing and privies, the telephone, photography, record players, radios, and television represent major capital investments for consumers. In order to sell the devices, manufacturers had to make them simple enough for almost anyone to operate. Then, in most cases, they had to provide materials—"software." The machine–the receiver or player—was seen in most instances as the major source of profit; the media were provided

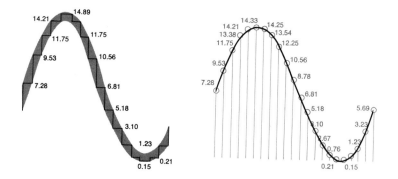

Figure 6-4. DIGITAL VERSUS ANALOGUE. The theory behind digital techniques is that *everything* can be quantified. Instead of producing an analoguous record of sounds or images (right), such as a phonograph groove or electromagnetic signal, digitized recordings sample that signal many times each second, convert the sample into whole numbers, and record those numbers (in binary form). There can be no question about the numbers. The digital curve looks rough here only because it has been simplified for illustrative purposes.

so that the machine had something to receive or play. Because the machines could be made fairly simply and cheaply and because the profit lay in the "hardware," it was thus useful to make the experience of media private so that the greatest number of machines could be sold.

We have already seen in Chapter 4 how this pattern operated in the development of the motion picture industry. Edison and the other originators of film developed the machinery, then provided films to be played on the machines. Because the machinery and its systems were complex and expensive there was little chance that projectors could be marketed as consumer durables and film remained a public rather than private art. Gradually, the center of economic power in film shifted from the manufacturer of the machinery to the exhibitor (the level of "retail sales"), then to the producer-distributors. In addition, at each stage film businessmen, whether manufacturers, exhibitors, producers, or distributors, naturally attempted to exercise monopoly control—a development later mirrored in the history of network radio and television.

Even before the rise of film, the inventions of the telephone and the amateur camera had foreshadowed this pattern of development. With both, the service and the machinery were intimately connected. Both also provided individual service rather than broad media of communication, which sets them apart structurally from such media as radio, records, and television. Interestingly, radio was considered for a long time simply an adjunct to the telephone—a device that could provide intercommunication, but only on a one-to-one level. Marconi demonstrated the effectiveness of his invention in 1899, but it wasn't until 1920 that broadcasting—the widespread dissemination of the signal to reach large numbers of listeners—was seen to be practicable. Ironically, the commercial potential was demonstrated almost accidently. Like many other amateur radio operators, Frank Conrad, a resident of Pittsburgh and a researcher for Westinghouse, was in the habit of transmitting program material—music, news, et cetera—as well as conversing with other "hams."

Late in September 1920, the Joseph Horne department store in Pittsburgh ran an advertisement in the Pittsburgh *Sun* that called attention to Conrad's amateur broadcasts and offered an "Amateur Wireless Set" for sale that could receive them. The response was immediate. Westinghouse officials, who had known of Conrad's hobby but had never given it much thought, now perceived the commercial value of broadcasting. As Erick Barnouw puts it in his invaluable history of broadcasting, *Tube of Plenty* (1975): "What had seemed an eccentric hobby, or a form of exhibitionism, or at best a quixotic enterprise pursued by visionaries . . . was suddenly seen as a sound business concept that could yield rich profits through the sale of receivers." Conrad was immediately put to work building the first commercial transmitter, which on October 27, 1920 was assigned the call letters KDKA. That station still operates.

At first, despite the immediate success of radio, broadcasting was still regarded as simply a minimal service necessary to instigate the purchase of receivers, where the profit was. The Radio Corporation of America (the descendant of Marconi's original company) joined together with AT&T, Westinghouse, General Electric, and the United Fruit Company (who had discovered early on that radio was useful for communicating with their wide-ranging empire of plantations) to form the RCA group monopoly. The practice of selling commercial time on radio developed almost accidentally. AT&T had been assigned the "radio telephony" sector of the market. In order to become involved in commercial production without breaking their monopoly agreement, AT&T invented what they called "toll radio" in 1922. Instead of broadcasting their own programs, they would simply rent out their studio to whoever wished to broadcast: the studio was likened to a telephone booth, in which the sender of the message pays the bill. WEAF in New York, which later became the cornerstone of the National Broadcasting Company, was the first such toll station. The response was minimal at first, but eventually it became clear that people not only were listening but would respond to advertising, and the success of commercial broadcasting was assured.

Throughout the thirties, forties, and fifties, this toll system dominated the structure of broadcasting, first in radio, then in television.

Although networks and stations did produce much of their own programming, they were essentially in the business of selling time to advertisers. Quite often these advertisers bought large blocks of time and their agencies produced the shows—hence, the *Ipana Troubadours, The A&P Gypsies, The Lux Radio Theatre, The Colgate Comedy Hour,* and so forth. Gradually it became clear that production simply tied up capital and could more profitably be left to independent entrepreneurs. During the 1960s, the television networks began to concentrate on distribution, themselves producing only News and Sports, which required ongoing organizations, and leaving most of the prime-time entertainment product to "independent" producers, many of whom, ironically, were subsidiaries of the motion picture studios.

The networks now not only do not have to tie up large amounts of capital in production, but they can also get away with paying the producers of the shows less than they cost. This strange state of affairs is made possible because the total real value of a successful television program is significantly greater than its one-time production cost. Producers hope to make their margin of profit on syndication sales to independent stations and export sales after the program has received the network imprimatur.

Around 1960, when this system of relying on independent producers had gained currency, the economic nexus of network television also changed. The networks still sold time to advertisers but it was measured in terms of actual minutes and seconds of commercial broadcast, not hours of programming. Thus, whereas an advertiser in 1952 might buy an hour of prime time on Tuesday evening for the next nine months and then put whatever programming he felt like sponsoring on the air to surround his commercial messages and attract an audience, by 1960 he was reduced to buying thirty seconds of ad time in a specific show produced by independents and controlled by the networks themselves.

This new system focused much more attention on the ratings. In the early days of TV a sponsor might very well finance a show that had a relatively small audience. His aim wasn't necessarily gross ratings points but prestige and influence. Thus, the so-called "Golden Age" of TV was marked by such relatively unpopular shows as *Hallmark's Hall of Fame, The U.S. Steel Hour,* and *Armstrong Circle Theater.*

But now that networks were controlling programming, the ratings game became all-important. Not only were individual shows closely ranked (the cost of advertising time within the top-ranked shows could be sold for more than the time in poorly-ranked shows), but each network's yearly average became the index of "success" or "failure." In most years since 1960, the difference in ratings averages between the first and second (and sometimes the third) network has been so small as to be statistically insignificant, but the psychology of ratings has been so obsessive that such meaningless point differences can still make millions of dollars of difference in advertising revenues.

Most observers agree that the quality of network television will not change significantly until the ratings system is either abolished or becomes moribund. It is unlikely that either the FCC or Congress will challenge a system the networks are comfortable with. Yet technological developments may very soon make the ratings game archaic. After all, if even a significant minority of television watchers own cassette recorders and therefore have the opportunity to decide themselves *when* they want to watch any particular TV program, the ratings battle becomes absurd: each show is in competition with every other show (as well as prerecorded discs and tapes) and no gross rating assures an advertiser that the show is even watched: it simply proves that someone *recorded* it, maybe to play it back later, maybe not. Finally, the technology of cassette recorders even today permits a viewer to skip commercials much as he might when reading a magazine or newspaper—this isn't possible with broadcast TV.

The main structural differences among the media are summarized in the chart on p. 362. The two economic factors—the nexus and the sales orientation—determine to a large extent how the media develop structurally. Other factors, such as access, control, and interaction—which we might call the political dimensions of the media—also have an effect, especially in regard to the manner in which each medium is used. The most salient social effect of the rise of the media has been the shift from interactive methods of communication to unidirectional methods. Many of the newer product inventions, it will be noted, shift the focus slightly back from unidirectional dominance to more equal interaction, a phenomenon which might have considerable political significance in the future. As more channels open up, as the technology becomes demystified, as access is allowed to the public at large, the media become more democratic. The difficulty is that while the technology may democratize the media, economic control is still highly concentrated—more obviously in other countries, in which radio and television are more or less government controlled, but no less effectively in the U.S. Production is relatively free of strictures, but distribution is still closely controlled by powerful economic interests. Anyone can produce a book, film, record, tape, magazine, or newspaper; few people can get their work read, seen, or heard by large numbers of people. So long as the work is specialized and directed to a sharply focused audience, this is no problem. But the writer, filmmaker, or "tapemaker" who wants to communicate with the general public often has considerable difficulty.

A close examination of the chart reveals some interesting facts. Physical items such as books, newspapers, magazines, records, and tapes have considerable advantage over the broadcast media. They are produced and distributed discretely, so the consumer can exercise choice more easily. The consumer also controls the experience. One can listen to a record, read a book, or watch a videodisc as frequently as one likes at whatever speed one prefers.

On the other hand, the salient characteristic of the broadcast media as opposed to the physical media is their circumscribed nature. Access is severely restricted, although recently the advent of cable television, which guarantees a limited amount of public access, and "talk" radio shows, which encourage listeners to phone in, have somewhat expanded opportunities. Nevertheless, unless he has his own tape recorder, the consumer is locked into the time schedule of the broadcast media and, because the distribution flow is continuous rather than discrete, he has little opportunity to control the experience. Channels, too, are strictly limited.

Newspapers and magazines present an interesting hybrid case: not only do they combine the sale of ad space and audience with the sale of the object itself, but—more important—they distribute their collections of information and entertainment in such a way that the reader has considerable control. The mosaic arrangement of these print media allows the reader the efficient luxury of what in computer terminology is called "real-time access." For instance, a newspaper reader can choose precisely which items he wants to read and can decide as well how long he wants to stay with each one, whereas someone watching television news is locked in to the time scheme of the broadcast and experiences the information precisely the same way as every other viewer. This, in general, is the most significant difference between print and electronic media. Because information in print is coded more strictly than media information, print is still the most efficient medium for communicating abstract information. Partly because the reader has such considerable control over the experience, far more information can be presented, and the structure of the print media makes it available in a more efficient manner: you can't thumb through a record, or skim a film.

THE TECHNOLOGY OF MECHANICAL AND ELECTRONIC MEDIA

Whether the eventual form of transmission is either broadcast or physical, all the mechanical and electronic media depend on one single

THE POLITICAL AND ECONOMIC RELATIONSHIPS OF MEDIA

MEDIUM	MEDIA ECONOMICS		MEDIA POLITICS				
	Nexus	Sales Orientation	Channels	Access	Interaction	Distribution Flow	Consumer Control
BOOKS	distribution	object	open	good	unidirectional	discrete	yes
NEWSPAPERS & MAGAZINES	prod./dist.	object, ad space, audience	open	good	unidirectional	semidiscrete mosaic	yes
FILM	distribution	entertainment	open	limited	unidirectional	discrete	some
RADIO	prod./dist.	ad time, audience	limited	limited	mainly unidirect.	continuous	no
CB	manufacture	equipment	limited	excellent	interactive	continuous	no
AUDIO DISCS	prod./dist.	object	open	fair	unidirectional	discrete	yes
AUDIO TAPES	production	object	open	good	unidirectional	discrete	yes
TELEVISION	dist. (prod.)	ad time, audience	closed	none	unidirectional	continuous	no
CABLE	distribution	entertainment	limited	some	mainly unidirect.	continuous	no
VIDEODISC	manufacture	equipment	open	limited	unidirectional	discrete	yes
VIDEOTAPE	manufacture	equipment	open	good	unidirectional	discrete	yes

Nexus: Where does the concentration of economic power lie? *Sales Orientation:* What is the primary product being sold? *Channels:* Are there a limited number of distribution channels? *Access:* How easy is it for someone to gain access to the medium? *Interaction:* Is the medium unidirectional or interactive? *Distribution Flow:* Are the items distributed singly or continuously? *Consumer Control:* Must the consumer/spectator/reader/listener adjust his schedule to the medium's, or can he control the time and location of the experience?

concept: the physics and technology of wave forms. Since our two primary senses—sight and hearing—also depend on wave physics, this is not surprising. Yet until Edison's phonograph, no way had ever been found to utilize this phenomenon artificially. The phonograph, as Edison conceived it, did not depend on any advanced developments in technology: it was a simple mechanical system involving no chemistry or electronics, or even any particularly difficult engineering. The essential components are the horn, which amplifies sound waves, the diaphragm, which translates sound waves into physical motion, the stylus, which transmits the physical motion to the recording medium, and the cylinder or disc—the recording medium that accepts and preserves the record of the sound. The governing concept here, as with all electronic media, is the technique of translating one wave form into another: in this case sound waves, whose medium is air, are translated into physical waves, whose medium is the wax cylinder or disc.

As ingenious as it was, Edison's early phonograph was also a limited instrument. Much quality was lost in the progression of the signal from horn to diaphragm to stylus to wax cylinder, then back again through stylus, diaphragm, and horn. Further improvements had to wait for the developing electronic technology in the early years of the twentieth century. Here, the history of the phonograph merges with the history of radio and telephony. Both radio and telephony are founded in electrical theory, but there is a significant conceptual difference between them: the telephone transmits its message through a limited channel—the wire—whereas radio performs essentially the same function by using the medium of electromagnetic radiation. Because the nature of the electromagnetic spectrum allows radio signals to be broadcast easily (a radio signal originates at a single point, but can be received anywhere within a broad area), radio seems at first to be a more advanced system than telephony, which is "narrowcast" (a telephone signal travels from any one point to any other single point). Yet, as we shall see, the advantages of the limited-channel telephone system are beginning to be appreciated. The wires of telephony, although difficult and expensive to install compared with radio's easily generated electromagnetic waves, nevertheless offer the prospect of two-way interactive communication, which is more difficult with radio. Cable television is moving in this direction.

Samuel Morse had patented a telegraph apparatus in 1840. It was a simple device for carrying a signal through wires via electrical energy. It had, however, only two "words": the current was either on, or off. Morse's dot-dash code made useful communication possible, but a more flexible system was needed. Bell's telephone added a significant dimen-

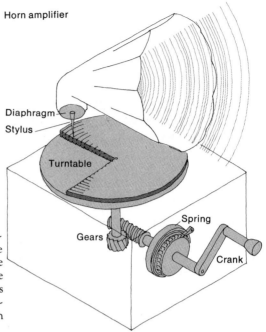

Figure 6-5. THE MECHANICAL PHO-
NOGRAPH. The crank supplies the
energy, the mainspring stores it, the
gears transmit it. The grooves of the
record store the signal, the stylus
transmits it, the diaphragm translates it from mechanical vibration
into sound, the horn amplifies it.

sion to electrical technology: it was the first invention to translate
sound waves into electrical waves and back again to sound. Bell began
with an amplifying horn similar in principle to Edison's, but he thought
to translate the sound waves into an electrical medium rather than a
physical medium. This enabled the telephone to transmit its message
immediately. The "microphone" consists of horn, diaphragm, and a
collection of carbon granules in direct contact with the diaphragm. As
the diaphragm moves in response to the sound waves that impinge upon
it, the carbon particles are compressed to a greater or lesser extent so
that their electrical resistance varies in response to the acoustic pressure. This variance produces corresponding fluctuations in an electrical
current passing through the carbon granules. At the other end of the
transmission, a "speaker" translates the electrical signal back into a
sound signal by a slightly different process: passed through an electro-
magnet, the electrical signal varies the intensity of the magnet, which
in turn controls the fluctuation of a metallic diaphragm whose movements re-create the sound waves.

By the 1890s, the telephone was in wide use. As important as it was,
Bell's microphone-speaker system would have had limited usefulness
without the concurrent development of complex and ingenious switching equipment and amplifying devices. The concept of amplification

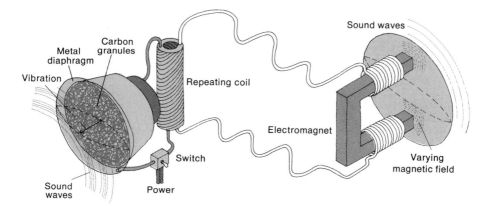

Figure 6-6. THE ELECTRICAL TRANSMISSION OF SOUND. The telephone is the simplest device for translating sound energy into electrical energy, then back again, but the principle described here is the basis for all sound transmission. The key concepts are the carbon granule construction of the microphone (or mouthpiece) which translates sound waves into electric waves, the repeating coil—a simple transformer—which acts as an amplifier, and the electromagnet-diaphragm combination of the loudspeaker (or earpiece) which translates the electrical signal back into sound.

that allowed the telephone signal to travel greater distances led directly to a host of twentieth-century electronic devices. The theory that developed out of the telephone switching system, which allowed any one phone in the system to be connected with any other, directly foreshadowed computer technology and modern systems theory.

Meanwhile, Heinrich Hertz, while conducting experiments that confirmed James Clerk Maxwell's electromagnetic theory, had discovered a way to produce electromagnetic radiation at will. The spectrum of electromagnetic radiation, which runs in frequency from 0 cycles per second as high as 10^{23} cycles per second includes a wide range of useful phenomena including visible light, heat, X rays, infrared radiation, ultraviolet radiation, and radio waves. It was the radio section of the spectrum that first intrigued inventors. Two facts were significant about electromagnetic radiation: first, that eletromagnetic waves needed no pre-existing physical medium (like sound waves)—they could be transmitted through a vacuum; second, that transmitters and receivers could be "tuned" to transmit or receive only waves of a certain frequency. A radio transmitter or receiver could thus be tuned to transmit or receive on any one of a large number of channels, a great advance over the telegraphic/telephonic systems, whose channels were limited to the number of wires attached to each and the sophistication of the switching system.

A young Italian, Guglielmo Marconi, was the first of a number of

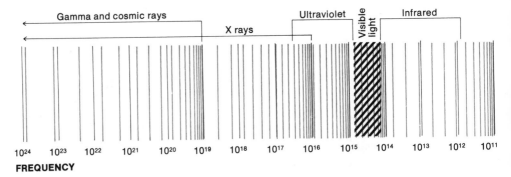

Figure 6-7. THE ELECTROMAGNETIC SPECTRUM. Since the speed of electromagnetic waves is 300,000 kilometers per second, most electromagnetic waves have extremely high frequencies. Even the longest radio waves—with wavelengths measured in kilometers—have frequencies on the order of hundreds of cycles per second. The shortest

experimenters to perfect a workable system of radiotelegraphy. In 1896 and 1897, he demonstrated his "wireless" telegraph in England, and soon powerful corporations were formed to exploit the commercial value of the invention. Unlike telegraph cables, radio signals were not subject to sabotage: the military value of the invention was seen immediately.

Yet, like Morse's system, Marconi's could not carry complex sound signals, only "on-off" code. The telephone translated sound waves into electrical waves that were carried in the medium of the wire, but the "wireless" already depended on a wave system as the medium; how could another wave system (the signal) be carried by the wave system of the medium? Reginald Fessenden, a Canadian, was one of the first to solve this problem. His idea was to superimpose the signal wave on the carrier wave; to "modulate" the carrier wave. This is the basic concept of radio and television. Since there are two variables associated with a wave—"amplitude" or strength, and "frequency" or "wavelength"—there were two possibilities for modulation: hence the current AM (Amplitude Modulation) and FM (Frequency Modulation) systems of broadcasting. (See p. 368.)

At first, Fessenden's theory seemed impractical. Lee DeForest's invention of the "audion" tube (1906) was crucial. It provided a simple way to modulate the carrier frequency. It was also very useful for the job of amplification. With the audion tube, electronics was born. The system, however, was still fairly crude. It became evident that the carrier frequency and its modulated signal had to be coaxed, filtered, strengthened, and otherwise aided. Edwin H. Armstrong's Regenerative Circuit and

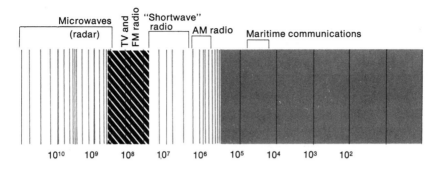

electromagnetic waves—gamma rays—have wavelengths measured in billionths of a centimeter, frequencies measured in sextillion cycles per second. The most important bands in the spectrum are those occupied by visible light and the radio spectrum, which is further divided arbitrarily into a number of bands allocated for special uses.

Superheterodyne Circuit (1912, 1918) were among the first and most important such devices. The idea that an electronic signal could be modified by circuitry became one of the most important concepts of the twentieth century. DeForest's audion vacuum tube was the workhorse of circuitry until the invention of the transistor in 1948 by John Bardeen, W. H. Brattain, and William Shockley. Much smaller and more reliable than the vacuum tubes, as well as cheaper to produce, the transistors opened up numerous new possibilities in circuitry. The complexity of the technology took another quantum jump in 1959 with the introduction of the Integrated Circuit. Produced chemically rather than mechanically, the Integrated Circuit did the work of boxes full of earlier electronic equipment in the space of chips smaller than a thumbnail.

Just as the developers of cinematography had always wanted to produce sound as well as image, so the early experimenters in radio wanted to broadcast images as well as sound. The difficulty was that, although both sound and light are wave phenomena, we perceive sound waves collectively while we perceive light waves in a sense discretely. The light waves coming from any one point in our field of vision might be as complex as all the sound waves in our "field of hearing." Because of this added complexity, light waves would have to be broken down somehow in order to be carried by radio wave forms. The solution to the problem was similar to the one adopted in printing technology: to break the continuous image into a sufficient number of discrete particles. At first, mechanical devices were tried. Paul Nipkow's invention, the "Nipkow disc" (1884) used a spiral array of perforations on a rotating disc to create a rapid scanning movement. As late as the early fifties, the CBS

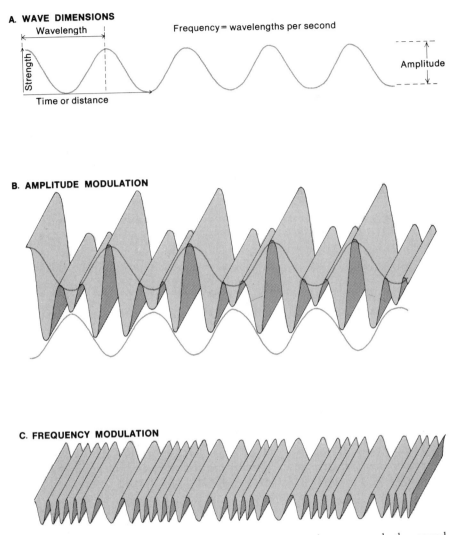

A. WAVE DIMENSIONS

Wavelength

Frequency = wavelengths per second

Strength

Time or distance

Amplitude

B. AMPLITUDE MODULATION

C. FREQUENCY MODULATION

Figure 6-8. WAVE MECHANICS AND SIGNAL MODULATION. Any wave, whether sound, light, or radio, is measured in three dimensions: amplitude, wavelength, and frequency. The amplitude is the strength of the wave. Wavelength and frequency are interconnected. Frequencies are measured in Hertz—cycles (or wavelengths) per second. Therefore, a sound wave with a length of 11 feet will have a frequency of 100 cps; likewise a sound wave 5½ feet long will have a frequency of 200 cps.

To modulate a signal means to impose another signal upon it. It's logical that there are two ways to do this: either modulate the amplitude, or modulate the frequency (which is the same thing as modulating the wavelength). AM is illustrated in B: the carrier wave is indicated by the shaded ribbon band. The program signal has been imposed upon it. FM is visualized in C.

Figure 6-9. ELECTRONIC "VALVES":
AUDION TO INTEGRATED CIRCUIT:
De Forest's invention was as valuable as it was ingenious. The audion tube amplifies a signal because
the grid acts as a continually varying electronic gate. Whatever signal the grid carries is impressed
upon the stronger current flowing
between cathode and anode. The
audion tube was the model for all
vacuum tubes—or "valves."

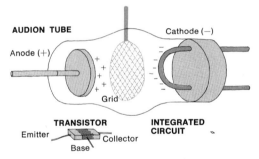

Beginning in the 1950s the transistor (left), drawn here lifesize, began to replace the
vacuum tube in most applications. The principle of operation is basically the same, but
it is more chemical than physical, and hence the transistor is much smaller and more
reliable, both great advantages. The integrated circuit, which combines numerous transistor circuits, is even smaller and is represented (lifesize) by the dot to the right.

color system utilized this mechanical technology. It worked quite well
for the color video cameras used in the Apollo moon program.

The eventual solution was, however, electronic rather than mechanical. The work of a Russian immigrant to the U.S., Vladimir K. Zwory-
kin, was essential. He developed both the "Iconoscope," a device for
receiving an image and translating it into an electronic signal, from
which most contemporary television cameras descend; and the "Kinescope," or Cathode Ray Tube, a device for translating the electronic
signal back into an image. In order to produce an image of sufficient
quality, it is necessary to break the picture down into at least 100,000
and preferably 200,000 "bits." These bits are called picture elements.
Like the dots produced in the printing of photographs by the halftone
screen, these picture elements, although discrete, are psychologically
understood as composing a continuous picture. In American television,
they are arrayed in a 525-line pattern. In European television, the
standard is 625 lines. As a result, the European image is sharper.

Unlike the printed photograph, the televised image moves. Therefore, the phenomenon of persistence of vision and the Phi effect come
into play, as they do in film. Again there is a slight difference between
European and American standards. European television operates at
twenty-five "frames" per second, American at thirty. In the iconoscope,
image orthicon, and vidicon camera tubes, all of which operate similarly, the image is projected optically onto a surface or screen within
the tube covered with the necessary number of picture elements in the
proper array, each of which has the capability of holding an electrical
charge. These charges are read by an electron beam, focused and con-

trolled by an electromagnetic lens, which scans the entire array twenty-five or thirty times each second. The signal that results carries a different value of brightness for each of 210,000 bits twenty-five or thirty times each second. The television signal is obviously much more complex than the radio signal.

In order to produce an image on its screen, the other essential component of the system, the Cathode Ray Tube (CRT), essentially reverses the process. The screen of the CRT is covered with a phosphorescent coating, any particle of which produces light when struck by a high energy beam of electrons. A "gun" at the opposite end of the tube produces this beam, varying its intensity according to the brightness value desired. The beam is controlled by a magnetic lens like the one in the camera tube that sweeps across 525 (or 625) lines thirty (or twenty-five) times each second. In reality, the system is slightly more complex. Just as a film projector shutter splits the light beam not only between frames but also in the middle of each frame to decrease the flicker effect, so the CRT electron gun actually divides each sweep into two components: it first sweeps the even-numbered lines, then returns to the top of the picture to sweep the odd-numbered lines, so that the phosphors of the screen surface fade more evenly from top to bottom between sweeps.

Color television is the same, only three times more complex. Like color printing, it extends the theory of the halftone to color psychology, creating the entire spectrum of color through various combinations of elemental color values. For television these elements are blue, red, and green. Color cameras consist either of three image orthicon tubes that, through a system of mirrors and filters, each read one of the basic colors, or of a single tube whose screen plate is masked in such a way that the picture elements are arranged in three separate sets. Likewise, the picture tube can consist of three separate electron guns, each scanning a different color, or one gun which scans each color consecutively. Figure 6-11 describes the system of masks, which can be observed by close examination of any color picture tube. Color was introduced commercially in the U.S. in 1953 and in Europe generally in the late sixties.

Interestingly, the developing technologies of image (film) and sound (radio) crossed paths in 1928, when both sound film and television were introduced. But while the sound film was immediately accepted, commercial television was delayed nearly twenty years. Partly, this delay was caused by technical reasons; mainly, it was the result first of economic decisions, then of the intervention of World War II.

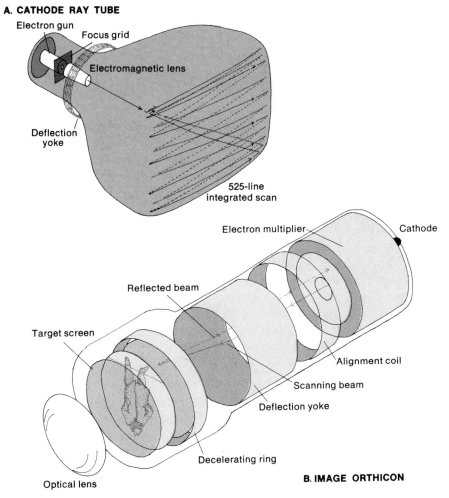

A. CATHODE RAY TUBE

Electron gun

Focus grid

Electromagnetic lens

Deflection yoke

525-line integrated scan

Electron multiplier

Cathode

Reflected beam

Target screen

Alignment coil

Scanning beam

Deflection yoke

Decelerating ring

Optical lens

B. IMAGE ORTHICON

Figure 6-10. THE CATHODE RAY TUBE AND THE IMAGE ORTHICON. Translating an optical image into an electronic signal is more difficult than the reverse operation. The cathode ray tube consists essentially, of an electron gun, a focusing arrangement (grid and lens), a deflection yoke, and a screen coated with picture element phosphors. The stream of electrons coming from the gun is focused into a tight beam by the grid and the electromagnetic lens. The deflection yoke causes the beam to scan in regular patterns. In the American television system, the scan consists of 525 lines (there are approximately 400 picture elements on each line). 30 times each second, the beam traces each of these lines (and returns in the "off" mode—hence the dotted lines). In order to provide the smoothest picture, however, the scan is "interlaced": that is, all odd numbered lines are scanned in the first half of the frame, then all even numbered lines. Two of these "fields" comprise each "frame."

The image orthicon camera tube is more complex. An optical lens focuses the image on the target screen which is covered with picture elements which can translate light energy into electronic energy. These various values are then read by the scanning beam which surveys the target screen in the same interlaced pattern as the cathode ray tube. The beam is reflected back into a device called an electron multiplier, an essential part of the system, whose job it is to amplify the very weak signal received from the face of the target screen. The sequential signal—carrying information about the differences in brightness of each of the 210,000 picture elements—is then broadcast to receivers.

Whereas film producers and distributors needed sound to counteract the threat of radio as an entertainment and information medium and revive a faltering market, their counterparts in broadcasting were involved with a relatively young medium, radio, which had not yet reached its full economic potential. As a result, there was no reason to rush into television production.

Beginning in 1925, phonograph technology began borrowing from the developing electronics of radio. Amplification and refinement circuitry both in recording and reproducing greatly enhanced the latitude of the phonograph. The introduction of the long-playing record (1948) and stereophonic reproduction (1958) were advances based on radio technology, as was, especially, the development of far more sophisticated "high-fidelity" circuitry during the 1960s. Yet the disc record had one basic drawback as a recording medium: it could not be edited. In the late 1940s and early 1950s, the perfection of magnetic tape as a recording medium changed this. Besides being a more precise medium (because it translated the electrical sound signal not into physical waves but into magnetic representations), it was also linear and therefore could be edited. Moreover, it presented the possibility of recording a performance on a number of separate tracks at the same time, which gave the sound engineer further control over the signal through the technique of mixing. Finally, because it was nearly as easy to record tape as to play it back, the technique of recording was opened up to wide numbers of individuals, greatly increasing access to the medium. In fact, economically tape was marketed primarily as a do-it-yourself medium rather than simply an alternative to the phonograph record.

Because the television signal is markedly more complex than a simple audio signal, it was a good ten years before tape technology was sophisticated enough to accommodate video. Once videotape was introduced in the 1960s, however, it not only changed the shape of commercial television, which had been limited to the choices of live presentation or film, but eventually opened up television—at least as a recording medium if not a broadcast medium—to wide numbers of people. The result has been the separate art of "video." Because it was basically an electromagnetic system, tape was eventually capable of being adapted to the complex video signal. What is surprising about the recent commercial introduction of video disc recordings is not that they do the job well, but that they do it at all. Two of the presently competing systems—the RCA and TeD systems—use records that combine electrical codes carried in a physical groove which a playback stylus must follow. The competing MCA/Phillips laser videodisc represents an interesting hybrid technology: its disc carries a visually encoded electromagnetic sig-

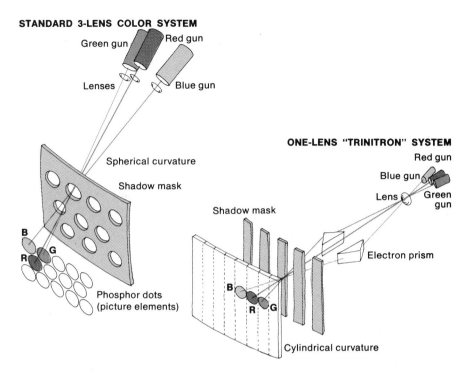

STANDARD 3-LENS COLOR SYSTEM

Green gun

Red gun

Lenses

Blue gun

Spherical curvature

Shadow mask

ONE-LENS "TRINITRON" SYSTEM

Red gun

Blue gun

Lens

Green gun

Shadow mask

Electron prism

B

R G

Phosphor dots
(picture elements)

B

R G

Cylindrical curvature

Figure 6-11. COLOR VIDEO SYSTEMS. The standard color system, illustrated at left, consists of three separate electron guns, three lenses, and a shadow mask which effectively blocks the electron beam from, for example, the blue gun, from striking any but the blue phosphors arranged on the surface of the screen. Precision of focus is crucial—so exacting in fact, that the force of gravity can deflect any color signal beam enough during its short journey from the gun to the screen to throw the color off. The Trinitron system, developed by the Sony Corporation, gets around this difficulty by aligning all color phosophors vertically, so that when the beam is pulled down slightly by the force of gravity it will nevertheless strike a dot of its own color. In addition, the prism system of the Trinitron allows all three beams to be focused through the same lens and deflection coil (neither of which is shown in these drawings). The theory is that, the larger the lens and coil, the more precise the focusing. A single lens can be larger then three separate lenses.

nal. In effect, it combines some of the best features of tape and disc. Moreover, by introducing laser technology to the media, it greatly increases efficiency, since light waves are of far higher frequencies than radio waves and can thus carry more information more easily.

The battle now going on between the rival videodisc technologies has been foreshadowed several times before: RCA and CBS both introduced differing versions of the long-playing record in the late forties. Both CBS's 33⅓rpm twelve-inch disc (developed by Peter Goldmark) and NBC's 45 rpm seven-inch disc eventually found applications, although the 33⅓ rpm disc had a more revolutionary effect on the medium. Several years later, the two competing giants of the broadcasting monopoly faced each other again over the question of a color system. RCA's all-electronic system quickly beat out CBS's partially mechanical system (also developed by Goldmark). In each case, the more radical technology was the more successful. If this holds true to form, RCA is about to lose the battle of the videodiscs to a new competitor, the combine of Phillips, essentially a Dutch company, and the U.S. media conglomerate, MCA.

RADIO AND RECORDS

Interestingly, there is not all that much difference structurally between radio and television. The esthetic and formal history of television since 1948 in the U.S. is consistent with the history of radio between 1922 and 1948 (although, since the advent of network television, radio has been forced to specialize esthetically). In a sense, it is more useful to speak of broadcasting, which includes both, than to differentiate too strongly between the two. Both serve the essential socializing function of mediating the world around us. Formerly isolated individuals and communities are brought into relatively intimate contact with a new, general cultural pattern. The problem is that the media are unidirectional, so that these cultural patterns, so thoroughly affective, tend to be controlled rather than free. Anyone who has ever watched an infant grow into a child with television as a surrogate mother can testify to the remarkable power of the electronic media in this respect. In helping to create new needs (for barbie dolls or fruit loops on the one hand, or continual fictional stimulation or the omnipresence of a human voice on the other), in inculcating shared values, and in defining the general shape of the culture, television and radio have no equals. The print media, because they do not have a human presence of their own, because the reader controls the experience, and because they must be actively decoded or read, have not a tenth the power of the electronic media, nor does film, which although it does have a presence and need not, strictly speaking, be decoded, nevertheless stands as a separate experience: it takes place in the movie house, not in the home.

This elemental force may be more clearly seen in contemporary radio than in television, since radio can be apprehended so much more easily (that is, it is not necessary actually to look at it). In this respect, radio

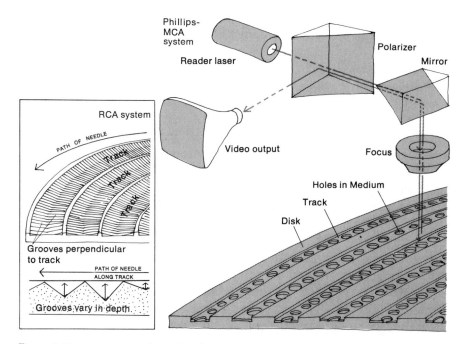

Figure 6-12. VIDEODISCS. Several videodisc technologies currently compete. The problem is to encode vast amounts of information on relatively limited areas. The RCA system (left) uses a physical groove and stylus which at first may appear similar to the standard audio disc, but the information is actually encoded differently. The stylus does not "bump" along the track but rather reads the varying depths of the track as electrical capacitances. The Phillips-MCA system uses laser coding. No physical stylus touches the disc. The laser reads the holes burned into the disc medium as digital information.

still serves as a model for television, a medium which, in contrast to film, puts more emphasis on the sound component than on the image. The essential purpose of radio is not only to tell stories and convey information, but also to create a pervasive aural environment. The ultimate product of this is Muzak, a continuous stream of carefully designed and programmed music constructed to create a specific mood: sound as architecture rather than meaning. Much of contemporary radio, whether talk or music, tends in this direction. Dead space is to be abhorred; what is important, as any disc jockey knows, is the continuous flow. Psychologically, radio serves a "stroking" function: it is artificial but very much needed company. Likewise, much of television is designed to accompany the flow of the day. Visual information, paradoxically, although often useful, is not necessary. There is no particular need to watch a talk show or television news, and most television drama is generally comprehensible without visual input. As a result, it is not uncommon for people to "read" a newspaper and "watch" television simultaneously.

It became clear early in the history of commercial radio that the concept of personality would dominate the medium. Even more than film, radio heightened the effect of celebrity because the 'variety' program allowed stars to be free of fictional, artificial roles and to play "themselves." What was significant about the vast majority of radio entertainment was that the shows were often indistinguishable from their stars. The basic form had been taken over from vaudeville, but the master of ceremonies now dominated the proceedings. Jack Benny, George Burns and Gracie Allen, Fred Allen, Bing Crosby, Edgar Bergen and Charlie McCarthy, Easy Aces, all followed a well-defined form—the basic characteristic of which was a seamless weave of fictional and real elements. The personas of the stars were simple and easily identified: Benny's stinginess, Gracie's peculiar logic, Fred Allen's homespun sarcasm—and these characteristics formed the skeletons of the shows. In each case, the star was himself as well as an actor in a plot. The radio show itself was quite often an element of the plot, a Pirandellian twist that still intrigues connoisseurs of radio.

By far the most common plot—possibly because it was every writer's nightmare—began with the premise that is "x" minutes to airtime when the star suddenly discovers there is no script for this week's program. Half an hour later, it doesn't matter anymore. Albert Brooks's brilliant parody of the radio comedy form, *The Albert Brooks Show*, uses this plot. During the course of the usually very thin plot, a parade of supporting players, a guest star, a singer, were introduced, did their turn with the star, then moved on. Fred Allen's "Allen's Alley" was probably the most blatant example of this basic technique.

Because there was no visual reality to distract from the story line, radio had a peculiar ability to compress narrative time and space. The cinematic term montage isn't applicable because the joints were undetectable. The musical term segue is more appropriate: radio segments followed each other continually and easily without a break. On the comedy and variety programs, at least, the star could move from a word of welcome to the audience through a brief scene "in character" with another actor into a commercial announcement and back out into the plot again without skipping a beat. Although it was much less easily accomplished in television, this segue technique was an important model for TV, in which "lead-ins" are an essential device.

While dramatic programs had much the same freedom as radio comedies, they were more circumspect in using it. It was felt that some semblance of realism had to be maintained to support the dramatic mood. Radio dramas were of two kinds: "serious" plays, such as could be heard on *Lux Radio Theatre, Inner Sanctum, Suspense,* and—most important—*The Mercury Theatre,* Orson Welles's company; and "serials," by far the dominant dramatic form and radio's most important contribution to dramatic esthetics. Serials (which could as easily be comic as dramatic) dated from the première of *Amos 'n' Andy* in 1929. Serials focused attention on continuing characters and allowed dramatic programs to tap the same rich vein of personality as the comedy shows. Such serials as *The Shadow, The Lone Ranger, The Whistler,* and *Sherlock Holmes* presented striking fictional personalities couched in an endless variety of plots. The concept of the serial quickly became popular on daytime radio. The soap opera domestic drama was one of the last of radio dramatic forms to disappear in the late fifties.

The soap opera (a very important genre, if difficult to deal with) and the evening serial dramatic program were different in kind, however. When television adopted the two forms, the vocabulary became more specific: the serial presents a continuing personality in a continuing story, whereas the series presents the same character in different stories, each complete in itself.

By the early thirties, the spectrum of radio entertainment was complete; it changed little during the next fifteen years. Comedy and musical variety programs dominated the network schedules; news and sports events took up considerable time; game shows and occasional talk shows, together with soap operas, serials, and occasional serious drama, filled the remainder of the airspace. In the 1950s, however, the networks turned their attention to the even more profitable medium of television, and radio responded by retreating to a defensible position. The major part of the schedules of non-network, independent local stations had always been dominatd by music and talk. As the networks lost interest in radio, this pattern became pervasive.

In addition, as modern marketing techniques began to demand specific audiences for advertisements, radio stations began to specialize instead of offering a mix of various entertainment services. This development was facilitated by the relatively large number of potential radio channels. An American city of any size now counts among its fifteen or twenty radio stations at least one devoted to each of the following major specialties: all-news, talk and call-in, rock, middle-of-the-road, country-and-western, and soul music. Larger cities often have stations that play classical music and jazz, as well. Although these stations serve small minorities, their audiences are usually "upscale," that is, heavily weighted in the higher income brackets, and are therefore attractive to advertisers.

As a medium, records have the potential to present as much variety of programming as radio. In actuality, however, the recording industry is essentially a partner of the music industry. Because radio comedy and drama have largely died out, the market for such performances on record is small. Nevertheless, there are occasional productions—utilizing the elaborate techniques of mixing and editing that were unavailable to radio in its heyday—which stand out. The albums of the The Firesign Theatre, Mike Nichols and Elaine May, Peter Sellers, and Albert Brooks are examples. As for music, the influence of modern recording techniques combined with the development of flexible electronic instrumentation has had a profound effect.

Both esthetically and economically, music is now more a recording art than a performance art. The record and radio provided means to package musical commodities so that they could be sold more efficiently and, as the technology of recording developed rapidly with the advent of tape and high-fidelity circuitry, it became clear that the record offered musicians an undreamed-of flexibility. At first, this new latitude resulted only in the gimmickry of double-tracking that characterized much popular music in the 1950s. The records of Les Paul and Mary Ford were landmarks in this respect. Then multiple-track recording systems began to yield much more sophisticated results. The remarkable success of the Beatles' *Sergeant Pepper's Lonely Hearts Club Band* album in 1967 marked a turning point. Most of the cuts on that album were so highly "worked" that they couldn't be performed live. From that point on, music has been "built" as often as it has been "played." Jean-Luc Godard investigated this phenomenon in his 1968 film of the Rolling Stones, *One Plus One*.

The development of progressive popular music on record was closely linked with the evolution of radio in the 1960s. FM radio, which provides sound reproduction notably superior to that of AM, had first been developed by Edwin H. Armstrong in 1933. He had foreseen a major reconversion of radio to the new much more faithful system, but David Sarnoff, head of the near-monopoly Radio Corporation of America, decided otherwise. Sarnoff was more interested in the marketing of television, felt that FM would compete with TV for badly needed capital, and did his best to block the acceptance of the new radio technology. He was more or less successful. Armstrong managed to start his own experimental FM broadcasts in the late thirties, but TV and FM were in competition not only for capital but also for the same high-level frequencies. Originally, channel 1 of the VHF frequencies had been set

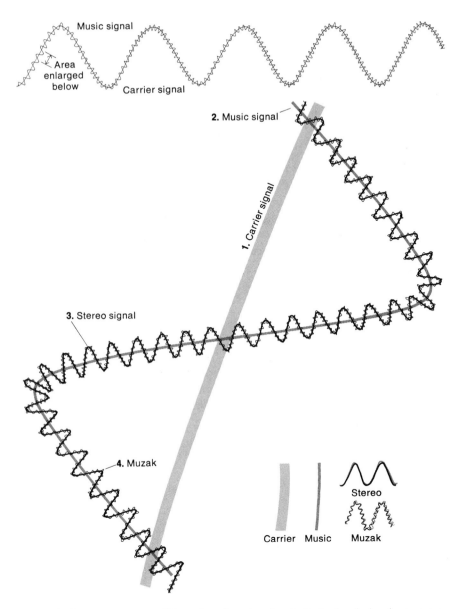

Figure 6-13. MULTIPLEXING. Wave form broadcasting is limited only by the imagina-tion. Just as the carrier wave supplies the base on which the signal is imposed (see p. 368) so the signal itself can be used as a carrier for a second signal, as it is in stereo "multiplexing." That signal, in turn, can be used as the carrier for a third signal (a fourth waveform). Some "Muzak" systems operate this way, their signal carried piggy-back on an FM stereo signal. Multiplexing is hard to visualize, but it works.

aside for FM. After the war, the Federal Communications Commission shifted the FM frequencies further up the spectrum, requiring a complete retooling and forcing FM to begin all over again. After long legal battles, Armstrong later committed suicide.

For years, FM was effectively dominated by AM networks and independent stations. Almost all FM programming was a duplication of AM transmission. In 1966, however, the FCC handed down a decision requiring owners of FM stations (who in most cases were AM entrepreneurs) to program FM separately from AM. For the first time, the full potential of FM could be realized. The more sophisticated radio medium soon found its proper subject matter in the new progressive rock music, and the two developed rapidly and symbiotically thereafter. Although it served smaller audiences than AM, FM attracted more sophisticated listeners and provided an attractive market for advertisers.

By the late seventies, FM had surpassed AM as the mass medium for advertising, a remarkable performance in less than fifteen years. As of 1980, the two formats divided the work of radio pretty much according to their capabilities: AM concentrated on talk and news, FM on music. In 1980, however, the FCC approved a long-awaited system of AM stereo, taking the unusual step of prescribing one of several competing technological systems. The aim is to redress the balance between FM and AM. The question is whether listeners will wish to invest in stereo AM when it simply duplicates the stereo FM they already have (even if they don't have to worry about differing systems). Chances are that, unless it is imposed on customers by radio manufacturers, AM stereo won't find much of a market.

Ironically, although the FCC required that television sound be FM, American networks and television manufacturers, reacting neurotically to the challenge of FM radio, have conscientiously ignored the FM potential for the sophisticated sound in television, providing most TV receivers with crude audio systems that would be embarrassing in even a good quality AM radio—this despite the fact that television has a strong esthetic dependence on sound. This has not been true in other countries: the Japanese network, NHK, for example, has been experimenting with stereophonic sound.

TELEVISION AND VIDEO

Essentially, television is more like radio than it is different from it. As with radio, the concept of flow is all-important; the product of both media is continuous and continuing, within both the smaller unit of the show and larger unit of day's or evening's programming. Moreover, because of the relatively poor quality of the televised image (as compared with theatrical film), TV depends heavily on its audio component. The curved screen, the lack of definition and contrast, the difficulties of broadcast reception, all work to minimize the effectiveness of the TV image. Visually, the density of information is low, which is made up for in part by a relatively compressed density of programming and sequencing. The segue and lead-in of radio are also of prime significance in the grammar of television: dead space and dead time are to be avoided at all costs: the flow must continue.

In 1961, a man named Newton Minow, who was chairman of the Federal Communications Commission, gained a certain degree of notoriety when he labelled American television "a vast wasteland." The phrase stuck. Even now, three television generations later, the "wasteland" is the metaphor of choice for most critics of this entertainment and information medium which is at the center of American life. Yet it may be more useful to describe TV not in terms of land but of water, as rather a vast, wine-dark sea of images and sounds that sometimes frightens because of its apparent sameness, but that, when examined more closely, reveals certain currents and eddies, occasional contradictory rip-tides, and—once in a great while—extraordinary phenomena like waterspouts and tsunami. Like the real sea, the TV sea has its laws.

There are eighty-two television channels available in each broadcast area of the United States. For various technical reasons, however, less than half of these are usable. Moreover, only twelve of the eighty-two are powerful VHF stations; the other seventy, operating on a different frequency band (UHF), are considerably weaker and therefore marginal operations at present. Only seven of the twelve VHF channels are in operation in any one area (and far fewer in most areas outside the major urban centers), a fact that has allowed the three oligopolistic commercial networks—NBC, CBS, and ABC—to dominate the airwaves both economically and esthetically since the commercial birth of television in 1946. NBC was formed in 1926 as a subsidiary of RCA, which itself had been erected as a monopolistic shelter corporation for General Electric, Westinghouse, AT&T and United Fruit. Originally, NBC operated two radio networks—NBC-Red and NBC-Blue—but in 1941 an FCC ruling had required NBC to divest itself of one of the two networks. NBC-blue was sold to the manufacturer of Lifesaver candies for $8 million and became ABC. CBS was founded in 1927 by the Columbia Phonograph Record Company, but was soon sold to a cigar manufacturer, Sam Paley, who turned it over to his son William. By

1950, Paley had built CBS into the most prominent network, and it dominated television until 1976 when the rise of ABC began.

Two basic limitations govern the nature of broadcast television and allow networks to dominate: one is the limited number of channels available, the other the limit of time. A television program director has only 168 hours at his disposal each week and his programs, moreover, must be in direct competition with those of the other networks. A newspaper reader can buy several papers and read them all carefully in sequence. A television viewer, however, can watch only one network news program at a time, and while he is watching it he is missing the others.

Because of the inherent limitations of time and channels, the three commercial networks have effective control over the airwaves, subject only to an occasional FCC ruling. Network programming begins at 7:00 A.M. each day and lasts, with occasional breaks for local shows, until 2:00 A.M. the next morning. The networks are not allowed to own outright more than a handful of local stations. Several FCC rulings have been directed to increasing the local affiliates' independence from networks (such as the Prime Time Access rule of the early seventies, which set aside certain hours for nonnetwork programming), but affiliates' connections with networks are extraordinarily lucrative and they are not likely to disregard the wishes of the networks very often.

As we have already noted, in the 1950s, the networks themselves produced most of their programming, often in conjunction with advertising agencies (and sponsors) to whom they had sold an entire time block outright.* As a rule, they no longer sell blocks of time or whole shows to advertisers, having found it more profitable to market the 13 or 14 percent of each hour reserved for advertising in small pieces ranging from ten to 120 seconds; 20- and 30-second spots dominate. The price of this time is now more than $200,000 per minute on the most popular shows, so a network's gross revenue for one prime-time evening schedule could conceivably reach $5 or $6 million.

The price the network can get for advertising time depends on the show's popularity as measured by ratings, the Neilsen rating being the most important. The networks, like contemporary magazines, are not therefore selling time so much as they are selling a particular audience. The result has been a shift from programming in the early 1960s devoted to "Middle America"—middle-aged, middle-class viewers in large

---

*In late 1976, NBC consented to the settlement of an antitrust suit which restricted both the number of network-owned programs and the financial interest it might have in entertainment programs owned by others. The other networks concurred later.

towns and rural areas—to programming in the 1970s directed at a younger, more urban, "upscale" audience with more disposable income.

Newspapers determine their advertising rates by ratings, too (as measured in circulation) but, significantly, a newspaper's circulation figures, no matter how they are broken down demographically, still reflect on the paper as a whole. In television, each show is rated, so that whereas a newspaper publisher can afford to carry unpopular material, a television programmer must judge the economic potential of each individual program. Subtle shifts in timing can produce huge increases in revenue, which makes television programming an interesting and increasingly sophisticated game to observe, quite unconnected with the content or value of the shows that are its raw material. During the 1974-75 season, for example, NBC lost out to CBS in total ratings (for the nineteenth year in a row) by less than a single Neilsen point, yet that slight difference was worth $17.5 million to the winner. ABC, with thirty fewer affiliates a perennial also-ran until the mid-seventies, hired personality Barbara Walters in 1976 at a record salary of $1 million per year. All Walters had to do to justify this sum was boost the ratings of ABC news by a single point. If she could increase the Neilsen by two points, ABC would make a 100 percent profit on the deal.

The networks produce their own news and public affairs programs mainly for the prestige it affords them (even though many news programs draw considerable revenue). CBS first established itself as a respectable challenger of NBC through its news coverage of World War II. All networks produce their own highly profitable sports programming as well (and late evening and early morning talk shows), but they rely on outside producers for the bulk of their prime-time entertainment product. The producers—many of them subsidiaries of the Hollywood studios—approach programming executives with ideas or outlines for a show. It the executive thinks the show may have potential, he approves expenses for the writing of a few scripts and the making of a pilot, which is often later recycled as a special or theatrical film. The pilot is tested with small audiences in preview theaters (and sometimes via cable). But its success in the tests doesn't in any way guarantee it a spot in the schedule, for the real art of network television lies in the complex game of scheduling.

It is not the gross popularity of each show that matters so much as its share of the audience watching television during its time period, or "slot." If, for example, both ABC and CBS have scheduled comedies for 8:00 P.M. Wednesday, NBC might just squeak through to win the period by "counter-programming" with an action show. In addition, a strong show has value as a lead-in (or less frequently as a lead-out) to a program that needs a boost, since television dials tend to follow Neilsen's laws of inertia. It follows that the structure of network television is unlike the structures of the entertainment and information media that have preceded it. Networks don't sell entertainment, as the Hollywood studios did; they sell audiences, whose size and quality depend almost as much on the talent and luck of the programming executive in placing shows effectively as they do on the inherent value of the shows. The programmer wants a show to fit the "sound" or "look" he is trying to create. We don't watch a show so often as we "watch television." The result is that elements of a show are more significant than the show as a whole. This structure is emphasized by the peculiar breakdown of shows into discrete segments by the practice of threading advertisements throughout the time slot rather than bunching them between programs as is done in some other countries.

The focus of critical attention, then, is the family of programs, each group identified by a particular style or rhythm, an attitude to character, a specific subtext or type of payoff. These characteristics have their roots in film or radio. In the thirties, film genres fit into a similar system yet, despite the practice of the double feature, each film was separate—individually as well as generically identifiable. The concept of genre is, as we shall see, much more intense and sophisticated in television.

As television history has progressed, this process of grouping shows into series and series into families has become more precise. We could crudely define several periods of television history this way: the late 1940s and early fifties are best remembered for their variety series, as the new medium quickly consumed large amounts of aging vaudeville talent, and radio comedy and variety programs were transferred en masse to the more profitable medium. This was the era of Ed Sullivan, Milton Berle, and (a little later) Sid Caesar who, with Imogene Coca, Mel Brooks, Carl Reiner, and Howard Morris, created one of the earliest and most interesting television programs, *Your Show of Shows*, produced by Max Liebman. Second only to Caesar in this period was Ernie Kovacs, who started on local stations in New York and Philadelphia. Kovacs, who died in 1962 perhaps before he had realized his full potential, was easily the most technically inventive television artist of the 1950s. In its perceptive use of the curious technology of the new medium, his work forecast later developments in independent video.

In the mid-fifties, television—as had film before it—turned to more respectable enterprises as it tried to establish a more mature reputation. This period, the adolescence of television, is remembered for its live, nonserial serious dramas, such as *Philco Playhouse, Studio One, Kraft*

Figure 6-14. The serial and series were less important in film than in radio and television. Here, Flash Gordon (Buster Crabbe) and his crew from the popular Universal film serial of the late 1930s, *Flash Gordon*. Many of the film serials were a staple in the early days of television and thus became part of the mythic memories of a second generation, as well. Recently, they have been revived for still a third generation of viewers.

Television Theatre, and *Playhouse 90*. The received critical opinion is that this was the "Golden Age" of television drama, yet it can be argued that the stagey pretensions of these individualized, theatrical productions were directly counterproductive. During this period, television writers and directors achieved some public status. Paddy Chayefsky, Reginald Rose, Tad Mosel, Robert Alan Aurthur, and Frank D. Gilroy, among others, developed reputations as writers that later stood them in good stead, while directors like John Frankenheimer, Franklin Schaffner, Sidney Lumet, and Arthur Penn later went on to successful careers in feature films.

The introduction of videotape techniques in the early sixties, together with the continuing shift from network production to production by outside agencies, marked an important turning point in television history. During this period, American TV developed the mix of standard forms by which we know it today. News and public affairs coverage, the prestigious items, were expanded. Profitable sports coverage

Figure 6-15. Howard Morris, Sid Caesar, Imogene Coca, and Carl Reiner in a sketch from *Your Show of Shows* (September 1953). (NBC.)

became more common and more popular as technical proficiency expanded. The instant replay, slow motion, and stop motion doubled the impact of professional sports. New leagues were formed in response to the growing interest. Football became the metaphor of choice for politicians. Talk shows, pioneered in the fifties by such personalities as Arthur Godfrey, Dave Garroway, Steve Allen, and Jack Paar, became a dominant television form with the rise of Johnny Carson (1962) and a host of imitators. The mix of talk, game shows, and soap opera was established as a standard for daytime television.

Meanwhile, prime-time entertainment had settled into the mix of half-hour comedy and hour-long action/drama series that we recognize

Figure 6-16. Morris, Caesar, Coca, and Reiner months later in what appears to be a reprise of the earlier sketch. The costumes and sets are more elaborate, but the gag's the same. (June 1954.) (NBC.)

today as its basic structure. Both types of programs were descendants of dominant radio forms: indeed, we can trace their genesis even further back to the movies' two-reel comedies and sixty- to seventy-minute action "programmers." But the forms took on new relevance in television. Jack Webb's *Dragnet* and Lucille Ball's *I Love Lucy* were basic models in the fifties. Webb established the concept of strong identification with the hero and the importance of location shooting in his seminal, magnificently stylized, "realistic" series about the work of Sergeant Friday of the Los Angeles Police Department. Ball established the dominant mode of the "situation comedy" by filming in front of a live

Figure 6-17. Kovac's famous library sketch. "Eugene" can't quite pour his milk straight into the glass. The camera is tilted so that it is square with the inclined set. (Notice the stagehand mopping up at the right.) (January 1957.) (*NBC.*)

audience and shooting with three cameras simultaneously. The three-camera technique dated from the earliest experiments with TV in the thirties, but Ball was the first to realize that immediate, "real-time" live television editing (in which the director monitors all cameras and makes instantaneous decisions about which image to use) could be combined with after-the-fact film editing.

Just as many of the best Hollywood films were made in the 1930s, before people were aware that they were inventing narrative forms that would last for forty years, so much of the best American television dates from the early sixties, when the patterns that were later to become highly stylized and defined were first being established. Generally, the action/drama shows organized themselves according to professions. (Jack Webb's influence is important in this respect, as well.) Police and Detective genres were action oriented (as were most Westerns); doctor,

Figure 6-18. The Army-McCarthy hearings in 1954 proved an important turning point for television news/public affairs departments. For the first time, the TV vision of the world became a major determining factor in American politics. As the hearings droned on, Senator Joseph McCarthy revealed himself as a sniggling, egomaniacal liar and the once great power he wielded evaporated quickly. Here he is advised by his counsel, Roy Cohn (left). His adversary, Joseph N. Welch, counsel for the Army, gained instant celebrity projecting the image of a wise, good humored, slightly sardonic judge. (The battle between McCarthy and Welch was more a contest of images than of issues.) Twenty years later, "country lawyer" Senator Sam Irvin projected an image similar to Welch's (and just as popular) as Chairman of the Senate Committee hearings on Watergate (*From Emile De Antonio's* Point of Order. *New Yorker Films. Frame enlargement from kinescope.*)

lawyer, teacher, and other profession shows were more idea-oriented. Even social workers and politicians were represented in the mid-sixties. The best of the profession programs by far were those produced in New York. Herbert Brodkin's *The Defenders* (E. G. Marshall and Robert Reed as lawyers) and David Susskind's *East Side, West Side* (George C. Scott and Cicely Tyson as social workers) are typical. As opposed to the majority of programs produced in Los Angeles, the New York shows were more successful on every count. They were far more likely to use location settings; they were more tightly written, with grittier characterizations and more irony; and they availed themselves of the large

Figure 6-19. Lucy and Ricky Ricardo in the front seat, Ethel and Fred Mertz in the back, on their way to California over the George Washington Bridge via rear projection. A symbolic move, as it turned out. (Lucille Ball, Desi Arnaz, Vivian Vance, William Frawley.) *I Love Lucy* set a style for situation comedy that persisted for twenty years. The show was lucrative enough to permit Desilu studios to become a major production company. (CBS.)

pool of acting talent in New York, while the Hollywood shows had little to draw on except starlets (of both sexes).

But as the 1960s wore on, and the movie studios began to exert more influence, New York television production all but disappeared. In the late sixties, American television settled into a dull rut: the more sophisticated the ratings game became, the less interesting were the products that acted as lures for massive audiences. During his tenure at CBS, program director James Aubrey set the style for this period: the aim was to use the technique of the lowest common denominator so as to offend the fewest possible potential members of an audience. To define the situation of TV comedy in the mid-sixties, we have only to name the most successful show of those years, Aubrey's *The Beverly Hillbillies*. In the late sixties, the renaissance of television in the seventies was prefigured by two 60-minute programs—*Laugh-In* and *The Smothers Comedy Brothers Hour*—both of which dealt in topical humor; both of which,

Figure 6-20. NEW YORK TELEFILMS: George C. Scott and Cicely Tyson in David Sus-skind's *East Side, West Side* (1963). This episode, #2 "The Sinner," was directed by Jack Smight and photographed by Jack Priestly. Scott's character, Neil Brock, was often impatient, sometimes wrong. He was permitted to fail, as well. The plan was to develop the character throughout the series, but *East Side, West Side* lasted only one season. (*David Susskind. Frame enlargement.*)

for varying reasons, burned out quickly. *Laugh-In,* although it developed a stable of interesting comic actors, was too frenzied and lacked direction. The Smothers Brothers, on the other hand, developed a reputation as political radicals through such acts of network defiance as reading the entire Declaration of Independence on the air.

During the sixties, too, the concept of the "spinoff" gained widespread acceptance. If a show was successful, it was because of the elements of the program rather than its wholeness. As a result, those elements could be duplicated, slightly rearranged, and put together again to form a second successful show. Television began to replicate itself.

In 1970, two programs debuted that set a new style for topical comedy, *The Mary Tyler Moore Show* and *All In the Family* (itself a spinoff of a popular British program *Till Death Us Do Part*). Within five years, these two programs were responsible for between twelve and fifteen spinoffs and imitations on the network schedules. Since the fifties, programs like these had been referred to as "sitcoms" (situation comedies), but the phrase is misleading. Their real value, as with the action/drama shows, involves character rather than situation. There is nothing inherently funny about a lower-middle-class family living in Queens (*All in the Family*), or about a single woman working for a television news program in Minneapolis (*Mary Tyler Moore*). There is something basically humorous about the characters that Caroll O'Connor and Mary Tyler Moore fashioned over the years and the ensemble playing of these two shows. They do not play themselves, but they have established extraordinarily strong characters. Again, as in radio, personality is the key. (*All in the Family* offered a striking lesson in sitcom character. In the first—pilot—show, Jean Stapleton's Edith Bunker was entirely different from the naïve, sweet, dopey "dingbat" that later became famous. This first try at Edith was more intelligent, more sardonic, and—it must have been clear to the producers and writers— entirely too self-confident to last long under Archie's roof. Had this early version of Edith continued, it would have been she that was spun-off, not relative Maude.)

The significance of character as opposed to plot, situation, or event is clear even in the actions shows, which are ostensibly devoted to event. The most successful detective heroes of the seventies, for example, were *Columbo* (Peter Falk), *Kojak* (Telly Savalas), and Jim Rockford (James Garner) of *The Rockford Files*. It isn't what these characters do that gets people to tune in week after week, but what they are. Such extraordinarily quirky characters would be out of place on the stage or in films, but they provide the quintessential television experience. We tune in week after week to be with them because we know what to expect.

The basic unit of television is not the show, but the series, which gives television an advantage in building character over every other narrative medium except perhaps the novel saga. This is also why TV is not so much a medium of stories as of moods and atmosphere. We tune in not to find out what is happening (for generally the same things are always happening), but to spend time with the characters.

Television is not only better equipped than most other media to deal with subtle development of character: it is also conversely poorly equipped to succeed with other basic dramatic elements. Because it is much less intense than cinema (it gives us less visual and audial information), action and spectacle come off more poorly than in the movie theater. And because it is measurably less intimate than live theater, it can't deal as well with the high drama of ideas and emotions.

There is one factor, however, that prevents American series from reaching their full potential in terms of character: until now, they have been open-ended. A successful series can run nearly forever. The result is that series characters, like Pirandello's, can become frozen in the eternal moment, never developing, never changing. A successful program simply has far too great a profit potential to be closed down for esthetic or dramatic reasons, even when it is perfectly clear to everyone, from viewers to actors to executives, that it has outlived its purpose. The twenty-five-year-old radio/television series *Gunsmoke* was cancelled in the mid-seventies not because Kitty, Doc, and Matt Dillion had lost their appeal, but because network executives had decided that Westerns drew a rural, middle-aged audience that wasn't as attractive to advertisers as it might be. Archie Bunker has continued as, first, his children left the show, then his wife left. In order to inject new life into the program in its tenth year, producers Norman Lear and Bud Yorkin thought it advisable to kill off Edith in the opening episode in 1980. The theory was that this would leave Archie free to find another woman.

Some successful comedies have partially avoided the open-end trap by generating a profusion of spinoffs, each of which altered the situation of the parent show. Two of the supporting players of *Mary Tyler Moore* (*Phyllis* and *Rhoda*) were given shows of their own in the mid-seventies. *All in the Family*, itself a spinoff, spun off *The Jeffersons* and *Maude*, which in turn spun off *Good Times* (thus a fourth-generation spinoff). Finally, the show spun off *itself* into *Archie Bunker's Place*.

In fact, of the twenty comedies in the 1975 schedule, all but three were spinoffs or imitations of *Mary Tyler Moore* or *All in the Family* or were produced by Moore (MTM Enterprises) or Norman Lear (Tandem Productions). By the mid-seventies, Lear, an independent, had grown so powerful that he was actually able to challenge the dominance of the networks by stringing together his own ad hoc chain of independent outlets for his parodic soap opera, *Mary Hartman, Mary Hartman*, one of the more significant ratings successes of the mid-seventies and a show originally rejected as too innovative by all the networks. In the late 1970s, television situation comedy sank close to the nadir of the mid-sixties as network programming executives became fascinated with simplistic sexual innuendo and pre-adolescent humor. Partly, this was the result of the success of *Happy Days* and *Welcome Back, Kotter*, which both drew on nostalgia for the fifties teenager lifestyle that appealed, apparently, both to the preteens intent upon reliving those days and their parents who remembered them. (Television was not alone in exploiting this nostalgia. *Saturday Night Fever* and *Grease* were both highly successful films of the late seventies—both starred John Travolta

Figure 6-21. The Smothers Brothers, Dick and Tom (1967). *The Smothers Comedy Brothers Hour* (sic) was not only politically alive and sharply satirical but also stylistically inventive during its short tenure, before it was cancelled by nervous CBS executives. (CBS.)

Figure 6-22. *Laugh-In* had little of the Smotherses' political consciousness and lasted longer. A collage of bits and pieces, one-liners, short sketches, blackouts, catch phrases, wordplay, cartoons, set pieces, and running jokes, it set a style considered typical of the sixties. It also gave an unusual opportunity to female performers, including Ruth Buzzi, Judy Carne, Joann Worley, and Goldie Hawn, pictured here, as well as Lily Tomlin. Its most famous guest performer, however, was one Richard M. Nixon, who appeared briefly one evening in 1968 to intone solemnly (and prophetically): "Sock it to *me?!*" (NBC.)

from *Kotter.* And *Grease* became the longest running Broadway show before it closed in 1980.)

Partly, too, the late-seventies sitcom drew on *Charlie's Angels,* a lightly dramatic hour whose main purpose was to exploit its three female stars who ran around a lot without bras. As a result, such programs gained the sobriquet "Jiggly Shows." Efforts like *Three's Company* and *Hello, Larry* prove beyond a doubt the validity of programmer Paul Klein's theory of "Least Objectionable Program." Klein, who was one of the chief programmers for NBC in the late seventies, realized that most people don't watch a specific television program (and thus don't judge individual shows on their worth), they watch television. Hence, they are likely to tune in the show that offends them least—and a light sitcom that will only demand half an hour from them and has a couple of pretty girls bouncing around and maybe some jokes (they don't have to be all that good) and some thinly-veiled double entendre will probably offend most people least.

The spectrum of action/drama shows is only a little more varied. Here one can identify four or five categories of shows, ranging from domestic exercises in nostalgia (*Walt Disney, The Waltons*) to the proto-fascist mayhem at the extreme end of the cop/private eye spectrum. During the 1975 season, which serves as a model, there were thirteen series that were best classified simply as "drama" (as opposed to "action") because they evinced little or no violence. These fall into two families: "corn" (*Walt Disney, The Waltons, Little House on the Prairie*)—there were seven in 1975—Doctor/Lawyer shows (six) often with interchangeable titles: *Doctor's Hospital, Medical Center, Medical Story.*

Most of the hour-long programs fell at the "action" end of the spectrum. At their best they were intriguing mysteries, at worst crude excuses for blood and guts. There were twenty-eight programs in this category in 1975: thirteen cop shows (*Columbo, Kojak,* et cetera), ten private eyes, from *Cannon* to *Ellery Queen,* and five that fit neither of these two categories: two science-fiction fantasies and three programs that at least offered the lure of more unusual professions: paramedics, truckers, and TV investigative reporters. Raymond Williams, whose *Television: Technology and Cultural Form* (1975) is an essential essay on the medium, duly calls attention to TV's obsessive preoccupation with "crime and illness."

During the late seventies, not much of importance happened in the action format aside from the already noted *Charlie's Angels*—which raised issues of sexism and will be noted historically for the brief but phenomenal stardom of Farrah Fawcett—and *The Rockford Files,* an elegant vehicle for veteran television actor James Garner.

We have been speaking, of course, about prime time network television exclusively. No account of the 1970s in American television would be complete without a mention of *Saturday Night Live,* the "experiment" which made the late-night time slot almost as profitable for NBC on Saturday as it was during the week when occupied by the venerable Johnny Carson.

Beginning in 1975, the show quickly gained a following among young people. It was, indeed, broadcast live (except when shows were repeated)—a remarkable fact in the late seventies—and this resulted in a spirit of impromptu immediacy that hadn't been seen for almost twenty years in network television. It also provided some of the best humor in America during the period, sometimes relevant, often more than simply witty. Most important, it set the tone of the generation, for better or worse.

Television has become an enormously popular pastime, entertainment, and medium. We tend to take its pervasive influence for granted, but it is a phenomenon worth remarking upon. Audiences for worldwide sports events, for example, are regularly measured in the hundreds of millions. Even an unsuccessful network series can draw ten- to twenty-million viewers per program. A local public affairs program so unpopular it can't even draw a measurable rating may still be reaching an audience larger than the circulation of many newspapers and magazines.

The economic system of television, depending on ratings, assures that the majority of programs satisfy certain needs and desires that by now are fairly well established. Much of popular television may be criticized from an elitist viewpoint as lacking in esthetics, but nevertheless the strong popularity of the best-rated shows speaks volumes about national taste. Television is the contemporary equivalent of folk literature; its most durable plots, situations, and characters are the stuff of developing myths. Indeed, not only drama series but comedies as well treat contemporary political, moral, and philosophical issues with a remarkable degree of intelligence. If they aren't sophisticated enough to compete with the best that is done in literature and film (an arguable proposition, anyway), it must be remembered that they regularly reach huge audiences, most of whom never would have had the chance to be exposed to the more elite arts.

Commentators on both the left and right of the political spectrum have often criticized the American television system for inculcating the values of a minority on the majority—and there is real substance to these criticisms. Yet on the whole, television—like any very popular medium—must be seen as generally reflecting shared cultural values. If cops and doctors seem to rule the airwaves, there may be good reasons for this state of affairs. As Sonny Grosso, a former New York City detective turned television writer and producer, points out, hospitals and station houses are the contemporary clearing houses for dramatic stories. As a result, they make excellent locations for plot-hungry series. The worst action shows are simply selling doses of violence, it's true, but the best television series—more often than might be expected— deal with relevant issues and contemporary characters.

Ironically, the most inventive form of American television in recent years has its roots not in TV but in films. Starved for product, the networks had turned in the early sixties to the vast backlog of Hollywood movies. Edited for reasons of time censorship, theatrical films were a major staple of the television diet throughout the decade, espe-

Figure 6-23. Larry Gelbart's 1980 experiment in "adult" television for NBC, *United States* attempted to do "serious" comedy in the half-hour format without audience or laughtrack. Some critics compared it favorably with Ingmar Bergman's series *Scenes from a Marriage,* others found it pretentious.

cially valuable because they had been presold. As the existing product began to run thin and as film producers turned to subjects seemingly unfit for television, the networks turned to producing films themselves. These are the awkwardly labelled "made-for-TV movies."

The trouble with made-for-television films was that, unlike the theatrical product, their telecasts were not supported by massive publicity. The networks discovered an ingenious solution to this problem. Trading on the striking identity between fiction and reality that characterizes the television experience, program executives developed the so-called "docudrama," a made-for-TV film based more or less loosely in current events and history, dealing with subjects already well known to viewers and thus in a sense presold. *The Missiles of October* (1974), which dramatized the 1962 Cuban missile crisis of John Kennedy's term as President, was among the first of these. *Fear on Trial* (1975) investigated the blacklisting by CBS in the mid-fifties of John Henry Faulk, a well-known commentator, and thus gave the genre a nice self-critical twist. *Brian's Song* (1971) was the true story of a football's player's battle

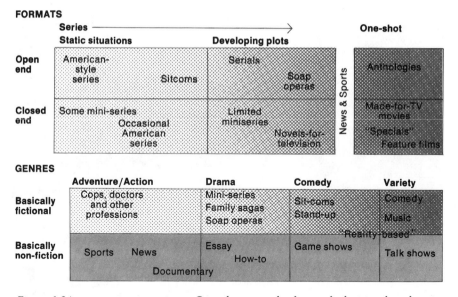

Figure 6-24. FORMATS AND GENRES. Over the years, the forms of television broadcasting have been refined and standardized. The variables include continuity, development, and organization (format); and fictional nature, quality, and approach (genre). In recent years, more attention has been paid to hybrid formats and genres: for example, the miniseries, in between a full series and a one-shot; and so-called "reality shows" which merge fiction with nonfiction.

with cancer and thus traded not only on the popular fascination with disease, but also on the mania for sports. Of course, the godfather of the docudrama was Orson Welles's historic radio program *The War of the Worlds* (1938), whose documentary techniques were so lifelike that hundreds of thousands of listeners thought we really were being invaded by Martians.

The second important development of the late seventies was the miniseries, sometimes aptly if awkwardly referred to as the Novel for television. After several experiments with this extended two-part or three-part movie-for-television (*QB VII*, for example) ABC enjoyed extraordinary ratings success with Alex Haley's *Roots*, broadcast in late January 1977 on eight consecutive evenings. The ABC management had thought so little of the cheaply produced series that it had scheduled it during a non-sweep period when it would have the least effect on network and local ratings. *Roots* was an extraordinary hit, however, and seven of its eight episodes were ranked in the top ten television shows of all time (sharing those hallowed precincts with the two parts of *Gone with the Wind,* which had been broadcast for the first time the previous fall, and that January's Superbowl).

A little more than a year later NBC's *Holocaust,* also taking as its subject a historical tragedy of epic proportions, received controversial critical notices and substantial ratings. The telecast of Francis Coppola's two *Godfather* films with a few minutes of extra footage re-edited in chronological order, during four evenings in November of 1977 is also worthy of mention. By the spring of 1978 the miniseries was well-established as a television format and the networks were involved in numerous productions of this sort.

In fact, the miniseries simply filled in the continuum between the one-shot hour-and-a-half made for-television-movie and the endless American style series. A television property (or theatrical film for that matter) can be couched, now, in numerous forms of various lengths and divisions. What unites all these formats—and separates them from the traditional formats— is their serial style; Their stories develop: an end is in sight (even if it is not always reached).

One effect of the novel-for-television style had been to revive the serial format in regular television programming. *Soap* has applied the serial to satirical situation comedy. In 1979, *Dallas*—an evening soap opera—met with popular approval. In a sense, *Dallas,* a family saga, is the real *Beacon Hill.* Several years earlier, CBS had attempted to duplicate PBS's success with English serial drama with that show, a notable failure. In more thoroughly American terms, the idea has been a success. This is only one evidence of the surprising influence British television has had on American TV.

While the esthetics of American television have largely been governed by the profit motive, such has not been the case with European television. While the American airwaves were being divided among the various factions of the network oligopoly, European channels were, in the main, reserved as public facilities and operated by state agencies. In Italy the agency, RAI, has been influential as coproducer of a number of interesting theatrical/TV films ventures. Directors like Ermanno Olmi and Roberto Rossellini have been sustained by this system. Likewise, the German state networks were instrumental in financing the renaissance in film in that country in recent years. In France, television has had both less influence on film and fewer successes on its own, although there have been occasional landmarks like *Les Gens de Mogador* (*The People of Mogador*), a twelve-part series of the early seventies that dealt with the lives of three generations of women between 1860 and 1914 and enjoyed extraordinarily popularity. In France in 1975, the break-up of the state network ORTF into three competing channels—

Television Française 1, Antenne 2, and France Régionale 3—two of which accept advertising, may mean that French TV will in future follow the British pattern.

Commercial television was introduced into Britain in 1955, joining the British Broadcasting Corporation's two channels that had been in operation since 1936. The unusual mix of commercial and public television in England has led to the most vital industry outside the U.S. Much of the British output is unremarkable, but beginning in the late sixties BBC and ITV (commercial) prestige series began to have a noticeable effect on world markets, eventually even influencing the developing shape of American TV. Partly this was the result of British traditions of independence, which left the BBC relatively free of the government censorship to which most other state-owned systems had to submit. At the same time, because it was financed through a user license fee (rather than by advertising or tax allotments), British public television was free from the constraints that that system of financing brought to American television, as well as relatively isolated from political censorship. Moreover, while in the U.S. filmmakers thought of television as a training ground, in Britain in the late sixties it also became a refuge for theatrical film directors who could no longer obtain financing.

The British dramatic series differs from the American series in several notable respects: first, and most important, it is close-ended; characters are allowed to grow, change, even die; there is no pressure to keep a series going after it has outlived its dramatic potential; time is allowed to pass. In addition, the British series depends less on a single top star and more on ensemble playing: there is a sense of community in most of the best series that is rare in American television. Finally, the British quickly discovered the similarities between the close-ended television series and the nineteenth-century novel saga, and recycled a number of them in the new medium. The twenty-six episodes of the BBC's version of John Galsworthy's *Forsyte Saga* made in 1967 were a major international success and opened world markets to British television. *War and Peace* (1972, twenty episodes and easily the best adaptation of that classic in any medium), Sartre's *Roads to Freedom* (1970, thirteen episodes), and Zola's *Nana* (1968, five episodes), all stand out in memory, but there were many others of considerable impact as well.

These were all adaptations of proven material. The BBC left it to the producers of British commercial television (mainly Granada and London Weekend) to come up with original series. *Upstairs/Downstairs* (1971–75, sixty-eight episodes), which chronicled the lives of a well-to-do family and its servants from 1900 to 1930, was a major international success. A *Family at War* (1970–71, fifty-two episodes), the less

Figure 6-25. TELEVISION FAMILIES. For a number of reasons, the family is an important element of television drama and comedy. The continuing nature of the series (whether open- or closed-ended) allows for the development of complex networks of interrelationships among characters. In addition, the domestic nature of the television experience suggests the family as a topic of interest, especially since "drawing room" drama, dependent on dialogue rather than imagery, intimate and psychological, fits the small screen very well. American television families tend to be simple, "nuclear": a mother, father, and one or two children. The "Ricardo"/Ball/Arnaz family, which literally grew up on television first in *I Love Lucy,* then *The Lucy Show,* is a typical example. There are countless others.

The twenty-six-episode British series *The Forsyte Saga,* (BBC, 1967), based on the six-book cycle by Victorian novelist John Galsworthy, was an enormous success worldwide. Pictured here sitting for a family portrait in the 1880s are the fifteen major characters. Irene (Nyree Dawn Porter), the heroine, is seated, center. To her left, in the foreground is Soames (Eric Porter), at first the villain of the piece, later its major character. Jo (Kenneth More) is second from the left in the back row. Throughout most of the series he is the sensible narrator.

glamorous saga of a family in Liverpool during World War II poised between middle and working classes, was less popular but more interesting dramatically. Frederic Raphael's *The Glittering Prizes* (1975, six episodes) followed the lives of a group of Cambridge students from the 1950s through the 1970s. Ken Loach's *Days of Hope* (1975, 4 episodes) followed a working-class family from the outbreak of World War I through the General Strike of 1926.

Loach is the leading practitioner of the British style of documentary

Figure 6-26. TELEVISION FAMILIES. American families are smaller, more abstract. Here, the Bunkers of Queens, New York, and *All in the Family* (Norman Lear and Bud Yorkin, 1971): Gloria (Sally Struthers), Edith (Jean Stapleton), Archie (Carroll O'Connor), Mike (Rob Reiner), with Betty Garrett.

drama, which is much more politically oriented than the American "real life stories," and one of the very few television directors who is able to inject some relevant politics into what is generally a medium notable for apolitical culture. Loach's *Cathy Come Home* (1966), written by Jeremy Sandford, a dramatization of housing problems, actually led to legislation. Several of his working-class telefilms—*The Rank and File* (1969) and *After a Lifetime* (1970), for example—rate among the most interesting British films produced for any medium in that period.

No account of British TV would be complete without a mention of *Monty Python's Flying Circus.* British dramatic series may just be more effective and eloquent versions of a mode of entertainment that is common in the U.S., but British comedy is a radical departure from the American style. *Monty Python,* a half-hour string of skits, animation, wordplay, satire, and silliness, recognized once and for all that the elementary particle of TV is the incident, not the show; that comedy can be at least as eloquent, dense, and rewarding as drama; and that "*nobody* expects the Spanish Inquisition."

The period of the late seventies proved less fertile for British television, both commercial and BBC. "Production values"—acting, direction, sets, costumes, and so on, were still at a high level but the

Figure 6-27. TELEVISION FAMILIES. The family as self-parody: the Hartman/Shumway clan of *Mary Hartman* (Norman Lear, 1976). Part soap opera, part satire, part neurotic psychodrama, *MH, MH* marked a satiric point of no return for the American television family.

concepts of the shows were not nearly so innovative as during the early seventies. Alfred Shaughnessy, producer of the long-running *Upstairs, Downstairs,* attempted to repeat his success with *The Duchess of Duke Street,* based on the life of chef and hoteliere Rosa Lewis. The latter program had the same Edwardian, First World War and 1930s settings and the same focus on class differences but on the whole it amounted to a pale copy of its predecessor. *I, Claudius,* from the Robert Graves books, met with considerable critical success. It marked a departure for British television, not being set in Britain during the Victorian or Edwardian periods. *The Pallisers,* based on the six-novel series by Anthony Trollope *was* set in the Victorian period—in fact, like its source, it remains perhaps the quintessence of Victorianism.

British comedy never achieved the heights of Monty Python in the late seventies, but nevertheless continued to produce exportable product. Many of these shows had the aid of ex-Pythons. Michael Palin and Terry Jones (and occasionally Eric Idle) wrote for *The Two Ronnies,* produced in the early seventies. That show, like most of British television comedy in the seventies (*Benny Hill* is another example) was much closer in spirit to British Music Hall traditions. Palin and Jones also wrote and produced *Ripping Yarns* (Palin starred), a series of six

Figure 6-28. TELEVISION FAMILIES. Rougher, not as popular, but altogether more vital and relevant than *The Forsyte Saga* was this independent British series, *A Family at War*, produced by Granada Television between 1971 and 1973. Fifty-two episodes long, *Family At War* followed the fortunes of the Ashton family of Liverpool through World War II. Often verging perilously close to soap opera, *A Family at War*, edited and conceived by John Finch, nevertheless managed more often than not to describe the British experience on the home front during the war with telling detail while it helped to analyze the roots of contemporary British class politics in that experience. Father Edwin Ashton (Colin Douglas), a miner's son who has married into the middle class, is seen in the center of the back row. Next to him is Sefton Briggs (John McKelvey), his brother-in-law, the very model of the bourgeois boss. (*Granada Television.*)

narrative parodies. Meanwhile, John Cleese, the first of the group to leave, was responsible for *Fawlty Towers* in which, with the aid of his wife and ex-wife, he portrayed the twitchy, choleric owner of a small, silly, pointless resort hotel.

By far the most successful British series of the late seventies fit no established genre. *Rock Follies* (1976–77), produced by Andrew Brown, directed by Brian Farnham and Jon Scoffield, with music by Andy McKay, was written and conceived by an American, Howard Schuman. *Rock Follies* followed the fortunes of a women's rock group ("The Little Ladies") through the commercial twists and turns of the hype-centered music business in the seventies. For wit, sharp characterization, irony, and relevance, the series has few peers. It also included some excellent original music, showing for the first time how the form of the musical could successfully and intelligently be adapted to television. (The show was immediately copied, not once, but three separate times, by American ripoffs. All died quickly.)

Figure 6-29. *Rock Follies:* Julie Covington, Charlotte Cornwell, and Rula Lenska as Dee, Anna, and "Q"—"The Little Ladies" group.

Rock Follies wasn't the only attempt at musical television in Britain in the seventies. *Pennies from Heaven* proved a novel frame for numerous early twentieth-century popular songs, as it followed the fortunes of a song-plugger in the thirties.

Many of these British series have been imported into the U.S. via the Public Broadcasting Service. A loosely linked chain of educational stations, PBS was started only in 1969. Serving as an alternative mainly in large cities and limited by its many UHF outlets, PBS depends on a trickle of government and foundation funds together with contributions from its member stations for its survival. Its member stations themselves must go through quarterly rituals of fund-raising. Almost as if by design, PBS has not yet been able to begin a full production schedule of its own. Most if its funds are devoted to news and public affairs programming such as *Wall Street Week*, its most widely seen program. After a couple of disastrous attempts at fiction programming (most notably *The Adams Chronicles*, which attempted to mimic the British style), PBS has settled down as the American outlet for the British networks. Nearly all of its most popular programs have been imports, and its fortunes are still inextricably linked to English television.

It is worth noting, by the way, that PBS is no longer the "noncom-

Figure 6-30. *Monty Python's Flying Circus* (BBC, 1969–1974). Here, the dirty fork sketch. Drawing on the traditions of British Music Hall as modified by the Goon Show of the 1950s, the Pythons created an ethereally abstract, yet often sharply pointed satirical style that gained wide audiences.

mercial" broadcasting system it might once have been intended to be. Nearly all of its shows are "underwritten" (a euphemism for "sponsored") by large corporations (notably Mobil and other oil companies) for which they receive a mention at the beginning and end of the programs—a form of low-key advertising precisely like that which characterized the earliest attempts at radio commercials, and a good buy considering the upscale, influential audience of PBS. Hamstrung by its increasing dependence on the corporations as well as its debt to government legislation, PBS has never been able to develop politically relevant programming to any significant degree—which is one reason British novelistic dramas are so popular.

In addition to such apolitical imports, PBS has also been successful with several BBC essay series, including Kenneth Clark's *Civilization* (1969) and Jacob Bronowski's *The Ascent of Man* (1973). The best original productions of PBS affiliates (Boston's WGBH and New York's WNET are the primary producers) have also been in the essay/documentary mode. Frederick Wiseman's investigations of contemporary institutions have already been mentioned in Chapter 4. Also of importance in this regard was *An American Family* (1973), produced by Craig Gilbert and filmed by Alan and Susan Raymond, twelve episodes of direct cinema about the Loud family of Santa Barbara, California. It's a sign of the poverty of the Public Broadcasting System that that show, despite its saturation publicity, didn't come close to the accomplishments of the later *Six American Families* (Paul Wilkes, 1977) which was produced by the commercial company, Westinghouse Broadcasting.

Because it is a continuing rather than a singular experience, television has an extraordinary ability to mediate between the viewer and reality. Films may last two, three, possibly four hours, during which time we live in their world. Television is on-going, never-ending, whether in the context of a single day's programming or in regard to the series and the serials that are its native forms. Moreover, television happens in our space, in our time. It becomes part of our reality. As a consequence, it mediates not only between the viewer and reality but also between reality and fiction. Because it is both an entertainment and an information medium, it sometimes becomes hard to distinguish between the essentially fictional nature of the first and the essentially nonfictional nature of the second. Much has been written about the socializing influence of TV—the effect repetitive violence has on children, the tendency of the television world to become the real reality for people addicted to it, and so on. The sum effect of this powerful medium may be that, as Raymond Williams says in *Television: Technology and Cultural Form*, it has made drama a part of life. "It is clearly one of the unique characteristics of advanced industrial societies," he writes, "that drama as an experience is now an intrinsic part of everyday life, *at a quantitative level which is so very much greater than any precedent as to seem a fundamental qualitative change*" (emphasis added). Drama, which even as late as the heyday of the movies was a separable experience, now for the first time in history occupies center stage. A shooting takes place on the street and people automatically turn to look for the cameras. Often there aren't any. The carnage of war, in living color, accompanies cocktails before dinner. It is immediately followed, without punctuation, by a commercial warning against "waxy yellow buildup." The commercial segues neatly into a police show, which, although an entirely fictional creation, assures its viewers that "everything you are about to see is true. Only the names have been changed to protect the innocent."

This mediated everyday life is also profitably exported. Both radio and television were closely connected with the military during their infancies. The U.S. Department of Defense now operates thirty-eight television stations and more than two-hundred radio transmitters world-wide. Far more powerful is the global syndication network pioneered by NBC, CBS, and ABC and taken over by the Hollywood conglomerates after a 1971 FCC decision ruled that the networks could no longer distribute programs they themselves had not produced. *Bonanza,* the most popular of U.S. programs in syndication during the mid-seventies, could be seen each week by more than 400 million viewers in ninety countries. The fourteen-year run of *Bonanza* included 359 episodes. Before its syndication run is ended, viewers may have spent more than 143 trillion personhours exposed to the values of the Cartwright family.

These are the numbers for a single program. Hundreds are in distribu-tion. UNESCO estimates that between 100,000 and 200,000 hours of American programming are available for export each year. In recent years, Warner Brothers has controlled fifty-two foreign subsidiaries op-erating in 117 countries, and MCA (Universal) had twenty-four sub-sidiaries dealing with 115 nations. Moreover, many of those national television systems were built outright by the manufacturing arms of the American networks, or else bought their equipment from them. Ameri-can advertising gets the message across, too. ABC's satellite coverage of the 1972 Olympic games was available to two billion people in 100 countries. As Erik Barnouw points out in *Tube of Plenty,* often the American syndicators effectively undercut native production, offering product at far lower rates than native producers can. The net result is cultural imperialism—even if often unintended—on an unprecedented scale.

The pervasive influence of television is a question of dramatic signifi-cance domestically as well as internationally. For many years, critiques of television have centered on the issue of subject matter—specifici-cally violence—as it affects viewers. The problem seem especially acute with regard to younger children. There is much evidence to prove that TV does in fact raise the violence quotient of everyday life (how could it not when it makes shootings, stabbings, and other acts of violence as American as cherry pie, as Rap Brown once said—and far more com-mon). There is also a convincing body of evidence to show that TV works as a safety valve, defusing potentially violent personalities. In the late seventies, lawyers for a boy accused of murder in Florida blamed his action in part on his exposure to television violence, and several girls accused of rape in California cited a made-for-television movie as their model. These defenses were not successful, but the issue was sharply drawn.

In the last few years television criticism has moved to a new level. In her 1977 book *The Plug-in Drug,* author Marie Winn shifted the focus of TV censure from the subject matter to the experience of the medium. The problem with TV, Winn contended, is not what it shows but how it shows it. She made a convincing argument that the medium inculcates passivity in children, and suggested that exposure to television might very well affect even the neurological development of small children. Winn discussed the effect of TV on language abilities and investigated its relationship to changed states of consciousness, but the crux of her argument—and it is a powerful one—lies in her critique of the destruction of family life by the presence of television. For Winn, the box has become a surrogate parent, taking over most of the work of presenting and developing social and ethical values and in the process achieving a much greater degree of authority than the child's biological parents. The title of her book is not meant to be metaphorical. Parents, she says, first use television precisely like a drug, to keep children quiet. Eventually the child becomes addicted and the box becomes a necessary, lifelong habit.

Now, many children do survive the television experience, but many too are affected deeply by it, and we still don't know to what degree or how, nor do we know what this will mean socially and politically. Much of the discussion of TV will center on this profound question during the next few years. Already the movement has begun to ban TV advertising to children under a certain age. That crusade may escalate. A year after Winn's book appeared its thesis was made to look positively conservative by ex-adman Jerry Mander's own wide-ranging diatribe against his former employer. The title of that work was, simply, *Four Arguments for the Elimination of Television.* Mander was serious. And others are too. In the end, that may be the only way to deal with this powerful force.

We have been speaking so far of broadcast television only. The development of portable, fairly inexpensive videotape equipment in the late sixties has led to new subcategory of television, usually referred to as "video." Easier to operate and often cheaper than film equipment, these devices have opened up a section of the medium to artists outside the network system. Because it is electronic, video has an extraordinary ability to manipulate images, a fact that has been exploited to full advantage by such conceptual artists as Nam June Paik, a pioneer experimenter in video. But video is not limited to the domain of pure visual arts. Often its most useful characteristic is its portability and relative unobtrusiveness—essential requirements for a flexible and responsive documentary medium. An underground group, Top Value

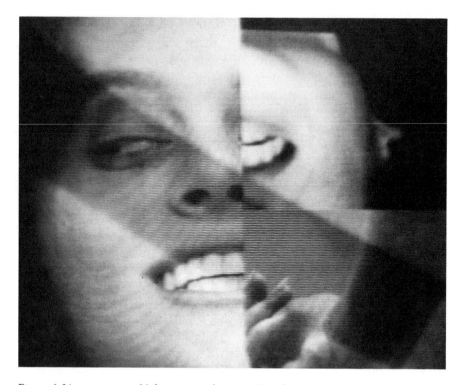

Figure 6-31. VIDEO ART. Video is *not* television. Broadcast is much less important than execution. If there is a general artistic medium now forming, it must be video: painters, sculptors, conceptual artists, theater people, musicians, dancers, and filmmakers have all moved into video. This is a frame from Hermine Freed's *Art Herstory* (1975, *Video and Television Review*, NET) which bears direct comparison with the stills in Figures 1-10, 2-11, 3-4, 3-8, 4-15, 4-16, 4-17, and 4-55. (*Photo: C. Brownie Harris, NET.*)

Television (TVTV) had noticeable success in this area of video in the mid-seventies. Their irreverent essays on the Watergate period (*Gerald Ford's America*, 1974) and other phenomena of the early seventies (*Lord of the Universe*, 1973, *Superbowl*, 1976) enabled them to break through into broadcast via PBS and NBC, before disbanding. As interesting as the recent developments in independent video are, however, the power and extent of commercial popular television are so enormous that video remains relatively inconsequential. Nevertheless, if videodisc systems succeed, and access to distribution is not too tightly controlled, video may multiply its effect a thousandfold in the next five years or so, as individuals and medium-sized organizations begin to wrest control of at least a section of the media spectrum from the entertainment and network conglomerates. Already, videocassette decks have freed those

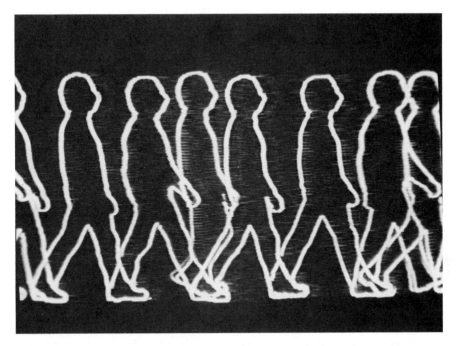

Figure 6-32. VIDEO ART. Filmmaker Ed Emshwiller's 1975 videotape *Crossings and Meetings* (*Video and Television Review*, NET. Photo: C. Brownie Harris).

families who can afford the machines from the demands of the network schedules. Not only does the cassette recorder allow viewer to schedule their own TV time, it also suggests the possibility that maybe, just maybe, it may not be so important to catch tonight's episode of *Dallas*. When a viewer must rely on evanescent broadcast scheduling, there is a strong urge to see the program, not to be left out. When the show has been safely captured on tape it becomes, in a sense, not necessary to watch it. When it's recorded we have control over it.

A CONCLUDING NOTE: MEDIA DEMOCRACY

It would be satisfying to conclude with a report that a new age of media lies ahead; that the unidirectional media, controlled by corporate interests, were about to be democratized and to become more interactive; that television, radio, records, and film were now about to graduate from being economic products whose function is profit, to artistic activities whose aim would be analysis, enlightenment, and communication. It would be satisfying to conclude on such an optimistic note—but would it be true?

Sixteen-mm and 8-mm film equipment, audio and video tape have greatly democratized the means of production in the electronic media during the last fifteen years, it's true, just as Xerox and neighborhood offset printing have opened up print media to much larger numbers of people. Yet the means of distribution are still controlled by solidly established economic interests. Technologically, the media are moving toward ever increasing simplicity, sophistication, and integration. Videotape is now used as a matter of course to aid in filming. Videodiscs should allow the same ease of access to the visual media that we enjoy with phonograph records and the print media. Yet, as the science of the media develops to the point where they become useful tools that everyone can use for intercommunication, the economics and politics of the media continue to militate against such democratic use.

In the early seventies, cable television, with its twenty to forty high-quality channels and the promise of more to come, seemed an inviting alternative. Yet cable distribution has been taken over by interests closely allied with the broadcasting industry, the Public Access channels are given lip service only, and cable now looks to be only a larger, more expensive version of the multifarious but ultimately uniform broadcast experience we know all too well.

In 1977, Warner Cable introduced the "Qube" system in Columbus, Ohio, on a test basis. With this computer-controlled cable network it is possible for viewers to "vote" by pressing one of twelve buttons on their home consoles (it is also possible to charge fees per program, since the computer knows to which cable channel a set is tuned). Yet, despite various highly publicized experiments, the main use to which the system is likely to be put is the painless ordering of products advertised on the cable channels.

In December of 1979, the Sony corporation announced that it intended to begin marketing home satellite dish antennas, not for $36,500 each, as the Neiman-Marcus catalogue had advertised that Christmas, but for less than $300 each, a price well within the range of most American families.

Such possibilities had been suggested as early as 1978 when Atlanta entrepreneur Ted Turner's successful local Channel 17 became the first "Superstation." Turner simply put the sports and movies carried by his station—and his commercials—on a satellite transponder, available to cable systems (and broadcast stations for that matter) across the country. He was followed quickly by other superstations, some of them

Figure 6-33. CURRENT SATELLITE PLACEMENT. A satellite in orbit at a height of 22,300 miles is geosynchronous; that is, it seems to hang stationary overhead since it is moving at the same speed as the surface of the earth. This makes the job of communicating with it much simpler since the earth station antennas needn't move to track it. Although the circumference of this orbit at the equator alone is more than 166,000 miles, we can now foresee the possibility of crowding. In the near future, nations will contend for satellite locations. More than 60 communications satellites are already operating in this orbit. In 1980, the FCC approved no less than 20 launch applications. Note: the map of satellite placement is not drawn to scale.

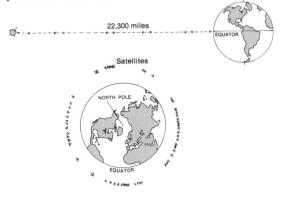

Figure 6-34. THE KEYPAD CONNECTION. This is Warner-Amex Cable's Qube III cable television tuner—or "keypad." (1980). Like earlier versions of Qube (introduced in 1977) it allows the cable television viewer to select a large variety of programming channels—some of which incur per-hour charges—and also to "talk back" to the cablecasting network. Unlike earlier versions, Qube III is designed to accomodate 110 channels and to permit data entry in order to take advantage of home data services Qube networks will offer. The Qube interactive system has come to dominate the burgeoning cable television industry during the last few years. It marks the shift of television service from entertainment to information. In 1980, more than 50 percent of standard

television sets sold in the U.S. were equipped with remote control keypads of a similar (but much simpler design). It wasn't that consumers had suddenly become exceptionally lazy; rather, manufacturers were preparing the market for teletext and viewdata services to be introduced in the early eighties—services that will require a data entry keypad.

Figures 6-35, 6-36. By 1980 videotape was quickly gaining on film as the chosen medium of "filmmakers" (and "tapemakers?"). John Keeler and Ruth Charney chose tape for *The Last Space Voyage of Wallace Ramsel*, shown on Public Television. Kathylee Hart plays a newswoman. The production gained from the immediacy of tape.

Edin and Ethel Velez used tape in a more unusual way for *Tule, The Cuna Indians of San Blas*, an anthropological essay, shot on location, about a tribe living in self-imposed isolation off the Atlantic Coast of Panama.

actually using programming "borrowed" without paying from local broadcast stations.

If the media mavens are to be believed, the typical American home of 1990 will be thoroughly saturated with all manner of electronic signals.

None of this is news. The pervasion of the media has been a common theme in science fiction ever since George Orwell's vision of *1984*: "The instrument, the telescreen, could be dimmed but there was no way of shutting it off completely." But the facts bear repeating: what we still choose to call "reality" is now largely determined for us. It is not only that someone else is telling our stories—it's also the kinds of stories they're telling.

Yet there are signs of hope. Technologies developed to be sold at a profit often have revolutionary implications never recognized by their inventors and exploiters. In the Soviet Union, for example, photocopying machines are as closely guarded as bank vaults: the prospects they offer enticingly for samizdat, or self-publishing, could topple the system of Soviet control of printed materials. In order for this to happen, the machines would have to be fairly wide-spread, however, and this will take time.

We have already noted the expanding channels for film distribution. The situation in television is even more fluid and chaotic—and where there's action, there's hope. Not all technological inventions succeed (remember CBS's vaunted EVR—electronic video recording—a system for home recording that was announced in 1971 and died shortly there-after, and remember, too, quadraphonic recording, which never caught the public imagination). But the technological ferment is so great at the moment that many if not all of these developments may survive—and some of them must have positive effects.

As of late 1980, the list of television possibilities included the follow-ing: cable systems reaching more than 25 percent of U.S. homes; multi-plying pay cable distribution services; pay broadcast premium channels; Qube and similar systems of interactive cable; superstation programming for cable systems and for broadcast channels; vastly increased satellite distribution systems which producers might use to plug directly into local station programming thereby bypassing network control; tape and disc distribution of most fictional programming; direct-to-home satellite broadcasting (which could work in conjunction with many of the above innovations); home computer systems; home computer terminals hooked up to the central data banks and to central film and video libraries via air, wire, and cable permitting individual subscribers to record and playback programs whenever they chose; systems like the British Teletext con-necting home telephones and televisions to central real-time data banks; fibre-optic cables offering thousands of times more channels, thereby multiplying the effect of most of the interconnections listed above; and electronic mail delivery systems run by the postal service, and by private corporations:

These are a few of the possibilities. There are others.

This enumeration, as lengthy and exciting as it may seem, is not offered as proof of the impending video revolution. Remember that such media utopias have been forecast in the past. Each time a new innovation is introduced its sponsors predict an age of universal peace and justice. It hasn't happened yet, It's wise to remember that—some-how—such technological wonders always seem to make a profit and thus serve the status quo. Yet, the potential for developments in media and communications during the next few years is so great that a certain measure of hope seems justified.

It is true that access to the means of production of the media, both print and nonprint, has become markedly more democratic during the last twenty years. It seems likely that access to the means of distribution will undergo a similar process of democratization during the next few years. If that does happen, the new age will have been foreshadowed by two unusual historical phenomena of the last fifteen years. During the late sixties and early seventies, a subculture of "phone freaks" and "computer freaks" developed—people who had a high degree of techni-cal knowledge about the electronic web that envelops us and the desire to use that knowledge to subvert the infinitely complex system. Often they played with the complexities of the phone system or (through it) with major computer systems for their own enjoyment: that the systems were vulnerable to their own esthetics entertained them. But on occasion they also manipulated the systems for political effect. They did much to demythologize the technology of communications. They proved that the media monolith was vulnerable.

A few years later, in an unrelated development, millions of Americans discovered Citizen's Band Radio. Popularized by the first oil and gas crisis of 1973–74, CB quickly blossomed into a phenomena of exciting proportions. The democratic vista it offered was one that would have thrilled even Walt Whitman.

I hear American singing, the varied carols I hear,

he wrote more than a century before,

Each singing what belongs to him or her and to none else. . .
Singing with open mouths their strong melodious songs.

In short, every one of us a broadcaster.

A STANDARD GLOSSARY FOR FILM AND MEDIA CRITICISM

This is by no means an exhaustive list of all the terms used by film-makers, writers, and cinephiles. The arts of film and media are peculiarly comprehensive and the language used to described their phenomena has developed haphazardly. Most of the terms used in criticism of film and media that are more closely associated with music, dance, drama, photography, or painting have been omitted here, as have many professional and technical terms that are of little use to viewers. When a technical term does appear, it is either because the technology has a direct bearing on our understanding of the experience of film and media, or because it is historically important.

An earlier version of this glossary was published by the American Film Institute in 1971. Its purpose was to elicit comments and criticism from a wide variety of writers and scholars, so that some standardization of the language of film criticism could be achieved. A second edition, incorporating those criticisms and corrections, appeared in 1975 under the auspices of New York Zoetrope. The present version, thoroughly revised and expanded to include the vocabulary of the media, is thus the result of a continuing process of refinement and redefinition. Comments, additions, and corrections are once again welcome. An expanded version is available separately.

Cross-references are set in small caps.

A

ABSOLUTE FILM   An ABSTRACT FILM that is nonrepresentational, using form and design to produce its effect and often describable as visual music. See COMPUTER FILM, LUMIA.

ABSTRACT FILM   An ABSOLUTE FILM or a film that presents recognizable images in such a way that the aim is more poetic than narrative.

ACADEMY APERTURE   The standard frame mask established by the Academy of Motion Picture Arts and Sciences in 1932. A ratio of width to height of 4:3, or 1.33:1. (See Figure 2-31). See also WIDESCREEN, TV MASK.

ACCELERATED MONTAGE   A sequence edited into progressively shorter shots to create a mood of tension and excitement. See PARALLEL ACTION.

ACCELERATED MOTION   See FAST MOTION.

ACCESS   The right to make use of a medium. Access to radio and television is strictly limited, while access to the print media is relatively more open. REAL-TIME access permits use of the medium instantaneously without intervening processing (such as publication).

ACTUAL SOUND   Sound whose source is an object or person in the scene. See COMMENTATIVE SOUND.

ADVERTISING   The attraction of public attention to a product or service: at its simplest, an advertisement is an announcement of fact; at its most complex, it creates a cultural value for the product. See PUBLIC RELATIONS.

AERIAL SHOT   A shot taken from a crane, plane, or helicopter. Not necessarily a moving shot. See CRANE SHOT.

AFFECTIVE FALLACY   A term used in twentieth-century literary criticism to suggest that it is an error to judge a work of art on the basis of its results, especially its emotional effect. Introduced by W. K. Wimsatt (*The Verbal Icon*). See INTENTIONAL FALLACY.

AFFECTIVE THEORY   Theory that deals with the effect of a work of art rather than its creation. Also called *Receptive Theory*. See GENERATIVE THEORY.

AFFILIATE   By law U.S. television networks are allowed to own outright only 5 VHF and 2 UHF BROADCASTING stations. The remainder of the network is composed of privately owned stations who distribute the network's programming operating under contract. They have leeway to disapprove shows.

ALBUM   A phonograph record production consisting of one or more LP records and at least 30 minutes in length. See SINGLE.

ALEATORY TECHNIQUE   An artistic technique that utilizes chance conditions and probability. In aleatory films, images and sounds are not planned in advance.

ALIENATION EFFECT   See ESTRANGEMENT EFFECT.

AM   Amplitude Modulation, a system of broadcasting in which the PROGRAM SIGNAL is imposed on the *carrier wave* by modifying the strength or amplitude of that signal. (See Figure 6-8.) See also FM, WAVE MECHANICS.

AMBIENT LIGHT   The natural light surrounding the subject, usually understood to be soft. See AVAILABLE-LIGHT PHOTOGRAPHY.

AMPLITUDE   See WAVE MECHANICS.

ANAMORPHIC LENS   A camera lens that squeezes a wide image to conform to the dimensions of standard frame width. The anamorphic lens on the projector then unsqueezes the image. See WIDESCREEN.

ANGLE OF VIEW   The angle subtended by the lens. WIDE-ANGLE lenses have broad angles of view, TELEPHOTO lenses have very narrow angles of view. (See Figure 2-9.) Not to be confused with CAMERA ANGLE.

ANIMATION   Methods by which inanimate objects are made to move on the screen, giving the appearance of life. These methods include drawing on the film itself, photographing CELLS (drawings) one at a time, and photographing concrete objects one frame at a time while adjusting their positions in between frames (PIXILLATION).

ANSWER PRINT   The first print of the completed film received back from the laboratory. Color values have been corrected, or TIMED. See MARRIED PRINT.

ARC LIGHT   Used both on the set and in projectors to provide high energy illumination. An electric current arcs across the gap between two pieces of carbon creating a very white, strong light with a COLOR TEMPERATURE close to 6000°K. See XENON LAMP, AVAILABLE-LIGHT PHOTOGRAPHY.

ARRIFLEX   A lightweight, portable camera introduced in the late 1950s and essential to the HAND-HELD technique of the NEW WAVE and the contemporary style of cinematography that followed in the sixties. The Arriflex was soon joined by many imitators. (See Figure 2-26.) See also MITCHELL.

ART   Originally the word was used to refer to any kind of skill, but gradually took on more specific meanings having to do with esthetic activity. It now refers generally to those endeavors that are not strictly useful. Includes the practical arts of design, environmental arts such as architecture, pictorial arts (painting, sculpture, drawing), dramatic arts, narrative arts, and musical arts. The various earlier senses of the word are still represented in a number of derivations: an "artisan" is a craftsperson; an "artiste" is a performing artist.

ART DIRECTOR   The designer, in charge of sets and costumes. Sometimes a major contributor to a film, play, or media presentation.

ART FILM   In the mid-fifties, a distinction grew up between the art film—often of foreign origin—with distinct esthetic pretentions, and the commercial film of the Hollywood tradition. Art films were shown in "art houses," usually small theaters catering to a discriminating clientele; commercial movies were shown in larger theaters. Although the range of film activity is at least as great today, the dichotomy between art and commercial film has largely died out. See FILM D'ART.

ARTICULATION   The linguist André Martinet suggested that languages have the power of double articulation; that is, the user of a language must be able to distinguish sounds as well as meanings. The smallest distinguishable units of sound are called PHONEMES; the smallest distinguishable units of meaning are called MONEMES. Christian Metz suggests that cinema does not have the power of double articulation, since signifier and signified are too closely connected. Umberto Eco, however, suggests that cinema is a "language" marked by triple articulation in which "figures" combine to form "signs," which then combine to form "semes."

A.S.A.   See EMULSION SPEED.

ASPECT RATION   The ratio of the width to the height of the film or television image. The formerly standard ACADEMY APERTURE is 1.33:1. WIDESCREEN ratios vary. In Europe 1.66:1 is most common, in the U.S., 1.85:1. ANAMORPHIC processes such as CINEMASCOPE and PANAVISION are even wider. 2.00:1 to 2.55:1. (See Figure 2-31.) See also VISTAVISION, TV MASK.

ASYNCHRONOUS SOUND   Sound which does not operate in unison with the image. See COMMENTATIVE SOUND, CONTRAPUNTAL SOUND. Compare SYNCHRONOUS SOUND.

ATTRACTION   Eisenstein's theory of film analyzes the image as a series or collection of attractions, each in a dialectical relationship with the others. Attractions were thus basic elements of film form, and the theory of attractions was a precursor to modern semiotic theory. See MONTAGE OF ATTRACTION.

AUDIO   (1) The sound portion of a transmission or broadcast. (2) Sound and recording arts in general. Soo VIDEO, VISUALS.

AUDION   The original name of Lee De Forest's VACUUM TUBE. The simplest type consists of two electrodes separated by a grid that can modify the current flowing between them, thus permitting amplification and modification of a signal. (See Figure 6-9.)

AUDIOPHILE   A person with some expertise in and appreciation of the AUDIO arts. See CINEPHILE.

AUTEUR   (1) The prime author of a film. (2) A director with a recognizable style. Compare METTEUR EN SCÈNE.

AUTEUR POLICY   The auteur policy postulates that one person, usually the director, has the artistic responsibility for a film and reveals a personal worldview through the tensions among style, theme, and the conditions of production. The net result is that films can be studied like novels or paintings—as clearly individual productions. The "politique des auteurs" (auteur policy) was first stated by François Truffaut in his article "Une certaine tendance du cinéma français," which appeared in the January 1954 issue of Cahiers du Cinéma. It became the policy for that journal and was elaborated on by other writers, mainly André Bazin. Andrew Sarris has been the main exponent of the auteur policy in the U.S. See PANTHÉON.

AVAILABLE-LIGHT PHOTOGRAPHY   Recent advances in the chemistry of FILM-STOCKS have produced materials with more sensitivity to light, making available-light photography more common. No artificial light is used; the cinematographer confines himself to PRACTICAL LIGHTING such as the sun and normal household lamps. (See Figure 2-15.) See also AMBIENT LIGHT.

AVANT GARDE   If ART is seen as progressing and developing chronologically, then it will by its nature reveal a cutting edge of artists—the avant garde—more intellectually and esthetically advanced than are their contemporaries. Recently, as a steady-state theory of art has developed, the concept of the avant garde has lessened in importance. Avant-garde films are generally nonnarrative in structure. See ABSOLUTE FILM, ABSTRACT FILM. POETIC FILM.

B

BACKLIGHTING   The main source of light is behind the subject, silhouetting it, and directed toward the camera. (See Figures 3-45, 3-46.) See also KEY LIGHT, FILLER LIGHT.

BACK PROJECTION   See REAR PROJECTION.

BAND   (1) A defined group of radio frequencies. (2) a CUT on a record.

BARN DOORS   "Blinders" placed on set lights to direct the flow of the lightbeam in a certain direction.

BEN DAY SCREEN   The array of dots or lines that, when used as a "filter," permits the decomposition of the continuous tones of a photograph into the pure blacks and whites used in printing. Invented by Benjamin Day. (See Figure 6-2.)

BIOGRAPH   American Mutoscope and Biograph, the company for which D. W. Griffith worked between 1908 and 1913.

BIOPIC   A filmed biography, especially of the sort produced by Warner Brothers in the 1930s and 1940s.

BIOSKOP   The camera/projector Max and Emil Skladanowsky developed in Germany.

BIRD   a SATELLITE.

BLACK COMEDY   A type of comedy popular during the late fifties and early sixties that dealt in macabre subjects, such as atomic war, murder, mutilation, and fatness. See SLAPSTICK, SCREWBALL.

BLAXPLOITATION   *Variety's* term for EXPLOITATION FILMS aimed at the Black market. See SEXPLOITATION.

BLIMP   A semipermanent soundproofing cover for the camera. Many cameras are now self-blimped; that is, constructed in such a way that they operate relatively noiselessly.

BLIND BIDDING   The practice of requiring exhibitors to bid for a film without having seen it. Now outlawed in an increasing number of states. See BLOCK BOOKING.

BLOCK BOOKING   The practice of requiring exhibitors to book a package of several films at once, usually including one or two they want, and many they don't. See BLIND BIDDING.

BLOCKBUSTER   Jargon term for a film that either is highly successful commercially or has cost so much to make that it must be extraordinarily popular in order to return a profit.

BLOOP   A small patch placed over a splice in a soundtrack or tape in order to cover the noise made by the splice moving across the sound HEAD.

BLUE SCREEN   A process of combining separate images using a TRAVELLING MATTE. (See Figures 2-48, 2-49.) See also CHROMA KEY.

BOOKING   The rental of a film. See DISTRIBUTION, EXHIBITION, BLIND BIDDING, BLOCK BOOKING.

BOOM   A travelling arm for suspending a microphone above the actors and outside the frame.

B PICTURE   When double features were the rule, quick, cheap pictures were made to fill the bottom of the double bill. The equivalent today is the MADE-FOR-TV MOVIE.

BRIDGING SHOT   A shot used to cover a jump in time or place or other discontinuity. Examples are falling calendar pages, railroad wheels, newspaper headlines, seasonal changes.

BROADCAST   Transmission over a wide area. See NARROWCAST, CABLE TELEVISION.

BUFF   A person with an unusual enthusiasm for a subject, especially regarding its details. (From the nickname of early New York volunteer firemen—hence enthusiasts—who wore buff-colored uniforms.)

C

CABLE TELEVISION   Television transmission via wire rather than broadcast radio waves. Originally developed to permit reception in areas where normal broadcasting was impeded by geographical conditions, cable has developed into a separate service providing a great many more channels as well as special services. See PUBLIC ACCESS TELEVISION, HOME BOX OFFICE, CATV, COAXIAL CABLE.

CAHIERS DU CINÉMA   A seminal film journal founded by André Bazin, Jacques Doniol-Valcroze, and Lo Duca in 1951. Godard, Truffaut, Chabrol, Rohmer, Rivette, and others wrote for it. See NEW WAVE, AUTEUR POLICY.

CALL-IN RADIO   See TALK RADIO.

CAMERA ANGLE   The angle at which the camera is pointed at the subject: low, high, or TILT. Not to be confused with ANGLE OF VIEW.

CAMERA LUCIDA   A device that permits the projection of a natural scene on a piece of drawing paper. (See Figure 2-3.) See also CAMERA OBSCURA.

CAMERA OBSCURA   One of the earliest antecedents of the photographic camera.

Literally, a "dark room" or box with a pinhole in one wall that acts as a lens to focus light rays on the opposite wall. (See Figure 2-2.) See also CAMERA LUCIDA.

CAMÉRA-STYLO   "Camera-pen." The phrase used by Alexandre Astruc to suggest that the art of film is equal in flexibility and range to older arts, such as the novel and the essay.

CANNED LAUGHTER   See LAUGHTRACK.

CARRIER WAVE   See WAVE MECHANICS.

CARTRIDGE   Specifically, a tape system in which the tape transport mechanism is enclosed and that operates with a single reel. The tape feeds off the interior of the reel and is wound continuously back onto the exterior. See CASSETTE.

CASSETTE   An enclosed tape system using two reels. See CARTRIDGE.

CATHODE RAY TUBE   A television picture tube or similar device. The face is coated with phosphors that are excited by an electron beam focused by an electromagnetic lens at the opposite end of the tube. (See Figure 6-10.)

CATV   "Community Antenna Television." CABLE TELEVISION designed to improve reception in problem areas. Subscribers are connected by cable to a master antenna located high enough to receive a good signal from the broadcast.

CB   "Citizen's Band" radio. The FCC sets aside certain frequencies in the radio band for use by persons with little or no formal training in broadcasting. CB transceivers permit both reception and transmission of signals in a limited area, usually one to ten miles.

CELEBRITY   In Daniel Boorstin's famous phrase, a celebrity is "known for being well-known."

CELL   Each of the thousands of individual drawings used in ANIMATION. To cut the work involved, combinations of cells may be used: one for the background, which doesn't change from frame to frame; one for the middle ground, which changes only a little; and one for the foreground, where most of the action takes place.

CENSORSHIP   Film and electronic media are normally exposed to a greater degree of censorship than is print. "Prior censorship," which forbids even the release of the film, is more damaging than the kind of censorship that challenges the exhibitor's right to continue showing the film after it has had a formal release. See RATINGS.

CHANGE-OVER CUE   Small dot or other mark in the top right-hand corner of the frame, often in series, that signals the projectionist to switch from one projector to another.

CHANNEL   A fixed band of frequencies set aside for television or radio transmission.

CHEMTONE   A process developed by TVC Laboratories that is a chemical equivalent to POST-FLASHING.

CHIAROSCURO   (kyahro-skooro) The technique of using light and shade in pictorial representation, or the arrangement of light and dark elements. The Italian words for "clear" and "dark."

CHOPSOCKY   Variety's term for martial arts or kung fu EXPLOITATION FILMS.

CHROMA KEY   An electronic television technique similar to BLUE SCREEN TRAVELING MATTE, which allows the melding of separate images.

CHROMINANCE   In order to produce a signal that is compatible for both black-and-white and color television reception, the information of the color signal must be separated in such a way that the color information (hue, saturation) is included in the chrominance part of the signal, while the black-and-white information (intensity) is included in the luminance part of the signal. See COLOR.

CINÉASTE   A filmmaker. More generally, anyone associated in a professional capacity with film.

CINECITTA (Cheenaycheetah) The major Roman studio complex.

CINÉMA DU PAPA François Truffaut's phrase for the type of established cinema against which the NEW WAVE reacted.

CINEMAGRAPHIC A general adjective, not in wide use, for the scientific study of film. See CINEMATOLOGY, FILMOLOGY.

CINEMA NOVO The Brazilian movement for a new cinema in the 1960s. See NEW WAVE, NEUE KINO.

CINEMASCOPE Twentieth Century-Fox's trade name for its ANAMORPHIC process; by extension, used to refer to anamorphic processes in general. See PANAVISION, VISTA-VISION.

CINEMATE A neologism, based on the model of "literate."

CINEMATHEQUE A film museum and library.

CINÉMATHÈQUE FRANÇAISE The world's largest film library and museum, located in Paris, founded by Henri Langlois. It has a collection of over 60,000 films. The availability of many of its old films is credited with having an important effect on the development of French film in the 1950s and 1960s.

CINÉMATOGRAPHE The Lumière Brothers' camera/projector. See also KINETO-GRAPH, BIOSKOP.

CINEMATOGRAPHER Also known as "director of photography" or, in England, "lighting cameraman." Responsible for the camera and lighting and, therefore, the quality of the image.

CINEMATOGRAPHY Motion picture photography. See PHOTOGRAPHY.

CINEMATOLOGY The study of film itself, as opposed to FILMOLOGY, which is the study of the economic, political, social, and technological causes and effects of film.

CINÉMA VÉRITÉ A word now often used loosely to refer to any kind of documentary technique, it originally signified a cinema that utilized lightweight equipment, two-person crews (camera and sound), and interview techniques. Jean Rouch was an important figure. See DIRECT CINEMA, DOCUMENTARY.

CINEPHILE A lover of cinema.

CINERAMA A WIDESCREEN process invented by Fred Waller, using three camera synchronized electronically. The first Cinerama film was *This Is Cinerama* (1952). In 1962, after *How the West Was Won*, the three-camera/projector curved screen system was abandoned in favor of a wide film ANAMORPHIC process marketed under the same name.

CINE-STRUCTURALISM The application of SEMIOTICS to cinema in an essentially sociological or ethnographic way. The British journal *Screen* was the most important center.

CLAPPER BOARD A chalkboard, photographed at the beginning of a shot, upon which are written the pertinent data for the shot. A clapstick on top of the board is snapped shut and the resultant sound and image are used later to synchronize picture and sound.

CLOSED CIRCUIT A television or radio system in which the program is not broadcast but rather distributed by wire to a limited number of receivers.

CLOSED-END SERIES A SERIES of program episodes of limited number, usually involving a more complex plot and more character development than does an OPEN-END SERIES.

CLOSEUP (1) Precisely, a shot of the subject's face only. (2) Generally, any close shot. (See Figure 3-48.)

COAXIAL CABLE The line, composed of a thin major element, insulation, and an outer conducting shell, by which television signals are carried between stations and in CABLE TELEVISION systems.

CODES, SUBCODES   In SEMIOTICS, the rules and sets of identifiable elements, an understanding of which allow us to interpret a film. Codes are analytic tools constructed after the fact.

COLD TYPE   Jargon for type set by photographic means. See PHOTOTYPOGRAPHY, HOT TYPE.

COLOR   Visible light is comprised of one section of the ELECTROMAGNETIC SPECTRUM. Perceived color is a function of the *wavelength* or *frequency* of the light. Beginning with the longest wavelengths and progressing toward the shortest, the visible spectrum includes the colors red, orange, yellow, green, blue, indigo, and violet. These are the basic *hues*. Two other measurable factors in the perception of color are *intensity* and *saturation*. The intensity of a color is a measure of its brightness (if it is a light source) or lightness (if it is a reflecting object). The saturation of a color is a measure of the vividness of its hue, or the degree of difference between the color and a gray of the same lightness or brightness. Color photography, cinematography, printing, and television are made possible by the fact that combinations of colors can produce other colors. The primary colors of a light source are red, green, and blue. The primaries for a reflecting object, such as pigment, are red, yellow, and blue. There is a further complication because color technology utilizes two complementary methods of mixing: additive and subtractive. For light sources, the additive primaries are red, green, and blue, while the subtractive primaries are magenta (a combination of red and blue), cyan (a combination of green and blue), and yellow. (See Figure 2-38.) See also TECHNICOLOR, EASTMANCOLOR, SOLARIZATION.

COLORCAST   A television broadcast in color.

COLORFLEX   Invented by Gerry Turpin, a system of POST-FLASHING that adds color to the image.

COLOR TEMPERATURE   A measure of the dominant spectrum of light produced by a light source. Lower color temperature light sources tend to the red end of the spectrum, while high color temperatures tend to the blue/violet end. Sunlight (ideal white light) has a color temperature 6000° Kelvin, for example, while incandescent house lamps have a more orange color temperature of about 3200° K. The human nervous system makes many automatic adjustments for variances in the spectrum of the light the eye perceives; FILMSTOCKS do not, so the cinematographer must make adjustments to correct for this limited response.

COMMENTATIVE SOUND   Sound whose source is outside the reality of the scene being shot. The opposite of ACTUAL SOUND. Compare ASYNCHRONOUS SOUND, CONTRAPUNTAL SOUND.

COMMUNICATIONS SATELLITES   See SATELLITE COMMUNICATIONS.

COMPILATION FILM   A film composed of SHOTS, SCENES, or SEQUENCES from other films.

COMPUTER FILM   A film in which a computer controls the visual information, usually via a CATHODE RAY TUBE display, and sometimes the sound. See ABSOLUTE FILM.

COMPUTER FREAK   A person who makes a hobby of manipulating and studying the complexities of computer systems.

CONCRETE MUSIC   Music composed directly on tape from a variety of naturally occurring sounds that may be modulated electronically before they are finally mixed. Introduced by Pierre Schaeffer of the Studio d'Essai of ORTF in 1948.

CONNOTATION   The suggestive or associative sense of an expression (word, IMAGE, SIGN) that extends beyond its strict literal definition. See DENOTATION.

CONTENT CURVE   A term used to denote the amount of time necessary for the average viewer to assimilate most of the meaning of a SHOT.

CONTINUITY   The script supervisor is in charge of the continuity of a film production, making sure that details in one shot will match details in another, even though the shots may be filmed weeks or months apart. The script supervisor also keeps detailed records of TAKES.

CONTRAPUNTAL SOUND   Sound used in counterpoint to the image. See PARALLEL SOUND, COMMENTATIVE SOUND.

CONTRAST   Used to refer to both the quality of the lighting of a scene and a characteristic of the FILMSTOCK. High-contrast lighting shows a stark difference between blacks and whites; low-contrast (or soft-contrast) lighting mainly emphasizes the midrange of grays. See GAMMA.

COOL AND HOT MEDIA   Marshall McLuhan's terms to indicate the relative degree of audience involvement in varying media. See his *Understanding Media.*

COSTS   Modern film and television budgets are complicated documents; there are professionals who specialize in compiling them. Three terms are important: "Above-the-line costs" include those expenses relating to the period before shooting begins, such as script costs, supervision, salaries of the cast, music, royalties and commissions, some taxes, and fixed costs. "Below-the-line costs" include expenses incurred during shooting and post-production work on the film: set construction, salaries of technical personnel, equipment rental, transportation, location costs, makeup, wardrobe, special effects and basic lab work, filmstock, editing, and so forth. "Negative cost" is the sum of above-the-line and below-the-line costs: in other words, the total amount necessary to produce the final edited and prepared negative of the film. Not included in the "negative cost" are expenses that the distributor of the film often shares with the producer: advertising, prints, promotion. They may run to considerable amounts.

COUNTER PROGRAMMING   In a three-network television system such as that operating in the U.S., any one network can often garner larger RATINGS than its competitors by programming against them. If, for example, both NBC and CBS have scheduled detective series for a particular time slot, ABC might "win" that period by programming a variety program against them. Since the first two networks will split the audience for that type of show, the third will have the remainder of the audience to itself, at least in theory. See LEAD IN, HAMMOCKING.

COVER SHOT   See MASTER SHOT.

CRANE SHOT   A shot taken from a crane, a device resembling the "cherrypickers" used by the telephone company to repair lines. (See Figure 3-51.)

CRAWL   The rolling CREDITS common to television, usually at the end of the program.

CREDITS   The list of technical personnel, cast, and crew of a film or program.

CROSS-CUTTING   Intermingling the shots of two or more scenes to suggest PARALLEL ACTION.

CROSSLIGHTING   Lighting from the side. See BACKLIGHTING.

CRT   See CATHODE RAY TUBE.

CUT   (1) In film and television, a switch from one image to another. (2) In disc recording, a band of grooves separated from other bands to provide an access reference point.

CUTAWAY   A shot inserted in a scene to show action at another location, usually brief, and most often used to cover breaks in the main TAKE, as in television and documentary interviews. See REACTION SHOT.

CUTTER   See EDITOR.

D

DAILIES   See RUSHES.

DAY AND DATING   BOOKING a film for a first or second run at several theaters at the same time. See EXHIBITION, SHOWCASE.

DAY FOR NIGHT   The practice of using filters to shoot night scenes during the day.

DÉCOUPAGE   The design of the film, the arrangement of its shots. "Découpage classique" is the French term for the old Hollywood style of seamless narration.

DEEP FOCUS   A technique favored by REALISTS, in which objects very near the camera as well as those far away are in focus at the same time. (See Figure 2-18.) See also SHALLOW FOCUS.

DEFINITION   As used in regard to FILMSTOCK, the word indicates the power of the film to define the elements of an image—a measure of the GRAIN. See RESOLUTION.

DEMOGRAPHICS   The study of the characteristics of a population. Advertisers use demographics to pinpoint specific, potentially profitable audiences in order to increase the efficiency of the advertising media. See UPSCALE.

DENOTATION   The strict literal definition of an expression (word, IMAGE, SIGN) as opposed to its CONNOTATION.

DENSITY   (1) The degree of darkness or EXPOSURE of a film image. (2) In theory, a measure of the amount of information an IMAGE or medium communicates.

DEPTH OF FIELD   The range of distances from the camera at which the subject is acceptably sharp. See FOCUS PLANE.

DETAIL SHOT   Usually more magnified than a CLOSEUP. A shot of a hand, eye, mouth, or subject of similar detail.

DEVELOPMENT   The chemical process that brings out the latent image in the FILM-STOCK. If a film has been UNDEREXPOSED it can later be OVERDEVELOPED to regain some of the balance between light and dark. In AVAILABLE-LIGHT color photography, it is often necessary to push the film a few "stops" in development (overdevelop it) in order to regain a balanced image. See EXPOSURE, SPEED, CHEMTONE.

DIACHRONIC   In linguistic theory, a phenomenon is diachronic when it consists of or depends upon a change in its state, usually across time. See SYNCHRONIC.

DIALECTICS   The system of thought that focuses on contradictions between opposing concepts; in the Marxian sense of the term, historical change occurs through the opposition of conflicting forces and ideas.

DIAPHRAGM   The device that controls the amount of light passing through a LENS. (See Figure 2-14.)

DIEGESIS   The DENOTATIVE material of film narrative, it includes, according to Metz, not only the narration itself, but also the fictional space and time dimensions implied by the narrative.

DIFFUSER   A gelatin plate that is placed in front of a light to change its quality. See SCRIM, GOBO, FLAG.

DIRECT CINEMA   The dominant style of DOCUMENTARY in the U.S. since the early

1960s. Like CINÉMA VÉRITÉ, it depends on lightweight, mobile equipment. Unlike cinéma vérité, it does not permit the filmmaker to become involved in the action and, in fact, is noted for its avoidance of narration.

DIRECTOR OF PHOTOGRAPHY   See CINEMATOGRAPHER.

DIRECT SATELLITE BROADCASTING   At present, although satellites are commonly used to transmit between major ground stations, none are equipped to broadcast directly to home television and radio receivers. Direct Satellite Broadcasting offers the prospect of instantaneous transmission to every receiver in the world.

DIRECT SOUND   The technique of recording sound simultaneously with image, direct sound has become much more feasible since the development of portable tape recorders and self-BLIMPED cameras. See CINÉMA VÉRITÉ, DIRECT CINEMA.

DISC, DISK   The disc recording configuration offers the advantage of cheap reproduction and instant access to any point in the recording. Its disadvantages are that it is highly susceptible to physical damage and that, because it is not linear, it cannot be edited satisfactorily. See TAPE, LIVE; MAGNETIC DISC, LASER DISC.

DISCOGRAPHY   An organized list of records, often by a particular performer.

DISKETTE   See FLOPPY DISC.

DISSOLVE   The superimposition of a FADE OUT over a FADE IN. Sometimes called a *lap dissolve*.

DISTRIBUTION   The dissemination of media; the intermediate stage between production and EXHIBITION (or reception).

DISTRIBUTION FLOW   The structure of distribution, can be either discrete (composed of separate independent units, such as books, records, or films) or continuous (in which case the units are linked together, as in television and radio). A third variation is the *mosaic*, which offers a number of immediate choices, as in newspaper and magazine layout or the separate channels of television. Distribution flow is also defined as either *unidirectional* or *interactive*, the latter allowing intercommunication between sender and receiver. Further, distribution is either BROADCAST or NARROWCAST.

DOCUDRAMA   Semifictionalized versions of actual events, docudramas became popular staples of American television in the early seventies.

DOCUMENTARY   A term with a wide latitude of meaning, basically used to refer to any film or program not wholly fictional in nature. The term was first popularized by John Grierson. See CINÉMA VÉRITÉ, DIRECT CINEMA, DOCUDRAMA.

DOLBY   A system of recording sound that greatly mutes the background noise inherent in film and tape reproduction. (See Figure 2-40.)

DOLLY   A set of wheels and a platform upon which the camera can be mounted to give it mobility. Also called "Crab Dolly."

DOLLY SHOT   A shot taken from a moving DOLLY. Almost synonymous in general usage with TRACKING SHOT. See FOLLOW SHOT.

DOMESTIC COMEDY   That form of television (and sometimes film) centering on interrelationships in the family unit.

DOMINANT   The controlling CODE or ATTRACTION in an image or montage. See SUBSIDIARY, INTRINSIC INTEREST.

DOUBLE-SYSTEM SOUND   The technique widely used today in which sound is recorded separately by a lightweight magnetic recorder that is physically separate from the camera although often linked to it for purposes of SYNCHRONIZATION. See SINGLE-SYSTEM SOUND.

DRAMATIZATION   A fictional representation of an actual event.

DUB   (1) To rerecord dialogue in a language other than the original. (2) To record dialogue in a specially equipped studio after the film has been shot. See LOOPING.

DUPE   (1) To print a duplicate negative from a positive print. Also, to print a duplicate REVERSAL print. (2) A print made in this manner. See GENERATION.

DYE TRANSFER   A system of printing film used in the TECHNICOLOR process in which ink-like dyes are applied to the FILMSTOCK in a manner similar to PLANO-GRAPHIC printing.

E

EASTMANCOLOR   The color FILMSTOCK now used almost universally. It employs a chemical process, not a DYE-TRANSFER process like TECHNICOLOR. There are many companies who process Eastman stock in their own ways, but the differences are minimal.

ÉCRITURE   The French semiological term for that quality of a work of art that is a combination of the artist's personal style and more general social, political, and historical concerns.

EDITING   See EDITOR.

EDITOR   The *cutter*. The person who determines the narrative structure of a film, in charge of the work of splicing the shots of a film together into final form. See MONTAGE, FINE CUT, ROUGH CUT.

EFFECTS TRACK   The soundtrack on which the sound effects are recorded prior to MIXING.

ELECTROMAGNETIC SPECTRUM   The entire range of radiation extending in frequency from 0 cycles per second (Hertz) to 10^{23} cycles per second (Hertz) and including cosmic rays, gamma rays, X rays, ultraviolet rays, visible light, infrared rays, microwaves, radio waves, heat, and electric currents. (See Figure 6-7.)

ELECTRON GUN   The device in a CATHODE RAY TUBE that supplies the electron beam.

EMULSION   The thin coating of chemicals, mounted on the base of the FILMSTOCK, that reacts to light.

EMULSION SPEED   A measure of the sensitivity of FILMSTOCK to light. Measured against a scale devised by the American Standards Association (A.S.A.). The faster the speed of the emulsion, the higher the A.S.A. number, and the greater the sensitivity to light. High-speed films generally have a rougher GRAIN than slow-speed films. See SPEED, DEFINITION, AVAILABLE-LIGHT PHOTOGRAPHY.

ENHANCEMENT   An electronic method of refining an audio or video recording or image using computer techniques. The computer extrapolates from basic information.

EPIC THEATRE   In Brecht's theory, theater that appeals more to the spectator's reason than to his feeling. See ESTRANGEMENT EFFECT, THEATER OF CRUELTY.

ESTABLISHING SHOT   Generally a LONG SHOT that shows the audience the general location of the scene that follows, often providing essential information, and orienting the viewer.

ESTRANGEMENT EFFECT   *Verfremdungseffekt*. Essential to Brecht's theory of theater, it keeps both audience and actors intellectually separate from the action of the drama. It provides intellectual distance. See EPIC THEATRE.

EVR   Electronic Video Recording. A system combining electronic and film techniques for home PLAYBACK, invented by Peter Goldmark. Discontinued in 1972.

EXCITER LAMP   The light source for the optical sound head that reads the SOUND-TRACK.

EXHIBITION   The final link in the film production chain See FIRST RUN, GENERAL RELEASE, SHOWCASE, FOUR-WALLING, DAY AND DATING, BLIND BIDDING, BLOCK BOOKING.

EXPLOITATION FILM   A film designed to profit by serving a particular need or desire of the audience. Examples: SEXPLOITATION, BLAXPLOITATION. Usually the term has a negative connotation.

EXPOSURE   A measure of the amount of light striking the surface of the film. Film can be intentionally *overexposed* to give a very light, washed out, dreamy quality to the print image, or it can be *underexposed* to make the image darker, muddy, and foreboding. See DEVELOPMENT.

EXPOSURE LATITUDE   A measure of a FILMSTOCK's flexibility in regard to EXPOSURE.

EXPRESSIONISM   Generally, the kind of film style that allows liberal use of technical devices and artistic distortion and in which the personality of the director is always paramount and obvious. See GERMAN EXPRESSIONISM, REALISM, NEOREALISM, FORMALISM.

EXTREME CLOSEUP   See DETAIL SHOT.

EXTREME LONG SHOT   A panoramic view of an exterior location photographed from a considerable distance, often as far as a quarter-mile away. (See Figure 3-48.) See also ESTABLISHING SHOT.

F

FADE IN   A punctuation device. The screen is black at the beginning; gradually the image appears, brightening to full strength. See DISSOLVE, FADE OUT, FOCUS OUT.

FADE OUT   The opposite of FADE IN. With the recent expansion of color filmmaking, some directors now choose to fade from or to a color other than black.

FAST MOTION   Also called *accelerated motion*. The film is shot at less that 24 frames per second so that when it is projected at the normal speed actions appear to move much faster. The camera is UNDERCRANKED. Often useful for comic effect.

FEATURE   (1) The main film of a multifilm program. (2) Any film considered to be full-length, i.e., 75 minutes or more. See SHORT.

FEED   The transmission of a television or radio program from network headquarters to individual stations, from which it is then BROADCAST.

FEEDBACK   (1) A basic phenomenon of electronic technology: in any system that has both input and output, the return of some of the output to the input. Useful for amplification and other applications. (2) *Interactive* communication. See DISTRIBUTION FLOW.

FIBER OPTICS TRANSMISSION   The distribution of a radio or television signal that is imposed on a visible light *carrier wave*. The light beam is carried by a thin glass filament and usually generated by a LASER. Because light wavelengths are very much shorter than radio wavelengths, they can carry considerably greater amounts of information. See CABLE TELEVISION, WAVE MECHANICS.

FIELD   In television, one of two equal parts into which a frame is divided in interlaced scanning. See RASTER.

FILLER LIGHT, FILL LIGHT   An auxiliary light, usually from the side of the subject, that can soften shadows and illuminate areas not covered by the KEY LIGHT. (See Figure 3-42.)

FILM CHAIN   The interlock between projector and television camera which translates 24-frame-per-second film into 30-frame-per-second video.

FILM CLIP   A short section of film taken out of context. A "quote."

FILM D'ART   The early movement in French film to produce records of more respectable stage productions. See ART FILM.

FILM GAUGE   FILMSTOCK is made in various widths, measured in millimeters: 35 mm stock is the standard for commercial feature films (although 16 mm is becoming more prominent); 65 mm and 70 mm stocks are used for major epical productions; 16 mm stock is the standard for most of the rest of the industry, including television newsfilm; 8 mm stock is becoming a possible alternative here, although previously it has been limited to amateur use. Super 8 mm and Super 16 mm greatly increase the available picture area in their respective gauges by making sprocket holes smaller or by eliminating one of the two rows of sprockets. (See Figure 2-32.)

FILMIC SPACE   A phrase not in wide use, which refers to the power of the film medium that makes possible the combination of shots of widely separated origins into a single framework of fictional space.

FILM NOIR   Originally a French term, now in common usage, to indicate a film with a gritty, urban setting that deals mainly with dark or violent passions in a downbeat way. Especially common in American cinema during the late forties and early fifties.

FILMOGRAPHY   A listing of films, on the model of "bibliography."

FILMOLOGY   The study and analysis of film as a social, political, and historical phenomenon. See CINEMATOLOGY.

FILMSTOCK   The raw material of film.

FILTER   (1) A plate of gelatin, glass, or plastic placed in front of the lens to alter the quality of the light. (2) An electronic device that alters the quality of sound or image.

FINAL CUT   The film as it will be released. The guarantee of final cut assures a filmmaker that the producer will not be able to revise the film after the filmmaker has finished it.

FINE CUT   The film in its final state, as opposed to ROUGH CUT.

FIRST RUN   One of several types of film distribution, the first run is the opening engagement, often at a limited number of theaters. A second run is often organized at a larger number of theaters. See GENERAL RELEASE, SHOWCASE, FOUR-WALLING, DAY AND DATING.

FISH-EYE LENS   An extremely WIDE-ANGLE LENS that has an ANGLE OF VIEW approaching 180 degrees. It greatly distorts the image.

FLAG   A device placed in front of a light to cast a shadow. See GOBO, SCRIM.

FLARE   When the light source is pointed directly at the camera, the optics of the LENS often produce in the image a haze, glow, or aura known as flare.

FLASHBACK   A SCENE or SEQUENCE (sometimes an entire film) that is inserted into a scene in "present" time and that deals with the past. The flashback is the past tense of film.

FLASH CUTTING   Editing the film into shots of very brief duration that succeed each other rapidly.

FLASH-FORWARD   On the model of FLASHBACK, scenes or shots of future time; the future tense of film.

FLASH FRAME   A shot of only a few frames duration—sometimes a single frame, which can just barely be perceived by the audience.

FLASHING   See POST-FLASHING.

FLAT LIGHTING   Low CONTRAST lighting. See GAMMA, POST-FLASHING.

FLICKER   In film projection, a cyclical fluctuation in the intensity of the light falling upon the screen, caused by the passage of the SHUTTER across the light beam. The psychological effect is caused by a projection rate of fewer frames per second than PERSISTENCE OF VISION is able to forge into a continuous image.

FLIP   A type of WIPE.

FLOPPY DISC   Inexpensive and widely used system of computer information storage which uses magnetic recording, but on a thin disc (7¾ inches in diameter or smaller) rather than on tape. The disc format offers the advantage of greatly increased accessibility. Also called *Diskette, Minidisc.*

FLUTTER   See WOW.

FM   Frequency Modulation, a system of broadcasting in which the PROGRAM SIGNAL is imposed on the *carrier wave* by modifying the frequency or wavelength of that signal. See AM, WAVE MECHANICS. (See Figure 6-8.)

F-NUMBER   The size of the opening of the DIAPHRAGM. The higher the F-number, the smaller the opening, and less light entering the camera. Also called *F-stop.* There also exists a system of measurement in *T-numbers,* which is a more accurate index of the amount of light actually striking the emulsion.

FOCAL LENGTH   The length of the lens, a measurement (usually in millimeters) of the distance from the center of the outside surface of the lens to the film plane. Long lenses are TELEPHOTO lenses, short lenses are WIDE-ANGLE lenses.

FOCUS   The sharpness of the image. A range of distances from the camera will be acceptably sharp. See DEEP FOCUS, SHALLOW FOCUS.

FOCUS IN, OUT   A punctuation device. The image gradually comes into focus or goes out of focus.

FOCUS PLANE   The plane in the scene being photographed upon which the lens is focused, measured as a distance from the film plane. See DEPTH OF FIELD.

FOCUS PULL   To refocus during a TAKE: to change the FOCUS PLANE. See RACK FOCUS, FOLLOW FOCUS.

FOLLOW FOCUS   To PULL FOCUS during a shot in order to follow a subject as it moves away from or toward the camera. See RACK FOCUS, FOLLOW SHOT.

FOLLOW SHOT   A TRACKING SHOT or ZOOM, which follows the subject as it moves.

FOOTAGE   A measurement of the amount of film actually shot or to be shot.

FORELENGTHENING   The linear distortion caused by a WIDE-ANGLE lens: the perception of depth is exaggerated. (See Figures 2-9, 2-11.)

FORESHORTENING   The distortion caused by a TELEPHOTO lens: the illusion of depth is compressed. (See Figures 2-9, 2-12.)

FORMALISM   (1) Concern with form over content. (2) The theory that meaning exists primarily in the form or language of a discourse rather than in the content or subject. (3) The Russian movement of the twenties that developed these ideas. See EXPRESSIONISM.

FORMAT   (1) The basic structure of a radio or television program. (2) The basic orientation of a radio station: Rock, Classical, All-News, Country, Talk, Educational, and the like. (3) A system of information storage, such as DISC, TAPE.

FORMATIVE THEORY   Theory that deals with form rather than function or subject.

FORMS, OPEN AND CLOSED   Closed forms suggest that the limits of the FRAME are the limits of artistic reality, while open forms suggest that reality continues outside the frame. (See Figures 3-31, 3-32.)

FOUR-WALLING   The practice of renting a film theater outright at a fixed rate rather than sharing in the proceeds with the owner or operator of the theater.

FPS   (1) Frames per second. (2) Feet per second.

FRAME   (1) Any single image on the film. (2) The size and shape of the image on the film, or on the screen when projected. (3) the compositional unit of film design. See FORMS, OPEN AND CLOSED.

FREE CINEMA   The nonfiction, DOCUMENTARY movement in film in Britain in the fifties, whose theory was developed by Karel Reisz, Tony Richardson, and Lindsay Anderson.

FREEZE FRAME   A freeze shot, which is achieved by printing a single frame many times in succession to give the illusion of a still photograph when projected.

FREQUENCY   See WAVE MECHANICS.

FRONT PROJECTION   A more precise and effective method of combining images than REAR PROJECTION. Live action is filmed against a highly reflective screen. An image from a slide or movie projector is projected on the screen by means of mirrors along the axis of the taking lens so that there are no visible shadows cast by the actors. Since the screen is exceptionally reflective, and since the live actors are well lit, no image from the projector is visible on the actors or props in front of the screen. The system was refined by Douglas Trumbull for Kubrick's *2001: A Space Odyssey.* (See Figures 2-46, 2-47.)

F-STOP   See F-NUMBER.

FULL SHOT   A shot of a subject that includes the entire body and not much else. (See Figure 3-48.)

FX   SOUND EFFECTS.

G

GAFFER   The chief electrician on the set; in charge of the lights. His assistant is the "best boy."

GAME SHOW   A popular type of radio/television program based on the parlor game as spectator entertainment.

GAMMA   The measurement of the contrast latitude of a FILMSTOCK. A high gamma signifies high contrast. (See Figure 2-36.)

GATE   The channel through which film passes in a camera or projector at the point at which it is exposed.

GAUGE   See FILM GAUGE.

GENERAL RELEASE   Widespread simultaneous exhibition of a film with as many as 1500 prints in circulation, as opposed to limited FIRST RUN.

GENERATION   The film in the camera when the shot is taken is "first generation." A print of this negative will be "second generation." An internegative made from this positive will be "third generation," and so on. Each generation marks a progressive deterioration in the quality of the image. (See Figure 2-30.)

GENERATIVE THEORY   Theory that deals with the phenomenon of the production of a film rather than the consumption of it. See AFFECTIVE THEORY.

GENRE   A type of film. Certain archetypal patterns, such as the Western, the Gangster, the Science Fiction film, and the Detective Story. See FILM NOIR.

GERMAN EXPRESSIONISM   Style of film common in Germany in the twenties, characterized by dramatic lighting, distorted sets, and symbolic action and character. The movement also involved painting and theater.

GEST   (pronounced "guest") In Brecht's theory of acting the Gest was the basic meaningful unit of the language of gesture.

GHOST IMAGE   (1) A type of double exposure in which one or more preceding frames are printed together with the main frame to give a multiple exposure. (2) The same effect in television reception caused by the reflection of signals from mountains or large buildings.

GLASS SHOT   A type of SPECIAL EFFECT in which part of the scene is painted on a clear glass plate mounted in front of the camera. (See Figure 2-44.)

GOBO   A wooden, opaque screen placed in front of a light in order to shield part of the subject from that light or to cast a shadow. See SCRIM.

GRAIN   A quality of the EMULSION of a film. Grainy emulsions, which have poor powers of DEFINITION, are sometimes preferred for their "realistic" connotations. The visibility of the grain varies inversely with the size of the FILM GAUGE and directly with the amount of OVERDEVELOPMENT.

GRAVURE   A type of printing that uses a depressed, engraved, intaglio surface to carry the ink rather than the raised, relief surface of LETTERPRESS. See also OFFSET.

GRIP   The person in charge of props on a set.

H

HALFTONE   The process of photoengraving using a BEN DAY SCREEN, which permits photographs to be reproduced by means of the printing press.

HAMMOCKING   The practice of situating a new or weak television program between two strong, established programs so that the audiences for the strong programs will lap over into the time period occupied by the weak program. See LEAD IN, LEAD-OUT.

HAND-HELD   Since the development of lightweight portable cameras, hand-held shots have become much more common.

HARDWARE, SOFTWARE   In computer and media terminology, hardware refers to relatively permanent equipment, such as cameras, lights, and editing tables; software is the term for consumable materials such as film, tape, and programming.

HARMONICS   The series of overtones that, when combined with the basic tone, give character and depth to sounds.

HEAD   (1) The beginning of a film. (2) The electromagnetic or optical device that reads a soundtrack or tape.

HERTZ   The contemporary term for "cycles per second." Frequencies are measured in Hertz.

HIGH KEY   A type of lighting arrangement in which the KEY LIGHT is very bright, often producing shadows.

HIGHLIGHTING   Sometimes pencil-thin beams of light are used to illuminate certain parts of the subject (most often the actress's eyes). (See Figure 3-44.)

HOLOGRAPHY   A system of photography using LASER light, which realistically duplicates the three-dimensions of space and PARALLAX.

HOME BOX OFFICE   Time-Life, Inc.'s proprietary name for the leading system of subscription cable television providing movies, sports, and special entertainment for an additional monthly fee.

HORSE OPERA   Nickname for a Western.

HOT TYPE   Jargon for metal movable type and LINOTYPE. See COLD TYPE.

HUE   See COLOR.

HUE MODULATION   A system for high fidelity optical SOUNDTRACKS in which the sound signal is carried by the modification of the color of the track.

HYPHENATE   Jargon for a filmmaker who fulfills more than one function, such as writer-director, actor-producer, or writer-producer.

I

IC   See INTEGRATED CIRCUIT.

ICON   In the Peirce/Wollen semiotics, a sign that represents its object mainly by its similarity to it. See INDEX, SYMBOL.

ICONOSCOPE   The earliest type of television camera tube. See IMAGE ORTHICON.

IMAGE   An image is both an optical pattern and a mental experience. (1) A single specific picture. (2) Generally, the VISUALS of film or media as opposed to sound. (3) A visual TROPE. (4) By extension, often a nonvisual trope; hence, we speak of aural, poetic, or musical "images."

IMAGE ORTHICON   The standard television camera tube. (See Figure 6-10.) See also CATHODE RAY TUBE.

INDEX   In the Peirce/Wollen system, a sign that represents its object by virtue of an existential bond. For example, a clock or a thermometer. See ICON, SYMBOL.

INFORMATION THEORY   Theory that deals with the transmission of messages, considering problems of distribution, transmission, and reception. In film, for example, Christian Metz identifies five separate channels of information: IMAGES, graphic representation (words read from the screen), recorded speech, recorded music, and recorded sound effects.

INSERT, INSERT SHOT   A DETAIL SHOT that gives specific and relevant information necessary to a complete understanding of the meaning of the scene. Examples: a letter, a tell-tale physical detail.

INTAGLIO PRINTING   A system of printing in which the printing surface is depressed. See RELIEF PRINTING, PLANOGRAPHIC.

INTEGRATED CIRCUIT   A highly miniaturized electronic system incorporating a number of otherwise separate elements (transistors, capacitors, etc.) in its design. See PRINTED CIRCUIT.

INTELSAT   International Telecommunications Satellite Consortium, established in 1964. Also the name of satellites launched by that organization.

INTENSITY   See COLOR.

INTENTIONAL FALLACY   The error of judging a work of art by its author's intentions. See AFFECTIVE FALLACY.

INTENTIONAL TECHNOLOGY   See TECHNOLOGICAL DETERMINISM.

INTERACTIVE MEDIUM   See DISTRIBUTION FLOW.

INTERCUT   See CROSS-CUT.

INTERMITTENT MOVEMENT   See PULL-DOWN MECHANISM.

INTERNEGATIVE   A negative prepared from a positive print especially for the purpose of producing other positive prints from it.

INTRINSIC INTEREST   A quality of an object or an area of the image that draws attention to it even though the design of the image does not. See DOMINANT.

IRIS IN, IRIS OUT   An old technique of punctuation that utilizes a DIAPHRAGM in front of the lens, which is opened (Iris In) or closed (Iris Out) to begin or end a scene. The iris can also be used to focus attention on a detail of the scene. See FOCUS IN, FADE IN.

J

JAMMING   The practice of broadcasting noise signals to interfere intentionally with the signal of a radio or a television station.

JUMP CUT   A cut that occurs within a scene rather than between scenes, to condense the shot. It can effectively eliminate dead periods, such as that between the time a character enters a room and the time he reaches his destination on the other side of the room. When used according to certain rules, jump cuts are unobtrusive. But in *Breathless*, Jean-Luc Godard deliberately inserted jump cuts in shots where they would be quite obvious. Obvious, obtrusive jump cuts are still uncommon, however. Not to be confused with MATCH CUT.

K

KENWORTHY   A highly flexible, servo-controlled CRANE apparatus that can be computer-programmed to photograph miniature sets in such a way that the proper corrections are made for the reduction in size of the subject. See LOUMA.

KEY LIGHT   The main light on a subject. Usually placed at a 45° angle to the camera-subject axis. See FILLER LIGHT, BACKLIGHT.

KEY-LIGHTING, HIGH OR LOW   In high key lighting, the key light provides all or most of the light in the scene. In low key lighting, the key light provides much less of the total illumination.

KINEME   Pier Paolo Pasolini's term for the basic unit of cinematic language.

KINESCOPE   A film record of a television show shot directly from a television screen (and therefore of poor quality).

KINETOGRAPH   Edison's projector. See BIOSKOP, CINÉMATOGRAPHE, KINETOSCOPE.

KINETOPHONE   Edison's sound film apparatus.

KINETOSCOPE   Edison's peephole viewer. (See Figure 2-6.)

KINO-EYE   One of the first CINÉMA VÉRITÉ approaches to film esthetics, developed by Dziga Vertov in the 1920s. His film *Man With a Movie Camera* is a famous example.

L

LANGUAGE, LANGUAGE SYSTEM   Unwieldy English equivalents of the French terms *langage* and *langue*, respectively. Cinema is a language because it is a means of communication, but it is not necessarily a language system because it doesn't follow the rules of written or spoken language.

LAP DISSOLVE   See DISSOLVE.

LASER   "Light Amplifaction by Stimulated Emission of Radiation," first developed in 1960. The laser produces a concentrated, pure beam of light whose various rays are synchronized. As a result, laser light behaves in unusual ways. It has applications in HOLOGRAPHY, which would be impossible without it, and in piped transmission of electromagnetic signals. See FIBER OPTICS.

LASER DISC   The Phillips-MCA Discovision system utilizes a system of recording that encodes a signal in light rather than magnetically (as in magnetic tape) or physically (as with the ordinary audio disc). The advantages are twofold: a great increase in capacity, and resistance to damage.

LATITUDE   See EXPOSURE LATITUDE.

LAUGHTRACK   Laughter, applause, and other audience reactions, usually artificially composed, that are added to a television program soundtrack in post-production. Also called *canned laughter*.

LEADER   (1) A piece of FILMSTOCK of uniform color, usually black, added to the HEAD or the TAIL of a reel. (2) A length of film showing countdown numbers, which is spliced to the beginning of a reel.

LEAD-IN, LEAD-OUT   (1) A transition, verbal or visual, into or out of a particular segment of a television or radio show. See SEGUE. (2) In programming, a show that precedes or follows another show. A popular lead-in will deliver a larger potential audience to the show that follows it. See also HAMMOCKING.

LENS   An optical lens bends light rays in order to focus them; a magnetic lens bends electron beams so that they can be controlled for the purposes of SCANNING. (See Figure 2-8.)

LETTERPRESS   The traditional method of printing using raised type. Each sheet is printed separately. See ROTARY PRESS, OFFSET, XEROGRAPHY.

LIBRARY SHOT   A STOCK SHOT.

LIGHTING   Early FILMSTOCKS were relatively insensitive. At first, only the sun could provide enough illumination. As a result, the earliest studios were built to rotate to catch the rays of the sun. Huge, unwieldy ARC LAMPS were the mainstays of cinematic lighting from the twenties until very recently when quartz lamps, together with filmstocks with much faster EMULSIONS, greatly increased the flexibility of the medium. Now, films shot entirely with AVAILABLE LIGHT are not uncommon, and complicated, controlled lighting has become a luxury rather than a necessity. The more light available, the smaller may be the opening of the DIAPHRAGM, and consequently the greater the DEPTH OF FIELD. Central to the calculation of EXPOSURE and lighting is the GAMMA, or CONTRAST of the filmstock, although recently developed techniques of PRE- and POST-FLASHING offer interesting ways of manipulating the contrast. Lighting remains one of the basic techniques of the film medium. See BACKLIGHTING, BARN DOORS, COLOR TEMPERATURE, DIFFUSER, FILLER LIGHT, GOBO, GAFFER, HIGHLIGHTING, KEY-LIGHTING.

LIGHTING CAMERAMAN   The British phrase for CINEMATOGRAPHER.

LIGHTSHOW   The projection of more or less abstract light patterns either moving or still, using numerous techniques including film. Lightshows were popular in the sixties as accompaniments to rock concerts.

LINKAGE   Pudovkin's term for MONTAGE. See EDITOR.

LINOTYPE   A typewriterlike machine that permits the casting of lines of type quickly and cheaply. See PHOTOTYPOGRAPHY.

LIP SYNC   Synchronization between the movement of the mouth and the words on the SOUNDTRACK.

LITHOGRAPHY   A printing system based on the fact that oil and water do not mix, so that printing surfaces and nonprinting surfaces can be PLANOGRAPHIC yet separate. See RELIEF, INTAGLIO.

LIVE   In television and radio a live broadcast is a broadcast in REAL TIME, as it happens. See DISC, TAPE.

LIVE RECORDING   A seeming contradiction in terms, "live recording" signifies that a record or tape was recorded on location, usually in front of an audience, rather than in a studio. The suggestion is that the performance has undergone a minimum of technical manipulation. See MIXING.

LONG SHOT   A long shot includes at least the full figures of the subjects, usually more. See FULL SHOT, EXTREME LONG SHOT.

LOOP   (1) The technique that permits the intermittent motion PULL-DOWN MECHANISM of the camera and projector to operate effectively. Loops of film before and after the mechanism allow continuous motion to be translated into intermittent motion. (2) A short piece of film joined end to end so as to repeat.

LOOPING   A technique of POST-DUBBING. The performer attempts to match dialogue to performance while watching a short piece of the scene formed into a loop.

LOUMA   A very flexible CRANE that is controlled by servomechanisms and that uses a television camera and MONITOR so the camera operator can control the camera from a distance. (See Figure 2-28.)

LP   A "long-playing" record that rotates at 33⅓ rpm; an ALBUM.

LUMIA   An electromechanical apparatus for producing cyclical moving patterns of light on a screen, invented by Thomas Wilfred. See LIGHT SHOW.

LUMINANCE   See CHROMINANCE.

M

McGUFFIN   Alfred Hitchcock's term for the device or plot element that catches the viewer's attention or drives the logic of the plot, especially in suspense films. According to Hitchcock, the McGuffin can be ignored as soon as it has served its purpose. Examples are the mistaken identity at the beginning of *North by Northwest* and the entire Janet Leigh subplot of *Psycho*.

MACROCINEMATOGRAPHY   The photographing of objects intermediate in size between those requiring magnification by a microscope and those which can be photographed by a normal lens.

MACRO LENS   A lens that can focus to very close distances, as little as 1 mm from the surface of the lens.

MACRO ZOOM LENS   A lens developed by the Canon corporation that can focus from 1 mm to infinity and can zoom as well. It permits unusual effects.

MADE-FOR-TV MOVIE   An awkward phrase for a type of filmed television, intermediate in style and construction between a dramatic program and a THEATRICAL FILM. See TELEFILM.

MAGNETIC DISC   As used for the storage of information in computer systems, the magnetic disc combines the technique of magnetic tape recording with the advantages, and accessibility of the disc configuration. See FLOPPY DISC.

MAGTRACK   Magnetic soundtrack on film, as opposed to OPTRACK—optical soundtrack.

MARRIED PRINT   A positive print of a film including both sound and image. See ANSWER PRINT.

MASK   (1) A shield placed before the camera lens to block off a part of the image. (2) A shield placed behind the projector lens to obtain the correct ASPECT RATIO. See TV MASK, MATTE SHOT.

MASTER   The original record or tape from which all record or tape copies are ultimately produced. Also used as a verb.

MASTER SHOT   A long TAKE of an entire scene, generally a relatively LONG SHOT that facilitates the assembly of component closer shots and DETAILS. The EDITOR can always fall back on the master shot: consequently, it is also called a *cover shot*.

MATCH CUT   A cut in which the two shots joined are linked by visual, aural, or metaphorical parallelism. Famous example: at the end of *North by Northwest*, Cary Grant is pulling Eva Marie Saint up the cliff of Mt. Rushmore; match cut to Grant pulling her up to a pullman bunk. (See Figure 3-60.) See also MONTAGE. Do not confuse with JUMP CUT.

MATERIALIST CINEMA   (1) A contemporary movement, mainly in AVANT-GARDE cinema, which celebrates the physical fact of film, camera, light, projector, and in which the materials of the art are in fact its main subject matter. Michael Snow, Tony Conrad, Paul Sharits, and Hollis Frampton are important figures in the movement. (2) The cinema of filmmakers such as Jean-Luc Godard and Roberto Rossellini, which combines some of the qualities of definition (1) with a strong conception of political change as dialectically materialistic, that is, as rooted in the basic conflicts of concrete economic realities.

MATTE SHOT   A matte is a piece of film that is opaque in part of the frame area. When printed together with a normal shot it masks part of the image of that shot and allows another scene, reversely matted, to be printed in the masked-off area. If the matte changes from frame to frame, the process is called TRAVELLING MATTE or BLUE SCREEN. (See Figures 2-48, 2-49.) See also CHROMA KEY.

MECHANICAL   Copy and artwork prepared to be photographed for PHOTOENGRAVING plates to be used in printing.

MEDIA   (singular: MEDIUM) Agencies or channels for the exchange, transmission, or dissemination of information. Especially "mass media," such as newspapers and magazines (print media), radio and television (electronic media).

MEDIA EVENT   An event staged to draw the particular attention of the media. The simplest and oldest example of a media event is the press conference. The development of television as the main social medium for news has led to more sophisticated media events such as the staged, acted dramatization (for example, politicians' visits to newsworthy sites), and the demonstration.

MEDIA IMAGE   The aura created in electronic and print media for an idea, company, product, concept, person, or political theory. See VALIDATION.

MEDIATE   (1) To serve as a vehicle for the transmission of information. (2) To change or modify that information in such a way that it fits the peculiar requirements of the print or electronic MEDIA.

MEDIUM SHOT   A shot intermediate between a CLOSEUP and a FULL SHOT.

MELODRAMA   Originally, simply a drama with music; more precisely, the type of nineteenth-century drama that centered on the simplistic conflict between heroes and villains. More recently, the word has come to signify any low-keyed drama, such as those dominating television.

METONYMY   In rhetoric, a common figure of speech that is characterized by the substitution of a word or concept closely associated with the object for the object itself (hence, "gun" for "gunman"). Generally, an associative device common in cinematic language. See INDEX, ICON, SYMBOL, SYNECDOCHE.

METTEUR EN SCÈNE   A modest—sometimes derogatory—term for "director." See AUTEUR.

MICROCINEMATOGRAPHY   Film photography through a microscope. See MACRO-CINEMATOGRAPHY.

MICROPHONE   A device that picks up sound waves, "focuses" them, and translates them into an electrical signal which can then be amplified.

MIMESIS   The Greek word for "imitation," a term important to the definition of REALISM.

MINICAM   A small, lightweight television camera which can be hand-held.

MINIDISC   See FLOPPY DISC.

MINIMAL CINEMA   A kind of extreme, simplified REALISM: Carl Dreyer, Robert Bresson, early Andy Warhol. Minimal dependence on the technical power of the medium.

MINISERIES   A CLOSED-END television SERIAL, usually based on a novel.

MIRROR SHOT   (1) A shot in a mirror. (2) A kind of GLASS SHOT.

MISE EN SCÈNE   The term usually used to denote that part of the cinematic process that takes place on the set, as opposed to MONTAGE, which takes place afterwards. Literally, the "putting-in-the-scene": the direction of actors, placement of cameras, choice of lenses, et cetera. Mise en scène is more important to REALISTS, montage to EXPRESSIONISTS.

MISE EN SHOT, MISE EN CADRE   The design of an entire shot, in time as well as space.

MITCHELL   The brand name of the most common type of Hollywood camera, a large, complex machine requiring several operators. (See Figure 2-25.) See also ARRIFLEX.

MIX   (1) Optical: A DISSOLVE. (2) Sound: The marriage of several separate recording tracks such as music, dialogue, and SOUND EFFECTS.

MIXING, MIXAGE   The general term for the work of the sound editor or mixer, who combines and edits various separate soundtracks into one final version. See MONTAGE.

MODEL SHOT   A shot using miniatures instead of the real objects or locations. Especially useful for staging great disasters. (See Figure 2-50.)

MODULATION   The principle that makes it possible for electromagnetic waves to transmit messages. Information is translated into waveforms which can then be imposed on a carrier wave. See WAVE MECHANICS, AM, FM.

MOGUL   One of the descendants of Baber, who conquered India in 1526, or a rich and powerful, often autocratic, person. The word is most often used in referring to the heads and owners of the great Hollywood studios.

MONAURAL   Single-source tape or disc sound reproduction, as compared with binaural STEREOPHONIC reproduction.

MONEME   The basic unit of formal choice in European linguistics.

MONITOR   A CATHODE RAY TUBE or television set connected directly to a camera.

MONTAGE   (1) Simply, EDITING. (2) Eisenstein's idea that adjacent shots should relate to each other in such a way that A and B combine to produce another meaning, C, which is not actually recorded on the film. (3) "Dynamic Cutting": a highly stylized form of editing, often with the purpose of providing a lot of information in a short period of time. See MIXING.

MONTAGE OF ATTRACTION   A concept associated with Eisenstein's theory of EDITING: the construction of a system of ATTRACTIONS.

MORPHEME   The basic unit of formal meaning in linguistics. See PHONEME, MONEME.

MORSE CODE   One of the earliest systems of MODULATION, the Morse code translates the Western alphabet into combinations of only two symbols: dots and dashes (short and long bursts of energy).

MOSAIC   See DISTRIBUTION FLOW.

MOTIF   A recurrent thematic element used in the development of an artistic work.

MOVIOLA   A brand of EDITING machine; also used generically. See STEENBECK.

MULTIPLE EXPOSURE   A number of images printed over each other. Not to be confused with MULTIPLE IMAGE. (See Figures 3-39, 3-40, 3-41.)

MULTIPLE IMAGE   A number of images printed beside each other within the same frame, often showing different camera angles of the same action, or separate actions. Also called SPLIT SCREEN.

MULTIPLEX   A technique of imposing one PROGRAM SIGNAL upon another to increase the channels available on each radio frequency. Multiplex is used for FM STEREOPHONIC and QUADRAPHONIC braodcasting as well as for the transmission of entirely separate programming, such as MUZAK.

MUSIC TRACK   One of three basic tracks, together with dialogue and EFFECTS, that are MIXED together to form the final SOUNDTRACK.

MUSIQUE CONCRÈTE   See CONCRETE MUSIC.

MUZAK   Specially programmed and performed music, designed to produce a useful mood or effect, then broadcast or reproduced by tape as an aural environment.

N

NAGRA   Brand name of a widely used portable sound tape recorder, important in the history of CINÉMA VÉRITÉ and DIRECT CINEMA.

NARRATION   Spoken description or analysis of action. See COMMENTATIVE SOUND.

NARRATIVE   Story; the linear, chronological structure of a story. An important concept in SEMIOLOGY.

NARRATIVE FILM   A film that tells a story, as opposed to POETIC FILM.

NARROWCAST   The distribution of a transmission to a limited, controlled audience. See BROADCAST.

NATURALISM   A theory of literature and film which supposes a scientific determinism such that the actions of a character are predetermined by biological, sociological, economic, or psychological laws. Often wrongly used as synonymous with REALISM, it does not mean simply "natural" in style.

NEGATIVE   A film that produces an inverse record of the light and dark areas of the photographed scene. See REVERSAL FILMSTOCK, POSITIVE, PRINT.

NEGATIVE COST   The cost of the finished film not including projection prints, publicity, distribution, and exhibition expenses. See COSTS.

NEGATIVE IMAGE   An image in which blacks are white and vice-versa. See SOLAR-IZATION.

NEILSEN   In the U.S., the most widely used RATINGS system, consisting of monitor boxes attached to the receiving sets of a DEMOGRAPHIC sample of viewers or listeners. The monitors can provide continuous, real-time information. See TRENDEX.

NEOREALISM   A style of filmmaking identified with Vittorio De Sica, Roberto Rossellini, and Luchino Visconti (among others) in Italy in the mid- and late 1940s. Characterized by political aims, the use of nonprofessional actors, location shooting, and some HAND-HELD camerawork. See REALISM.

NETWORK   A system of interconnected BROADCAST stations. See AFFILIATE.

NEUE KINO (DAS)   German Cinema since 1968.

NEW AMERICAN CINEMA   The "personal" cinema of independent filmmakers in the U.S. since World War II. Characterized by a lyric, poetic, experimental approach.

NEWSCAST   A news broadcast.

NEWSHOLE   The space in a newspaper, or magazine, or the time in a broadcast, alloted to news as opposed to advertising and commercials. In a successful newspaper, the newshole may be as small as 20 percent.

NEWSREEL   THEATRICAL FILM news report or, by extension, any filmed actuality.

NEW WAVE, NOUVELLE VAGUE   (1) Godard, Truffaut, Chabrol, Rohmer, Rivette, et al. Strictly, filmmakers who began as critics on CAHIERS DU CINÉMA in the 1950s and who were influenced by André Bazin. (2) The term is also used more loosely to refer to either (a) all the young French filmmakers of the 1960s, or (b) any new group of filmmakers.

NICKELODEON   The earliest film theaters; the admission price was originally five cents.

NIPKOW DISK   Invented in 1884 by Paul Nipkow: a spinning disc on which are arranged spiral patterns of apertures that permit a light beam to SCAN.

NONTHEATRICAL DISTRIBUTION   Distribution of films to schools, universities, clubs, and other essentially nonprofit organizations. Nontheatrical distribution has grown considerably since 1965; some films make larger profits in this market than in the theatrical or commercial market.

NOVELIZATION   A novel made from a film or SCREENPLAY. See TIE-IN.

O

OFFSET   A PLANOGRAPHIC printing process in which ink is transferred from the printing plate to the paper by means of flat rubber "offset" rollers. When combined with contemporary PHOTOENGRAVING techniques, offset is a quick, inexpensive, and easily accessible means of printing. See LETTERPRESS, GRAVURE, XEROGRAPHY.

ONE-REELER   A film of ten to twelve minutes in length.

OPEN-END SERIES   An unlimited SERIES, one which has a narrative scheme that leads to no particular conclusion. See CLOSED-END SERIES.

OPEN UP   (1) To open up a lens means to increase the opening of the DIAPHRAGM to permit more light into the camera. (2) To open up a narrative means to provide scenes or sequences in other than the main location. It is often thought that plays, when filmed, must be "opened up."

OPTICAL   An operation accomplished in the laboratory rather than on the SET or in the cutting room. Examples: DISSOLVES, FREEZE FRAMES, WIPES, GHOST IMAGES, and MATTE SHOTS.

OPTICAL PRINTER   The machine that duplicates prints of a film. Many operations of a technical nature are performed on the optical printer, including OPTICALS, the balancing of color values (see TIMING), and the correction of CONTRAST.

OPTRACK   Optical soundtrack on film, as opposed to MAGTRACK—magnetic sound-track.

ORTHICON   See IMAGE ORTHICON.

ORTHOCHROMATIC   A type of black-and-white FILMSTOCK that is sensitive to the blue and green areas of the spectrum. See PANCHROMATIC.

OUT OF SYNC   An expression used to indicate that sound and image are not in locked synchronization.

OUT-TAKE   A TAKE that is not used in the FINE CUT of the film.

OVERCRANK   To speed up a camera; to shoot at more than the normal 24 frames per second, so that the resulting image will appear in slow motion. See UNDERCRANK.

OVERDEVELOPMENT   See DEVELOPMENT.

OVEREXPOSURE   See EXPOSURE.

OVERLAP SOUND   A cut in which the cut in the SOUNDTRACK is not synchronous with the cut in the image. Often used in REACTION SHOTS.

OVER-THE-SHOULDER SHOT   A shot commonly used in dialogue scenes in which the speaker is seen from the perspective of a person standing just behind and a little to one side of the listener, so that parts of the head and shoulder of the listener are in the frame, as well as the head of the speaker.

P

PACE   The rhythm of a film.

PAN   Movement of the camera from left to right or right to left around the imaginary vertical axis that runs through the camera. See TILT, ROLL. A panning shot is sometimes confused with a TRACKING SHOT, which is quite different. (See Figure 2-23.) See also CAMERA ANGLE.

PAN AND SCAN   The technique of reframing used to prepare WIDESCREEN and ANAMORPHIC films for television projection in the standard television ASPECT RATIO of 1.33:1.

PANAVISION   Now the most widely used ANAMORPHIC process, it has largely super-seded other similar processes such as CINEMASCOPE. "Super Panavision" utilizes 70 mm filmstock, unsqueezed; "Ultra Panavision" uses 70 mm stock with 1:1.25 squeeze ratio.

PANCHROMATIC   A type of black-and-white film that is equally responsive to all the colors of the visible spectrum. See ORTHOCHROMATIC.

PANTHEON   The system of rating directors in hierarchical categories common to the AUTEUR POLICY. Pantheon directors are the highest rated.

PARADIGM   In SEMIOLOGY, a unit of potential, as opposed to actual, relationship.

The paradigm describes "what elements or statements go with what"; the SYN-TAGMA, "what follow what."

PARALLAX   The apparent change in position of a viewed object, caused by differences in perspective or point of view. Parallax is useful in providing a sense of depth to otherwise two-dimensional representations, especially in cinema when it is a function of the moving camera. Parallax is a problem for photographers who sight their images through a viewfinder rather than the taking lens. The solution is the REFLEX CAMERA.

PARALLEL ACTION   A device of narrative in which two scenes are observed in parallel by CROSS-CUTTING. Also called *parallel montage*. See ACCELERATED MONTAGE.

PARALLEL MONTAGE   See PARALLEL ACTION.

PARALLEL SOUND   Sound that matches its accompanying image. Compare CONTRAPUNTAL SOUND, OVERLAP SOUND.

PAYOLA   The practice of paying a radio disc jockey to play a certain record. See PLUGOLA.

PAY TELEVISION   Any of several systems of television financed by charges to the viewer rather than by advertising. See CABLE TELEVISION, HOME BOX OFFICE.

PERSISTENCE OF VISION   The physiological phenomenon that makes cinema and television possible. An image is retained on the retina of the eye for a short period after it is seen so that, if another image takes its place soon enough, the illusion of motion can be created. See PHI EFFECT.

PERSONA   From the Latin for "mask." A character in a literary, cinematic, or dramatic work. More precisely, the psychological image of the character that is created, especially in relationship to other levels of reality.

PERSONALITY   In the media sense, a performer who doesn't act, but "is," whose value lies in the PERSONA or image created and projected. See CELEBRITY.

PHI EFFECT, PHI PHENOMENON   The psychological perception of motion which is caused by the displacement of two objects seen in quick succession in neighboring positions. Compare with PERSISTENCE OF VISION, which is physiologically rather than psychologically defined.

PHONE FREAK   A person who makes a hobby of manipulating and studying the complexities of the telephone system. Similarly, COMPUTER FREAK.

PHONEME   In linguistics, the smallest unit of speech or sound that is identifiable (the unit of the "signifier"). See MONEME, MORPHEME.

PHONOGRAPH   A device, either wholly mechanical, mechanical-electrical, or mechanical-electronic, for recording and playing back sound signals on a wax or plastic DISC. (See Figure 6-5.)

PHOTOCOPY   See REPROGRAPHY.

PHOTOENGRAVING   A photographic process for making a printing plate. Any original material, such as typescript, previously printed page, or line drawing can be reproduced quickly. See OFFSET, HALFTONE.

PHOTOGENIC   Attractive as a subject for photography.

PHOTOGRAM   From the French; a STILL.

PHOTOGRAPHY   Literally "light-writing." Any system of recording images, especially those which use chemical technology. Although CINEMATOGRAPHY is the more precise term for motion picture photography, the more general term, photography, is often used synonymously: one speaks of photographing a motion picture rather than "cinematographing" it, for example.

PHOTOLITHOGRAPHY   An OFFSET printing process using PHOTOENGRAVED plates that are PLANOGRAPHIC. See TYPOGRAPHY.

PHOTOTELEGRAPHY   The transmission of photographs via TELEGRAPHY.

PHOTOTYPOGRAPHY   The reproduction of TYPOGRAPHIC materials, such as printing plates, via photographic means. Rather than utilizing metal type, phototypography depends on stored film images of the letters and symbols to be reproduced. See PHOTOENGRAVING.

PICTURE ELEMENT   Any one of the hundreds of thousands of individual, coded areas of light and shade which go to make up a television image.

PILOT   A sample television program prepared to test the concept of a planned SERIES. Today, pilots are often recycled as MADE-FOR-TV or THEATRICAL FILMS.

PIRANDELLIAN   An adjective derived from the name of the twentieth-century playwright Luigi Pirandello, whose plays investigated the subtle differences between fiction and reality and described a world system in which illusion and actuality combined in intricate ways to produce a continuum of VERISIMILITUDE.

PIXILLATION   A technique of ANIMATION in which real objects, people, or events are photographed in such a way that the illusion of continuous, real movement is broken, either by photographing one frame at a time or later printing only selected frames from the continuously-exposed negative. Example: some films by Norman McLaren.

PLANOGRAPHIC   Systems of printing in which the image is essentially the same height as the nonprinting area. LITHOGRAPHY is planographic.

PLAYBACK   The act or process of replaying a record or tape.

PLUG   A mention of a commercial product or service within the context of a show, program, or film production. See ADVERTISING.

PLUGOLA   The practice of paying a film, television, or radio PERSONALITY, star, producer, or director in order to obtain a PLUG. See PAYOLA.

POETIC FILM   Non-NARRATIVE FILM, often experimental. Jonas Mekas's phrase to distinguish NEW AMERICAN CINEMA from the general run of commercial, narrative fiction film.

POINT OF VIEW SHOT   A shot which shows the scene from the point of view of a character. Often abbreviated 'pov."

POLITIQUE DES AUTEURS   See AUTEUR POLICY.

PORN, PORNO   Pornographic film exploiting sex.

POSITIVE   A film record in which lights and darks conform to the reality of the scene photographed; a projection print. See NEGATIVE, REVERSAL.

POST-DUBBING   See DUB.

POST-FLASHING   A technique in which color FILMSTOCK is exposed, after shooting, to a neutral gray light source of a predetermined level and uniform density in order to mute the INTENSITY of the colors for a more realistic effect, to decrease the CONTRAST range of the FILMSTOCK to aid in AVAILABLE-LIGHT photography, or to bring out detail in shadow areas. See PREFLASHING, COLORFLEX, CHEMTONE.

POST-SYNCHRONIZATION   Recording the sound after the picture has been shot. See LOOPING.

PRACTICAL LIGHTING   (1) Normal light fixtures, such as common household incandescent bulbs. (2) The technique of using such fixtures for AVAILABLE-LIGHT photography.

PRACTICAL SET   A realistically built set in which doors, windows, and equipment actually work, or a real location. A practical set does not have WILD WALLS.

PRE-FLASHING   The same as POST-FLASHING except that the FILMSTOCK is exposed before shooting rather than after. Pioneered by Freddie Young in *The Deadly Affair* (1966).

PRESENCE   The quality of intelligence, character, or personality a performer projects via the media. See PHOTOGENIC, TELEGENIC.

PRIME TIME   The hours when most television sets are in use and which therefore offer advertisers the greatest potential audience. In the Eastern U.S., 7:30 P.M. to 11:00 P.M.

PRIME-TIME ACCESS RULE   The FCC's 1971 ruling that forbids NETWORKS from providing more than an average of three hours of prime-time programming per evening. The ruling was designed to open up prime time to local programming. The effect, however, was that local broadcasters turned en masse to SYNDICATED programming.

PRINT   A POSITIVE copy of a film.

PRINTED CIRCUIT   A miniaturized electronic circuit whose interconnections are printed on a circuit board. Devices such as transistors, resistors, and capacitors can then be plugged into the circuit rather than painstakingly wired in.

PROBLEMATIC   A Marxian concept. The theoretical or ideological framework in which any word or concept must be understood and considered.

PROCESS SHOT   REAR PROJECTION, MATTE SHOTS, OPTICALS, and the like.

PROGRAMMER   (1) The executive in charge of PROGRAMMING at a NETWORK or station. (2) A B PICTURE; a minor film made to fill a program.

PROGRAMMING   The art and science of designing a television or radio schedule to obtain maximum audiences DEMOGRAPHICALLY determined to appeal to ADVERTISERS.

PROGRAM SIGNAL   The signal that carries the actual program information and that is imposed on the *carrier wave*. See WAVE MECHANICS.

PROMO   A television or radio "house ad" or announcement advertising upcoming programs.

PROP   Any physical item used in a play or film: chairs, tables, eyeglasses, books, pens, et cetera.

PROPERTY   (1) A PROP. (2) Any one of a number of possible versions of either a fictional or nonfictional story—in manuscript, playscript, typescript, or book form—that has potential commercial value in the MEDIA. Properties can be recycled many times. *Cabaret*, for example, began as a book of short stories (Christopher Isherwood's *Berlin Stories*), which became the play *I Am a Camera*, which became the film *I Am a Camera*, which became the musical play *Cabaret*, which was the source of the record album, film, and soundtrack album of the same title: one property seven exploitations.

PUBLIC ACCESS TELEVISION   Channels set aside on CABLE systems for use by any member of the public. See ACCESS.

PUBLIC RELATIONS, PUBLICITY   Nonspecific ADVERTISING devoted to promoting ideas, people, images, products and services.

PULL-BACK SHOT   A TRACKING SHOT or ZOOM that moves back from the subject to reveal the context of the scene.

PULL-DOWN MECHANISM   The device that makes INTERMITTENT MOVEMENT possible: usually a Maltese cross gear (Figure 2-20) or a cam-mounted claw that pulls each frame into position in the aperture of the projector and holds it steady while the SHUTTER opens, then closes. The invention of a practical pull-down mechanism, which made cinema possible, is usually credited to Thomas Armat. Recently, the development of rotating prism apertures have obviated the need for pull-down mechanisms. In such systems (found notably in high-speed cameras and modern editing tables such as the STEENBECK), the film moves continuously rather than intermittently past the aperture while the prism continually redirects the light beam toward the lens.

PULL FOCUS   See FOCUS PULL.

PUSH DEVELOPMENT   Overdevelopment. See DEVELOPMENT.

PUSHOVER   A type of WIPE in which the succeeding image appears to push the preceding image off the screen.

Q

QUADRAPHONIC SOUND   A development of STEREOPHONIC reproduction that uses four channels of information rather than two either in FM MULTIPLEX broadcasting, discs, or tapes. Two channels feed front speakers with basic stereophonic signals while the two remaining channels feed back speakers with slightly different signals to provide an environmental ROOM SOUND. Introduced by the recording industry in 1972, quadraphonic sound did not have the anticipated impact on the stereo marketplace. It waned quickly.

QUBE   Warner Cable's name for its pioneering TWO-WAY CABLE system introduced in Columbus, Ohio, in 1977.

QUINTAPHONIC SOUND   A film SOUNDTRACK system that provides five channels of sound information: three in front, two behind. See STEREOPHONIC, QUADRAPHONIC.

R

RACK FOCUSING   A technique that uses SHALLOW FOCUS (shallow DEPTH OF FIELD) to direct the attention of the viewer forcibly from one subject to another. Focus is pulled, or changed, to shift the FOCUS PLANE, often rapidly, sometimes several times within the shot.

RADIO   (1) From the Latin for "the emission of beams." The transmission of information such as a PROGRAM SIGNAL encoded on a *carrier wave* within the RADIO SPECTRUM of the ELECTROMAGNETIC SPECTRUM. (2) More colloquially, any broadcast of sound without picture. See WAVE MECHANICS.

RADIOGRAPH   An image produced on a radiosensitive surface, such as photographic film, by radiation other than visible light.

RADIO SPECTRUM   The complete range of ELECTROMAGNETIC frequencies used for radio, radar, and television. The spectrum runs from about ten kiloHertz (10,000 cycles per second) to 300,000 megaHertz (300,000 million cycles per second) and includes the following areas: very low frequency (vlf): 10 to 30 kHz; low frequency (lf): 30 to 300 kHz; medium frequency (mf): 300 to 3,000 kHz; high frequency (hf): 3,000 to 30,000 kHz; very high frequency (vhf): 30 to 300 mHz; ultra high frequency (uhf): 300 to 3,000 mHz; super high frequency (shf): 3,000 to 30,000 mHz; and extremely high frequency (ehf): 30,000 to 300,000 mHz. AM radio transmitters operate in the medium frequency band; FM radio, and television channels 2 through

13 in the very high frequency band; television channels 14 through 83 in the ultra high frequency band.

RADIOTELEGRAPHY   The transmission of TELEGRAPH messages by RADIO signals rather than wires.

RADIOTELEPHONY   The transmission of TELEPHONE messages by RADIO signals rather than wires.

RAPPORTS DE PRODUCTION   In Marxian thought, the relationships in the productive system between producer, distributor, and consumer.

RASTER   The predetermined patterns of television SCANNING lines that provide uniform coverage of the image. (See Figure 2-1F.) See also FIELD.

RATINGS   (1) In cinema, systems of classification based on sexual or violence factors. The British Board of Film Censors bestows three types of certificates: U (Universal); A (Adult, prohibited to children under 16 unless accompanied by an adult); and X (unsuitable for children under 16). In the U.S., the Motion Picture Producers of America (MPAA) rates films in four categories: G (General); PG (Parental Guidance suggested for children); R (Restricted to persons under 18 unless accompanied by an adult); and X (Prohibited to persons under 18). (2) Systems of calculating audience size for television and radio programs. See NEILSEN, TRENDEX.

RATIO   See SHOOTING RATIO, ASPECT RATIO.

REACTION SHOT   A shot that cuts away from the main scene or speaker in order to show a character's reaction to it. See CUTAWAY.

REACTIVE TECHNOLOGY   *Unidirectional* technology. See DISTRIBUTION FLOW.

REALISM   In film, that attitude opposed to EXPRESSIONISM that emphasizes the subject as opposed to the director's view of the subject. Usually concerns topics of a socially conscious nature, and uses a minimal amount of technique. See NEOREALISM, MINIMAL CINEMA, FORMALISM.

REAL TIME   A concept borrowed from computer technology. The actual time during which a process or event occurs. A LIVE broadcast occurs in real time, for example.

REAL-TIME ACCESS   See ACCESS.

REAR PROJECTION   A process in which a background scene is projected onto a translucent screen behind the actors so it appears that the actors are in that location. Superseded at present by FRONT PROJECTION and MATTE techniques, both more effective systems. (See Figures 2-45, 6-19.)

RECEPTIVE THEORY   AFFECTIVE THEORY. See also GENERATIVE THEORY.

RECORD FILM   A film that provides a duplicate representation of the subject photographed with no pretense to artistic content.

REEL   A holder for film or tape. The feed reel supplies the film or tape; the take-up reel gathers it in.

REEL TO REEL   A tape recorder that uses open reels of tape rather than closed CASSETTES or CARTRIDGES.

REFLEX CAMERA   A camera that incorporates a mirrored shutter so that the cameraman can observe the scene through the TAKING LENS rather than a separate VIEWFINDER, thereby eliminating problems of PARALLAX distortion and greatly enhancing the photographer's ability to judge the elements of the scene. (See Figure 2-21.)

REGENERATIVE CIRCUIT   First developed by Edwin Armstrong, an amplification circuit that uses the principle of FEEDBACK to strengthen the incoming signal.

RELATIONAL EDITING   Editing of shots to suggest a conceptual association between shots. See MONTAGE OF ATTRACTION.

RELEASE PRINT   A print ready for DISTRIBUTION and SCREENING. See also GENERATION.

RELIEF PRINTING   A system of printing in which the printing surface is raised. See INTAGLIO PRINTING, PLANOGRAPHIC.

REPRO   Copy prepared to be photographed for PHOTOENGRAVING plates to be used in printing.

REPROGRAPHY   Chemical or electrophotographic systems of image-transfer printing, such as XEROGRAPHY and similar systems. See OFFSET, LETTERPRESS.

RERUN   A rebroadcast of a television program.

RESOLUTION   The ability of a lens to define visual details, usually measured as the number of lines per millimeter that can be separately identified. See DEFINITION.

RESPONSE TIME   In the technology of sound reproduction, the minimum amount of time necessary for a system of amplifier and speaker to reproduce sound and therefore a measure of the acuity of the system.

REVERSAL FILMSTOCK   A stock whose emulsion will print POSITIVE after exposure and development.

REVERSE ANGLE   (1) A SHOT from the opposite side of a subject. (2) In a dialogue scene, a SHOT of the second participant.

REVERSE MOTION   The film is run through the camera backwards so that when it is later run through the projector in the normal manner the illusion will be created that time is running backwards.

ROLL   The movement of the camera around the axis that runs longitudinally from the lens to the subject. (See Figure 2-23.) See also TILT, PAN.

ROOM SOUND, ROOM NOISE, ROOM TONE   (1) The particular quality of sound in a certain location, mainly a matter of reverberation and echoes. (2) The basic, underlying sound present in a location, such as clocks, traffic, activity. Room sound is often recorded WILD and later mixed with dialogue and effects.

ROTARY PRESS PRINTING   Curved printing plates are attached to a rotating cylinder to permit continuous rather than intermittent operation of the press. Rolls of paper rather than individual sheets feed the press. Pages are cut later. Rotary presses can operate at very high speeds. See LETTERPRESS, OFFSET.

ROTOSCOPING   A SPECIAL EFFECTS technique which uses individual MATTES photographed frame by frame, similar in effect to a TRAVELLING MATTE.

ROUGH CUT   The first assembly of a film, prepared by the editor from the selected TAKES, which are joined in the order planned in the script. Finer points of timing and montage are left to a later stage.

RUSHES   Prints of TAKES that are made immediately after a day's shooting so that they can be examined before the next day's shooting begins. Also called *dailies*. See ANSWER PRINT.

S

SACCADE   The flick movement of the eye from one position to another that occurs not only when reading words but also when reading images and real scenes. (See Figure 3-5.)

SAFE ACTION AREA   See TV MASK.

SATELLITE COMMUNICATIONS   A satellite placed in geosynchronous orbit

22,300 miles above the equator, will remain stationary with respect to the earth permitting sending and receiving antennas to be permanently aimed at it. TRANS-PONDERS on the satellite receive earth signals, amplify them, and retransmit them. Satellite technology for telephone, television, and information transmission has grown rapidly during the last five years and has had a marked effect on the structure of the television industry.

SATURATION   See COLOR.

SCANNING   In television, the movement of the electron beam in regular patterns to cover the mosaic of receptor cells in the camera or the pattern of phosphor PICTURE ELEMENTS on the screen of the CATHODE RAY TUBE. See FIELD, RASTER.

SCENARIO   (1) An outline for a SCREENPLAY. (2) A complete screenplay. See TREAT-MENT.

SCENE   A complete unit of film narration. A series of SHOTS (or a single shot) that take place in a single location and that deal with a single action. A relatively vague term. See SHOT, SEQUENCE.

SCHUFFTAN PROCESS   An obsolete process that combined a MIRROR SHOT with a MODEL SHOT to produce a composite image.

SCOPE   Abbreviation of CINEMASCOPE, and by extension all ANAMORPHIC processes.

SCORE   The music for a film.

SCREEN   (1) The surface on which a film or television image is projected. (2) A method of printing in which ink is forced through a fabric screen to make the desired impression, the blank areas having been covered with an opaque material to prevent the ink from coming through. (3) A glass plate etched with crossed lines used to make HALFTONE patterns. See BEN DAY. (4) (verb) To project a film for a limited audience.

SCREENPLAY   The script of a film or television show, usually but not necessarily including rough descriptions of camera movements as well as dialogue. Formerly "photoplay." See SCENARIO, TREATMENT, TELEPLAY, DÉCOUPAGE.

SCREWBALL COMEDY   A type of comedy prevalent in the 1930s and typified by frenetic action, wisecracks, and sexual relationships as an important plot element. Usually about upper-class characters and therefore often involving opulent sets and costumes as visual elements. *It Happened One Night* (1934), *Easy Living* (1937), and *Bringing Up Baby* (1938) are prime examples. Highly verbal, as opposed to its predecessor, the SLAPSTICK comedy. See also BLACK COMEDY.

SCRIM   An opaque plate placed in front of a light in order to cast a particular shadow, usually to create the illusion of natural lighting. See GOBO, DIFFUSER.

SCRIPT GIRL   An obsolete term for the script supervisor. See CONTINUITY.

SECOND UNIT   An auxiliary film crew whose job is to shoot material, such as foreign location backgrounds or special shots, not handled by the first unit.

SEG   *Special effects generator*, a piece of electronic equipment that allows a television TECHNICAL DIRECTOR to create FADES, DISSOLVES, WIPES, SPLIT SCREENS and the like in real time.

SEGMENT   A basic unit of the television program, especially of the type of show unique to radio and television.

SEGUE   (pronounced seg-way) (1) a bridging element from one SEGMENT to another in television or radio. (2) A smooth, seamless musical change of key.

SEMIOCLASM   Roland Barthes's term for the destruction of the connotations and denotations of the cultural language that is necessary before those languages can be rebuilt afresh.

SEMIOLOGY, SEMIOTICS   Theory of criticism pioneered by Roland Barthes in literature and Christian Metz, Umberto Eco, and Peter Wollen in film. It uses the theories of modern linguistics, especially Ferdinand de Saussure's concept of signification, as a model for the description of the operation of various cultural languages, such as film, television, kinesics (body language), and written and spoken languages. See SYNTAGMA, PARADIGM, DIEGESIS.

SEQUENCE   A basic unit of film construction consisting of one or more SCENES that form a natural unit. An ambiguous term. See SHOT, SEQUENCE SHOT.

SEQUENCE SHOT   A long, usually complex shot, often including complicated camera movements and action. Also called Plan-séquence.

SERIAL   In both films and television, a continuing story told in episodes, each of which has a specific place in the narrative. A serial has a definite beginning, middle, and end, as opposed to a SERIES.

SERIES   A continuing string of television or radio programs or films, with each episode sharing basic situations and characters but divorced from the others in terms of plot. The series may be either OPEN-ENDED or CLOSE-ENDED. See SERIAL, SPECIAL.

SET   The location of a scene, usually artificially constructed on a SOUND STAGE.

SET-UP   A camera and lighting position. When large, unwieldy cameras and lights are used, the number of different set-ups required can become an important economic factor.

SEXPLOITATION   Jargon term for sex EXPLOITATION film or PORN.

SHALLOW FOCUS   A technique that utilizes shallow DEPTH OF FIELD to create a shallow FOCUS PLANE, usually in order to direct the attention of the viewer to the subject or action in that plane. (See Figure 2-17.) See also DEEP FOCUS, RACK FOCUS, FOLLOW FOCUS.

SHOOTING RATIO   The ratio between film actually exposed in the camera during shooting to film used in the final cut. A shooting ratio of ten to one or more is not uncommon.

SHORT   A film usually less than thirty minutes in length. See also FEATURE.

SHORT-CIRCUIT SIGN   According to Christian Metz, the condition of the cinematic SIGN in which the SIGNIFIER is the same as the SIGNIFIED.

SHOT   A single piece of film, however long or short, without cuts, exposed continuously. A film may be composed of more than a thousand shots or it may seem to be a single shot. See SCENE, SEQUENCE, TAKE, CLOSEUP, CAMERA ANGLE, PAN, ZOOM, and DETAIL, FULL, LONG, MEDIUM, EXTREME LONG, ESTABLISHING, TWO-, AERIAL, POINT OF VIEW, MASTER, FOLLOW, STOCK, DOLLY, TRACKING, and INSERT SHOTS.

SHOWCASE   Multiple exhibition of a film in a selected number of theaters. See FIRST RUN, FOUR-WALLING, GENERAL RELEASE.

SHUTTER   The device that opens and closes an aperture on a camera or projector.

SIGN   In SEMIOLOGY, the basic unit of signification composed of the *signifier* (which carries the meaning) and the *signified* (which is the concept or thing signified). In written language, for example, the word "tree" is the signifier, the idea of the tree the signified; the whole sign is comprised of both elements. In cinema, the signified, the idea of the tree, remains the same, but the signifier, the image (or even the sound) of the tree is much more complex. See MONEME, PHONEME, MORPHEME, SHORT-CIRCUIT SIGN.

SIGNAL   In the electronic media, the coded message of the program that is imposed on the *carrier wave*. See WAVE MECHANICS.

SIGNIFIED   See SIGN.

SIGNIFIER   See SIGN.

SINGLE   A short record, usually 45 rpm, seven-inch diameter, with one song on each side. See ALBUM.

SINGLE-SYSTEM SOUND   A system often used for news film, consisting of a camera that includes a recording HEAD and FILMSTOCK, one edge of which is striped with magnetic recording material. See DOUBLE-SYSTEM SOUND.

SITCOM   Situation comedy; a type of program, first in radio, then television, usually a half hour in length, which is centered on a limited number of characters—often a family—located in a particular situation. See DOMESTIC COMEDY.

SLAPSTICK   A type of comedy, widely prevalent during the silent film era, which depends on broad physical action and pantomime for its effect rather than verbal wit or character dialogue. See SCREWBALL COMEDY.

SLATE   See CLAPPER BOARD.

SLOW MOTION   The camera is OVERCRANKED, so that the film runs through faster than the normal 24 frames per second, so that when it is later projected at the normal rate the action will take more time than in reality. See FAST MOTION.

SOAP OPERA   A type of continuing, never-ending serialized drama pioneered in radio, later a staple of daytime television, which deals with basically domestic situations, eveyday problems, and common middle-class characters—usually house-wives. Almost always daily in frequency, the soap opera soon evolves an extraordi-narily involuted and tangled plot since so much is made to happen to so few so often. Soap operas were often sponsored by soap and detergent products, hence the name.

SOCIALIST REALISM   The Stalinist dogma of art that is neither particularly socialist nor particularly realistic, but which insists that Art serve the purposes of the State.

SOFT FOCUS   Filters, vaseline, or specially constructed lenses soften the delineation of lines and points, usually to create a romantic effect.

SOFTWARE   See HARDWARE.

SOLARIZATION   A chemical or electronic process of reversal or shift of the color spectrum so that blues become yellow, reds cyan, and greens magenta. See COLOR.

SOUND   See ACTUAL, ASYNCHRONOUS, CONTRAPUNTAL, COMMENTATIVE, SYNCHRO-NOUS, OVERLAP, PARALLEL, CONCRETE, and DIRECT SOUND.

SOUND EFFECTS   All those created sounds that are not dialogue or music. See SOUNDTRACK.

SOUND STAGE   A specially constructed building in which SETS can be built for studio filming.

SOUNDTRACK   Optical soundtracks operate by the modulation of a beam of light tha creates a band on the film that widens and narrows to encode the information of the signal. Magnetic soundtracks, like tape recordings, encode the information electromagnetically on a specially prepared surface. The final soundtrack, whether optical or magnetic, is usually a mixture of several primary tracks—effects, dialogue, and music. (See Figures 2-1A, 2-39.) See also STEREOPHONIC SOUND, QUINTA-PHONIC SOUND, AUDIO.

SPAGHETTI WESTERN   A European Western, usually filmed in Spain or Italy and popularized in the 1960s by the films of Sergio Leone.

SPECIAL   A single television program that is not part of a series, serial, or other continuing structure.

SPECIAL EFFECTS   A broad term for a wide range of devices and processes, includ-ing some kinds of work performed by stunt men, MODEL SHOTS, OPTICALS, in-camera effects, MATTE SHOTS, REAR PROJECTION, SOLARIZATION, NEGATIVE IMAGE, and much more.

SPECIAL EFFECTS GENERATOR   See SEG.

SPEED   (1) Camera and projector speed: the standard for sound films is 24 frames per second; for silent films, between 16 and 18 fps; for American television, 30 fps; for all other television, 25 fps. (2) Lens speed: a measure of the ability of a lens to capture and admit light: the faster the lens, the more light admitted. See F-NUMBER. (3) Emulsion speed: the ability of an EMULSION to capture and fix light. The faster the speed of the emulsion, the less light is needed for a proper exposure.

SPINOFF   A television series created out of elements (usually characters, but sometimes situations) of an earlier series.

SPLICE   The physcial joint between two pieces of film.

SPLIT SCREEN   Two or more separate images within the frame, not overlapping. Accomplished on an OPTICAL PRINTER (for film) and a SEG (for television). See MULTIPLE IMAGE.

SPOTLIGHTING   Lighting a particular, often very small, area for effect.

SPROCKETS   (1) The regularly spaced and shaped holes in FILMSTOCK that enable the film to be mechanically advanced. (2) The gears which engage the sprocket holes and drive the film.

SQUIB   A very small explosive charge in a capsule, used to simulate a gunshot or the like.

STATION BREAK   The required interruption of radio and television programming in order to identify the station broadcasting.

STEADICAM   The invention of cameraman Garrett Brown (developed in conjunction with Cinema Prodcuts, Inc.) this is a system which permits hand-held filming with an image steadiness comparable to TRACKING SHOTS. A vest redistributes the weight of the camera to the hips of the cameraman; a spring-loaded arm damps the motion of the camera; a video monitor frees the cameraman from the eyepiece. Because it replaces expensive and time-consuming dolly tracks, the Steadicam should result in lower produciton costs. First used by Haskell Wexler on *Bound for Glory* (1975).

STEENBECK   A particular brand of modern editing table that is much more flexible than the old standard MOVIOLA. (See Figure 2-41.)

STEREOPHONIC SOUND   In reality, sound is heard from many sources and the binaural ability of the two ears creates a sense of dimensionality. Stereophonic sound, which uses two or more speakers and tracks, approximates the binaural experience. Stereophonic headphones come closest to mimicking reality, since each ear then hears only one track. See QUADRAPHONIC SOUND.

STEREOSCOPY   Photography utilizing two separate, paired images—one for each eye—to re-create a sense of depth in the image. There are, however, many psychological and technical problems that contemporary stereoscopy cannot overcome. "Orthostereoscopy" is normal stereoscopic vision. "Hyperstereoscopy" increases the distance between the cameras to more than the distance between human eyes, creating the illusion of depth where human eyes could not perceive it. "Pseudoscopic stereoscopy" reverses the left image with the right, creating complicated psychological reactions. "Pseudostereoscopy" consists of those techniques—overlapping, PARALLAX, and movement in the frame, for example—which two-dimensional photography uses to create the illusion of depth. See HOLOGRAPHY.

STILL   A single photograph; more precisely, a frame enlargement or similar publicity photograph from a film. A PHOTOGRAM.

STOCK   See FILMSTOCK.

STOCK SHOT   (1) A *library shot,* one which is literally borrowed from a collection, such as World War II shots or jet planes in flight, or ESTABLISHING SHOTS of New York City. (2) Any unimaginative or common shot that looks as if it might as well have been a library shot.

STOP-MOTION PHOTOGRAPHY   A technique in which the camera operates one frame at a time, allowing objects to be adjusted between frames. Responsible for much trick photography. See FAST MOTION, PIXILLATION.

STORY BOARD   A series of drawings and captions (sometimes resembling a comic strip) that shows the planned shot divisions and camera movements of the film—its DÉCOUPAGE.

STROBOSCOPE   A light that flashes on and off in precisely timed cycles. The rate can be varied, which sometimes produces dangerous psychological effects, such as epileptic attacks. Some AVANT-GARDE films experiment with stroboscopic effects.

STRUCTURALISM   The study of society, psychology, and related phenomena as arrangements of parts, usually called CODES. Closely allied with SEMIOLOGY, structuralism is more ethnographic than linguistic.

STRUCTURALIST FILM   A film in which the codes and structures of social arrangements are evident. See CINE-STRUCTURALISM, MATERIALIST CINEMA.

SUBCODE   See CODE.

SUBJECTIVE CAMERA   A style that allows the viewer to observe events from the point of view of either a character or the PERSONA of the author. See POINT OF VIEW SHOT.

SUBSIDIARY   A minor interest of the image, often controlled by the DOMINANT.

SUNDAY GHETTO   Jargon for the time periods on Sunday when few television sets are in use and in which NETWORKS commonly schedule their public service programming.

SUPERHETERODYNE CIRCUIT   A radio circuit, invented by Edwin Armstrong, that mixes a signal generated within the receiver with an incoming PROGRAM SIGNAL for the purposes of amplification.

SUPERIMPOSITION   See MULTIPLE EXPOSURE.

SURFACE NOISE   The basic random sound level inherent in any recording medium—film, tape, or disc. See also DOLBY.

SURREALISM   (1) A movement in painting and film during the 1920s best represented in film by the work of Salvador Dali and Luis Buñuel. (2) A film style reminiscent of that movement, either fantastic or psychologically distortive.

SWISH PAN   Also called flick pan, zip pan, whip pan. A PAN in which the intervening scene moves past too quickly to be observed. It approximates psychologically the action of the human eye as it moves from one subject to another. See SACCADE.

SYMBOL   (1) In the Peirce/Wollen system, a SIGN that demands neither resemblance to its object nor any existential bond with it, but operates by pure convention. See INDEX, ICON. (2) More generally, something that represents something else by resemblance, association, or convention.

SYMPTOMATIC TECHNOLOGY   See TECHNOLOGICAL DETERMINISM.

SYNC, SYNCHRONIZATION   Mechanical, electric, electronic, or crystal clock devices are used to keep sound and picture in proper relationship to each other. See LIP SYNC.

SYNCHRONIC   In SEMIOLOGICAL theory, a phenomenon is synchronic when all its elements belong to the same moment in time and do not depend on a change of state across time. See DIACHRONIC.

SYNCHRONOUS SOUND   Sound whose source is visible in the frame of the image or whose source is understandable from the context of the image. Compare ASYNCHRONOUS SOUND, COMMENTATIVE SOUND.

SYNDICATION   An alternative to NETWORK distribution of television and radio programming. Programs are sold by the producer or distributor directly to the local stations rather than the networks.

SYNECDOCHE   In rhetoric, a common figure of speech in which a part signifies the whole (or the whole a part), hence a "motor" is understood to be an "automobile." Generally, a metaphorical device basic to cinematographic language. Closely associated with the similar concept of METONYMY. See INDEX, ICON, SYMBOL.

SYNTAGMA   A SEMIOLOGICAL term. A unit of actual rather than potential relationship. Syntagmatic relationships exist between the present elements of a shot or a statement in film. The syntagma describes what follows what, rather than what goes with what. Contrast with PARADIGM.

T

TAIL   The end of a reel of film.

TAKE   A version of a SHOT. A filmmaker shoots one or more takes of each shot or SET-UP. Only one of each group of takes appears in the final film.

TAKING LENS   The LENS which transmits the image to be photographed. On some cameras, a separate lens is used for the VIEWFINDER. See REFLEX CAMERA.

TALKING HEADS   Jargon for a television news SEGMENT or documentary sequence in which subjects simply talk to the camera.

TALK RADIO   A radio format consisting of conversations between a host and performer or PERSONALITY. Telephone calls from members of the audience are often accepted.

TALK SHOW   (1) A common type of television program consisting of light interviews, conversation, and occasional performances or news items. (2) A TALK RADIO show.

TAPE   A mode of recording that is linear and editable, using a thin, flexible plastic base coated with electromagnetic particles. See DISC, LIVE.

TECHNICAL DIRECTOR   The television crew member in charge of control-room decisions—such as which camera to use when—during the ʹ ıping or broadcast of a show.

TECHNICOLOR   The first successful color film system. *Becky Sharp* (1935) was the first full Technicolor FEATURE. In 1942, Technicolor Corporation introduced the "Monopack" system, which required only one camera and therefore made color filming flexible, but it was not until the late sixties that color became the norm and black-and-white the exception. By that time, the Technicolor technology had been superseded by EASTMANCOLOR, yet Technicolor continued to survive as a process because it used DYE-TRANSFER technology and therefore gave better color values and a much longer lasting print than did Eastman's straight chemical process. Since the late 1970's Technicolor has been moribund. The only plant that still processes Technicolor is in China.

TECHNISCOPE   See WIDESCREEN.

TECHNOLOGICAL DETERMINISM   A theory of the relationship between technology and society that sees the historical development of technology as separate and independent of social, political, and economic forces. In this view, technologies arise independently, and *then* determine the shape of societies associated with them. *Symptomatic technology* also assumes that research and technology are self-generating, but sees their development in a slightly different way: historically, according to this theory, technologies become symptomatic of their societies. *Intentional technology*, on the other hand, views technological phenomena as the direct products of social, political, and economic forces.

TELECINE   The FILM CHAIN.

TELEFILM   Originally, any filmed program prepared for television broadcast. Recently, the word has taken on some of the connotations of MADE-FOR-TV MOVIE, an awkward term that telefilm may soon replace.

TELEGENIC   Attractive as a subject for television.

TELEGRAPHY   Literally, "writing at a distance." A system of communication by wire or broadcast (RADIOTELEGRAPHY) that translates messages into simple coded signals. See MORSE CODE, TELEPHONY.

TELEMETRY   Literally, "measurement at a distance." The technology of monitoring scientific instruments and measuring devices at great distances by either wire or radio.

TELEPHONY   Literally, "sound at a distance." A two-way, interactive system of communication by voice rather than coded message using wires or broadcast (RADIO-TELEPHONY).

TELEPHOTO LENS   A lens with a long FOCAL LENGTH that acts like a telescope to magnify distant objects. It has a very narrow ANGLE OF VIEW and flattens depth perception. See FORESHORTENING, WIDE-ANGLE LENS.

TELEPLAY   (1) A play specially written for television. (2) Any script for a television program, on the model of SCREENPLAY.

TELEVISION   Literally, "sight at a distance." A system of *unidirectional* communication of images and sounds by either wires or broadcast. See CABLE TELEVISION.

THEATRE OF CRUELTY   Antonin Artaud's theory of theater that emphasizes the stage as a concrete physical space requiring its own physical language. By "cruelty" Artaud meant a theater that was "difficult," that insisted on the involvement of the spectator in the theatrical process, that was free from "subjugation to the text," and that returned to basic, mystical, cathartic qualities. See EPIC THEATRE.

THEATRICAL DISTRIBUTION   The distribution of films through commercial exhibitors, as opposed to NONTHEATRICAL DISTRIBUTION.

THEATRICAL FILM   A film made to be seen in theaters rather than on television, in classrooms, or elsewhere.

THIRD CINEMA   Fernando Solanas's and Octavio Getino's theory of cinema as neither consumer goods nor avant-garde experiment, but rather an instrument of revolutionary consciousness whose products "the System cannot assimilate."

THIRD WORLD CINEMA   The cinema of the developing nations of Latin America, Africa, and Asia.

TIE-IN   Any commercial venture that is connected to a film or media program; most often, the simultaneous release of a NOVELIZATION or a soundtrack album.

TILT SHOT   The camera tilts up or down, rotating around the axis that runs from left to right through the camera head. See PAN, ROLL.

TIME-LAPSE PHOTOGRAPHY   Extreme FAST MOTION. A typical speed might be 1 frame every 30 seconds so that 24 hours of REAL TIME would be compressed, when projected, into 2 minutes of film time. As a scientific tool, time-lapse photography makes it possible to study activities, such as the opening of a flower, which occur too slowly in nature to allow us to perceive them. The opposite of time-lapse photography is extreme SLOW MOTION, which has a similar use in studying phenomena that occur too quickly in nature to be observed.

TIME SLOT   In radio and television, a structured time period into which a show must fit. In the U.S., time slots are generally measured in half hours.

TIMING   The process of correcting and matching color values in various shots and scenes shot at different times of the day, in different places, or under different lighting conditions so that the PRINT will be uniform. See ANSWER PRINT.

T-NUMBER   See F-NUMBER.

TODD-AO   A WIDESCREEN system using 65 mm film.

TONE   (1) A general term for photographic CONTRAST. (2) The musical quality of a sound.

TOPLIGHTING   Lighting from above the subject.

TRACK   (1) The SOUNDTRACK. (2) Any one of a number of separate parallel recording channels on TAPE that can be played together or separately and later MIXED or modified in a number of ways. (3) The rails on which a camera moves for a TRACKING SHOT.

TRACKING SHOT   Generally, any shot in which the camera moves from one point to another either sideways, in, or out. The camera can be mounted on a set of wheels that move on TRACKS or on a rubber-tired DOLLY, or it can be HAND-HELD. Also called "travelling shot."

TRAILER   A short publicity film, usually describing an upcoming program.

TRANSISTOR   A semiconductor device that, like a VACUUM TUBE, can amplify or otherwise modify an electronic signal. Because the transistor is so much smaller and more durable than its predecessor the vacuum tube, it has had a profound effect on electronic technology.

TRANSPONDER   An electronic device which receives a signal, amplifies it, and retransmits it, as, for example, on communications satellites.

TRAVELLING MATTE   A MATTE SHOT in which the matte changes from frame to frame to follow the action. See CHROMA KEY.

TRAVELLING SHOT   See TRACKING SHOT.

TRAVELOGUE   A film or television program whose main function is to show scenes from exotic locales.

TREATMENT   A general description of a film, somewhat longer than a simple outline but shorter than a full SCREENPLAY. See SCENARIO.

TRENDEX   One of the major U.S. radio and television RATINGS services, based on random telephone surveys. Arbitron is another. See NEILSEN.

TROPE   Any artistic device, such as a figure of speech or a symbol; a CONNOTATIVE twist or turn in meaning. As a comprehensive art, film can avail itself of the tropes of many other arts. In addition, it has tropes that are unique: the SWISH PAN, for example, or RACK FOCUSING.

TRUCKING SHOT   See TRACKING SHOT.

TV MASK   A mask used in the camera viewfinder to block off those areas that will not be reproduced on the curved rectangle of a television screen. The area within the mask is the *safe action area.*

TWO-REELER   A film lasting approximately twenty minutes. During the silent period, more often than not a comedy. See ONE-REELER.

TWO-SHOT   A shot of two people. Likewise, three-shot. (See Figures 3-27, 3-28.)

TWO-WAY CABLE   Cable television system in which a computer monitors receiving sets allowing viewers to "talk back." Using a console, subscribers can choose specific programs for which they will be charged separately (since the computer knows what they are watching). They can also respond to simple multiple-choice questions with the results of the poll displayed immediately. Warner-Amex Cable's QUBE system was the first commercial two-way cable.

TYPAGE   Eisenstein's theory of casting, which eschews professional actors in favor of "types" or representative characters.

TYPOGRAPHY   Literally, "writing by type." The composition of printed materials. The simplest and earliest form of typography uses movable type as the direct printing agent, as in LETTERPRESS. Moveable type can also be cast to produce a "stereotype" plate, which can then be used as the printing agent. The plate can be curved to fit a ROTARY PRESS. Movable type can furthermore be used to print a REPRO from which a PHOTOENGRAVING plate can be made which is then used as a printing agent. Recently, PHOTOTYPOGRAPHY, in which film negatives of the letter forms replace metal movable type, has come to dominate typography.

Four major processes are used in printing: LETTERPRESS uses a relief image in which the letter forms are raised; GRAVURE uses intaglio, in which the letter forms are depressed; SCREEN and OFFSET (lithography) are planographic; that is, the letter forms are essentially the same height as the nonprinting areas.

U

UNDERCRANK   To slow down a camera; to shoot at less than the normal 24 frames per second so that the image, when projected at 24 fps, will appear in FAST MOTION. See OVERCRANK.

UNDEREXPOSURE   See EXPOSURE.

UNDERGROUND FILM   Independent film, made without connection to the usual sources of funding and distribution, usually on small budgets; noncommercial cinema. See AVANT GARDE, NEW AMERICAN CINEMA.

UNIDIRECTIONAL MEDIUM   See DISTRIBUTION FLOW.

UNIFRANCE   A quasi-governmental French film export agency.

UNITALIA   A quasi-governmental Italian film export agency.

UPSCALE   In DEMOGRAPHICS, the group of young, upwardly mobile people with sophisticated tastes and relatively large amounts of disposable income whose presence in an audience is greatly valued by advertisers and whose tastes, therefore, increasingly affect television programming.

V

VACUUM TUBE   A glass tube that is either evacuated or filled with an inert gas and that provides a proper atmosphere for the electronic manipulation of a signal imposed on a grid between cathode and anode. See AUDION, TRANSISTOR.

VALIDATION   The peculiar ability of the media to define an acceptable social reality and therefore, in part, to govern what we consider true or "real."

VERFREMDUNGSEFFEKT   See ESTRANGEMENT EFFECT.

VERISIMILITUDE   The quality of appearing to be true or real; a more precise descriptive term than REALISM, since the latter word has special theoretical connotations in film and the arts.

VERISM   General realism in art, literature, and film.

VIDEO   (1) The picture portion of a television signal. See AUDIO. (2) Independent television art, usually on TAPE, often produced for CLOSED-CIRCUIT distribution rather than commercial BROADCAST.

VIDEODISC   Either of several competing systems of videorecording. The MCA/Phillips systems records the signal on a plastic disc in light waves, using lasers. The RCA system inscribes the signal electromechanically. The TeD system is entirely mechanical.

VIDEOTAPE   A TAPE system of television recording. Professional systems use 2-inch wide tape; amateur and semiprofessional systems use ½-inch and ¾-inch tape.

VIEWFINDER   Specifically, the eyepiece through which the camera operator observes the image. Non-REFLEX cameras have separate optical systems for viewfinder and TAKING LENS.

VIGNETTE   A MASKING device, often with soft edges. (See Figure 3-30.) See also IRIS.

VISTAVISION   Paramount's answer to Twentieth Century-Fox's CINEMASCOPE in the fifties. A non-ANAMORPHIC process in which no action took place at the top or bottom of the screen so that exhibitors with different aperture masks could choose their own ASPECT RATIO from 1.33 to 2.0. The NEGATIVE was made on 70 mm stock and reduced to 35 mm during printing to reduce graininess.

VISUALS   The IMAGES of a film as opposed to its SOUNDTRACK.

VITAGRAPH   J. Stuart Blackton's early film company; a competitor to Edison's VITASCOPE and the BIOGRAPH company.

VITASCOPE   The projecting version of Edison's KINETOSCOPE exhibition machine.

VOICE-OVER   The narrator's voice when the narrator is not seen, especially in television commercials. See COMMENTATIVE SOUND.

W

WAVELENGTH   See WAVE MECHANICS.

WAVE MECHANICS   Wave forms require a medium through which to be transmitted. Sound waves travel in air or water. Light and radio waves travel in the electromagnetic spectrum of particles. Any wave has two dimensions: the vertical—*amplitude*, or strength; and the horizontal—*wavelength*. The length of the wave is inversely proportional to its *frequency*, measured in cycles per second (also known as Hertz): the longer the wave, the lower the frequency. Receivers can be tuned to particular frequencies, thus making it possible for even narrow bands of the electromagnetic spectrum to carry numerous, separable signals. The PROGRAM SIGNAL is imposed on the *carrier wave* in either of two basic ways: either by the modulation of the amplitude (AM) or the modulation of the frequency (FM) of the wave. (See Figure 6-8.) See also ELECTROMAGNETIC SPECTRUM.

WIDE-ANGLE LENS   A lens with a very broad ANGLE OF VIEW, it increases the illusion of depth and also exaggerates linear distortion. See FISH-EYE LENS, TELEPHOTO LENS, FORELENGTHENING.

WIDESCREEN   Any one of a number of ASPECT RATIOS of 1.66:1 or greater. Almost all theatrical films today are widescreen. Widescreen processes are not necessarily ANAMORPHIC; some processes simply mask the top and bottom of the aperture during shooting or projection in order to increase the aspect ratio. *Techniscope* utilizes a two-hole PULL-DOWN MECHANISM (rather than the 35-mm standard four-hole pull-down) in order not to waste filmstock while shooting. The resulting negative is then printed in a standard four-hole format for projection. The most common nonanamorphic widescreen ratios in use today are 1.66:1 (European) and 1.85:1 (American). (See Figure 2-31.) See also CINEMASCOPE, PANAVISION, VISTAVISION.

WILD RECORDING   Recording sound separately from images, usually in order to obtain usable tapes of sound effects, such as ROOM SOUND.

WILD SHOOTING   Shooting a sound film without recording the sound simultaneously. See POST-SYNCHRONIZAITON, DIRECT SOUND.

WILD SOUND   Sound recorded separately from images.

WILD WALLS   The walls of a set that have been constructed in such a way that they can easily be moved to facilitate the positioning of the camera. Camera angles are thus obtained that would not be possible on a PRACTICAL SET.

WIPE   An OPTICAL effect in which an image appears to "wipe off" the preceding image. Very common in the thirties; less so today. See FADE-OUT, DISSOLVE, IRIS-OUT.

WIRELESS   Radio.

WORK PRINT   A quick print made from the NEGATIVE, often without having been corrected in any way, which is used for screening RUSHES, assembling a ROUGH CUT, and other preliminary editorial work.

WOW AND FLUTTER   Distortion in the sound produced by tape, disc, or film soundtrack, caused by variations in motor speeds.

X

XENON LAMP   An enclosed lamp filled with the inert gas xenon, which produces a very bright light of controlled COLOR TEMPERATURE and which has replaced the ARC LIGHT in most cinematic applications.

XEROGRAPHY   An instant electrophotographic printing process. "Xerox" is a trade name for the first and most successful of a number of similar processes that are often grouped together under this generic title. See OFFSET, LETTERPRESS, ROTARY, GRAVURE.

Z

ZIP PAN   See SWISH PAN.

ZOETROPE   From the Greek for "life" plus "turning"; an early antecedent of the Cinématographe consisting of a cylinder with a series of photographs or illustrations on the interior and regularly spaced slits through which one observed the drawings in sequence. (See Figure 2-5.)

ZOOM   A shot using a lens whose FOCAL LENGTH is adjusted during the shot. The focal lengths of which the lens is capable range from WIDE ANGLE to TELEPHOTO. Zooms are sometimes used in place of TRACKING SHOTS, but the differences between the two are significant. (See Figures 2-13 and 3-50.)

READING ABOUT FILM AND MEDIA

As late as 1970 the number of books published annually on film and related subjects was small enough to permit a student of film to keep up with the scholarship in this new academic field. It was even possible, if one were so inclined, to read just about everything that appeared in print. That is quite clearly no longer the case. During the 1970s, film and media developed rapidly as subjects of academic and critical inquiry. This biliography is designed as a guide to the basic materials available in the field as well as an introduction to further reading on subjects raised in *How to Read a Film.* To facilitate its use, the bibliography has been divided into sections.

Part One, "A Basic Library," is divided into six sections, corresponding to the chapters of *How To Read a Film:*

1. Film as an Art
2. The Technology of Film and Media
3. The Language of Film
4. Film History
5. Film Theory and Practical Criticism
6. Media

Because the Film History section is itself so inclusive, it has been further divided into subsections:

A. The Economics and Politics of Film
B. General Historical Studies
C. Specific Major Periods
D. Genres and Specific Topics
E. The Documentary
F. National Cinemas
G. Films and Filmmakers
H. Filmscripts

Part Two, "Film Information," is a guide to research materials, journals, encyclopedias, indexes, and the like. It is organized in five sections:

7. Film Lists and Encyclopedias
8. Film Book Bibliographies
9. Guides to Periodical Literature
10. Miscellaneous Guides
11. Journals and Magazines

The Appendix concludes with a "Bibliographical Note." Thirty-three selected titles have been marked with a • in the margin. These books aren't *necessarily* the most influential, but taken together they form a well-rounded, useful, and interesting basic library in film and media.

PART ONE: A BASIC LIBRARY

1. FILM AS AN ART

Allen, Don, ed. *The Book of the Cinema.* London: Chris Milsome, New York: Crown, 1979. An illustrated introduction. Includes chapters by Monaco, Maurice Hatton, Tom Milne, David Robinson, and others.

Artaud, Antonin. *The Theater and Its Double.* New York: Grove Press, 1958.

Auerbach, Erich. *Mimesis: The Representation of Reality in Western Literature.* New York: Doubleday, 1957.

Barsacq, Léon. *Caligari's Cabinet and Other Grand Illusions: A History of Film Design.* New York: New American Library, 1976.

Baxandall, Lee. *Radical Perspectives on the Arts.* London: Pelican, 1972.

Bluestone, George, *Novels into Film.* Berkeley: University of California Press, 1968.

Brecht, Bertolt. *Brecht on Theatre.* Edited and translated by John Willett. New York: Hill and Wang, 1964.

Gombrich, E. H. *Art and Illusion.* 2nd ed. Princeton: Princeton University Press, 1961.

Gouldner, Alvin W. *The Dialectic of Ideology and Technology.* New York: Seabury Press, 1976.

Horace. *Ars Poetica.*

Horton, Andrew, and Joan Magretta, eds. *Modern European Filmmakers and the Art of Adaptation.* New York: Frederick Ungar, 1980.

Hurt, James. *Focus on Film and Theatre.* Englewood Cliffs, N.J.: Prentice-Hall, 1974.

Manvell, Roger. *Shakespeare and the Film.* New York: Praeger, 1971.

Mesthene, Emmanuel. *Technological Change: Its Impact on Man and Society.* New York: New American Library, 1970.

Mumford, Lewis. *Technics and Civilization.* 1934. Reprint. New York: Harcourt, Brace and World, 1966.

Newhall, Beaumont. *The History of Photography.* New York: The Museum of Modern Art, 1964.

Nicoll, Allardyce. *Film and Theatre.* London, 1936. Reprint. New York: Arno Press, 1972. An early, standard study.

Peary, Gerald, and Roger Shatzkin, eds. *The Classic American Novel and the Movies.* New York: Frederick Ungar, 1977.

Pildas, Ave. *Movie Palaces.* New York: Clarkson N. Potter 1979.

Prendergast, Roy M. *Film Music: A Neglected Art.* New York: Norton, 1977.

Rohmer, Eric. *Six Moral Tales.* New York: The Viking Press, 1980.

Rosenblum, Ralph, and Robert Karen. *When the Shooting Stops . . . the Cutting Begins: A Film Editor's Story.* New York: The Viking Press, 1979.

Thomas, Tony, ed. *Film Score: The View from the Podium.* Cranbury, N.J.: A. S. Barnes, 1979.

Tynan, Kenneth. *Show People.* New York: Simon and Schuster, 1980.

Vardac, A. Nicholas. *From Stage to Screen.* Reprint. New York: Benjamin Bloom, 1968.

●Williams, Raymond. *Keywords: A Vocabulary of Culture and Society.* New York: Oxford University Press, 1976.

Yacowar, Maurice. *The Modern American Novel and the Movies.* New York: Frederick Ungar, 1978.

2. THE TECHNOLOGY OF FILM AND MEDIA

Brosnan, John. *Movie Magic: The Story of Special Effects in the Cinema.* New York: New American Library, 1974, 1976.

Campbell, Russell, ed. *Photographic Theory for the Motion Picture Cameraman.* Cranbury, N.J.: A. S. Barnes, 1970.

————, ed. *Practical Motion Picture Photography.* Cranbury, N.J.: A. S. Barnes, 1970.

Ceram, C.W. *Archeology of the Cinema.* New York: Harcourt, Brace and World, 1965. The prehistory of film.

Clarke, Charles G., A.S.C. *Professional Cinematography.* Los Angeles: American Society of Cinematographers, 1968. Hollywood orthodoxy.

Dickson, W.K., and Antonia Dickson. *History of the Kinetograph, Kinetoscope, and Kinetophonograph.* Twickenham, Middlesex, 1895. Reprint. New York: Arno Press, 1970. By one of the fathers of film.

Ellul, Jacques. *The Technological Society.* New York: Vintage, 1964.

Ferkiss, Victor C. *Technological Man: The Myth and the Reality.* New York: Mentor, 1969.

Fielding, Raymond. *Focal Encyclopedia of Film and T.V. Techniques.* New York: Hastings House, 1969. Recommended.

————. *Technique of Special Effects Cinematography.* New York: Hastings House, 1973.

————, ed. *A Technological History of Motion Pictures and Television.* Berkeley: University of California Press, 1967. A valuable collection of documents.

Laybourne, Kit. *The Animation Book: A Complete Guide to Animated Filmmaking from Flip-Books to Sound Cartoons.* New York: Crown Publishers, 1979.

Limbacher, James. *Four Aspects of the Film.* New York: Arno, 1978. Invaluable for its discussion of color, sound, 3-D, and widescreen processes.

Lipton, Lenny. *Independent Filmmaking.* New York: Straight Arrow, 1973. A valuable compendium.

Malkiewicz, J. Kris. *Cinematography.* New York: Van Nostrand Reinhold, 1973.

Maltin, Leonard, ed. *Behind the Camera: The Cinematographer's Art.* New York: Signet, 1971.

Marner, Terence St. John, ed. *Directing Motion Pictures.* Cranbury, N.J.: A. S. Barnes, 1972.

————, ed. *Film Design.* Cranbury, N.J.: A. S. Barnes, 1974. Art direction, set and costume design.

Miller, Arthur C., and Walter Strenge, eds. *American Cinematographer Manual.* 3rd ed. Los Angeles: American Society of Cinematographers, 1969. A valuable technical reference manual, not an introductory text.

Wheeler, Leslie. *Principles of Cinematography.* 4th ed. New York: Fountain Press, 1971.

3. THE LANGUAGE OF FILM

Armes, Roy. *Film and Reality.* New York: Penguin, 1974. A quick survey.

•Arnheim, Rudolf. *Art and Visual Perception: A Psychology of the Creative Eye.* Berkeley: University of California Press, 1954. A general text in the visual arts that has much to say about film.

————. *Visual Thinking.* Berkeley: University of California Press, 1969.

•Berger, John. *Ways of Seeing.* London: BBC and Penguin Books, 1972. A book based on Berger's BBC series on advertising and art. Highly recommended.

Bobker, Lee R. *Elements of Film.* 2nd ed. New York: Harcourt Brace Jovanovich, 1974.

Bordwell, David, and Kristin Thompson. *Film Art: An Introduction.* Reading, Mass.: Addison-Wesley, 1979. Introductory text.

•Braudy, Leo. *The World in a Frame.* New York: Anchor, 1976.

Dick, Bernard F. *The Anatomy of Film.* New York: St. Martin's Press, 1978. Introductory text.

Eidsvik, Charles. *Cineliteracy: Film Among the Arts.* New York: Random House, 1978. Introductory text.

Gessner, Robert. *The Moving Image: A Guide to Cinematic Literacy.* New York: Dutton, 1970. One of the better introductions to the art.

Giannetti, Louis. *Understanding Movies.* 2nd ed. Englewood Cliffs, N.J. Prentice-Hall, 1976. Useful basic text. Recommended.

Godard, Jean-Luc. "Montage, mon beau souci." In *Godard on Godard,* edited by Tom Milne, New York: Viking Press, 1972.

Huss, Roy, and Norman Silverstein. *The Film Experience.* New York: Delta, 1968. A good introduction.

Jacobs, Lewis, ed. *The Movies as Medium.* New York: Farrar, Straus & Giroux, 1970. A text composed of articles by various authors.

Johnson, Lincoln. *Film: Space, Time, Light and Sound.* New York: Holt, Rinehart and Winston, 1974.

Nilsen, Vladimir. *Cinema as Graphic Art.* New York: Hill and Wang, 1973. A standard.

Perkins, V.F. *Film as Film: Understanding and Judging Movies.* New York: Penguin, 1972. Highly recommended, it reflects modern cinematic theory.

Reisz, Karel. *The Technique of Film Editing.* 2nd enlarged ed. New York: Amphoto/Hastings House, 1968. A "how to" book for film editors, it has been esthetically influential. Recommended.

Scientific American. *Image, Object and Illusion.* Introduction by Richard Held. San Francisco: W. H. Freeman, 1974.

Sharples, Win, Jr. "The Aesthetics of Film Sound." *Filmmakers Newsletter* 8:5 (March 1975).

Spottiswoode, Raymond R. *Film and Its Techniques.* Berkeley: University of California Press, 1951. Reprint 1965. Rather out of date, but a classic in its time. Good on technical matters.

———. *A Grammar of Film.* Berkeley: University of California Press, 1950.

Stephenson, Ralph, and J.R. Debrix. *The Cinema as Art.* New York: Penguin, 1965. Still a useful introduction.

Talbot, Daniel, ed. *Film: An Anthology.* Berkeley: University of California Press, 1967. First published in 1959 and still a useful general collection.

See also Bazin, Eco, Metz, and Wollen entries in Section 5.

4A. FILM HISTORY: THE ECONOMICS AND POLITICS OF FILM

Balio, Tino, ed. *The American Film Industry.* Madison: University of Wisconsin Press, 1976.

Bentley, Eric. *Thirty Years of Treason.* New York: Viking, 1971. The blacklisting period.

Bergman, Andrew. *We're in the Money.* New York: Harper & Row, 1973. The 1930s in America.

Bogle, Donald. *Toms, Coons, Mulattoes, Mammies and Bucks.* New York: Viking, 1973. Images of Blacks in American movies.

Ceplair, Larry and Steve Englund. *The Inquisition in Hollywood: Politics in the Film Community.* New York: Doubleday, 1980.

•Cripps, Thomas. *Slow Fade to Black: The Negro in American Film, 1900–1942.* New York: Oxford University Press, 1977. A seminal study.

Deming, Barbara. *Running Away from Myself: Dream Portrait of America Drawn from the Films of the Forties.* New York: Viking, 1969. Important sociologically oriented study.

Dyer, Richard. *Stars.* London: British Film Institute, and New York: New York Zoetrope, 1979.

Geduld, Harry M. *Birth of the Talkies.* Bloomington: Indiana University Press, 1975.

Guback, Thomas H. *The International Film Industry.* Bloomington: Indiana University Press, 1969. Out of print, but invaluable study of international film economics.

Haskell, Molly. *From Reverence to Rape.* New York: Penguin, 1974. One of several recent studies of women and film. Recommended.

Huaco, George A. *The Sociology of Film Art.* New York: Basic Books, 1965. A standard text on the subject.

Leab, Daniel J. *From Sambo to Superspade.* Boston: Houghton Mifflin, 1975. The Black image in film.

MacCann, Richard, ed. *Film and Society.* New York: Scribners, 1963.

———. *The People's Films: Political History of the U.S. Government Pictures.* New York: Hastings House, 1973.

Manvell, Roger. *Films and the Second World War.* Cranbury, N.J.: A. S. Barnes, 1974.

Mayer, Michael F. *The Film Industries.* 2nd ed. New York: Hastings House, 1973, 1979. By a lawyer, the best book available on the business of film.

•Monaco, James. *American Film Now: The People, the Power, the Money, the Movies.* New York: Oxford University Press and New American Library, 1979. Includes appendices, bibliography, and charts.

Murray, James. *To Find an Image: Black Films from Uncle Tom to Superfly*. Indianapolis: Bobbs-Merrill, 1973.

Pye, Michael. *Moguls: Inside the Business of Show Business*. New York: Holt, Rinehart and Winston, 1980.

Schickel, Richard. *His Picture in the Papers: A Speculation on Celebrity in America, Based on the Life of Douglas Fairbanks, Sr.* New York: Charterhouse, 1973. An interesting essay on a neglected phenomenon.

Schumach, Murray. *The Face on the Cutting Room Floor: The Story of Movie and Television Censorship*. New York: Da Capo Press, 1957, 1975.

Shindler, Colin. *Hollywood Goes to War*. London: Routledge & Kegan Paul, 1979.

Sklar, Robert. *Movie-Made America: A Cultural History of American Movies*. New York: Random House, 1975.

Talbot, David, and Barbara Zheutlin. *Creative Differences: Profiles of Hollywood Dissidents*. Boston: South End Press, 1978. Political activists, past and present: a significant study.

Thomson, David. *America in the Dark*. New York: William Morrow, 1977. Recommended.

•Vogel, Amos. *Film as a Subversive Art*. New York: Random House, 1975. Recommended.

Wolfenstein, Martha, and Nathan Leites. *Movies: A Psychological Study*. New York: Atheneum, 1960. Reprint 1970.

Wood, Michael. *America in the Movies*. New York: Basic Books, 1975. An important essay on the politics and style of American movies. Recommended.

4B. FILM HISTORY: GENERAL HISTORICAL STUDIES

Armes, Roy. *A Critical History of British Cinema*. New York: Oxford University Press, 1978.

Braudy, Leo, and Morris Dickstein. *Great Film Directors: A Critical Anthology*. New York: Oxford University Press, 1978.

Brownlow, Kevin. *The War, the West, and the Wilderness*. New York: Knopf, 1979. Recommended.

Clair, René. *Cinema Yesterday and Today*. New York: Dover, 1972. A personal view.

Cowie, Peter, ed. *A Concise History of the Cinema*. 2 vols. Cranbury, N.J.: A. S. Barnes, 1970. Recommended. Short, but useful.

————. *Eighty Years of Cinema*. Cranbury, N.J.: A. S. Barnes, 1975.

Dickinson, Thorold. *A Discovery of Cinema*. New York: Oxford University Press, 1971. Recommended.

Ellis, Jack C. *A History of Film*. Englewood Cliffs, N.J.: Prentice-Hall Inc., 1979. Text.

Everson, William K. *American Silent Film*. New York: Oxford University Press, 1978. A valuable history.

Fell, John L. *A History of Films*. New York: Holt, Rinehart and Winston, 1979. Text.

Hampton, Benjamin. *History of the American Film Industry from Its Beginnings to 1931*. 1931. Reprint. New York: Dover, 1970.

Jacobs, Lewis, ed. *The Emergence of Film Art*. New York: Hopkinson and Blake, 1970. Forty-two selections arranged chronologically from Méliès to Mekas.

————. *Introduction to the Art of the Movies*. New York: Noonday, 1960. Thirty-six essays written between 1910 and 1960 and arranged chronologically.

•Mast, Gerald. *A Short History of the Movies*. 2nd ed. Indianapolis: Bobbs-Merrill, 1976.

Montagu, Ivor. *Film World.* New York: Penguin, 1964. A standard work. Still useful.

Rhode, Eric. *A History of Cinema.* New York: Hill and Wang, 1975.

Robinson, David. *The History of World Cinema.* New York: Stein and Day, 1974.

Rotha, Paul, and Richard Griffith. *The Film Till Now.* New York: Twayne, 1960. First published in 1930, updated several times since, this is an early classic of film scholarship.

Stanley, Robert H. *The Celluloid Empire: A History of the American Movie Industry.* New York: Hastings House, 1978.

•Thomson, David. *A Biographical Dictionary of Film.* New York: Morrow, 1976. Excellent essays on star personas.

Wright, Basil. *The Long View.* New York: Knopf, 1975. A weighty history but possibly too idiosyncratic.

4C. FILM HISTORY: SPECIFIC MAJOR PERIODS

Anger, Kenneth. *Hollywood Babylon.* Reprint. New York: Delta, 1975. A classic of gossip.

Apra, Adriano, and Patrizia Pistagnesi, eds. *The Fabulous Thirties: Italian Cinema 1929–1944.* Rome: Electa International Publishing Group, 1979. An interesting approach.

Barr, Charles. *Ealing Studios.* Woodstock, N.Y.: Overlook Press, 1980.

Barnes, John. *Beginnings of the Cinema in England.* New York: Barnes & Noble, 1976.

•Brownlow, Kevin. *The Parade's Gone By.* New York: Ballantine, 1968. Recommended. Early film history.

Cameron, Ian, ed. *Second Wave.* New York: Praeger, 1970. Essays on Makavejev, Skolimowski, Oshima, Guerra, Rocha, Groulx, Lefebvre, Straub.

Chanan, Michael. *The Dream That Kicks: The Prehistory and Early Years of the Cinema in Britain.* London: Routledge & Kegan Paul, 1979.

Cowie, Peter. *Fifty Major Filmmakers.* London: Tantivy, 1975.

———, ed. *Hollywood 1920–1970.* Cranbury, N.J.: A. S. Barnes, 1975.

Dowdy, Andrew. *The Films of the Fifties.* New York: Morrow, 1973.

Gelmis, Joseph, ed. *The Film Director as Superstar.* New York: Doubleday, 1970. Interviews with contemporary filmmakers, all conducted by Gelmis.

Harcourt, Peter. *Six European Directors.* New York: Penguin, 1974. Eisenstein, Renoir, Buñuel, Bergman, Fellini, Godard.

Harvey, Sylvia. *May '68 and Film Culture.* London: British Film Institute; and New York: New York Zoetrope, 1978. Recommended.

Hennebelle, Guy. *15 Ans du cinéma mondial.* Paris: Editions du Cerf, 1975.

Houston, Penelope. *The Contemporary Cinema.* New York: Penguin, 1963. Recommended. A good introduction and survey, if a bit dated.

Jacobs, Diane. *Hollywood Renaissance.* New York: Delta Books, 1980. Rev. ed. Coppola, Scorsese, Ritchie, and the generation of the seventies.

McCarthy, Todd, and Charles Flynn, eds. *Kings of the B's: Working within the Hollywood System.* New York: Dutton, 1975. Anthology of studies of 'B' directors.

•Monaco, James F. *The New Wave: Truffaut, Godard, Chabrol, Rohmer, Rivette.* New York: Oxford University Press, 1976.

Parrish, Robert. *Growing Up in Hollywood.* New York: Harcourt, Brace, Jovanovich, 1976.

Petley, Julian. *Capital and Culture: German Cinema 1933–1945*. London: British Film Institute; and New York: New York Zoetrope, 1979.

Powdermaker, Hortense. *Hollywood: The Dream Factory*. New York: Arno Press, 1924, 1979.

Pye, Michael, and Lynda Myles. *The Movie Brats: How the Film Generation Took Over Hollywood*. London: Faber & Faber, New York: Holt, Rinehart and Winston, 1979. Comments on Coppola, Lucas, DePalma, Milius, Scorsese, Spielberg, and others.

Ramsaye, Terry. *A Million and One Nights*. New York: Simon & Schuster, 1926. Early cinema.

Slide, Anthony, *Early American Cinema*. Cranbury, N.J.: A. S. Barnes, 1970.

———. *Early Women Directors: Their Role in the Development of the Silent Cinema*. Cranbury, N.J.: A. S. Barnes, 1977.

•Taylor, John Russell. *Cinema Eye, Cinema Ear*. New York: Hill and Wang, 1964. A landmark in its approach to film as a serious art; surveys the European scene in the sixties.

———. *Directors and Directions: Cinema for the Seventies*. New York: Hill and Wang, 1975. Chabrol, Pasolini, Anderson, Kubrick, Warhol/Morrissey, S. Ray, Jancsó, Makavejev.

Wagenknecht, Edward. *Movies in the Age of Innocence*. New York: Ballantine, 1971. Early cinema.

Walker, Alexander. *The Shattered Silents: How the Talkies Came To Stay*. New York: William Morrow, 1979.

4D. FILM HISTORY: GENRES AND SPECIFIC TOPICS

Balio, Tino. *United Artists: The Company Built by the Stars*. Madison: University of Wisconsin Press, 1976.

Battcock, Gregory, ed. *The New American Cinema*. New York: Dutton, 1967.

Brosnan, John *Future Tense: The Cinema of Science Fiction*. New York: St. Martin's Press, 1978.

Clarens, Carlos. *Crime Movies: From Griffith to The Godfather and Beyond*. New York: Norton, 1980.

Cook, Jim and Mike Lewington, eds. *Images of Alcoholism*. London: BFI; New York: New York Zoetrope, 1979.

•Corliss, Richard. *Talking Pictures: Screenwriters in the American Cinema*. New York: Viking, 1973.

Cripps, Thomas. *Black Film as Genre*. Bloomington: Indiana University Press, 1979.

Durgnat, Raymond. *The Crazy Mirror*. New York: Delta, 1969. About Hollywood.

Dyer, Richard, et al. *Gays and Film*. London: British Film Institute; and New York: New York Zoetrope, 1977.

Everson, William K. *The Bad Guys*. New York: Citadel, 1964.

———. *The Detective in Film*. New York: Citadel, 1972.

Eyles, Allen. *The Western*. Cranbury, N.J.: A. S. Barnes, 1975.

Fenin, George N., and William K. Everson. *The Western: From Silents to the Seventies*. 2nd ed. New York: Grossman, 1973. Recommended.

Frayling, Christopher. *Spaghetti Westerns: Cowboys and Europeans from Karl May to Sergio Leone*. Boston: Routledge & Kegan Paul, 1980.

French, Philip. *Westerns: Aspects of a Movie Genre.* New York: Oxford University Press, 1977.

Geduld, Harry M., ed. *Authors on Film.* Bloomington: Indiana University Press, 1972. A farrago of bits and pieces from Tolstoy to James Baldwin. Forty-one items.

————, ed. *Filmmakers on Filmmaking.* Bloomington: Indiana University Press, 1967. Thirty pieces by filmmakers ranging from Lumière to Anger.

Glaessner, Verina, *Kung-Fu: Cinema of Vengeance.* New York: Bounty, 1973.

Higham, Charles. *Hollywood Cameramen.* Bloomington: Indiana University Press, 1970.

————. *Warner Brothers.* New York: Scribners, 1975.

Kaplan, E. Ann, ed. *Women in Film Noir.* London: British Film Institute; and New York: New York Zoetrope, 1978. Useful collection.

Kawin, Bruce F., *Mindscreen: Bergman, Godard, and First-Person Film.* Princeton, N.J.: Princeton University Press, 1978. A theory of narration.

Kay, Karyn, and Gerald Peary, eds. *Women and the Cinema: A Critical Anthology.* New York: Dutton, 1977.

Kerr, Walter, *The Silent Clowns.* New York: Knopf, 1975. Recommended.

Kitses, Jim. *Horizons West.* Bloomington: Indiana University Press, 1970. One of the first practical applications of semiological theories.

Kolker, Robert Phillip. *A Cinema of Loneliness: Penn, Kubrick, Coppola, Scorsese, Altman.* New York: Oxford University Press, 1980.

Lawder, Standish D. *The Cubist Cinema.* New York: New York University Press, 1973.

Leyda, Jay. *Films Beget Films.* New York: Hill and Wang, 1965. A study of compilation films.

McArthur, Colin. *Underworld U.S.A.* New York: Viking, 1972.

Mast, Gerald *The Comic Mind.* Indianapolis: Bobbs-Merrill, 1973.

Mellen, Joan. *Big Bad Wolves: Masculinity in American Films.* New York: Pantheon, 1978.

Morin, Edgar. *Les Stars.* Paris: Editions du Seuil, 1972. New edition of this classic work.

Nash, Constance, and Virginia Oakley. *The Screenwriter's Handbook (Writing for the Movies).* New York: Barnes & Noble, 1978.

O'Connor, John E., and Martin Jackson, eds. *American History/American Film: Interpreting the Hollywood Image.* New York: Frederick Ungar, 1978.

Patterson, Lindsay, ed. *Black Films and Filmmakers.* New York: Dodd, Mead, 1975.

Renan, Sheldon. *An Introduction to the American Underground Film.* New York: Dutton, 1967.

Rubinstein, Leonard. *The Great Spy Films: A Pictorial History.* Secaucus, N.J.: Citadel Press, 1979.

Saleh, Dennis. *Science Fiction Gold: Classic Films of the Fifties.* New York: McGraw-Hill, 1979.

Schrader, Paul. *Transcendental Style in Film: Ozu, Bresson, Dreyer.* Berkeley: University of California Press, 1972.

Silver, Alain. *The Samurai Film.* Cranbury, N.J.: A. S. Barnes, 1975.

———— and Elizabeth Wald. *Film Noir: An Encyclopedic Reference to the American Style.* Woodstock, N.Y.: Overlook Press, 1980.

Sitney, P. Adams, ed. *Film Culture Reader.* New York: Praeger, 1970. From the magazine devoted to New American Cinema.

————. *Visionary Film: The American Avant-Garde 1943–1978.* 2nd ed. New York: Oxford University Press, 1979. A seminal study. Recommended.

Solomon, Stanley J. *Beyond Formula: American Film Genres.* New York: Harcourt Brace Jovanovich, 1976. An interesting approach.

Stephenson, Ralph. *Animation in the Cinema.* Cranbury, N.J.: A. S. Barnes, 1966.

Taylor, John Russell, and Arthur Jackson. *The Hollywood Musical.* New York: McGraw-Hill, 1971.

Turan, Kenneth, and Stephen F. Zito. *Sinema: American Pornographic Films and the People Who Make Them.* New York: Praeger, 1974.

Vallance, Tom. *The American Musical.* Cranbury, N.J.: A. S. Barnes, 1970.

Wright, Will. *Six Guns and Society: A Structural Study of the Western.* Berkeley: University of California Press, 1975.

Youngblood, Gene. *Expanded Cinema.* New York: Dutton, 1970. New directions; the cinematic forms of the future. Recommended.

4E. FILM HISTORY: THE DOCUMENTARY

Aldgate, Anthony. *Cinema & History: British Newsreels and the Spanish Civil War.* London: Scolar Press, 1979.

•Barnouw, Erik. *Documentary: A History of the Non-Fiction Film.* New York: Oxford University Press, 1974. A basic history. Recommended.

Barsam, Richard. *Non-Fiction Film: A Critical History.* New York: Dutton, 1973. A good introduction.

Fielding, Raymond. *The American Newsreel: 1911–1967.* Norman: University of Oklahoma Press, 1972.

Jacobs, Lewis, ed. *The Documentary Tradition: From Nanook to Woodstock.* New York: Hopkinson and Blake, 1971. Ninety-six pieces on documentaries.

Lovell, Alan, and Jim Hillier. *Studies in Documentary.* New York: Viking, 1972.

Mamber, Stephen. *Cinéma Vérité in America.* Boston: M.I.T. Press, 1974.

Marcorelles, Louis. *Living Cinema.* New York: Praeger, 1972. Study of Direct Cinema and Concrete Cinema.

Sussex, Elizabeth. *The Rise and Fall of British Documentary.* Berkeley: University of California Press, 1975.

4F. FILM HISTORY: NATIONAL CINEMAS

Anderson, Joseph L., and Donald Richie. *Japanese Film: Art and Industry.* New York: Grove, 1969. A basic text.

Armes, Roy. *French Cinema Since 1946.* 2 vols. 2nd enlarged ed. Cranbury, N.J.: A. S. Barnes, 1970. A useful monograph. The second volume deals with the New Wave.

———. *French Film.* Cranbury, N.J.: A. S. Barnes, 1970.

———. *Patterns of Realism: Italian Neo-Realist Cinema.* Cranbury, N.J.: A. S. Barnes, 1971.

Barnouw, Erik, and S. Krishnaswamy. *Indian Film.* 2nd ed. New York: Oxford University Press, 1980.

Betts, Ernest. *The Film Business: A History of the British Cinema 1896–1972.* New York: Pitman, 1973.

Björkman, Stig. *Film in Sweden: The New Directors.* Cranbury, N.J.: A. S. Barnes, 1976.

Bock, Audie. *Japanese Film Directors*. New York: Kodansha International, 1978.

Burch, Nöel. *To the Distant Observer: Form and Meaning in the Japanese Cinema*. Berkeley: University of California Press, 1979.

Chanan, Michael, ed. *Chilean Cinema*. London: British Film Institute; and New York: New York Zoetrope, 1976.

Cowie, Peter. *Dutch Cinema: An Illustrated History*. Cranbury, N.J.: A. S. Barnes, 1979.

———. *Screen Series: Sweden 1*. Cranbury, N.J.: A. S. Barnes, 1970. An efficient summary.

Durgnat, Raymond. *A Mirror for England*. New York: Praeger, 1971.

Eisner, Lotte. *The Haunted Screen*. Berkeley: University of California Press, 1974. The German cinema.

Everson, William K. *The American Movie*. New York: Atheneum, 1963.

Feldman, Seth, and Joyce Nelson, eds. *Canadian Film Reader*. Toronto: Peter Martin Associates; and New York: New York Zoetrope, 1977. Essays on Canadian film.

Hochman, Stanley, ed. *American Film Directors: A Library of Film Criticism*. New York: Ungar, 1974. Arranged as an encyclopedia: 61 directors, filmographies, index of critics and films.

Hull, David S. *Films in the Third Reich*. New York: Simon & Schuster, 1969.

Jacobs, Lewis. *The Rise of the American Film*. New York: Columbia University Teachers College Press, 1939.

Kracauer, Siegfried. *From Caligari to Hitler: A Psychological History of the German Film*. Princeton, N.J.: Princeton University Press, 1947. A classic study. Recommended.

Leiser, Irwin, *Nazi Cinema*. New York: Collier, 1975.

Leprohon, Pierre. *Italian Cinema*. New York: Praeger, 1966.

Leyda, Jay. *Dian Ying: Electric Shadows: An Account of Films and the Film Audience in China*. Boston: M.I.T. Press, 1972. Recommended.

•———. *Kino: History of Russian and Soviet Film*. New York: Collier, 1960. Recommended.

Liehm, Antonin J. *Closely Watched Films: The Czechoslovak Experience*. White Plains, N.Y.: International Arts and Sciences Press, 1974. Recommended.

——— and Mira Liehm. *The Most Important Art: Eastern European Films after 1945*. Berkeley: University of California Press, 1977.

Manvell, Roger. *New Cinema in Britain*. New York: Dutton, 1969. Monograph.

———. *New Cinema in Europe*. New York: Dutton, 1966. Monograph.

———. *New Cinema in the U.S.A.* New York: Dutton, 1968. Monograph.

———, and Heinrich Frankel. *The German Cinema*. New York: Praeger, 1971. A useful introduction.

Mellen, Joan. *Voices from the Japanese Cinema*. New York: Liveright, 1975. A collection of interviews.

———. *The Wave at Genji's Door: Japan Through Its Cinema*. New York: Pantheon, 1976.

Morris, Peter. *Embattled Shadows: A History of Canadian Cinema 1895–1939*. Montreal: McGill—Queens University Press, 1978.

Myerson, Michael. *Memories of Underdevelopment; The Revolutionary Films of Cuba*. New York: Grossman, 1973. Script of the film plus an essay on Cuban cinema.

Richie, Donald. *Japanese Film*. New York: Doubleday, 1971.

•Sarris, Andrew. *The American Cinema: Directors and Directions: 1929–1968*. New York: Dutton, 1968. Sarris's "Pantheon," blurbs on a great number of directors, plus index.

Schnitzer, Luda; Jean Schnitzer; and Marcel Martin. *Cinema in Revolution: the Heroic Era of Soviet Film.* New York: Hill and Wang, 1973. Soviet cinema.

Skvorecky, Josef. *All the Bright Young Men and Women: A Personal History of the Czech Cinema.* Toronto: Peter Martin Associates, 1971.

4G. FILM HISTORY: FILMS AND FILMMAKERS

ALDRICH, ROBERT

Combs, Richard, ed. *Robert Aldrich.* London: British Film Institute; and New York: New York Zoetrope, 1978.

ALLEN, WOODY

Lax, Eric. *On Being Funny: Woody Allen and Comedy.* New York: Charterhouse, 1975.

Palmer, Miles. *Woody Allen.* New York: Lippincott & Crowell, 1980.

Yacowar, Maurice. *Loser Take All: The Comic Art of Woody Allen.* New York: Frederick Ungar, 1979.

ALTMAN, ROBERT

Kass, Judith. *Robert Altman.* New York: Popular Library, 1978.

ANTONIONI, MICHELANGELO

Cameron, Ian and Robin Wood. *Antonioni.* New York: Praeger, 1969. Monograph.

Huss, Roy, ed. *Focus on "Blow-Up."* Englewood Cliffs, N.J.: Prentice-Hall, 1971.

Leprohon, Pierre. *Michelangelo Antonioni.* New York: Simon & Schuster, 1963.

BERGMAN, INGMAR

Björkman, Stig, Torsten Manns, and Jonas Sima. *Bergman on Bergman.* Translated by Paul Britten Austin. New York: Touchstone/Simon & Schuster. 1973. Interview.

Kaminsky, Stuart, and Joseph F. Hill, eds. *Ingmar Bergman: Essays in Criticism.* New York: Oxford University Press, 1975.

Simon, John. *Ingmar Bergman Directs.* New York: Harcourt Brace Jovanovich, 1972. Intensive rather than comprehensive.

Steene, Birgitta. *Ingmar Bergman.* New York: Twayne, 1968.

Wood, Robin. *Ingmar Bergman.* New York: Praeger, 1969. Recommended.

•Young, Vernon. *Cinema Borealis: Ingmar Bergman and the Swedish Ethos.* New York: Avon, 1971. One of the more interesting approaches to Bergman. Recommended.

BOGART, HUMPHREY

Benchley, Nathaniel. *Bogart.* Boston: Little, Brown, 1975. One of few recommendable studies of stars' careers.

BRESSON, ROBERT

Cameron, Ian, ed. *The Films of Robert Bresson.* New York: Praeger, 1969.

BUÑUEL, LUIS

Durgnat, Raymond. *Luis Buñuel.* Berkeley: University of California Press, 1970.

Mellen, Joan, ed. *The World of Luis Buñuel: Essays in Criticism.* New York: Oxford University Press, 1978.

CAPRA, FRANK

Capra, Frank. *The Name above the the Title.* New York: Bantam, 1971. Memoirs.

CHABROL, CLAUDE

Wood, Robin, and Michael Walker. *Claude Chabrol.* New York: Praeger, 1970.

CHAPLIN, CHARLES

•Chaplin, Charles. *My Autobiography.* New York: Pocket Books, 1966. Recommended.

Tyler, Parker, *Chaplin, Last of the Clowns.* New York: Horizon Press, 1972.

COCTEAU, JEAN

Fraigneau, André. *Cocteau on the Film.* 1954. Reprint. New York: Dover, 1972. Recorded conversations.

Gilson, René. *Jean Cocteau.* New York: Crown, 1964.

COSTARD, HELLMUTH

Dawson, Jan. *The Films of Hellmuth Costard.* London: Riverside Studios; and New York: New York Zoetrope, 1979.

CUKOR, GEORGE

Lambert, Gavin. *On Cukor.* New York: Capricorn Books, 1973.

DREYER, CARL

Nash, Mark. *Dreyer.* London: British Film Institute; and New York: New York Zoetrope, 1977.

Milne, Tom. *The Cinema of Carl Dreyer.* Cranbury, N.J.: A. S. Barnes, 1971.

Skoller, Donald, ed. *Dreyer in Double Reflection.* New York: Dutton, 1973. Translation of Dreyer's *Om Filmen.*

EISENSTEIN, SERGEI

Barna, Yon. *Eisenstein.* Boston: Little, Brown, 1973.

Eisenstein, Sergei. *Notes of a Film Director.* Reprint. New York: Dover, 1970.

————. *The Complete Films of Eisenstein,* New York: Dutton, 1974.

————, and Upton Sinclair. *The Making and Unmaking of "Que Viva Mexico."* Bloomington: Indiana University Press, 1970.

Montagu, Ivor. *With Eisenstein in Hollywood.* New York: International, 1967. Reminiscences.

FASSBINDER, RAINER WERNER

Rayns, Tony, ed. *Fassbinder,* 2nd ed. London: British Film Institute; and New York: New York Zoetrope, 1976, 1980.

FELLINI, FEDERICO

Bondanella, Peter, ed. *Federico Fellini: Essays in Criticism.* New York: Oxford University Press, 1978.

Fellini, Federico. *Fellini on Fellini.* Translated by Isabel Quigley. New York: Delacorte, 1976.

Rosenthal, Stuart. *Cinema of Federico Fellini.* Cranbury, N.J.: A. S. Barnes, 1976.

FLAHERTY, ROBERT

Calder-Marshall, Arthur. *The Innocent Eye.* New York: Penguin, 1970.

FORD, JOHN

McBride, Joseph, and Michael Wilmington. *John Ford.* Reprint. New York: DaCapo, 1976.

Sarris, Andrew. *The John Ford Movie Mystery.* Bloomington: Indiana University Press, 1977.

Sinclair, Andrew. *John Ford.* New York: The Dial Press, 1978.

FRANJU, GEORGES

Durgnat, Raymond. *Franju.* Berkeley: University of California Press, 1967.

FULLER, SAMUEL

Garnham, Nicholas. *Samuel Fuller.* New York: Viking, 1971.

GODARD, JEAN-LUC

Brown, Royal S., ed. *Focus on Godard.* Englewood Cliffs, N.J.: Prentice-Hall, 1972. Useful collection.

Cameron, Ian, ed. *The Films of Jean-Luc Godard.* New York: Praeger, 1969. Collection of essays.

Collet, Jean. *Jean-Luc Godard.* New York: Crown, 1968.

Godard, Jean-Luc. *Godard On Godard.* Edited by Tom Milne. New York: Viking, 1972.

MacBean, James Roy. *Film and Revolution.* Bloomington: Indiana University Press, 1975. Includes several major essays on Godard. Recommended.

Mussman, Toby, ed. *Jean-Luc Godard.* New York: Dutton, 1968. Collection of essays.

•Roud, Richard. *Jean-Luc Godard.* Bloomington: Indiana University Press, 1969. A seminal critical work. Recommended.

GRIFFITH, D. W.

Geduld, Harry M., ed. *Focus on D. W. Griffith.* Englewood Cliffs, N.J.: Prentice-Hall, 1971.

Henderson, Robert, M. *D. W. Griffith: His Life and Work.* New York: Oxford University Press, 1972.

————. *D. W. Griffith: The Years at Biograph.* New York: Noonday, 1970.

Silva, Fred, ed. *Focus on "The Birth of a Nation."* Englewood Cliffs, N.J.: Prentice-Hall, 1971.

Wagenknecht, Edward, and Anthony Slide. *The Films of D. W. Griffith.* New York: Crown, 1976.

HAWKS, HOWARD

McBride, Joseph, ed. *Focus on Howard Hawks.* Englewood Cliffs, N.J.: Prentice-Hall, 1972.

Wood, Robin. *Howard Hawks.* New York: Doubleday, 1968.

HITCHCOCK, ALFRED

Durgnat, Raymond. *Strange Case of Alfred Hitchcock.* Boston: M.I.T. Press, 1975.

Rohmer, Eric, and Claude Chabrol. *Hitchcock: The First 44 Films.* Trans. Stanley Hochman. New York: Frederick Ungar, 1978.

Spoto, Donald. *The Art of Alfred Hitchcock: Fifty Years of His Motion Pictures.* New York: Hopkinson and Blake, 1976.

Taylor, John Russell. *Hitch: The Life and Times of Alfred Hitchcock.* New York: Berkley, 1977.

•Truffaut, François, and Helen Scott. *Hitchcock.* New York: Simon & Schuster, 1966. Landmark book-length interview. Recommended.

Wood, Robin. *Hitchcock's Films.* Cranbury, N.J.: A. S. Barnes, 1969. Selective.

HUSTON, JOHN

Pratley, Gerald. *The Cinema of John Huston.* Cranbury, N.J.: A. S. Barnes, 1976.

Ross, Lillian. *Picture.* New York: Avon, 1952. A classic piece of journalism on the filming of John Huston's *Red Badge of Courage.*

IVENS, JORIS

Iven, Joris. *The Camera and I.* New York: International, 1969. Memoirs.

Delmar, Rosalind. *Joris Ivens: Fifty Year of Filmmaking.* London: British Film Insitute; and New York: New York Zoetrope, 1979.

KAZAN, ELIA

Ciment, Michel. *Kazan on Kazan.* New York: Viking, 1973. "Oral history."

KEATON, BUSTER

Lebel, J. P. *Buster Keaton.* Cranbury, N.J.: A. S. Barnes, 1967.

Moews, Daniel. *Keaton: The Silent Features.* Berkeley: University of California Press, 1977.

KLUGE, ALEXANDER

Dawson, Jan. *Alexander Kluge & The Occasional Work of a Female Slave.* New York: New York Zoetrope, 1977.

KUBRICK, STANLEY

Agel, Jerome. *The Making of "2001."* New York: Signet, 1970. A chatty compendium in the style of the "non-book" popular in the sixties.

Clarke, Arthur C. *Lost Worlds of "2001."* New York: Signet, 1972. The screenwriter's journal of his experiences.

Dumont, Jean-Paul, and Jean Monod. *Le Foetus Astral.* Paris: Editions Christian Bourgeois, 1970. One of the earliest full-length structuralist studies of a film (*2001*).

Kagan, Norman. *Cinema of Stanley Kubrick.* New York: Grove, 1975.

Nabakov, Vladimir. *Lolita: A Screenplay.* New York: McGraw-Hill, 1975. Not strictly about the film, this is Nabakov's original screenplay, which differs considerably from the final film. Comparison is interesting.

Walker, Alexander. *Stanley Kubrick Directs.* New York: Harcourt Brace Jovanovich, 1971.

KUROSAWA, AKIRA

Richie, Donald. *Films of Akira Kurosawa.* Berkeley: University of California Press, 1965.

LANG, FRITZ

Jensen, Paul M. *The Cinema of Fritz Lang.* Cranbury, N.J.: A. S. Barnes, 1969.

LOSEY, JOSEPH

Leahy, James. *The Cinema of Joseph Losey.* Cranbury, N.J.: A. S. Barnes, 1967.

Milne, Tom, ed. *Losey on Losey.* New York: Doubleday, 1968. "Oral history."

LUBITSCH, ERNST

Weinberg, Herman. *The Lubitsch Touch.* New York: Dutton, 1971.

MELVILLE, JEAN-PIERRE

Nogueira, Rui. *Melville.* New York: Viking, 1971. "Oral history."

MURNAU, F. W.

Eisner, Lotte. *Murnau.* Berkeley: University of California Press, 1973.

OPHULS, MAX

Willemen, Paul, ed. *Ophuls.* London: British Film Institute; and New York: New York Zoetrope, 1978.

OZU, YASUJIRO

Richie, Donald. *Ozu.* Berkeley: University of California Press, 1975.

PENN, ARTHUR

Cawelti, John G., ed. *Focus on "Bonnie and Clyde."* Englewood Cliffs, N.J.: Prentice-Hall, 1972.

Wood, Robin. *Arthur Penn.* New York: Praeger, 1969.

PREMINGER, OTTO

Pratley, Gerald. *The Cinema of Otto Preminger.* Cranbury, N.J.: A. S. Barnes, 1971.

RAY, SATYAJIT

Seton, Marie. *Portrait of a Director: Satyajit Ray.* Bloomington: Indiana University Press, 1971.

Wood, Robin. *The Apu Trilogy.* New York: Praeger, 1971.

RENOIR, JEAN

Bazin, André. *Jean Renoir.* Edited by François Truffaut. New York: Simon & Schuster, 1973. Recommended.

Braudy, Leo. *Jean Renoir.* New York: Doubleday, 1972. Recommended

Durgnat, Raymond. *Jean Renoir.* Berkeley: University of California Press, 1975.

Gilliatt, Penelope. *Jean Renoir: Essays, Conversations, Reviews.* New York: McGraw-Hill, 1975.

Leprohon, Pierre. *Jean Renoir*. New York: Crown, 1971.

Renoir, Jean. *My Life and My Films*. New York: Atheneum, 1974.

Sesonske, Alexander. *Jean Renoir: The French Films 1924–1939*. Cambridge: Harvard University Press, 1980.

RESNAIS, ALAIN

Armes, Roy. *The Cinema of Alain Resnais*. Cranbury, N.J.: A. S. Barnes, 1968.

Monaco, James. *Alain Resnais: The Role of Imagination*. London: Secker & Warburg, 1978; and New York: Oxford University Press, 1979. Includes a chapter on Resnais's "non-films."

Ward, John. *Alain Resnais or the Theme of Time*. New York: Doubleday, 1968. Recommended.

ROSSELLINI, ROBERTO

Guarner, José Luis. *Rossellini*. New York: Praeger, 1970.

ROUCH, JEAN

Eaton, Mick, ed. *Anthropology-Reality-Cinema: The Films of Jean Rouch*. London: British Film Institute; and New York: New York Zoetrope, 1979.

STRAUB, JEAN-MARIE

Roud, Richard. *Straub*. New York: Viking, 1972. Recommended.

TATI, JACQUES

Maddock, Brent. *The Films of Jacques Tati*. Metuchen, N.J.: Scarecrow Press, 1977.

TRUFFAUT, FRANÇOIS

Allen, Don. *Truffaut*. New York: Viking, 1974.

Braudy, Leo, ed. *Focus on "Shoot the Piano Player."* Englewood Cliffs, N.J.: Prentice-Hall, 1972.

Crisp, C. G. *François Truffaut*. New York: Praeger, 1972.

Insdorf, Annette. *François Truffaut*. Boston: Twayne Publishers, 1978.

Petrie, Graham. *The Cinema of François Truffaut*. Cranbury, N.J.: A. S. Barnes, 1970.

VIGO, JEAN

Salles Gomes, P. E. *Jean Vigo*. Berkeley: University of California Press, 1971.

Smith, John M. *Jean Vigo*. New York: Praeger, 1972.

VISCONTI, LUCHINO

Nowell-Smith, Geoffrey. *Luchino Visconti*. New York: Doubleday, 1968.

VON STERNBERG, JOSEF

Weinberg, Herman. *Josef Von Sternberg*. New York: Dutton, 1967.

VON STROHEIM, ERICH

Curtis, Thomas Quinn. *Von Stroheim*. New York: Farrar, Straus & Giroux, 1971.

Weinberg, Herman. *Stroheim: A Pictorial Record of His Nine Films*. New York: Dover, 1975.

WAJDA, ANDRZEJ

Michalek, Boleslaw. *The Cinema of Andrzej Wajda*. Cranbury, N.J.: A. S. Barnes, 1973.

WELLES, ORSON

Bazin, André. *Orson Welles*. New York: Holt, Rinehart and Winston,

Cowie, Peter, *The Cinema of Orson Welles*. Cranbury, N.J.: A. S. Barnes, 1973.

Gottesman, Ronald, ed. *Focus on "Citizen Kane."* Englewood Cliffs, N.J.: Prentice-Hall, 1971.

———, ed. *Focus on Orson Welles*. Englewood Cliffs, N.J.: Prentice-Hall, 1975.

Higham, Charles. *The Films of Orson Welles*. Berkeley: University of California Press, 1970.

Kael, Pauline. *The Citizen Kane Book*. Boston: Little, Brown, 1972. Includes the script and Kael's important essay on the genesis of the film. Recommended.

McBride, Joseph. *Orson Welles*. New York: Viking, 1972.
Naremore, James. *The Magic World of Orson Welles*. New York: Oxford University Press, 1978.
WENDERS, WIM
Dawson, Jan. *Wim Wenders*. New York: New York Zoetrope, 1977.

MISCELLANEOUS

Sarris, Andrew, ed. *Interviews with Film Directors*. New York: Avon/Bard, 1967. A compendium of often important interviews. Recommended.
Schickel, Richard, ed. *The Men Who Made the Movies*. New York: Atheneum 1975. Eight interviews by Schickel based on the television program.

SERIES

G.K. Hall publishes a series of "Reference and Resource Guides" on various directors. Twayne and Monarch also have series of monographs devoted to directors. Indiana University Press has discontinued their "Filmguide" series of anthologies on specific films. Prentice-Hall no longer publishes their "Focus On" series devoted to filmmakers, films, and genres.

4H. FILM HISTORY: FILMSCRIPTS

More than one hundred filmscripts are now available in American editions. That number, as impressive as it is, obviously represents only a very small percentage of American and foreign films worthy of the close study for which scripts are necessary. Moreover, because of the unencouraging attitudes of the Hollywood studios and conglomerates, relatively few American filmscripts are in print.

There isn't room here to list all the scripts in print, but a few notes about the publishers should indicate the variety of the sources available.

The popular paperback publishers (Signet, Ballantine, *et al.*) produce occasional scripts of popular films. The texts are often untrustworthy, verging on novelizations.

Grove Press pioneered in the production of carefully edited filmscripts in the late sixties and has published more than thirteen contemporary European classics to date.

Viking Press was responsible for six volumes of M-G-M films.

Simon & Schuster imported the extensive Lorrimer series of classic and modern filmscripts from London. The collection numbered more than forty.

Grossman produced a limited series of volumes, each of which included several scripts by a single director.

Farrar, Straus & Giroux were responsible for the publication of some scripts of recent American films.

Avon published the Film Classics Library edited by Richard J. Anobile, limited to popular classics.

Harper & Row's Icon series consisted of volumes that survey national cinemas.

Random House has published a number of Woody Allen's scripts.

Southern Illinois University Press and University of Wisconsin Press publish scripts on a regular basis.

Easily the most extensive, the most accurate, and the most useful series of scripts is that produced in French by *L'Avant-Scène du Cinéma*. Issued monthly and sold by subscription, *L'Avant-Scène* now numbers more than 200 scripts of European, American, and Third World films, each of which is well illustrated with frame enlargements and accompanied by critical apparatus—including scripts of short films and synopses of additional features. So far, nothing like *L'Avant Scène* exists in English.

5. FILM THEORY AND PRACTICAL CRITICISM

Adler, Renata. *A Year in the Dark*. New York: Random House, 1969. This "journal" of Adler's year on the *Times* provides an interesting mirror of the work of the daily critic.

Agee, James. *Agee on Film. Vol. I: Criticism; Vol. 2: Screenplays*. Reprint. New York: Grosset, 1969. Possibly the most important American film reviewer of the early years. Vol. 1 recommended.

Andrew, Dudley. *André Bazin*. New York: Oxford University Press, 1978. An important and engaging study of the man and his thought. Highly recommended.

———. *The Major Film Theories: An Introduction*. New York: Oxford University Press, 1976. The best available one-volume introduction to film theory. Highly recommended.

Arnheim, Rudolf. *Film as Art*. Berkeley: University of California Press, 1957. A classic exposition of expressionist theory. Recommended.

Balázs, Béla. *Theory of the Film*. 1952. Reprint. New York: Dover, 1970.

Barsam Richard. *Nonfiction Film Theory*. New York: Dutton, 1980.

Barthes, Roland. *Elements of Semiology/Writing Degree Zero*. Translated by Annette Lavers and Colin Smith. Boston: Beacon, 1968. Barthes, essentially a literary critic, should be basic reading for anyone interested in semiology. Recommended.

———. *Mythologies*. Translated by Annette Lavers. New York: Hill and Wang, 1972.

Bazin, André. *What is Cinema?* 2 vols. Selected and translated by Hugh Gray. Berkeley: University of California Press, 1967, 1971. Selections from the multi-volume *Que'est-ce que le cinéma?* Essential.

———. *The Cinema of Cruelty*. New York: Okpaku Communications, 1977.

Bellour, Raymond; Thierry Kuntzel; and Christian Metz, eds. "Psychanalyse et cinéma," *Communications 23*. Paris: Seuil, 1975. Psychoanalytic French semiology.

Benjamin, Walter. *Illuminations*. Edited by Hannah Arendt. New York: Schocken, 1968. Essays from the 1930s by one of the leading dialectical critics. See especially "The Work of Art in the Age of Mechanical Reproduction." Recommended.

Bettetini, Gianfranco. *The Language and Technique of the Film*. The Hague: Mouton, 1973. One of the leading Italian semioticians.

Burch, Noel. *The Theory of Film Practice*. New York: Praeger, 1973. One of the two important English-language books on semiological approaches.

Cameron, Ian, ed. *Movie Reader*. New York: Praeger, 1972. Thirty-three articles on various topics which first appeared in the highly respected magazine *Movie*: includes the *Movie* "Pantheon."

Cavell, Stanley. *The World Viewed: Reflections on the Ontology of Film*. New York: Viking, 1971. Recommended.

Denby, David. *Awake in the Dark: An Anthology of American Film Criticism 1915 to the Present*. New York: Random House, 1977.

Dovzhenko, Alexander. *The Poet as Filmmaker: Selected Writings.* Edited and translated by Marco Carynnyk. Boston: M.I.T. Press, 1973.

Eco, Umberto. *The Semiotic Threshhold.* The Hague: Mouton, 1973.

———. *A Theory of Semiotics.* Bloomington: University of Indiana Press, 1976. Seminal.

Eisenstein, Sergei. *Film Essays and a Lecture.* New York: Praeger, 1970.

———. *Film Form.* New York: Harcourt, Brace and World, 1949. Essential and basic.

———. *Film Sense.* New York: Harcourt, Brace and World, 1947. Essential and basic.

Ellis, John, ed. *Screen Reader One: Cinema/Ideology/Politics.* London: S.E.F.T.; New York: New York Zoetrope, 1977. Selections from the influential journal.

Farber, Manny. *Negative Space.* New York: Praeger, 1971. The "outsider" point of view.

Ferguson, Otis. *The Film Criticism of Otis Ferguson.* Edited by Robin Wilson. Philadelphia: Temple University Press, 1973.

Gidal, Peter, ed. *Structural Film Anthology,* 2nd ed. London: British Film Institute; and New York: New York Zoetrope, 1978. Important collection of documents.

Gilliatt, Penelope. *Unholy Fools.* New York: Viking, 1973.

Godard, Jean-Luc. *Godard on Godard.* Translated by Tom Milne. New York: Viking, 1972. Difficult reading, but essential. A thorough anthology of Godard's work as a critic 1950–1967.

Greene, Graham. *Graham Greene on Film: Collected Film Criticism 1935–39.* New York: Simon & Schuster, 1972.

Grierson, John. *Grierson on Documentary.* Edited by Forsyth Hardy. New York: Praeger, 1971.

Hammond, Paul, ed. *The Shadow and Its Shadow: Surrealist Writings on Cinema.* London: British Film Institute; and New York: New York Zoetrope, 1978. Important collection of documents.

Henderson, Brian. *A Critique of Film Theory.* New York: Dutton, 1980. Recommended.

Jameson, Fredric. *Marxism and Form.* Princeton, N.J.: Princeton University Press, 1971. Not about cinema. Despite the density of the prose, an important introduction to dialectical criticism. Recommended.

———. *The Prison-House of Language.* Princeton, N.J.: Princeton University Press, 1972. A useful introduction to semiotics and related areas.

Jay, Martin. *The Dialectical Imagination.* Boston: Little, Brown, 1973. A survey of the Frankfurt school.

Kael, Pauline. *Deeper into Movies.* New York: Bantam, 1974. Kael is probably the most thoroughly collected periodical critic.

———. *Going Steady.* New York: Bantam, 1971.

———. *I Lost It at the Movies.* New York: Bantam, 1965.

———. *Kiss Kiss Bang Bang.* New York: Bantam, 1968.

———. *Reeling.* Boston: Little, Brown, 1976.

———. *When the Lights Go Down.* New York: Holt, Rinehart and Winston, 1980.

Kauffmann, Stanley. *Figures of Light.* New York: Harper & Row, 1971. Film criticism and the literary sensibility.

———. *Living Images.* New York: Harper & Row, 1975.

———. *A World on Film.* New York: Harper & Row, 1966.

———, and Bruce Henstell, eds. *American Film Criticism: From the Beginnings to "Citizen Kane."* New York: Liveright, 1972. A very useful anthology. Wide ranging and thorough.

Kracauer, Siegfried. *Theory of Film: The Redemption of Physical Reality.* New York: Oxford University Press, 1960. An essential exposition of realist theory. Recommended.

Kuleshov, Lev. *Kuleshov on Film.* Berkeley: University of California Press, 1975.

Lacan, Jacques. *Ecrits: A Selection.* New York: Norton, 1977. An introduction to Lacan's work in English.

Lane, Michael, ed. *Introduction to Structuralism.* New York: Basic Books, 1970. Not specifically about film, but a useful introduction.

Lindsay, Vachel, *The Art of the Moving Pictures.* 1915. Reprint. New York: Liveright, 1970. The poet examines the young art of movies.

Lorentz, Pare. *Lorentz on Film.* New York: Harcourt Brace Jovanovich, 1975. The filmmaker as critic.

MacCann, Richard D., ed. *Film: A Montage of Theories.* New York: Dutton, 1966. Forty essays by filmmakers and critics. Recommended.

McConnell, Frank. *The Spoken Seen: Film and the Romantic Imagination.* Baltimore: Johns Hopkins University Press, 1975.

————. *Storytelling and Mythmaking: Images from Film and Literature.* New York: Oxford University Press, 1979. An interesting theory of narrativity.

Macdonald, Dwight. *On Movies.* New York: Berkley, 1971. Macdonald's limited foray into film criticism provides a useful view of the essentially political sensibility confronting the art.

Mast, Gerald. *Film/Cinema/Movie.* New York: Harper Colophon, 1977.

————, and Marshall Cohen, eds. *Film Theory and Criticism.* New York: Oxford University Press, 1974. A very useful collection of theoretical texts. Highly recommended.

Mekas, Jonas. *Movie Journal: Rise of the New American Cinema: 1959–1971.* New York: Macmillan, 1972. The chronicler of the "New American Film" underground and champion of nonnarrative film.

Metz, Christian. *Film Language: A Semiotics of the Cinema.* Translated by Michael Taylor. New York: Oxford University Press, 1974. An English version of the first volume of Metz's two-volume *Essais sur la signification au cinéma.* Paris: Editions Klincksieck, 1968, 1972. Metz is the premiere theoretician of cinema semiotics. (The reader should be advised that his thought has progressed since *Film Language* was written.) Recommended.

————. *Language and Cinema.* Translated by Donna Jean Umiker-Sebeok. The Hague: Mouton, 1974. English version of *Langage et cinéma.* Paris: Larousse, 1971.

Münsterberg, Hugo. *The Film: A Psychological Study.* 1916. Reprint. New York: Dover, 1970. One of the earliest approaches to film psychology.

Murray, Edward. *Nine American Film Critics.* New York: Ungar, 1975. Surveys recent critical approaches.

National Society of Film Critics. *Film 67/68:* 1968; *Film 68/69:* 1969; *Film 69/70:* 1970; *Film 70/71:* 1971. New York: Simon & Schuster. *Film 72/73:* 1973; *Film 73/74:* 1974. Indianapolis: Bobbs-Merrill. A yearly anthology of review by the members of N.S.F.C.

Neale, Steven. *Genre.* London: British Film Institute; New York: New York Zoetrope, 1980.

Nichols, Bill, ed. *Movies and Methods.* Berkeley: University of California Press, 1977. A very important anthology of contemporary criticism. Highly recommended.

Nizhny, Vladimir. *Lessons with Eisenstein.* New York: Hill and Wang, 1962.

Potamkin, Harry Alan. *The Compound Cinema: The Film Writings of Harry Alan Potamkin.* Ed. Lewis Jacobs. New York: Teachers College Press, 1978. One of the more important critics of the 1930s.

Pudovkin, V.I. *Film Technique and Film Acting.* 1929, 1937. Reprint. New York: Grove, 1970. Next to Eisenstein, the most important of the Soviet theorists.

Rohdie, Sam, ed. "Cinema Semiotics and the Work of Christian Metz," *Screen* 14:1/2 Spring/Summer 1973). A landmark collection of essays in English.

Sarris, Andrew. *Confessions of a Cultist.* New York: Simon & Schuster, 1970. With Kael, the most influential of the American critics; popularizer of the auteur theory in America.

————. *The Primal Screen: Essays on Film and Related Subjects.* New York: Simon & Schuster, 1973.

————. *Politics and Cinema.* New York: Columbia University Press, 1979. Despite title, a collection of various pieces from the seventies.

Simon, John. *Movies into Films: Film Criticism 1967–70.* New York: Dial Press, 1971. The critic as hero; best representative of the conservative esthetic.

————. *Private Screenings.* New York: Berkley, 1967.

Solanas, Fernando, and Octavio Getino. "Towards a Third Cinema." *Cinéaste* IV:3 (1970).

Sontag, Susan. *Against Interpretation.* New York: Delta, 1966. More a cultural critic than a film reviewer, Sontag's books are listed in this section because of her influence in popularizing modern French theoretical developments.

————. *Styles of Radical Will.* New York: Farrar, Straus & Giroux, 1970. Important essays on Godard and Bergman.

Truffaut, François. *The Films in My Life.* New York: Grove Press, 1978.

Tudor, Andrew. *Theories of Film.* New York: Viking, 1973. Useful survey.

Tyler, Parker. *Classics of the Foreign Film.* New York: Citadel, 1962.

————. *Hollywood Hallucination.* 1944. Reprint. New York: Simon & Schuster, 1970.

————. *Magic and Myth in the Movies.* 1947. Reprint. New York: Grove, 1970.

————. *Screening the Sexes: Homosexuality in the Movies.* New York: Doubleday, 1973.

————. *Sex, Psyche, Etc. in the Film.* New York: Penguin, 1971.

————. *The Shadow of an Airplane Climbs the Empire State Building: A World Theory of Film.* New York: Doubleday, 1973.

————. *Underground Film.* New York: Grove, 1969.

Warshow, Robert. *The Immediate Experience.* 1962. Reprint. New York: Atheneum, 1970. Next to Agee, the most important critic of film's adolescence. Especially useful on film as popular art.

•Wollen, Peter. *Signs and Meaning in the Cinema.* 2nd ed. New York: Viking, 1972. The most important original semiological study in English. Recommended.

Young, Vernon. *On Film.* New York: Quadrangle, 1973. An unusual approach: Young combines auteurism with ethnography.

6. MEDIA

Altick, Richard D. *The English Common Reader: A Social History of the Mass Reading Public, 1800–1900.* Chicago: University of Chicago Press, 1963.

Arlen, Michael. *Living Room War: Writings About Television.* New York: The Viking Press, 1969.

Barnouw, Erik. *A History of Broadcasting in the United States.* New York: Oxford University Press. Vol. 1: *A Tower in Babel,* 1966. Vol. 2: *The Golden Web,* 1968. Vol. 3: *The Image Empire,* 1970. The standard work on the subject. Recommended.

————. *Tube of Plenty: The Evolution of American Television.* New York: Oxford University Press, 1975. A one-volume revision of *A History of Broadcasting in the United States.* Highly recommended.

————. *The Sponsor: Notes on a Modern Potentate.* New York: Oxford University Press, 1978. A short and pithy analysis.

Brooks, John. *Telephone: The First Hundred Years.* New York: Harper & Row, 1976.

Brown, Les. *Television: The Business Behind the Box.* New York: Harcourt Brace Jovanovich, 1972.

Carnegie Commission on the Future of Public Broadcasting. *A Public Trust: The Landmark Report.* New York: Bantam Books, 1979.

Caughie, John, ed. *Television: Ideology and Exchange.* London: British Film Institute; New York: New York Zoetrope, 1978.

Chapple, Steve, and Reebee Garofalo. *Rock 'n' Roll Is Here To Pay: The History and Politics of the Music Industry.* Chicago: Nelson-Hall, 1977. An excellent survey.

Compaine, Benjamin M., ed. *Who Owns the Media? Concentration of Ownership in the Mass Communications Industry.* New York: Harmony, 1979, 1980. See especially Thomas Guback's chapter on theatrical film.

Comstock, George, et al. *Television and Human Behavior.* New York: Columbia University Press, 1978.

Fornatale, Peter, and Joshua E. Mills. *Radio in the Television Age.* Woodstock, N.Y.: Overlook Press, 1980.

Friendly, Fred. *Due to Circumstances Beyond Our Control.* New York: Random House, 1967.

Gans, Herbert. *Deciding What's News.* New York: Random House, 1979.

Garnham, Nicholas. *Structures of Television.* 2nd ed. London: British Film Institute; New York: New York Zoetrope, 1978.

Gedin, Per. *Literature in the Market Place.* Woodstock, N.Y.: The Overlook Press, 1977.

Gitlin, Todd. *The Whole World Is Watching: Mass Media in the Making and Unmaking of the New Left.* Berkeley: University of California Press, 1980.

Greenfield, Jeff. *Television: The First Fifty Years.* New York: Harry N. Abrams, 1977. Essentially an expensive picture book, but Greenfield's text provides an excellent introduction.

Harris, Jay S., ed. *TV Guide: The First 25 Years.* New York: New American Library, 1980.

Heller, Caroline. *Broadcasting and Accountability.* London: British Film Institute; New York: New York Zoetrope, 1978.

Innis, Harold. *The Bias of Communication.* Toronto: University of Toronto Press, 1951, 1973. Seminal.

McArthur, Colin. *Television and History.* London: British Film Institute; New York: New York Zoetrope, 1978.

McLuhan, Marshall. *Understanding Media: The Extensions of Man.* New York: McGraw-Hill, 1964. Controversial and often unintelligible, but seminal.

Maddox, Brenda. *Beyond Babel: New Directions in Communications.* Boston: Beacon Press, 1972.

Mander, Jerry. *Four Arguments for the Elimination of Television.* New York: Morrow, 1978. An absolutist approach to the problem, but provocative.

Mankiewicz, Frank, and Joel Swerdlow. *Remote Control: Television and the Manipulation of American Life.* New York: Times Books, 1978. Recommended.

Mayer, Martin. *About Television.* New York: Harper & Row, 1974.

Miller, Jonathan. *Marshall McLuhan*. New York: Viking Press, 1971.

Monaco, James, *et al. Celebrity: Who Gets It, How They Use It, Why It Works*. New York: Delta Books, 1978. Includes analysis of star images of the seventies.

———. *Media Culture: Television, Books, Radio, Records, Magazines, Newspapers, Movies*. New York: Delta Books, 1978, 1980. Includes a special section "Who Owns the Media?" and extensive appendices.

Moody, Kate. *Growing Up on Television: A Report to Parents*. New York: Times Books, 1980.

Mueller, Claus. *The Politics of Communication*. New York: Oxford University Press, 1973.

The Network Project *Notebooks*. 1. *Domestic Communications Satellites* (October 1972); 2. *Directory of the Networks* (February 1973); 3: *Control of Information* (March 1973); 4: *Office of Telecommunications Policy—The White House Role in Domestic Communications* (April 1973); 5: *Cable Television* (June 1973); 6: *Down Sesame Street* (November 1973); 7: *The Case Against Satellites* (Spring 1974); 8: *Cable Television—End of a Dream* (Summer 1974); 9: *Government Television* (Autumn 1974); 10: *Global Salesman* (Winter 1975). 101 Earl Hall, Columbia University, New York. 10027.

Newcomb, Horace, ed. *The Critical View: Television*. New York: Oxford University Press, 1976.

———. *TV: The Most Popular Art*. New York: Doubleday, 1974.

Palmer, Tony. *All You Need Is Love: The Story of Popular Music*. New York: Grossman Publishers, 1976.

Powers, Ron. *The Newscasters: The News Business as Show Business*. New York: St. Martin's Press, 1977.

Schiller, Herbet I. *Mass Communications and American Empire*. Boston: Beacon Press, 1969.

Schneider, Ira, and Beryl Korot. *Video Art*. New York: Harcourt Brace Jovanovich, 1976.

Schwartz, Tony. *The Responsive Chord: How Radio and TV Manipulate You. . . .* New York: Anchor, 1973.

Shamberg, Michael, and the Raindance Corp. *Guerrilla Television*. New York: Holt, Rinehart and Winston, 1972.

Shanks, Bob. *The Cool Fire: How To Make It in Television*. New York: Norton, 1976.

Shapiro, Andrew. *Media Access*. Boston: Little, Brown, 1976.

Smith, Anthony. *The Newspaper: An International History*. London: Thames and Hudson, 1979. An introduction.

———. *Goodbye Gutenberg: The Newspaper Revolution of the Eighties*. New York: Oxford University Press, 1980.

Smith, Ralph Lee. *The Wired Nation: Cable TV: The Electronic Communications Highway*. New York: Harper & Row, 1972.

Smithsonian Institution. *History of Music Machines*. New York and London: Drake Publishers, 1975. Intro. by Erik Barnouw.

Sontag, Susan. *On Photography*. New York: Farrar, Straus & Giroux, 1977.

•Tebbel, John. *The Media in America*. New York: Mentor, 1974. Traces the development of print and electronic media.

Tunstall, Jeremy. *The Media Are American*. London: Constable; New York: Columbia University Press, 1977.

Veith, Richard. *Talk-Back TV: Two-Way Cable Television*. Blue Ridge Summit, PA: TAB Books, 1976.

Williams, Raymond. *Communications*. 3rd ed. London: Penguin, 1976.
●————. *Television: Technology and Cultural Form*. New York: Schocken, 1975. Recommended.
Williamson, Judith. *Decoding Advertisements: Ideology and Meaning in Advertising*. London: Marion Boyars, 1978. An interesting approach.
●Winn, Marie. *The Plug-in Drug: Television, Children, and the Family*. New York: Viking and Bantam, 1977. An influential book.
Wright, John W. *The Commercial Connection: Advertising and the American Mass Media*. New York: Delta Books, 1979. A useful collection of articles, with appendices.
————, *et al. Edsels, Luckies, and Frigidaires: Advertising the American Way*. New York: Delta Books, 1978. An intriguing collection of historical advertisements.

PART TWO: INFORMATION

7. LISTS AND ENCYCLOPEDIAS

FILM

●*A Biographical Dictionary of Film*. David Thomson. London: Secker and Warburg; New York: Morrow, 1975, 1976. Interesting personal views.
Cinema: A Critical Dictionary: The Major Filmmakers. Richard Roud, ed. 2 vols. London: Secker & Warburg; New York: Viking, 1980.
The Film Encyclopedia. Ephraim Katz. New York: Lippincott/Crowell, 1979.
●*The Filmgoer's Companion*, 6th ed. Leslie Halliwell. New York: Hill and Wang, 1977. A basic general guide.
Halliwell's Film Guide. Leslie Halliwell. London: Granada, 1977. 2nd ed. 1980.
International Encyclopedia of Film. Edited by Roger Manvell and Lewis Jacobs. New York: Crown, 1972.
The Oxford Companion to Film. Edited by Liz-Anne Bawden. New York: Oxford University Press, 1976.
Who's Who in American Film Now. James Monaco and Sharon Boonshoft. New York: New York Zoetrope, 1980. A guide to credits and careers of more than 1200 actors, actresses, and filmmakers.
The World Encyclopedia of Film. Edited by Tim Cawkwell and John M. Smith. New York: A&W Visual Library, 1972.
The New York Times Directory of the Film. New York: Arno Press, 1970, 1974. A computer-generated name index to *Times* film reviews.
Dictionary of Films, Dictionary of Filmmakers. Georges Sadoul. Translated and updated by Peter Morris. Berkeley: University of California Press, 1972. Personal views.
TV Movies. Annual. Leonard Maltin. New York: New American Libary, 1980. 10,000 entries with capsule descriptions. No filmographical data.
Movies on TV. Annual. Steven. H. Scheuer. New York: Bantam Books, 1980. 9,000 entries. Plot summaries but no filmographcal information.
Screen Series. Various authors. London: Tantivy Press; New York: A. S. Barnes, 1969–1970. Volumes on Japan, Sweden, France, Germany, Eastern Europe, and other topics.

Directory of Films By and/or About Women. Berkeley: Women's Historical Research Center, 1972.

The British Film Catalogue 1895/1970. Denis Gifford. New York: McGraw-Hill, 1973. 15,000 entries; a complete list.

The American Film Institute Catalogue of Motion Pictures Produced in the U.S. Part I: Feature Films 1921/1930 (2 vols.), *Part II: Feature Films 1961/1970.* 1971, 1976. A reputedly complete catalogue.

Film Book Series: vol. 1: Directors; vol. 2: Screenwriters and Producers; vol. 3: Technicians; vol. 4: Actors. London: Saint James Press; New York: St. Martin's Press, 1976, 1977, 1978, 1979.

World Filmography. London: Tantivy, 1976. 640 pp. A yearly compilation.

RADIO

The Big Broadcast 1920–1950. Frank Buxton and Bill Owen. New York: Avon Books, 1972. A reference guide to radio.

Tune in Yesterday: The Ultimate Encyclopedia of Old-Time Radio: 1925–1976. John Dunning. Englewood Cliffs, N.J.: Prentice-Hall, 1976.

TELEVISION

The Complete Directory to Prime Time Network TV Shows 1946–Present. Tim Brooks and Earle Marsh. New York: Ballantine, 1979.

The Complete Encyclopedia of Television Programs. Vincent Terrace. Cranbury, N.J.: A. S. Barnes, 1976.

•*The New York Times Encyclopedia of Television.* Les Brown. New York: Times Books, 1977. An invaluable reference.

TV Guide Almanac. New York: Ballantine, 1979.

TV Annual. Steven Scheuer. New York: Macmillan, 1979.

TV Season 74–75, TV Season 75–76, et cetera. Nina David. Phoenix, Arizona: The Oryx Press, 1976. . . . . Annual.

8. BOOK BIBLIOGRAPHIES

Basic Books in the Mass Media. Eleanor Blum. Urbana: University of Illinois Press, 1972. A basic bibliography.

Cinema Booklist. George Rehrauer. Metuchen, N.J.: Scarecrow Press, 1972. *Supplement One,* 1974. *Supplement Two,* 1976. The standard bibliographical guide to film literature.

Film Criticism: An Index to Critics' Anthologies. Richard Heinzkill. Metuchen, N.J.: Scarecrow Press, 1975.

Literature of the Film. Alan Dyment. London: White Lion Publishers, 1975.

Moving Pictures: An Annotated Guide to Selected Film Literature. Eileen Sheahan. Cranbury, N.J.: A. S. Barnes, 1978.

9. GUIDES TO PERIODICAL LITERATURE

Of the seven guides to periodical literature in film that are now available, three limit themselves to film magazines, one is mainly devoted to film magazines but includes material from occasional general publications, one concentrates on general magazines, and one covers a wide range of both specialist and general periodicals. Of the three that concentrate on film journals, two are limited to English-language magazines. Each is therefore useful in its own way, although there is considerable overlapping.

International Index to Film Periodicals. Sponsored by Fédération internationale des archives du film (FIAF). Yearly. *Vol. 1: 1972.* Edited by Karen Jones. New York: R. R. Bowker, 1973. 344 pp. *Vol. 2: 1973.* Edited by Michael Moulds. New York: R. R. Bowker, 1974. 395 pp. *Vol. 3: 1974.* Edited by Karen Jones. London: Saint James Press; New York: St. Martin's Press, 1975. 517 pp. The standard index to film periodicals; covers foreign-language journals as well as English.

The Film Index: A Bibliography. Vol. 1: The Film As Art. Edited by Harold Leonard. 1941. Reprint. New York: Arno Press, 1970. An early classic guide.

The New Film Index. Edited by Richard Dyer MacCann and Edward S. Perry. New York: Dutton, 1975. 600 pp. Covers 38 film magazines in English as well as occasional other journals from 1930 to 1970. Together with the FIAF yearly volumes, comprises a basic research tool.

The Critical Index. John C. and Lana Gerlach. New York: Teachers' College Press. 1974. 726 pp. Computer-generated bibliography of articles on film in English, 1946–1973. 22 periodicals covered. Available inexpensively in paperback.

Index to Critical Film Reviews in British and American Film Periodicals; Index to Critical Reviews of Books About Film: 1930–1972. 2 vols. Stephen E. Bowles. New York: Burt Franklin Co., 1975. Approximately 700 pp. The index of book reviews is unique.

A Guide to Critical Reviews, Part 4: Bibliography of Critical Reviews of Feature Length Motion Pictures Released from October 1927 through 1963. James R. Salem. 2 vols. Metuchen, N.J.: Scarecrow Press, 1971. 12,000 entries.

Retrospective Index to Film Periodicals 1930–1971. Linda Batty. New York: R. R. Bowker, 1975. Companion to the FIAF yearly indexes listed above. 20 English-language periodicals covered.

Motion Picture Directors: A Bibliography of Magazine and Periodical Articles, 1900–1969. Mel Schuster. Metuchen, N.J.: Scarecrow Press, 1973. 418 pp.

Film Literature Index. Edited by Vincent J. Aceto, Jane Graves and Fred Silva. Albany, N.Y.: Filmdex, Inc. A quarterly subject/author index covering more than 300 film periodicals in various languages and 125 English-language general interest magazines.

The New York Times Film Reviews 1913–1968. 6 vols. New York: Arno Press, 1970. A complete reprinting covering more than 17,000 films together with a cumulative index.

The New York Times Film Reviews 1913–1970: A One-Volume Selection. Edited by George Amberg. New York: Quadrangle, 1971. 495 pp.

The Drama Scholar's Index to Plays and Filmscripts: A Guide to Plays and Filmscripts in Selected Anthologies, Series, and Periodicals. Gordon Samples. Metuchen, N.J.: Scarecrow Press, 1974. 460 pp.

10. MISCELLANEOUS GUIDES

American Film Institute Guide to College Courses in Film and Television. 7th ed. Washington, D.C.: American Film Institute, 1980.

Ash, René. *The Motion Picture Film Editor.* Metuchen, N.J.: Scarecrow Press, 1974. 193 pp. Credits of 652 film editors.

Beattie, Eleanor. *The Handbook of Canadian Film,* 2nd ed. Toronto: Peter Martin Associates; and New York: New York Zoetrope, 1977.

Corliss, Richard, ed. *The Hollywood Screenwriters.* New York: Avon, 1972. Includes a 35 pp. filmography for 50 screenwriters.

•Cowie, Peter, ed. *International Film Guide.* Yearly, 1964 to present. London: Tantivy Press; New York: A. S. Barnes. One of the most useful film references. Includes five "directors of the year," essays on cinema production in each of 48 countries, and essays on topics ranging from film music, TV in Canada and Europe, and animation, to subtitling, film schools, and alternative cinema. Highly recommended.

Enser, A. G. S., ed. *Filmed Books and Plays: 1928–1974.* New York: Academic Press, 1974. A list of books and plays from which films have been made.

Georgakas, Dan, *et al. In Focus: A Guide to Using Films.* New York: Cine Information and New York Zoetrope, 1980.

Gianakos, Larry. *Television Drama Series Programming: A Comprehensive Chronicle, 1959–1975.* Metuchen, N.J.: Scarecrow Press, 1979.

Klotman, Phyllis Rauch. *Frame by Frame: A Black Filmography.* Bloomington: Indiana University Press, 1979.

Limbacher, James L. *Feature Films on 8 mm and 16 mm.* 4th ed. New York: R. R. Bowker, 1974, A bookers' guide.

Marill, Alvin H. *Movies Made for Television: The Telefeature and the Miniseries 1964–79.* New York: Arlington House, 1979.

Michael, Paul *The Great American Movie Book.* Englewood Cliffs, N.J.: Prentice-Hall, 1980.

Peyton, Patricia, ed. *Reel Change: A Guide to Social Issue Films.* San Francisco: The Film Fund; New York: New York Zoetrope, 1980. A catalogue of films with political and social themes.

Powers, Ann. *Blacks in American Movies.* Metuchen, N.J.: Scarecrow Press, 1974, 167 pp.

Ragan, David. *Who's Who in Hollywood 1900–76.* New York: Arlington House, 1977.

Rovin, Jeff. *The Signet Book of Movie Lists.* New York: Signet, 1979.

Steinberg, Cobbett. *Film Facts.* New York: Facts on File, 1980.

Thompson, Hilary, *et al.,* eds. *1951–1976: British Film Institute Productions: A Catalogue of Films Made Under the Auspices of the Experimental Film Fund 1951–1966 and the Production Board 1966–1976.* London: British Film Institute, 1977.

Truitt, Evelyn. *Who Was Who On Screen: 1920–1971.* New York: R. R. Bowker, 1974. 480 pp. 6,000 screen personalities.

Van Daalen, Nicholas. *The Book of Movie Lists.* New York: Dutton, 1980.

Van Nooten, S. I., ed. *Vocabulaire du Cinéma/Film Vocabulary/Film Woordenlijst . . .* 6th ed. The Hague: Netherlands Information Service, 1974. Distributed in the U.S. by Pflaum. 900 film terms in French, English, Dutch, Italian, German, Spanish, and Danish.

World Radio T.V. Handbook. New York: Billboard Publications, published yearly.

11. JOURNALS AND MAGAZINES

At one time or another, more than 500 film magazines have been published in the English language alone. As many as 200 survive today. This is a carefully selected list that includes nearly all the magazines currently indexed plus a few others which, although small in circulation, are growing in influence.

BIBLIOGRAPHICAL AND FILMOGRAPHICAL

Monthly Film Bulletin. British Film Institute. 81 Dean Street, London W1V6AA. Monthly. Credits, synopses, and reviews of all feature films released in the U.K. A standard reference.

Filmfacts. Box 213, Village Station, New York 10014. Fortnightly. A checklist of all feature films released in the U.S. with summaries of major reviews.

Film Dope. 5 Norman Court, Little Heath, Potters Bar, Hertfordshire EN6 1HY, England. Quarterly. A serial dictionary of film.

LEADING GENERAL CRITICAL MAGAZINES

American Film. Circ.: 100,000. Edited by Antonio Chemasi. American Film Institute, Kennedy Center, Washington, DC 20006. Monthly.

Sight and Sound. Circ.: 35,000. Edited by Penelope Houston. British Film Institute, 81 Dean Street, London W1V 6AA. Quarterly.

Film Comment. Circ.: 28,000. Edited by Richard Corliss. Film Society of Lincoln Center, 1865 Broadway, New York 10023. Bimonthly.

Film Quarterly. Circ.: 9,000. Edited by Ernest Callenbach. University of California Press, Berkeley, CA 94720. Quarterly.

OTHER GENERAL CRITICAL MAGAZINES

American Cinematographer. Edited by Herb Lightman. P.O. Box 2230, Hollywood, CA 90028. The leading technical journal.

Cineaste. Edited by Gary Crowdus. 333 Sixth Avenue, New York 10014. Recommended.

Film Library Quarterly. Edited by William Sloan. Box 348, Radio City Station, New York 10019.

Journal of Popular Film. University Hall 101, Bowling Green State University, Bowling Green, Ohio 43403. Quarterly.

Jump Cut. Edited by Chuck Kleinhans and John Hess. 3138 West Schubert, Chicago, IL 60647. Bimonthly. Recommended.

MOVIE. Edited by Ian Cameron. 25 Lloyd Baker Street, London, WC1X 9AT. Quarterly.

Movietone News. Edited by Richard T. Jameson. Seattle Film Society. 5236 18th Avenue N.E., Seattle, WA 98105. Monthly. Recommended.

SCREEN. 29 Old Compton Street, London W1V 5PL. Quarterly. The major semiological journal in English.

The Velvet Light Trap. Arizona Jim Co-op. 602 Club, 602 University Avenue, Madison, WI 53703. Quarterly.

MEDIA JOURNALS

Washington Journalism Review. Edited by Ray White. 3122 M St., N.W., Washington, DC 20007. Since the demise of MORE this is the most useful general media magazine.

Emmy: The Magazine of the Academy of Television Arts and Sciences. Edited by Pamela E. Gates. 4605 Lankershim Blvd., North Hollywood, CA 91602. Quarterly.

Columbia Journalism Review. Columbia University, New York 10027.

Variety. 154 West 46th St, New York 10036. Exceptionally useful, extensive, and smart coverage of film, television, and radio.

Publishers Weekly. 1180 Avenue of the Americas, New York 10036. Extensive coverage
   of book publishing.
Panorama. 850 Third Ave., New York 10022. General coverage of television of a fairly
   high level.

IN MEMORIAM
Two important magazines ceased publication in the late seventies. MORE: *The Media
Magazine* covered journalism, print and nonprint, with verve and intelligence. *Take
One* dealt with film in all its variety with wit and humor. Both are missed.

12. A BIBLIOGRAPHICAL NOTE

Publishers specializing in books on film and media include Simon & Schuster, Viking,
Crown, Dutton, Indiana University Press, University of California Press, Arno, Avon,
A. S. Barnes, and Oxford University Press, among others in the U.S., and Tantivy and
Secker and Warburg in London. Many of the most useful studies have been printed in
series of monographs by a number of these publishers.

In London major film bookstores include:
   Larry Edmunds Bookshop. 6658 Hollywood Blvd., Hollywood, CA 90028.
   Cinemabilia. 10 West 13th Street, New York 10011.
   Cinebooks. 642 Yonge Street, Toronto, Ontario M4Y 1Z8
   The Gotham Book Mart. 41 West 47th Street, New York 10036.
   Cinema Books. 701 Broadway East, Seattle, WA 98102.
   Limelight Bookstore. 1803 Market Street, San Francisco, CA 94114.
   Movie Madness. 1642 Massachusetts Avenue, Cambridge, MA 02138.
   Westwood Bookstore. 1021 Broxton Avenue, Los Angeles, CA 90024.

In London major film bookstores are:
   Cinema Bookshop. 13–14 Great Russell Street, WC1.
   The Motion Picture Bookshop at the NFT. South Bank, SE1 8XT.
   A. Zwemmer. 78 Charing Cross Road, London WC2.

APPENDIX III

FILM AND MEDIA: A CHRON- OLOGY

130 A.D. Ptolemy of Alexandria discovers the phenomenon of persistence of vision.

1250 Leon Battista Alberti invents forerunner of camera obscura.

1456 August 24. Heinrich Cremer finishes binding the first Gutenberg bibles, first books to be printed with movable type.

1700s Rise of newspapers and journals.

1800s Development of widespread literacy in England and elsewhere in Europe, and development as a consequence of mass media culture of books, magazines, and newspapers.

1810 König's steam-powered printing press.

1827 March 16. The first Black newspaper, *Freeman's Journal,* appears.

1834 Zoetrope, based on an ancient invention, patented.

1839 Daguerreotype and Talbottype announced.

1840 Morse's telegraph.

1846 Hoe's rotary press.

1850 Photographic magic lantern slides come into use.

1867 Sholes invents typewriter, to be exploited by Remington.

1873 Muybridge's experiments begin in photography of motion. He is successful in 1877.

1876 Bell's telephone.

1877 Edison's phonograph.
      Reynaud's Praxinoscope.

1880 *New York Graphic* prints the first halftone photographs.

1884 Eastman's roll paper photographic medium.
      Mergenthaler's linotype.
      The Nipkow disc introduces the concept of scanning.

1889 Development of Eastman's flexible roll film medium for photography.
      Dickson demonstrates Kinetophone to Edison.

1891–94 Development of the Kinetoscope private viewer.

1895 December 28. Lumières' first public showing of Cinematographe films at Grand Café, Boulevard des Capucines, Paris.

Max Skladănowsky completes Bioskop projector.

1896–1915: The Birth of Film

1896 April 23. Edison's first show at Koster and Bial's Music Hall, New York.

September 2. Marconi demonstrates wireless telegraphy in England.

Dickson forms American Mutoscope and Biograph Company.

1897 Edison begins patent infringement suits.

May. Fire at film showing at Bazar de la Charité takes 140 lives.

Edwin Porter joins Edison's company.

1899 James Stuart Blackton founds Vitagraph Company.

1900 At the Paris Exposition, embryonic color and sound film systems are demonstrated.

Danish telephone engineer Valdemar Poulsen patents "telegraphone," a wire recording system.

1901 First transatlantic wireless transmission, by Marconi from England to Newfoundland.

Queen Victoria's funeral reported via film.

Fessenden begins experiments in voice transmission.

1902 Méliès's *Voyage to the Moon.*

T. L. Tally's Electric Theatre opens in Los Angeles.

Pathé opens studio at Vincennes.

1903 Porter's *Life of an American Fireman* and *The Great Train Robbery.*

1905 Hepworth's *Rescued by Rover.*

1906 De Forest invents Audion vacuum tube.

Biograph 14th Street Studio opens in Manhattan.

1907 Griffith begins work in film as an actor.

1908 Émile Cohl (in France) and Winsor McKay (in U.S.) begin work in animation.

Pathé leads industry in abandoning outright sales of film in favor of rentals.

Film d'art movement begins in France.

1909 The Motion Picture Patents Company is founded, soon followed by the General Film Company (distributors). Patent wars begin.

1910 Griffith and his company begin wintering in Los Angeles. The locus of major film activity shifts from New York to Los Angeles within the next few years.

1911 Max Sennett's first Keystone comedy produced.

1912 Armstrong's regenerative circuit developed.

Warner brothers begin producing films; Fox company and Universal formed.

British Board of Film Censors formed.

First fan magazines appear.

1913   Italian epics *Quo Vadis?* and *Cabiria* suggest value of feature-length films.

1915   Griffith's *The Birth of a Nation* signals beginning of new period in film history.

Vachel Lindsay's *The Art of the Moving Picture* published.

1916–1930: The Silent Film, the Births of Radio and Sound Film

1916   Griffith's *Intolerance*.

Münsterberg's *The Photoplay: A Psychological Study* published.

1917   UFA formed in Germany.

Kuleshov's workshop begins in Soviet Union.

1918   Armstrong's Superheterodyne circuit makes radio a commercial possibility.

1919   United Artists formed. Star system dominant in film industry.

General Electric creates Radio Corporation of America to take over monopoly of American Marconi Company.

Soviet film industry nationalized.

Tri-Ergon sound-on-film system patented in Germany.

Wiene's *Cabinet of Dr. Caligari*. German Expressionist movement begins.

1920   American domination of world film industry established.

Emigration of filmmakers to Hollywood starts.

KDKA begins broadcasting in Pittsburgh.

1922   August 28. 5:15 P.M. The first radio commercial: Mr. Blackwell, for the Queensboro Corp. on AT&T's WEAF in New York.

Lang's *Dr. Mabuse*.

Vertov's *Kino-Pravda*.

Flaherty's *Nanook of the North*.

BBC begins informally in Britain.

1923   Stiller's *Saga of Gösta Berling*, starring Greta Garbo.

Stroheim's *Greed*, forerunner of contemporary realism.

Time—first "newsmagazine"—begins publication.

1924   Columbia Pictures founded, M-G-M consolidated.

Léger's *Ballet Mécanique*.

1925   London Film Society founded; film study develops in France.

Eisenstein' *Battleship Potemkin*.

1926   August 6. Vitaphone (sound-on-record) premier: *Don Juan*.

November 15. 8 P.M. to 12:25 A.M. NBC begins network broadcasting with a program from the roof of the Waldorf-Astoria in New York featuring the New York Symphony, the New York Oratorio Society, Will Rogers, Weber & Fields, and Vincent Lopez. Twenty-five stations in 21 cities broadcast the program.

Pudovkin's *Film Technique* published.

Rudolph Valentino dies.

1927   British Cinematograph Act provides for a quota system.

BBC chartered.

U.S. Radio Act creates Federal Radio Commission (later F.C.C.).

Roxy Theatre opens in New York.

April. Fox Movietone News begins, using sound-on-film system.

October 6. Warner Brothers' *The Jazz Singer*, with music and several talking sequences, first popular sound success.

CBS formed.

German inventor Pfleumer devises magnetic tape system.

1928 RKO Radio Pictures Corporation formed by G.E./Westinghouse/R.C.A. combine to exploit R.C.A.'s sound patents in film.

Television introduced.

Massive transition to sound leads to increased influence of banking interests in film production.

Crossley Radio Survey ratings begin. First published 1930.

First "all-talking" picture: *Lights of N.Y.*

Dreyer's *Passion of Joan of Arc.*

Vertov's *Man With a Movie Camera.*

Dali and Buñuel's *Un Chien Andalou*

1929 Hitchcock's *Blackmail* first British dialogue film.

Mamoulian's *Applause* one of the first successful musicals.

Marx Brothers' first film, *The Coconuts*, presages massive exodus of Broadway talent to Hollywood.

Amos 'n' Andy becomes first popular NBC network series.

Conversion to sound has resulted in nearly twofold increase in box office admission in two years. (1927: 60 million patrons; 1929: 110 million.)

Electrical transcription introduced to radio.

1930 Production Code instituted, but laxly enforced.

Necessity of foreign-language versions for export results in second wave of influx of European talent to Hollywood.

Clair's *Sous les toits de Paris* first French sound film.

Von Sternberg's *Blue Angel*, with Marlene Dietrich.

Disney's first *Silly Symphony.*

U.S. brings antitrust suit against RCA and its patent allies.

Grierson, Rotha, Wright, and Jennings involved in British documentary movement.

1931–1945: The Great Age of Hollywood and Radio

1931 Hecht and MacArthur's play *The Front Page* is filmed by Lewis Milestone. It marks the continued growth in importance of newspapers as a cultural medium.

Wellman's *Public Enemy* marks rise of Gangster genre.

Chaplin's *City Lights* filmed with music-only soundtrack.

Dracula and *Frankenstein*, emblems of the Horror genre.

Murnau and Flaherty collaborate on semidocumentary *Tabu.*

1932 Hawks, Hughes, and Hecht collaborate on *Scarface*, major Gangster film.

Post-dubbing techniques put into practice, greatly facilitating the shooting of sound films.

Radio City Music Hall, the ultimate movie palace, opens in the Radio City complex, home of RCA, in Rockefeller Center.

Venice Film Festival—first of its kind—begins.

Busby Berkeley's choreography for *42nd Street* establishes a style for the musical of the 1930s.

Lubitsch's *Trouble in Paradise* confirms the Paramount style of sophisticated comedy for the decade.

1933 Astaire and Rogers in *Flying Down to Rio* establish a mode of urbane sophistication which marks most entertainments of the 1930s.

Cooper and Schoedsack's *King Kong* evokes racial fears to establish a popular myth.

Arnheim's *Film as Art* published.

German film industry under Nazi control.

British Film Institute founded.

Armstrong develops FM radio.

First "Fireside Chats" by President Roosevelt utilize radio medium.

1934 Breen strengthens censorship under Production Code.

Capra's *It Happened One Night*, major early Screwball comedy, along with Hawks's *Twentieth Century*.

Riefenstahl's *Triumph of the Will* celebrates Nazi mystique.

British Government involved in financing documentaries.

Flaherty completes *Man of Aran*.

1935 Technicolor three-strip process comes into use.

De Rochemont's March of Time series of documentaries begins.

"Audimeter"—device for radio broadcast ratings—invented.

1936 BBC begins television service (to be interrupted by the war).

Cinémathèque Française founded by Henri Langlois.

Chaplin's *Modern Times*.

Capra's *Mr. Deeds Goes to Town* marks cycle of American populist films.

Renoir's *Le Crime de M. Lange*.

Life magazine debuts.

1937 Renoir's *Grand Illusion*.

Arriflex lightweight 35 mm camera—the first with reflex shutter—introduced.

1938 Eisentein's *Alexander Nevsky*.

Michael Balcon takes over production at Ealing Studios.

October 31. Welles's *War of the Worlds* radio broadcast.

1939 National Film Board of Canada founded.

Hollywood's greatest year: Selznick's *Gone With The Wind* and M-G-M's *The Wizard of Oz* (both directed by Victor Fleming) become classics of entertainment fantasy.

John Ford's *Stagecoach*, classic Western.

Renoir's *Rules of the Game*.

April 30. President Roosevelt appears in a telecast at the World's Fair in New York marking the inauguration of regular television service in the U.S.

June 19. Pocket Books, a new company partly owned by Simon & Schuster, puts ten pocketsize paper-covered books priced at 25 cents each on sale at Macy's and a few Manhattan newsstands. The paperback revolution begins.

August 26. First major league baseball telecast: a doubleheader between the Brooklyn Dodgers and Cincinnati Reds.

1940 January 12. First American television network broadcast on WNBT-TV, New York, and WRGB-TV, Schenectady.

August. CBS demonstrates their color television system, developed by Peter Goldmark.

Hitchcock moves to Hollywood.

Murrow's broadcasts from London during the Blitz dramatize news value of radio.

1941 Renoir moves to Hollywood.

Ford's *The Grapes of Wrath*, from Steinbeck novel.

Huston's *The Maltese Falcon* establishes his reputation, Bogart's, and the Detective genre.

Welles's *Citizen Kane*, "the great American movie."

1942 Noel Coward's *In Which We Serve* marks paradoxical revitalization of British film during the war.

Capra's *Why We Fight* series of effective documentary propaganda.

1943 Maya Deren's *Meshes of the Afternoon* marks renewed development of the American avant garde.

First wire sound recorders in use in the military.

Due to antitrust suit, ABC created out of NBC's second network.

1944 Technicolor Monopack system first used for features.

1945 Rossellini's *Rome, Open City* and De Sica's *Shoeshine* mark Neorealism.

De Rochemont applies semidocumentary style to fiction in *House on 92nd Street*.

Murrow reports from Buchenwald.

German tape recorders captured.

1946–1960: The Growth of Television
_____

1946 February 14. The War Department announces the development of EN-IAC (Electronic Numerical Integrator and Computer). For the first time, electronic speed is applied to numerical tasks. The device covers 15,000 square feet of the basement of the Moore School of Electronic Engineering at the University of Pennsylvania.

American film industry's best year at the box office: $1.7 billion in receipts.

Cannes Film Festival founded.

Paramount antitrust suit begins.

American television begins broadcasting; BBC resumes.

Hawks's *The Big Sleep* presages Film Noir genre.

Wyler's *The Best Years of Our Lives*, popular study of the effects of war.

Hitchcock's *Notorious*.

1946 June 19. First television network sponsor: Gillette, Joe Louis vs. Billy Conn boxing match.

1947 House Un-American Activities Committee begins hearings on "Communist influence in Hollywood."

Lee Strasberg founds Actor's Studio.

Capra's *It's A Wonderful Life*, last in populist tradition.

1948 Astruc's essay on "caméra-stylo" published.

Howard Hughes buys RKO.

Black radio stations begin broadcasting.

Transistor developed.

Milton Berle's *Texaco Star Theatre* begins television comedy format.

Ed Sullivan's *Toast of the Town* begins television variety format.

1948 June 21. Goldmark's LP record unveiled.

1949 Donen and Kelly's *On the Town*: new style Musical.

"Stop the Music," first TV quiz show, debuts.

For the first time, more paperback books are sold than hardcovers.

1950 Blacklist in radio and television in full swing.

Cocteau's *Orpheus*.

Ophüls's *La Ronde*.

Wilder's *Sunset Boulevard*.

Sid Caesar, Imogene Coca begin *Your Show of Shows*.

1951 Murrow and Friendly begin *See It Now* series.

Paramount signs consent decree on antitrust suit.

I Love Lucy begins, success indicates film can work in television.

Jack Webb's *Dragnet* premiers.

NBC's *Today* program begins, mixing news and features.

Nyby's *The Thing* among first paranoid science-fiction films of the decade.

Kurosawa's *Rashomon* successful at Venice Film Festival.

Cahiers du Cinéma founded.

First coast-to-coast television broadcast via AT&T's coaxial cable.

1952 Community Antenna television, precursor of cable, begins.

Kelly and Donen's *Singin' in the Rain*.

Zinnemann's *High Noon*, "adult" Western.

Decca purchases Universal.

Sony develops stereo broadcasting in Japan.

Cinerama debuts.

Eastmancolor system introduced.

Nixon's televised "Checkers" speech.

1953 January 19. Desi Arnaz, Jr., is born the same day that the episode of *I Love Lucy* in which his fictional alter ego is born is telecast.

RKO liquidated by owner, General Tire Corp.

CinemaScope and 3-D introduced.

Hitchcock's *Rear Window*.

Chayevsky's *Marty* on *Goodyear Television Playhouse* signals the heyday of live television drama.

1954 January 1. NBC broadcasts Festival of Roses parade in color: first network colorcast.

January 1. NTSC Standard color broadcasting begins in the U.S.

January. Truffaut's essay, "Une certaine tendance du cinéma français" published in *Cahiers du Cinéma.*

Fellini's *La Strada,* international success.

Kazan's *On the Waterfront* assures Brando's success.

See It Now broadcast on Senator McCarthy has significant public effect.

Televised Army-McCarthy hearings result in McCarthy's disgrace and beginning of the end for the blacklist.

Disney and Warner Bros. contract to produce for ABC.

1955 Satyajit Ray's *Pather Panchali* introduces Indian film to West.

Commercial (ITV) channel begins broadcasting in Britain.

Nicholas Ray's *Rebel Without a Cause* sets the tone for the late fifties. James Dean dies.

The Village Voice founded. It will be a major force in the counterculture until 1970.

U.S. Census Bureau reports that 67 percent of all U.S. homes have television. TV income surpasses radio income by the end of the year.

1956 Release of hundreds of pre-1948 feature films to television signals the new relationship between film and broadcasting industries.

Ford's *The Searchers,* his most complex Western.

Bergman's *The Seventh Seal,* internationally successful.

November 30. First use of videotape in television: the West Coast feed of *Douglas Edwards With the News,* CBS.

1957 RKO studios sold to Desilu for television production.

Pocket transistor radios introduced.

1958 Stereophonic records and phonographs first marketed.

Hitchcock's *Vertigo.*

1959 Hitchcock's *North by Northwest.*

Birth of the New Wave: Truffaut's *400 Blows,* Resnais's *Hiroshima Mon Amour.*

Fellini's *La Dolce Vita,* together with other films released this year, marks a turning point in world cinema.

Cassavetes's *Shadows* suggests the possibility of a more personal American cinema.

Decca/Universal merges with MCA talent agency.

First regular series color broadcasts: *Bonanza*, NBC.

1960 Godard debuts with *Breathless*.

Reisz's *Saturday Night and Sunday Morning*, first major British working-class film.

Hitchcock's *Psycho*.

Videotape in use.

First demonstration of laser device, by Hughes Aircraft Co.

Leacock-Pennebaker's *Primary* first major Direct Cinema production, indicates new directions for documentary.

Kracauer's *Theory of Film: Redemption of Physical Reality* published.

Antonioni's *L'Avventura*.

Rouch's *Chronique d'un été*, first film of cinéma vérité.

In-flight movies introduced on airlines.

Screen Actors Guild strikes Hollywood to gain share of residual rights for films sold to television.

1961–1980: The Media World

1961 Buñuel's *Viridiana* marks his return to Europe.

Bergman begins his trilogy with *Through a Glass Darkly*.

Directors trained in television move into film.

September. NBC introduces theatrical movies into prime-time scheduling with *How To Marry a Millionaire*, on *Saturday Night at the Movies*.

1962 Truffaut's *Jules and Jim*.

Dr. No (Terrence Young) begins James Bond genre.

Subscription television experiments begin in California.

Johnny Carson takes over NBC's late-night talkshow; this type of programming grows in importance throughout the sixties.

Ernie Kovacs, inventive television comedian, dies at age 42.

Telstar 1 launched.

Fellini's 8½.

All-Channel rule of the FCC goes into effect requiring all television sets sold in the U.S. to be equipped to receive UHF.

1963 Kubrick's *Dr. Strangelove*.

Swedish Film Institute founded.

Holography demonstrated, developed by Ein Leith and Juris Upatnieks, based on work by Dennis Gabor in 1947.

1964 Godard's *A Married Woman* develops cinema as essay.

McLuhan's *Understanding Media* published.

Antonioni's *Red Desert*

Lester's *A Hard Day's Night* with The Beatles helps establish the new rock.

1965 Super-8 mm film format introduced for amateur market.

April 6. "Early Bird" satellite, Intelsat I, is launched. It is the first

commercial communications satellite and also the first geosynchronous communications satellite.

CBS joins NBC as an all-color network. ABC follows a few months later
marking completion of conversion from black and white.

1966   Godard's *2 or 3 Things I Know About Her.*

Rossellini continues work in television with *The Rise to Power of Louis
XIV.*

Bergman's *Persona* and Antonioni's *Blow-Up* draw new intellectual interest to film.

Loach's television film *Cathy Come Home* results in changes in British
housing laws.

Gulf & Western buys Paramount.

FCC ruling requires separate programming on FM stations. FM develops
rapidly in the next few years, drawing on the new rock music.

1967   The *World-Journal-Tribune,* a New York newspaper which was the result
of a merger of no less than seven papers, dies after little more than
year.

Seven Arts buys Warner Bros.

Corporation for Public Broadcasting formed to develop Public Television
network.

Transamerica Corporation buys United Artists.

Multitrack recording techniques are perfected.

Frederick Wiseman begins his career as documentarist for National Educational Television.

Public Broadcasting Laboratory develops magazine/essay format.

Smothers Brothers introduce a new sophistication and relevance to television comedy.

BBC's *Forsyte Saga* becomes a worldwide success over the next few years
and establishes the televised novel as a powerful new form.

Flashing techniques are introduced which significantly expand latitude
of filmstock.

Penn's *Bonnie and Clyde* sets a pattern of antiheroes which continues
through the seventies.

Lester's *Petulia* investigates the newly developing consciousness of the
sixties.

Sjoman's *I Am Curious—Yellow* breaks new ground in the depiction of
sexual activities and excites censorship furor.

American Film Institute founded.

Nam June Paik exhibits video works at the Howard Wise Gallery, New
York.

1968   Film an important arena for discussion during the political events of May
and June in France.

Television coverage of "police riots" at the Democratic National Convention in August equally influential. "The whole world is watching,"
the demonstrators chant.

Czech film renaissance cut short by Soviet invasion of Czechoslovakia.

Laugh-In experiments with new form of television comedy.

Kubrick's *2001: A Space Odyssey* pioneers many new special effects techniques, including front projection.

Kodak introduces 5254 color stock.

Fellini produces *A Director's Notebook* for television.

Rohmer reached international audiences with intellectual *My Night at Maud's*.

Christian Metz's *Essais sur la signification au cinéma* published.

FCC's "Carterfone" decision allows telephone customers to hook up own equipment to Bell lines.

1969 Growth of Xerox and offset as "instant" printing systems available to individuals and small groups continues.

Development of phototypesetting accelerates.

General interest magazines continue to decline, as special interest magazines experience rapid growth.

Sesame Street premiers, utilizing TV commercial techniques to teach basic skills.

Seven Arts/Warner Bros. merges with Kinney National Services.

Swiss film experiences a renaissance beginning with the production of Tanner's *La Salamandre*.

Peter Wollen's *Signs and Meaning in the Cinema* published.

Hill's *Butch Cassidy and the Sundance Kid* marks the continued decline in women's roles in the sixties and presages a raft of male bonding friendships in films of the seventies.

Hopper's *Easy Rider* marks the explosion of the short-lived genre of youth films.

Peckinpah's *The Wild Bunch* forecasts increasing violence in film.

Glauber Rocha's *Antonio Das Mortes* signals new interest in Third World Cinema.

Costa-Gavras's *Z* sets a new style for political melodrama.

ABC telecasts Harold Robbins's *The Survivors*, first novel-for-television.

1970 The economic recession reinforces the trend toward fewer and fewer American films produced each year.

American interests—which had recently provided as much as 90 percent of the capital for the British film industry—pull out precipitously due to the recession. British filmmakers emigrate to the U.S., or turn to television.

Kluge, Fassbinder, Schlöndorff establish Das Neue Kino on world screens. Television coproduction important.

Mary Tyler Moore Show marks renaissance of situation comedy.

Robert Altman consolidates his reputation with *M.A.S.H.*—later a popular television series.

Wadleigh's *Woodstock* sets a new style for concert musicals.

The growth of film study begins to accelerate in the U.S.

May. MGM auctions its heritage.

Sony sells Portapak half-inch portable videotape system. Video movement begins.

1971 Van Peebles's *Sweet Sweetback's Baadasssss Song* signals the establishment of the Black film.

Marcel Ophuls's *The Sorrow and the Pity* (originally a television program) excites new interest in the documentary interview form as personal essay.

Cable television systems, supplying nonbroadcast product, continue rapid expansion.

All in the Family, based on a British series, is Norman Lear's first television success.

FCC institutes Prime Time Access rule, ostensibly limiting networks to 3 hours of programming per evening in prime-time.

Computer memory chips introduced which can hold 1000 bits of information each.

FCC authorizes "specialized common carriers" to compete with AT&T in providing long-distance private lines to customers.

Word processing computers begin to have an effect on office procedures.

1972 Quadraphonic disc system introduced. The public rexponse is minimal.

Life magazine ceases publication.

Bertolucci's *Last Tango in Paris* is considered a mature treatment of sex.

Godard and Gorin finish Dziga-Vertov experiments with *Tout Va Bien.* Godard turns to video.

Canada's Anik I is launched, first domestic communications satellite.

FCC approves common carrier satellite services.

Coppola's *The Godfather* becomes the most profitable film of all time, to date.

1973 Growth of Citizen's Band (CB) radio greatly accelerated by first oil crisis.

Warner Bros.' *The Exorcist* marks renewed interest in shock effect of film.

1974 M-G-M opts out of film business, sells studio, sets, and costumes.

Home Box Office, a pay-television channel, is marketed through cable systems.

A Roper poll shows that, for the first time, television is the prime source of news for most people, having surpassed newspapers.

Watergate hearings televised.

Eastman introduces 5247 color stock.

Women begin moving into film and video en masse.

Computer memory chips now hold 4000 bits.

Bergman directs six-part *Scenes from a Marriage* for television.

Westar, the first U.S. domestic communications satellite, is launched.

1975 January. The Altair 8800 is the first personal computer offered for sale to public.

Dolby film sound system introduced.

French television reorganized into three networks, two of which accept advertising.

Networks agree on self-censorship "Family Time" provision.

Altman's *Nashville* released.

Bergman's *Face to Face*.

Jaws sets box office records, disaster genre.

Davis's *Hearts and Minds*, documentary on Vietnam.

FCC requires television set manufacturers to build sets with click-stop UHF tuning comparable to VHF tuning.

Steadicam is used for the first time, by Haskell Wexler on *Bound for Glory*.

1976 Bergman leaves Sweden.

South Africa is the last nation of any size to begin television service.

By end of 1976, U.S. networks sell all prime advertising time for 1977.

ABC places first in ratings for first time.

Home videotape Betamax cassette system introduced by Sony.

Bertolucci's *1900*.

More audio cassettes are sold this year than 8-track cartridges.

During the last eighteen months RCA and AT&T have launched their Satcom and Comstar satellites, respectively, marking the maturity of satellite communications systems.

1977 January 23–30. *Roots* is broadcast on ABC, setting ratings records. Six of the eight episodes will rank among the top ten television shows of all time.

April 27. Edwin Land of Polaroid Corp. demonstrates Polavision, instant movie system, for immediate sale.

For the first time, NBC News uses more tape than film.

Computer memory chips now hold 16,000 bits of information: 16 times more powerful than five years previously.

Autumn. The David Begelman affair focuses public attention on shady Hollywood business practices. Within eighteen months, the public loses interest.

Critical and commercial success of Woody Allen's *Annie Hall* marks slight shift of film industry away from Hollywood, toward New York.

George Lucas's *Star Wars* is released, quickly becomes highest grossing film of all time.

ABC displaces CBS as leading American network in terms of ratings and advertising revenues. CBS had held the number one position almost without exception since the early fifties. A significant number of NBC and CBS affiliates defect to ABC.

Rise of disco music culminates in popularity of the film *Saturday Night Fever*.

1978 *Saturday Night Fever*, a highly successful film, nevertheless earns more from soundtrack album sales than from the box office.

January. Orion Pictures Corporation Studio is formed by five former top executives of United Artists. By in effect renting Warner Bros.' distribution system, Orion avoids start-up costs of over $250 million.

April. *Variety* publishes its first "Vidcassette" review, of *Lectric Lady Disco*, which claims to be the first show produced specifically for the home videotape market.

Fred Silverman, formerly head of programming at both CBS and ABC when those networks ranked first in the ratings game, moves to NBC as president.

Releases of *Grease* and *Superman* reinforce blockbuster psychology.

October 4. In a live network broadcast of a television match on CBS Jimmy Connors uses the expletive "bullshit." No complaints are received.

October 5. In an episode of *Taxi* the word "bastard" is used.

Times of London is struck. (The paper will not appear again until a year later.)

December. Phillips-MCA begins test-marketing their videodisc player in Atlanta and Seattle.

1979 Canada and Australia emerge as film powers.

February 17. On *Saturday Night Live* (NBC) Gilda Radner performs a parody of singer Patti Smith. The song she sings is dedicated to Mick Jagger, and includes the refrain: "Are you woman, are you man/I'm your biggest fucked-up fan." The lyrics are garbled but the refrain is clear. According to the *New York Times* two days later, NBC received 160 calls during and right after the show. "75 found Miss Radner's language 'disgusting;' but 85, the network said, thought she was 'a fabulous and very talented lady.' "

The China Syndrome foreshadows events at Three Mile Island several weeks before they actually occur.

Success of "small" films like *Meatballs, Starting Over, Breaking Away,* and *Kramer vs Kramer* marks shift away from blockbusters, despite *Star Trek: The Motion Picture,* reputed to have cost $40 million, and *Apocalypse Now,* $30 million.

A Melbourne, Australia, television station offers the first 3-D service.

For the first time in more than twenty years, revenues in the recording industry are down. Several conglomerates move to sell their record companies.

August 15. Francis Coppola's *Apocalypse Now* is finally released accompanied by an extraordinary publicity campaign.

October. The Ladd Company is formed by former top executives of Twentieth Century-Fox, continuing the decentralization of Hollywood executive power that began eighteen months earlier with the formation of Orion Pictures Corp.

The Intel Corporation introduces a magnetic bubble memory chip capable of storing one million bits of information. Price: approximately $2,000.

1980 Continued development of word processing equipment suggests new more efficient methods of typesetting for books, newspapers, and magazines.

Home dish antennas to receive satellite signals are offered to the public at reasonable cost.

Screen Actors Guild strikes Hollywood film and television studios to gain share of future tape, disc, satellite, and other ancillary rights.

Godard returns to feature films with *Sauve qui peut la vie.*

INDEX

A number of film titles which are cited (mainly in Chapter 4) for purposes of identification only are not listed here. None of the Appendices are indexed. Check the Glossary and Chronology for further information. Terms which appear in the Glossary as well the main text are, however, noted here with an asterisk.

A

ABC, 381
abstraction, 5, 8, 31
Academy aperture, 149, 154
Academy of Motion Picture Arts and
    Sciences, 86
Academy ratio, 86
acting, 148
action-drama shows, 395
actors, 33, 154, 198, 201, 222
Adorno, T. W., 14
advertising, 215, 354, 382*
"The Aesthetics of Film Sound": 182
Africa, 282
Agee, James, 344
Al Hazen, 54, 73
Alberini, Filoteo, 200, 237
Albers, Joseph, 6
The Albert Brooks Show, 376
Aldrich, Robert, 254
Alea, Tomas Gutierrez, 279
Alexander Nevsky, 39, 326
Alice Doesn't Live Here Anymore, 227
Alice in the Cities, 290
Alien, 273
Alienation effect: see Verfremdungseffekt
All in the Family, 391–92

Allen, Fred, 181, 376
Allen, Gracie, 376
Allen, Karen, 305
Allen, Penny, 302
Allen, Woody, 170, 299
Almond, Paul, 280
Altman, Robert, 65, 103, 296
AM, 366, 378*
An American Family, 407
American Film, 345
The American Friend, 290
The American Game, 302
American Gigolo, 304
American Graffiti, 182, 295
American Indians, 226
An American in Paris, 256
American Mutoscope and Biograph
    Company, 200
American Zoetrope, 295
Amos 'n' Andy, 377
amplification, 364, 372
amplitude, 50, 366*
amplitude modulation, 366, 378*
anamorphic, 87, 149*
Anderson, Lindsay, 270
Andersson, Bibi, 29, 171
Andrew, J. Dudley, 315
angle, 164, 172*